THE HOME
OF THE
BLIZZARD

THE HOME OF THE BLIZZARD

A Heroic Tale of Antarctic Exploration and Survival

BY SIR DOUGLAS MAWSON

ILLUSTRATED WITH MAPS

With 260 Full-Page and Smaller Illustrations By
Dr. E. A. Wilson and Other Members of the Expedition,
Photogravure Frontispieces, 12 Plates in Facsimile from
Dr. Wilson's Sketches, Panoramas, and Maps

Skyhorse Publishing

Skyhorse Publishing books may be purchased in bulk at special discounts for sales promotion, corporate gifts, fund-raising, or educational purposes. Special editions can also be created to specifications. For details, contact the Special Sales Department, Skyhorse Publishing, 307 West 36th Street, 11th Floor, New York, NY 10018 or info@skyhorsepublishing.com.

Skyhorse® and Skyhorse Publishing® are registered trademarks of Skyhorse Publishing, Inc.®, a Delaware corporation.

Visit our website at www.skyhorsepublishing.com.

10 9 8 7 6 5 4 3 2 1

Library of Congress Cataloging-in-Publication Data

Mawson, Douglas, Sir, 1882-1958.
    The home of the blizzard : a heroic tale of antarctic exploration and survival / Sir Douglas Mawson.
        p. cm.
    Summary: "Sir Douglas Mawson records his historic expedition to explore uncharted land in Antarctica. Pitted against formidable natural forces, he and his team faced unrelenting natural forces as they traverse the previously unexplored King George V Land directly south of Australia"–Provided by publisher.
    ISBN 978-1-62087-409-7 (pbk. : alk. paper)

    1. Mawson, Douglas, Sir, 1882-1958–Travel. 2. Australasian Antarctic Expedition (1911-1914) 3. Antarctica–Discovery and exploration. I. Title.
    GV8501911.M32 A2 2012 919.89–dc23
                        2012033058

Printed in United States of America

TO THOSE WHO MADE IT POSSIBLE

THE SUBSCRIBERS AND CO-OPERATORS

TO THOSE WHO MADE IT A SUCCESS

MY COMRADES

AND TO

THOSE WHO WAITED

Contents

Author's Preface

THE OBJECT OF THIS BOOK IS TO PRESENT A connected narrative of the Expedition from a popular and general point of view. The field of work is a very extensive one, and I feel that this account provides a record inadequate to our endeavours. However, I am comforted by the fact that the lasting reputation of the Expedition is founded upon the scientific volumes which will appear in due course.

Allusion to the history of Antarctic exploration has been reduced to a minimum, as the subject has been ably dealt with by previous writers. This, and several other aspects of our subject, have been relegated to special appendices in order to make the story more readable and self-contained.

A glossary of technicalities is introduced for readers not familiar with the terms. In the same place is given a list of animals referred to from time to time. There, the common name is placed against the scientific name, so rendering it unnecessary to repeat the latter in the text.

The reports handed to me by the leaders concerning the work of sledging journeys and of the respective bases were in the main clearly and popularly written. Still it was necessary to make extensive excisions so as to preserve a "balance" of justice in all the accounts, and to keep the narrative within limits. I wish to assure the various authors of my appreciation of their contributions.

Mr. Frank Hurley's artistic taste is apparent in the numerous photographs. We who knew the circumstances can warmly testify to his perseverance under conditions of exceptional difficulty. Mr. A. J. Hodgeman is responsible for the cartographical work, which occupied his time for many months. Other members of the Expedition have added treasures to our collection of illustrations; each of which is acknowledged in its place.

To Dr. A. L. McLean, who assisted me in writing and editing the book, I am very greatly indebted. To him the book owes any literary style it may possess. Dr. McLean's journalistic talent was discovered by me when he occupied the post of Editor of the *Adelie Blizzard*, a monthly volume which helped to relieve the monotony of our second year in Adelie Land. For months he was constantly at work, revising cutting down or amplifying the material of the story.

Finally, I wish to express my thanks to Dr. Hugh Robert Mill for hints and criticisms by which we have profited.

DOUGLAS MAWSON

London, Autumn 1914.

Foreword

Nor on thee yet
Shall burst the future, as successive zones
Of several wonder open on some spirit
Flying secure and glad from heaven to heaven.
—Browning

THE AIM OF GEOGRAPHICAL EXPLORATION HAS, IN these days, interfused with the passion for truth. If now the ultimate bounds of knowledge have broadened to the infinite, the spirit of the man of science has quickened to a deeper fervour. Amid the finished ingenuities of the laboratory he has knitted a spiritual entente with the moral philosopher, viewing:

The narrow creeds of right and wrong, which fade
Before the unmeasured thirst for good.

Science and exploration have never been at variance; rather, the desire for the pure elements of natural revelation lay at the source of that unquenchable power the "love of adventure."

Of whatever nationality the explorer was always emboldened by that impulse, and, if there ever be a future of decadence, it will live again in his ungovernable heritage.

Eric the Red; Francis Drake—the same ardour was kindled at the heart of either. It is a far cry from the latter, a born marauder, to the modern scientific explorer. Still Drake was a hero of many parts, and though a religious bigot in present acceptation, was one of the enlightened of his age. A man who moved an equal in a court of Elizabethan manners was not untouched by the glorious ideals of the Renaissance.

Yet it was the unswerving will of a Columbus, a Vasco da Gama or a Magellan which created the devotion to geographical discovery, per se, and made practicable the concept of a spherical earth. The world was opened in imaginative entirety, and it now remained for the geographer to fill in the details brought home by the navigator.

It was long before Thule the wondrous ice-land of the North yielded her first secrets, and longer ere the Terra Australis of Finné was laid bare to the prying eyes of Science.

Early Arctic navigation opened the bounds of the unknown in a haphazard and fortuitous fashion. Sealers and whalers in the hope of rich booty ventured far afield, and, ranging among the mysterious floes or riding out fierce gales off an ice-girt coast, brought back strange tales to a curious world. Crudely embellished, contradictory, yet alluring they were; but the demand for truth came surely to the rescue. Thus, it was often the whaler who forsook his trade to explore for mere exploration's sake. Baffin was one of those who opened the gates to the North.

Then, too, the commercial spirit of the generations who sought a North West Passage was responsible for the incursions of many adventurers into the new world of the ice.

Strangely enough, the South was first attacked in the true scientific spirit by Captain Cook and later by Bellingshausen. Sealing and whaling ventures followed in their train.

At last the era had come for the expedition, planned, administered, equipped and carried out with a definite objective. It is characteristic of the race of men that the first design should have centred on the Pole—the top of the earth, the focus of longitude, the magic goal, to reach which no physical sacrifice was too great. The heroism of Parry is a type of that adamant persistence which has made the history of the conquest of the Poles a volume in which disaster and death have played a large part. It followed on years of polar experience, it resulted from an exact knowledge of geographical and climatic conditions, a fearless anticipation, expert information on the details of transport—and the fortune of the brave— that Peary and Amundsen had their reward in the present generation.

Meanwhile, in the wake of the pioneers of new land there were passing the scientific workers born in the early nineteenth century. Sir James Clark Ross is an epitome of that expansive enthusiasm which was the keynote of the life of Charles Darwin. The classic *The Voyage of the Beagle* (1831–36) was a triumph of patient rigorous investigation conducted in many lands outside the polar circles.

The methods of Darwin were developed in the *Challenger* Expedition (1872) which worked even to the confines of the southern ice. And the torch of the pure flame of Science was handed on. It was the same consuming ardour which took Nansen across the plateau of Greenland, which made him resolutely propound the theory of the northern ice-drift, to maintain it in the face of opposition and ridicule and to plan an expedition down to the minutest detail in conformity therewith. The close of the century saw Science no longer the mere appendage but the actual basis of exploratory endeavour.

Disinterested research and unselfish specialization are the phrases born to meet the intellectual demands of the new century.

The modern polar expedition goes forth with finished appliances, with experts in every department—sailors, artisans, soldiers and students in medley; supremely, with men who seek risk and privation—the glory of the dauntless past. A. L. M.

Introduction

ONE OF THE OFT-REPEATED QUESTIONS FOR WHICH I usually had a ready answer, at the conclusion of Sir Ernest Shackleton's Expedition (1907–09) was, "Would you like to go to the Antarctic again?" In the first flush of the welcome home and for many months, during which the keen edge of pleasure under civilized conditions had not entirely worn away, I was inclined to reply with a somewhat emphatic negative. But, once more a man in the world of men, lulled in the easy repose of routine, and performing the ordinary duties of a workaday world, old emotions awakened. The grand sweet days returned in irresistible glamour, faraway "voices" called:

> . . . *from the wilderness, the vast and Godlike spaces,*
> *The stark and sullen solitudes that sentinel the Pole.*

There always seemed to be something at the back of my mind, stored away for future contemplation, and it was an idea which largely matured during my first sojourn in the far South. At times, during the long hours of steady tramping across the trackless snow-fields, one's thoughts flow in a clear and limpid stream, the mind is unruffled and composed and the passion of a great venture springing suddenly before the imagination is sobered by the calmness of pure reason. Perchance this is true of certain moments, but they are rare and fleeting. It may have been in one such phase that I suddenly found myself eager for more than a glimpse of the great span of Antarctic coast lying nearest to Australia.

Professor T. W. E. David, Dr. F. A. Mackay and I, when seeking the South Magnetic Pole during the summer of 1908–09, had penetrated farthest into that region on land. The limiting outposts had been defined by other expeditions; at Cape Adare on the east and at Gaussberg on the west.

Between them lay my "Land of Hope and Glory," of whose outline and glacial features the barest evidence had been furnished. There, bordering the Antarctic Circle, was a realm far from the well-sailed highways of many of the more recent Antarctic expeditions.

The idea of exploring this unknown coast took firm root in my mind while I was on a visit to Europe in February 1910. The prospects of an expedition operating to the west of Cape Adare were discussed with the late Captain R. F. Scott and I suggested that the activities of his expedition might be arranged to extend over the area in question. Finally he decided that his hands were already too full to make any definite proposition for a region so remote from his own objective.

Sir Ernest Shackleton was warmly enthusiastic when the scheme was laid before him, hoping for a time to identify himself with the undertaking. It was in some measure due to his initiative that I felt impelled eventually to undertake the organization and leadership of an expedition.

For many reasons, besides the fact that it was the country of my home and Alma Mater, I was desirous that the Expedition should be maintained by Australia. It seemed to me that here was an opportunity to prove that the young men of a young country could rise to those traditions which have made the history of British Polar exploration one of triumphant endeavour as well as of tragic sacrifice. And so I was privileged to rally the "sons of the younger son."

A provisional plan was drafted and put before the Australasian Association for the Advancement of Science at their meeting held at Sydney in January 1911, with a request for approval and financial assistance. Both were unanimously granted, a sum of £1000 was voted and committees were formed to co-operate in the arrangement of a scientific programme and to approach the Government with a view to obtaining substantial help.

The three leading members of the committees were Professor Orme Masson (President), Professor T. W. Edgeworth David (President Elect) and Professor G. C. Henderson (President of the Geographical Section). All were zealous and active in furthering the projects of the Expedition.

Meanwhile I had laid my scheme of work before certain prominent Australians and some large donations** had been promised. The sympathy and warm-hearted generosity of these gentlemen was an incentive for me to push through my plans at once to a successful issue.

I therefore left immediately for London with a view to making arrangements there for a vessel suitable for polar exploration, to secure

----

** *Refer to Finance Appendix.*

sledging dogs from Greenland and furs from Norway, and to order the construction of certain instruments and equipment. It was also my intention to gain if possible the support of Australians residing in London. The Council of the University of Adelaide, in a broad-minded scientific spirit, granted me the necessary leave of absence from my post as lecturer, to carry through what had now resolved itself into an extensive and prolonged enterprise.

During my absence, a Committee of the Australasian Association for the Advancement of Science approached the Commonwealth Government with an appeal for funds. Unfortunately it was the year (1911) of the Coronation of his Majesty King George V, and the leading members of the Cabinet were in England, so the final answer to the deputation was postponed. I was thus in a position of some difficulty, for many requirements had to be ordered without delay if the Expedition were to get away from Australia before the end of the year.

At length, through the kindness of Lord Northcliffe, the columns of the *Daily Mail* were opened to us and Sir Ernest Shackleton made a strong appeal on our behalf. The Royal Geographical Society set the seal of its approval on the aims of the Expedition and many donations were soon afterwards received.

At this rather critical period I was fortunate in securing the services of Captain John King Davis, who was in future to act as Master of the vessel and Second in Command of the Expedition. He joined me in April 1911, and rendered valuable help in the preliminary arrangements. Under his direction the SY *Aurora* was purchased and refitted.

The few months spent in London were anxious and trying, but the memory of them is pleasantly relieved by the generosity and assistance which were meted out on every hand. Sir George Reid, High Commissioner for the Australian Commonwealth, I shall always remember as an ever-present friend. The preparations for the scientific programme received a strong impetus from well-known Antarctic explorers, notably Dr. W. S. Bruce, Dr. Jean Charcot, Captain Adrian de Gerlache, and the late Sir John Murray and Mr. J. Y. Buchanan of the *Challenger* Expedition. In the dispositions made for oceanographical work I was indebted for liberal support to H.S.H. the Prince of Monaco.

In July 1911 I was once more in Australia, a large proportion of my time being occupied with finance, the purchase and concentration of stores and equipment and the appointment of the staff. In this work I was aided by Professors Masson and David and by Miss Ethel Bage, who throughout this busy period acted in an honorary capacity as secretary in Melbourne.

Time was drawing on and the funds of the Expedition were wholly inadequate to the needs of the moment, until Mr. T. H. Smeaton, M.P., introduced a deputation to the Hon. John Verran, Premier of South Australia. The deputation, organized to approach the State Government for a grant of £5000, was led by the Right Hon. Sir Samuel Way, Bart., Chief Justice of South Australia and Chancellor of the Adelaide University, and supported by Mr. Lavington Bonython, Mayor of Adelaide, T. Ryan, M.P., the Presidents of several scientific societies and members of the University staff. This sum was eventually forthcoming and it paved the way to greater things.

In Sydney, Professor David approached the State Government on behalf of the Expedition for financial support, and, through the Acting Premier, the Hon. W. A. Holman, £7000 was generously promised. The State of Victoria through the Hon. W. Watt, Premier of Victoria, supplemented our funds to the extent of £6000.

Upheld by the prestige of a large meeting convened in the Melbourne Town Hall during the spring, the objects of the Australasian Antarctic Expedition were more widely published. On that memorable occasion the Governor-General, Lord Denman, acted as chairman, and among others who participated were the Hon. Andrew Fisher (Prime Minister of the Commonwealth), the Hon. Alfred Deakin (Leader of the Opposition), Professor Orme Masson (President A.A.A.S. and representative of Victoria), Senator Walker (representing New South Wales) and Professor G. C. Henderson (representing South Australia).

Soon after this meeting the Commonwealth Government voted £5000, following a grant of £2000 made by the British Government at the instance of Lord Denman, who from the outset had been a staunch friend of the Expedition.

At the end of October 1911 all immediate financial anxiety had passed, and I was able to devote myself with confidence to the final preparations.

Captain Davis brought the *Aurora* from England to Australia, and on December 2, 1911, we left Hobart for the South. A base was established on Macquarie Island, after which the ship pushed through the ice and landed a party on an undiscovered portion of the Antarctic Continent. After a journey of fifteen hundred miles to the west of this base another party was landed and then the *Aurora* returned to Hobart to refit and to carry out oceanographical investigations, during the year 1912, in the waters south of Australia and New Zealand.

In December 1912 Captain Davis revisited the Antarctic to relieve the two parties who had wintered there. A calamity befell my own sledging party, Lieut. B. E. S. Ninnis and Dr. X. Mertz both lost their lives and my arrival back at Winter Quarters was delayed for so long, that the *Aurora* was forced to leave five men for another year to prosecute a search for the missing party. The remainder of the men, ten in number, and the party fifteen hundred miles to the west were landed safely at Hobart in March 1912.

Thus the prearranged plans were upset by my non-return and the administration of the Expedition in Australia was carried out by Professor David, whose special knowledge was invaluable at such a juncture.

Funds were once more required, and, during the summer of 1912, Captain Davis visited London and secured additional support, while the Australasian Association for the Advancement of Science again successfully approached the Commonwealth Government (The Right Hon. J. H. Cook, Prime Minister). In all, the sum of £8000 was raised to meet the demands of a second voyage of relief.

The party left on Macquarie Island, who had agreed to remain at the station for another year, ran short of food during their second winter. The New Zealand Government rendered the Expedition a great service in dispatching stores to them by the *Tutanekai* without delay.

Finally, in the summer of 1913, the *Aurora* set out on her third cruise to the far South, picking up the parties at Macquarie Island and in the Antarctic, carried out observations for two months amid the ice and reached Adelaide late in February 1914.

Throughout a period of more than three years Professors David and Masson—the fathers of the Expedition—worked indefatigably and unselfishly in its interests. Unbeknown to them I have taken the liberty to reproduce the only photographs at hand of these gentlemen, which action I hope they will view favourably. That of Professor David needs some explanation: It is a snapshot taken at Relief Inlet, South Victoria Land, at the moment when the Northern Party of Shackleton's Expedition, February 1909, was rescued by the SY *Nimrod*.

In shipping arrangements Capt. Davis was assisted throughout by Mr. J. J. Kinsey, Christchurch, Capt. Barter, Sydney, and Mr. F. Hammond, Hobart.

Such an undertaking is the work of a multitude and it is only by sympathetic support from many sources that a measure of success can be expected. In this connexion there are many names which I recall with warm gratitude. It is impossible to mention all to whom the Expedition is indebted, but I trust that none of those who have taken a prominent part will fail to find an acknowledgment somewhere in these volumes.

I should specially mention the friendly help afforded by the Australasian Press, which has at all times given the Expedition favourable and lengthy notices, insisting on its national and scientific character.

With regard to the conduct of the work itself, I was seconded by the whole-hearted co-operation of the members, my comrades, and what they have done can only be indicated in this narrative.

CHAPTER I

The Problem and Preparations

NOTWITHSTANDING THE FACT THAT IT HAS been repeatedly stated in the public press that the Australasian Antarctic expedition had no intention of making the South Geographical Pole its objective, it is evident that our aims were not properly realized by a large section of the British public, considering that many references have appeared in print attributing that purpose to the undertaking. With three other Antarctic expeditions already in the field, it appeared to many, therefore, that the venture was entirely superfluous.

The Expedition had a problem sketched in unmistakable feature, and the following pages will shortly set forth its historical origin and rationale.

The Antarctic problem** assumed its modern aspect after Captain Cook's circumnavigation of the globe in high southern latitudes, accomplished between 1772 and 1775. Fact replaced the fiction and surmise of former times, and maps appeared showing a large blank area at the southern extremity of the earth, where speculative cartographers had affirmed the existence of habitable land extending far towards the Equator. Cook's voyage made it clear that if there were any considerable mass of Antarctic land, it must indubitably lie within the Antarctic Circle, and be subjected to such stringent climatic conditions as to render it an unlikely habitation for man.

Cook's reports of seals on the island of South Georgia initiated in the Antarctic seas south of America a commercial enterprise, which is still carried on, and has incidentally thrown much light upon the geography of the South Polar regions. Indeed, almost the whole of such information, prior to the year 1839, was the outcome of sealing and whaling projects.

** *Dr. H. R. Mill has compiled a complete account of Antarctic exploration in his "Siege of the South Pole." Refer also to the Historical Appendix for an abridged statement.*

About the year 1840, a wave of scientific enthusiasm resulted in the dispatch of three national expeditions by France, the United States, and Great Britain; part at least of whose programmes was Antarctic exploration. Russia had previously sent out an expedition which had made notable discoveries.

The contributions to knowledge gained at this period were considerable. Those carried back to civilization by the British expedition under Ross, are so well known that they need not be described. The French under Dumont D'Urville and the Americans under Wilkes visited the region to the southward of Australia—the arena of our own efforts—and frequent references will be made to their work throughout this story.

What has been termed the period of averted interest now intervened, before the modern movement set in with overpowering insistence. It was not till 1897 that it had commenced in earnest. Since then many adventurers have gone forth; most of the prominent civilized nations taking their share in exploration. By their joint efforts some, at least, of the mystery of Antarctica has been dispelled.

It is now a commonplace, largely in the world of geographical concerns, that the earth has still another continent, unique in character, whose ultimate bounds are merely pieced together from a fragmentary outline. The continent itself appears to have been sighted for the first time in the year 1820, but no human being actually set foot on it until 1895. The Belgian expedition under de Gerlache was the first to experience the Antarctic winter, spending the year 1898 drifting helplessly, frozen in the pack-ice, to the southward of America. In the following year a British expedition under Borchgrevinck, wintering at Cape Adare, passed a year upon the Antarctic mainland.

The main efforts of recent years have been centred upon the two more accessible areas, namely, that in the American Quadrant** which is prolonged as a tongue of land outside the Antarctic Circle, being consequently less beset by ice; secondly, the vicinity of the Ross Sea in the Australian Quadrant. It is because these two favoured domains have for special reasons attracted the stream of exploration that the major portion

---

** *For convenience, the Antarctic regions may be referred to in four main divisions, corresponding with the quadrants of the hemisphere. Of the several suggestions thrown out by previous writers, the one adopted here is that based on the meridian of Greenwich, referring the quadrants to an adjacent continent or ocean. Thus the American Quadrant lies between 0° and 90° W., the African Quadrant between 0° and 90° E., and the Australian Quadrant between 90° and 180° E. The fourth division is called the Pacific Quadrant, since ocean alone lies to the north of it.*

Virgin Solitudes

of Antarctica is unknown. Nevertheless, one is in a position to sketch broad features which will probably not be radically altered by any future expeditions.

Certain it is that a continent approaching the combined areas of Australia and Europe lies more or less buried beneath the South Polar snows; though any statement of the precise area is insufficient for a proper appreciation of the magnitude, unless its elevated plateau-like character be also taken into consideration. It appears to be highest over a wide central crown rising to more than ten thousand feet. Of the remainder, there is little doubt that the major portion stands as high as six thousand feet. The average elevation must far exceed that of any other continent, for, with peaks nineteen thousand feet above sea-level, its mountainous topography is remarkable. Along the coast of Victoria Land, in the Australian Quadrant, are some of the most majestic vistas of alpine scenery that the world affords. Rock exposures are rare, ice appearing everywhere except in the most favoured places.

Regarding plant and animal life upon the land there is little to say. The vegetable kingdom is represented by plants of low organization such as mosses, lichens, diatoms and algae. The animal world, so far as true land-forms are concerned, is limited to types like the protozoa (lowest in the organic scale), rotifera and minute insect-like mites which lurk hidden away amongst the tufts of moss or on the under side of loose stones. Bacteria, most fundamental of all, at the basis, so to speak, of animal and vegetable life, have a manifold distribution.

It is a very different matter when we turn to the life of the neighbouring seas, for that vies in abundance with the warmer waters of lower latitudes. There are innumerable seals, many sea-birds and millions of penguins. As all these breed on Antarctic shores, the coastal margin of the continent is not so desolate.

In view of the fact that life, including land-mammals, is abundant in the North Polar regions, it may be asked why analogous forms are not better represented in corresponding southern latitudes. Without going too deeply into the question, it may be briefly stated, firstly, that a more widespread glaciation than at present prevails invested the great southern continent and its environing seas, within recent geological times, effectually exterminating any pre-existing land life. Secondly, since that period the continent has been isolated by a wide belt of ocean from other lands, from which restocking might have taken place after the manner of the North Polar regions. Finally, climatic conditions in the Antarctic are, latitude for latitude, much more severe than in the Arctic.

With regard to climate in general, Antarctica has the lowest mean temperature and the highest wind-velocity of any land existing. This naturally follows from the fact that it is a lofty expanse of ice-clad land circumscribing the Pole, and that the Antarctic summer occurs when the earth is farther from the sun than is the case during the Arctic summer.

There are those who would impatiently ask, "What is the use of it all?" The answer is brief.

The polar regions, like any other part of the globe, may be said to be paved with facts, the essence of which it is necessary to acquire before knowledge of this special zone can be brought to even a provisional exactitude. On the face of it, polar research may seem to be specific and discriminating, but it must be remembered that an advance in any one of the departments into which, for convenience, science is artificially divided, conduces to the advantage of all. Science is a homogeneous whole. If we ignore the facts contained in one part of the world, surely we are hampering scientific advance. It is obvious to every one that, given only a fraction of the pieces, it is a much more difficult task to put together a jig-saw puzzle and obtain an idea of the finished pattern than were all the pieces at hand. The pieces of the jig-saw puzzle are the data of science.

Though it is not sufficiently recognized, the advance of science is attended by a corresponding increase in the creature comforts of man. Again, from an economic aspect, the frozen South may not attract immediate attention. But who can say what a train of enterprise the future may bring?

Captain James Cook, on his return to London after the circumnavigation of Antarctica, held that the far-southern lands had no future. Yet, a few years later, great profits were being returned to Great Britain and the United States from sealing-stations established as a result of Cook's own observations. At the present day, several whaling companies have flourishing industries in the Antarctic waters within the American Quadrant.

Even now much can be said in regard to the possibilities offered by the Antarctic regions for economic development, but, year by year, the outlook will widen, since man is constantly resorting to subtler and more ingenious artifice in applying Nature's resources. It will be remembered that Charles Darwin, when in Australia, predicted a very limited commercial future for New South Wales. But the mastery of man overcame the difficulties which Darwin's too penetrating mind foresaw.

What will be the role of the South in the progress of civilization and in the development of the arts and sciences, is not now obvious. As sure as there is here a vast mass of land with potentialities, strictly limited at

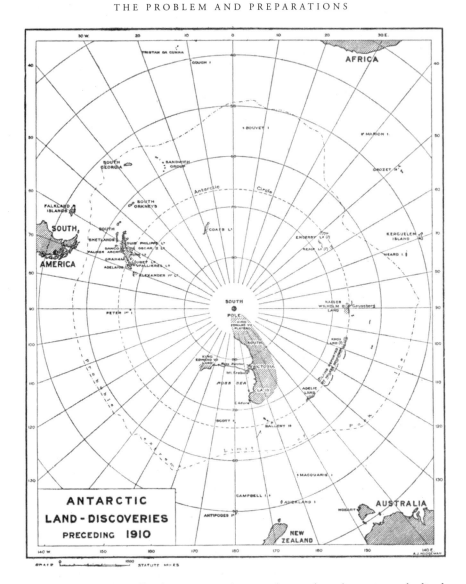

present, so surely will it be cemented some day within the universal plinth of things.

An unknown coast-line lay before the door of Australia. Following on the general advance of exploration, and as a sequel to several important discoveries, the time arrived when a complete elucidation of the Antarctic problem was more than ever desirable. In the Australian Quadrant, the broad geographical features of the Ross Sea area were well known, but of the remainder and greater portion of the tract only vague and imperfect reports could be supplied.

Before submitting our plans in outline, it will be as well to review the stage at which discovery had arrived when our Expedition came upon the scene.

The coast-line of the eastern extremity of the Australian Quadrant, including the outline of the Ross Sea and the coast west-north-west of Cape Adare as far as Cape North, was charted by Ross and has been amplified by seven later expeditions. In the region west of Cape North, recent explorers had done little up till 1911. Scott in the *Discovery* had disproved the existence of some of Wilkes's land; Shackleton in the *Nimrod* had viewed some forty miles of high land beyond Cape North; lastly, on the eve of our departure, Scott's *Terra Nova* had met two patches of new land—Oates Land—still farther west, making it evident that the continent ranged at least two hundred and eighty miles in a west-north-west direction from Cape Adare.

Just outside the western limit of the Australian Quadrant lies Gaussberg, discovered by a German expedition under Drygalski in 1902. Between the most westerly point sighted by the *Terra Nova* and Gaussberg, there is a circuit of two thousand miles, bordering the Antarctic Circle, which no vessel had navigated previous to 1840.

This was the arena of our activities and, therefore, a synopsis of the voyages of early mariners will be enlightening.

Balleny, a whaling-master, with the schooner *Eliza Scott* of one hundred and fifty-four tons, and a cutter, the *Sabrina* of fifty-four tons, was the first to meet with success in these waters. Proceeding southward from New Zealand in 1839, he located the Balleny Islands, a group containing active volcanoes, lying about two hundred miles off the nearest part of the mainland and to the north-west of Cape Adare. Leaving these islands, Balleny sailed westward keeping a look-out for new land. During a gale the vessels became separated and the *Sabrina* was lost with all hands. Balleny in the *Eliza Scott* arrived safely in England and reported doubtful land in 122° E. longitude, approximately. Dr. H. R. Mill says: "Although the name of the cutter *Sabrina* has been given to an appearance of land at this point, we cannot look upon its discovery as proved by the vague reference made by the explorers."

On January 1, 1840, Dumont D'Urville sailed southward from Hobart in command of two corvettes, the *Astrolabe* and the *Zelée*. Without much obstruction from floating ice, he came within sight of the Antarctic coast, thenceforth known as Adelie Land. The expedition did not set foot on the mainland, but on an adjacent island. They remained in the vicinity of the coast for a few days, when a gale sprang up which was hazardously

The Wall of the Antarctic Continent

Finner Whales of the South

weathered on the windward side of the pack-ice. The ships then cruised along the face of flat-topped ice-cliffs, of the type known as barrier-ice or shelf-ice, which were taken to be connected with land and named Cote Clarie. As will be seen later, Cote Clarie does not exist.

Dr. H. R. Mill sums up the work done by the French expedition during its eleven days' sojourn in the vicinity of the Antarctic coast:

"D'Urville's discoveries of land were of but little account. He twice traced out considerable stretches of a solid barrier of ice, and at one point saw and landed upon rocks in front of it; but he could only give the vaguest account of what lay behind the barrier."

Wilkes of the American expedition proceeded south from Sydney at the close of 1839. His vessels were the *Vincennes*, a sloop of war of seven hundred and eighty tons, the *Peacock*, another sloop of six hundred and fifty tons, the *Porpoise*, a gun-brig of two hundred and thirty tons and a tender, the *Flying Fish* of ninety-six tons. The scientists of the expedition were precluded from joining in this part of the programme, and were left behind in Sydney. Wilkes himself was loud in his denunciation both of the ships and of the stores, though they had been specially assembled by the naval department. The ships were in Antarctic waters for a period of forty-two days, most of the time separated by gales, during which the crews showed great skill in navigating their ill-fitted crafts and suffered great hardships.

Land was reported almost daily, but, unfortunately, subsequent exploration has shown that most of the landfalls do not exist. Several soundings made by Wilkes were indicative of the approach to land, but he must have frequently mistaken for it distant ice-masses frozen in the pack. Experience has proved what deceptive light-effects may be observed amid the ice and how easily a mirage may simulate reality.

Whatever the cause of Wilkes's errors, the truth remains that Ross sailed over land indicated in a rough chart which had been forwarded to him by Wilkes, just before the British expedition set out. More recently, Captain Scott in the *Discovery* erased many of the landfalls of Wilkes, and now we have still further reduced their number. The *Challenger* approached within fifteen miles of the western extremity of Wilkes's Termination Land, but saw no sign of it. The *Gauss* in the same waters charted Kaiser Wilhelm II Land well to the south of Termination Land, and the eastward continuation of the former could not have been visible from Wilkes's ship. After the voyage of the *Discovery*, the landfalls, the existence of which had not been disproved, might well have been regarded as requiring confirmation before their validity could be recognised.

The only spot where rocks were reported *in situ* was in Adelie Land, where the French had anticipated the Americans by seven days. Farther west, earth and stones had been collected by Wilkes from material embedded in floating masses of ice off the coast of his Knox Land. These facts lend credence to Wilkes's claims of land in that vicinity. His expedition did not once set foot on Antarctic shores, and, possibly on account of the absence of the scientific staff, his descriptions tend to be inexact and obscure. The soundings made by Wilkes were sufficient to show that he was probably in some places at no great distance from the coast, and, considering that his work was carried out in the days of sailing-ships, in unsuitable craft, under the most adverse weather conditions, with crews scurvy-stricken and discontented, it is wonderful how much was achieved. We may amply testify that he did more than open the field for future expeditions.

After we had taken into account the valuable soundings of the *Challenger* (1872), the above comprised our knowledge concerning some two thousand miles of prospective coast lying to the southward of Australia, at a time when the plans of the Australasian Expedition were being formulated.

The original plans for the Expedition were somewhat modified upon my return from Europe. Briefly stated, it was decided that a party of five men should be stationed at Macquarie Island, a sub-antarctic possession of the Commonwealth. They were to be provided with a hut, stores and a complete wireless plant, and were to prosecute general scientific investigations, co-operating with the Antarctic bases in meteorological and other work. After disembarking the party at Macquarie Island, the *Aurora* was to proceed south on a meridian of 158° E. longitude, to the westward of which the Antarctic programme was to be conducted.

Twelve men, provisioned and equipped for a year's campaign and provided with wireless apparatus, were to be landed in Antarctica on the first possible opportunity at what would constitute a main base. Thereafter, proceeding westward, it was hoped that a second and a third party, consisting of six and eight men respectively, would be successively established on the continent at considerable distances apart. Of course we were well aware of the difficulties of landing even one party, but, as division of our forces would under normal conditions secure more scientific data, it was deemed advisable to be prepared for exceptionally favourable circumstances.

Macquarie Island, a busy station in the days of the early sealers, had become almost neglected. Little accurate information was to be had regarding it, and no reliable map existed. A few isolated facts had been gathered of its geology, and the anomalous fauna and flora *sui generis* had been but partially described. Its position, eight hundred and fifty miles south-south-east of Hobart, gave promise of valuable meteorological data relative to the atmospheric circulation of the Southern Hemisphere and of vital interest to the shipping of Australia and New Zealand.

As to the Antarctic sphere of work, it has been seen that very little was known of the vast region which was our goal. It is sufficient to say that almost every observation would be fresh material added to the sum of human knowledge.

In addition to the work to be conducted from the land bases, it was intended that oceanographic investigations should be carried on by the *Aurora* as far as funds would allow. With this object in view, provision was made for the necessary apparatus which would enable the ship's party to make extensive investigations of the ocean and its floor over the broad belt between Australia and the Antarctic continent. This was an important branch of study, for science is just as much interested in the greatest depths of the ocean as with the corresponding elevations of the land. Indeed, at the present day, the former is perhaps the greater field.

The scope of our intentions was regarded by some as over-ambitious, but knowing

> *How far high failure overleaps the bound*
> *Of low successes,*

and seeing nothing impossible in these arrangements, we continued to adhere to them as closely as possible, with what fortune remains to be told.

To secure a suitable vessel was a matter of fundamental importance. There was no question of having a ship built to our design, for the requisite expenditure might well have exceeded the whole cost of our Expedition. Accordingly the best obtainable vessel was purchased, and modified to fulfil our requirements. Such craft are not to be had in southern waters; they are only to be found engaged in Arctic whaling and sealing.

The primary consideration in the design of a vessel built to navigate amid the ice is that the hull be very staunch, capable of driving into the pack and of resisting lateral pressure, if the ice should close in around it.

So a thick-walled timber vessel, with adequate stiffening in the framework, would meet the case. The construction being of wood imparts a certain elasticity, which is of great advantage in easing the shock of impacts with floating ice. As has been tragically illustrated in a recent disaster, the ordinary steel ship would be ripped on its first contact with the ice. Another device, to obviate the shock and to assist in forging a way through the ice-floe, is to have the bow cut away below the water-line. Thus, instead of presenting to the ice a vertical face, which would immediately arrest the ship and possibly cause considerable damage on account of the sudden stress of the blow, a sloping, overhanging bow is adopted. This arrangement enables the bow to rise over the impediment, with a gradual slackening of speed. The immense weight put upon the ice crushes it and the ship settles down, moving ahead and gathering speed to meet the next obstacle.

Of importance second only to a strong hull is the possession of sails in addition to engines. The latter are a *sine qua non* in polar navigation, whilst sails allow of economy in the consumption of coal, and always remain as a last resort should the coal-supply be exhausted or the propeller damaged.

The *Aurora*, of the Newfoundland sealing fleet, was ultimately purchased and underwent necessary alterations. She was built in Dundee in 1876, but though by no means young was still in good condition and capable of buffeting with the pack for many a year. Also, she was not without a history, for in the earlier days she was amongst those vessels which hurried to the relief of the unfortunate Greely Expedition.

The hull was made of stout oak planks, sheathed with greenheart and lined with fir. The bow, fashioned on cutaway lines, was a mass of solid wood, armoured with steel plates. The heavy side-frames were braced and stiffened by two tiers of horizontal oak beams, upon which were built the 'tween decks and the main deck. Three bulkheads isolated the fore-peak, the main hold, the engine-room and the after living-quarters respectively.

A hull of such strength would resist a heavy strain, and, should it be subjected to lateral pressure, would in all probability rise out of harm's way. However, to be quite certain of this and to ensure safety in the most extreme case it is necessary that the hull be modelled after the design adopted by Nansen in the *Fram*.

The principal dimensions were, length one hundred and sixty-five feet, breadth thirty feet, and depth eighteen feet.

The registered tonnage was three hundred and eighty-six, but the actual carrying capacity we found to be about six hundred tons.

The engines, situated aft, were compound, supplied with steam from a single boiler. The normal power registered was ninety-eight horse-power, working a four-bladed propeller, driving it at the rate of sixty or seventy revolutions per minute (six to ten knots per hour).

Steam was also laid on to a winch, aft, for handling cargo in the main hold, and to a forward steam-windlass. The latter was mainly used for raising the anchor and manipulating the deep-sea dredging-cable.

The ship was square on the foremast and schooner-rigged on the main and mizen masts.

13

Between the engine-room bulkhead and the chain and sail locker was a spacious hold. Six large steel tanks built into the bottom of the hold served for the storage of fresh water and at any time when empty could be filled with seawater, offering a ready means of securing emergency ballast.

On the deck, just forward of the main hatch, was a deckhouse, comprising cook's galley, steward's pantry and two laboratories. Still farther forward was a small lamp-room for the storage of kerosene, lamps and other necessaries. A lofty fo'c'sle-head gave much accommodation for carpenters, shipwrights and other stores. Below it, a capacious fo'c'sle served as quarters for a crew of sixteen men.

Aft, the chart-room, captain's cabin and photographic dark-room formed a block leading up to the bridge, situated immediately in front of the funnel. Farther aft, behind the engine-room and below the poop deck, was the ward-room(,) a central space sixteen feet by eight feet, filled by the dining-table and surrounded by cabins with bunks for twenty persons.

From the time the *Aurora* arrived in London to her departure from Australia, she was a scene of busy activity, as alterations and replacements were necessary to fit her for future work.

In the meantime, stores and gear were being assembled. Purchases were made and valuable donations received both in Europe and Australia. Many and varied were the requirements, and some idea of their great multiplicity will be gained by referring to the appendices dealing with stores, clothing and instruments.

Finally, reference may be made in this chapter to the staff. In no department can a leader spend time more profitably than in the selection of the men who are to accomplish the work. Even when the expedition has a scientific basis, academic distinction becomes secondary in the choice of *men*. Fiala, as a result of his Arctic experience, truly says, "Many a man who is a jolly good fellow in congenial surroundings will become impatient, selfish and mean when obliged to sacrifice his comfort, curb his desires and work hard in what seems a losing fight. The first consideration in the choice of men for a polar campaign should be the moral quality. Next should come mental and physical powers."

For polar work the great desideratum is tempered youth. Although one man at the age of fifty may be as strong physically as another at the age of twenty, it is certain that the exceptional man of fifty was also an exceptional man at twenty. On the average, after about thirty years of age, the elasticity of the body to rise to the strain of emergency diminishes, and, when forty years is reached, a man, medically speaking, reaches his acme. After that, degeneration of the fabric of the body slowly and maybe imperceptibly

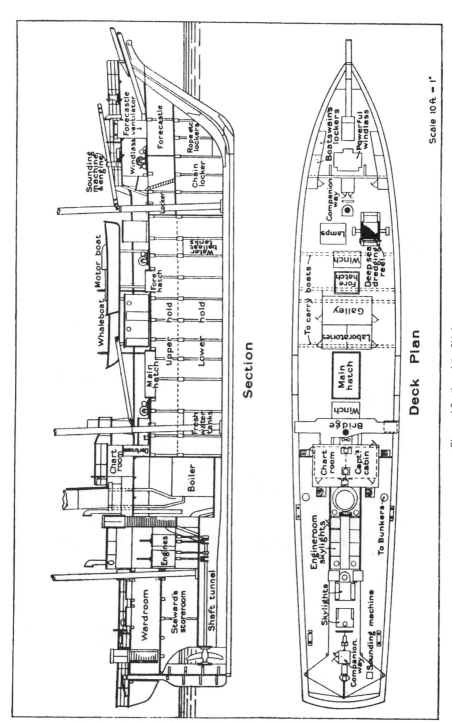

Section

Sounding machine & engine
Forecastle ventilator
Forecastle
Windlass engine
Rope etc lockers
Chain locker
Locker
Water ballast tanks
Whaleboat
Motor boat
Fore hatch
Main hatch
Upper hold
Lower hold
Fresh water tanks
Chart room
Darkroom
Boiler
Engines
Wardroom
Steward's storeroom
Shaft tunnel

Deck Plan

Boatswains lockers
Powerful windlass
Companion way
Lamps
To carry boats
Winch
Deep sea dredging reel
Fore hatch
Galley
Laboratories
Main hatch
Winch
Bridge
Chart room
Capt's cabin
To Bunkers
Engineroom skylights
Skylights
Sounding machine
Companion way

Scale 10 ft = 1"

Plan and Section of the SY *Aurora*

sets in. As the difficulties of exploration in cold regions approximate to the limit of human endurance and often enough exceed it, it is obvious that the above generalizations must receive due weight.

The *Aurora* Crossing the Equator, August 1911

But though age and with it the whole question of physical fitness must ever receive primary regard, yet these alone in no wise fit a man for such an undertaking. The qualifications of mental ability, acquaintance with the work and sound moral quality have to be essentially borne in mind. The man of fifty might then be placed on a higher plane than his younger companion.

With regard to alcohol and tobacco, it may be maintained on theoretical grounds that a man is better without them, but, on the other hand, his behaviour in respect to such habits is often an index to his self-control.

Perfection is attained when every man individually works with the determination to sacrifice all personal predispositions to the welfare of the whole.

Ours proved to be a very happy selection. The majority of the men chosen as members of the land parties were young graduates of the Commonwealth and New Zealand Universities, and almost all were representative of Australasia. Among the exceptions was Mr. Frank Wild, who was appointed leader of one of the Antarctic parties. Wild had distinguished himself in the South on two previous occasions, and now is in the unique position of being, as it were, the oldest resident of Antarctica. Our sojourn together at Cape Royds with Shackleton had acquainted me with Wild's high merits as an explorer and leader.

Lieutenant B. E. S. Ninnis of the Royal Fusiliers, Dr. X. Mertz, an expert ski-runner and mountaineer, and Mr. F. H. Bickerton in charge of the air-tractor sledge, were appointed in London. Reference has already been made to Captain Davis: to him were left all arrangements regarding the ship's complement.

A "Who's who" of the staff appears as an appendix.

Frank Wild

CHAPTER II

The Last Days at Hobart and the Voyage to Macquarie Island

"Let us probe the silent places, let us seek what luck betide us;
Let us journey to a lonely land I know.
There's a whisper on the night-wind, there's a star agleam to guide us.
And the Wild is calling, calling—Let us go."

—Service

IT WILL BE CONVENIENT TO PICK UP THE THREAD of our story upon the point of the arrival of the *Aurora* in Hobart, after her long voyage from London during the latter part of the year 1911.

Captain Davis had written from Cape Town stating that he expected to reach Hobart on November 4. In company with Mr. C. C. Eitel, secretary of the Expedition, I proceeded to Hobart, arriving on November 2.

Early in the morning of November 4 the Harbour Board received news that a wooden vessel, barquentine-rigged, with a crow's-nest on the mainmast, was steaming up the D'Entrecasteaux Channel. This left no doubt as to her identity and so, later in the day, we joined Mr. Martelli, the assistant harbour-master, and proceeded down the river, meeting the *Aurora* below the quarantine ground.

We heard that they had had a very rough passage after leaving the Cape. This was expected, for several liners, travelling by the same route, and arriving in Australian waters a few days before, had reported exceptionally heavy weather.

Before the ship had reached Queen's Wharf, the berth generously provided by the Harbour Board, the Greenland dogs were transferred to the quarantine ground, and with them went Dr. Mertz and Lieutenant

Ninnis, who gave up all their time during the stay in Hobart to the care of those important animals. A feeling of relief spread over the whole ship's company as the last dog passed over the side, for travelling with a deck cargo of dogs is not the most enviable thing from a sailor's point of view. Especially is this the case in a sailing-vessel where room is limited, and consequently dogs and ropes are mixed indiscriminately.

Evening was just coming on when we reached the wharf, and, as we ranged alongside, the Premier, Sir Elliot Lewis, came on board and bade us welcome to Tasmania.

Captain Davis had much to tell, for more than four months had elapsed since my departure from London, when he had been left in charge of the ship and of the final arrangements.

At the docks there had been delays and difficulties in the execution of the necessary alterations to the ship, in consequence of strikes and the Coronation festivities. It was so urgent to reach Australia in time for the ensuing Antarctic summer, that the recaulking of the decks and other improvements were postponed, to be executed on the voyage or upon arrival in Australia.

Captain Davis seized the earliest possible opportunity of departure, and the *Aurora* dropped down the Thames at midnight on July 27, 1911. As she threaded her way through the crowded traffic by the dim light of a thousand flickering flames gleaming through the foggy atmosphere, the dogs entered a protest peculiar to their "husky" kind. After a short preliminary excursion through a considerable range of the scale, they picked up a note apparently suitable to all and settled down to many hours of incessant and monotonous howling, as is the custom of these dogs when the fit takes them. It was quite evident that they were not looking forward to another sea voyage. The pandemonium made it all but impossible to hear the orders given for working the ship, and a collision was narrowly averted. During those rare lulls, when the dogs' repertoire temporarily gave out, innumerable sailors on neighbouring craft, wakened from their sleep, made the most of such opportunities to hurl imprecations in a thoroughly nautical fashion upon the ship, her officers, and each and every one of the crew.

On the way to Cardiff, where a full supply of coal was to be shipped, a gale was encountered, and much water came on board, resulting in damage to the stores. Some water leaked into the living quarters and, on the-whole, several very uncomfortable days were spent. Such inconvenience at the outset undoubtedly did good, for many of the crew, evidently not prepared for emergency conditions, left at Cardiff. The scratch crew with which the *Aurora* journeyed to Hobart composed for the most part of replacements made at Cardiff, resulted in some permanent appointments of unexpected value to the Expedition.

At Cardiff the coal strike caused delay, but eventually some five hundred tons of the Crown Fuel Company's briquettes were got on board, and a final leave taken of English shores on August 4.

Cape Town, the only intermediate port of call, was reached on September 24, after a comparatively rapid and uneventful voyage. A couple of days sufficed to load coal, water and fresh provisions, and the course was then laid for Hobart.

Rough weather soon intervened, and Lieutenant Ninnis and Dr. Mertz, who travelled out by the *Aurora* in charge of the sledging-dogs, had their time fully occupied, for the wet conditions began to tell on their charges.

On leaving London there were forty-nine of these Greenland, Esquimaux sledging-dogs of which the purchase and selection had been made through the offices of the Danish Geographical Society. From Greenland they were taken to Copenhagen, and from thence transhipped to London, where Messrs. Spratt took charge of them at their dog-farm until the date of departure. During the voyage they were fed on the finest dog-cakes, but they undoubtedly felt the need of fresh meat and fish to withstand the cold and wet. In the rough weather of the latter part of the voyage water broke continually over the deck, so lowering their vitality that a number died from seizures, not properly understood at the time. In each case death was sudden, and preceded by similar symptoms. An apparently healthy dog would drop down in a fit, dying in a few minutes, or during another fit within a few days. Epidemics, accompanied by similar symptoms, are said to be common amongst these dogs in the Arctic regions, but no explanation is given as to the nature of the disease. During a later stage of the Expedition, when nearing Antarctica, several more of the dogs were similarly stricken. These were examined by Drs. McLean and Jones, and the results of post-mortems showed that in one case death was due to gangrenous appendicitis, in two others to acute gastritis and colitis.

The dog first affected caused some consternation amongst the crew, for, after being prostrated on the deck by a fit, it rose and rushed about snapping to right and left. The cry of "mad dog" was raised. Not many seconds had elapsed before all the deck hands were safely in the rigging, displaying more than ordinary agility in the act. At short intervals, other men, roused from watch below appeared at the fo'c'sle companion-way. To these the situation at first appeared comic, and called forth jeers upon their faint-hearted shipmates. The next moment, on the dog dashing into view, they found a common cause with their fellows and sprang aloft. Ere

Ginger and Her Family on the Voyage from London

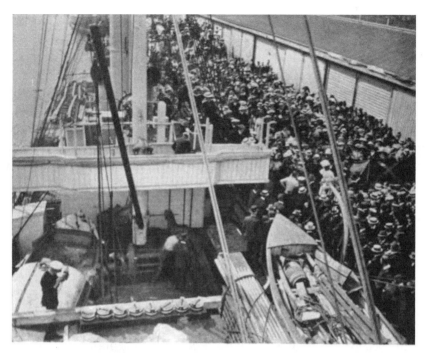

Queen's Wharf, Hobart, an Hour Before Sailing, December 2, 1911

The Last View of Hobart Nestling Below Mt. Wellington

many minutes had elapsed the entire crew were in the rigging, much to the amusement of the officers. By this time the dog had disappeared beneath the fo'c'sle head, and Mertz and Ninnis entered, intending to dispatch it. A shot was fired and word passed that the deed was done: thereupon the crew descended, pressing forward to share in the laurels. Then it was that Ninnis, in the uncertain light, spying a dog of similar markings wedged in between some barrels, was filled with doubt and called out to Mertz that he had shot the wrong dog. In a flash the crew had once more climbed to safety. It was some time after the confirmation of the first execution that they could be prevailed upon to descend.

Several litters of puppies were born on the voyage, but all except one succumbed to the hardships of the passage.

The voyage from Cardiff to Hobart occupied eighty-eight days.

The date of departure south was fixed for 4 PM on Saturday, December 2, and a truly appalling amount of work had to be done before then.

Most of the staff had been preparing themselves for special duties; in this the Expedition was assisted by many friends.

A complete, detailed acknowledgment of all the kind help received would occupy much space. We must needs pass on with the assurance that our best thanks are extended to one and all.

Throughout the month of November, the staff continued to arrive in contingents at Hobart, immediately busying themselves in their own departments, and in sorting over the many thousands of packages in the great Queen's Wharf shed. Wild was placed in charge, and all entered heartily into the work. The exertion of it was just what was wanted to make us fit, and prepared for the sudden and arduous work of discharging cargo at the various bases. It also gave the opportunity of personally gauging certain qualities of the men, which are not usually evoked by a university curriculum.

Some five thousand two hundred packages were in the shed, to be sorted over and checked. The requirements of three Antarctic bases, and one at Macquarie Island were being provided for, and consequently the most careful supervision was necessary to prevent mistakes, especially as the omission of a single article might fundamentally affect the work of a whole party. To assist in discriminating the impedimenta, coloured bands were painted round the packages, distinctive of the various bases.

It had been arranged that, wherever possible, everything should be packed in cases of a handy size, to facilitate unloading and transportation; each about fifty to seventy pounds in weight.

In addition to other distinguishing marks, every package bore a different number, and the detailed contents were listed in a schedule for reference.

Concurrently with the progress of this work, the ship was again overhauled, repairs effected, and many deficiencies made good. The labours of the shipwrights did not interfere with the loading, which went ahead steadily during the last fortnight in November.

The tanks in the hold not used for our supply of fresh water were packed with reserve stores for the ship. The remainder of the lower hold and the bunkers were filled with coal. Slowly the contents of the shed diminished as they were transferred to the 'tween decks. Then came the overflow. Eventually, every available space in the ship was flooded with a complicated assemblage of gear, ranging from the comparatively undamageable wireless masts occupying a portion of the deck amidships, to a selection of prime Australian cheeses which filled one of the cabins, and pervaded the ward-room with an odour which remained one of its permanent associations.

Yet, heterogeneous and ill-assorted as our cargo may have appeared to the crowds of curious onlookers, Captain Davis had arranged for the stowage of everything with a nicety which did him credit. The complete effects of the four bases were thus kept separate, and available in whatever order was required. Furthermore, the removal of one unit would not break the stowage of the remainder, nor disturb the trim of the ship.

At a late date the air-tractor sledge arrived. The body was contained in one huge case which, though awkward, was comparatively light, the case weighing much more than the contents. This was securely lashed above the maindeck, resting on the fo'c'sle and two boat-skids.

As erroneous ideas have been circulated regarding the "aeroplane sledge," or more correctly "air-tractor sledge," a few words in explanation will not be out of place.

This machine was originally an R.E.P. monoplane, constructed by Messrs. Vickers and Co., but supplied with a special detachable, sledge-runner undercarriage for use in the Antarctic, converting it into a tractor for hauling sledges. It was intended that so far as its role as a flier was concerned, it would be chiefly exercised for the purpose of drawing public attention to the Expedition in Australia, where aviation was then almost unknown. With this object in view, it arrived in Adelaide at an early date accompanied by the aviator, Lieutenant Watkins, assisted by Bickerton. There it unfortunately came to grief, and Watkins and Wild narrowly escaped death in the accident. It was then decided to make no attempt to fly in the Antarctic; the wings were left in Australia and Lieutenant Watkins returned to England. In the meantime, the machine was repaired and forwarded to Hobart.

Air-tractors are great consumers of petrol of the highest quality. This demand, in addition to the requirements of two wireless plants and a motor-launch, made it necessary to take larger quantities than we liked of this dangerous cargo. Four thousand gallons of "Shell" benzine and one thousand three hundred gallons of "Shell" kerosene, packed in the usual four-gallon export tins, were carried as a deck cargo, monopolizing the whole of the poop-deck.

For the transport of the requirements of the Macquarie Island Base, the SS *Toroa*, a small steam-packet of one hundred and twenty tons, trading between Melbourne and Tasmanian ports, was chartered. It was arranged that this auxiliary should leave Hobart several days after the *Aurora*, so as to allow us time, before her arrival, to inspect the island, and to select a suitable spot for the location of the base. As she was well provided with passenger accommodation, it was arranged that the majority of the land party should journey by her as far as Macquarie Island.

The Governor of Tasmania, Sir Harry Barron, the Premier, Sir Elliot Lewis, and the citizens of Hobart extended to us the greatest hospitality during our stay, and, when the time came, gave us a hearty send-off.

Saturday, December 2 arrived, and final preparations were made. All the staff were united for the space of an hour at luncheon. Then began the final leave-taking. "God speed" messages were received from far and wide, and intercessory services were held in the Cathedrals of Sydney and Hobart.

We were greatly honoured at this time by the reception of kind wishes from Queen Alexandra and, at an earlier date, from his Majesty the King.

Proud of such universal sympathy and interest, we felt stimulated to greater exertions.

On arrival on board, I found Mr. Martelli, who was to pilot us down the river, already on the bridge. A vast crowd blockaded the wharf to give us a parting cheer.

At 4 PM sharp, the telegraph was rung for the engines, and, with a final expression of good wishes from the Governor and Lady Barron, we glided out into the channel, where our supply of dynamite and cartridges was taken on board. Captain G. S. Nares, whose kindness we had previously known, had the HMS *Fantome* dressed in our honour, and lusty cheering reached us from across the water.

As we proceeded down the river to the Quarantine Station where the dogs were to be taken off, Hobart looked its best, with the glancing sails of pleasure craft skimming near the foreshores, and backed by the stately, sombre mass of Mount Wellington. The "land of strawberries and cream," as the younger members of the Expedition had come to regard it, was for ever to live pleasantly in our memories, to be recalled a thousand times during the adventurous months which followed. Mr. E. Joyce, whose name is familiar in connexion with previous Antarctic expeditions, and who had travelled out from London on business of the Expedition, was waiting in mid-stream with thirty-eight dogs, delivering them from a ketch. These were passed over the side and secured at intervals on top of the deck cargo.

The engines again began to throb, not to cease until the arrival at Macquarie Island. A few miles lower down the channel, the Premier, and a number of other friends and well-wishers who had followed in a small steamer, bade us a final adieu.

Behind lay a sparkling seascape and the Tasmanian littoral; before, the blue southern ocean heaving with an ominous swell. A glance at the barograph showed a continuous fall, and a telegram from Mr. Hunt, Head of the Commonwealth Weather Bureau, received a few hours previously, informed us of a storm-centre south of New Zealand, and the expectation of fresh south-westerly winds.

The piles of loose gear presented an indescribable scene of chaos, and, even as we rolled lazily in the increasing swell, the water commenced to run about the decks. There was no time to be lost in securing movable articles and preparing the ship for heavy weather. All hands set to work.

On the main deck the cargo was brought up flush with the top of the bulwarks, and consisted of the wireless masts, two huts, a large motor-launch, cases of dog biscuits and many other sundries. Butter to the extent of a couple of tons was accommodated chiefly on the roof of the main deck-house, where it was out of the way of the dogs. The roof of the chart-house, which formed an extension of the bridge proper, did not escape, for the railing offered facilities for lashing sledges; besides, there was room for tide-gauges, meteorological screens, and cases of fresh eggs and apples. Somebody happened to think of space unoccupied in the meteorological screens, and a few fowls were housed therein.

On the poop-deck there were the benzine, sledges, and the chief magnetic observatory. An agglomeration of instruments and private gear rendered the ward-room well nigh impossible of access, and it was some days before everything was jammed away into corners. An unoccupied five-berth cabin was filled with loose instruments, while other packages were stowed into the occupied cabins, so as to almost defeat the purpose for which they were intended.

The deck was so encumbered that only at rare intervals was it visible. However, by our united efforts everything was well secured by 8 PM.

It was dusk, and the distant highlands were limned in silhouette against the twilight sky. A tiny, sparkling lamp glimmered from Signal Hill its warm farewell. From the swaying poop we flashed back, "Good-bye, all snug on board."

Onward with a dogged plunge our laden ship would press. If *Fram* were "Forward," *she* was to be hereafter our *Aurora* of "Hope"—the Dawn of undiscovered lands.

Home and the past were effaced in the shroud of darkness, and thought leapt to the beckoning South—the "land of the midnight sun."

During the night the wind and sea rose steadily, developing into a full gale. In order to make Macquarie Island, it was important not to allow the ship

A Big, Following Sea

Mclean Walking Aft in Rough Weather

Cruising Along the West Coast of Macquarie Island

to drive too far to the east, as at all times the prevailing winds in this region are from the west. Partly on this account, and partly because of the extreme severity of the gale, the ship was hove to with head to wind, wallowing in mountainous seas. Such a storm, witnessed from a large vessel, would be an inspiring sight, but was doubly so in a small craft, especially where the natural buoyancy had been largely impaired by overloading. With an unprecedented quantity of deck cargo, amongst which were six thousand gallons of benzine, kerosene and spirit, in tins which were none too strong, we might well have been excused a lively anxiety during those days. It seemed as if no power on earth could save the loss of at least part of the deck cargo. Would it be the indispensable huts amidships, or would a sea break on the benzine aft and flood us with inflammable liquid and gas?

By dint of strenuous efforts and good seamanship, Captain Davis with his officers and crew held their own. The land parties assisted in the general work, constantly tightening up the lashings and lending "beef," a sailor's term for man-power, wherever required. For this purpose the members of the land parties were divided into watches, so that there were always a number patrolling the decks.

Most of us passed through a stage of sea-sickness, but, except in the case of two or three, it soon passed off. Seas deluged all parts of the ship. A quantity of ashes was carried down into the bilge-water pump and obstructed the steam-pump. Whilst this was being cleared, the emergency deck pumps had to be requisitioned. The latter were available for working either by hand-power or by chain-gearing from the after-winch.

The deck-plug of one of the fresh-water tanks was carried away and, before it was noticed, sea-water had entered to such an extent as to render our supply unfit for drinking. Thus we were, henceforth, on a strictly limited water ration.

The wind increased from bad to worse, and great seas continued to rise until their culmination on the morning of December 5, when one came aboard on the starboard quarter, smashed half the bridge and carried it away. Toucher was the officer on watch, and no doubt thought himself lucky in being, at the time, on the other half of the bridge.

The deck-rings holding the motor-launch drew, the launch itself was sprung and its decking stove-in.

On the morning of December 8 we found ourselves in latitude 49° 56' S. and longitude 152° 28' E., with the weather so far abated that we were able to steer a course for Macquarie Island.

During the heavy weather, food had been prepared only with the greatest difficulty. The galley was deluged time and again. It was enough to dishearten any cook, repeatedly finding himself amongst kitchen debris of all kinds, including pots and pans full and empty. Nor did the difficulties end in the galley, for food which survived until its arrival on the table, though not allowed much time for further mishap, often ended in a disagreeable mass on the floor or, tossed by a lurch of more than usual suddenness, entered an adjoining cabin. From such localities the elusive *pièce de rèsistance* was often rescued.

As we approached our rendezvous, whale-birds** appeared. During the heavy weather, Mother Carey's chickens only were seen, but, as the wind abated, the majestic wandering albatross, the sooty albatross and the mollymawk followed in our wake.

Whales were observed spouting, but at too great a distance to be definitely recognized.

At daybreak on December 11 land began to show up, and by 6 AM we were some sixteen miles off the west coast of Macquarie Island, bearing on about the centre of its length.

In general shape it is long and narrow, the length over all being twenty-one miles. A reef runs out for several miles at both extremities of the main island, reappearing again some miles beyond in isolated rocky islets: the Bishop and Clerk nineteen miles to the southward and the Judge and Clerk eight miles to the north.

The land everywhere rises abruptly from the sea or from an exaggerated beach to an undulating plateau-like interior, reaching a maximum elevation of one thousand four hundred and twenty-five feet. Nowhere is there a harbour in the proper sense of the word, though six or seven anchorages are recognized.

The island is situated in about 55° S. latitude, and the climate is comparatively cold, but it is the prevalence of strong winds that is the least desirable feature of its weather.

Sealing, so prosperous in the early days, is now carried on in a small way only, by a New Zealander, who keeps a few men stationed at the island during part of the year for the purpose of rendering down sea elephant and penguin blubber. Their establishment was known to be at the north end of the island near the best of the anchorages.

Captain Davis had visited the island in the *Nimrod*, and was acquainted with the three anchorages, which are all on the east side and sheltered from the prevailing westerlies. One of the old-time sealers had reported a cove suitable for small craft at the south-western corner, but the information

---

** *For the specific names refer to Appendix which is a glossary of special and unfamiliar terms.*

was scanty, and recent mariners had avoided that side of the island. On the morning of our approach the breeze was from the south-east, and, being favourable, Captain Davis proposed a visit.

By noon, Caroline Cove, as it is called, was abreast of us. Its small dimensions, and the fact that a rocky islet for the most part blocks the entrance, at first caused some misgivings as to its identity.

A boat was lowered, and a party of us rowed in towards the entrance, sounding at intervals to ascertain whether the *Aurora* could make use of it, should our inspection prove it a suitable locality for the land station.

We passed through a channel not more than eighty yards wide, but with deep water almost to the rocks on either side. A beautiful inlet now opened to view. Thick tussock-grass matted the steep hillsides, and the rocky shores, between the tide-marks as well as in the depths below, sprouted with a profuse growth of brown kelp. Leaping out of the water in scores around us were penguins of several varieties, in their actions reminding us of nothing so much as shoals of fish chased by sharks. Penguins were in thousands on the uprising cliffs, and from rookeries near and far came an incessant din. At intervals along the shore sea elephants disported their ungainly masses in the sunlight. Circling above us in anxious haste, sea-birds of many varieties gave warning of our near approach to their nests. It was the invasion by man of an exquisite scene of primitive nature.

After the severe weather experienced, the relaxation made us all feel like a band of schoolboys out on a long vacation.

A small sandy beach barred the inlet, and the whaleboat was directed towards it. We were soon grating on the sand amidst an army of Royal penguins; picturesque little fellows, with a crest and eyebrows of long golden-yellow feathers. A few yards from the massed ranks of the penguins was a mottled sea-leopard, which woke up and slid into the sea as we approached.

Several hours were spent examining the neighbourhood. Webb and Kennedy took a set of magnetic observations, while others hoisted some cases of stores on to a rocky knob to form a provision depot, as it was quickly decided that the northern end of the island was likely to be more suitable for a permanent station.

The Royal penguins were almost as petulant as the Adelie penguins which we were to meet further South. They surrounded us, pecked at our legs and chattered with an audacity which defies description. It was discovered that they resented any attempt to drive them into the sea, and it was only after long persuasion that a bevy took to the water. This was a sign of a general capitulation, and some hundreds immediately followed, jostling each other in their haste, squawking, whirring their flippers, splashing and churning the water, reminding one of a crowd of miniature surf-bathers. We followed the files of birds marching inland, along the course of a tumbling stream, until at an elevation of some five hundred feet, on a flattish piece of ground, a huge rookery opened out—acres and acres of birds and eggs.

In one corner of the bay were nests of giant petrels in which sat huge downy young, about the size of a barn-door fowl, resembling the grotesque, fluffy toys which might be expected to hang on a Christmas-tree.

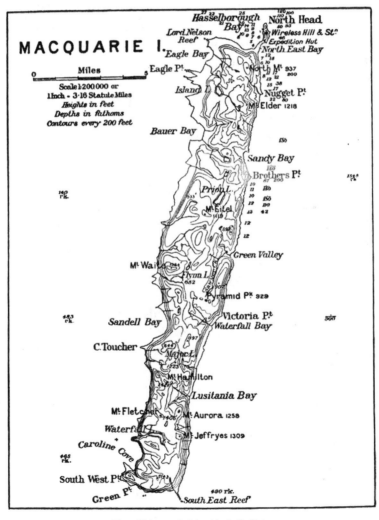

Map of Macquarie Island by L. R. Blake

Here and there on the beach and on the grass wandered bright-coloured Maori hens. On the south side of the bay, in a low, peaty area overgrown with tussock-grass, were scores of sea elephants, wallowing in bog-holes or sleeping at their ease.

Sea elephants, at one time found in immense numbers on all sub-antarctic islands, are now comparatively rare, even to the degree of extinction, in many of their old haunts. This is the result of ruthless slaughter prosecuted especially by sealers in the early days. At the present time Macquarie Island is more favoured by them than probably any other known locality. The name by which they are popularly known refers to their elephantine proportions and to the fact that, in the case of the old males, the nasal regions are enormously developed, expanding when in a state of excitement to form a short, trunk-like appendage. They have been recorded up to twenty feet in length, and such a specimen would weigh about four tons.

Arriving on the *Aurora* in the evening, we learnt that the ship's company had had an adventure which might have been most serious. It appeared that after dropping us at the entrance to Caroline Cove, the ship was allowed to drift out to sea under the influence of the off-shore wind. When about one-third of a mile north-west of the entrance, a violent shock was felt, and she slid over a rock which rose up out of deep water to within about fourteen feet of high-water level; no sign of it appearing on the surface on account of the tranquil state of the sea. Much apprehension was felt for the hull, but as no serious leak started, the escape was considered a fortunate one. A few soundings had been made proving a depth of four hundred fathoms within one and a half miles of the land.

A course was now set for the northern end of the island. Dangerous-looking reefs ran out from many headlands, and cascades of water could be seen falling hundreds of feet from the highlands to the narrow coastal flats.

The anchorage most used is that known as North-East Bay, lying on the eastern side of a low spit joining the main mass of the island, to an almost isolated outpost in the form of a flat-topped hill—Wireless Hill—some three-quarters of a mile farther north. It is practically an open roadstead, but, as the prevailing winds blow on to the other side of the island, quiet water can be nearly always expected.

However, when we arrived at North-East Bay on the morning following our adventure; a stiff south-east breeze was blowing, and the wash on the beach put landing out of the question. Captain Davis ran in as near the coast as he could safely venture and dropped anchor, pending the moderation of the wind.

A Giant Petrel on the Nest

A Young Giant Petrel on the Nest. Caroline Cove

The Wreck of the *Clyde*

On the leeward slopes of a low ridge, pushing itself out on to the southern extremity of the spit, could be seen two small huts, but no sign of human life. This was not surprising as it was only seven o'clock. Below the huts, upon low surf-covered rocks running out from the beach, lay a small schooner partly broken up and evidently a recent victim. A mile to the southward, fragments of another wreck protruded from the sand.

We were discussing wrecks and the grisly toll which is levied by these dangerous and uncharted shores, when a human figure appeared in front of one of the huts. After surveying us for a moment, he disappeared within to reappear shortly afterwards, followed by a stream of others rushing hither and thither; just as if he had disturbed a hornets' nest. After such an exciting demonstration we awaited the next move with some expectancy.

Planks and barrels were brought on to the beach and a flagstaff was hoisted. Then one of the party mounted on the barrel, and told us by flag signals that the ship on the beach was the *Clyde*, which had recently been wrecked, and that all hands were safely on shore, but requiring assistance. Besides the shipwrecked crew, there were half a dozen men who resided on the island during the summer months for the purpose of collecting blubber.

The sealers tried repeatedly to come out to us, but as often as it was launched their boat was washed up again on the beach, capsizing them into the water. At length they signalled that a landing could be made on the opposite side of the spit, so the anchor was raised and the ship steamed round the north end of the island, to what Captain Davis proposed should be named Hasselborough Bay, in recognition of the discoverer of the island. This proved an admirable anchorage, for the wind remained from the east and south-east during the greater part of our stay.

The sealers pushed their boat across the spit, and, launching it in calmer water, came out to us, meeting the *Aurora* some three miles off the land. The anchor was let go about one mile and a half from the head of the bay.

News was exchanged with the sealers. It appeared that there had been much speculation as to what sort of a craft we were; visits of ships, other than those sent down specially to convey their oil to New Zealand, being practically unknown. For a while they suspected the *Aurora* of being an alien sealer, and had prepared to defend their rights to the local fishery.

All was well now, however, and information and assistance were freely volunteered. They were greatly relieved to hear that our auxiliary vessel, the *Toroa* was expected immediately, and would be available for taking the ship-wrecked crew back to civilization.

Owing to the loss of the *Clyde*, a large shipment of oil in barrels lay piled upon the beach with every prospect of destruction, just at a time when the realization of its value would be most desirable, to make good the loss sustained by the wreck. I decided, therefore, in view of their hospitality, to make arrangements with the captain of the *Toroa* to take back a load of the oil, upon terms only sufficient to recoup us for the extension of the charter.

In company with Ainsworth, Hannam and others, I went ashore to select a site for the station. As strong westerly winds were to be expected during the greater part of the year, it was necessary to erect buildings in the lee of substantial break-winds. Several sites for a hut convenient to a serviceable landing-place were inspected at the north end of the beach. The hut was eventually erected in the lee of a large mass of rock, rising out of the grass-covered sandy flat at the north end of the spit.

It would have been much handier in every way, both in assembling the engines and masts and subsequently in operating the wireless station, had the wireless plant been erected on the beach adjacent to the living-hut. On the other hand, a position on top of the hill had the advantage of a free outlook and of increased electrical potential, allowing of a shorter length of mast. In addition the ground in this situation proved to be peaty and sodden, and therefore a good conductor, thus presenting an excellent "earth" from the wireless standpoint. In short, the advantages of the hill-site outweighed its disadvantages. Of the latter the most obvious was the difficult transportation of the heavy masts, petrol-engine, dynamo, induction-generator and other miscellaneous gear, from the beach to the summit—a vertical height of three hundred feet.

To facilitate this latter work the sealers placed at our disposal a "flying fox" which ran from sea level to the top of Wireless Hill, and which they had erected for the carriage of blubber. On inspecting it, Wild reported that it was serviceable, but would first require to be strengthened. He immediately set about effecting this with the help of a party.

Hurley now discovered that he had accidentally left one of his cinematograph lenses on a rock where he had been working in Caroline Cove. As it was indispensable, and there was little prospect of the weather allowing of another visit by the ship, it was decided that he should go on a journey overland to recover it. One of the sealers, Hutchinson by name, who had been to Caroline Cove and knew the best route to take, kindly volunteered to accompany Hurley. The party was eventually increased by the addition of Harrisson, who was to keep a look-out for matters of biological interest. They started off at noon on December 13.

Although the greater part of the stores for the Macquarie Island party were to arrive by the *Toroa* there were a few tons on board the *Aurora*. These and the dogs were landed as quickly as possible. How glad the poor animals were to be once more on solid earth! It was out of the question to let them loose, so they were tethered at intervals along a heavy cable, anchored at both ends amongst the tussock-grass. Ninnis took up his abode in the sealers' hut so that he might the better look after their wants, which centred chiefly on sea elephant meat, and that in large quantities. Webb joined Ninnis, as he intended to take full sets of magnetic observations at several stations in the vicinity.

Bickerton and Gillies got the motor-launch into good working order, and by means of it the rest of us conveyed ashore several tons of coal briquettes, the benzine, kerosene, instruments and the wireless masts, by noon on December 13.

Everything but the requirements of the wireless station was landed on the spit, as near the north-east corner as the surf would allow. Fortunately, reefs ran out from the shore at intervals, and calmer water could be found in their lee. All gear for the wireless station was taken to a spot about half a mile to the north-west at the foot of Wireless Hill, where the "flying fox" was situated. Just at that spot there was a landing-place at the head of a charming little boat harbour, formed by numerous kelp-covered rocky reefs rising at intervals above the level of high water. These broke the swell, so that in most weathers calm water was assured at the landing-place.

This boat harbour was a fascinating spot. The western side was peopled by a rookery of blue-eyed cormorants; scattered nests of white gulls relieved the sombre appearance of the reefs on the opposite side: whilst Gentoo penguins in numbers were busy hatching their eggs on the sloping ground beyond. Skua-gulls and giant petrels were perched here and there amongst the rocks, watching for an opportunity of marauding the nests of the non-predacious birds. Sea elephants raised their massive, dripping heads in shoal and channel. The dark reefs, running out into the pellucid water, supported a vast growth of a snake-like form of kelp, whose octopus-like tentacles, many yards in length, writhed yellow and brown to the swing of the surge, and gave the foreground an indescribable weirdness. I stood looking out to sea from here one evening, soon after sunset, the launch lazily rolling in the swell, and the *Aurora* in the offing, while the rich tints of the afterglow paled in the south-west.

I envied Wild and his party, whose occupation in connexion with the "flying fox" kept them permanently camped at this spot.

The *Toroa* made her appearance on the afternoon of December 13, and came to anchor about half a mile inside the *Aurora*. Her departure had been delayed by the bad weather. Leaving Hobart late on December 7, she had anchored off Bruni Island awaiting the moderation of the sea. The journey was resumed on the morning of the 9th, and the passage made in fine weather. She proved a handy craft for work of the kind, and Captain Holliman, the master, was well used to the dangers of uncharted coastal waters.

Within a few minutes of her arrival, a five-ton motor-boat of shallow draught was launched and unloading commenced.

Those of the staff arriving by the *Toroa* were housed ashore with the sealers, as, when everybody was on board, the *Aurora* was uncomfortably congested. Fifty sheep were taken on shore to feed on the rank grass until our departure. A large part of the cargo consisted of coal for the *Aurora*. This was already partly bagged, and in that form was loaded into the launches and whale-boats; the former towing the latter to their destination. Thus a continuous stream of coal and stores was passing from ship to ship, and from the ships to the several landing-places on shore. As soon as the after-hold on the *Toroa* was cleared, barrels of sea elephant oil were brought off in rafts and loaded aft, simultaneously with the unloading forward.

We kept at the work as long as possible—about sixteen hours a day including a short interval for lunch. There were twenty-five of the land party available for general work, and with some assistance from the ship's crew the work went forward at a rapid rate.

On the morning of the 15th, after giving final instructions to Eitel, who had come thus far and was returning as arranged, the *Toroa* weighed anchor and we parted with a cheer.

The transportation of the wireless equipment to the top of the hill had been going on simultaneously with the un-loading of the ships. Now, however, all were able to concentrate upon it, and the work went forward very rapidly.

All the wireless instruments, and much of the other paraphernalia of the Macquarie Island party had been packed in the barrels, as it was expected that they would have to be rafted ashore through the surf. Fortunately, the weather continued to "hold" from an easterly direction, and everything was able to be landed in the comparatively calm waters of Hasselborough Bay; a circumstance which the islanders assured us was quite a rare thing. The wireless masts were rafted ashore. These were of oregon pine, each composed of four sections.

Digging the pits for bedding the heavy, wooden "dead men," and erecting the wireless masts, the engine-hut and the operating-hut provided plenty of work for all. Here was as busy a scene as one could witness anywhere—some with the picks and shovels, others with hammers and nails, sailors splicing ropes and fitting masts, and a stream of men hauling the loads up from the sea-shore to their destination on the summit.

Some details of the working of the "flying fox" will be of interest. The distance between the lower and upper terminals was some eight hundred feet. This was spanned by two steel-wire carrying cables, secured above by "dead men" sunk in the soil, and below by a turn around a huge rock which outcropped amongst the tussock-grass on the flat, some fifty yards from the head of the boat harbour. For hauling up the loads, a thin wire line, with a pulley-block at either extremity, rolling one on each of the carrying wires, passed round a snatch-block at the upper station. It was of such a length that when the loading end was at the lower station, the counterpoise end was in position to descend at the other. Thus a freight was dispatched to the top of the hill by filling a bag, acting as counterpoise, with earth, until slightly in excess of the weight of the top load; then off it would start gathering speed as it went.

Several devices were developed for arresting the pace as the freight neared the end of its journey, but accidents were always liable to occur if the counterpoise were unduly loaded. Wild was injured by one of these brake-devices, which consisted of a bar of iron lying on the ground about thirty yards in front of the terminus, and attached by a rope with a loose-running noose to the down-carrying wire. On the arrival of the counterpoise at that point on the wire, its speed would be checked owing to the drag exerted. On the occasion referred to, the rope was struck with such velocity that the iron bar was jerked into the air and struck Wild a solid blow on the thigh. Though incapacitated for a few days, he continued to supervise at the lower terminal.

The larger sections of the wireless masts gave the greatest trouble, as they were not only heavy but awkward. A special arrangement was necessary for all loads exceeding one hundredweight, as the single wire carrier-cables were not sufficiently strong. In such cases both carrier-cables were lashed together making a single support, the hauling being done by a straight pull on the top of the hill. The hauling was carried out to the accompaniment of chanties, and these helped to relieve the strain of the Work. It was a familiar sight to see a string of twenty men on the hauling-line scaring the skua-gulls with popular choruses like "A' roving" and "Ho, boys, pull her along." In calm weather the parties at either terminal could communicate by shouting but were much assisted by megaphones improvised from a pair of leggings.

Considering the heavy weights handled and the speed at which the work was done, we were fortunate in suffering only one breakage, and that might have been more serious than it proved. The mishap in question occurred to the generator. In order to lighten the load, the rotor had been taken out.

The Boat Harbour—Hassleborough Bay

The North End of Macquarie Island Showing Wireless Hill. The Living-Hut Is at the North End of the Isthmus, with North-East Bay on the Right and Hassleborough Bay on the Left Side.

When almost at the summit of the hill, the ascending weight, causing the carrying-wires to sag unusually low, struck a rock, unhitched the lashing and fell, striking the steep rubble slope, to go bounding in great leaps out amongst the grass to the flat below. Marvellous to relate, it was found to have suffered no damage other than a double fracture of the end-plate casting, which could be repaired. And so it was decided to exchange the generators in the two equipments, as there would be greater facilities for engineering work at the Main Base, Adelie Land. Fortunately, the other generator was almost at the top of the ship's hold, and therefore accessible. The three pieces into which the casting had been broken were found to be sprung, and would not fit together. However, after our arrival at Adelie Land, Hannam found, curiously enough, that the pieces fitted into place perfectly—apparently an effect of contraction due to the cold—and with the aid of a few plates and belts the generator was made as serviceable as ever.

In the meantime, Hurley, Harrisson, and the sealer, Hutchinson, had returned from their trip to Caroline Cove, after a most interesting though arduous journey. They had camped the first evening at The Nuggets, a rocky point on the east coast some four miles to the south of North-East Bay. From The Nuggets, the trail struck inland up the steep hillsides until the summit of the island was reached; then over pebble-strewn, undulating ground with occasional small lakes, arriving at the west coast near its southern extremity. Owing to rain and fog they overshot the mark and had to spend the night close to a bay at the south-end. There Hurley obtained some good photographs of sea elephants and of the penguin rookeries.

The next morning, December 15, they set off again, this time finding Caroline Cove without further difficulty. Harrisson remained on the brow of the hill overlooking the cove, and there captured some prions and their eggs. Hurley and his companion found the lost lens and returned to Harrisson securing a fine albatross on the way. This solitary bird was descried sitting on the hill side, several hundreds of feet above sea-level. Its plumage was in such good condition that they could not resist the impulse to secure it for our collection, for the moment not considering the enormous weight to be carried. They had neither firearms nor an Ancient Mariner's cross-bow, and no stones were to be had in the vicinity—when the resourceful Hurley suddenly bethought himself of a small tin of meat in his haversack, and, with a fortunate throw, hit the bird on the head, killing the majestic creature on the spot.

Shouldering their prize, they trudged on to Lusitania Bay, camping there that night in an old dilapidated hut; a remnant of the sealing days. Close by there was known to be a large rookery of King penguins; a variety of penguin with richly tinted plumage on the head and shoulders, and next in size to the Emperor—the sovereign bird of the Antarctic Regions. The breeding season was at its height, so Harrisson secured and preserved a great number of their eggs. Hutchinson kindly volunteered to carry the albatross in addition to his original load. If they had skinned the bird, the weight would have been materially reduced, but with the meagre appliances at hand, it would undoubtedly have been spoiled as a specimen. Hurley, very ambitiously, had taken a heavy camera, in addition to a blanket and other sundries. During the rough and wet walking of the previous day, his boots had worn out and caused him to twist a tendon in the right foot, so that he was not up to his usual form, while Harrisson was hampered with a bulky cargo of eggs and specimens.

Saddled with these heavy burdens, the party found the return journey very laborious. Hurley's leg set the pace, and so, later in the day, Harrisson decided to push on ahead in order to give us news, as they had orders to be back as soon as possible and were then overdue. When darkness came on, Harrisson was near The Nuggets, where he passed the night amongst the tussock-grass. Hurley and Hutchinson, who were five miles behind, also slept by the wayside. When dawn appeared, Harrisson moved on, reaching the north-end huts at about 9 AM. Mertz and Whetter immediately set out and came to the relief of the other two men a few hours later.

Fatigue and the lame leg subdued Hurley for the rest of the day, but the next morning he was off to get pictures of the "flying fox" in action. It was practically impossible for him to walk to the top of the hill, but not to be baffled, he sent the cinematograph machine up by the "flying fox," and then followed himself. Long before reaching the top he realized how much his integrity depended on the strength of the hauling-line and the care of those on Wireless Hill.

During the latter part of our stay at the island, the wind veered to the north and north-north-east. We took advantage of this change to steam round to the east side, intending to increase our supply of fresh water at The Nuggets, where a stream comes down the hillside on to the beach. In this, however, we were disappointed, for the sea was breaking too heavily on the beach, and so we steamed back to North-East Bay and dropped anchor. Wild went off in the launch to search for a landing-place but found the sea everywhere too formidable.

Signals were made to those on shore, instructing them to finish off the work on the wireless plant, and to kill a dozen sheep—enough for our needs for some days.

The ship was now found to be drifting, and, as the wind was blowing inshore, the anchor was raised, and with the launch in tow we steamed round to the calmer waters of Hasselborough Bay. At the north end of the island, for several miles out to sea along the line of a submerged reef, the northerly swell was found to be piling up in an ugly manner, and occasioned considerable damage to the launch. This happened as the *Aurora* swung around; a sea catching the launch and rushing it forward so that it struck the stern of the ship bow-on, notwithstanding the fact that several of the men exerted themselves to their utmost to prevent a collision. On arrival at the anchorage, the launch was noticeably settling down, as water had entered at several seams which had been started.

After being partly bailed out, it was left in the water with Hodgeman and Close aboard, as we wished to run ashore as soon as the weather improved. Contrary to expectation the wind increased, and it was discovered that the *Aurora* was drifting rapidly, although ninety fathoms of chain had been paid out. Before a steam-winch** was installed, the anchor could be raised only by means of an antiquated man-power lever-windlass. In this type, a see-saw-like lever is worked by a gang of men at each extremity, and it takes a long time to get in any considerable length of chain. The chorus and chanty came to our aid once more, and the long hours of heaving on the fo'c'sle head were a bright if strenuous spot in our memories of Macquarie Island. In course of time, during which the ship steamed slowly ahead, the end came in sight—'Vast heaving!—but the anchor was missing. This put us in an awkward situation, for the stock of our other heavy anchor had already been lost. There was no other course but to steam up and down waiting for the weather to moderate. In the meantime, we had been too busy to relieve Close and Hodgeman, who had been doing duty in the launch, bailing for five hours, and were thoroughly soaked with spray. All hands now helped with the tackle, and we soon had the launch on board in its old position near the main hatch.

These operations were unusually protracted for we were short handed; the boatswain, some of the sailors and most of the land party being marooned on shore. We were now anxious to get everybody on board and to be off. The completion of their quarters was to be left to the Macquarie Island party, and it was important that we should make the most of the southern season. The wind blew so strongly, however, that there was no immediate prospect of departure.

The ship continued to steam up and down. On the morning of December 23 it was found possible to lower the whale-boat, and Wild went off with a complement of sturdy oarsmen, including Madigan,

---

** *Fitted on return to Sydney after the first Antarctic cruise.*

Moyes, Watson and Kennedy, and succeeded in bringing off the dogs. Several trips were made with difficulty during the day, but at last all the men, dogs and sheep were brought off.

Both Wild and I went with the whale-boat on its last trip at dusk on the evening of December 23. The only possible landing-place, with the sea then running, was at the extreme north-eastern corner of the beach. No time was lost in getting the men and the remainder of the cargo into the boat, though in the darkness this was not easily managed. The final parting with our Macquarie Island party took place on the beach, their cheers echoing to ours as we breasted the surf and "gave way" for the ship.

The *Aurora* Anchored in Hassleborough Bay. In the Foreground Giant Seaweed Is Swinging in the Wash of the Surge.

A Wanderer Albatross at Rest on the Water

Hunter Tickles a Sleeping Baby Sea Elephant

CHAPTER III

From Macquarie Island to Adelie Land

T HE MORNING FOLLOWING OUR FAREWELL TO
Ainsworth and party at the north end of the island found us
steaming down the west coast, southward bound.

Our supply of fresh water was scanty, and the only resource was to
touch at Caroline Cove. As a matter of fact, there were several suitable
localities on the east coast, but the strong easterly weather then prevailing
made a landing impossible.

On the ship nearing the south end, the wind subsided. She then crept
into the lee of the cliffs, a boat was dropped and soundings disclosed a deep
passage at the mouth of Caroline Cove and ample water within. There was,
however, limited space for manoeuvring the vessel if a change should occur
in the direction of the wind. The risk was taken; the *Aurora* felt her way
in, and, to provide against accident, was anchored by Captain Davis with
her bow toward the entrance. Wild then ran out a kedge anchor to secure
the stern.

During the cruise down the coast the missing stock of our only anchor
had been replaced by Gillies and Hannam. Two oregon "dead men," bolted
together on the shank, made a clumsy but efficient makeshift.

Two large barrels were taken ashore, repeatedly filled and towed off to
the ship. It was difficult at first to find good water, for the main stream
flowing down from the head of the bay was contaminated by the penguins
which made it their highway to a rookery. After a search, an almost dry
gulley bed was found to yield water when a pit was dug in its bed. This spot
was some eighty yards from the beach and to reach it one traversed an area
of tussocks between which sea elephants wallowed in soft mire.

A cordon of men was made and buckets were interchanged, the full
ones descending and the empty ones ascending. The barrels on the beach

were thus speedily filled and taken off by a boat's crew. At 11 PM darkness came, and it was decided to complete the work on the following day.

As we rowed to the ship, the water was serenely placid. From the dark environing hills came the weird cries of strange birds. There was a hint of wildness, soon to be forgotten in the chorus of a Varsity song and the hearty shouts of the rowers.

About 2 AM the officer on watch came down to report to Captain Davis a slight change in the direction of the breeze. At 3 AM I was again awakened by hearing Captain Davis hasten on deck, and by a gentle bumping of the ship, undoubtedly against rock. It appeared that the officer on watch had left the bridge for a few minutes, while the wind freshened and was blowing at the time nearly broadside-on from the north. This caused the ship to sag to leeward, stretching the bow and stern cables, until she came in contact with the kelp-covered, steep, rocky bank on the south side. The narrow limits of the anchorage were responsible for this dangerous situation.

All hands were immediately called on deck and set to work hauling on the stern cable. In a few minutes the propeller and rudder were out of danger. The engines were then started slowly ahead, and, as we came up to the bower anchor, the cable was taken in. The wind was blowing across the narrow entrance to the Cove, so that it was advisable to get quickly under way. The kedge anchor was abandoned, and we steamed straight out to sea with the bower hanging below the bows. The wind increased, and there was no other course open but to continue the southward voyage.

The day so inauspiciously begun turned out beautifully sunny. There was additional verve in our Christmas celebration, as Macquarie Island and the Bishop and Clerk, in turn, sank below the northern horizon.

During the stay at the island little attention had been given to scientific matters. All our energies had been concentrated on speedily landing the party which was to carry out such special work, so as to allow us to get away south as soon as possible. Enough had been seen to indicate the wide scientific possibilities of the place.

For some days we were favoured by exceptional weather; a moderate breeze from the north-east and a long, lazy swell combining to make our progress rapid.

The sum of the experiences of earlier expeditions had shown that the prevailing winds south of 60° S. latitude were mainly south-easterly, causing a continuous streaming of the pack from east to west. Our obvious expedient on encountering the ice was to steam in the same direction as this drift. It had been decided before setting out that we would confine ourselves to the region west of the meridian of 158° E. longitude. So it was intended to reach the pack, approximately in that meridian, and, should we be repulsed, to work steadily to the west in expectation of breaking through to the land.

Regarding the ice conditions over the whole segment of the unknown tract upon which our attack was directed, very little was known. Critically examined, the reports of the American squadron under the command of Wilkes were highly discouraging. D'Urville appeared to have reached his landfall without much hindrance by ice, but that was a fortunate circumstance in view of the difficulties Wilkes had met. At the western limit of the area we were to explore, the Germans in the *Gauss* had been irrevocably trapped in the ice as early as the month of February. At the eastern limit, only the year before, the *Terra Nova* of Scott's expedition, making a sally into unexplored waters, had sighted new land almost on the 158th meridian, but even though it was then the end of summer, and the sea was almost free from the previous season's ice, they were not able to reach the land on account of the dense pack.

In the early southern summer, at the time of our arrival, the ice conditions were expected to be at their worst. This followed from the fact that not only would local floes be encountered, but also a vast expanse of pack fed by the disintegrating floes of the Ross Sea, since, between Cape Adare and the Balleny Islands, the ice drifting to the north-west under the influence of the south-east winds is arrested in an extensive sheet. On the other hand, were we to wait for the later season, no time would remain for the accomplishment of the programme which had been arranged. So we were forced to accept things as we found them, being also prepared to make the most of any chance opportunity.

In planning the Expedition, the probability of meeting unusually heavy pack had been borne in mind, and the three units into which the land parties and equipment were divided had been disposed so as to facilitate the landing of a base with despatch, and, maybe, under difficult circumstances. Further, in case the ship were frozen in, "wireless" could be installed and the news immediately communicated through Macquarie Island to Australia.

At noon on December 27 whales were spouting all round us, and appeared to be travelling from west to east. Albatrosses of several species constantly hovered about, and swallow-like Wilson petrels—those nervous rangers of the high seas—would sail along the troughs and flit over the crests of the waves, to vanish into sombre distance.

Already we were steaming through untravelled waters, and new discoveries might be expected at any moment. A keen interest spread throughout the ship. On several occasions, fantastic clouds on the horizon gave hope of

land, only to be abandoned on further advance. On December 28 and 29 large masses of floating kelp were seen, and, like the flotsam met with by Columbus, still further raised our hopes.

The possibility of undiscovered islands existing in the Southern Ocean, south of Australia and outside the ice-bound region, kept us vigilant. So few ships had ever navigated the waters south of latitude 55°, that some one and a quarter million square miles lay open to exploration. As an instance of such a discovery in the seas south of New Zealand may be mentioned Scott Island, first observed by the *Morning*, one of the relief ships of the British Expedition of 1902.

The weather remained favourable for sounding and other oceanographical work, but as it was uncertain how long these conditions would last, and in view of the anxiety arising from overloaded decks and the probability of gales which are chronic in these latitudes, it was resolved to land one of the bases as soon as possible, and thus rid the ship of superfluous cargo. The interesting but time-absorbing study of the ocean-depths was therefore postponed for a while.

With regard to the Antarctic land to be expected ahead, many of Wilkes's landfalls, where they had been investigated by later expeditions, had been disproved. It seemed as if he had regarded the northern margin of the solid floe and shelf-ice as land; perhaps also mistaking bergs, frozen in the floe and distorted by mirage, for ice-covered land. Nevertheless, his soundings, and the light thrown upon the subject by the Scott and Shackleton expeditions, left no doubt in my mind that land would be found within a reasonable distance south of the position assigned by Wilkes. Some authorities had held that any land existing in this region would be found to be of the nature of isolated islands. Those familiar with the adjacent land, however, were all in favour of it being continental—a continuation of the Victoria Land plateau. The land lay to the south beyond doubt; the problem was to reach it through the belt of ice-bound sea. Still, navigable pack-ice might be ahead, obviating the need of driving too far to the west.

"Ice on the starboard bow!" At 4 PM on December 29 the cry was raised, and shortly after we passed alongside a small caverned berg whose bluish-green tints called forth general admiration. In the distance others could be seen. One larger than the average stood almost in our path. It was of the flat-topped, sheer-walled type, so characteristic of the Antarctic regions; three-quarters of a mile long and half a mile wide, rising eighty feet above the sea.

A Weather-Worn Snow-Berg

A Grottoed Iceberg

It has been stated that tabular bergs are typical of the Antarctic as opposed to the Arctic. This diversity is explained by a difference in the glacial conditions. In the north, glaciation is not so marked and, as a rule, coastal areas are free from ice, except for valley-glaciers which transport ice from the high interior down to sea-level. There, the summer temperature is so warm that the lower parts of the glaciers become much decayed, and, reaching the sea, break up readily into numerous irregular, pinnacled bergs of clear ice. In the south, the tabular forms result from the fact that the average annual temperature is colder than that prevailing at the northern axis of the earth. They are so formed because, even at sea-level, no appreciable amount of thawing takes place in midsummer. The inland ice pushes out to sea in enormous masses, and remains floating long before it "calves" to form bergs. Even though its surface has been thrown into ridges as it was creeping over the uneven land, all are reduced to a dead level or slightly undulating plain, in the free-floating condition, and are still further effaced by dense drifts and repeated falls of snow descending upon them. The upper portion of a table-topped berg consists, therefore, of consolidated snow; neither temperature nor pressure having been sufficient to metamorphose it into clear ice. Such a berg in old age becomes worn into an irregular shape by the action of waves and weather, and often completely capsizes, exposing its corroded basement.

A light fog obscured the surrounding sea and distant bergs glided by like spectres. A monstrous block on the starboard side had not been long adrift, for it showed but slight signs of weathering.

The fog thickened over a grey swell that shimmered with an oily lustre. At 7 PM pack-ice came suddenly to view, and towards it we steered, vainly peering through the mists ahead in search of a passage. The ice was closely packed, the pieces being small and wellworn. On the outskirts was a light brash which steadily gave place to a heavier variety, composed of larger and more angular fragments. A swishing murmur like the wind in the tree-tops came from the great expanse. It was alabaster-white and through the small, separate chips was diffused a pale lilac coloration. The larger chunks, by their motion and exposure to wind and current, had a circle of clear water; the deep sea-blue hovering round their water-worn niches. Here and there appeared the ochreous-yellow colour of adhering films of diatoms.

As we could not see what lay beyond, and the pack was becoming heavier, the ship was swung round and headed out.

Steering to the west through open water and patches of trailing brash, we were encouraged to find the pack trending towards the south. By pushing through bars of jammed floes and dodging numerous bergs, twenty miles were gained due southwards before the conditions had changed. The fog cleared, and right ahead massive bergs rose out of an ice-strewn sea. We neared one which was a mile in length and one hundred feet in height. The heaving ocean, dashing against its mighty, glistening walls, rushed with a hollow boom into caverns of ethereal blue; gothic portals to a cathedral of resplendent purity.

The smaller bergs and fragments of floe crowded closer together, and the two men at the wheel had little time for reverie. Orders came in quick succession—"Starboard! Steady!" and in a flash—"Hard-a-port!" Then repeated all over again, while the rudder-chains scraped and rattled in their channels.

Gradually the swell subsided, smoothed by the weight of ice. The tranquillity of the water heightened the superb effects of this glacial world. Majestic tabular bergs whose crevices exhaled a vaporous azure; lofty spires, radiant turrets and splendid castles; honeycombed masses illumined by pale green light within whose fairy labyrinths the water washed and gurgled. Seals and penguins on magic gondolas were the silent denizens of this dreamy Venice. In the soft glamour of the midsummer midnight sun, we were possessed by a rapturous wonder—the rare thrill of unreality.

The ice closed in, and shock after shock made the ship vibrate as she struck the smaller pieces full and fair, followed by a crunching and grinding as they scraped past the sides. The dense pack had come, and hardly a square foot of space showed amongst the blocks; smaller ones packing in between the larger, until the sea was covered with a continuous armour of ice. The ominous sound arising from thousands of faces rubbing together as they gently oscillated in the swell was impressive. It spoke of a force all-powerful, in whose grip puny ships might be locked for years and the less fortunate receive their last embrace.

The pack grew heavier and the bergs more numerous, embattled in a formidable array. If an ideal picture, from our point of view it was impenetrable. No "water sky" showed as a distant beacon; over all was reflected the pitiless, white glare of the ice. The *Aurora* retreated to the open sea, and headed to the west in search of a break in the ice-front. The wind blew from the south-east, and, with sails set to assist the engines, rapid progress was made.

The southern prospect was disappointing, for the heavy pack was ranged in a continuous bar. The over-arching sky invariably shone with that yellowish-white effulgence known as "ice blink," indicative of continuous ice, in contrast with the dark water sky, a sign of open water, or a mottled sky proceeding from an ice-strewn but navigable sea.

A Typical Table-Topped Névé Berg Originating from Floating Shelf Ice

An Antarctic Iceberg with a Reticulation of Crevasses on Its Tilted Surface. This Berg Had No Doubt Taken Its Origin from the Ice of the Coastal Cliffs of Adelie Land.

Though progress can be made in dense pack, provided it is not too heavy, advance is necessarily very slow—a few miles a day, and that at the expense of much coal. Without a well-defined "water sky" it would have been foolish to have entered. Further, everything pointed to heavier ice-conditions in the south, and, indeed, in several places we reconnoitred, and such was proved to be the case. Large bergs were numerous, which, on account of being almost unaffected by surface currents because of their ponderous bulk and stupendous draught, helped to compact the shallow surface-ice under the free influence of currents and winds. In our westerly course we were sometimes able to edge a little to the south, but were always reduced to our old position within a few hours. Long projecting "tongues" were met at intervals and, when narrow or open, we pushed through them.

Whales were frequently seen, both rorquals and killers. On the pack, sea-leopards and crab-eater seals sometimes appeared. At one time as many as a hundred would be counted from the bridge and at other moments not a single one could be sighted. They were not alarmed, unless the ship happened to bump against ice-masses within a short distance of them. A small sea-leopard, shot from the fo'c'sle by a well-directed bullet from

In Pack-Ice

Wild, was taken on board as a specimen; the meat serving as a great treat for the dogs.

On January 2, when driving through a tongue of pack, a halt was made to "ice ship." A number of men scrambled over the side on to a large piece of floe and handed up the ice. It was soon discovered, however, that the swell was too great, for masses of ice ten tons or more in weight swayed about under the stern, endangering the propeller and rudder—the vulnerable parts of the vessel. So we moved on, having secured enough fresh-water ice to supply a pleasant change after the somewhat discoloured tank-water then being served out. The ice still remained compact and forbidding, but each day we hoped to discover a weak spot through which we might probe to the land itself.

On the evening of January 2 we saw a high, pinnacled berg, a few miles within the edge of the pack, closely resembling a rocky peak; the transparent ice of which it was composed appeared, in the dull light, of a much darker hue than the surrounding bergs. Another adjacent block exhibited a large black patch on its northern face, the exact nature of which could not be ascertained at a distance. Examples of rock debris embedded in bergs had already been observed, and it was presumed that this was a similar case. These were all hopeful signs, for the earthy matter must, of course, have been picked up by the ice during its repose upon some adjacent land.

At this same spot, large flocks of silver-grey petrels were seen resting on the ice and skimming the water in search of food. As soon as we had entered the ice-zone, most of our old companions, such as the albatross, had deserted, while a new suite of Antarctic birds had taken their place. These included the beautiful snow petrel, the Antarctic petrel, and the small, lissome Wilson petrel—a link with the bird-life of more temperate seas.

On the evening of January 3 the wind was blowing fresh from the south-east and falling snow obscured the horizon. The pack took a decided turn to the north, which fact was particularly disappointing in view of the distance we had already traversed to the west. We were now approaching the longitude of D'Urville's landfall, and still the pack showed no signs of slackening. I was beginning to feel very anxious, and had decided not to pass that longitude without resorting to desperate measures.

The change in our fortunes occurred at five o'clock next morning, when the Chief Officer, Toucher, came down from the bridge to report that the atmosphere was clearing and that there appeared to be land-ice near by. Sure enough, on the port side, within a quarter of a mile, rose a massive barrier of ice extending far into the mist and separated from the ship by a little loose pack-ice. The problem to be solved was, whether it was the seaward face of an ice-covered continent, the ice-capping of a low island or only a flat-topped iceberg of immense proportions.

By 7 AM a corner was reached where the ice-wall trended southward, limned on the horizon in a series of bays and headlands. An El Dorado had opened before us, for the winds coming from the east of south had cleared the pack away from the lee of the ice-wall, so that in the distance a comparatively clear sea was visible, closed by a bar of ice, a few miles in extent. Into this we steered, hugging the ice-wall, and were soon in the open, speeding along in glorious sunshine, bringing new sights into view every moment.

The wall, along the northern face, was low—from thirty to seventy feet in height—but the face along which we were now progressing gradually rose in altitude to the south. It was obviously a shelf-ice formation (or a glacier-tongue projection of it), exactly similar in build, for instance, to the Great Ross Barrier so well described by Ross, Scott, and others. At the north-west corner, at half a dozen places within a few miles of each other, the wall was puckered up and surmounted by semi-conical eminences, half as high as the face itself. These peculiar elevations were unlike anything previously recorded and remained unexplained for a while, until closer inspection showed them to be the result of impact with other ice-masses—a curious but conceivable cause.

On pieces of broken floe Weddell seals were noted. They were the first seen on the voyage and a sure indication of land, for their habitat ranges over the coastal waters of Antarctic lands.

A large, low, dome-topped elevation, about one mile in diameter, was passed on the starboard side, at a distance of two miles from the long ice-cliff. This corresponded in shape with what Ross frequently referred to as an "ice island," uncertain whether it was a berg or ice-covered land. A sounding close by gave two hundred and eight fathoms, showing that we were on the continental shelf, and increasing the probability that the "ice island" was aground.

Birds innumerable appeared on every hand: snow petrels, silver petrels, Cape pigeons and Antarctic petrels. They fluttered in hundreds about our bows. Cape pigeons are well known in lower latitudes, and it was interesting to find them so far south. As they have chessboard-like markings on the back when seen in flight, there is no mistaking them.

The ice-wall or glacier-tongue now took a turn to the south-east. At this point it had risen to a great height, about two hundred feet sheer. A fresh wind was blowing in our teeth from the south-south-east, and beyond this

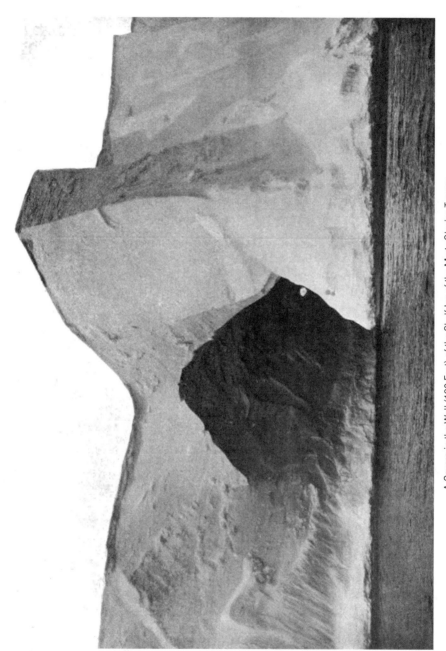

A Cavern in the Wall (120 Feet) of the Shelf Ice of the Mertz Glacier-Tongue

point would be driving us on to the cliffs. We put the ship about, therefore, and made for the lee side of the "ice island."

In isolated coveys on the inclined top of the "island" were several flocks, each containing hundreds of Antarctic petrels. At intervals they would rise into the air in clouds, shortly afterwards to settle down again on the snow.

Captain Davis moved the ship carefully against the lee wall of the "island," with a view of replenishing our water supply, but it was unscalable, and we were forced to withdraw. Crouched on a small projection near the water's edge was a seal, trying to evade the eyes of a dozen large grampuses which were playing about near our stern. These monsters appeared to be about twenty-five feet in length. They are the most formidable predacious mammals of the Antarctic seas, and annually account for large numbers of seals, penguins, and other cetaceans. The sea-leopard is its competitor, though not nearly so ferocious as the grampus, of whom it lives in terror.

The midnight hours were spent off the "ice island" while we wafted for a decrease in the wind. Bars of cirrus clouds covered the whole sky— the presage of a coming storm. The wind arose, and distant objects were blotted out by driving snow. An attempt was made to keep the ship in shelter by steaming into the wind, but as "ice island" and glacier-tongue were lost in clouds of snow, we were fortunate to make the lee of the latter, about fourteen miles to the north. There we steamed up and down until the afternoon of January 5, when the weather improved. A sounding was taken and the course was once more set for the south.

The sky remained overcast, the atmosphere foggy, and a south-south-east wind was blowing as we came abreast of the "ice island," which, by the way, was discovered to have drifted several miles to the north, thus proving itself to be a free-floating berg. The glacier-tongue on the port side took a sharp turn to the east-south-east, disappearing on the horizon. As there was no pack in sight and the water was merely littered with fragments of ice, it appeared most likely that the turn in the glacier-tongue was part of a great sweeping curve ultimately joining with the southward land. On our south-south-east course we soon lost sight of the ice-cliffs in a gathering fog.

On the afternoon of January 6 the wind abated and the fog began to clear. At 5 PM a line of ice confronted us and, an hour later, the *Aurora* was in calm water under another mighty ice face trending across our course. This wall was precisely similar to the one seen on the previous evening, and might well have been a continuation of it. It is scarcely credible that when the *Aurora* came south the following year, the glacier-tongue first discovered had entirely disappeared. It was apparently nothing more than a huge iceberg measuring forty miles in length. Specially valuable, as clearing

A Glimpse from Within the Cavern (Shown in the Preceding Illustration)

up any doubt that may have remained, was its re-discovery the following year some fifty miles to the north-west. Close to the face of the new ice-wall, which proved to be a true glacier-tongue, a mud bottom was found at a depth of three hundred and ninety-five fathoms.

While we were steaming in calm water to the south-west, the massive front, serrated by shallow bays and capes, passed in magnificent review. Its height attained a maximum of one hundred and fifty feet. In places the sea had eaten out enormous blue grottoes. At one spot, several of these had broken into each other to form a huge domed cavern, the roof of which hung one hundred feet above the sea. The noble portico was flanked by giant pillars.

The glacier-tongue bore all the characters of shelf-ice, by which is meant a floating extension of the land-ice.** A table-topped berg in the act of formation was seen, separated from the parent body of shelf-ice by a deep fissure several yards in width.

At 11 PM the *Aurora* entered a bay, ten miles wide, bounded on the east by the shelf-ice wall and on the west by a steep snow-covered promontory rising approximately two thousand feet in height, as yet seen dimly in hazy outline through the mist. No rock was visible, but the contour of the ridge was clearly that of ice-capped land.

There was much jubilation among the watchers on deck at the prospect. Every available field-glass and telescope was brought to bear upon it. It was almost certainly the Antarctic continent, though, at that time, its extension to the east, west and south remained to be proved. The shelf-ice was seen to be securely attached to it and, near its point of junction with the undulating land-ice, we beheld the mountains of this mysterious land haloed in ghostly mist.

While passing the extremity of the western promontory, we observed an exposure of rock, jutting out of the ice near sea-level, in the face of a scar left by an avalanche. Later, when passing within half a cable's length of several berg-like masses of ice lying off the coast, rock was again visible in black relief against the water's edge, forming a pedestal for the ice. The ship was kept farther offshore, after this warning, for though she was designed to buffet with the ice, we had no desire to test her resistance to rock.

The bottom was very irregular, and as an extra precaution, soundings were taken every few minutes. Through a light fog all that could be seen landwards was a steep, sloping, icy surface descending from the interior, and terminating abruptly in a seaward cliff fifty to two hundred feet in height.

The ice-sheet terminating in this wall presented a more broken surface than the floating shelf-ice. It was riven and distorted by gaping crevasses; an indication of the rough bed over which it had travelled.

Towards midnight another bay was entered and many rocky islets appeared on its western side. The engines were stopped for a few hours, and the voyage was resumed in clearer weather on the following morning.

** *Subsequently this shelf-ice formation was found to be a floating glacier-tongue sixty miles in length, the seaward extension of a large glacier which we named the Mertz Glacier.*

All day we threaded our way between islands and bergs. Seals and penguins swam around, the latter squawking and diving in a most amusing manner.

Cautiously we glided by an iceberg, at least one hundred and fifty feet high, rising with a faceted, perpendicular face chased with soft, snowy traceries and ornamented with stalactites. Splits and rents broke into the margin, and from each streamed the evanescent, azure vapour. Each puncture and tiny grotto was filled with it, and a sloping cap of shimmering snow spread over the summit. The profile-view was an exact replica of a battleship, grounded astern. The bold contour of the bow was perfect, and the massive flank had been torn and shattered by shell-fire in a desperate naval battle. This berg had heeled over considerably, and the original water-line ran as a definite rim, thirty feet above the green water. From this rim shelved down a smooth and polished base, marked with fine vertical striae.

Soundings varied from twenty to two hundred fathoms, and, accordingly, the navigation was particularly anxious work.

Extending along about fifteen miles of coast, where the inland ice came down steeply to the sea, was a marginal belt of sea, about two or three miles in width, thickly strewn with rocky islets. Of these some were flat and others peaked, but all were thickly populated by penguins, petrels and seals. The rocks appeared all to be gneisses and schists.

Later that night we lay off a possible landing-place for one of our bases, but, on more closely inspecting it in the morning, we decided to proceed farther west into a wide sweeping bay which opened ahead. About fifty miles ahead, on the far side of Commonwealth Bay, as we named it, was a cape which roughly represented in position Cape Decouverte, the most easterly extension of Adelie Land seen by D'Urville in 1840. Though Commonwealth Bay and the land already seen had never before been sighted, all was placed under the territorial name of Adelie Land.

The land was so overwhelmed with ice that, even at sea-level, the rock was all but entirely hidden. Here was an ice age in all earnestness; a picture of Northern Europe during the Great Ice Age some fifty thousand years ago. It was evident that the glaciation of Adelie Land was much more severe than that in higher Antarctic latitudes, as exampled on the borders of the Ross Sea; the arena of Scott's, Shackleton's and other expeditions. The temperature could not be colder, so we were led to surmise that the snowfall must be excessive. The full truth was to be ascertained by bitter experience, after spending a year on the spot.

I had hoped to find the Antarctic continent in these latitudes bounded by a rocky and attractive coast like that in the vicinity of Cape Adare;

The Mertz Glacier Tongue, at a Point 50 Miles from the Land.

the nearest well-explored region. It had proved otherwise, only too well endorsing the scanty information supplied by D'Urville and Wilkes of the coastline seen by them. A glance at the austere plateau and the ice-fettered coast was evidence of a rigid, inhospitable climate. It was apparent, too, that only a short summer could be expected in these latitudes, thus placing limitations upon our operations.

If three bases were to be landed it was important that they should be spread at sufficiently wide intervals. If one were placed in Adelie Land, the ship would probably have to break through the pack in establishing each of the other two bases. Judging by our previous experience there was no certain prospect of this being effected. The successful landing of three bases in suitable positions, sufficiently far apart for advantageous co-operation in geographical, meteorological and other observations, had now become problematical. In addition, one of the parties was not as strong as I would have liked, considering what would be undoubtedly its strenuous future.

For some days the various phases of the situation had occupied my mind, and I now determined to risk two bases, combining the smallest of the three parties with the Main Base. Alterations in the personnel of the third party were also made, by which the Main Base would be increased in strength for scientific work, and the other party under the leadership of Wild would be composed of men of specially good sledging calibre, besides being representative of the leading branches of our scientific programme.

We had a splendid lot of men, and I had no difficulty in choosing for Wild seven companions who could be relied upon to give a good account of themselves. It was only by assuring myself of their high efficiency that I could expect to rest from undue anxiety throughout the year of our separation. The composition of the two parties was as follows:

Main Base: R. Bage, F. H. Bickerton, J. H. Close, P. E. Correll, W. H. Hannam, A. J. Hodgeman, J. G. Hunter, J. F. Hurley, C. F. Laseron, C. T. Madigan, A. L. McLean, X. Mertz, H. D. Murphy, B. E. S. Ninnis, F. L. Stillwell, E. N. Webb, L. H. Whetter and myself.

Western Party: G. Dovers, C. T. Harrisson, C. A. Hoadley, S. E. Jones, A. L. Kennedy, M. H. Moyes, A. D. Watson, and F. Wild (leader).

I was now anxious to find a suitable location for our Main Base; two reasons making it an urgent matter. The first was, that as we advanced to the west we were leaving the South Magnetic Pole, and I was anxious to have our magnetographs running as near the latter as possible. Secondly, we would be daily increasing our distance from Macquarie Island, making wireless communication more uncertain.

At noon on January 8, while I was weighing the pros and cons with Captain Davis, Wild came in to say that there was a rocky exposure about fifteen miles off on the port side, and suggested altering our course to obtain a better view of it.

Just after 4 PM, when the ship was about one mile from the nearest rocks, the whale-boat was lowered and manned. We rowed in with the object of making a closer investigation. From the ship's deck, even when within a mile, the outcrop had appeared to project directly from under the inland ice-sheet. Now, however, we were surprised to find ourselves amongst an archipelago of islets. These were named the Mackellar Islets, in remembrance of one who had proved a staunch friend of the Expedition.

Weddell seals and Adelie penguins in thousands rested upon the rocks; the latter chiefly congregated upon a long, low, bare islet situated in the centre. This was the largest of the group, measuring about half a mile in length; others were not above twenty yards in diameter. As we came inshore, the main body of the archipelago was found to be separated by a mile and a half from the mainland. A point which struck us at the time was that the islets situated on the southern side of the group were capped by unique masses of ice; resembling iced cakes. Later we were able to see them in process of formation. In the violent southerly hurricanes prevalent in Adelie Land, the spray breaks right over them. Part of it is deposited and frozen, and by increments the icing of these monstrous "cakes" is built up. The amount contributed in winter makes up for loss by thawing in midsummer. As the islets to windward shelter those in their lee, the latter are destitute of these natural canopies.

Soundings were taken at frequent intervals with a hand lead-line, manipulated by Madigan. The water was on the whole shallow, varying from a few to twenty fathoms. The bottom was clothed by dense, luxuriant seaweed. This rank growth along the littoral was unexpected, for nothing of the kind exists on the Ross Sea coasts within five or six fathoms of the surface.

Advancing towards the mainland, we observed a small islet amongst the rocks, and towards it the boat was directed. We were soon inside a beautiful, miniature harbour completely land-locked. The sun shone gloriously in a blue sky as we stepped ashore on a charming ice-quay—the first to set foot on the Antarctic continent between Cape Adare and Gaussberg, a distance of one thousand eight hundred miles.

Wild and I proceeded to make a tour of exploration. The rocky area at Cape Denison, as it was named, was found to be about one mile in

The *Aurora* in Commonwealth Bay; the Rising Plateau of Adelie Land in the Distance

The Invaluable Motor-Launch; Left to Right, Hamilton, Bickerton, and Blake

The Whale-Boat with Passengers for the Shore; Wild at the Steering Oar

length and half a mile in extreme width. Behind it rose the inland ice, ascending in a regular slope and apparently free of crevasses—an outlet for our sledging parties in the event of the sea not firmly freezing over. To right and left of this oasis, as the visitor to Adelie Land must regard the welcome rock, the ice was heavily crevassed and fell sheer to the sea in cliffs, sixty to one hundred and fifty feet in height. Two small dark patches in the distance were the only evidences of rock to relieve the white monotony of the coast.

In landing cargo on Antarctic shores, advantage is generally taken of the floe-ice on to which the materials can be unloaded and at once sledged away to their destination. Here, on the other hand, there was open water, too shallow for the *Aurora* to be moored alongside the ice-foot. The only alternative was to anchor the ship at a distance and discharge the cargo by boats running to the ideal harbour we had discovered. Close to the boat harbour was suitable ground for the erection of a hut, so that the various impedimenta would have to be carried only a short distance. For supplies of fresh meat, in the emergency of being marooned for a number of years, there were many Weddell seals at hand, and on almost all the neighbouring ridges colonies of penguins were busy rearing their young.

As a station for scientific investigations, it offered a wider field than the casual observer would have imagined. So it came about that the Main Base was finally settled at Cape Denison, Commonwealth Bay.

We arrived on board at 8 PM, taking a seal as food for the dogs. Without delay, the motor-launch was dropped into the water, and both it and the whale-boat loaded with frozen carcasses of mutton, cases of eggs and other perishable goods.

While some of us went ashore in the motor-launch, with the whale-boat in tow, the *Aurora* steamed round the Mackellar Islets seeking for a good anchorage under the icy barrier, immediately to the west of the boat harbour. The day had been perfect, vibrant with summer and life, but towards evening a chill breeze sprang up, and we in the motor-launch had to beat against it. By the time we had reached the head of the harbour, Hoadley had several fingers frost-bitten and all were feeling the cold, for we were wearing light garments in anticipation of fine weather. The wind strengthened every minute, and showers of fine snow were soon whistling down the glacier. No time was lost in landing the cargo, and, with a rising blizzard at our backs, we drove out to meet the *Aurora*. On reaching the ship a small gale was blowing and our boats were taken in tow.

The first thing to be considered was the mooring of the *Aurora* under the lee of the ice-wall, so as to give us an opportunity of getting the boats aboard. In the meantime they were passed astern, each manned by several hands to keep them bailed out; the rest of us having scrambled up the side. Bringing the ship to anchor in such a wind in uncharted, shoal water was difficult to do in a cool and methodical manner. The sounding machine was kept running with rather dramatic results; depths jumping from five to thirty fathoms in the ship's length, and back again to the original figure in the same distance. A feeling of relief passed round when, after much manoeuvring, the anchor was successfully bedded five hundred yards from the face of the cliff.

Just at this time the motor-launch broke adrift. Away it swept before a wind of forty-five miles per hour. On account of the cold, and because the engine was drenched with sea-water, some difficulty was found in starting the motor. From the ship's deck we could see Bickerton busily engaged with it. The rudder had been unshipped, and there was no chance of replacing it, for the boat was bobbing about on the waves in a most extraordinary manner. However, Whetter managed to make a jury-rudder which served the purpose, while Hunter, the other occupant, was kept laboriously active with the pump.

They had drifted half a mile, and were approaching the rocks of an islet on which the sea was breaking heavily. Just as every one was becoming very apprehensive, the launch began to forge ahead, and the men had soon escaped from their dangerous predicament. By the united efforts of all hands the boats were hoisted on board and everything was made as "snug" as possible.

The wind steadily increased, and it seemed impossible for the anchor to hold. The strain on the cable straightened out a steel hook two inches in diameter. This caused some embarrassment, as the hook was part of the cable attachment under the fo'c'sle-head. It is remarkable, however, that after this was adjusted the ship did not lose her position up to the time of departure from Adelie Land.

Though we were so close under the shelter of a lofty wall, the waves around us were at least four feet in height and when the wind increased to sixty-five and seventy miles per hour, their crests were cut off and the surface was hidden by a sheet of racing spindrift.

Everything was securely lashed in readiness for going to sea, in case the cable should part. Final arrangements were then made to discharge the cargo quickly as soon as the wind moderated.

Two days had elapsed before the wind showed any signs of abatement. It was 8 PM on January 10 when the first boat ventured off with a small cargo, but it was not till the following morning that a serious start was

First Steps in the Formation of the Main Base Station; Landing of Stores and Equipment at the Head of the Boat Harbour, Cape Denison. In the Distance Men Are to Be Seen Sledging the Materials to the Site Selected for the Erection of the Hut.

A View of a Rocky Stretch of the Adelie Land Coast West of Commonwealth Bay

made. In good weather, every trip between the ship and the boat harbour, a distance of a mile, meant that five or six tons had been landed. It was usual for the loaded launch to tow both whale-boats heavily laden and, in addition, a raft of hut timbers or wireless masts. Some of the sailors, while engaged in building rafts alongside the ship, were capsized into the water and after that the occupation was not a popular one.

Ashore, Wild had rigged a derrick, using for its construction two of the wireless royal masts. It was thus possible to cope with the heavier packages at the landing-place. Of the last-named the air-tractor sledge was by far the most troublesome. With plenty of manual labour, under Wild's skilful direction, this heavy machine was hoisted from the motor-launch, and then carefully swung on to the solid ice-foot.

Captain Davis superintended the discharging operations on the ship, effected by the crew and some of the land party under the direction of the ship's officers. Wild supervised conveyance ashore, and the landing, classification, and safe storage of the various boat-loads. Gillies and Bickerton took alternate shifts in driving the motor-launch. The launch proved invaluable, and we were very glad that it had been included in the equipment, for it did a remarkable amount of work in a minimum of time.

In view of the difficulty of embarking the boats, if another hurricane should arise, tents were erected ashore, so that a party could remain there with the boats moored in a sheltered harbour.

Everything went well until just before midnight on January 12, when the wind again swept down. Wild, four of the men and I were forced to remain ashore. We spent the time constructing a temporary hut of benzine cases, roofed with planks; the walls of which were made massive to resist the winds. This structure was henceforth known as the "Benzine Hut."

The barometer dropped to 28.5 inches and the wind remained high. We were struck with the singular fact that, even in the height of some of these hurricanes, the sky remained serene and the sun shone brightly. It had been very different when the ship was amongst the pack a few miles to the north, for, there, cloudy and foggy conditions had been the rule. The wind coming to us from the south was dry; obviously an argument for the continental extension of the land in that direction.

At 2 AM on January 15 a pre-arranged whistle was sounded from the *Aurora*, advising those of us ashore that the sea had moderated sufficiently to continue unloading. Wild sped away in the launch, but before he had reached the ship the wind renewed its activity. At last, after 2 PM on the same day it ceased, and we were able to carry on work until midnight, when the wind descended on us once more. This time, eighteen men remained

ashore. After twelve hours there was another lull, and unloading was then continued with only a few intermissions from 1 PM on January 16 until the afternoon of January 19.

Never was landing so hampered by adverse conditions, and yet, thanks to the assiduous application of all, a great assortment of materials was safely embarked. Comprised among them were the following: twenty-three tons of coal briquettes, two complete living-huts, a magnetic observatory, the whole of the wireless equipment, including masts, and more than two thousand packages of general supplies containing sufficient food for two years, utensils, instruments, benzine, kerosene, lubricating oils an air-tractor and other sledges.

Then came the time for parting. There was a great field before Wild's party to the west, and it was important that they should be able to make the most of the remainder of the season. My great regret was that I could not be with them. I knew that I had men of experience and ability in Davis and Wild, and felt that the work entrusted to them was in the best

A Panoramic View Looking South from Near the Hut. In the Distance Are the Slopes of the Inland Ice-Sheet. In the Foreground Is the Terminal Moraine. Between the Rocks and the Figure Is a Zone Where Rapid Thawing Takes Place in the Summer Owing to the Amount of Dirt Contained in the Ice.

A Panoramic View Looking North Towards the Sea. In the Middle of the Picture Is Round Lake. The Hut Is Towards the Left-Hand Side and the Anemograph Is on the Hill. The Men Are Practising Ski Running.

of hands. Through the medium of wireless telegraphy I hoped to keep in touch with the Macquarie Island party, the Western Base,** and the ship itself, when in Australian waters.

It was my idea that Wild's party should proceed west and attempt to effect a landing and establish a western wintering station at some place not less than four hundred miles west of Adelie Land. On the way, whenever opportunity presented itself, they were to cache provisions at intervals along the coast in places liable to be visited by sledging parties.

The location of such caches and of the Western Base, it was hoped, would be communicated to us at the Main Base, through the medium of wireless telegraphy from Hobart.

All members of the land parties and the ship's officers met in the wardroom. There were mutual good wishes expressed all round, and then we celebrated previous Antarctic explorers, more especially D'Urville and Wilkes. The toast was drunk in excellent Madeira presented to us by Mr. J. T. Buchanan, who had carried this sample round the world with him when a member of the celebrated *Challenger* Expedition.

The motor-launch was hoisted and the anchor raised. Then at 8.45 PM on January 19 we clambered over the side into one of the whale-boats and pushed off for Cape Denison, shouting farewells back to the *Aurora*. Several hours later she had disappeared below the north-western horizon, and we had set to work to carve out a home in Adelie Land.

** *They were supplied with masts and a receiving set sufficiently sensitive to pick up messages from a distance of five or six hundred miles.*

CHAPTER IV

New Lands

L
EAVING THE LAND PARTY UNDER MY CHARGE AT
Commonwealth Bay on the evening of January 19, the *Aurora* set
her course to round a headland visible on the north-western horizon.
At midnight the ship came abreast of this point and continued steaming
west, keeping within a distance of five miles of the coast. A break in the icy
monotony came with a short tract of islets fronting a background of dark
rocky coastline similar to that at Cape Denison but more extensive.

Some six miles east of D'Urville's Cape Discovery, a dangerous reef was
sighted extending at right angles across the course. The ship steamed along
it and her soundings demonstrated a submerged ridge continuing some
twelve miles out to sea. Captain Davis's narrative proceeds:

"Having cleared this obstacle we followed the coastline to the west from
point to point. Twelve miles away we could see the snow-covered slopes
rising from the seaward cliffs to an elevation of one thousand five hundred
feet. Several small islands were visible close to a shore fringed by numerous
large bergs.

"At 10 PM on January 20, our progress to the west was stopped by a fleet
of bergs off the mainland and an extensive field of berg-laden pack-ice,
trending to the north and north-east. Adelie Land could be traced continuing
to the west. Where it disappeared from view there was the appearance of a
barrier-formation, suggestive of shelf-ice, running in a northerly direction.
Skirting the pack-ice on a north and north-west course, we observed the
same appearance from the crow's-nest on January 21 and 22."

The stretch of open, navigable, coastal water to the north of Adelie
Land, barred by the Mertz Glacier on the east and delimited on the west
by more or less compact ice, has been named the D'Urville Sea. We
found subsequently that its freedom from obstruction by ice is due to the

persistent gales which set off the land in that locality. To the north, pack-ice in variable amount is encountered before reaching the wide open ocean.

The existence of such a "barrier-formation,"** as indicated above, probably resting on a line of reef similar to the one near Cape Discovery, would account for the presence of this ice-field in practically the same position as it was seen by D'Urville in 1840.

At a distance, large bergs would be undistinguishable from shelf-ice, appearances of which were reported above.

Quoting further: "We were unable to see any trace of the high land reported by the United States Squadron (1840) as lying to the west and south beyond the compact ice.

"At 1.30 AM on the 23rd the pack-ice was seen to trend to the south-west. After steaming west for twenty-five miles, we stood south in longitude 132° 30' E, shortly afterwards passing over the charted position of Cote Clarie. The water here was clear of pack-ice, but studded with bergs of immense size. The great barrier which the French ships followed in 1840 had vanished. A collection of huge bergs was the sole remnant to mark its former position.

"At 10 AM, having passed to the south of the charted position of D'Urville's Cote Clarie, we altered course to S. 10° E. true. Good observations placed us at noon in latitude 65° 2' S. and 132° 26' E. A sounding on sand and small stones was taken in one hundred and sixty fathoms. We sailed over the charted position of land east of Wilkes's Cape Carr in clear weather.

"At 5.30 PM land was sighted to the southward—snowy highlands similar to those of Adelie Land but greater in elevation.

"After sounding in one hundred and fifty-six fathoms on mud, the ship stood directly towards the land until 9 PM. The distance to the nearest point was estimated at twenty miles; heavy floe-ice extending from our position, latitude 65° 45' S. and longitude 132° 40' E., right up to the shore. Another sounding realized two hundred and thirty fathoms, on sand and small stones. Some open water was seen to the south-east, but an attempt to force a passage in that direction was frustrated.

"At 3 AM on the 24th we were about twelve miles from the nearest point of the coast, and further progress became impossible. The southern slopes

---

** An analysis of the data derived from the later voyages of the Aurora makes it practically certain that there is a permanent obstacle to the westerly drift of the pack-ice in longitude 137° E. There is, however, some uncertainty as to the cause of this blockage. An alternative explanation is advanced, namely, that within the area of comparatively shallow water, large bergs are entrapped, and these entangle the drifting pack-ice.

were seamed with numerous crevasses, but at a distance the precise nature of the shores could not be accurately determined."

To this country, which had never before been seen, was given the name of Wilkes's Land; as it is only just to commemorate the American Exploring Expedition on the Continent which its leader believed he had discovered in these seas and which he would have found had Fortune favoured him with a fair return for his heroic endeavours.

"We steered round on a north-westerly course, and at noon on January 24 were slightly to the north of our position at 5.30 AM on the 23rd. A sounding reached one hundred and seventy fathoms and a muddy bottom. Environing us were enormous bergs of every kind, one hundred and eighty to two hundred feet in height. During the afternoon a westerly course was maintained in clear water until 4 PM, when the course was altered to S. 30° W., in the hope of winning through to the land visible on the southern horizon."

At 8 PM the sky was very clear to the southward, and the land could be traced to a great distance until it faded in the south-west. But the ship had come up with the solid floe-ice once more, and had to give way and steam along its edge. This floating breakwater held us off and frustrated all attempts to reach the goal which we sought.

"The next four days was a period of violent gales and heavy seas which drove the ship some distance to the north. Nothing was visible through swirling clouds of snow. The *Aurora* behaved admirably, as she invariably does in heavy weather. The main pack was encountered on January 29, but foggy weather prevailed. It was not until noon on January 31 that the atmosphere was sufficiently clear to obtain good observations. The ship was by this time in the midst of heavy floe in the vicinity of longitude 119° E., and again the course had swung round to south. We had soon passed to the south of Balleny's Sabrina Land without any indication of its existence. Considering the doubtful character of the statements justifying its appearance on the chart, it is not surprising that we did not verify them.

"At 11 AM the floes were found too heavy for further advance. The ship was made fast to a big one and a large quantity of ice was taken on board to replenish the fresh-water supply. A tank of two hundred gallons' capacity, heated within by a steam coil from the engine-room, stood on the poop deck. Into this ice was continuously fed, flowing away as it melted into the main tanks in the bottom of the ship.

"At noon the weather was clear, but nothing could be discerned in the south except a faint blue line on the horizon. It may have been a "lead"

In Open Pack-Ice

The Face of the Shackleton Ice-Shelf 100 Miles North of the Mainland. Each Strongly-Marked Horizontal Band on the Sheer Wall Represents a Year's Snowfall.

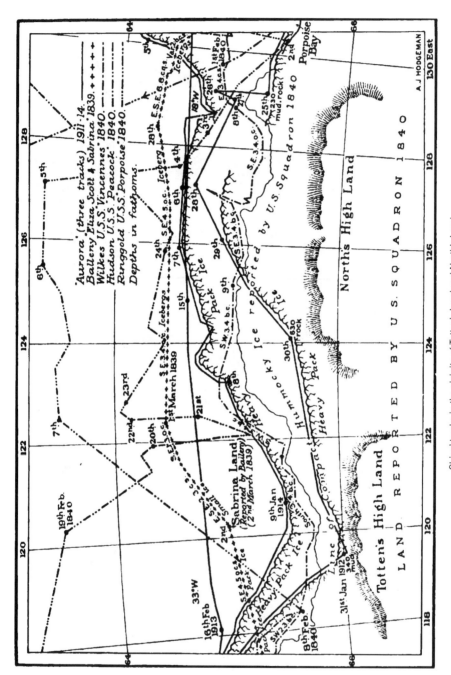

Ships' tracks in the vicinity of Totten's Land and North's Land

of water, an effect of mirage, or even land-ice—in any case we could not approach it."

The position as indicated by the noon observations placed the ship within seven miles of a portion of Totten's High Land in Wilkes's charts. As high land would have been visible at a great distance, it is clear that Totten's High Land either does not exist or is situated a considerable distance from its charted location. A sounding was made in three hundred and forty fathoms.

Towards evening the *Aurora* turned back to open water and cruised along the pack-ice. A sounding next day showed nine hundred and twenty-seven fathoms.

It was about this time that a marked improvement was noted in the compass. Ever since the first approach to Adelie Land it had been found unreliable, for, on account of the proximity to the magnetic pole, the directive force of the needle was so slight that very large local variations were experienced.

The longitude of Wilkes's Knox Land was now approaching. With the exception of Adelie Land, the account by Wilkes concerning Knox Land is more convincing than any other of his statements relating to new Antarctic land. If they had not already disembarked, we had hoped to land the western party in that neighbourhood. It was, therefore, most disappointing when impenetrable ice blocked the way, before Wilkes's "farthest south" in that locality had been reached. Three determined efforts were made to find a weak spot, but each time the *Aurora* was forced to retreat, and the third time was extricated only with great difficulty. In latitude 65° 5' S. longitude 107° 20' E., a sounding of three hundred fathoms was made on a rocky bottom. This sounding pointed to the probability of land within sixty miles.

Repulsed from his attack on the pack, Captain Davis set out westward towards the charted position of Termination Land, and in following the trend of the ice was forced a long way to the north.

At 7.40 AM, February 8, in foggy weather, the ice-cliff of floating shelf-ice was met. This was disposed so as to point in a north-westerly direction and it was late in the day before the ship doubled its northern end. Here the sounding wire ran out for eight hundred and fifty fathoms without reaching bottom. Following the wall towards the south-south-east, it was interesting at 5.30 PM to find a sounding of one hundred and ten fathoms in latitude 64° 45'. A line of large grounded bergs and massive floe-ice was observed ahead trailing away from the ice-wall towards the north-west.

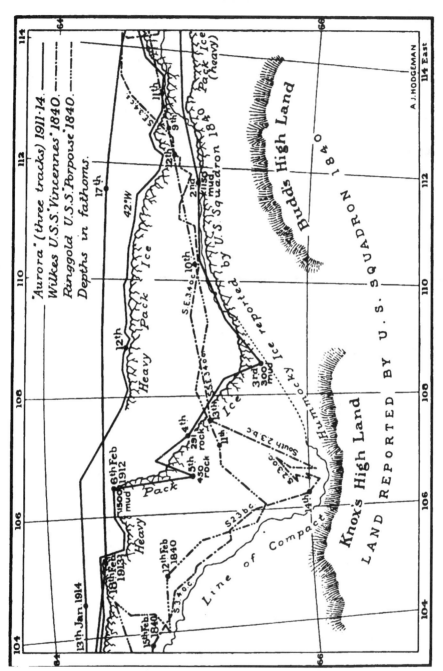

Ships' Tracks in the Vicinity of Knox Land and Budd Land

On plotting the observations, it became apparent that the shelf-ice was in the form of a prolonged tongue some seven miles in breadth. As it occupied the position of the "Termination Land" which has appeared on some charts, (after Wilkes) it was named Termination Ice-Tongue.

A blizzard sprang up, and, after it had been safely weathered in the lee of some grounded bergs, the *Aurora* moved off on the afternoon of February 11. The horizon was obscured by mist, as she pursued a tortuous track amongst bergs and scattered lumps of heavy floe. Gradually the sea became more open, and by noon on February 12 the water had deepened to two hundred and thirty-five fathoms. Good progress was made to the south; the vessel dodging icebergs and detached floes.

The discovery of a comparatively open sea southward of the main pack was a matter of some moment. As later voyages and the observations of the Western Party showed, this tract of sea is a permanent feature of the neighbourhood. I have called it the Davis Sea, after the captain of the *Aurora*, in appreciation of the fact that he placed it on the chart.

At noon, on February 13, in latitude 65° 54 ½' S. longitude 94° 25' E., the western face of a long, floating ice-tongue loomed into view. There were five hundred fathoms of water off its extremity, and the cliffs rose vertically to one hundred feet. Soon afterwards land was clearly defined low in the south extending to east and west. This was thenceforth known as Queen Mary Land.

The sphere of operations of the German expedition of 1902 was near at hand, for its vessel, the *Gauss*, had wintered, frozen in the pack, one hundred and twenty-five miles to the west. It appeared probable that Queen Mary Land would be found to be continuous[**] with Kaiser Wilhelm II Land, which the Germans had reached by a sledging journey from their ship across the intervening sea-ice.

The *Aurora* followed the western side of the ice-tongue for about twenty miles in a southerly direction, at which point there was a white expanse of floe extending right up to the land. Wild and Kennedy, walking several miles towards the land, estimated that it was about twenty-five miles distant. As the surface over which they travelled was traversed by cracks and liable to drift away to sea, all projects of landing there had to be abandoned; furthermore, it was discovered that the ice-tongue, alongside of which the ship lay, was a huge iceberg. A landing on it had been contemplated, but was now out of question.

The main difficulty which arose at this juncture was the failing coal-supply. It was high time to return to Hobart, and, if a western base was to be formed at all, Wild's party would have to be landed without further delay.

[**] *Such was eventually proved to be the case.*

After a consultation, Davis and Wild decided that under the circumstances an attempt should be made to gain a footing on the adjacent shelf-ice, if nothing better presented itself.

The night was passed anchored to the floe, on the edge of which were numerous Emperor penguins and Weddell seals. A fresh south-easterly wind blew on February 14, and the ship was kept in the shelter of the iceberg. During the day enormous pieces were observed to be continually breaking away from the berg and drifting to leeward.

Captain Davis continues: "At midnight there was a strong swell from the north-east and the temperature went down to 13°F. At 4 AM, February 15, we reached the northern end of the berg and stood first of all to the east, and then later to the south-east.

"At 8.45 AM, shelf-ice was observed from aloft, trending approximately north and south in a long wall. At noon we came up with the floe-ice again, in about the same latitude as on the western side of the long iceberg. Land could be seen to the southward. At 1 PM the ship stopped at the junction of the floe and the shelf-ice."

Wild, Harrison and Hoadley went to examine the shelf-ice with a view to its suitability for a wintering station. The cliff was eighty to one hundred feet in height, so that the ice in total thickness must have attained at least as much as six hundred feet. Assisted by snow-ramps slanting down on to the floe, the ascent with ice-axes and alpine rope was fairly easy.

Two hundred yards from the brink, the shelf-ice was thrown into pressure-undulations and fissured by crevasses, but beyond that was apparently sound and unbroken. About seventeen miles to the south the rising slopes of ice-mantled land were visible, fading away to the far east and west.

The ice-shelf was proved later on to extend for two hundred miles from east to west, ostensibly fusing with the Termination Ice-Tongue, whose extremity is one hundred and eighty miles to the north. The whole has been called the Shackleton Ice-Shelf.

Wild and his party unanimously agreed to seize upon this last opportunity, and to winter on the floating ice.

The work of discharging stores was at once commenced. To raise the packages from the floe to the top of the ice-shelf, a "flying-fox" was rigged.

"A kedge-anchor was buried in the sea-ice, and from this a two-and-a-half-inch wire-hawser was led upwards over a pair of sheer-legs on top of the cliff to another anchor buried some distance back. The whole was set taut by a tackle. The stores were then slung to a travelling pulley on the wire, and hauled on to the glacier by means of a rope led through a second pulley on the sheer-legs. The ship's company broke stores out of the hold

The *Aurora* Anchored to Thick Floe-Ice 100 Miles North of the Western Base, Queen Mary Land. In This Region the Annual Snowfall Is Very Heavy, So That It Is Possible That the Great Thickness of Floe Is Due to the Accumulation of One Year.

and sledged them three hundred yards to the foot of an aerial, where they were hooked on to the travelling-block by which the shore party, under Wild, raised them to their destination."

"It was most important to accelerate the landing as much as possible, not only on account of the lateness of the season—the *Gauss* had been frozen in on February 22 at a spot only one hundred and seventy miles away—but because the floe was gradually breaking up and floating away. When the last load was hoisted, the water was lapping within ten yards of the 'flying-fox'."

A fresh west-north-west wind on February 17 caused some trouble. Captain Davis writes:

"February 19. The floe to which we have been attached is covered by a foot of water. The ship has been bumping a good deal to-day. Notwithstanding the keen wind and driving snow, every one has worked well. Twelve tons of coal were the last item to go up the cliff."

In all, thirty-six tons of stores were raised on to the shelf-ice, one hundred feet above sea-level, in four days.

"February 20. The weather is very fine and quite a contrast to yesterday. We did not get the coal ashore a moment too soon, as this morning the ice marked by our sledge tracks went to sea in a north-westerly direction, and this afternoon it is drifting back as if under the influence of a tide or current. We sail at 7 AM to-morrow.

A Berg with Inclusions of Mud and Rock. Long. 10° E.

The "Flying-Fox" Viewed from the Floe-Ice Below the Brink of the Shelf-Ice on Which the Western Party Wintered

"I went on to the glacier with Wild during the afternoon. It is somewhat crevassed for about two hundred yards inland, and then a flat surface stretches away as far as the eye can see. I wished the party 'God-speed' this evening, as we sail early to-morrow."

Early on February 21, the ship's company gave their hearty farewell cheers, and the *Aurora* sailed north, leaving Wild and his seven companions on the floating ice.

The bright weather of the immediate coastal region was soon exchanged for the foggy gloom of the pack.

"February 21, 11 PM. We are now passing a line of grounded bergs and some heavy floe-ice. Fortunately it is calm, but in the darkness it is difficult to see an opening. The weather is getting thick, and I expect we shall have trouble in working through this line of bergs.

"February 22. I cannot explain how we managed to clear some of the bergs between 11 PM last night and 3 AM this morning. At first stopping and lying-to was tried, but it was soon evident that the big bergs were moving and would soon hem us in: probably in a position from which we should be unable to extricate ourselves this season.

"So we pushed this way and that, endeavouring to retain freedom at any cost. For instance, about midnight I was 'starboarding' to clear what appeared to be the loom of a berg on the starboard bow, when, suddenly, out of the haze a wall seemed to stretch across our course. There was no room to turn, so 'full speed astern' was the only alternative. The engines responded immediately, or we must have crashed right into a huge berg. Until daylight it was ice ahead, to port and to starboard—ice everywhere all the time. The absence of wind saved us from disaster. It was a great relief when day broke, showing clearer water to the northward."

On February 23, the *Aurora* left the shelter of Termination Ice-Tongue, and a course was set nearly true north. There was a fresh breeze from the north-east and a high sea. The ship was desperately short of ballast and the coal had to be carefully husbanded. All movable gear was placed in the bottom of the ship, while the ashes were saved, wetted and put below. The ballast-tanks were found to be leaking and Gillies had considerable trouble in making them watertight.

The distance from the Western Base in Queen Mary Land to Hobart was two thousand three hundred miles, through the turbulent seas of the fifties and forties. It was the end of a perilous voyage when the *Aurora* arrived in Hobart with nine tons of coal.

On March 12, the captain's log records:

"The *Aurora* has done splendidly, beating all attempts of the weather to turn her over. We had two heavy gales during the first week of March, but reached Hobart safely to-day, passing on our way up the Derwent the famous Polar ship, *Fram*, at anchor in Sandy Bay. Flags were dipped and a hearty cheer given for Captain Amundsen and his gallant comrades who had raised the siege of the South Pole."

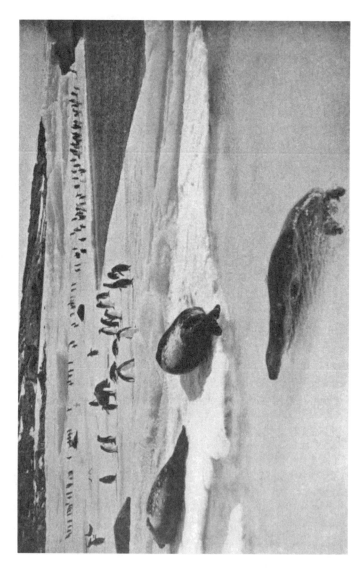

Summer at the Boat Harbour, Cape Denison

An Adelie Penguin on the Nest Defending Her Eggs

First Days in Adelie Land

THE OVERCROWDED WHALE-BOAT DISGORGED its cargo at 10 PM on the ice-quay at Cape Denison. The only shelter was a cluster of four tents and the Benzine Hut, so the first consideration was the erection of a commodious living-hut.

While the majority retired to rest to be ready for a fresh burst of work on the morrow, a few of us discussed the preliminary details, and struck the first blows in the laying of the foundations.

A site for the living-hut was finally approved. This was a nearly flat piece of rocky ground of just sufficient size, partially sheltered on the southern side by a large upstanding rock. Other points to recommend it were, proximity to the boat harbour and to a good sledging surface; the ice of the glacier extending to the "front door" on the western side. Several large rocks had to be shifted, and difficulty was anticipated in the firm setting of the stumps. The latter were blocks of wood, three feet in length, embedded in the ground, forming the foundation of the structure. Unfortunately, no such thing as earth or gravel existed in which to sink these posts, and the rock being of the variety known as gneiss, was more than ordinarily tough.

Since two parties had combined, there were two huts available, and these were to be erected so that the smaller adjoined and was in the lee of the larger. The latter was to be the living-room; the former serving as a vestibule, a workshop and an engine-room for the wireless plant. Slight modifications were made in the construction of both huts, but these did not affect the framework. After the completion of the living-hut, regular scientific observations were to commence, and the smaller hut was then to be built as opportunity offered.

Nothing has so far been said about the type of hut adopted by our Antarctic stations. As the subject is important, and we had expended much thought thereon before coming to a final decision, a few remarks will not be out of place.

Strength to resist hurricanes, simplicity of construction, portability and resistance to external cold were fundamental. My first idea was to have the huts in the form of pyramids on a square base, to ensure stability in heavy winds and with a large floor-area to reduce the amount of timber used. The final type was designed at the expense of floor-space, which would have been of little use because of the low roof in the parts thus eliminated. In this form, the pyramid extended to within five feet of the ground on the three windward sides so as to include an outside veranda. That veranda, like the motor-launch, was a wonderful convenience, and another of the many things of which we made full use. It lent stability to the structure, assisted to keep the hut warm, served as a store-house, physical laboratory and a dog-shelter.

Round the outside of the three veranda walls boxes of stores were stacked, so as to continue the roof-slope to the ground. Thus, the wind striking the hut met no vertical face, but was partly deflected; the other force-component tending to pin the building to the ground.

All three huts were essentially of the same construction. The largest, on account of its breadth, had four special supporting posts, symmetrically placed near the centre, stretching from the ground to the roof framework. The only subdivisions inside were a small vestibule, a photographic darkroom and my own room. This rough idea I had handed over to Hodgeman, leaving him to complete the details and to draw up the plans. The frame timbers he employed were stronger than usual in a building of the size, and were all securely bolted together. The walls and roof, both inside and outside, were of tongued and grooved pine-boards, made extra wind-proof by two courses of tarred paper. As rain was not expected, this roofing was sufficient. There were four windows in the roof, one on each side of the pyramid. We should thereby get light even though almost buried in snow.

The largest hut was presented by the timber merchants of Sydney, and proved its astonishing strength during the winter hurricanes. The smallest was purchased in Adelaide, the third was built and presented by Messrs. Anthony of Melbourne.

On the morning of January 20 all were at work betimes. As we were securely isolated from a trades hall, our hours of labour ranged from 7 AM till 11 PM.

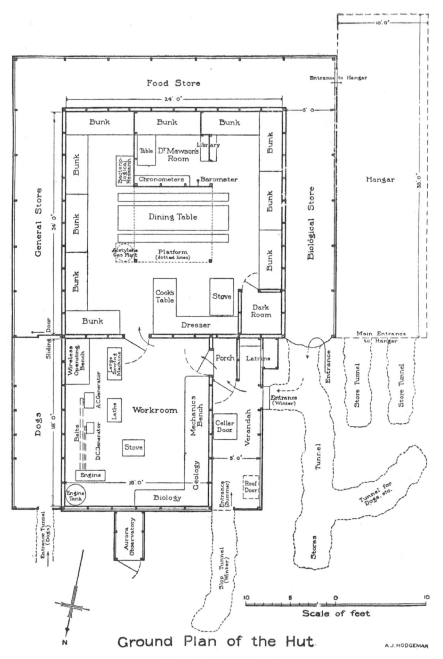

Ground Plan of the Hut. A.J. HODGEMAN

Plan of the Hut, Adelie Land

Dynamite was to be used for blasting out the holes for the reception of the stumps, and so the steel rock-drills were unpacked and boring commenced. This was easier than it appeared, because the rock was much traversed by cracks. By the end of the day a good deal of damage had been done to the rock, at the expense of a few sore fingers and wrists caused by the sledge-hammers missing the drills. The work was tedious, for water introduced into the holes had a habit of freezing. The metal drills, too, tended to be brittle in the cold and required to be tempered softer than usual. Hannam operated the forge, and picks and drills were sent along for pointing; an outcrop of gneiss serving as an anvil.

Among other things it was found difficult to fire the charges, for, when frozen, dynamite is not readily exploded. This was overcome by carrying the sticks inside one's pocket until the last moment. In the absence of earth or clay, we had no tamping material until some one suggested guano from the penguin rookeries, which proved a great success.

Next day the stumps were in place; most of them being fixed by wedges and other devices. Cement was tried, but it is doubtful if any good came of it, for the low temperature did not encourage it to set well. By the evening, the bottom plates were laid on and bolted to the tops of the stumps, and everything was ready for the superstructure.

The Living-Hut, Nearing Completion. The Tents and Shelter Built of Benzine Cases Used as Temporary Quarters Are Shown.

The Completion of the Hut—Cheering the Union Jack as It Was Hoisted on the Flag Pole

On January 22, while some were busy with the floor-joists and wall-frames, others carried boulders from the neighbouring moraine, filling in the whole space between the stumps. These were eventually embedded in a mass of boulders, as much as three feet deep in places. By the time both huts were erected, nearly fifty tons of stones had been used in the foundations—a circumstance we did not regret at a later date.

Hodgeman was appointed clerk of works on the construction, and was kept unusually busy selecting timber, patrolling among the workmen, and searching for his foot-rule which had an unaccountable trick of vanishing in thin air.

Hannam had various occupations, but one was to attend to the needs of the inner man, until the completion of the hut. There is no doubt that he was regarded at this time as the most important and popular member of the party, for our appetites were abnormally good. About an hour before meals he was to be seen rummaging amongst the cases of provisions, selecting tins of various brands and hues from the great confusion. However remote their source or diverse their colour, experience taught us that only one preparation would emerge from the tent-kitchen. It was a multifarious stew. Its good quality was undoubted, for a few minutes after the "dinner-bell rang" there was not a particle left. The "dinner-bell" was

Adelie Penguins at Home, Cape Denison

a lusty shout from the master cook, which was re-echoed by the brawny mob who rushed madly to the Benzine Hut. Plates and mugs were seized and portions measured out, while the diners distributed themselves on odd boxes lying about on the ice. Many who were accustomed to restaurants built tables of kerosene cases and dined *al fresco*. After the limited stew, the company fared on cocoa, biscuits—"hard tack"—and jam, all *ad libitum*.

On those rare summer days, the sun blazed down on the blue ice; skua gulls nestled in groups on the snow; sly penguins waddled along to inspect the building operations; seals basked in torpid slumber on the shore; out on the sapphire bay the milk-white bergs floated in the swell. We can all paint our own picture of the good times round the Benzine Hut. We worked hard, ate heartily and enjoyed life.

By the evening of January 24 the floor and outside walls were finished, and the roof-frame was in position. Work on the roof was the coldest job of all, for now there was rarely an hour free from a cold breeze, at times reaching the velocity of a gale. This came directly down from the plateau, and to sit with exposed fingers handling hammer and nails was not an enviable job. To add to our troubles, the boards were all badly warped from being continually wet with sea-water on the voyage. However, by judicious "gadgetting," as the phrase went, they were got into place.

The windward roof was up on January 25, and several of us camped in sleeping-bags under its shelter. Already Hannam had unpacked the large range and put the parts together in the kitchen. Henceforth the cooking operations were simplified, for previously a sledging-cooker had been used.

Mention of the stove recalls a very cold episode. It happened that while our goods were being lifted from the boats to the landing-stage, a case had fallen into the harbour. When the parts of the stove were being assembled, several important items were found to be missing, and it was thought that they might compose the contents of the unknown case lying in the kelp at the bottom of the bay.

Laseron and I went on board the whale-boat one day at low water, and located the box with a pole, but though we used several devices with hooks, we were unable to get hold of it. At last I went in, and, standing on tip-toe, could just reach it and keep my head above water. It took some time to extricate from the kelp, following which I established a new record for myself in dressing. The case turned out to be full of jam, and we had to make a new search for the missing parts. I do not think I looked very exhilarated after that bath, but strange to say, a few days later Correll tried an early morning swim which was the last voluntary dip attempted by any one.

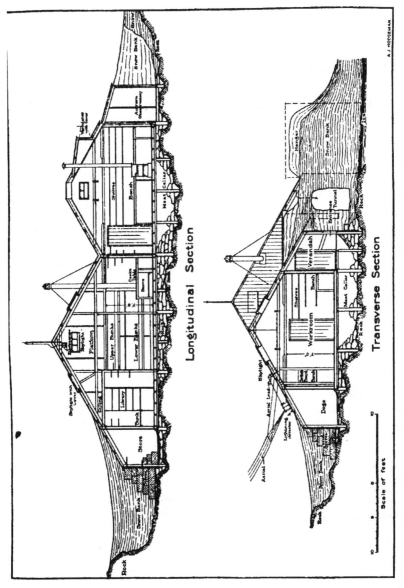

Sections Across the Hut, Adelie Land

The enthusiasm of the builders rose to its highest pitch as the roof neared completion, and we came in sight of a firm and solid habitation, secure from the winds which harassed us daily. A dozen hammers worked at once, each concentrated upon a specific job. The ardour with which those engaged upon the ceiling inside the hut plied their nails resulted in several minor casualties to those sitting on the roof, deeply intent on the outer lining. A climax was reached when McLean, working on the steeply inclined roof, lost his footing and, in passing, seized hold of the wire-stay of the chimney as a last hope. Alas, that was the only stay, and as he proceeded over the end of the roof into a bank of snow, Ninnis, within the hut, convinced that nothing less than a cyclone had struck the building, gallantly held on to the lower hot section amidst a shower of soot.

Everybody was in the best of spirits, and things went ahead merrily. On January 30 the main building was almost completed, and all slept under its roof. Bunks had been constructed, forming a double tier around three sides of the room. For the first time since coming ashore we retired to sleep in blankets; fur sleeping-bags had been previously used. That night the sky which had been clear for a fortnight banked up with nimbus cloud, and Murphy, who was sleeping under a gap in the roof, woke up next morning to find over him a fine counterpane of snow. He received hearty congratulations all round.

Regular meteorological observations began on February 1. The various instruments had been unpacked as soon as the outer shell of the Hut was completed. The barometer and barograph were kept running inside. Outside there were two large screens for the reception of a number of the instruments. It was important to erect these as near the Hut as possible. The standard thermometer, thermograph and hygrograph were to occupy one of the screens, a convenient site for which was chosen about twenty yards to the east. Close by there was also a nephoscope for determining the motion of clouds. The immediate vicinity of the Hut, being a gully-like depression, was unsuitable for the wind and sunshine recorders. A more distant site, on a rocky ridge to the east, was chosen for these. There were set up a recording anemometer (wind-velocity meter), a sunshine-meter and the second screen containing the anemograph (wind-direction recorder).

Madigan was to take charge of the meteorological observations and he, assisted by Ninnis and Mertz, erected the two screens and mounted the instruments. Special care was taken to secure the screens against violent winds. Phosphor-bronze wire-stays, with a breaking strength of one ton, were used, attached to billets of wood driven into fissures in the rock. Strong as these wires were, several breakages had to be replaced during the year.

Webb was busy with the magnetic work. For this two huts were to be erected; the first for "absolute" determinations, the second for housing the recording instruments—the magnetographs. Distant sites, away from the magnetic disturbances of the Hut, were chosen. Webb and Stillwell immediately set to work as soon as they could be spared from the main building. For the "absolute hut" there were only scrap materials available; the "magnetograph house," alone, had been brought complete. They had a chilly job, for as the days went by the weather steadily became worse. Yet in a little over a week there were only the finishing touches to make, and the first observations were started.

It was now necessary to institute a routine of night-watchmen, cooks and messmen. The night-watchman's duties included periodic meteorological observations, attention to the fire in the range, and other miscellaneous duties arising between the hours of 8 PM and 8 AM. The cook prepared the meals, and the messman of the day rendered any assistance necessary. A rotation was adopted, so arranged that those most actively engaged in scientific observations were least saddled with domestic duties. Thus each contributed his equivalent share of work.

Whilst others were occupied finishing off the interior of the hut, Whetter and Close sledged the cases of stores across from the landing-stage, classified them and stacked them against the veranda walls. An additional barricade was constructed of flour cases, in the form of a wall, which increased the breadth of the rocky break-wind on the southern side.

Murphy, who was in charge of all the stores, saw that a good stock of food was accessible in the veranda. Here he put up shelves and unpacked cases, so that samples of everything were at hand on the shortest notice. Liquids liable to freeze and burst their bottles were taken into the Hut.

Already we had several times seized the opportunity of a calm hour to take out the whale-boat and assist Hunter to set traps and make a few hauls with the hand-dredge. Even in five fathoms, bright red and brown star-fish had been caught in the trap, as well as numerous specimens of a common Antarctic fish known as *Notothenia*. In ten fathoms and over the results were better, though in no case was the catch so abundant as one would expect from the amount of life in the water. The luxuriant kelp probably interfered with the proper working of the traps. Fish of the same species as the above were caught on a hand-line.

Hunter, our biologist, was very unfortunate in crushing some of his fingers while carrying a heavy case. This accident came at a time when he had just recovered from a severe strain of the knee-joint which he suffered during our activities in the Queen's Wharf shed at Hobart. Several of us were just going out to the traps one afternoon when the casualty occurred. Hunter was very anxious to go, so we waited until McLean had sewn up a couple of his fingertips.

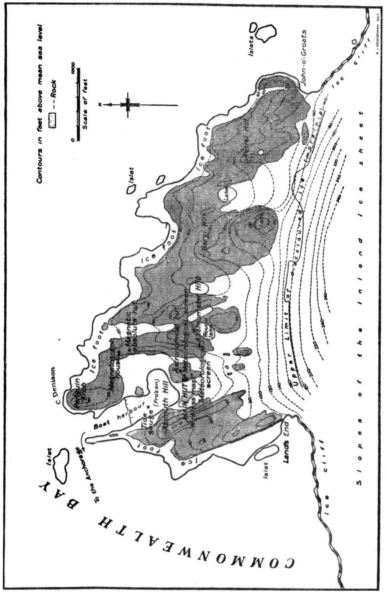

The Vicinity of the Main Base, Adelie Land

Weddell, and with them occasional crab-eater seals, were at this time always to be found in numbers sleeping on the ice-foot around the boat harbour. It appeared as if we would have plenty of meat throughout the year, so I waited until the building was completed before laying in a stock. The penguins, however, were diminishing in numbers fast and the young birds in the rookeries had grown very large and were beginning to migrate to warmer regions. Several parties, therefore, raided them and secured some hundreds for the winter.

Giant petrels and skua gulls swarmed in flocks round the seals' and penguins' carcases. These scavengers demolish an incredible amount of meat and blubber in a short time. It is a diabolical sight to witness a group of birds tearing out the viscera of a seal, dancing the while with wings outspread.

During the afternoon of February 11 Webb came in with the news that a sea elephant was making its way over the rocks near the shore. We rushed out in time to see it standing over Johnson, one of the dogs, who, true to his name, did not look abashed. Attracted by more formidable antagonists, the monster left Johnson and came towards us. He was a fair-sized male with a good skin, so we shot him before he had time to get back into the sea. His measurements were seventeen feet six inches in length and twelve feet in maximum circumference.

With the temperature well below freezing-point, skinning is cold work in the wind, and must be done before the animal has time to freeze stiff. A number of us set to work flaying. In order to move the mountain of flesh a Westing purchase and a "handy-billy" (rope and block purchase) had to be rigged. It was several hours before everything was disposed of; the skin and skull for the biological collection and the meat and blubber for the dogs. Ninnis and Mertz, who were the wardens of the dogs, cut up about one ton of meat and blubber, and stored it as a winter reserve for their charges.

It may be mentioned that sea elephants are sub-antarctic in distribution, and only rarely have these animals been observed on the shores of the Antarctic continent. As far as I am aware, the only other occasion of such an occurrence was noted by Captain Scott in McMurdo Sound. Wilkes reported many of them on the pack-ice to the north of the Balleny Islands, so possibly they have a stronghold in that vicinity.

The dogs, ever since their arrival ashore, had been chained up on the rocks below the Hut. The continuous wind worried them a good deal, but they had a substantial offset to the cold in a plentiful supply of seal-meat. On the whole, they were in a much better condition than when they left the *Aurora*. Nineteen in all, they had an odd assemblage of names, which seemed to grow into them until nothing else was so suitable: Basilisk, Betli, Caruso, Castor, Franklin, Fusilier, Gadget, George, Ginger, Ginger Bitch, Grandmother, Haldane, Jappy, John Bull, Johnson, Mary, Pavlova, Scott and Shackleton. Grandmother would have been better known as

A View of the Main Base Hut in February 1912, Just Prior to Its Completion. Within a Few Days of the Taking of This Picture the Hut Became So Buried in Packed Snow That Ever Afterwards Little Beyond the Roof Was to Be Seen.

Grandfather. He was said to have a grandmotherly appearance; that is why he received the former name. The head dog was Basilisk, and next to him came Shackleton.

Early in February, after having experienced nothing but a succession of gales for nearly a month, I was driven to conclude that the average local weather must be much more windy than in any other part of Antarctica. The conditions were not at all favourable for sledging, which I had hoped to commence as soon as the Hut was completed. Now that the time had arrived and the weather was still adverse, it seemed clear that our first duty was to see everything snug for the winter before making an attempt.

Hannam, assisted by Bickerton, Madigan and others, had laid heavy and firm foundations for the petrol-motor and generator. The floor of the smaller room was then built around these bed-plates, and last of all came the walls and roof. Murphy, Bage and Hodgeman were chiefly responsible for the last-named, which was practically completed by February 10. Minor additions and modifications were added after that date. Meanwhile, Hannam continued to unpack and mount the instruments forming the wireless plants. Along one wall and portion of another, in the outer hut, a bench was built for mechanical work and for scientific purposes. This was in future to be the work-room.

Our home had attained to a stage of complex perfection. To penetrate to the inside hut, the stranger reverently steps through a hole in the snow to the veranda, then by way of a vestibule with an inner and outer door he has invaded the privacy of the work-room, from which with fear and trembling he passes by a third door into the sanctum sanctorum. Later, when the snow-tunnel system came into vogue, the place became another Labyrinth of Minos.

The three doors were fitted with springs to keep them shut unless they were jammed open for ventilation, which was at once obtained by opening an aperture in the cooking-range flue. A current of air would then circulate through the open doors. The roof windows were immovable and sealed on the inside by a thick accumulation of ice. An officer of public health, unacquainted with the climate of Adelie Land, would be inclined to regard the absence of more adequate ventilation as a serious omission. It would enlighten him to know that much of our spare time, for a month after the completion of the building, was spent in plugging off draughts which found their way through most unexpected places, urged by a wind-pressure from without of many pounds to the square foot.

Excepting the small portion used as an entrance-porch, the verandas were left without any better flooring than well-trodden snow. In the boarded floor of the porch was a trap-door which led down into a shallow cellar extending under a portion of the work-room. The cellar was a refrigerating chamber for fresh meat and contained fifteen carcases of mutton, besides piles of seal-meat and penguins.

In preparation for our contemplated sledging, masts, spars and sails were fitted to some of the sledges, rations were prepared and alterations made to harness and clothing. Soon a sledge stood packed, ready to set out on the first fine day.

For several days in succession, about the middle of February, the otherwise continuous wind fell off to a calm for several hours in the evening. On those occasions Mertz gave us some fine exhibitions of skiing, of which art he was a consummate master. Skis had been provided for every one, in case we should have to traverse a country where the snow lay soft and deep. From the outset, there was little chance of that being the case in wind-scoured Adelie Land. Nevertheless, most of the men seized the few opportunities we had to become more practiced in their use. My final opinion, however, was that if we had all been experts like Mertz, we could have used them with advantage from time to time.

The end of February approached. We were fully prepared for sledging, and were looking forward to it with great expectation. The wind still continued, often rising to the force of a hurricane, and was mostly accompanied by snow.

One evening, when we were all at dinner, there was a sudden noise which drowned the rush of the blizzard. It was found that several sledges had been blown away from their position to the south of the Hut, striking the building as they passed. They were all rescued except one, which had already reached the sea and was travelling rapidly toward Australia.

Mertz, Bage and I had taken advantage of a lull to ascend the ice-slope to the south, and to erect a flag-pole at a distance of two miles. Besides being a beacon for sledging parties, it was used for ablation measurements. These were determinations of the annual wasting of the ice-surface, whether by evaporation, melting, or wind-abrasion.

Webb and Stillwell, assisted by others, had commenced to build the Magnetograph House. Dr. Chree, of the British National Physical Laboratory, had arranged that the German Antarctic Expedition, several observatories in low latitudes and our own Expedition, should take special "quick runs," synchronously, twice each month. A "quick run" was

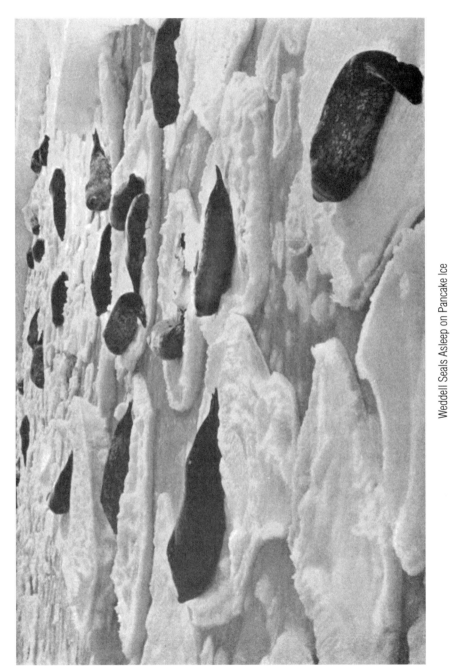

Weddell Seals Asleep on Pancake Ice

Adelie Penguin After Weathering a Severe Blizzard. Observe the Lumps of Ice Adhering to It

a continuous, careful observation made over a period of two hours, on a more searching time-scale than usual. Until the Magnetograph House was established this could not be done efficiently, and so the construction of this hut was pushed on as quickly as possible.

Many other schemes required our attention, and there was not a spare moment for any one. Though we chafed at the delay in sledging, there was some consolation in the fact that the scientific programme was daily becoming more and more complete.

The Weathered Cliffs of a Glacier Sheet Pushing Out into the Frozen Sea East of Cape Denison

CHAPTER VI

Autumn Prospects

A S FAR AS WE COULD SEE, THE INLAND ICE WAS AN unbroken plateau with no natural landmarks. From the hinterland in a vast solid stream the ice flowed, with heavily crevassed downfalls near the coast. Traversing this from north to south was a narrow belt, reasonably free from pitfalls, running as a spur down to the sea. To reach the Hut in safety it would be necessary for sledging parties returning from the interior to descend by this highway. The problem was to locate the path. Determinations of latitude and longitude would guide them to the neighbourhood of Commonwealth Bay, but the coastline in the vicinity of Winter Quarters, with the rocks and islets, would not come into view until within two miles, as above that point the icy slopes filled the foreground up to the distant berg-studded horizon. Delays in reaching the Hut owing to the difficult descent might have serious consequences, for provisions are usually short near the conclusion of a sledging journey.

The necessity of making artificial landmarks was, therefore, most obvious. Already we had a flagstaff two miles to the south. It was now my intention to run a line of similar marks backwards to the plateau.

Bage, Madigan and I were to form a reconnoitring party to plant these flags, and to make a journey of a few days' duration into the hinterland, to see its possibilities, and with a view to an extended sledging campaign to commence as soon as possible after our return. It was decided not to make use of the dogs until later in the year, when they would be in better form.

The wind continued, accompanied by more or less drift-snow. This appeared to be the settled state of the weather. We decided to move out as soon as a moderate phase should occur.

On the afternoon of February 28 the weather cleared up for several hours, and we decided to leave on the following day. The wind resumed operations once more, but fell off late on February 29, when we made a start. We intended to get the packed sledge up the first steep slope, there to leave it until the morrow. The drift was slight and low, flowing along like a stream below our knees. Bickerton, Hurley and Mertz assisted us with the hauling. At a distance of a little more than a mile, at an elevation of five hundred feet, the sledge was anchored and we returned to the Hut for the night.

Next morning the weather cleared still more, and we left just before noon. Three miles out, a mast and flag were erected, when our companions of the day before, who had again assisted us, turned back. At five and a half miles the brow of the main rise was reached, and the gradient became much flatter beyond it. The elevation was found to be one thousand five hundred feet.

To the south nothing was visible but a great, wan, icy wilderness. To the north a headland appeared on either hand, each about twenty-five miles away, and between them lay an expanse of sea dotted with many bergs. The nearer portions of the coast, together with the Mackellar Islets, were lost to view on account of the curvature of the foreground.

During most of the day we had travelled over a surface of clear ice, marked by occasional scars where fissuring, now healed, had at some time taken place. Beyond the three-mile flag, however, the ice was gashed at frequent intervals, producing irregular crevasses, usually a few yards in length and, for the most part, choked with snow. At five and a half miles we were on the edge of a strip of snow, half a mile across, whose whiteness was thrown in dazzling contrast against the foil of transparent, dark ice.

It was dusk, and light drift commenced to scud by, so, as this was a suitable place to erect a flag, we decided to camp for the night. Some hours later I woke up to hear a blizzard blowing outside, and to find Madigan fumbling amongst some gear at the head-end of the tent. From inside my bag I called out to inquire if there was anything wrong, and received a reply that he was looking for the primus-pricker. Then he slipped back into his sleeping-bag, and all became quiet, except for the snow beating against the tent. So I presumed that he had found it. Revolving the incident in my mind, and dimly wondering what use he could have for a primus-pricker in the middle of the night, I again fell asleep. In the morning the blizzard was still blowing, accompanied by a good deal of drift. On inquiry I found that Madigan knew nothing of his midnight escapade. It was a touch of somnambulism.

It would serve no useful purpose to go on in thick drift, for the main object of our journey was to define the best route through the crevassed zone; and that could only be done on a clear day. I decided, accordingly, that if the weather did not improve by noon to leave the sledge with the

An Evening View from Cape Denison

The Head of a Weddell Seal

A Weddell Seal Scratching Himself. "Drat Those Fleas!"

gear and walk back to the Hut, intending to make another attempt when conditions became more settled.

Whilst the others erected a flagstaff and froze the legs of a drift-proof box (containing a thermograph) into the ice, I made lunch and prepared for our departure. The tent was taken down and everything lashed securely on the sledge.

It was nearly 3 PM when we set out in thick drift, and in two hours we were at the Hut; the weather having steadily improved as we descended. On comparing notes with those at home it appeared that we, at the fifteen hundred feet level, had experienced much more wind and drift than they at sea-level.

Webb and his assistants were beginning to make quite a display at the Magnetograph House. The framework, which had already been erected once, to be demolished by the wind, was now strongly rebuilt and was ready for the outside covering of boards.

From the night of our return to March 8 there was a high wind accompanied by much drift; for some hours it continued at eighty miles per hour, the mean temperature being about 15° F., with a minimum of 5° F.

Up to this date the dogs had been kept on the chain, on account of their depredations amongst the seals and penguins. The severe weather now made it necessary to release them. Thenceforth, their abode for part of the day was inside the veranda, where a section was barricaded-off for their exclusive use. Outside in heavy drift their habit was to take up a position in the lee of some large object, such as the Hut. In such a position they were soon completely buried and oblivious to the outside elements. Thus one would sometimes tread on a dog, hidden beneath the snow; and the dog often showed less surprise than the offending man. What the dogs detested most of all during the blizzard-spells was the drift-snow filling their eyes until they were forced to stop and brush it away frantically with their paws. Other inconveniences were the icy casing which formed from the thawing snow on their thick coats, and the fact that when they lay in one position, especially on ice, for any length of time they become frozen down, and only freed themselves at the expense of tufts of hair. In high winds, accompanied by a low temperature, they were certainly very miserable, unless in some kind of shelter.

Several families were born at this time, but although we did everything possible for them they all perished, except one; the offspring of Gadget. This puppy was called "Blizzard." It was housed for a while in the veranda and, later on, in the Hangar. Needless to say, Blizzard was a great favourite and much in demand as a pet.

On the night of March 7, Caruso, who had been in poor condition for some time, was found to have a gaping wound around the neck. It was a clean cut, an inch deep and almost a foot in length. The cause was never satisfactorily explained, though a piece of strong string embedded in the wound evidently made the incision. Caruso was brought inside, and, whilst Whetter administered chloroform, McLean sewed up the wound. After careful attention for some days, it healed fairly well, but as the dog's general health was worse, it was deemed advisable to shoot him.

The outer shell of the Magnetograph House was nearly completed, affording a protection for those who worked on the interior linings. When completed, the walls and roof consisted of two coverings of tongued and grooved pine boards and three layers of thick tarred paper.

While there still remained a breach in the wall, Hurley repaired there with his cinematograph camera and took a film showing the clouds of drift-snow whirling past. In those days we were not educated in methods of progression against heavy winds; so, in order to get Hurley and his bulky camera back to the Hut, we formed a scrum on the windward side and with a strong "forward" rush beat our formidable opponent.

On March 8 the blizzard died away and a good day followed. All hands joined in building a solid stone outside of the Magnetograph House. This piece of work, in which thirty tons of rock were utilized, was completed on the following day. The wall reached almost to the roof on every side. The unprotected roof was lagged with sacks and sheep-skins and, after this had been effected, the hut became practically windtight. The external covering controlled the influx of cold from the penetrating winds, and, on the other hand, the conduction of the sun's warmth in summer. Thus a steady temperature was maintained; a most desirable feature in a magnetograph house. Webb had the instruments set up in a few days, and they were working before the end of the month.

After the calm of March 8, the wind steadily increased and became worse than ever. Madigan, who was in charge of the whale-boat, kept it moored in the boat-harbour under shelter of the ice-foot. An excursion was made to the fish traps, buoyed half a mile off shore, on February 8, and it was found that one had been carried away in the hurricane. The other was brought in very much battered. That night it was decided at the first opportunity to haul up the boat and house it for the winter. Alas! the wind came down again too quickly, increasing in force, with dense drift. It was still in full career on the 12th, when Madigan came in with the news that the boat had disappeared. It was no fault of the rope-attachments for they were securely made and so we were left to conclude that a great mass of ice had broken away from the overhanging shelf and carried everything before it.

The regularity of the high-velocity winds was already recognized as one of the most remarkable features of Adelie Land. By itself such wind would have been bad enough, but, accompanied by dense volumes of drifting snow, it effectually put a stop to most outdoor occupations.

The roof and walls of the veranda being covered with a single layer of tongued and grooved boards, the snow drove through every chink. The cases outside were a partial protection, but the cracks were innumerable, and in the course of twenty-four hours the snow inside had collected in deep drifts. This required to be shovelled out each day or the veranda would have been entirely blocked.

Much time was spent endeavouring to make it drift-tight; but as the materials at our disposal were very limited, the result was never absolutely satisfactory. The small veranda serving as an entrance-porch was deluged with snow which drove in past the canvas doorway. The only way to get over this trouble was to shovel out the accumulations every morning. On one occasion, when Close was night-watchman, the drift poured through in such volume that each time he wished to go outside it took

him half an hour to dig his way out. On account of this periodic influx, the vestibule doorway to the workroom was moved to the other end of the wall, where the invading snow had farther to travel and was consequently less obstructive.

One advantage of the deposit of snow around the Hut was that all draughts were sealed off. Before this happened it was found very difficult to keep the inside temperature up to 40° F. A temperature taken within the Hut varied according to the specific position in reference to the walls and stove. That shown by the thermometer attached to the standard barometer, which was suspended near the centre of the room, was taken as the "hut temperature." Near the floor and walls it was lower, and higher, of course, near the stove. On one occasion, in the early days, I remember the "hut temperature" being 19° F., notwithstanding the heat from the large range. Under these conditions the writing-ink and various solutions all over the place froze, and, when the night-watchman woke up the shivering community he had many clamorous demands to satisfy. The photographer produced an interesting product from the dark room—a transparent cast of a developing-dish in which a photographic plate left overnight to wash was firmly set.

We arranged to maintain an inside temperature of 40° F.; when it rose to 50° F. means were taken to reduce it. The cooking-range, a large one

The Meteorologist with an Ice-Mask

Where the Plateau Descends to Commonwealth Bay

designed to burn anthracite coal, was the general warming apparatus. To raise the temperature quickly, blocks of seal blubber, of which there was always a supply at hand, were used. The coal consumption averaged one hundred pounds a day, approximately, this being reduced at a later date to seventy-five pounds by employing a special damper for the chimney. The damper designed for ordinary climates allowed too much draught to be sucked through during the high winds which prevailed continually.

The chimney was fitted with a cowl which had to be specially secured to keep it in place. During heavy drifts the cowl became choked with snow and ice, and the Hut would rapidly fill with smoke until some one, hurriedly donning burberrys, rushed out with an ice-axe to chip an outlet for the draught. The chimney was very short and securely stayed, projecting through the lee side of the roof, where the pressure of the wind was least felt.

The first good display of aurora polaris was witnessed during the evening of March 12, though no doubt there had been other exhibitions obscured by the drift. As the days went by and the equinox drew near, auroral phenomena were with few exceptions visible on clear evenings. In the majority of cases they showed up low in the northern sky.

In the midst of a torment of wind, March 15 came as a beautiful, sunny, almost calm day. I remarked in my diary that it was "typical Antarctic weather," thinking of those halcyon days which belong to the climate of the southern shores of the Ross Sea. In Adelie Land, we were destined to find, it was hard to number more than a dozen or two in the year.

A fine day! the psychological effect was remarkable; pessimism vanished, and we argued that with the passing of the equinox there would be a marked change for the better. Not a moment was lost: some were employed in making anchorages for the wireless masts; others commenced to construct a Hangar to house the air-tractor sledge.

In building the Hangar, the western wall of the Hut was used for one side; the low southern end and the western wall were constructed of full and empty cases, the lee side was closed with a tarpaulin and blocks of snow and over all was nailed a roof of thick timber—part of the air-tractor's case. To stiffen the whole structure, a small amount of framework, in the form of heavy uprights, was set in the ground. The dimensions inside were thirty-four feet by eleven feet; the height, eleven feet at the northern and six feet at the southern end. As a break-wind a crescent-shaped wall of benzine cases was built several yards to the south. As in the case of the veranda, it was very difficult to make the Hangar impervious to drift; a certain quantity of snow always made its way in, and was duly shovelled out.

Seals had suddenly become very scarce, no doubt disgusted with the continuous winds. Every one that came ashore was shot for food. Unfortunately, the amount of meat necessary for the dogs throughout the winter was so great that dog-biscuits had to be used to eke it out.

Only a few penguins remained by the middle of March. They were all young ones, waiting for the completion of their second moult before taking to the sea. The old feathers hung in untidy tufts, and the birds were often in a wretched plight owing to the wind and drift-snow. Many were added to the bleaching carcases which fill the crevices or lie in heaps on ancient rookeries among the rocky ridges. None were free from the encumbrance of hard cakes of snow which often covered their eyes or dangled in pendent icicles from their bodies. The result was very ludicrous.

Hurley obtained some excellent photographs of the seals and penguins, as of all other subjects. So good were they that most of us withdrew from competition. His enthusiasm and resourcefulness knew no bounds. Occasional days, during which cameras that had been maltreated by the wind were patched up, were now looked upon as inevitable. One day, when Webb and Hurley were both holding on to the cinematograph camera, they were blown away, with sundry damages all around. It was later in the year when Hurley with his whole-plate camera broke through the sea-ice—a sad affair for the camera.

The good conditions on the 15th lasted only a few hours, and back came the enemy as bad as ever. On the 18th the wind was only thirty

Maccormick Skua Gull on the Nest with Egg

Chick of Maccormick Skua Gull on the Nest

miles per hour, giving us an opportunity of continuing the buildings outside. It was only by making the most of every odd hour when the weather was tolerable that our outdoor enterprises made any headway. Sometimes when it was too windy for building we were able to improve our knowledge of the neighbourhood.

A glance at Stillwell's map is instructive as to the extent and character of the rocky area. It is devoid of any forms of vegetation sufficiently prominent

Protection—Adelie Penguin and Chick

to meet the casual eye. Soil is lacking, for all light materials and even gravel are carried away by the winds. The bare rock rises up into miniature ridges, separated by valleys largely occupied by ice-slabs and lakelets. Snow fills all the crevices and tails away in sloping ramps on the lee side of every obstacle. In midsummer a good deal thaws, and, re freezing, is converted into ice. The highest point of the rock is one hundred and forty feet. The seaward margin is deeply indented, and the islets off shore tell of a continuation of the rugged, rocky surface below the sea. On the northern faces of the ridges, fronting the ice-foot, large, yellowish patches mark the sites of penguin rookeries. These are formed by a superficial deposit of guano which never becomes thick, for it blows away as fast as it accumulates. Standing on the shore, one can see kelp growing amongst the rocks even in the shallowest spots, below low-water level.

To the south, the rocks are overridden by the inland ice which bears down upon and overwhelms them. The ice-sheet shows a definite basal moraine, which means that the lowest stratum, about forty feet in thickness, is charged with stones and earthy matter. Above this stratum the ice is free from foreign matter and rises steeply to several hundred feet, after which the ascending gradient is reduced.

The continental glacier moves down to the sea, regularly but slowly; the rate of movement of some portions of the adjacent coastal ice cliffs was found to be one hundred feet per annum. The rocky promontory at Winter Quarters, acting as an obstacle, reduces the motion of the ice to an annual rate measured in inches only. Perhaps the conditions now prevailing are those of a comparative "drought," for there is clear evidence that our small promontory was at one time completely enveloped. In a broad way this is illustrated by the topography, but the final proof came when Stillwell and others discovered rock-faces polished and grooved by the ice.

Whatever "ice-floods" there may have been in the past, the position of the margin of the glacier must have remained for a long period in its present situation. The evidence for this is found in the presence of a continuous, terminal moraine, at or just in advance of the present ice-front. This moraine, an accumulation of stones of all kinds brought to their present resting-place by the ice-sheet, was in itself a veritable museum. Rocks, showing every variety in colour and form, were assembled, transported from far and wide over the great expanse of the continent.

Stillwell found these moraines a "happy hunting-ground" for the geologist. His plane-table survey and rock collections are practical evidence of work carried out in weather which made it seldom short of an ordeal.

The story of the buried land to the south is in large measure revealed in the samples brought by the ice and so conveniently dumped. Let us swiftly review the operations leading to the deposition of this natural museum.

As the ice of the hinterland moves forward, it plucks fragments from the rocky floor. Secure in its grip, these are used as graving-tools to erode its bed.

The Grey Rock Hills at Cape Denison

121

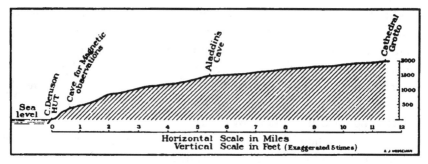

A Section of the Coastal Slope of the Continental Ice-Sheet Inland from Winter Quarters, Adelie Land

Throwing its whole weight upon them it grinds and scratches, pulverizes and grooves. The rocky basement is gradually reduced in level, especially the softer regions. The tools are faceted, polished and furrowed, for ever moving onwards. Finally, the rock-powder or "rock-flour," as it is termed, and the boulders, thenceforth known as "erratics," arrive at the terminal ice-face. Here, the melting due to the sun's heat keeps pace with the "on-thrust" and some of the erratics may remain stationary, or else, floating in the sea, a berg laden with boulders breaks off and deposits its load in the depths of the ocean. Each summer the ice-face above the rocks at Winter Quarters thawed back a short distance and the water ran away in rivulets, milky-white on account of the "rock-flour" in suspension. The pebbles and boulders too heavy to be washed away remained behind to form the moraine.

The "erratics" comprised a great variety of metamorphic and igneous rocks, and, on a more limited scale, sedimentary types. Amongst the latter were sandstones, slates, shales and limestones.

Apart from the moraines, the rock exposed *in situ* was mainly a uniform type of gneiss, crumpled and folded, showing all the signs of great antiquity—pre-Cambrian, in the geological phrase. Relieving the grey sheen of the gneiss were dark bands of schist which tracked about in an irregular manner. Sporadic quartz veins here and there showed a light tint. They were specially interesting, for they carried some less common minerals such as beryl, tourmaline, garnet, coarse mica and ores of iron, copper and molybdenum. The ores were present in small quantities, but gave promise of larger bodies in the vicinity and indicated the probability of mineral wealth beneath the continental ice-cap.

The Lower Moraine, Composed of Water Worn Boulders, Cape Denison

An Ice-Polished Surface, Cape Denison

The Boat Harbour in March. The Hut Is Seen Dimly Through Light Drift

CHAPTER VII

The Blizzard

THE EQUINOX ARRIVED, AND THE ONLY INDIC-
ation of settled weather was a more marked regularity in the winds.
Nothing like it had been reported from any part of the world. Any
trace of elation we may have felt at this meteorological discovery could not
compensate for the ever-present discomforts of life. Day after day the wind
fluctuated between a gale and a hurricane. Overcast skies of heavy nimbus
cloud were the rule and the air was continually charged with drifting snow.

Lulls of a singular nature occasionally relieved the monotony. During
these visitations the sequence of events could almost be predicted; indeed,
they would often occur at the same time on several succeeding days.

On March 19 the first well-marked lull intervened at the height of a gale.
On that day the wind, which had been blowing with great force during the
morning, commenced to subside rapidly just after noon. Towards evening,
the air about the Hut was quite still except for gusts from the north and
rather frequent "whirlies."

This was the name adopted for whirlwinds of a few yards to a hundred
yards or more in diameter which came to be regarded as peculiar to the
country. Similar disturbances have been observed in every part of the
world, but seldom possessed of the same violence and regularity as is the
case in Adelie Land.

The whirlies tracked about in a most irregular manner and woe
betide any light object which came in their path. The velocity of the
wind in the rotating column being very great, a corresponding lifting
power was imparted to it. As an illustration of this force, it may be
mentioned that the lid of the air-tractor case had been left lying on
the snow near the Hut. It weighed more than three hundredweights,
yet it was whisked into the air one morning and dropped fifty yards
away in a north-easterly direction. An hour afterwards it was picked
up again and returned near its original position, this time striking the

125

rocks with such force that part of it was shivered to pieces. Webb and Stillwell watched the last proceeding at a respectful distance.

Again, the radius of activity of these whirlies was strictly limited; objects directly in their path only being disturbed. For instance, Laseron one day was skinning at one end of a seal and remained in perfect calm, while McLean, at the other extremity, was on the edge of a furious vortex.

Travelling over the sea the whirlies displayed fresh capabilities. Columns of brash-ice, frozen spray and water-vapour were frequently seen lifted to heights of from two hundred to four hundred feet, simulating water spouts.

Reverting to the afternoon of March 19. Beyond the strange stillness of the immediate vicinity, broken occasionally by the tumult of a passing, wandering whirly, an incessant, seething roar could be heard. One could not be certain from whence it came, but it seemed to proceed either from the south or overhead. Away on the icy promontories to the east and west, where the slopes were visible, mounting to an altitude of several thousand feet, clouds of drift-snow blotted out the details of the surface above a level of about six hundred feet. It certainly appeared as if the gale, for some reason, had lifted and was still raging overhead. At 7.30 PM the sound we had heard, like the distant lashing of ocean waves, became louder. Soon gusts swept the tops of the rocky ridges, gradually descending to throw up the snow at a lower level. Then a volley raked the Hut, and within a few minutes we were once more enveloped in a sea of drifting snow, and the wind blew stronger than ever.

The duration of the lulls was ordinarily from a few minutes to several hours; that of March 19 was longer than usual. In the course of time, after repeated observations, much light was thrown on this phenomenon. On one occasion, a party ascending the ice slopes to the south met the wind blowing at an elevation of four hundred feet. At the same time snow could be seen pouring over the "Barrier" to the west of the Winter Quarters, and across a foaming turmoil of water. This was evidently the main cause of the seething roar, but it was mingled with an undernote of deeper tone from the upland plateau—like the wind in a million tree-tops.

In the early spring, while we were transporting provisions to the south, frequent journeys were made to higher elevations. It was then established that even when whole days of calm prevailed at the Hut, the wind almost without exception blew above a level of one thousand feet. On such occasions it appeared that the gale was impelled to blow straight out from the plateau slopes over a lower stratum of dead-air. An explanation was thereby afforded of the movement of condensation clouds which appeared in the zenith at these times. A formation of delicate, gauzy clouds developed at a low altitude, apparently in still air, but doubtless at the base of a hurricane stratum. Whirling round rapidly in eddying flocculi, they quickly tailed away to the north, evaporating and disappearing.

The auditory sense was strangely affected by these lulls. The contrast was so severe when the racking gusts of an abating wind suddenly gave way to intense, eerie silence, that the habitual droning of many weeks would still reverberate in the ears. At night one would involuntarily wake up if the wind died away, and be loth to sleep "for the hunger of a sound." In the open air the stillness conveyed to the brain an impression of audibility, interpreted as a vibratory murmur.

During one hour on March 22 it blew eighty-six miles. On the morning of that day there was not much snow in the air and the raging sea was a fearful sight. Even the nearest of the islands, only half a mile off the land, was partially hidden in the clouds of spray. What an impossible coast this would be for the wintering of a ship!

Everybody knows that the pressure exerted by a wind against an object in its path mounts up in much greater proportion than the velocity of the wind. Thus may be realized the stupendous force of the winds of Adelie Land in comparison with those of half the velocity which fall within one's ordinary experience. As this subject was ever before us, the following figures quoted from a work of reference will be instructive. The classification of winds, here stated, is that known as the "Beaufort scale." The corresponding velocities in each case are those measured by the "Robinson patent" anemometer; our instrument being of a similar pattern.

Beyond the limits of this scale, the pressures exerted rise very rapidly. A wind recorded as blowing at the rate of a hundred miles per hour exerts a pressure of about twenty-three pounds per square foot of surface exposed to it. Wind above eighty miles per hour is stated to "prostrate everything."

The mileages registered by our anemometer were the mean for a whole hour, neglecting individual gusts, whose velocity much exceeded the average and which were always the potent factors in destructive work.

Obviously the greatest care had to be taken to secure everything. Still, articles of value were occasionally missed. They were usually recovered, caught in crevices of rock or amongst the broken ice. Northward from the Hut there was a trail of miscellaneous objects scattered among the hummocks and pressure-ridges out towards Penguin Hill on the eastern

Beaufort Scale.		Velocities in miles per hour.	Pressures in lbs. per square foot of area.	Apparent effect.
0	Calm	2	0.02	May cause smoke to move
1	Light air	4	0.06	from the vertical Moves the leaves of trees
2	Light breeze	7	0.19	Moves small branches
3	Gentle breeze	10	0.37	of trees
4	Moderate breeze	14	0.67	and blows up dust
5	Fresh breeze	19	1.16	Good sailing breeze and makes
6	Strong breeze	25	1.90	white caps
7	Moderate gale	31	2.81	Sways trees and breaks small
8	Fresh gale	37	3.87	branches
9	Strong gale	44	5.27	Dangerous for sailing-
10	Whole gale	53	7.40	vessels
11	Storm	64	10.40	Prostrates exposed tress and
12	Hurricane	77	14.40	frail houses

side of the boat harbour: tins of all kinds and sizes, timber in small scraps, cases and boards, paper, ashes, dirt, worn-out finnesko, ragged mitts and all the other details of a rubbish heap. One of the losses was a heavy case which formed the packing of part of the magnetometer. Weighted-down by stones this had stood for a long time in what was regarded as a safe place. One morning it was discovered to be missing. It was surmised that a hurricane had started it on an ocean voyage during the previous day. Boxes in which Whetter used to carry ice for domestic requirements were as a rule short-lived. His problem was to fill the boxes without losing hold of them, and the wind often gained the ascendancy before a sufficient ballast had been added. We sometimes wondered whether any of the flotsam thus cast upon the waters ever reached the civilized world.

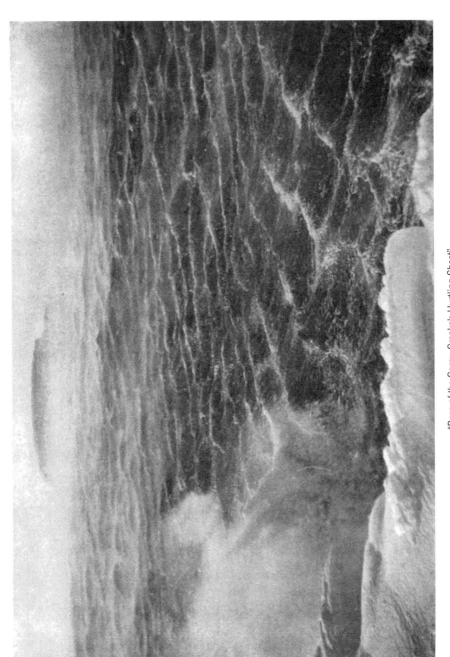

"Race of the Spray-Smoke's Hurtling Sheet"

Walking Against a Strong Wind

Picking Ice for Domestic Purposes in a Hurricane Wind. Note the High Angle at Which Webb Is Leaning on the Wind

Whatever has been said relative to the wind-pressure exerted on inanimate objects, the same applied, with even more point, to our persons; so that progression in a hurricane became a fine art. The first difficulty to be encountered was a smooth, slippery surface offering no grip for the feet. Stepping out of the shelter of the Hut, one was apt to be immediately hurled at full length down wind. No amount of exertion was of any avail unless a firm foothold had been secured. The strongest man, stepping on to ice or hard snow in plain leather or fur boots, would start sliding away with gradually increasing velocity; in the space of a few seconds, or earlier, exchanging the vertical for the horizontal position. He would then either stop suddenly against a jutting point of ice, or glide along for twenty or thirty yards till he reached a patch of rocks or some rough sastrugi.

Of course we soon learned never to go about without crampons on the feet. Many experiments in the manufacture of crampons were tried with the limited materials at our disposal. Those designed for normal Antarctic conditions had been found unserviceable. A few detachable pairs made of wrought iron with spikes about one and a half inches in length, purchased in Switzerland, gave a secure foothold. Some of the men covered the soles of their boots with long, bristling spikes and these served their purpose well. Ice-nails, screwed into the soles without being riveted on plates, were liable to tear out when put to a severe test, besides being too short. Spikes of less than an inch in length were inadequate in hurricanes. Nothing devised by us gave the grip of the Swiss crampons, but, to affix them, one had to wear leather boots, which, though padded to increase their warmth, had to be tightly bound by lashings compressing the feet and increasing the liability to frost-bite.

Shod with good spikes, in a steady wind, one had only to push hard to keep a sure footing. It would not be true to say "to keep erect," for equilibrium was maintained by leaning against the wind. In course of time, those whose duties habitually took them out of doors became thorough masters of the art of walking in hurricanes—an accomplishment comparable to skating or skiing. Ensconced in the lee of a substantial break-wind, one could leisurely observe the unnatural appearance of others walking about, apparently in imminent peril of falling on their faces.

Experiments were tried in the steady winds; firmly planting the feet on the ground, keeping the body rigid and leaning over on the invisible support. This "lying on the wind," at equilibrium, was a unique experience. As a rule the velocity remained uniform; when it fluctuated in a series of gusts, all our experience was likely to fail, for no sooner had the correct angle for the maximum velocity been assumed than a lull intervened—with the obvious result.

This particular record illustrates a day of constant high velocity wind. In the case of the upper chart each rise of the pen from the bottom to the top of the paper indicates that another 100 miles of wind has passed the instrument. The regularity of these curves shows the steadiness of the wind. It will be observed that the average velocity for twenty-four hours was 90.1 miles, and the maximum of the average hourly velocities throughout that period was ninety-seven miles. The lower chart, the record of the direction from which the wind blew, is marked only by a single broad bar in the position of South-by-East, the wind not having veered in the slightest degree.

Before the art of "hurricane-walking" was learnt, and in the primitive days of ice-nails and finnesko, progression in high winds degenerated into crawling on hands and knees. Many of the more conservative persisted in this method, and, as a compensation, became the first exponents of the popular art of "board-sliding." A small piece of board, a wide ice flat and a hurricane were the three essentials for this new sport.

Wind alone would not have been so bad; drift snow accompanied it in overwhelming amount. In the autumn overcast weather with heavy falls of snow prevailed, with the result that the air for several months was seldom free from drift. Indeed, during that time, there were not many days when objects a hundred yards away could be seen distinctly. Whatever else happened, the wind never abated, and so, even when the snow had ceased falling and the sky was clear, the drift continued until all the loose accumulations on the hinterland, for hundreds of miles back, had been swept out to sea. Day after day deluges of drift streamed past the Hut, at times so dense as to obscure objects three feet away, until it seemed as if the atmosphere were almost solid snow.

At the time of plotting only the above two months were available, but they are enough to illustrate the unusually severe winter conditions of Adelie Land. The data for Cape Royds is that supplied by the Shackleton Expedition. The solid black line refers to Adelie Land, the broken line to Cape Royds. It will be noted that whereas the average temperature conditions are closely similar at both stations, only on three days during the period did the average wind velocity at Cape Royds reach that of the lowest daily value of Adelie Land.

Picture drift so dense that daylight comes through dully, though, maybe, the sun shines in a cloudless sky; the drift is hurled, screaming through

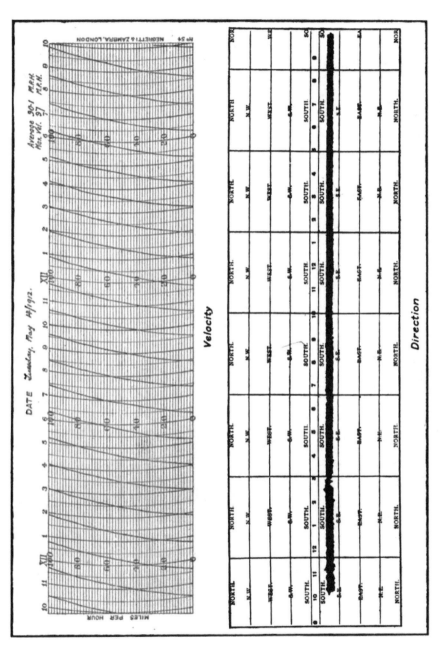

A Copy of the Wind-Velocity (Anemometer) and the Wind Direction (Anemograph) for a Period of Twenty-Four Hours, Adelie Land

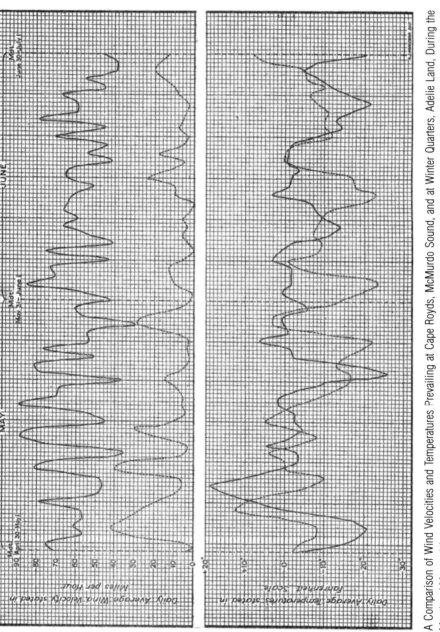

A Comparison of Wind Velocities and Temperatures Prevailing at Cape Royds, McMurdo Sound, and at Winter Quarters, Adelie Land, During the Months of May and June

space at a hundred miles an hour, and the temperature is below zero, Fahrenheit.** You have then the bare, rough facts concerning the worst blizzards of Adelie Land. The actual experience of them is another thing.

Shroud the infuriated elements in the darkness of a polar night, and the blizzard is presented in a severer aspect. A plunge into the writhing storm-whirl stamps upon the senses an indelible and awful impression seldom equalled in the whole gamut of natural experience. The world a void, grisly, fierce and appalling. We stumble and struggle through the Stygian gloom; the merciless blast—an incubus of vengeance—stabs, buffets and freezes; the stinging drift blinds and chokes. In a ruthless grip we realize that we are

> poor windlestraws
> *On the great, sullen, roaring pool of Time.*

It may well be imagined that none of us went out on these occasions for the pleasure of it. The scientific work required all too frequent journeys to the instruments at a distance from the Hut, and, in addition, supplies of ice and stores had to be brought in, while the dogs needed constant attention.

Every morning, Madigan visited all the meteorological instruments and changed the daily charts; at times having to feel his way from one place to the other. Attending to the exposed instruments in a high wind with low temperature was bad enough, but with suffocating drift difficulties were increased tenfold.

Around the Hut there was a small fraternity who chose the outside veranda as a rendezvous. Here the latest gossip was exchanged, and the weather invariably discussed in forcible terms. There was Whetter, who replenished the water-supply from the unfailing fountain-head of the glacier. For cooking, washing clothes and for photographic and other purposes, eighteen men consumed a good deal of water, and, to keep up with the demand, Whetter piled up many hardly-won boxes of ice in the veranda. Close unearthed coal briquettes from the heap outside, shovelled tons of snow from the veranda and made himself useful and amiable to every one. Murphy, our stand-by in small talk, travel, history, literature and what not, was the versatile storeman. The store in the veranda was continually invaded by similar snow to that which covered the provision boxes outside. To keep the veranda cleared, renew the supplies and satisfy

---

** *Temperatures as low as −28° F. (60° below freezing-point) were experienced in hurricane winds, which blew at a velocity occasionally exceeding one hundred miles per hour. Still air and low temperatures, or high winds and moderate temperatures, are well enough; but the combination of high winds and low temperatures is difficult to bear.*

the demands of the kitchen required no other than Murphy. Ninnis and Mertz completed the "Veranda Club," to which honorary members from within the Hut were constantly being added.

The meteorological instruments, carefully nursed and housed though they were, were bound to suffer in such a climate. Correll, who was well fitted out with a lathe and all the requirements for instrument-making, attended to repairs, doing splendid service. The anemometer gave the greatest trouble, and, before Correll had finished with it, most of the working parts had been replaced in stronger metal.

When the recording sheets of the instruments had been successfully changed, the meteorologist packed them in a leather bag, strapped on his shoulders, so that they would not be lost on the way to the Hut. As soon as he arrived indoors the bag was opened and emptied; the papers being picked out from a small heap of snow.

It was a fortunate thing that no one was lost through failing to discover the Hut during the denser drifts. Hodgeman on one occasion caused every one a good deal of anxiety. Among other things, he regularly assisted Madigan by relieving him of outdoor duties on the day after his night-watch, when the chief meteorologist was due for a "watch below." It was in the early autumn—few of us, then, were adepts at finding our way by instinct—that Hodgeman and Madigan set out, one morning, for the anemometer. Leaving the door of the Hut, they lost sight of each other at once, but anticipated meeting at the instrument. Madigan reached his destination, changed the records, waited for a while and then returned, expecting to see his companion at the Hut. He did not appear, so, after a reasonable interval, search parties set off in different directions.

The wind was blowing at eighty miles per hour, making it tedious work groping about and hallooing in the drift. The sea was close at hand and we realized that, as the wind was directly off shore, a man without crampons was in a dangerous situation. Two men, therefore, roped together and carefully searched round the head of the boat harbour; one anchoring himself with an ice-axe, whilst the other, at the end of the rope, worked along the edge of the sea. Meanwhile Hodgeman returned to the Hut, unaided, having spent a very unpleasant two hours struggling from one landmark to another, his outer garments filled with snow.

The fact that the wind came steadily from the same direction made it possible to steer, otherwise outdoor operations would not have been conducted so successfully. For instance, Webb, who visited the Magnetograph House, a quarter of a mile distant, at least once a day, made his way between various "beacons" by preserving a definite bearing on the wind. His journeys were rendered all the more difficult because they were frequently undertaken at night.

In struggling along through very dense drifts one would be inclined to think that the presence of the sun was a matter of small concern. As a matter of fact there was, during the day, a good deal of reflected white light and a dark object looms up within a yard or two. In darkness there was nothing to recognize. So Webb would often run by dead reckoning on to the roof of the Hut, and would then feel his way round it till he caught the glimmer of a hurricane lantern coming through the veranda entrance.

I had always the greatest admiration for the unfailing manner in which those responsible for the tidal, magnetic and meteorological work carried out their duties.

As a measure of the enormous amount of drift, we set about constructing a gauge, which, it was hoped, would give us a rough estimate of the quantity passing the Hut in a year. Hannam, following the approved design, produced a very satisfactory contrivance. It consisted of a large drift-tight box, fitted on the windward side with a long metal cone, tapering to an aperture three-quarters of an inch in diameter. The drift-laden air entered the aperture, its speed was checked on entering the capacious body of the gauge and consequently the snow fell to the bottom of the box and the air passed out behind through a trap-door. The catch was taken out periodically through a bolted lid, the snow was melted, the resulting water measured and its weight calculated.

In thick drifts, one's face inside the funnel of the burberry helmet became rapidly packed with snow, which, by the warmth of the skin and breath, was changed into a mask of ice. This adhered firmly to the rim of the helmet and to the beard and face. The mask became so complete that one had to clear away obstructions continually from the eyes. It was not easy to remove the casing of ice, outside in the wind, because this could only be done slowly, with bare fingers exposed. An experienced man, once inside the Hut, would first see that the ice was broken along the rim of the helmet; otherwise, when it came to be hastily dragged off, the hairs of the beard would follow as well. As soon as the helmet was off the head, the icicles hanging on the beard and glazing the eyelashes were gradually thawed by the fingers and removed. The above treatment was learned by experience.

The abrasion-effects produced by the impact of the snow particles were astonishing. Pillars of ice were cut through in a few days, rope was frayed, wood etched and metal polished. Some rusty dog-chains were exposed to

Leaning upon the Wind; Madigan Near the Meteorological Screen

it, and, in a few days, they had a definite sheen. A deal box, facing the wind, lost all its painted bands and in a fortnight was handsomely marked; the hard, knotty fibres being only slightly attacked, whilst the softer, pithy laminae were corroded to a depth of one-eighth of an inch.

The effect of constant abrasion upon the snow's surface is to harden it, and, finally, to carve ridges known as sastrugi. Of these much will be said when recounting our sledging adventures, because they increase so much the difficulties of travelling.

Even hard, blue ice may become channelled and pitted by the action of drift. Again, both névé and ice may receive a wind-polish which makes them very slippery.

Of the effect of wind and drift upon rock, there was ample evidence around Winter Quarters. Regarded from the north, the aspect of the rocks was quite different from that on the southern side. The southern, windward faces were on the whole smooth and rounded, but there was no definite polish, because the surface was partly attacked by the chipping and splitting action of frost. The leeward faces were rougher and more disintegrated. More remarkable still were the etchings of the non-homogeneous banded rocks. The harder portions of these were raised in relief, producing quite an artistic pattern.

Stillwell Collecting Geological Specimens in the Wind

In the Blizzard; Getting Ice for Domestic Purposes from the Glacier Adjacent to the Hut

In regard to the drift, a point which struck me was the enormous amount of cold communicated to the sea by billions of tons of low-temperature snow thrown upon its surface. The effect upon the water, already at freezing-point, would be to congeal the surface at once. Whilst the wind continued, however, there was no opportunity for a crust to form, the uppermost layers being converted into a pea-soup-like film which streamed away to the north.

A description of the drifts of Adelie Land would not be complete without mentioning the startling electrical effects which were sometimes observed. The first record of these was made by McLean, when on night-watch on March 22. While taking the observations at midnight, he noticed St. Elmo's fire, a "brush discharge" of electricity, on the points of the nephoscope. As the weather became colder this curious phenomenon increased in intensity. At any time in the drift, an electroscope exposed outside became rapidly charged. A spark gap in a vacuum, connected with a free end of wire, gave a continuous discharge. At times, when the effects were strong, the night-watchman would find the edges and wire stays of the screen outlined in a fashion reminiscent of a pyrotechnic display or an electric street-advertisement. The corners of boxes and points of rock glowed with a pale blue light. The same appeared over points on the clothing, on the mitts and round the funnel of the helmet. No sensation was transmitted to the body from these points of fire, at least nothing sufficiently acute to be felt, with the drift and wind lashing on the body outside. However, the anemograph several times discharged a continuous

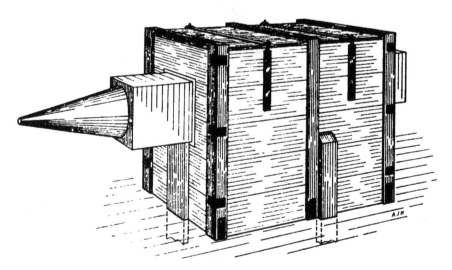

The Drift Gauge

stream of sparks into Madigan's fingers while he was changing the records. Once these sparks reached half an inch in length, and, as his fingers were bared for the work, there was no mistaking the feeling.

For regular observations on the subject, Correll fixed a pointed collector—a miniature lightning-conductor—above the flagpole on the summit of the roof. A wire was led through an insulator, so that the stream of electricity could be subjected to experiment in the Hut. Here a "brush" of blue light radiated outwards to a distance of one inch. When a conductor was held close to it, a rattling volley of sparks immediately crossed the interval and the air was pervaded with a strong smell of ozone. Of course sparks were not always being emitted by the collector, and it was important to determine the periods of activity. To ensure this, Hurley devised an automatic arrangement, so that an electric bell was set ringing whenever a current was passing; the night-watchman would then note the fact in the log-book. However, the bell responded so often and so vigorously that it was soon dismantled for the benefit of sleepers. It was singular that the "brush discharge" was sometimes most copious when the atmosphere was filled with very fine drift, and not necessarily during dense drift.

After what has been said, it will be obvious that the drift-laden hurricanes of the country were more than ordinarily formidable. They scarcely seemed to provide a subject for poetic inspiration; still the following effusion appeared by McLean, Editor of the *Adelie Blizzard*:—

THE BLIZZARD

A snow-hush brooding o'er the grey rock-hills!
A world of silence, ominous, that fills
The wide seascape of ice-roofed islands, rolls
To ether-zones that gird the frigid Poles!

Realm of purest alabaster-white,
Wreathed in a vast infinitude of light;
The royal orb swings to thy summer gaze
A glitt'ring azure world of crystal days.

The lorn bird-voices of an unseen land—
No hue of forest, gleam of ocean sand—
Rise in a ceaseless plaint of raucous din,
On northern tides the bergs come floating in.

The wind-sprites murmuring in hinter-snow—

The pent heart-throbbings of the wan plateau—
Wing through the pulsing spell thrown o'er the sea,
In wild and shrieking blizzard minstrelsy.

Swirl of the drift-cloud's shimm'ring sleet;
Race of the spray-smoke's hurtling sheet;
Swelling trail of the streaming, sunbright foam,
Wafting sinuous brash to an ice-field home.
Eddy-wraiths o'er the splintered schist—
Torrent spume down the glacier hissed!
Throbbing surge of the ebbing seaward gust,
Raping stillness vast in its madd'ning lust.

Lotus-floe 'neath the Barrier brink,
Starting sheer—a marble blink—
Pelting shafts from the show'ring arrow-blast
Strike—ill the blackened flood seethe riven past.

Glow of the vibrant, yellow west
Pallid fades in the dread unrest.
Low'ring shades through the fury-stricken night
Rack the screaming void in shudd'ring might.

Requiem peace from the hinter-snows
Soft as river music flows.
Dawn in a flushing glamour tints the sea;
Serene her thrill of rhythmic ecstasy.

Sledging was out of the question. Indeed, we recognized how fortunate we were not to have pushed farther south in March. Had we advanced, it is more than likely that provisions would have been exhausted before we could have located the Hut in the sea of drift. Our hopes were now centred on midwinter calms.

Looking through my diary, I notice that on March 24, "we experienced a rise in spirits because of the improved weather." I find the average velocity of the wind for that day to have been forty-five miles per hour, corresponding to a "strong gale" on the Beaufort scale. This tells its own story.

When the high wind blew off shore, there was no backswell, on account of the pack-ice to the north quelling the sea. The arrival of a true ocean swell meant that the pack had been dispersed. On March 24 such appears to have been the case, for then, during the day, a big northerly swell set in, dashing over the ice-foot and scattering seaweed on the rocks.

After the equinox, the temperatures remained in the vicinity of zero, Fahrenheit. The penguins took to the sea, and, save for the glimpse of an occasional petrel on the wing, the landscape was desolate.

It was high time that our programme of construction was completed, but, however much we tried, it was impossible to do a great deal in winds exceeding fifty miles an hour. By taking advantage of days freest from drift, the exterior of the Hangar was completed by April 6. After the air-tractor sledge had been moved inside, the snow was piled so high on the leeward face, that the shelter became naturally blocked with a rampart of snow which served admirably in place of the wall of tarpaulin which we originally intended to use.

Bickerton could now proceed at leisure to make any necessary alterations. The Hangar was also used as a store for many articles which had been crowded into odd corners or rescued from the snow outside. To increase its size, tunnels were afterwards driven into the bank of snow and timber was stowed in these so as to be safe from burial and loss.

The building was finished just in the nick of time. Snow came down so thickly that had the falls occurred a few days earlier, the cases from which the place was constructed would have been effectually buried and the construction made an impossibility.

But for the wind, the Hut would have been lost to sight. Still, it was completely surrounded by massive drifts, and the snow was driven by the wind past the canvas flap and through the entrance, until the veranda became choked.

Close, who was night-watchman during the early morning hours of April 7, had the greatest difficulty in getting outside to attend to his duties. To dig his way through the entrance, reach the instruments and to return occupied a whole hour.

We were inundated with snow; even a portion of the roof was buried. The situation required immediate attention; so it was decided to make a tunnel connecting the entrance veranda with the store veranda. From the north-western end of the latter, an out-draught had established itself, preserving a vertical funnel-like opening in the snow bank, always free for entrance or exit. This proved a fortunate accident.

Further, a second tunnel, over twenty feet in length, was driven out from the original entrance with a view to reaching the surface at a point beyond the lee of the Hut. It was thought that the scouring effect of the

An Incident in March Soon After the Completion of the Hut: Hodgeman, the Night Watchman, Returning from His Rounds Outside, Pushes His Way into the Veranda Through the Rapidly Accumulating Drift Snow.

Mertz in the Snow Tunnels on His Way to the Interior of the Hut with a Box of Ice for the Melters

Mertz Emerging from the Trap-Door in the Roof

wind, there, would keep the opening of the tunnel free of drift. But when completed, it filled rapidly with snow and had to be sealed. It was then used to receive slop-water. While the fever for excavation was at its height, Whetter drove, as an off-shoot to the first, another tunnel which came to be used as a nursery for the pups.

At this stage, to leave the Hut, it was necessary to crawl through a low trap-door in the wall of the inside or entrance veranda; the way then led to the connecting tunnel and onwards to the store veranda; finally one climbed through a manhole in the snow into the elements without. From the store veranda there was access to the Hangar by a hinged door in the common wall, and, as an additional convenience, a trap-door was made in the roof of the inner veranda to be used during spells of clear weather or in light drift.

The old landmarks became smothered in snow, making the Hut's position a matter of greater uncertainty. A journey by night to the magnetic huts was an outing with a spice of adventure.

Climbing out of the veranda, one was immediately swallowed in the chaos of hurtling drift, the darkness sinister and menacing. The shrill wind fled by—

> . . .the noise of a drive of the Dead,
> Striving before the irresistible will
> Through the strange dusk of this, the Debatable land
> Between their place and ours.

Unseen wizard hands clutched with insane fury, hacked and harried. It was "the raw-ribbed Wild that abhors all life, the Wild that would crush and rend."

Cowering blindly, pushing fiercely through the turmoil, one strove to keep a course to reach the rocks in which the huts were hidden—such and such a bearing on the wind—so far. When the rocks came in sight, the position of the final destination was only deduced by recognising a few surrounding objects.

On the return journey, the vicinity of the Hut would be heralded by such accidents as tripping over the "wireless" ground wires or kicking against a box or a heap of coal briquettes. These clues, properly followed up, would lead to the Hut itself, or at least to its shelving roof. In the very thick drifts it was even possible to stand on portions of the roof without any notion of the fact. Fossicking about, one kept on the alert for the feel of woodwork. When found and proved to be too extensive to be a partially buried box, it might safely be concluded to be some part of the roof, and only required to be skirted in order to reach the vertical entrance. The lost man often discovered this pitfall by dropping suddenly through into the veranda.

At the entrance to the tunnel, the roar of the tempest died away into a rumble, the trap-door opened and perhaps the strains of the gramophone would come in a kind of flippant defiance from the interior. Passing through the vestibule and work-room one beheld a scene in utter variance with the outer hell. Here were warm bunks, rest, food, light and companionship—for the time being, heaven! Outside, the crude and naked elements of a primitive and desolate world flowed in writhing torrents.

The night-watchman's duty of taking the meteorological observations at the screen adjacent to the Hut was a small matter compared with the foregoing. First of all, it was necessary for him to don a complete outfit of protective clothing. Dressing and undressing were tedious, and absorbed a good deal of time. At the screen, he would spend a lively few minutes wrestling in order to hold his ground, forcing the door back against the pressure of wind, endeavouring to make the light shine on the instruments, and, finally, clearing them of snow and reading them. For illumination a hurricane lantern wrapped in a calico wind-shield was first used, to be displaced later by an electrical signalling-lamp and, while the batteries lasted, by a light permanently fixed by Hannam in the screen itself. To assist in finding the manhole on his return, the night-watchman was in the habit of leaving a light burning in the outer veranda.

I remember waking up early one morning to find the Hut unusually cold. On rising, I discovered Hurley also awake, busy lighting the fire which had died out. There was no sign of Correll, the night-watchman, and we found that the last entry in the log-book had been made several hours previously. Hurley dressed in full burberrys and went out to make a search, in which he was soon successful.

It appeared that Correll, running short of coal during the early morning hours, had gone out to procure some from the stack. While he was returning to the entrance, the wind rolled him over a few times, causing him to lose his bearings. It was blowing a hurricane, the temperature was −7° F., and the drift-snow was so thick as to be wall-like in opacity. He abandoned his load of coal, and, after searching about fruitlessly for some time in the darkness, he decided to wait for dawn. Hurley found him about twenty yards from the back of the Hut.

The suppression of outdoor occupations reacted in an outburst of indoor work. The smaller room had been well fitted up as a workshop, and all kinds of schemes were in progress for adapting our sledging-gear and

Winter Quarters, Adelie Land

instruments to the severe conditions. Correll worked long hours to keep up with the demands made upon him. Nobody was idle during the day, for, when there was nothing else to be done, there always remained the manufacture and alteration of garments and crampons.

As soon as the wind abated to a reasonable velocity, there was a rush to the outside jobs. Lulls would come unexpectedly, activity inside ceased, and the Hut, as seen by a spectator, resembled an ants' nest upon which a strange foot had trodden: eighteen men swarming through the manhole in rapid succession, hurrying hither and thither.

The neighbouring sea still remained free from an ice-crust. This, of course, did not mean that freezing was not going on continuously. On the contrary, the chilling was no doubt accelerated, but the bulk of the ice was carried off to the north as fast as it was formed. Quantities, however, remained as ground-ice, anchored to the kelp and stones on the bottom. Gazing down through the clear waters one saw a white, mamillated sheath covering the jungle of giant seaweed, recalling a forest after a heavy snowfall. The ice, instead of being a dead weight bearing down the branches, tended to float, and, when accumulated in large masses, sometimes succeeded in rising to the surface, uprooting and lifting great lengths of seaweed with it. One branching stem, found floating in the harbour, measured eighteen feet in length.

Whenever a temporary calm intervened, a skin of ice quickly appeared over the whole surface of the water. In the early stages, this formation consisted of loose, blade-like crystals, previously floating freely below the surface and rising by their own buoyancy. At the surface, if undisturbed, they soon became cemented together. For example, during a calm interval on April 6, within the interval of an hour, an even crust, one inch thick, covered the sea. But the wind returned before the ice was sufficiently strong to resist it, and it all broke up and drifted away to the north, except a piece which remained wedged firmly between the sides of the boat harbour.

In the calm weather, abundant "worms" freely swimming, jelly-fish, pteropods and small fish were observed. Traps were lowered along the edge of the harbour-ice and dredgings were made in every possible situation. The bulk of the biological collecting was effected under circumstances in which Hunter and Laseron might well have given up work in disgust. For instance, I noted in my diary that on May 16, with an off shore wind of forty-three miles per hour, they and several others were dredging from the edge of the slippery bay-ice. The temperature at the time was −2° F.

During April the head of the boat harbour froze over permanently, the ice reaching a thickness of eighteen inches in ten days. By that time it was strong enough to be suitable for a tide-gauge. This was one of

Working in the Hurricane Wind, Adelie Land

Getting Ice for Domestic Purposes. Whetter Picking; Madigan with the Ice-Box

Bage's charges, destined to take him out for many months in fair and foul weather.

There were several occasions in April when the velocity of the wind exceeded ninety miles an hour. On the evening of the 26th, the wind slackened, and for part of the 27th had almost fallen to a calm. This brought the optimists to the fore, once again, with the theory that the worst was over. The prediction was far from being fulfilled, for, as the days passed, the average velocity steadily rose. On May 11 the average for the twenty-four hours was eighty miles per hour. By that time the Hut had been further protected by a crescent of cases, erected behind the first break-wind. In height this erection stood above the Hangar, and, when the snow became piled in a solid ramp on the leeward side, it was more compact than ever. Inside the Hut extra struts were introduced, stiffening the principal rafters on the southern side. It was reassuring to know that these precautions had been taken, for, on May 15, the wind blew at an average velocity of ninety miles per hour throughout the whole twenty-four hours.

Having failed to demolish us by dogged persistence, the hurricane tried new tactics on the evening of May 24, in the form of a terrific series of Herculean gusts. As we learned afterwards, the momentary velocity of these doubtless approached two hundred miles per hour. At 11.30 PM the situation was cheerfully discussed, though every one was tuned up to a nervous pitch as the Hut creaked and shuddered under successive blows. It seemed very doubtful whether the roof would resist the gusts, and the feasibility of the meat cellar as a last haven of refuge was discussed. After the passage of each gust, the barometer dropped, rising again immediately afterwards. Similar pulsations of the barometer were observed many times later in the year. The maximum sudden movement noted was one-fifth inch. Had the interior of the Hut been more freely in communication with the outside air, instead of resembling a hermetically sealed box, the "kicks" would undoubtedly have been much greater.

Cyclonic gusts were repeated a few days after, when the upper tiers of boxes composing the break-wind were thrown down and pebbles from the moraine were hurled on the roof. The average velocity of the wind for each of the three autumn months was as follows: March, 49 miles per hour; April, 51.5 miles per hour, and May 60.7 miles per hour.

On May 1 the temperatures became lower, so that it was difficult to move about in the gales without the face getting frost-bitten. Our usual remedy when this occurred was to hold a mitt over the part affected; thus sheltered, its circulation of blood was soon re-established, unless the cold

were very intense. In the extremities—the fingers and toes—warmth was not so easily restored.

Returning from attending the instruments at noon on May 22, Madigan, according to the usual habit, before taking off his wind-proof clothes, commenced clearing away the ice adhering to his helmet and face. One white patch refused to leave the side of his face, until some one observed that it was a frost-bite, and acquainted him of the fact. Frost-bites that day were excusable enough, for the wind was blowing between ninety-five and hundred miles per hour, there was dense drifting snow and a temperature of –28° F.

We had found an accursed country. On the fringe of an unspanned continent along whose gelid coast our comrades had made their home— we knew not where—we dwelt where the chill breath of a vast, Polar wilderness, quickening to the rushing might of eternal blizzards, surged to the northern seas. Already, and for long months we were beneath "frost-fettered Winter's frown."

The Ice-Cliff Coastline East of Winter Quarters

Madigan's Frostbitten Face

CHAPTER VIII

Domestic Life

OUR HEARTH AND HOME WAS THE LIVING-HUT and its focus was the stove. Kitchen and stove were indissolubly linked, and beyond their pale was a wilderness of hanging clothes, boots, finnesko, mitts and what not, bounded by tiers of bunks and blankets, more hanging clothes and dim photographs between the frost-rimed cracks of the wooden walls.

One might see as much in the first flicker of the acetylene through a maze of hurrying figures, but as his eyes grew accustomed to the light, the plot would thicken: books orderly and disorderly, on bracketed shelves, cameras great and small in motley confusion, guns and a gramophone-horn, serpentine yards of gas-tubing, sewing machines, a microscope, rows of pint-mugs, until—thud! he has obstructed a wild-eyed messman staggering into the kitchen with a box of ice.

The wilderness was always inhabited, so much so that it often became a bear-garden in which raucous good humour prevailed over everything.

Noise was a necessary evil, and it commenced at 7.30 AM, with the subdued melodies of the gramophone, mingled with the stirring of the porridge-pot and the clang of plates deposited none too gently on the table. At 7.50 AM came the stentorian: "Rise and shine!" of the night-watchman, and a curious assortment of cat-calls, beating on pots and pans and fragmentary chaff. At the background, so to speak, of all these sounds was the swishing rush of the wind and the creaking strain of the roof, but these had become neglected. In fact, if there were a calm, every one was restless and uneasy.

The seasoned sleeper who survived the ten minutes' bombardment before 8 o'clock was an unusual person, and he was often the Astronomer Royal. Besides his dignified name he possessed a wrist-watch, and there was never a movement in his mountain of blankets until 7.59 AM, unless the jocular night-watchman chose to make a heap of them on the floor. To calls like "Breakfast all ready! Porridge on the table getting cold!" seventeen persons in varying stages of wakefulness responded. No one was guilty of an elaborate toilet, water being a scarce commodity. There were adherents of the snow-wash theory, but these belonged to an earlier and warmer epoch of our history.

For downright, tantalizing cheerfulness there was no one to equal the night-watchman. While others strove to collect their befuddled senses, this individual prated of "wind eighty miles per hour with moderate drift and brilliant St. Elmo's fire." He boasted of the number of garments he had washed, expanded vigorously on bread making—his brown, appetizing specimens in full public view—told of the latest escapade among the dogs, spoke of the fitful gleams of the aurora between 1.30 and 2 AM, of his many adventures on the way to the meteorological screen and so forth; until from being a mere night-watchman he had raised himself to the status of a public hero. For a time he was most objectionable, but under the solid influence of porridge, tinned fruit, fresh bread, butter and tea and the soothing aroma of innumerable pipes, other public heroes arose and ousted this upstart of the night. Meanwhile, the latter began to show signs of abating energy after twelve hours' work. Soon some wag had caught him having a private nap, a whispered signal was passed round and the unfortunate hero was startled into life with a rousing "Rise and shine!" in which all past scores were paid off.

Every one was at last awake and the day began in earnest. The first hint of this came from the messman and cook who commenced to make a Herculean sweep of the pint-mugs and tin plates. The former deferentially proceeded to scrape the plates, the master-cook presiding over a tub of boiling water in which he vigorously scoured knives, forks and spoons, transferring them in dripping handfuls to the cleanest part of the kitchen-table. Cooks of lyric inclination would enliven the company with the score of the latest gramophone opera, and the messman and company would often feel impelled to join in the choruses.

The night-watchman had sunk into log-like slumber, and the meteorologist and his merry men were making preparations to go abroad. The merry men included the ice-carrier, the magnetician, the two wardens of the dogs, the snow-shoveller and coal-carrier and the storeman. The rest subdivided themselves between the living-hut at 45° F. and the outer Hut below freezing-point, taking up their endless series of jobs.

The merry men began to make an organized raid on the kitchen. Around and above the stove hung oddments like wolf-skin mitts, finnesko, socks,

Correll

Bage

Hunter

Bickerton

McLean

Hodgeman

A Winter Afternoon Scene in the Hut. From the Left: Mertz, Mclean, Madigan, Hunter, Hodgeman. High on the Left Is the Acetylene Generator

Taking a Turn in the Kitchen Department. Hunter, Hodgeman, Bage. The Doorway on the Right Is the Entrance to the Workroom

stockings and helmets, which had passed from icy rigidity through sodden limpness to a state of parchment dryness. The problem was to recover one's own property and at the same time to avoid the cook scraping the porridge saucepan and the messman scrubbing the table.

The urbane storeman saved the situation by inquiring of the cook: "What will you have for lunch?" Then followed a heated colloquy, the former, like a Cingalese vendor, having previously made up his mind. The argument finally crystallized down to lambs' tongues and beetroot, through herrings and tomato sauce, fresh herrings, kippered herrings, sardines and corn beef.

The second question was a preliminary to more serious business; "What would you like for dinner?"

Although much trouble might have been saved by reference to the regulation programme, which was composed to provide variety in diet and to eliminate any remote chance of scurvy, most cooks adopted an attitude of surly independence, counting it no mean thing to have wheedled from the storeman a few more ounces of "glaxo," another tin of peas or an extra ration of penguin meat. All this chaffering took place in the open market-place, so to speak, and there was no lack of frank criticism from bystanders, onlookers and distant eavesdroppers. In case the cook was worsted, the messman sturdily upheld his opinions, and in case the weight of public opinion was too much for the storeman, he slipped on his felt mitts, shouldered a Venesta box and made for the tunnel which led to the store.

He reaches an overhead vent admitting a cool torrent of snow, and with the inseparable box plunges ahead into darkness. An hour later his ruddy face reappears in the Hut, and a load of frosted tins is soon unceremoniously dumped on to the kitchen table. The cook in a swift survey notes the absence of penguin meat. "That'll take two hours to dig out!" is the storeman's rejoinder, and to make good his word, proceeds to pull off blouse and helmet. By careful inquiry in the outer Hut he finds an ice-axe, crowbar and hurricane lantern. The next move is to the outer veranda, where a few loose boards are soon removed, and the storeman, with a lithe twist, is out of sight.

We have pushed the tools down and, following the storeman, painfully squeezed into an Arcadia of starry mounds of snow and glistening plaques of ice, through which project a few boulders and several carcasses of mutton. The storeman rummages in the snow and discloses a pile of penguins, crusted hard together in a homogeneous lump. Dislodging a couple of penguins appears an easy proposition, but we are soon disillusioned. The storeman seizes the head of one bird, wrenches hard, and off it breaks as brittle as a stalactite. The same distracting thing happens to both legs, and the only remedy is to chip laboriously an icy channel around it.

In a crouching or lying posture, within a confined space, this means the expenditure of much patience, not to mention the exhaustion of all invective. A crowbar decides the question. One part of the channel is undermined, into this the end of the crowbar is thrust and the penguin shoots up and hits the floor of the Hut.

The storeman, plastered with snow, reappears hot and triumphant before the cook, but this dignitary is awkwardly kneading the dough of wholemeal scones, and the messman is feeding the fire with seal-blubber to ensure a "quick" oven. Every one is too busy to notice the storeman, for, like the night-watchman, his day is over and he must find another job.

Jobs in the Hut were the elixir of life, and a day's cooking was no exception to the rule. It began at 7 AM, and, with a brief intermission between lunch and afternoon tea, continued strenuously till 8.30 PM Cooks were broadly classified as "Crook Cooks" and "Unconventional Cooks" by the eating public. Such flattering titles as "Assistant Grand Past Master of the Crook Cooks' Association" or "Associate of the Society of Muddling Messmen" were not empty inanities; they were founded on solid fact— on actual achievement. If there were no constitutional affiliation, strong sympathy undoubtedly existed between the "Crook Cooks' Association" and "The Society of Muddling Messmen." Both contained members who had committed "championships."

"Championship" was a term evolved from the local dialect, applying to a slight mishap, careless accident or unintentional disaster in any department of Hut life. The fall of a dozen plates from the shelf to the floor, the fracture of a table-knife in frozen honey, the burning of the porridge or the explosion of a tin thawing in the oven brought down on the unfortunate cook a storm of derisive applause and shouts of "Championship! Championship!"

Thawing-out tinned foods by the heroic aid of a red-hot stove was a common practice. One day a tin of baked beans was shattered in the "port" oven, and fragments of dried beans were visible on the walls and door for weeks. Our military cook would often facetiously refer to "platoon-firing in the starboard oven."

One junior member of the "Crook Cooks' Association" had the hardihood to omit baking powder in a loaf of soda-bread, trusting that prolonged baking would repair the omission. The result was a "championship" of a very superior order. Being somewhat modest, he committed it through the trap-door to the

A Corner of the Hut—Bage Mending His Sleeping Bag. The Bunks in Two Tiers Around the Wall Are Almost Hidden by the Clothing Hanging from the Ceiling.

A Winter Evening at the Hut. Standing Up: Mawson, Madigan, Ninnis, and Correll. Sitting Round the Table from Left to Right: Stillwell, Close, Mclean, Hunter, Hannam, Hodgeman, Murphy, Lasebon, Bickerton, Mertz, and Bage

mercy of the wind, and for a time it was lost in the straggling rubbish which tailed away to the north. Even the prowling dogs in their wolfish hunger could not overcome a certain prejudice. Of course some one found it, and the public hailed it with delight. A searching inquiry was made, but the perpetrator was never discovered. That loaf, however, like the proverbial bad penny, turned up for months. When the intricate system of snow-tunnels was being perfected, it was excavated. In the early summer, when the aeroplane was dug out of the Hangar, that loaf appeared once more, and almost the last thing we saw when leaving the Hut, nearly two years after, was this petrifaction on an icy pedestal near the Boat Harbour.

No one ever forgot the roly-poly pudding made without suet; synthetic rubber was its scientific name. And the muddling messman could never be surpassed who lost the cutter of the sausage machine and put salt-water ice in the melting-pots.

There appeared in the columns of The *Adelie Blizzard* an article by the meteorologist descriptive of an occasion when two members of the "Crook Cooks' Association" officiated in the kitchen:

TEREBUS AND ERROR IN ERUPTION

An 'Orrible Affair in One Act

By a Survivor

Dramatis Personae

Crook Cooks:

TEREBUS

ERROR

Other Expedition Members

Scene: Kitchen, Winter Quarters. *Time*: 5.30 PM.

ERROR. Now, Terebus, just bring me a nice clean pot, will you?

A Morning in the Workshop. From Left to Right: Hodgeman, Hunter, Lasebon, Correll, and Hannam. The Petrol Engine Part of the Wireless Plant on the Right

Welding by Thermit in the Workroom, Adelie Land. Bickerton, Correll, Hannam and Mawson

TEREBUS [*from his bunk*]. Go on, do something yourself!

ERROR. Do something? I've done everything that has been done this afternoon.

TEREBUS. Well, you ought to feel pretty fresh.

ERROR. And all the melting-pots are empty and I'm not going to fill them. Besides, it's not in the regulations.

Voices. Who's going crook? Error!

[TEREBUS *climbs from his bunk and exit for ice.* ERROR *attempts to extricate a pot from the nails in the shelves. Loud alarums.*

Voices. Champ-ion-ship!

[*Alarums without. Loud cries of "Door!" Enter* TEREBUS *with box of ice; fills all the pots on the stove.*

ERROR. Good heavens, man, you've filled up the tea water with ice.

TEREBUS [*with hoarse laugh*]. Never mind, they won't want so much glaxo to cool it.

ERROR [*who has meanwhile been mixing bread*]. What shall we bake the bread in? I believe it is considered that a square tin is more suitable for ordinary ovens, but, on the other hand, Nansen in his *Farthest North* used flat dishes.

TEREBUS. Use a tin. There'll be less surface exposed to the cold oven.

ERROR. What's all this water on the floor? I thought my feet seemed cold. Some one must have upset a bucket.

TEREBUS. Oh, it's one of the taps turned on. Never mind, there's plenty more ice where that came from. Get your sea-boots.

[*Enter* METEOROLOGICAL STAFF *and others with snow-covered burberrys, mitts, etc., crowd kitchen and hang impedimenta round the stove. Great tumult.*

TEREBUS. Here, out of the kitchen. This isn't the time to worry the cooks.

ERROR. Take those burberrys away, please, old man. They're dripping into the soup.

TEREBUS. Give it some flavour at least.

[*Great activity in the crater of* ERROR *while* TEREBUS *clears the kitchen.* ERROR *continues stirring Soup and tapioca custard on the stove. Strong smell of burning.*

VOICES [*in peculiarly joyful chorus*]. Something burning!

ERROR [*aside to* TEREBUS]. It's all right. It will taste all right. Say it's cloth on the stove.

TEREBUS. Somebody's burberrys burning against the stove!!

[*General rush to the stove.*

TEREBUS. It's all right, I've taken them away.

[*Interval, during which much* sotto voce *discussion is heard in the kitchen.*

ERROR. We haven't put the spinach on to thaw and it's after six o'clock.

TEREBUS. Warm it up and put it on the table with the tin-openers.

ERROR. I'm afraid that's against the regulations. Put it in the oven and shut the door.

[TEREBUS *does so. Later, terrific explosion, followed by strong smell of spinach.*

VOICES. What's the matter? Terebus in eruption!

TEREBUS [*wiping spinach off his face*]. Nothing wrong. Only a tin of spinach opened automatically.

ERROR. It's plastered all over the oven and on everything.

TEREBUS. Don't worry, it will be served up with the baked penguin.

[*Period of partial quiescence of* TEREBUS *and* ERROR, *which is regarded as an evil omen.*

ERROR [*in persuasive tone*]. Have you made the tea, old boy? It's nearly half-past six.

[TEREBUS *takes off the lid of the tea-boiler, peers inside, making a scoop with his hand.*

ERROR. Here, don't do that. Mind your hands.

TEREBUS. It's all right, it's not hot.

ERROR. What shall we do, then? We'll never keep them quiet if we are late with the tea.

TEREBUS. Put the tea in now. It will be warmed up by the second course.

[TEREBUS *puts the infusers in the pot and stirs them round.*

ERROR. Taste it.

[BOTH *taste with a dirty spoon.*

TEREBUS. Tastes like your soup—'orrible!

ERROR. There's nothing wrong with the soup. You attend to the tea.

TEREBUS. I think we'll have coffee. Pass the coffee and I'll put that in and bring it to the boil. The coffee will kill the taste of the tea.

ERROR. Hope you make it stronger than that.

[*During quiescent stage while each is thinking of a retort, 6.30 PM arrives, and the soup is put on the table. Interval elapses during which the victims are expected to eat the soup.*

VOICES [*in loud chant from the table*]. How did you do it, Error?

TEREBUS [*after a suitable period*]. Any one like any more soup?

A VOICE. Couldn't risk it, Governor.

TEREBUS. Bowls up! Lick spoons!

[*Bowls are cleared away and baked penguin is put on the table.*

ERROR. Cooks have got their penguin, gentlemen.

[*Suspicious glances exchanged at table. Later, monotonous chant goes up, preceded by a soft "One, two, three." "Didn't scrape the blubber off, Error."*

[*Plates cleared away and scraped into dogs' bucket. ERROR takes tapioca custard from oven in two dishes.*

ERROR [*aside to* TEREBUS]. Take some out of this one for us and don't forget to put that dish in front of the Doctor, because I spilled soda in the other.

[TEREBUS *takes two large helpings out and puts rest on table as directed.*

TEREBUS. You need not remember the cooks, gentlemen.

A VOICE. Don't want to, if I can manage it.

ERROR [*aside to* TEREBUS]. Put on the Algerian sweets, and then we can have ours.

TEREBUS [*taking several handfuls*]. We'll put these aside for perks.

[*The sweets on the table,* TEREBUS *and* ERROR *retire to kitchen to have their dinner.*

ERROR. Is this my pudding? It's only an ordinary share.

[TEREBUS *is too busy to reply, and further eruption is prevented by the temporary plugging of* ERROR.

Cooking, under the inspiration of Mrs. Beeton, became a fine art:

> *On bones we leave no meat on,*
> *For we study Mrs. Beeton.*

So said the song. On birthdays and other auspicious occasions dishes appeared which would tempt a gourmet. Puff-pastry, steam-puddings, jellies and blancmanges, original potages and *consommés*, seal curried and spiced, penguin delicately fried, vegetables reflavoured, trimmed and adorned were received without comment as the culinary standard rose.

Birthdays were always greeted with special enthusiasm. Speeches were made, toasts were drunk, the supple boards of the table creaked with good things, cook and messman vied with each other in lavish hospitality, the Hut was ornate with flags, every man was spruce in his snowiest cardigan and neck-cloth, the gramophone sang of music-hall days, the wind roared its appreciation through the stove-pipe, and rollicking merriment was supreme. On such occasions the photographer and the biologist made a genial combination.

The dark-room was the nursery of the topical song. There, by lantern or candle-stump, wit Rabelaisian, Aristophanic or Antarctic was cradled into rhyme. From there, behind the scenes, the comedian in full dress could step before the footlights into salvoes of savage applause. "A Pair of Unconventional Cooks are we, are we," and the famous refrain, "There he is, that's him," were long unrivalled in our musical annals.

Celebrations were carried on into the night, but no one forgot the cook and the messman. The table was cleared by many willing hands, some brought in ice and coal or swept the floor, others scraped plates or rinsed out mugs and bowls. Soon, everything had passed through the cauldron of water, soap and soda to the drying-towels and on to the shelves. The main crowd then repaired with pipes and cigars to "Hyde Park Corner," where the storeman, our *raconteur par excellence*, entertained the smokers' club. A mixed concert brought the evening to the grand finale—"Auld Lang Syne."

After events of this character, the higher shelves of the kitchen, in the interstices between thermographs, photographic plates ink bottles, and Russian stout, abounded with titbits of pie crust, blancmange, jelly, Vienna

rusks, preserved figs, and other "perks." Such "perks," or perquisites, were the property of the presiding cook or night-watchman and rarely survived for more than a day.

The mania for celebration became so great that reference was frequently made to the almanac. During one featureless interval, the anniversary of the First Lighting of London by Gas was observed with extraordinary *éclat*.

The great medium of monetary exchange in the Hut was chocolate. A ration of thirty squares was distributed by the storeman every Saturday night, and for purposes of betting, games of chance, "Calcutta sweeps" on the monthly wind-velocity and general barter, chocolate held the premier place.

At the "sweeps," the meteorologist stood with a wooden hammer behind the table, and the gaming public swarmed on the other side. Numbers ranging from "low field" and forty-five to sixty-five and "high field" were sold by auction to the highest bidder. Excitement was intense while the cartographer in clerical glasses worked out the unknown number.

As a consequence of wild speculation, there were several cases of bankruptcy, which was redeemed in the ordinary way by a sale of the debtor's effects.

Two financiers, indifferent to the charms of chocolate, established a corner or "Bank" in the commodity. "The Bank," by barter and usurious methods, amassed a great heap of well-thumbed squares, and, when accused of rapacity, invented a scheme for the common good known as "Huntoylette." This was a game of chance similar to roulette, and for a while it completely gulfed the trusting public. In the reaction which followed, there was a rush on "The Bank," and the concern was wound up, but the promoters escaped with a large profit in candles and chocolate.

Throughout the winter months, work went on steadily even after dinner, and hours of leisure were easy to fill. Some wrote up their diaries, played games, or smoked and yarned; others read, developed photos, or imitated the weary cook and went to bed. The MacKellar Library, so called after the donor, was a boon to all, and the literature of polar exploration was keenly followed and discussed. Taste in literature varied, but among a throng of eighteen, the majority of whom were given to expressing their opinions in no uncertain terms—there were no rigid conventions in Adelie Land—every book had a value in accordance with a common standard.

There was not a dissenting voice to the charm of *Lady Betty across the Water*, and the reason for this was a special one. The sudden breath of a world of warmth and colour, richness and vivacity and astute, American freshness amid the somewhat grim attractions of an Antarctic winter was too much for every one. Lady Betty, in the realm of bright images, had

a host of devoted admirers. Her influence spread beyond the Hut to the plateau itself. Three men went sledging, and to shelter themselves from the rude wind fashioned an ice-cavern, which, on account of its magical hues and rare lustre, could be none other than "Aladdin's Cave." Lady Betty found her hero in a fairy grotto of the same name.

Lorna Doone, on the other hand, was liked by many. Still there were those who thought that John Ridd was a fool, a slow, obtuse rustic, and so on, while Lorna was too divine and angelic for this life.

The War of the Carolinas took the Hut by storm, but it was a "nine days' wonder" and left no permanent impression on the thinking community. Mostly, the story was voted delightfully funny, but very foolish and farcical after all. A few exclusive critics predicted for it a future.

Then there was *The Trail of '98*. For power and blunt realism there was nothing like it, but the character of the hero was torn in the shreds of debate. There was general agreement on two points: that the portrayal of

In the Catacombs. Ninnis on the Right

169

Bage and His Tide Gauge Which Was Erected on the Frozen Bay Ice

Raising the Lower Section of the Northern Wireless Mast

the desolate Alaskan wild had a touch of "home," and that the heroine was a "true sport."

All those who had ever hauled on the main braces, sung the topsail-halliard chanty, learned the intricate Matty Walker, the bowline-and-a-bite and a crowd of kindred knots, had a warm spot for any yarn by Jacobs. Night after night, the storeman held the audience with the humorous escapades of *Ginger Dick*, *Sam* and *Peter Russet*.

And lastly, there was a more serious, if divided interest in *Virginibus Puerisque*, *Marcus Aurelius*, *The Unveiling of Lhassa*—but the list is rather interminable.

The whole world is asleep except the night-watchman, and he, having made the bread, washed a tubful of clothes, kept the fire going, observed and made notes on the aurora every fifteen minutes and the weather every half-hour, and, finally, having had a bath, indulges in buttered toast and a cup of coffee.

The Hut is dark, and a shaded burner hangs by a canvas chair in the kitchen. The wind is booming in gusts, the dogs howl occasionally in the veranda, but the night-watchman and his pipe are at peace with all men. He has discarded a heavy folio for a light romance, while the hours scud by, broken only by the observations. The romance is closed, and he steals to his bunk with a hurricane lamp and finds a bundle of letters. He knows them well, but he reads them—again!

Pearly light rises in the north-east through the lessening drift, and another day has come.

CHAPTER IX

Midwinter and Its Work

WITH THE ADVENT OF THE FATEFUL IDES OF March, winter ii had practically set in, and work outside had a chequered career. When a few calm hours intervened between two blizzards a general rush was made to continue some long-standing job. Often all that could be done was to clear the field for action, that is, dig away large accumulations of snow. Then the furies would break loose again, and once more we would play the waiting game, meanwhile concerning ourselves with more sedentary occupations.

There was a familiar cry when, for some meteorological reason, the wind would relapse into fierce gusts and then suddenly stop, to be succeeded by intense stillness. "Dead calm, up with the wireless masts!" Every one hastily dashed for his burberrys, and soon a crowd of muffled figures would emerge through the veranda exit, dragging ropes, blocks, picks, and shovels. There was no time to be lost.

So the erection of the wireless masts began in earnest on April 4, continued feverishly till the end of the month, suffered a long period of partial cessation during May and June, was revived in July and August, and, by September 1, two masts, each consisting of a lower-mast and top-mast, had been raised and stayed, while between them stretched the aerial. For four weeks messages were sent out, and many of them were caught by Macquarie Island. Nothing was heard in Adelie Land, although, between certain hours, regular watches were kept at the receiver. The aerial was about sixty-five feet from the ground, and it was resolved to increase its height by erecting the top-gallant masts; but before anything considerable could be done, a terrific gust of wind on October 13 broke three wire-stays, and down came the mast, broken and splintered by the fall. That is a brief résumé of the fortunes of the "wireless" during the first year.

During February and March there were various other operations of more immediate importance which prevented concentration of our workers on the erection of the masts. There were many odd jobs to finish about the Hut, the Magnetograph House and Absolute Hut were "under way," the air-tractor sledge had to be efficiently housed, and all these and many other things could be done in weather during which it was out of question to hoist a mast into position. At first we were fastidious and waited for a calm, but later, as we grew more impatient, a top-mast was actually hauled up in a wind of thirty miles per hour, with gusts of higher velocity. Such work would sometimes be interrupted by a more furious outbreak, when all ropes would be secured and everything made as ship-shape as possible.

On March 15 the following note was made: "The wind was on the cool side just after breakfast. A few loads of wireless equipment were sledged up to the rocks at the back of the Hut, and by the time several masts were carried to the same place we began to warm to the work. One of Hannam's coils of frozen rope (one hundred and twenty fathoms) had become kinked and tangled, so we dragged it up the ice-slope, straightened it out and coiled it up again. Several 'dead men' to hold the stays were sunk into ice-holes, and, during the afternoon, one mast was dragged into position by a willing crowd. Rocks were sledged to and packed around the 'dead men' in the holes to make them compact. Towards sundown snow clouds filled the northern sky and a blizzard sprang up which is now doing sixty miles per hour. We philosophically expect another week cooped up in the Hut."

It took a long time to establish the twenty good anchorages necessary for the masts. Within a radius of eighty yards from the centre, ice-holes were dug, cairns of heavy boulders were built and rocky prominences dynamited off to secure an efficient holding for the stout "strops" of rope. April 24 was a typical day: "We spent the morning fixing up 'strops' for the wireless masts. The wind was blowing strongly in fifty- to sixty-mile gusts with drift, but most of the fellows 'stuck at it' all day. It was cold work on the hands and feet. Handling picks and shovels predisposes to frost-bite. Several charges of dynamite were fired in one hole wherein a mast will be stepped."

Each mast, of oregon timber, was in four sections. The lowest section was ten inches square and tapered upwards to the small royal mast at a prospective height of one hundred and twenty feet. At an early stage it was realized that we could not expect to erect more than three sections. Round the steel caps at each doubling a good deal of fitting had to be done, and Bickerton, in such occupation, spent many hours aloft throughout the year. Fumbling with bulky mitts, handling hammers and spanners, and manipulating nuts and bolts with bare hands, while suspended in a boatswain's chair in the wind, the man up the mast had a difficult and miserable task. Bickerton was the hero of all such endeavours. Hannam directed the other workers who steadied the stays, cleared or made fast the ropes, pulled and stood by the hauling tackle and so forth.

One day the man on the top-mast dislodged a heavy engineering hammer which he thought secure. No warning was given, as he did not notice that it had fallen. It whizzed down and buried itself in the snow, just grazing the heads of Close and Hodgeman.

The ropes securing the aerial and running through various blocks were in constant danger of chafing during the frequent hurricanes, from their proximity to the mast and stays, or from friction on the sharp edges of the blocks. Unknown to us, this had happened to a strong, new manilla rope by which Murphy was being hauled to the top of the lower-mast. It gave way, and, but for another rope close by, which he seized to break his fall, an accident might have ensued.

Frost-bites were common. There were so many occasions when one had to stand for a long time gripping a rope, pulling or maintaining a steady strain, that fingers would promptly become numb and feet unbearably cold. The usual restorative was to stamp about and beat the chest with the hands—an old sailor's trick. Attempting to climb to a block on the top-gallant mast one day, McLean had all his fingers frost-bitten at the same time.

In May the weather was atrocious, and in June building the Astronomical Hut and digging ice-shafts on the glacier absorbed a good many hands. In July, despite the enthusiasm and preparation for sledging, much was done. On August 10 the long looked-for top-mast of the southern mast became a reality:

"We were early astir—about 7 AM—while the pink coloration of dawn was stealing over the peaceful Barrier. For once, after months, it was perfectly still. We hurried about making preparations—hauled Bickerton up to the cross-trees and awaited the moment when we should raise the top-mast. We pulled it up half-way and Bickerton affixed a pin in its centre, above which two stays were to be attached. Suddenly, down came the wind in terrific gusts and, after securing the stays, the job had to be given up. . . . We were just about to have lunch when the wind ceased as suddenly as it had begun. We all sallied out once more, and, this time, completed the job, though for a while the top-mast was in imminent peril of being blown away by a sharp northerly gust."

Next day the aerial was hoisted in a wind of sixty miles per hour, but the strain was so severe on the block, upwind, that it carried away. Fortunately the insulators of the aerial were entangled by the stays in their fall to ground, otherwise some one may have been hurt, as there were a dozen men almost directly below.

Six days after this accident, August 17, the top-mast halliard of the down-wind mast frayed through, and as a stronger block was to be affixed for the aerial, some one had to climb up to wire it in position. Bickerton improvised a pair of climbing irons, and, after some preliminary practice, ascended in fine style.

Finally, by September 30, the aerial was at such a height as to give hope that long-distance messages might be despatched. There was a certain amount of suppressed excitement on the evening of that day when the engine started and gradually got up speed in the dynamo. The sharp note of the spark rose in accompanying crescendo and, when it had reached its highest pitch, Hannam struck off a message to the world at large. No response came after several nights of signalling, and, since sledging had usurped every other interest, the novelty soon wore off.

"Atmospherics"—discharges of atmospheric electricity—and discharges from the drift-snow were heard in the wireless receiver.

Bage at the Door of His Astronomical Transit House

Webb and His Magnetograph House

At Work on the Air-Tractor Sledge in the Hangar; Bage, Ninnis, and Bickerton

Webb Adjusting the Instruments in the Magnetograph House

While messages were being sent, induction effects were noted in metallic objects around the Hut. A cook at the stove was the first to discover this phenomenon, and then every one conceived a mania for "drawing" sparks. A rather stimulating experience—the more so as it usually happened unexpectedly and accidentally—was to brush one's head against one of the numerous coils of flexible metal gas-piping festooned about the place. Sparks immediately jumped the interval with startling effect.

October 13, the day when the mast blew down, was known in wireless circles as Black Sunday. All had worked keenly to make the "wireless" a success, and the final event was considered to be a public misfortune. However, the honours were to be retrieved during the following year.

It fell to the lot of most of the Staff that they developed an interest in terrestrial magnetism. For one thing every man had carried boulders to the great stockade surrounding the Magnetograph House. Then, too, recorders were regularly needed to assist the magnetician in the absolute Hut. There, if the temperature were not too low and the observations not too lengthy, the recorder stepped out into the blizzard with the conviction that he had learned something of value, and, when he sat down to dinner that night, it was with a genial sense of his own altruism. In his diary he would write it all up for his own edification.

It would be on this wise: The Earth's magnetic force, which is the active agent in maintaining the compass-needle in the magnetic meridian** at any particular spot, acts, not as is popularly supposed, in a horizontal plane, but at a certain angle of inclination with the Earth's surface. The nearer the magnetic poles the more nearly vertical does the freely suspended needle become. At the South Magnetic Pole it assumes a vertical position with the south end downwards; at the North Magnetic Pole it stands on its other end. At the intermediate positions near the equator the whole force is exerted, swinging the needle in the horizontal plane, and in such regions ordinary ships' compasses pivoted to move freely only in a horizontal plane give the greatest satisfaction. On approaching the magnetic poles, compasses become sluggish, for the horizontal deflecting force falls off rapidly. The force, acting in a vertical direction, tending to make the needle dip, correspondingly increases, but is of no value for navigation purposes. However, in the scientific discussion of terrestrial magnetism, both the horizontal and vertical components as well as the absolute value of the total force are important, and the determination of these "elements" is the work of the magnetician. Affecting the average values of the "magnetic elements" at any one spot on the Earth's surface are regular diurnal oscillations, apparent only by the application of very delicate methods of observation: also there are sudden large irregular movements referred to as magnetic storms; the latter are always specially noticeable when unusually bright auroral phenomena are in progress.

The observations made in the "Absolute Hut," carried out at frequent intervals and on each occasion occupying two men for several hours together, are necessary to obtain standard values as a check upon the graphic record of the self-recording instruments which run day and night in the "Magnetograph House."

But this is another story. Three hours, sitting writing figures in a temperature of –15° F., is no joke. The magnetician is not so badly off, because he is moving about, though he often has to stop and warm his fingers, handling the cold metal.

The Magnetograph House had by far the most formidable name. The Hut, though it symbolized our all in all, sounded very insignificant unless it were repeated with just the right intonation. The Absolute Hut had a superadded dignity. The Hangar, in passing, scarcely seemed to have a right

---

** *The magnetic meridian is the straight line joining the North and South Magnetic Poles and passing through the spot in question.*

to a capital H. The Transit House, on the other hand, was the only dangerous rival to the first mentioned. But what's in a name?

If the Magnetograph House had been advertised, it would have been described as "two minutes from the Hut." This can easily be understood, for the magnetician after leaving home is speedily blown over a few hillocks and sastrugi, and, coming to an ice-flat about one hundred and fifty yards wide, swiftly slides over it, alighting at the snow-packed door of his house. The outside porch is just roomy enough for a man to slip off burberrys and crampons. The latter are full of steel spikes, and being capable of upsetting magnetic equilibrium, are left outside. Walking in soft finnesko, the magnetician opens an inner door, to be at once accosted by darkness, made more intense after the white glare of the snow. His eyes grow accustomed to the blackness, and he gropes his way to a large box almost concealing the feeble glimmer of a lamp. The lamp is the source of the light, projected on to small mirrors attached to the magnetic needles of three variometers. A ray of light is reflected from the mirrors for several feet on to a slit, past which revolves sensitized photographic paper folded on a drum moving by clockwork. The slightest movements of the suspended needles are greatly magnified, and, when the paper is removed and developed in a dark-room, a series of intricate curves denoting declination, horizontal intensity and vertical force, are exquisitely traced. Every day the magnetician attends to the lamp and changes papers; also at prearranged times he tests his "scale values" or takes a "quick run."

To obtain results as free as possible from the local attraction of the rocks in the neighbourhood, Webb resolved to take several sets of observations on the ice-sheet. In order to make the determinations it was necessary to excavate a cave in the glacier. This was done about three-quarters of a mile south of the Hut in working shifts of two men. A fine cavern was hewn out, and there full sets of magnetic observations were taken under ideal conditions.

On sledging journeys the "dip" and declination were both ascertained at many stations, around and up to within less than half a degree of the South Magnetic Pole.

While the wind rushed by at a maddening pace and stars flashed like jewels in a black sky, a glow of pale yellow light overspread the north-east horizon—the aurorae. A rim of dark, stratus cloud was often visible below the light which brightened and diffused till it curved as a low arc across the sky. It was eerie to watch the contour of the arc break, die away into a delicate pallor and reillumine in a travelling riband. Soon a long ray, as from a searchlight, flashed above one end, and then a row of vertical streamers ran out from the arc, probing upwards into the outer darkness. The streamers waxed and waned, died away to be replaced and then faded into the starlight. The arc lost its radiance, divided in patchy fragments, and all was dark once more.

This would be repeated again in a few hours and irregularly throughout the night, but with scenic changes behind the great sombre pall of the sky. North-west, northeast, and south-east it would elusively appear in nebulous blotches, flitting about to end finally in long bright strands in the zenith, crossing the path of the "milky way."

By the observer, who wrote down his exact observations in the meteorological log, this was called a "quiet night."

At times the light was nimble, flinging itself about in rich waves, warming to dazzling yellow-green and rose. These were the nights when "curtains" hung festooned in the heavens, alive, rippling, dancing to the lilt of lightning music. Up from the horizon they would mount, forming a vortex overhead, soundless within the silence of the ether.

A "brilliant display," we would say, and the observer would be kept busy following the track of the evanescent rays.

Powerless, one was in the spell of an all-enfolding wonder. The vast, solitary snow-land, cold-white under the sparkling star-gems; lustrous in the radiance of the southern lights; furrowed beneath the icy sweep of the wind. We had come to probe its mystery, we had hoped to reduce it to terms of science, but there was always the "indefinable" which held aloof, yet riveted our souls.

The aurora was always with us, and almost without exception could be seen on a dark, driftless night. The nature of the aurora polaris has not yet been finally demonstrated, though it is generally agreed to be a discharge of electricity occurring in the upper, more rarefied atmosphere. The luminous phenomena are very similar to those seen when a current of electricity is passed through a vacuum tube.

One receives a distinct impression of nearness, watching the shimmering edges of the "curtains" in the zenith, but all measurements indicate that they never descend nearer than a few miles above the land-surface.

Careful records were taken to establish a relation between magnetic storms and aurorae, and a good deal of evidence was amassed to support the fact that auroral exhibitions correspond with periods of great magnetic disturbance. The displays in Adelie Land were found to be more active than those which occur in higher latitudes in the Ross Sea.

The Alpine-Glow. *Cape Denison.*

An occupation which helped to introduce variety in our life was the digging of ice-shafts. For the purpose of making observations upon its structure and temperature various excavations were made in the sea-ice, in the ice of the glacier, and in that of the freshwater lakes. The work was always popular. Even a whole day's labour with a pick and shovel at the bottom of an ice-hole never seemed laborious. It was all so novel.

A calm morning in June, the sky is clear and the north ablaze with the colours of sunrise—or is it sunset? The air is delicious, and a cool waft comes down the glacier. A deep ultramarine, shading up into a soft purple hue, blends in a colour-scheme with the lilac plateau. Two men crunch along in spiked boots over snow mounds and polished sastrugi to the harbour-ice. The sea to the north is glazed with freezing spicules, and over it sweep the petrels—our only living companions of the winter. It is all an inspiration; while hewing out chunks of ice and shovelling them away is the acute pleasure of movement, exercise.

The men measure out an area six feet by three feet, and take a preliminary temperature of the surface-ice by inserting a thermometer in a drilled hole. Then the ice begins to fly, and it is not long before they are down one foot. Nevertheless it would surprise those acquainted only with fresh water ice to find how tough, sticky and intractable is sea-ice. It is always well to work on a definite plan, channelling in various directions, and then removing the intervening lumps by a few rough sweeps of the pick. At a depth of one foot, another temperature is taken, and some large samples of the ice laid by for the examination of their crystalline structure. This is repeated at two feet, and so on, until the whole thickness is pierced to the sea-water beneath. At three feet brine may begin to trickle into the hole, and this increases in amount until the worker is in a puddle. The leakage takes place, if not along cracks, through capillary channels, which are everywhere present in sea-ice.

It is interesting to note the temperature gradually rise during the descent. At the surface the ice is chilled to the air-temperature, say −10° F., and it rises in a steep gradient to approximately 28° F.; close to the freezing-point of sea water. The sea-ice in the boat-harbour varied in thickness during the winter between five and seven feet.

In contrast with sea-ice, the ice of a glacier is a marvel of prismatic colour and glassy brilliance. This is more noticeable near the surface when the sun is shining. Deep down in a shaft, or in an ice-cavern, the sapphire reflection gives to the human face quite a ghastly pallor.

During the high winds it was always easy to dispose of the fragments of ice in the earlier stages of sinking a shaft. To be rid of them, all that

A Calm Noon in Winter, Cape Denison

The Ridged Surface of a Lake Frozen During a Blizzard

was necessary was to throw a shovelful vertically upwards towards the lee-side of the hole, the wind then did the rest. Away the chips would scatter, tinkling over the surface of the glacier. Of course, when two men were at work, each took it in turns to go below, and the one above, to keep warm, would impatiently pace up and down. Nevertheless, so cold would he become at times that a heated colloquy would arise between them on the subject of working overtime. When the shaft had attained depth, both were kept busy. The man at the pit's mouth lowered a bucket on a rope to receive the ice and, in hauling it up, handicapped with clumsy mitts, he had to be careful not to drop it on his companion's head.

The structural composition of ice is a study in itself. To the cursory glance a piece of glacier-ice appears homogeneous, but when dissected in detail it is found to be formed of many crystalline, interlocking grains, ranging in size from a fraction of an inch to several inches in diameter. A grain-size of a half to one inch is perhaps commonest in Antarctic glacier-ice.

The history of Antarctic glacier-ice commences with the showers of snow that fall upon the plateau. The snow particles may be blown for hundreds of miles before they finally come to rest and consolidate. The consolidated snow is called *névé*, the grains of which are one-twenty-fifth to one hundredth of an inch in diameter, and, *en masse*, present a dazzling white appearance on account of the air spaces which occupy one-third to one-half of the whole. In time, under the influence of a heavy load of accumulated layers of *névé*, the grains run together and the air spaces are eliminated. The final result is clear, transparent ice, of a more or less sapphire-blue colour when seen in large blocks. It contains only occasional air-bubbles, and the size of the grains is much increased.

Lake-ice, freezing from the surface downwards, is built up of long parallel prisms, like the cells of a honey-comb on a large scale. In a lakelet near the Hut this was beautifully demonstrated. In some places cracks and fissures filled with snow-dust traversed the body of the ice, and in other places long strings of beaded air-bubbles had become entangled in the process of freezing. To lie down on the clear surface and gaze "through the looking-glass" to the rocky bottom, twenty feet below, was a glimpse into "Wonderland."

In the case of sea-ice, the simple prismatic structure is complicated owing to the presence of saline matter dissolved in the sea water. The saline tracts between the prisms produce a milky or opalescent appearance. The prisms are of fresh water ice, for in freezing the brine is rejected and forced to occupy the interstices of the prisms. Water of good drinking quality can be obtained by allowing sea water ice to thaw partially. The brine, of lower freezing-point, flows away, leaving only fresh water ice behind. In this way blocks of sea-ice exposed to the sun's rays are relieved of their salty constituents, and crumble into pellucid gravel when disturbed.

A popular subject commanding general interest, apart from the devoted attention of specialists, was zoological collecting. Seals and birds were made the prey of every one, and dredging through the sea-ice in winter and spring was always a possible diversion.

It was a splendid sight to watch the birds sailing in the high winds of Adelie Land. In winds of fifty to seventy miles per hour, when with good crampons one had to stagger warily along the ice-foot, the snow petrels and Antarctic petrels were in their element. Wheeling, swinging, sinking, planing and soaring, they were radiant with life—the wild spirits of the tempest. Even in moderate drift, when through swirling snow the vistas of sea whitened under the flail of the wind, one suddenly caught the silver flash of wings and a snow petrel glided past.

But most memorable of all were certain winter mornings of unexpected calm, when ruddy clouds tessellated the northern sky and were mirrored in the freezing sea. Then the petrels would be *en fête*, flying over from the east following the line of the Barrier, winding round the icy coves, darting across the jutting points and ever onward in their long migration. In the summer they flew for weeks from the west—a never-ending string of snow, silver-grey and Antarctic petrels, and Cape pigeons. The silver-grey petrels and Cape pigeons were only abroad during that season and were accompanied by skua gulls, giant petrels, Wilson petrels, and penguins. The penguins remained in Adelie Land for the longest period—almost six months, the skua gulls and giant petrels for five months, and the rest for a shorter period—the tolerable season of midsummer.

Birds that haunt the wide oceans all make use of the soaring principle in flight, some much more than others. The beautiful sliding sweep of the albatross is the most familiar example. With wings outspread, it is a miniature aeroplane requiring no engines, for the wind itself supplies the power. A slight movement of the tail-feathers and wing-tips controls its balance with nice precision. Birds employing this method of flight find their home in the zone of continuous steady winds which blow across the broad wastes of the southern seas.

Many petrels on the wing were shot during the winter. Laseron, who prepared the skins of our Adelie Land collection, determined, in the case of a number of specimens, the ratio of weight to horizontal area exposed to the wind. This subject is one which has lately exercised the curiosity of aviators. The ratios are those evolved by nature, and, as such, should be wellnigh perfect. Below is appended a table of the results obtained.

WEIGHT OF CERTAIN ANTARCTIC BIRDS IN RELATION TO WING AREAS (Stated in pounds per square foot of wing surface)

Each is the mean of several determinations by Laseron

Giant petrel 3.5
Albatross 2.4
Antarctic petrel 2.1
Skua gull 1.6
Snow petrel 1.1
Wilson petrel 0.6

Values from a book of reference quoted for comparison
Bat 0.1
Sparrow 0.4
Wild goose 1.7

* * *

During the winter, for a long period, no seals ventured ashore, though a few were seen swimming in the bay. The force of the wind was so formidable that even a heavy seal, exposed in the open, broadside-on, would be literally blown into the water. This fact was actually observed out on the harbour-ice. A Weddell seal made twelve attempts to land on a low projecting shelf—an easy feat under ordinary circumstances. The wind was in the region of eighty-five miles per hour, and every time the clumsy, ponderous creature secured its first hold, back it would be tumbled. Once it managed to raise itself on to the flat surface, and, after a breathing spell, commenced to shuffle towards the shelter of some pinnacles on one side of the harbour. Immediately its broad flank was turned to the wind it was rolled over, hung for a few seconds on the brink, and then splashed into the sea. On the other hand, during the spring, a few more ambitious seals won their way ashore in high winds; but they did not remain long in the piercing cold, moving uneasily from place to place in search of protecting hummocks and finally taking to the water in despair. Often a few hours of calm weather was the signal for half a dozen animals to land. The wind sooner or later sprang up and drove them back to their warmer element.

Under the generic name, seal, are included the true or hair seals and the sea-bears or fur seals. Of these the fur seals are sub-polar in distribution, inhabiting the cold temperate waters of both hemispheres, but never living amongst the polar ice. The southern coast of Australia and the sub-antarctic islands were their favourite haunts, but the ruthless slaughter of the early days practically exterminated them. From Macquarie Island, for example, several hundred thousand skins were taken in a few years, and of late not a single specimen has been seen.

Closely related to the fur seals are the much larger animals popularly known as sea-lions. These still exist in great numbers in south temperate waters. Both are distinguished from the hair seals by one obvious characteristic: their method of propulsion on land is by a "lolloping" motion, in which the front and hind flippers are used alternately. The hair seals move by a caterpillar-like shuffle, making little or no use of their flippers; and so, the terminal parts of their flippers are not bent outwards as they are in the fur seals and sea-lions.

Of the hair seals there are five varieties to be recognized in the far South. The Weddell seals, with their mottled-grey coats, are the commonest. They haunt the coasts of Antarctica and are seldom found at any distance from them. Large specimens of this species reach nine and a half feet in length.

The crab-eater seal, a smaller animal, lives mostly on the pack-ice. Lying on a piece of floe in the sunshine it has a glistening, silver-grey skin—another distinguishing mark being its small, handsome head and short, thin neck. Small crustaceans form its principal food.

The Ross seal, another inhabitant of the pack-ice, is short and bulky, varying from a pale yellowish-green on the under side to a dark greenish-brown on the back. Its neck is ample and bloated, and when distended in excitement reminds one of a pouter-pigeon. This rare seal appears to subsist mainly on squid and jelly-fish.

The sea-leopard, the only predacious member of the seal family, has an elongated agile body and a large head with massive jaws. In general it has a mottled skin, darker towards the back. It lives on fish, penguins and seals. Early in April, Hurley and McLean were the first to obtain proof that the sea-leopard preyed on other seals. Among the broken floe-ice close beneath the ice-cliffs to the west of Winter Quarters, the wind was driving the dead body of a Weddell seal which swept past them, a few yards distant, to the open water. Then it was that a sea-leopard was observed tearing off and swallowing great pieces of flesh and blubber from the carcase.

The last variety of hair seal, the sea elephant, varies considerably from the preceding. Reference has already been made to the species earlier in the narrative. The habitat of these monstrous animals ranges over the cold, south-temperate seas; sea elephants are but occasional visitors to the ice-bound regions. Although they have been exterminated in many other places, one of their most populous resorts at the present day is Macquarie Island.

In the case of all the hair seals a layer of blubber several inches in thickness invests the body beneath the skin and acts as a conserver of warmth. They are largely of value for the oil produced by rendering down the blubber. The pelts are used for leather.

The operation of skinning seals for specimens, in low temperatures and in the inevitable wind, was never unduly protracted. We were satisfied merely to strip off the skin, leaving much blubber still adhering to it. In this rough condition it was taken into the work-room of the Hut to be cleaned. The blubber froze, and then had the consistency of hard soap and was readily severed from the pelt. It was found that there exuded amongst the frozen blubber a thin oil which remained liquid when collected and exposed to low temperatures. This oil was used to lubricate the anemometer and other instruments exposed outside.

A Lively Scene in the Vicinity of an Antarctic Petrel Rookery, Cape Hunter

A Weddell Seal Swimming Below the Ice-Foot

A Rascally Sea Leopard Casting a Wicked Eye over the Broken Floe at Land's End. Main Base

The main part of the biological work lay in the marine collections. Hunter with the small hand-dredge brought up abundant samples of life from depths ranging to fifty fathoms. In water shallower than ten fathoms the variety of specimens was not great, including seaweeds up to eighteen or more feet in length, a couple of forms of starfish, various small mollusca, two or three varieties of fish, several sea-spiders, hydroids and lace corals, and, in great profusion, worms and small crustaceans. In deeper waters the life became much richer, so that examples of almost every known class of marine animals were represented.

Early in June the sea bottom in depths less than ten fathoms had become so coated with ice that dredging in shallow water was suspended.

Floating or swimming freely were examples of pteropods, worms, crustaceans, ostracods, and jelly-fish. These were easily taken in the hand-net.

In those regions where ice and water are intermingled, the temperature of the water varies very slightly in summer and winter, remaining approximately at freezing-point. In summer the tendency to heating is neutralized by a solution of some of the ice, and in winter the cold is absorbed in the production of a surface layer of ice. This constancy of the sea's temperature is favourable to organic life. On land there is a wide range in temperature, and only the meagre mosses and lichens, and the forms of insect life which live among them can exist, because they have developed the capacity of suspending animation during the winter. The fresh-water lakelets were found to be inhabited by low forms of life, mainly microscopic. Among these were diatoms, algae, protozoa, rotifera, and bacteria.

The last-named were investigated by McLean and were found to be manifold in distribution. Besides those from the intestines of animals and birds, cultures were successfully made from the following natural sources: lichen soil, moss soil, morainic mud, guano, ice and snow. The results may open some new problems in bacteriology.

Of recent years much attention has been given to the study of parasites—parasitology. Parasites may be external, on the skin; internal, in the alimentary canal; or resident, in the corpuscles of the blood. In tropical countries, where there is great promiscuity of life, one is led to expect their almost universal presence. But in polar regions, where infection and intimate co-habitation for long periods are not the rule, while the climate is not favourable to organic existence, one would be surprised to find them in any great number. The fact remains that internal parasites were found in the intestine of every animal and fish examined, and in all the birds except the Wilson petrel. External parasites were present on every species of bird and seal, though individuals were often free of them. This was so in the case of the Adelie penguins. It is a demonstration of the protective warmth of the feathers that Emperor penguins may harbour insect parasites in great numbers. It is only less wonderful than the fact that they are able to rear their young during the Antarctic winter. A large number of blood-slides were prepared and stained for examination for blood-parasites.

A Crab-Eater Seal; Common Amongst the Pack-Ice

The Rare Ross Seal

Searching for "fleas" amongst the feathers of birds and the hair of seals, or examining the viscera for "worms" is neither of them a pleasant occupation. To be really successful, the enthusiasm of the specialist is necessary. Hunter allowed no opportunities to pass and secured a fine collection of parasites.

Amongst other work, McLean carried out monthly observations on six men, determining the colour-index and haemoglobin value of their blood over a period of ten months. The results showed a distinct and upward rise above the normal.

Among societies privileged to see the daily paper and to whom diversity and change are as the breath of life, the weather is apt to be tabooed as a subject of conversation. But even the most versatile may suddenly find themselves stripped of ideas, ignominiously reduced to the obvious topic. To us, instead of being a mere prelude to more serious matters, or the last resort of a feeble intellect, it was the all-engrossing theme. The man with the latest hare-brained theory of the causation of the wind was accorded a full hearing. The lightning calculator who estimated the annual tonnage of drift-snow sweeping off Adelie Land was received as a futurist and thinker. Discussion was always free, and the subject was never thrashed out. Evidence on the great topic accumulated day by day and month by month; yet there was no one without an innate hope that winter would bring calm weather or that spring-time, at least, must be propitious.

Meanwhile the meteorologist accepted things as he found them, supplied the daily facts of wind-mileage and direction, amount of drift, temperature and so forth, which were immediately seized by more vivacious minds and made the basis of daring speculations.

The daily facts were increased by the construction of a new instrument known as the puffometer. It was entirely a home-made contrivance, designed to measure the speed of heavy gusts of wind. A small aluminium sphere was arranged to blow out at the end of a light cord exerting tension on a calibrated spring. The pull was transferred to a lever carrying a pencil, which travelled across a disk of carbonized paper. The disk, moving by clockwork, made a complete revolution every hour. The recording parts of the instrument were enclosed in a snow-proof box in which there was a small aperture on the leeward side, through which ran the cord attachment of the sphere. This may give a rough idea of the apparatus employed to measure the momentary velocity of the cyclonic gusts. The idea is not an original one, having been previously applied for use on kites.

It was not always possible to use the puffometer in the strongest gusts because these were often transient, occurring unexpectedly or during the night; while it took a little time to get the instrument into running order. Even in daylight, with the landscape clear of drift, it was a time-absorbing and difficult task to secure a record.

Two men start from the Hut with iron crampons and a full complement of clothes and mitts. Outside they find themselves in a rushing torrent of air, pulsating with mighty gust-waves. Lowered from the estate of upright manhood, they humbly crawl, or make a series of crouching sprints between the gusts. Over the scattered boulders to the east of the Hut, across a patch of polished snow they push to the first low ridge, and there they stop for breath. Up on the side of "Annie Hill," in the local phrase, the tide sweeps by with fiendish strength, and among the jagged rocks the man clutching the puffometer-box has a few desperate falls. At last both

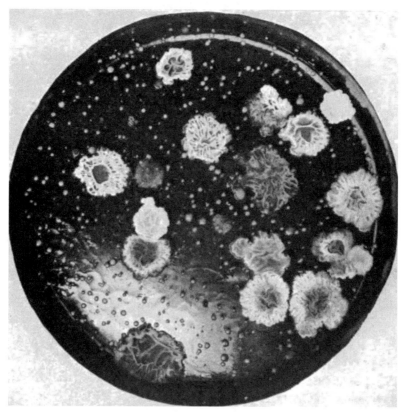

One of Mclean's Cultures; Bacteria and Moulds; Illustrating Micro-Organisms in the Hut

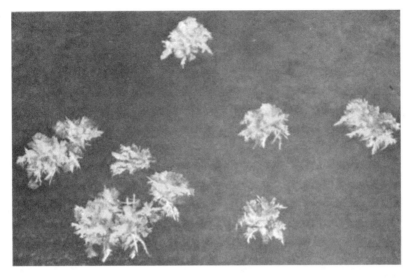

Ice Flowers on the Newly Formed Sea-Ice

clamber slowly to an eminence where a long steel pipe has been erected. To the top of this the puffometer is hauled by means of a pulley and line. At the same time the aluminium sphere is released, and out it floats in the wind tugging at the spring.

The puffometer was left out for an hour at a time, and separate gusts up to one hundred and fifty and one hundred and eighty miles per hour were commonly indicated. I remember the final fate of this invention. While helping to mount it one day, the wind picked me up clear of the ground and dashed myself and the instrument on some rocks several yards away. The latter was badly damaged, but thick clothing saved me from serious injury.

The average velocity for the day 66.9 miles per hour, and the maximum of the average hourly velocities, ninety-six miles.

The steadiness of the temperature was a subject for debate. The stronger the wind blew, the less variation did the thermometer show. Over a period of several days there might be a range of only four or five degrees. Ordinarily, this might be expected of an insular climate, but in our case it depended upon the fact that the wind remained steady from the interior of the vast frigid continent. The air which flowed over the Hut had all passed through the same temperature-cycle. The atmosphere of the interior, where the plateau stood at an elevation of, say, eight thousand feet, might have a temperature $-45°$ F. As the air flowed northwards over Adelie Land to the sea, it would rise slowly in temperature owing to the

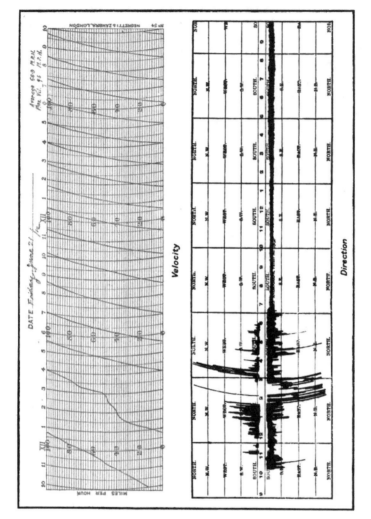

The Wind Velocity and Wind Direction Charts for Midwinter's Day, When the Steady South-by-East Gale was Broken After Noon by a Welcome Lull—the Wind Veering the While all Round the Compass.

increased barometric pressure consequent on the descending gradient of the plateau. At sea-level the temperature of the river of air would be, approximately, −20° F.

Such a rise in temperature due to compression is a well-known phenomenon, referred to as the Foehn effect.

The compression of the atmosphere during the gusts affected the air temperature so considerably that, coincident with their passage, the mercury column could often be seen rising and falling through several degrees. The uniform conditions experienced during steady high winds were not only expressed by the slight variation in the temperature, but often in a remarkably even barometric curve. Thus on July 11 the wind-velocity for twenty-four hours was, throughout, seventy miles per hour; the temperature remaining within a few degrees of −21° F., and the barometric curve did not show as much range as one-twentieth of an inch.

In attending to the many instruments and in gathering the voluminous meteorological data, Madigan had his hands very full. Throughout two years he carried on the work capably and thoroughly. It was difficult to keep the instruments free from the penetrating snow and in good running order. The Robinson anemometer was perhaps the greatest source of worry. Repairs and readjustments were unavoidable, as the instrument was constantly working at high pressure. In order that these might be carried out efficiently, the whole apparatus had to be carried down to the Hut. Here, Bickerton and Correll were continually in consultation with the meteorologist on the latest breakdown. Cups were blown off several times, and one was lost and replaced with difficulty. Most aggravating of all was a habit the clocks developed of stopping during the colder spells. The old-fashioned method of boiling them was found of assistance, but it was discovered that the best treatment was to put them through successive baths of benzene and alcohol.

The most chronic sufferer throughout the vicissitudes of temperature was the clock belonging to Bage's tide-gauge. Every sleeper in the Hut who was sensitive to ticking knew and reviled that clock. So often was it subjected to warm, curative treatment in various resting-places that it was hunted from pillar to post. A radical operation by Correll—the insertion of an extra spring—became necessary at last. Correll, when not engaged designing electroscopes, improving sledge-meters and perfecting theodolites, was something of a specialist in clocks. His advice on the subject of refractory time-pieces was freely asked and cheerfully given. By perseverance and unlimited patience, the tide-gauge down on the harbour-ice was induced to supply a good series of unbroken records.

The rise and fall of the tide is coincident with the movements of a perpendicular wire to which the *Float* is attached. The *Wheel* is revolved, and through wire connections (indicated above) displaces vertically the *Pen*. This traces a record on paper folded on the *Drum* which is driven by clockwork. In all weathers, the box was enveloped in drift-proof canvas.

Antarctica is a world of colour, brilliant and intensely pure. The chaste whiteness of the snow and the velvet blackness of the rocks belong to days of snowy nimbus enshrouding the horizon. When the sky has broken into cloudlets of fleece, their edges are painted pale orange, fading or richly glowing if the sun is low. In the high sun they are rainbow-rimmed.

Madigan Visiting the Anemograph Screen in a High Wind

The Puffometer, Designed to Record Maximum Gust Velocities

An Enormous Cone of Snow Piled Up by the Blizzards Under the Coastal Cliffs

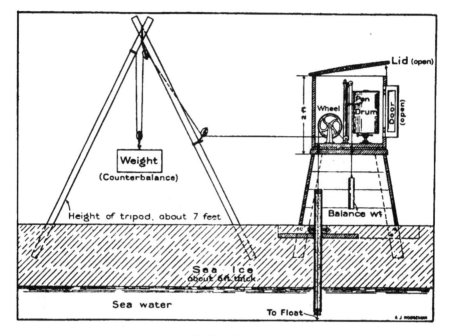

The Tide-Gauge

The clouds have opened into rifts and the sun is setting in the north-west. The widening spaces in the zenith are azure, and low in the north they are emerald. Scenic changes are swift. Above the mounting plateau a lofty arch of clear sky has risen, flanked by roseate clouds. Far down in the south it is tinged with indigo and ultramarine, washed with royal purple paling onwards into cold violet and greyish-blue.

Soon the north is unveiled. The liquid globe of sun has departed, but his glory still remains. Down from the zenith his colours descend through greenish-blue, yellowish-green, straw-yellow, light terra-cotta to a diffuse brick-red; each reflected in the dull sheen of freezing sea. Out on the infinite horizon float icebergs in a mirage of mobile gold. The Barrier, curving to east and west, is a wall of delicate pink overlaid with a wondrous mauve—the rising plateau. A cold picture—yet it awakens the throb of inborn divinity.

Despite contrary predictions, there were some enjoyable days in June. Occupation had to be strenuous, making the blood run hot, otherwise the wind was apt to be chill. So the Transit House was founded, and there were many volunteers to assist Bage in carrying the tons of stones which formed its permanent base. The nearest large collection of boulders was twenty yards away, on the edge of a moraine, but these after a while became

"Antarctica is a world of colour, brilliant and intensely pure . . ." *Commonwealth Bay.*

exhausted. Plenty of rocks actually showed above the surface, but the majority were frozen-in, and, when of suitable size, could only be moved by a heavy crowbar. Some of the men, therefore, dislodged the rocks, while others carried them.

When Bage was wondering how long the supply would last, Ninnis and Mertz came to the rescue with sledges and dog-teams. Boxes were piled on to the sledges and away the teams went, careering across the ice-flat towards the Magnetograph House close to which there were many heaps of stones, wind-swept and easily displaced. Soon a regular service was plying to the foundations, and, at the same time, the dogs were being trained. This occupation was continued, weather permitting, for several weeks before Midwinter's Day. Thus the drivers gained experience, while the animals, with a wholesome dread of the whip, became more responsive to commands. Eagerly the huskies strained at their traces with excited yelps. The heavily laden sledges would break out and start off with increasing speed over the rough ice. The drivers, running at full speed, jumped on the racing loads—Mertz in the lead shouting some quaint yodel song; Ninnis, perhaps, just behind upbraiding a laggard dog.

Midwinter's Day! For once, the weather rose to the occasion and calmed during the few hours of the twilight-day. It was a jovial occasion, and we celebrated it with the uproarious delight of a community of eighteen young men unfettered by small conventions. The sun was returning, and we were glad of it. Already we were dreaming of spring and sledging, summer and sledging, the ship and home. It was the turn of the tide, and the future seemed to be sketched in firm, sure outline. While the rest explored all the ice-caves and the whole extent of our small rocky "selection," Hannam and Bickerton shouldered the domestic responsibilities. Their *menu du dîner* to us was a marvel of gorgeous delicacies. After the toasts and speeches came a musical and dramatic programme, punctuated by choice gramophone records and rowdy student choruses. The washing-up was completed by all hands at midnight. Outside, the wind was not to be outdone; it surpassed itself with an unusual burst of ninety-five miles per hour.

Menu du Diner

Escoffier Potage à la Reine

Noisettes de Phoque
Haricot Verts
Champignons en Sauce Antarctique

Pingouin à la Terre Adélie
Petits Pois à la Menthe
Pommes Nouvelles

Asperges au Beurre Fondu

Plum Pouding Union Jack

Pâté de Groseilles

Desserts

Café

Claret Tintara

Burgundy Chauvenet 1898

Port Köpke

During dinner the Blizzard will render the usual accompaniments – The Tempest. For Ever and Ever etc

Midwinter Day Menu at the Main Base, Adelie Land, 1912

The Preparation of Sledging Equipment

THE WORLD OF FASHION INSISTS ON ITS MINUTE vagaries in dress not always with an eye to utility and an explorer in the polar regions is a very fastidious person, expending a vast amount of care on his attire, but with the sole idea of comfort, warmth, and usefulness. The clothes he wears are many and often cumbersome, but they have gradually been perfected to meet the demands of the local weather conditions. After a sojourn in the ice-lands, he returns to civilization with a new concept of the value of dress. At last he can stand still without being reminded that his feet are chilly; he experiences the peculiar sensation of walking about in an airily light suit, in glove-tight boots, without helmet or mitts. It gives him such a delicious feeling of freedom that his energy is unbounded and life is a very pleasant and easy thing. Then it is that he can turn in retrospect to the time in exile, appreciate his altered circumstances and recall the many ingenuities which were evolved to make him master of his environment.

It is sufficient to say that we found the proposition of clothing one of unusual interest. Any one who was not a practised needleman and machinist was handicapped for a time, until he fell into the ways of the through-and-through and blanket-stitch, thimbles, shuttles, spools and many other things he had once affected to despise as belonging to the sphere of women's work. It was not long before he was an enthusiast in many arts attaining to a stage of independence, in which he patented new ideas and maintained them in hot opposition to the whole community of the Hut. On some fundamental points all were in agreement, and one of them was that Adelie Land was the country *par excellence* for the wind-proof, drift-tight burberry.

Outside all other garments the burberry gabardine was worn. The material was light and loosely fitting, but in wind and drift it had to be hermetically sealed, so to speak, for the snow crept in wherever there was an aperture. The trousers were of double thickness, as they were exposed to the greatest wear. Attached by large buttons, toggles or lampwick braces, they reached as high as the lower part of the chest. Below, they had lamp-wick lashings which were securely bound round the uppers of boots or finnesko. In walking, the trousers would often work off the leather boots, especially if they were cut to a tailor's length, and snow would then pour up the leg and down into the boots in a remarkably short time. To counteract this, Ninnis initiated the very satisfactory plan of sewing a short length of canvas on to the boots to increase the length of the upper.

The burberry helmet and blouse were either in one piece or separate. For use round the Hut, in thick drifts, the combination of helmet and blouse was handy and time-saving. For sledging, when low temperatures and strong winds might be expected all the time, it met the conditions well; there being no necessity to worry about keeping the neck drift-tight. Under ordinary circumstances it was very convenient to have a blouse and helmet detached, as one so often could wear the former with a well-padded woollen helmet and be reduced only as a last resource to wearing the burberry helmet.

The blouse was roomy, giving great freedom of movement. Around the neck was a draw-string, which bunched in the jacket tightly over the lower part of the helmet. There was also a draw-string round the waist. It was here that we had the greatest difficulty in making the garment fit snow-tight. If simply tied, the blouse would soon slip up from below, especially if one were working with pick and shovel, carrying cases or blocks of ice. To obviate this, some of the men sewed loops or tags of lamp-wick on to the sides of the trousers, to connect with corresponding attachments on the blouse. As an additional security, others wore an outside belt which was, even if the blouse slipped up for some distance, a line of defence against the drift-snow.

The burberry helmet completely enclosed the head except for the face, which remained uncovered at the bottom of a funnel stiffened by several rings of copper-wire. Lampwick, the universal polar "cord," was sewn in short strips in front of the ears and tied at the back of the head, firmly securing the helmet. Since the voyage of the *Discovery* (1901–1904) lamp-wick had been used widely in sledging on account of its width, softness, comparative warmth and because of the fact that ordinary cord is not so easy to manipulate in cold weather. Large buttons of leather or bone were not nearly so popular as small, smooth lengths of stick engaging cross-wise with loops of cord—known as toggles, which became quite a mania with some members of the Expedition. Whetter, for instance, was known as the "Toggle King," because of the multitude of these stick-and-cord appendages which hung from every part of his clothing.

Under the burberrys thick, but light, suits of Jaeger fleece were worn. They combined trousers and a sleeveless coat, over which a woollen jersey was worn. In calm weather these with underclothing were all-sufficient, but in the average fifty-mile wind at any temperature in the neighbourhood of zero Fahrenheit, they felt distinctly porous.

In less windy weather the luxury of discarding burberrys, either partly or wholly, was an indulgence which gave great satisfaction.

Finnesko were the favourite foot-gear—soft and commodious reindeer-skin fur boots. Once these were stuffed with Lapp saennegras or manilla fibre, and the feet covered with several pairs of socks, cold could be despised unless one were stationary for some time or the socks or padding became damp. Even though the padding were wet, violent exercise kept the temperature "balance" in the warm direction, especially if one were also under the stimulus of a recent hot meal.

Of course, on smooth ice or polished snow in even moderate winds it was useless to try and keep one's feet in finnesko, although practice gave great agility in calmer weather. As already indicated, spiked crampons on approved models, tested on the glacier-slopes in a hurricane wind, were almost always worn encasing the finnesko. With so many coverings the feet often became uncomfortably hot, and for odd jobs about the Hut and not far abroad spiked leather boots gave most satisfaction.

There were various coverings for the hands: felt mitts, mittens, instrument-gloves and wolfskin mitts.

The first were used in conjunction with fingerless mittens. The wear and tear on these was greater than on any other item of clothing. It was a common sight to see them ragged, canvas-covered, patched, repatched and again repatched, to be at last reluctantly thrown away. There were two compartments in a single glove, one for the thumb and the other for the fingers. It is much easier to keep the fingers warm when in contact with one another than by having them in separate stalls.

Instrument-gloves of wool were used for delicate manipulations, as a partial protection, since they reduced the stinging chill of cold metal at low temperatures.

Wolfskin mitts are unexcelled for use in cold windy weather. Their shaggy external hair entangles the drift-snow, which thaws, soaks the skin and refreezes until the mitt is stiff as buckram. This is their main disadvantage.

The Cliffs at Land's End, Cape Denison. On the Brow of the Cliff in Front of the Figure (Mertz) Is a Good Example of a Snow Cornice

On the Frozen Sea in a Cavern Eaten Out by the Waves Under the Coastal Ice-Cliffs

These mitts or rather gauntlets were made longer in the arms than usual so as to overlap the burberry sleeves and keep the wrists warm.

Lambskin mitts with the wool facing inwards were very useful and wore well for occupations like hauling on ropes and lifting cases.

Like every other movable thing, mitts had to be made fast to prevent them blowing away. So they were slung round the neck by a yoke of lamp-wick. The mittened hand could then be removed with the assurance that the outer mitt would not be far away when it was wanted, no matter how hard the wind blew.

There has been much discussion as to the relative merits of fur and woollen clothing. After all the question has resolved itself into one of personal predilection. It has been claimed that furs are warmer and lighter. The warmth follows from the wind-proof quality of the hide which, unfortunately, also tends to retain moist exhalations from the body. In Adelie Land, the only furs we used were finnesko, wolfskin mitts and sleeping-bags of reindeer skins.

As in every part of the equipment, modifications had to be made in the circular Willesden-drill tents. To facilitate their erection in the perpetual winds they were sewn permanently on to the five bamboo poles, instead of being thrown over the latter previously set in position. Thus the tents opened like large conical umbrellas. A rawhide loop was fixed to the middle one of the three windward legs and, when raising a tent during a high wind, it was the usual thing for a man to be inside gripping the loop to pin down the windward legs and at the same time, kicking out the two leeward legs. On hard surfaces, holes were dug to receive the ends of the poles; at other times they were pressed home into the snow by the man inside the tent.

When pitched, the tent was held down by blocks of snow or ice, helped by spare food-bags, which were all piled round on a broad flounce. Ventilators, originally supplied with the tents, had to be dispensed with on account of the incessant drift. The door of the tent was an oval funnel of burberry material just large enough to admit a man and secured by a draw-string.

Strips of calico and webbing were sewn over the insides of the light tents to strengthen them for sledging in the summer. For heavy weather we also had japara sail-cloth tents with Willesden canvas flounces. These gave one a feeling of greater security and were much more wind-proof, but unfortunately twice as heavy as the first-mentioned.

A floor-cloth of light Willesden canvas covered the surface of snow or ice in the interior of the tent; performing when sledging the alternative office of a sail.

In order to cut snow, névé or ice to pile on the flounce, a pick and spade had to be included in the sledging equip meet. As a rule, a strong, pointed shovel weighing about six pounds answers very well; but in Adelie Land, the surface was so often wind-swept ice, polished porcelain-snow, or hard névé that a pick was necessary to make any impression upon it. It was found that a four-pound spade, carefully handled, and a four-pound miner's pick provided against all emergencies.

Our sledges were similar to those of other British Antarctic expeditions; of eleven- and twelve-foot lengths. The best were Norwegian, made of ash and hickory. Others built in Sydney, of Australian woods, were admirably suited for special work. Those made of mountain-ash had the advantage of being extremely light, but the runners wore out quickly on ice and hard névé. Sledges of powellized spotted gum were very strong and stood plenty of rough usage, but were heavier than those procured in Norway. A decking of bamboo slats secured by copper-wire to the crossbars was usually employed.

A light bamboo mast and spar were fitted to each sledge. Immediately in front of the mast came the "cooker-box," containing in respective compartments the primus and a bottle of spirit for lighting it, as well as spare prickers, openers and fillers for the kerosene tins, repair outfits and other odd articles. The cooker-boxes were of Venesta board, with hinged lids secured by chocks and overlapped by japara cloth to exclude as much drift-snow as possible. An instrument-box was secured to the sledge near the rear and just forward of a Venesta or aluminium tray on which the kerosene contained in one-gallon tins was carried. In several cases the tray was widened to receive as well a case containing a dip-circle. Rearmost of all was a wooden crosspiece to which the shaft of the sledge-meter was attached through a universal joint. On the middle section of the sledge between the cooker-box and instrument-box, sleeping-bags, food-bags, clothes-bags, tent, alpine rope, theodolite legs, and other articles, were arranged, packed and immovably stiffened by buckled straps passing from side to side.

Sledging harness for both men and dogs was constructed of canvas. In the former case, a wide belt of triple thickness encircled the body at the hips, sewn to braces of narrower strips passing over the shoulders, while hauling-rope was attached to the belt behind. The strength of the whole depended on the care bestowed in sewing the parts together, and, since his life might depend upon it, no one made anything else but a thorough job of his harness.

Ninnis and Mertz ran a tailoring business for the dogs, who were brought one by one into the outer Hut to be measured for harness. After many lengths had been cut with scissors the canvas bands were put through and sewn together on the large sewing-machine and then each dog was fitted and the final alterations were made. The huskies looked quite smart in their "suits."

Upon the primus heater, alone, did we rely for cooking the meals on sledging journeys. First used for purposes of sledging by Dr. Nansen in his journey across Greenland, the primus is only economically managed after some practice. To light a primus in a draughty tent at a low temperature calls for some forbearance before one is a thorough master of the art. A sledging cook will often make a disagreeable *faux pas* by extinguishing the primus in the preparation of hoosh. This is most readily done by lowering too quickly the outside cover over the rest of the cooker. Fumes of vaporizing kerosene soon fill the tent and when matches are found, the cooker pulled to pieces, the primus relighted and the choking vapours have cleared, one is apt to think that all is well. The hoosh is quite as successful as usual, but the cocoa, made from water in the annulus, has a tincture of kerosene which cannot be concealed.

In the "Nansen Cooker," which we used, a maximum result is secured from the heat of the primus. The hot gases from the combustion of the kerosene, before they escape into the outside air, have to circulate along a tortuous path, passing from the hot interior to the colder exterior compartments, losing heat all the time. Thus a hot hoosh is preparing in the central vessel side by side with the melting of snow for cocoa or tea in the annulus. By the combination of "Nansen Cooker" and primus stove one gallon of kerosene oil properly husbanded is made to last for twelve days in the preparation of the ordinary ration for three men.

The subject of food is one which requires peculiar consideration and study. It is assumed that a polar expedition must carry all its food-stuffs in that variety and quantity which may approximately satisfy normal demands. Fortunately, the advance of science has been such that necessaries like vegetables, fruit, meats and milk are now preserved so that the chances of bacterial contamination are reduced to a minimum. A cold climate is an additional security towards the same end.

Speaking generally, while living for months in an Antarctic hut, it is a splendid thing to have more than the mere necessaries of life. Since one is cut off from the ordinary amenities of social existence, it is particularly necessary that equipment and *food* should be of the very best; in some measure to replace a lack which sooner or later makes itself keenly felt. Explorers, after all, are only mortal.

Luxuries, then, are good in moderation, and mainly for their psychological effect. After a spell of routine, a celebration is the natural sequel, and if there are delicacies which in civilization are more palatable than usual, why not take them to where they will receive a still fuller and heartier appreciation? There is a corresponding rise in the "tide of life" and

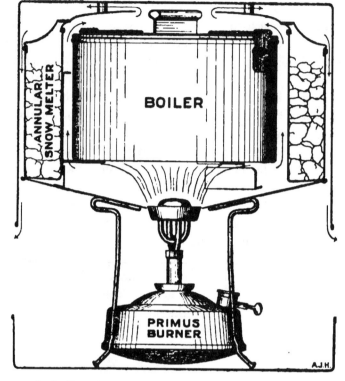

Section Through a Nansen Sledging Cooker Mounted on the Primus

the ennui of the same task, in the same place, in the same *wind*, is not so noticeable. So we did not forget our asparagus and jugged hare.

In the matter of sledging foods, one comes down to a solid basis of dietetics. But even dietetics as a science has to stand aside when actual experience speaks. Dietetics deals with proteins, carbohydrates, fats, and calories: all terms which need definition and comprehension before the value of a sledging ration can be fundamentally understood. When the subject was first introduced into table conversation at the Hut, it was regarded somewhat suspiciously as "shop." But it gradually won interest simply because it was of such vital concern.

In sledging there is undoubtedly a critical allowance which will yield the best results. Circumstances alter cases, and the correct ration under one set of conditions cannot be expected to coincide with that in another situation. Thus, the journey may be conducted under conditions of great cold or of comparative warmth, by man-hauling or auxiliary power, at sea-level or on an altitude, through regions where there is a reasonable hope of securing additions of meat by the way, or across barren tracts devoid of game. In each instance particular demands must be supplied.

In selecting the articles of diet, idiosyncrasies of individuals should be consulted in reason, and under no consideration should anything be taken which bears the slightest stigma of contamination. It remains, then, to discriminate those foods which contribute the greatest amount of nutriment for a given weight, and which, inter se, preserve a proper dietetic balance. Variety is very desirable, provided that there is no important sacrifice in nutrient value. The proof of a wisely selected ration is to find at the end of a long sledge journey that the sole craving is for an increase in the ration. Of course, such would be the ideal result of a perfect ration, which does not exist.

Considering that an ordinary individual in civilization may only satisfy the choice demands of his appetite by selecting from the multifarious bill of fare of a modern restaurant, it will be evident that the same person, though already on the restricted diet of an explorer, cannot be suddenly subjected to a sledging ration for any considerable period without a certain exercise of discipline.

For example, the Eastern Coastal Party, sledging at fairly high temperatures over the sea-ice, noted that the full ration of hoosh produced at times a mild indigestion, they drank much liquid to satisfy an intense thirst and on returning to the Hut found their appetites inclined to tinned fruit and penguins' eggs. Bickerton's and Bage's parties, though working at a much higher altitude, had a similar experience. The former, for instance, could not at first drink the whole allowance of thick, rich cocoa without a slight nausea. The latter saved rations during the first two weeks of their journey, and only when they rose to greater heights and were in fine condition did they appreciate the ration to the full. Again, even when one becomes used to the ration, the sensation of full satisfaction does not last for more than an hour. The imagination reaches forward to the next meal, perhaps partly on account of the fact that marching is often monotonous and the scenery uninspiring. Still, even after a good evening hoosh, the subconscious self may assert itself in food-dreams. The reaction from even a short sledging trip, where food has been plentiful, is to eat a good deal, astonishing in amount to those who for the time being have lived at the Hut.

It may appear that a serious case is being made against the polar sledging ration. On the whole, it was found to be excellent and the best that experience had been able to devise. Entering the polar zones, one must not be over-fastidious, but take it as a matter of course that there will be self-denial and deprivation of small luxuries.

The energy exerted by man, and the requirements of tissue-building are derived from the organic compounds known as proteins,** fats and carbohydrates, though in a slight degree from other substances, most important of which are minute quantities of mineral matter.

A calorie as used in dietetics is the amount of heat required to raise the temperature of one kilogramme of water at 0° C. to 1° C. The heat-value of food-stuffs, stated in calories, can be quickly reckoned when chemical analyses stating their protein, fat and carbohydrate contents are available. It has been ascertained that one gramme of protein or carbohydrate yields 4.1 calories, whilst the same amount of fat produces 9.3 calories. Thus the value of fat-containing foods in a sledging ration is at once apparent.

Theoretically, any of the three classes of foods mentioned might be thought to supply adequate energy, if taken in sufficient amount. Practically, however, protein and carbohydrate are essential, and it is better to have a mixture of all three. So, in concentrating foods for sledging, the largest possible proportion of fat, compatible with other considerations, is included.

Ordinarily, a normal man consumes some four or five pounds weight of solid food per diem, of which 50 per cent., it is rather surprising to learn, is water. When sledging, one has the satisfaction of knowing that all but the smallest quantity of the food dragged is solid nutriment. The water is added when the meals are cooked. It is just in this artificial addition that the sledging ration is not perfect, though as a synthesis it satisfies the demands of dietetics. Food containing water, as cooked meat oozing with its own gravy is a more palatable thing than dried meat-powder to which boiling water has been added. In the same way, a dry, hard biscuit plus liquid is a different thing from a spongy loaf of yeast bread with its high percentage of water. One must reckon with the psychic factor in eating. When sledging, one does not look for food well served as long as the food is hot, nourishing and filling. So the usage of weeks and a wolfish appetite make hoosh a most delicious preparation; but when the days of an enforced ration are over, the

---

** *The* proteins *are complex nitrogenous compounds which are preeminent in fulfilling the two functions of a food: to form tissue and to produce work and heat. As examples may be quoted, myosin the chief protein of ordinary meat or muscle, ovalbumin one of the proteins of egg-white, casein belonging to milk and cheese, and gluten a protein-mixture in flour.*
Fats *are organic non-nitrogenous substances obtained from both animal and vegetable sources, e.g. butter and olive oil.*
The carbohydrates *are compounds of carbon with hydrogen and oxygen in a certain proportion, e.g. cane-sugar and starch.*
Mineral matters *are inorganic, being chlorides, carbonates or phosphates of calcium, sodium and potassium.*

Ice Stalactites Draping the Foreshores

A Grotto of "Mysteries"

desire for appetizing well-served food reasserts itself. The body refuses to be treated merely as an engine.

The daily polar sledging ration for one man has been concentrated to a figure just above two pounds in weight, For instance, in recent Antarctic expeditions, Scott, in 1903, used 34.7 ozs., Shackleton in 1908 used 34.82 ozs. and our own amounted to 34.25 ozs. Exclusive of tea, pepper and salt, Shackleton's ration and that adopted by Wild at the Western Base and ourselves in Adelie Land were identical—34 ozs. Reverting to earlier explorers, for the sake of comparisons, McClintock in 1850 brought his minimum down to 42 ozs., Nares in 1875 to 40 ozs., Greely in 1882 to 41.75 ozs., and Abruzzi in 1900 to 43.5 ozs.

Our allowance was made up as follows, the relative amounts in the daily sledging ration for one man being stated: plasmon biscuit, 12 ozs.; pemmican, 8 ozs.; butter, 2 ozs.; plasmon chocolate, 2 ozs.; glaxo (dried milk), 5 ozs.; sugar, 4 ozs.; cocoa, 1 oz.; tea, .25 oz. It will be instructive to make a short note on each item.

Plasmon biscuit was made of the best flour mixed with 30 per cent. of plasmon powder. Each biscuit weighed 2.25 ozs., and was made specially thick and hard to resist shaking and bumping in transit as well as the rough usage of a sledging journey. The effect of the high percentage of plasmon, apart from its nutritive value, was to impart additional toughness to the biscuit, which tested our teeth so severely that we should have preferred something less like a geological specimen and more like ordinary "hard tack," The favourite method of dealing with these biscuits was to smash them with an ice-axe or nibble them into small pieces and treat the fragments for a while to the solvent action of hot cocoa. Two important proteins were present in this food: plasmon, a trade-name for casein, the chief protein of milk, and gluten, a mixture of proteins in flour.

The pemmican we used consisted of powdered dried beef (containing the important protein, myosin) and 50 per cent. of pure fat in the form of lard. The large content of fat contributes to its high caloric value, so that it is regularly included in sledging diets. Hoosh is a stodgy, porridge-like mixture of pemmican, dried biscuit and water, brought to the boil and served hot. Some men prefer it cooler and more dilute, and to this end dig up snow from the floor of the tent with their spoons, and mix it in until the hoosh is "to taste," Eating hoosh is a heightened form of bliss which no sledger can ever forget.

Glaxo is a proprietary food preparation of dried milk, manufactured in New Zealand. It is without doubt an ideal food for any climate where concentration is desirable and asepsis cannot be neglected. The value of milk as an all-round food is well known. It contains protein as casein, fat as cream and in fine globules, carbohydrate as lactose (milk sugar) and mineral substances whose importance is becoming more recognized. At the Western Base, Wild's party invented glaxo biscuits; an unbaked mixture of flour and dried milk, which were in themselves a big inducement to go sledging. At the Hut, making milk from the dried powder required some little experience. Cold water was added to the dried powder, a paste was made and warm or hot water poured in until the milk was at the required strength. One of the professional "touches" was to aerate the milk, after mixing, by pouring it from jug to jug.

Butter, although it contains nearly 20 per cent. of water is a food of high heat-value and is certainly more easily digested than fat, such as dripping, with a higher melting-point. Ours was fresh Victorian butter, packed in the ordinary export boxes, and carried to the Antarctic on the open bridge of the *Aurora*. With a sheath-knife, the sledging cook cut off three small chunks of two ounces each from the frozen butter every day at lunch. To show how the appetite is affected by extreme cold, one feels that butter is a wholesome thing just in itself, being more inclined to eat a pound than two ounces.

Sugar—the carbohydrate, sucrose—has special qualities as a food since it is quickly assimilated, imparting within a few minutes fresh energy for muscular exertion. Athletes will support this; in fact, a strong solution of sugar in water is used as a stimulant in long-distance running and other feats of endurance. Wild, for instance, found as a matter of experience that chocolate was preferable to cheese as a sledging food, even though similar weights had approximately the same food-value.

Cocoa and tea were the two sledging beverages. The cocoa was used for two meals, the first and the last in the day, and the tea for lunch. Both contain stimulating alkaloids, theobromine and caffeine, and fat is a notable constituent of cocoa. Of course, their chief nourishing value, as far as we were concerned, lay in the glaxo and sugar added.

Lastly, plasmon chocolate is a preparation of pure chocolate (a mixture of ground cocoa, white sugar and starch) with the addition of 10 per cent. of plasmon.

As food for the dogs, there was nothing better than dried seal-steaks with the addition of a little blubber. Ordinary pemmican is readily eaten, but not appreciated by the dogs in the same way as seal meat. To save weight, the meat was dried over the stove without heating it sufficiently to cook it. By this measure, almost 50 per cent. in weight was saved.

The Hut was all agog with movement and bustle on the days when rations were being made up and packed. Starting from the earliest stage in the process, there would be two men in the outer Hut grinding plasmon biscuit into powder. One would turn away for dear life and the other smash the biscuit with a hammer on a metal slab and feed continuously into the grinder. The atmosphere would be full of the nauseous vapours of blubber arising from dishes on the stove where seal meat was drying for the dogs. Ninnis and Mertz superintended in this department, in careless moments allowing the blubber to frizzle and diffuse its aroma through the Hut.

Inside, spread along the eighteen-foot table would be the weighers, the bag-makers or machinists, and the packers. The first made up a compound of cocoa, glaxo and sugar—cocoa compound; mixed glaxo and sugar and stirred together, pemmican and biscuit—pemmican compound. These were weighed and run into calico bags, rapidly supplied by several machinists farther along the table. In spare moments the weighers stowed chocolate, whole biscuits, butter and tea into 190 sacks of various sizes. Lastly, the packers had strong canvas tanks, as they were called, designed to hold food for a week and a fortnight respectively. Into these the rations were carefully distributed, butter in the centre, whole biscuits near the top. Then the tanks were tightly closed, and one man operated with palm and sail-needle, sewing them up with twine. At the same time, a side-line was run in pemmican which was removed semi-frozen from the air-tight tins, and shaved into small pieces with a strong sheath-knife. Butter, too, arrived from the refrigerator-store and was subdivided into two-ounce or pound lumps.

Meanwhile, other occupations were in full swing. An amateur cobbler, his crampon on a last, studded its spiked surface with clouts, hammering away in complete disregard of the night-watchman's uneasy slumbers. The big sewing-machine raced at top-speed round the flounce of a tent, and in odd corners among the bunks were groups mending mitts, strengthening sleeping-bags and patching burberrys. The cartographer at his table beneath a shaded acetylene light drew maps and sketched, the magnetician was busy on calculations close by. The cook and messman often made their presence felt and heard. In the outer Hut, the lathe spun round, its whirr and click drowned in the noisy rasp of the grinder and the blast of the big blow-lamp. The last-named, Bickerton, "bus-driver" and air-tractor expert, had converted, with the aid of a few pieces of covering tin, into a forge. A piece of red-hot metal was lifted out and thrust into the vice; Hannam was striker and Bickerton holder. General conversation was conducted in shouts, Hannam's being easily predominant.

The sum total of sounds was sufficient for a while to make every one oblivious to the clamour of the restless wind.

The Relief of Wild's Party. The *Aurora* Approaching the Floe at the Western Base, February 1913

Pacing the Deck: Capt. John King Davis and Capt. James Davis

CHAPTER XI

Spring Exploits

I F THE "WINTER CALMS" WERE A DELUSION, THERE were at least several beautifully clear, moderately calm days in June. The expectation of colder weather had been realized, and by the end of the month it was a perceptible fact that the sun had definitely turned, describing a longer arc when skimming the distant fleets of bergs along the northern horizon. Thus on June 28 the refracted image of the sun rose into visibility about eleven o'clock, heralded by a vivid green sky and damask cloud and by one o'clock had disappeared.

On the same day every one was abroad, advancing the wireless masts another stage and digging ice-shafts. Stillwell commenced a contoured plane-table survey of the neighbourhood of Winter Quarters. He continued this with many breaks during the next few months and eventually completed an accurate and valuable map, undeterred by the usual series of frost-bites.

There was much anticipated of July, but the wind soughed on and the temperature decreased. Just to demonstrate its resource, the wind maintained ninety-seven miles per hour for six hours on July 19, while the puff-anemometer indicated several "breaks" of one hundred and fifty miles per hour.

July 21 was cold, calm and clear. For the first time after many weeks the sun was mildly warm, and all felt with a spring of optimism that a new era had begun. The sea which had been kept open by the wind was immediately overspread with thin, dark ice, which in a few hours was dotted with many ice-flowers aggregates of fern-like, sprouting fronds similar to small bouquets or rosettes. Soon the surface had whitened and thickened and by next morning was firm enough to hold a man out beyond the nearest island. The wind did not allow this state of affairs to last for long, for by lunch-time it had hurried away the wide floes and raged across a foaming sea.

We still considered the question of sledging, and I decided that if there were the slightest prospect of accomplishing anything, several of us would start before the end of July on a short journey. The month, however, closed with nothing to commend it. The night-watchman for July 29 says:

"Amundsen," One of the Sledge Dogs Sent Down to Us from Amundsen's South Polar Expedition

At the Foot of a Snow Ramp Beneath the Coastal Ice-Cliffs, Commonwealth Bay

"The moon was wonderfully bright to-night, encircled by a complete halo. It appeared to hang suspended like a silver globe in the dark blue sky. The stars flash and sparkle and seem much nearer here than in Australia. At midnight the wind blew at ninety miles per hour, so that it was no easy job getting to the screen in slippery finnesko. Away in the north there was a dense cloud of spray and sea-smoke, and the wind screamed past the Hut. The 'St. Elmoscope' was buzzing merrily in the roof all the time."

Ninnis and Mertz with a team of dogs managed, on the morning of the 29th, to get several loads of forty pounds over the first steep rise of the glacier to Webb's magnetic ice-cave against a "blow" of seventy miles per hour.

August 1 was marked by a hurricane, and the celebration in the evening of Swiss Confederation Day. Mertz was the hero of the occasion as well as cook and master of ceremonies. From a mysterious box he produced all kinds of quaint conserves, and the menu soared to unknown delicacies like "Potage à la Suisse, Choucroute garnie aux saucission de Berne, Purée de foie gras trufée, and Leckerley de Bâle." Hanging above the buoyant assembly were the Cross of Helvetia and the Jack of Britannia.

It was not till August 8 that there was any indication of improvement. The sun was bright, the barometer was steady, the wind fell to forty miles an hour and a fine radiant of cirrus cloud spread out fan-like from the north; the first from that direction for months.

On the afternoon of August 9, Ninnis, Madigan and I set off with a team of dogs against a forty-mile wind in an attempt to push to the south. Darkness was coming on when we sighted a bamboo pole, three and a quarter miles south of the Hut, and camped. The dogs pulled well up the steep slopes, but the feet of several were cut by the sharp edges of the wind-worn ice.

Very heavy gusts swept by in the early morning hours of the 10th and when the time came to get out of our sleeping-bags it fell calm for a short space. We had taken down the tent and had started to move away, when back rushed the wind, strong and steady. Still we pushed on with our willing team and by a piece of good fortune reached the sledge which had been abandoned in the autumn, five and a half miles from the Hut, and of whose fate in the winter's hurricanes we had made all kind of conjectures.

On its leeward side there was a ramp of very hard snow slanting down from the top of the sledge. To windward the low pedestal of ice on which the runners stood was hollowed out, and the wood of the rails and cross-bars, the leather straps, tent, floor-cloth and canvas food-tanks were all bleached and worn. The aluminium cooker, strapped on its box, was brightly polished on the weather side by the dry, drifting snow impelled by the furious winds. A thermograph, left behind in the autumn, was found to be intact and indicated a temperature of −35° F.—the lowest for the eight days during which it had run. The remains of Madigan's plum-pudding of the autumn were unearthed and found in splendid condition. That evening it was thawed out over the primus and we demolished it, after a pause of over five months since having the first cut.

At this spot the steepest grades of the ascent to the plateau were left behind, and it appeared to be a strategic point from which to extend our sledging efforts. The main difficulty was that of pitching camp in the prevailing winds on a surface of ice. To obviate this, the only expedient was to excavate a shelter beneath the ice itself; and there was the further consideration that all sledging parties would be able to make use of such a haven and save extra wear on their tents.

On the morning of August 11 Madigan and Ninnis commenced to sink a deep vertical trench, at one end of which a room was hewn out large enough to accommodate three men. The job was finished on the following day, and we struck the tent and moved to our new abode. The tent was spread over the vertical shaft which served as the entrance.

It was a great relief to be in a strong room, with solid walls of ice, in place of the cramped tent flapping violently in the wind. Inside, the silence was profound; the blizzard was banished. Aladdin's Cave it was dubbed—a truly magical world of glassy facets and scintillating crystals.

Shelves were chipped out at a moment's notice for primus stove, spirit bottle, matches, kerosene and other oddments. At one side a small hole was cut to communicate with a narrow fissure which provided ventilation without allowing the entrance of drift snow. Whatever daylight there was

At Aladdin's Cave. The Vertical Passage Leading Down into the Cave Itself Is Situated Immediately Behind the Figure on the Right

Beneath the Surface of the Plateau. Bage Preparing a Meal in Aladdin's Cave in August

Laseron and Hunter Using the Collapsible Steel Handcart in Preparing for Dredging on the Frozen Sea

Greenland Sledging Dogs—"John Bull" and "Ginger"—Tethered on the Rocks Adjacent to the Hut

filtered through the roof and walls without hindrance. A small crevasse opened near at hand and was a natural receptacle for rubbish. The purest ice for cooking could be immediately hacked from the walls without the inconvenience of having to don one's burberrys and go outside for it. Finally, one neatly disposed of spare clothes by moistening the corner of each garment and pressing it against the wall for a few seconds, where it would remain hanging until required. The place, in fact, was simply replete with conveniences. We thoroughly enjoyed the night's rest in Aladdin's Cave, notwithstanding alarming cracks proceeding occasionally from the crevasses around.

Madigan and Ninnis dug a shelter for the dogs, which spent their time curled up so as to expose as little surface as possible to the biting wind. Their thick coats did not adhere to a snow surface, but readily became frozen down to ice, so that an ice-axe would have to be used to chip them free.

On August 13, though there was a steady, strong wind blowing, we continued our advance to the south. The dogs hated to face wind, but, on the whole, did better than expected. In the afternoon, when only eight miles south of Winter Quarters and at an altitude of two thousand feet, dark and lowering clouds formed overhead, and I decided to give up any idea of going farther out, for the time being. We had provisions for a few days only, and there was every indication of thick, drifting weather, during which, in the crevassed ice of that vicinity, it would not be advisable to travel.

After depoting a pick, shovel and some pemmican, we started back, thinking it might be possible to reach the Hut the same night. However, driven by a strong wind over a polished, slippery surface split into small crevasses, down a grade which steepened quickly, we required to have all our senses vigilant. Two of the dogs remained in harness and the rest were allowed to run loose ahead. These two strained every effort to catch up to their companions.

We retarded the sledge as much as possible and all went well for a few minutes. Then the wind slewed the sledge, the runners struck an irregularity in the surface and the whole capsized. This happened repeatedly, until there was nothing to do but loose the two remaining dogs and drag the sledge ourselves. The dogs were soon lost to sight, except Pavlova, who remained with us all the time. As the hours of light were short in August, darkness had come before Aladdin's Cave was reached, and it was with some relief that we saw the sledge, flag-pole and the expectant dogs suddenly loom up in front. The sleeping-bags and other gear were passed down into the Cave and the dogs were fed.

When the doorway was opened in the morning, August 14, a blizzard with dense drifting snow was in full progress. As it was not possible to see any distance, and as our quarters were very comfortable, we decided to wait for another day. Madigan and Ninnis went out and fed the dogs, who were all snugly curled up in beds of snow.

The weather was no better on the 15th, but, as we were only five and a half miles from the Hut, which was more comfortable and where there was much work to be done, it seemed a shame to remain cooped up in idleness. Madigan and Ninnis were both strongly in favour of making a dash for the Hut, so we set off.

The sledge having been dug out, one man went in front to keep the course and two men brought up the rear, holding back the load. With long-spiked Swiss crampons we could hold up very well on the ice. In dense drift it was not a simple matter to steer a correct course for the Hut and it was essential not to deviate, as the rocky foreshores near which it stood extended only for a mile east and west; on either side abutting on vertical ice-cliffs. With a compelling force like a prance at our backs, it was not a nice thing to contemplate finding ourselves on the brink of a precipice.

The wind, however, was steady, and we knew at what angle to steer to keep a rough course; and we were also helped by a number of small crevasses between three and five and a half miles which ran approximately north and south.

Half a mile had been covered before we remarked the absence of the dogs which had been left to follow. We had taken for granted that they would follow us, and were so fully occupied after starting that their absence had passed unnoticed. It would be difficult to locate them if we returned; the weather would improve in a few days; if they felt hungry they would come down of their own accord. So we decided to go on without them.

At two miles from the Hut the drift thinned out and the wind became more gusty. Between the gusts the view ahead opened out for a considerable distance, and the rocks soon showed black below the last steep fall.

Back at the Hut it was arranged that if the dogs did not return in a reasonable time, Bage, Mertz and Hurley should go up to Aladdin's Cave in search of them.

They made a great effort to get away next morning. The sledge was hauled for one thousand one hundred yards up to the magnetic ice-cave against a bitter torrent of air rushing by at eighty-two miles an hour. Here they retreated exhausted.

On the 17th the wind was gauged at eighty-four miles an hour, and nothing could be done. Dense drift and ferocious wind continued until the morning of August 21, and still none of the dogs had come home.

Bage, Hurley and Mertz took advantage of a slight lull to start off at 6.30 AM As they did not return that night we presumed they were making good headway.

The drift was thick and the wind high for four days, and it was not until the morning of the 25th that the weather showed clearer and more promising. At 2 PM Bage and his companions arrived at the Hut bringing all the dogs except Grandmother, who had died of exhaustion. Aladdin's Cave had been difficult to find in the driving snow, which had thickened after the first few miles. They actually passed close to it when Mertz, between the gusts, sighted Castor jumping about, fully alive to the approaching relief. The other dogs were found curled up in the snow, in a listless, apathetic state; apparently in the same positions when left seven days before. They had made no attempt to break into several bags of provisions lying close at hand, preferring to starve rather than expose their faces to the pelting drift. All were frozen down except Basilisk and Castor. Pavlova was in the best condition, possibly because her last meal had been an extra full one; a reward for remaining with us when the others had bolted. Grandmother was in the worst condition, and, despite all efforts at revival, died four hours after. As the poor brutes were very weak after their long fast and exposure, they were taken into the Cave and fed on warm hoosh. Everything possible was done for them, and in return the party passed a very miserable time cramped in such a small space with six dogs. The accommodation was slightly increased by enlarging the Cave.

Five days of calm weather! It could scarcely be credited, yet September came with such a spell. They gave us great opportunities, and, for once, a vision of what perfect Antarctic days might be. The sea speedily froze over and extended our territory to the north. Every day we dredged among the tide-cracks, until Hunter and Laseron had material enough to sort and bottle for weeks. Seals came up everywhere, and the dogs gorged on much-needed meat and blubber. Three large Weddells were shot near the "Eastern Barrier" on September 1, and hauled up an ice-cliff eighty feet high to the rocks above. Work on the wireless masts went on apace, and the geologist was abroad with his plane-table every day. Webb and Bage, after a protracted interval, were able to take star observations for time, in order to check the chronometers.

Mertz, Ninnis, Whetter and Laseron, with a team of dogs sledged a big load of food-stuffs to Aladdin's Cave on September 1. At the Cave the dogs were let loose, but instead of running back to the Hut, lingered about and finally had to be led down the slope. On being loosed again, several rushed back to the Cave and were only brought along by force. That night, Scott and Franklin, two kindred spirits, were not present at "roll-call."

On September 3, McLean, Whetter and Close took more provisions to Aladdin's Cave. They reported light drift and wind on the highlands, while at sea-level it was clear and calm.

The sea-ice was by then thick and safe. About half a mile off shore a very successful dredging was made in fifty fathoms; the bottom at this depth simply teemed with life. At first, the dredge, rope-coils, tub, picks and other necessary implements were dragged about on a sledge, but the sledge was hauled only with great difficulty and much exertion over the sticky, new sea-ice. As a substitute a portable, steel handcart was advantageously employed, although, owing to its weight, tide-cracks and rotten areas had to be crossed at a run. On one occasion a flimsy surface collapsed under it, and Hunter had a wetting before it was hauled on to firmer ice.

On September 4 there was a cloud radiant from the northwest, indicative of a change in the weather. Ninnis, Mertz and Murphy transported more food-bags and kerosene to Aladdin's Cave. They found Franklin one and a half miles south of the Hut lying on the ice quite well, but there was no sign of Scott. Both dogs were seen on the 1st of the month, when they were in a locality south-east of the Hut, where crevasses were numerous. It seemed most probable that Scott had lost his life in one of them. The party visiting the Cave reported a considerable amount of snow drifting above a level of one thousand feet.

There was another day of successful dredging, and, about four o'clock, while several men were still out on the ice, whirlies with great columns of drift came steadily down the glacier, pouring over the seaward cliffs. In a few minutes the snow-clouds were round the Hut and the wind was not long in working up to eighty miles per hour. The dredging party reached the land just in time; and the sea-ice drifted away to the north. Thus ended one of the most remarkable periods of fine weather experienced by us in Adelie Land, only to be excelled in the height of summer.

The possibility of such a spell being repeated fired us with the hope that after all a reasonable amount of sledging could be accomplished in the spring. Three parties were chosen to reconnoitre in different directions and to test the sledging gear. As we were far from being confident in the weather, I made it clear that no party should penetrate farther than fifty miles from the Hut, nor remain away longer than a fortnight.

Webb, McLean and Stillwell, the southern reconnoitring party, were the first to set off, leaving on September 7 against a wind of fifty-six miles per hour. Between them they had only one pair of good spiked crampons, and it was a hard, five hours' drag up to Aladdin's Cave. A tent which had been spread over the entrance to keep out snow was picked up here. It had suffered punctures and small tears from crampons, and, as the next day was one of boisterous wind, the party spent it repairing the tent and endeavouring to take magnetic observations. The latter had to be abandoned owing to the instrument becoming iced up.

Next afternoon the wind fell to the forties, and the party struggled on to the south for three miles two hundred yards and camped, as it was necessary to make a search for a small depot of pemmican tins, a pick and a shovel left by us in the vicinity in August. The drift cleared at noon on the 11th, and the bamboo pole marking the depot appeared a quarter of a mile away on the right. The pick, shovel and flag were secured and another afternoon's march against a fifty-mile wind with a temperature at −20° F. brought the party three and a quarter miles further, to a point eleven and three-quarter miles south of the Hut. The wind rose to the eighties during the night, and there were many small holes in the tent which provided more ventilation than was agreeable. As the wind was too strong for travelling on the 12th, it was decided to make a cave in case of accident to the tent.

A tunnel was driven into the sloping surface of the ice towards a crevasse about a foot wide. It was a good ten hours' job in tough ice before the crevasse was reached. Into the fissure all the hewn ice was thrown instead of being laboriously shovelled up through the tunnel. The "Cathedral Grotto" was soon finished, the tent was struck and the party made themselves comfortable inside. The cavern was found to be a very draughty place with a crevasse along one wall, and it was difficult to keep warm in one-man sleeping-bags. The crevasse was accordingly closed with ice and snow. That evening and on several subsequent occasions McLean took blood-pressure observations.

During the next three days the wind was so strong that Webb's were the only crampons in which any efficient marching could be done. The time was spent in building a high break-wind of ice-blocks, a pit being excavated on the windward side in which Webb took a full set of magnetic observations. Within the "Grotto" the instrument rapidly became coated with ice-crystals; in the open air this difficulty did not arise, but others had to be overcome. It was exceedingly cold work at −20° F. in a sixty-mile wind, both for Webb and his recorder Stillwell.

There seemed no hope of going forward, so the depot flag was hoisted and a fortnight's provisions and kerosene stowed in the lee of the break-wind. It was a furious race back to the Hut *via* Aladdin's Cave with a gusty, seventy-five-mile wind in the rear. McLean and Stillwell actually skied along on their short blunt crampons, while Webb did his best to brake behind.

The second party comprised Ninnis, Mertz, and Murphy, who went to the south-east, leaving on September 11. After a hard fight to Aladdin's Cave, the wind approaching fifty miles an hour, they diverged to the south-east. On the 12th they made steady progress up the slope of the glacier, delayed by many small crevasses. The surface was so rough that the nuts on the sledge-meter soon became loose and it was necessary to stop every quarter of a mile to adjust them. The day's march was a solid five and three quarter miles against a fifty-mile wind.

On the 13th Ninnis's record proceeds as follows:

"The sky was still clear but the wind had increased to sixty-five miles per hour, the temperature standing at −17° F.

"We kept on the same course; the glacier's slope being steeper. Mertz was as usual wearing leather boots and mountaineering crampons, otherwise progress would have been practically impossible; the finnesko crampons worn by Murphy and myself giving very little foothold. Travelling was very slow indeed, and when we camped at 4 PM, two and a half miles was all that had been covered.

"At 9.15 AM (September 14) the wind practically dropped, and we advanced under perfect conditions."

They had not gone far, however, before the wind suddenly increased so that only about four and a half miles were completed in the day. That

The Mackellar Islets Viewed from an Elevation of 800 Feet on the Mainland

evening, curiously enough, it fell calm for a time; then there was a period of alternating violent winds and calm.

On Sunday, September 15, it was impossible for them to move, as a hurricane raged outside. The tent was very much damaged by the wind, but in that state it managed to stand up till next morning. In the meantime all three fully dressed themselves and lay in their three-man sleeping-bag ready to take to the road at a moment's notice.

The next morning, at a distance of eighteen miles southeast of the Hut, there was nothing for it but to make for Aladdin's Cave, which was safely reached by a forced march of twelve and three-quarter miles, with a furious wind partly abeam. On the way the sledge was blown sideways on to the lids of many wide crevasses, which, fortunately for the party, were strong at that season of the year.

From the realistic reports of the two parties which had returned it was evident that Madigan and his companions, Close and Whetter who had set out on the 12th to the west were having a bad time. But it was not till the 23rd, after a week of clear skies, low temperatures and unceasing drift-free wind that we began to feel apprehensive about them.

September 24 and 25 were punctuated by several intervals of calm during which it was judged the party would have been able to travel.

On the morning of September 26 Ninnis and Mertz, with a team of dogs, set off up the hill to Aladdin's Cave to deposit some provisions and to scan the horizon for any sign of the sledgers. On the way they fell in with them descending the slopes, very worn and frost-bitten.

They had a thrilling story to tell, and, when it was known that the party had reached fifty miles to the west, everybody crowded round to listen. The wind average at the Hut during their fortnight of absence was fifty-eight miles per hour, implying worse conditions on the plateau. Madigan gave the facts:

"After leaving Aladdin's Cave on the 12th we continued due south, lunching at 2 PM on the site of Webb's first camp. Our troubles had already begun; the wind averaging sixty miles an hour all day with a temperature at noon of −14° F.

"As a few tears appeared in the tent during the night, we saw that it would not be advisable to put it up next day for lunch, so we had a cold meal, crouched in the lee of the sledge. This custom was found to economize time, as we became so cold eating our fare of biscuit, chocolate and butter that we got moving again as soon as possible. The great disadvantage was that there was nothing to drink between the morning and evening meals.

"We sewed up the rents in the tent during the halt, having to use bare fingers in the open. About four stitches at a time were as much as one man could manage, and then the other two took their turns.

"The next day was the only comparatively calm period of the two weeks of travelling. The wind was in the vicinity of thirty miles per hour, and, going west, we reached a spot, twenty miles 'out,' on a snow-covered surface, by nightfall.

"A steady seventy-five-mile wind blew all day on the 15th at right angles to our course, accompanied by a thick, low drift. The surface was partially consolidated snow, very hard and smooth. Sometimes the sledge would grip and we could pull straight ahead. Then, suddenly, it would slide away sideways down wind and often pull us off our feet with a sudden vicious jerk. Most of the time we were dragging in a south-westerly direction to make the sledge run west, stumbling through the drift with the sledge now behind us, now sliding away to leeward, often capsizing and requiring to be laboriously righted and sometimes repacked.

"After many experiments, we found the best device was to have two men on the bow-rope, about twenty feet long, and one with about ten feet of rope attached to the rear of the sledge. The man on the tail-rope, usually Whetter, found it very difficult to keep his feet, and, after a score of falls in stinging drift with incidental frost-bites on fingers and cheeks, he did not feel exactly cheerful.

"By 4 PM on the 15th we had reached twenty-five miles and were exhausted. We pitched camp at an early hour, partly influenced by the fact that it was a special occasion—Close's birthday! Some port wine had been slipped in to provide against that 'emergency.' On taking the precious bottle from the instrument-box, I found that the cork was out, and, for one awful moment, thought the bottle was empty. Then I realized that the wine had frozen solid and had pushed the cork out by its expansion on solidification.

"At last, the tent safely pitched and hoosh and cocoa finished, the moment came to drink to Close's health and happiness. The bottle had stood on the top of the cooker while the meal was being prepared, but the wine was still as solid as ever. After being shaken and held over the primus for a good half-hour it began to issue in lumps. Once the lumps were secured in mugs the rest of the thawing was easy. Finally, we toasted Close and his wife (in far Australia) in what we voted to be the finest draught it had ever been our good fortune to drink. In the morning a cairn was made of the snow-blocks which were taken from the tent-skirt, and it was surmounted with the bottle, being called 'Birthday Camp.'

"During September 16 my right eyelid became frostbitten. I noticed that it was hard and refused to shut, so I rubbed vigorously to bring it round. However, it swelled and blistered badly and the eye remained closed for two days.

"From twenty to fifty miles 'out', the surface was névé with areas of sastrugi up to three feet in height. No crevasses were noticed. At twenty-eight miles out, we lost sight of the sea, and at forty miles an altitude of four thousand five hundred feet was reached.

"We turned out at 6 AM every morning and were on the move by 9 AM Lunch only took half an hour and was a most uncomfortable meal. As we sat in the lee of the sledge, the surface-drift swirled up in our faces like fine sand. We never camped before 6 PM and were obliged to consider five miles a good day's run.

"Pitching camp took nearly an hour. Blocks of snow were cut and arranged in a semicircle, within which the tent was laid with its peak upwind. It sounds simple enough, but, as we had to take off crampons so as not to tread on the tent, our difficulties were enormously increased by having to move about wearing finnesko on a smooth surface in a high wind. One man crawled into the tent, and, at a given signal, the other two raised the peak while the former held on to the upwind leg and kicked the other legs into place with his feet. The others then quickly piled food-tanks and blocks of snow on to the skirt, calling out as soon as there was enough to hold it down, as the man gripping the bamboo leg inside would soon have 'deadly cold' fingers. It was always a great relief when the tent was up.

"Almost every night there was some sewing to do, and it was not long before every one's fingers were in a bad state. They became, especially near the tips, as hard as wood and devoid of sensation. Manipulating toggles and buttons on one's clothing gave an immense amount of trouble, and it always seemed an interminable time before we got away in the morning. Our lowest temperature was −35° F., early on September 18.

"We were fifty miles 'out' on September 19 on a white, featureless plain. Through low drift we had seen very little of our surroundings on the march. A bamboo pole with a black flag was raised, a mound was built, and a week's provisions for three men and two gallons of kerosene were cached.

"In the morning there was a howling eighty-mile blizzard with dense drift, and our hopes of an early start homeward were dispelled. We feared for the safety of the tent, knowing that if it had gone during that 'blow' our hopes of getting back to the Hut would have been small.

"The wind continued all day and the next night, but, to our joy, abated on the 21st to fifty miles an hour, permitting us to travel.

"Through a seventy-five-miler on the 22nd and a quieter day on the 23rd, we picked up our half-way mound at Birthday Camp on September 24. On the same night the long-suffering sledge-meter, much battered, gave up recording.

"At 3 AM I was awakened by something striking me on the head. I looked out of the sleeping-bag and found that the tent had fallen in on us. The lashing at the apex had carried away and the poles upwind were almost flat. The cap was gone, and one side of the tent was split from top to bottom. I awakened the others, and Whetter and I got out, leaving Close inside to hang on to the bag. Luckily we had kept on our burberrys in case of accidents. For once the entrance had not to be unfastened, as there was a ready-made exit. The poles were roughly bound together with an alpine rope and anchored to a pick on the windward side. It was blowing about eighty miles an hour, but fortunately there was no drift. When daylight came the tent was found to be hopelessly ruined, and to light the primus was impossible, though the wind had abated to thirty-five miles an hour.

"We ate some frozen food and pushed on, hoping to find Aladdin's Cave before dark, so that we should not have to spend a night without a tent. After a struggle of thirteen miles over rough ice we came, footsore and worn out, to Aladdin's Cave. Close's feet were badly blistered, and both my big toes had become frost-bitten at the fifty-mile camp, giving me a good deal of trouble on the way back.

"Never was the Cave a more luxurious place. The cooker was kept busy far into the night, while we drank and smoked and felt happy."

The successful conclusion of this journey in the face of the most adverse weather conditions was something upon which Madigan, Whetter and Close could well feel proud, for in its way it must be a record in the sledging world. They were indeed badly frost-bitten; Madigan's great toes having suffered most of all. Whetter's chief injury was a wound under the chin occasioned by a pair of scissors handled by Madigan to free Whetter's helmet on an occasion when it was firmly frozen to his face.

On October 1, Mertz, Hurley and Ninnis made a gallant attempt to rescue two dogs, Basilisk and Franklin, which had remained at Aladdin's Cave on September 26, after accompanying them there with a load of provisions. At the Hut there was no drift, but during the ascent it became thicker, and the wind stronger, forcing them at last to turn back.

Two days later another attempt was made by Ninnis and Mertz, and, in dense drift, after wandering about for a long time they happened on the Cave, to find that the dogs were not there, though spots were discovered where they had evidently been sleeping in the snow. Coming back disconsolately, they found that the dogs had reached the Hut not long before them. Apparently the two vagrants, hearing Ninnis and Mertz blundering about in the drift in search of the depot, had decided that it was time to return home. We concluded that the ways of these Greenland dogs were past finding out.

October came with a deluge of snow and transient hours of bright sunlight, during which the seals would make a temporary landing and retire again to the water when their endurance was exhausted. Snow petrels flew in great numbers about the rocks in the evening, seeking out their old nest-crevices. Seeing these signs of returning life, every one was in great expectation of the arrival of the penguins.

On the night of the 11th, Hurley, Laseron, Hunter and Correll made an innovation by presenting a small farce to an audience which had been starved of dramatic entertainment for a long time, and consequently showed tremendous appreciation.

The first penguin came waddling up the ice-foot against a seventy-mile wind late on the afternoon of October 12. McLean brought the bird back to the Hut and the newcomer received a great ovation. Stimulated by their success on the previous night and the appearance of the first penguin, the theatrical company added to their number, and, dispensing with a rehearsal, produced an opera, "The Washerwoman's Secret" (Laseron). Part of the Hut was curtained off as a combined green-room and dressing-room; the kitchen was the stage; footlights twinkled on the floor; the acetylene limelight beamed down from the rafters, while the audience crowded on a form behind the dining-table, making tactless remarks and steadily eating chocolate.

The typed programmes advertised the following:

THE WASHERWOMAN'S SECRET
(*Opera in Five Acts*)
DRAMATIS PERSONAE

Dr. Stakanhoiser (Tenor)	"Hoyle"	Hurley
Chevalier De Tintail (Fiver)	"Johnny"	Hunter
Baron De Brent (Basso)	"Joe"	Laseron
Count Hoopenkoff (Barrowtone)	"Little Willie"	Correll
Madam Fuclose (Don't Sing)	"Also Joe"	Laseron
Jemima Fuclose (Soprano)	"Dad"	Mclean
Dr. Stakanhoiser's Dog	"Monkey"	Greenland Pup
Village Idiot	"Bick"	Bickerton
Orchestra	"Stillwater Willie"	Stillwell

Snow Petrels Preparing to Nest, Cape Denison

A Snow Petrel on the Nest

Adelie Penguins Diving into the Sea in Quest of Food

Adelie Penguins Jumping on to the Floe

ACT I

SCENE: *Room in poorer part of Berlin*: MADAM FUCLOSE *in bed dying:* JEMIMA *at table washing clothes*

Song   "When Sparrows Build"   JEMIMA

[Knock at door. Enter Dr. STAKANHOISER.

Song: "I vas a Doctor"

[Attends MADAM FUCLOSE, *who, when dying, tells him that* JEMIMA *is not her daughter, but the Princess of Adeliana, whom she has rescued in Paris during the Revolution.*

Death Scene and Chorus: "Who Killed my Mother?"

ACT II
SCENE: *Beneath* JEMIMA'S *window*

[Enter Dr. STAKANHOISER *disguised as organ grinder.*

Song: "Vurds der Likum"   Dr. S.

*[*JEMIMA *opens window and throws flour on* DOCTOR.
[Enter BARON DE BRENT, *kicks* DOCTOR *out.*

Song: "Baron of Brent"

*[*BARON *makes love to* JEMIMA, *who laughs at him.*

Duet: "Wilt love me"   JEMIMA
and BARON

[Enter CHEVALIER DE TINTAIL, *who denounces the* BARON *as already having four wives. The* BARON *goes off, muttering revenge.*

Song: "I'm in love with a wonderful lady"   CHEVALIER

[The CHEVALIER *makes love to* JEMIMA, *who loves him in return.*

Chorus: "Jemima"

ACT III

SCENE: *Conspirators' Chamber*

[Enter DOCTOR, *who hides behind a barrel.*
[Enter COUNT HOOPENKOFF, *who amuses himself playing a piccolo.*

[*Enter* BARON. *They discuss plot to kidnap Princess, which is overheard by DOCTOR.*

[*Enter Ghost, who frightens conspirators away.*

Chorus: "Little Willie Smith"

ACT IV

SCENE: JEMIMA's *room*

[*The* CHEVALIER DE TINTAIL *is waiting.*

Song: "I want you to see my Girl"   CHEVALIER

[*Enter* JEMIMA. *Love scene.*

[*Enter* DOCTOR, *who discloses the plot he has heard and tells* JEMIMA *of her high descent. The* CHEVALIER *and the* DOCTOR *hide, and the two villains, by means of a ladder, enter the room. The heroes spring from their hiding-place and the villains are ejected.*

Chorus: "There is a Wash-House"

ACT V

SCENE: *Conspirators' Chamber*

[*The* BARON *and* COUNT *enter by different doors. They accuse each other of having betrayed the plot. Duel follows in which both are killed.*

Duet: "Mort de Botheo"   COUNT *and* BARON

[*All the others rush in. The two lovers come together and the* DOCTOR *says,* "God bless you, my children."

Chorus: "Auld Lang Syne"   COMPANY *and* AUDIENCE
And
GOD SAVE THE KING

Played by the Society for the Prevention of the Blues.

Saturday, October 12, 1912.
ADELIE HALL

Admission Free. Children Half Price.

October 13 was known as Black Sunday. We were all seated at dinner and the Hut was quivering in the tornado-like gusts which followed a heavy "blow" reaching a maximum hourly average of ninety-one miles.

242

One mighty blast was followed by a crack and the sound of a heavy falling body. For a moment it was thought that something had happened to the Hut. Then the messman ran out to the trap-door and saw that the northern wireless mast had disappeared.

The weather showed but meagre signs of improvement, but the penguins came up in great numbers. They were in groups all along the ice-foot in the lee of rocks and icy pinnacles. They climbed up to their old resorts, and in a few days commenced to build nests of small pebbles. Skua gulls mysteriously appeared, snow petrels hovered along the rocky ridges and odd seals landed on the wind-raked harbour ice. Silver-grey and Antarctic petrels flew along the shore with occasional Cape pigeons. If the weather were indifferent to the fact, the birds did not forget that spring had come.

A Weddell seal calved on the bay-ice on October 18. For a week the pup had a miserable time in winds ranging mostly about the seventies, with the temperature below zero Fahrenheit. At last it became so weak that it thawed a hole in the soft, sludgy ice and could not extricate itself. Both it and the mother were killed and skinned for the biological collection.

On all but the worst days a gang of men worked with picks and shovels digging out the Hangar, so that Bickerton could test the air-tractor sledge. The attack was concentrated upon a solid bank of snow and ice into which heaps of tins and rubbish had been compactly frozen. In soft snow enormous headway can be made in a short space of time, but in that species of conglomerate, progress is slow. Eventually, a cutting was made by which the machine could pass out. The rampart of snow was broken through at the northern end of the Hangar, and the sledge with its long curved runners was hauled forth triumphantly on the 25th. From that time onwards Bickerton continued to experiment and to improve the contrivance.

On October 21 there was a marked thaw inside the Hut. The frost along all the cracks dissolved into water and ran down the walls over pictures, on to book-shelves and bunks. The thick caking of ice on the windows dripped continually, coming away in layers at lunch-time and scattering among the diners at both ends of the table. Every available bucket and tub was in use, and small tin-gutters hooked under each window had to be emptied at frequent intervals.

Stillwell came in during the afternoon bearing an albino penguin with a prettily mottled head; a curious freak of which the biologists immediately took possession. The penguins now swarmed along the foreshores, those not settling down in the rookeries wandering about in small crowds, occasionally

visiting the Hut and exploring among the rocks or up the slippery glacier. Murphy was heard, at this time, to advance a theory accounting for the fact that Adelie penguins never made their nests on a scale more elaborate than a collection of stones. He submitted that anything else would be blown away. To support the contention, he stated that as soon as the female lays her egg, she places a stone on top to weight it down. The biologists kept a dignified silence during the discussion.

On the 21st an Emperor penguin landed on the harbour ice, and, early in November, two more were captured. These imperial birds are very rare on the coasts of Adelie Land, owing to the fact that their winter breeding-grounds in Antarctica are selected in spots where climatic conditions are comparatively good.

October closed with an average wind velocity of 56.9 miles per hour. Yet the possibility of summer sledging was no longer remote. The sun was high, spells of calm were longer and more frequent, and, with the certain knowledge that we should be on the plateau in November, the sledging parties were chosen, schemes of exploration were discussed, and the last details for an extensive campaign completed.

CHAPTER XII

Across King George V Land

We yearned beyond the skyline.

—Kipling

O CTOBER HAD PASSED WITHOUT OFFERING ANY opportunities for sledging, and we resolved that in defiance of all but the worst weather a start would be made in November. The *Aurora* was due to arrive early in January 1913 and the time at our disposal for exploration was slipping away rapidly.

The investigation by sledging journeys of the coastline to the eastward was regarded as of prime importance, for our experience in the *Aurora* when in those longitudes during the previous year was such as to give little promise of its ever being accomplished from the sea.

Westward, the coast was accessible from the sea; at least for some distance in that direction. Madigan's journey in the springtime had demonstrated that, if anything, the land to the west was steeper, and consequently more windy conditions might be expected there. Further, it was judged that information concerning this region would be forthcoming from the ship, which had cruised westward after leaving Adelie Land in January 1912. The field in that direction was therefore not so promising as that to the east.

Mertz in an Icy Ravine

Mertz and Ninnis Arrive with the Dogs at Aladdin's Cave

On this account the air-tractor sledge, of somewhat doubtful utility, was detailed for use to the westward of Winter Quarters, and, as it was obvious that the engine could only be operated in moderately good weather, its final departure was postponed until December.

The following is a list of the parties which had been arranged and which, now fully equipped, were on the tiptoe of expectation to depart.

(1) A Southern Party composed of Bage (leader), Webb and Hurley. The special feature of their work was to be magnetic observations in the vicinity of the South Magnetic Pole.

(2) A Southern Supporting Party, including Murphy (leader), Hunter and Laseron, who were to accompany the Southern Party as far as possible, returning to Winter Quarters by the end of November.

(3) A Western Party of three men—Bickerton (leader), Hodgeman and Whetter—who were to traverse the coastal highlands west of the Hut. Their intention was to make use of the air-tractor sledge and the departure of the party was fixed for early December.

(4) Stillwell, in charge of a Near Eastern Party, was to map the coastline between Cape Denison and the Mertz Glacier-Tongue, dividing the work into two stages. In the first instance, Close and Hodgeman were to assist him; all three acting partly as supports to the other eastern parties working further afield. After returning to the Hut at the end of November for a further supply of stores, he was to set out again with Close and Laseron in order to complete the work.

(5) An Eastern Coastal Party composed of Madigan (leader), McLean and Correll was to start in early November with the object of investigating the coastline beyond the Mertz Glacier.

(6) Finally, a Far-Eastern Party, assisted by the dogs, was to push out rapidly overland to the southward of Madigan's party, mapping more distant sections of the coastline, beyond the limit to which the latter party would be likely to reach.

As the plans for the execution of such a journey had of necessity to be more provisional than in the case of the others, I determined to undertake it, accompanied by Ninnis and Mertz, both of whom had so ably acquitted themselves throughout the Expedition and, moreover, had always been in charge of the dogs.

November opened with more moderate weather, auguring still better conditions for midsummer. Accordingly November 6 was fixed as the date of final departure for several of the parties. The evening of November 5 was made a special occasion: a farewell dinner, into which everybody entered very heartily.

On the morning of the 6th, however, we found a strong blizzard raging and the landscape blotted out by drift-snow, which did not clear until the afternoon of the following day.

At the first opportunity, Murphy, Hunter and Laseron (supporting the Southern Party) got away, but found the wind so strong at a level of one thousand feet on the glacier that they anchored their sledge and returned to the Hut for the night.

The next morning saw them off finally and, later in the day, the Near-Eastern Party (Stillwell, Close and Hodgeman) and the Eastern Coastal Party (Madigan, McLean and Correll) got under way, though there was still considerable wind.

My own party was to leave on the 9th for, assisted by the dogs, we could easily catch up to the other eastern parties, and it was our intention not to part company with them until all were some distance out on the road together.

The wind increased on the 9th and the air became charged with drift, so we felt sure that those who preceded us would still be camped at Aladdin's Cave, and that the best course was to wait.

At this date the penguin rookeries were full of new-laid eggs, and the popular taste inclined towards omelettes, in the production of which Mertz was a past master. I can recall the clamouring throng who pressed round for the final omelette as Mertz officiated at the stove just before we left on the 10th.

It was a beautiful calm afternoon as the sledge mounted up the long icy slopes. The Southern Party (Bage, Webb and Hurley) were a short distance in advance, but by the help of the dogs we were soon abreast of them. Then Bickerton, who had given Bage's party a pull as far as the three-mile post, bade us good-bye and returned to the Hut where he was to remain in charge with Whetter and Hannam until the return of Murphy's party.

At Aladdin's Cave, while some prepared supper, others selected tanks of food from the depot and packed the sledges. After the meal, the Southern

Party bade us farewell and set off at a rapid rate, intending to overhaul their supporting party on the same evening at the Cathedral Grotto, eleven and three-quarter miles from the Hut. Many finishing touches had to be put to our three sledges and two teams of dogs, so that the departure was delayed till next morning.

We were up betimes and a good start was made before anything came of the overcast sky which had formed during the night. The rendezvous appointed for meeting the others, in case we had not previously caught them up, was eighteen miles south-east of Aladdin's Cave. But, with a view to avoiding crevasses as much as possible, a southerly course was followed for several miles, after which it was directed well to the east. In the meantime the wind had arisen and snow commenced to fall soon after noon. In such weather it was impossible to locate the other parties, so a halt was made and the tent pitched after eight miles.

Five days of wind and drift followed, and for the next two days we remained in camp. Then, on the afternoon of the 13th, the drift became less dense, enabling us to move forward on an approximate course to what was judged to be the vicinity of the rendezvous, where we camped again for three days.

Comfortably ensconced in the sleeping-bags, we ate only a small ration of food; the savings being carefully put away for a future "rainy day." Outside, the dogs had at first an unpleasant time until they were buried in snow which sheltered them from the stinging wind. Ninnis and Mertz took turns day by day attending to their needs.

The monotony and disappointment of delay were just becoming acute when the wind fell off, and the afternoon of November 16 turned out gloriously fine.

Several excursions were immediately made in the neighbourhood to seek for the whereabouts of the other parties, but all were unsuccessful. At length it occurred to us that something serious might have happened, so we left our loads and started back at a gallop for Aladdin's Cave with two empty sledges, Mertz careering ahead on skis over the sastrugi field.

Shortly afterwards two black specks were seen away in the north; a glance with the binoculars leaving no doubt as to the identity of the parties. We returned to the loads, and, having picked them up, made a course to the east to intercept the other men.

It was a happy camp that evening! with the three tents pitched together, while we compared our experiences of the previous six days and made plans for the outward journey.

Our sledge-meter had already suffered through bumping over rough ice and sastrugi, and an exchange was made with the stronger one on Stillwell's sledge. A quantity of food was also taken over from him and the loads were finally adjusted.

The details and weights of the equipment on the three sledges belonging to my party are sufficiently interesting to be set out at length below. Most of the items were included in the impedimenta of all our parties, but slight variations were necessary to meet particular stances or to satisfy the whim of an individual.

TOTAL LOAD	lb.	oz.
The Principal Sledge, 11ft. long, 45 lb.		
Fittings for Same: Instrument-box 7 lb. 5 oz.; cooker-box, 7 lb. 6 oz.; kerosene-tray, 3 lb.; mast-attachment, 2 lb. 8 oz.; mast, 1 lb. 15 oz.; spar, 1 lb. 8 oz.; decking (canvas and bamboo), 3 lb. 5 oz.; rigging, 7.5 oz.; 5 leather straps, 5lb.:	77	6.5
Drill Tent, strengthened and attached to poles, also floor-cloth, 33 lb. Spare drill cover, 11 lb. 8 oz.:	44	8
Sleeping-bags, 3 one-man bags:	30	0
Cooking gear: Nansen cooker, 11 lb. 3 oz.; 3 mugs, 1 lb. 8 oz., 2 tins, 10 oz.; scales, 0.5 oz.; 3 spoons, 1.5 oz.; matches, 13.5 oz., and damp-proof tin to hold same, 3.7 oz.; "Primus" heater, full, 3 lb. 10 oz.; "Primus" prickers, 2.5 oz.; "Primus" repair outfit, 2 oz.; kerosene tin openers and pourers, 4.5 oz.; spirit for "Primus" in tin, 5 lb. 14 oz., also a ready bottle, full, 1 lb. 5 oz.:	25	14.2
Repair Outfit: Spare copper wire, rivets, needles, thread, etc., 1 lb. 14.5 oz.; set of 12 tools, 15.5 oz.; requirements for repairing dog-harness and medically treating the dogs, 3 lb. 8 oz.:	6	6
Medical Outfit: 6 "Burroughs & Wellcome" first field dressings absorbent cotton wool; boric wool; pleated lint; pleated bandages, roll bandages; adhesive tape; liquid collodion; "tabloid" ophthalmic drugs for treating snow-blindness; an assortment of "tabloid" drugs for general treatment; canvas case containing scissors, forceps, artery-forceps, scalpel, surgical needles and silk, etc.:	2	12.3

	lb.	oz.

Photographic outfit: A 1/4-plate, long, extension-camera in a case, with special stiffening board and 36 cut films, 4 lb. 4.5 oz.; adaptor to accommodate camera to theodolite legs, 2 oz.; a water-tight tin with 14 packets, each containing 12 cut films, 3 lb. 10 oz.: **8 0.5**

Surveying Requirements: A 3" transit theodolite in case, 5 lb. 14 oz.; legs for the same, 3 lb. 6 oz.; sledge-meter, 8 lb.; Tables from Nautical Almanack and book of Logarithmic Tables, 1 lb. 3 oz.; 2 note books, 1 lb. 6 oz.; angle-books, 5 oz.; map-tube, 10 oz.; maps, 6.5 oz.; pencils, 1.5 oz.; dividers and rubber, 1.5 oz.; protractor and set-square, 0.5 oz.; prismatic compass and clinometer, 8.5 oz.; sun-compass (Bage's), 1.5 oz.: **22 0**

Other Instruments: Zeiss prismatic binoculars X.12, 1 lb. 13.5 oz.; hypsometer, 2 lb. 1 oz.; 2 ordinary and 2 small minimum thermometers, 10 oz.; specimen labels, 1 oz.: **4 9.5**

Rifle, 22-bore with cover and cleaner, 3 lb. 3.7 oz.; ammunition, 1 lb. 6 oz.; sheath knife, 5.5 oz.; sharpening stone, 1.5 oz.; fishing line and hooks, 3.5 oz.: **4 14.7**

Waterproof Clothes-bag, 4 lb. 8 oz., containing 9 pairs of finnesko stuffed with saennegrass, 21 lb.; extra saennegrass, 3 lb.; 3 private kit-bags containing spare clothing, etc., 39 lb.; 4 extra rolls of lampwick for lashings, 1 lb. 3.5 oz.: **64 3.5**

Odd Gear: Pick, 4 lb. 5 oz.; 2 spades, 8 lb. 4 oz.; ice-axe, 2 lb. 4 oz.; alpine rope (20 metros) 3 lb.; skis (1 pair), 11 lb.; ski-stick, 1 lb. 1 oz.; ski-boots (2 pairs), 6 lb.; attachable crampons for the same, 4 lb.; finnesko-crampons (3 pairs), 9 lb.; 3 man-harnesses, 6 lb. 8 oz.; man-hauling tow-rope, 1 lb. 1 oz.; flags, 9.5 oz.; a water-proof bag to hold oddments, 4 lb. 8 oz.: **61 8.5**

Beacons: A depot-flag and bamboo pole, 5 lb.; a special metal depot-beacon, mast, flag and stays, 16 lb.; 2 damp-proof tins for depositing records at depots, 7.5 oz.: **21 7.5**

	lb.	oz.
Other Sledges: A second sledge decked with Venesta boarding and fitted with straps:	55	0
A Third Sledge, 12 ft. long and strong rope lashings (spare spars mentioned elsewhere acting as decking):	60	0
Fuel: Kerosene, 6 gallons in one-gallon tins:	60	0
Food: Man Food: 9 weeks' supplies for 3 men on the ration scale; also 25 lb. weight of special foods— 'perks':	475	0
Dog Food: Dried seal meat, blubber and pemmican; also the weight of the tin and bag-containers:	700	0
Total:	1723	11.3

Madigan's and Stillwell's parties broke trail to the east on the morning of the 17th while we were still attending to the sledges and dogs preparatory to departure. It was decided that Gadget, a rather miserable animal, who had shown herself useless as a puller thus far, should be killed. The following dogs then remained:—Basilisk, Shackleton, Ginger Bitch, Franklin, John Bull, Mary, Haldane, Pavlova, Fusilier, Jappy, Ginger, George, Johnson, Castor, Betli and Blizzard.

We went in pursuit of the other six men over a surface of rough sastrugi. The dogs, who were in fine fettle, rushed the sledges along, making frantic efforts to catch up to the parties ahead, who showed as black specks across the white undulating plain.

At noon all lunched together, after which we separated, shaking hands warmly all round and interchanging the sledgers' "Good luck!" Our dogs drew away rapidly to the east, travelling on a slight down grade; the other two parties with their man-hauled sledges following in the same direction. The surface was splendid, the weather conditions were ideal, the pace, if anything, too rapid, for capsizes were apt to occur in racing over high sastrugi. Any doubts as to the capability of the dogs to pull the loads were dispelled; in fact, on this and on many subsequent occasions, two of us were able to sit, each one on a sledge, while the third broke trail ahead.

In sledging over wide, monotonous wastes with dogs as the motive power, it is necessary to have a forerunner, that is, somebody to go ahead and point the way, otherwise the dogs will run aimlessly about. Returning over old tracks, they will pull along steadily and keep a course. In Adelie Land we had no opportunity of verifying this, as the continuous winds soon obliterated the impression of the runners.

Mertz Emerging from Aladdin's Cave

If the weather is reasonably good and food is ample, sledging dogs enjoy their work. Their desire to pull is doubtless inborn, implanted in a long line of ancestors who have faithfully served the Esquimaux. We found that the dogs were glad to get their harnesses on and to be led away to the sledge. Really, it was often a case of the dog leading the man, for, as soon as its harness was in place, the impatient animal strained to drag whatever might be attached to the other end of the rope. Before attaching a team of dogs to a sledge, it was necessary to anchor the latter firmly, otherwise in their ardour they would make off with it before everything was ready.

There can be no question as to the value of dogs as a means of traction in the Polar regions, except when travelling continuously over very rugged country, over heavily crevassed areas, or during unusually bad weather. It is in such special stances that the superiority of man-hauling has been proved. Further, in an enterprise where human life is always at stake, it is only fair to put forward the consideration that the dogs represent a reserve of food in case of extreme emergency.

We continued due eastwards until five o'clock on the afternoon of the 17th at an altitude of two thousand six hundred feet. On the crest of a ridge, which bore away in distinct outline, on our left, a fine panorama of coastal scenery was visible. Far off on the eastern horizon the Mertz Glacier

The Dogs Enjoy Their Work

Tongue discovered itself in a long wall touched in luminous bands by the south-western sun. A wide valley fell away in front, and beyond it was a deep indentation of the coastline, which would make it necessary for us to follow a more southerly course in order to round its head.

I determined to convey to the other parties my intentions, which had become more defined on seeing this view; and, in the meantime, we halted and treated ourselves to afternoon tea. This innovation in the ordinary routine was extended to a custom by saving a portion of the lunch ration for a "snack" at 5 PM on all days when the weather was moderately good. As latitude sights were required at midday and longitude shots at 5 PM, the arrangement was very convenient, for, while one of us made tea, the other two took the observations.

About 6 PM the two man-hauled sledges came up with us, our plans for the future were reviewed and the final instructions were given. We bade our comrades adieu and, turning to the south-east, descended quickly down a long slope leading into the valley. The sky was overcast and it was almost impossible to see the irregularities of the surface. Only a dull-white glare met the eyes, and the first indication of a hillock was to stub one's toes against it, or of a depression to fall into it. We pulled up the dogs at 7.30 PM after covering thirteen and a quarter miles in the day.

At 9.45 AM on November 18 everything was ready for a fresh start. The other parties could be seen rapidly bearing down on us under full sail, but our willing teams had soon dragged the three sledges over an eminence and out of their sight.

It was a lovely day; almost like a dream after the lengthy months of harassing blizzards. A venturesome skua gull appeared at lunch time, just as an observation for latitude was being taken. By the time Ninnis had unpacked the rifle the bird had flown away.

The direction of the sastrugi was found to vary from that which obtained farther west, owing to a slight swing in the direction of the prevailing wind. The irregularities in the coastline account for this; the wind tending to flow down to sea-level by the nearest route.

To the north-west, behind us, a projecting ridge of rock—Madigan Nunatak—came into sight. From the camp of the previous evening it had evidently been hidden from view by an undulation in the surface.

During the afternoon it was noted that the surface had become very deeply eroded by the wind, troughs three feet in depth being common, into which the sledges frequently capsized. Each of us took it in turn to run ahead, jumping from one sastruga to another. As these were firm and polished by the constant wind, one often slipped with a sudden shock to the ground. Our bodies were well padded with clothing and we were beginning to get into good form, so that these habitual tumbles were taken with the best grace we could muster. I surprised myself during the afternoon, when my turn came as forerunner, by covering two and a half miles at a jog-trot without a break. The grade was slightly downhill and the sledges moved along of their own accord, accelerated by jerks from the dogs, gliding at right angles to the knife-edge crests of the snow-waves.

The roughness of the surface was not without its effect on the sledge-meter, which had to be repaired temporarily. It was a matter of some inconvenience that after this date its records were erroneous and approximate distances were only obtained by checking the readings against absolute observations made for latitude and longitude.

At 5.30 PM a dark object stood in salient relief above the white contour of the snowy sky-line on the right. Suppressing our excitement, we pressed on eagerly, changing course so as to approach it. At nine o'clock it resolved itself into the summit of an imposing mountain rising up from a mysterious valley. Aurora Peak, as it was named, was to be a prominent landmark for several days to come.

All were ready to be on the move at 8.45 AM on November 19. While Mertz and Ninnis built a cairn of snow, I wrote a note to be left on it in a tin, containing instructions to Stillwell in case he should happen on the locality.

The weather was good and the temperatures were high, ranging at this time (one month from midsummer) between zero and 18 degrees F. When we camped for lunch the air was quite calm and the sun's rays were extremely warm.

The surface became softer and smoother as the afternoon lengthened until Mertz was tempted to put on his skis. He then became forerunner for the remainder of the day.

Mertz, who was skilled in the use of skis, found them of great service on this and on many future occasions. At such times he would relieve Ninnis and myself in the van. On the other hand, over deeply furrowed sastrugi or blue ice, or during a strong wind, unless it were at our backs, skiing was impossible.

Owing to a steeper down grade, the sledges were now commencing to run more freely and improvised brakes were tried, all of which were ineffectual in restraining the dogs. The pace became so hot that a small obstacle would capsize the sledge, causing it to roll over and over down the slope. The dogs, frantically pulling in various directions to keep ahead of the load, became hopelessly entangled in their traces and were dragged along unresistingly until the sledge stopped of its own accord or was arrested by one of us. At length, most of the dogs were allowed to run loose, and, with a man holding on behind and a couple of dogs pulling ahead, the loads were piloted down a steep slope for several miles.

The evening camp was situated at the crest of the last but steepest fall into a wide glacial valley which was clearly seen to sweep northwards past the eastern side of Aurora Peak. Looking back we could define our track winding down in the bed of a long shallow valley, while, uprising on either hand near the rim of the plateau were crevassed bluffs where the ice of the tableland streamed abruptly over the underlying crags.

Ninnis had a touch of snow-blindness which rapidly improved under treatment. The stock cure for this very irritating and painful affection is to place first of all tiny "tabloids" of zinc sulphate and cocaine hydrochloride under the eyelids where they quickly dissolve in the tears, alleviating the smarting, "gritty" sensation which is usually described by the sufferer. He then bandages the eyes and escapes, if he is lucky, into the darkness of his sleeping-bag.

In certain lights one is sure to be attacked more or less severely, and coloured glasses should be worn continually. Unfortunately, goggles are sometimes impracticable on account of the moisture from the breath covering the glasses with an icy film or driving snow clogging them and obscuring the view. For such contingencies narrow slots of various shapes are cut in plates or discs of wood or bone in the Esquimaux fashion.

Speeding East

A Distant View of Aurora Peak from the West

The amount of light reaching the eye can thus be reduced to the limit of moderately clear vision.

The morning of the 20th broke with wind and drift which persisted until after noon. Already everything had been packed up, but, as there was a steep fall in front and crevasses were not far distant, we decided not to start until the air was clear of snow.

When at last a move was possible, it became evident that the dogs could not be trusted to pull the sledges down to the edge of the glacier. So they were tethered to ice-axes while we lowered the sledges one by one, all three checking their speed, assisted by rope brakes round the runners. Finally, the impatient dogs were brought down and harnessed in their accustomed places.

Rapid travelling now commenced over a perfectly smooth surface, sloping gently to the bed of the glacier. Mertz shot ahead on skis, and our column of dogs and sledges followed quickly in his trail.

From this day forward our "order of procession" was as follows:— Behind the forerunner came a team of dogs dragging two sledges joined together by a short length of alpine rope. Bringing up the rear were the rest of the dogs dragging the third sledge. Each team pulled approximately equal weights; the front load being divided between two sledges. Except when taking my turn ahead, I looked after the leading team, Ninnis or Mertz, as the case might be, driving the one behind.

We skirted Aurora Peak on its south-eastern side. The mountain rose to a height of about seventeen hundred feet on our left, its steep sides being almost completely snow-clad.

The wide depression of the Mertz Glacier lay ahead, and on its far side the dim outline of uprising icy slopes was visible, though at the time we could not be certain as to their precise nature.

As the sledges passed Aurora Peak, Blizzard and Ginger Bitch ran alongside. The former had hurt one of her forefeet on the previous day during the "rough-and-tumble" descending into the valley. Ginger Bitch was allowed to go free because she was daily expected to give birth to pups. As she was such a good sledge-dog we could not have afforded to leave her behind at the Hut, and later events proved that the work seemed actually to benefit her, for she was at all times the best puller and the strongest of the pack. However, in permitting both dogs to run loose that afternoon, there was an element of danger which we had not sufficiently appreciated.

Suddenly, without any warning, half of my dogs dropped out of sight, swinging on their harness ropes in a crevasse. Next moment I realized that the sledges were in the centre of a bridge covering a crevasse, twenty-five feet wide, along the edge of which part of the team had broken through.

We spent many anxious moments before they were all hauled to the daylight and the sledge rested on solid ground. There were other crevasses about and almost immediately afterwards Ginger Bitch and Blizzard had broken through into a fissure and were frantically struggling to maintain their hold on the edge. They were speedily rescued; following which Ginger Bitch gave birth to the first of a large litter of pups. After this second accident we decided to camp.

During the morning of November 21 there was a good deal of wind and drift which made travelling rather miserable. Occasionally open crevasses would break the surface of the snow.

When the light at last improved, a nunatak was observed some fifteen miles or more to the south rising out of the glacier—Correll Nunatak. Ahead of us was a glittering line of broken ice, stretching at right angles to our path. Studded about on the icy plain were immense cauldrons, like small craters in appearance. Then an area dotted over with ice mounds approached and crevasses became correspondingly more numerous. The dogs frequently broke through them but were easily extricated in every instance.

Camp was pitched for lunch in the vicinity of many gaping holes leading down into darkness, places where the bridges over large crevasses had fallen in. Mertz prepared the lunch and Ninnis and I went to photograph an open crevasse near by. Returning, we diverged on reaching the back of the tent, he passing round on one side and I on the other. The next instant I heard a bang on the ice and, swinging round, could see nothing of my companion but his head and arms. He had broken through the lid of a crevasse fifteen feet wide and was hanging on to its edge close to where the camera lay damaged on the ice. He was soon dragged into safety. Looking down into the black depths we realized how narrowly he had escaped. As the tent was found to encroach partly on the same crevasse, it may be imagined that we did not dally long over the meal.

In the afternoon the weather became clear and fine, but, as if to offset this, the broken surface became impassable. The region was one of sérac where the glacier was puckered up, folded and crushed. After several repulses in what seemed to be promising directions, we were finally forced to camp, having ten miles to our credit.

Whilst Mertz fed the dogs and prepared hoosh, Ninnis and I roped up and went off to search for a passage.

All around, the glacier was pressed up into great folds, two hundred feet in height and between one quarter and a third of a mile from crest to crest. The ridges of the folds were either domes or open rifts partly choked with snow. Precipitous ice-falls and deep cauldrons were encountered everywhere. To the north the glacier flattened out; to the south it was more rugged.

In this chaos we wandered for some miles until a favourable line of advance had been discovered for the march on the following day.

The first three miles, on the 22nd, were over a piece of very dangerous country, after which our prospects improved and we came to the border of a level plain.

There Mertz slipped on his skis, went ahead and set a good pace. Although the sky had become overcast and snow fell fitfully, our progress was rapid towards the rising slopes of the land on the eastern side of the glacier. Over the last three miles of the day's journey the surface was raised in large, pimply masses surrounded by wide fissures. Into one of the fissures, bridged by snow, Ninnis's sledge fell, but fortunately jammed itself just below the surface. As it was, we had a long job getting it up again, having to unpack the sledge in the crevasse until it was light enough to be easily manipulated. Despite the delay, our day's run was sixteen and a half miles.

At 8 AM on the 23rd everything was in readiness for a fresh start. Moderate drift and wind descended from the hills and there were yet three miles of hidden perils to be passed. With the object of making our advance less dangerous, various devices were employed.

First of all the towing rope of the rear sledge was secured to the back of the preceding sledge. This arrangement had to be abandoned because the dogs of Ninnis's team persisted in entangling themselves and working independently of the dogs in front. Next, all the sledges were joined together with all the dogs pulling in front. The procession was then so long that it was quite unmanageable on account of the tortuous nature of our track through the labyrinth. In the long run, it was decided that our original method was the best, provided that special precautions were taken over the more hazardous crossings.

The usual procedure was, that the forerunner selected the best crossing of a crevasse, testing it with a ski-stick. The dog teams were then brought up to the spot and the forerunner went over the snow-bridge and stood on the other side, sufficiently far away to allow the first team to cross to him and to clear the crevasse. Then the second team was piloted to safety before the forerunner had resumed his position in front. This precaution was very necessary, for otherwise the dogs in the rear would make a course direct for wherever the front dogs happened to be, cutting across corners and most probably dragging their sledge sideways into a crevasse; the likeliest way to lose it altogether.

Often enough the dogs broke through the snow-bridges on the morning of the 23rd, but only once were matters serious, when Ninnis's sledge, doubtless on account of its extra weight, again broke through a lid of snow and was securely jammed in a crevasse just below the surface.

On this occasion we were in a serious predicament, for the sledge was in such a position that an unskilful movement would have sent it hurling into the chasm below. So the unpacking of the load was a tedious and delicate operation. The freight consisted chiefly of large, soldered tins, packed tightly with dried seal meat. Each of these weighed about ninety pounds and all were most securely roped to the sledge. The sledge was got up and reloaded without the loss of a single tin, and once more we breathed freely.

A valley almost free of crevasses was chosen as the upward track to the plateau. We threw in our weight hauling with the dogs, and had a long, steep drag over furrowed névé, pitching the tent after a day's journey of twelve miles.

On waking up on November 24 I found that my watch had stopped. I had been so tired on the previous evening that I had fallen asleep without remembering to wind it. The penalty of this accident was paid in my being forced to take an extra set of observations in order to start the watch again at correct time relative to the Hut.

Besides the observations for position, necessary for navigation, sets of angles were taken from time to time to fix the positions of objects of interest appearing within the field of view, while the magnetic variation was obtained at intervals. In this work Ninnis always assisted me. Mertz boiled the hypsometer when necessary to ascertain our elevation above sea-level. The meteorological conditions were carefully noted several times each day for future comparison with those of other parties and of Winter Quarters.

The day's work on November 24 brought us high up on the slopes. Away to the north-west Aurora Peak was still visible, standing up like a mighty beacon pointing the way back to the Hut. Below lay the Mertz Glacier extending out to sea as a floating tongue beyond the horizon. Inland, some twenty miles to the south, it mounted up in seamed and riven "cataracts" to a smooth, broad and shallow groove which wound into the ice-cap. Ahead, on our south-east course, the ground still rose, but to the north-east the ice-sheet fell away in long wide valleys, at the extremity of some of which icebergs were visible frozen into distant sea-ice.

The tent was raised at 10 PM in a forty-mile wind with light drift; temperature 10° F. The altitude of this camp was two thousand three hundred and fifty feet.

One of the worst features of drift overnight is that sledges and dogs become buried in snow and have to be dug out in the morning. Thus on the 25th it was 10 AM before we got away in a strong wind, with flying snow, across fields of sastrugi.

The dogs detested the wind and, as their heads were so near the ground, they must have found the incessant stream of thick drift very tantalizing. The snow became caked over their eyes so that every few minutes they had to scrape it away with their paws or rub their faces on the ground.

We stopped at 6 PM after a miserable day, covering sixteen miles in all.

November 26 broke overcast, the light being bad for travelling and the wind still strong. Nevertheless we set out at 10 AM through falling snow.

As the day progressed the wind subsided and Mertz was able to put on his skis over a surface which sloped gradually away to the east. The light was diffused uniformly over the irregularities of snow and ice so that depressions only a few feet away were invisible. Black objects, on the other hand, stood out with startling distinctness, and our attention was soon arrested by a hazy, dark patch which appeared in front and to the left. At first there was much doubt as to its nature, but it was soon clear that it must be a group of rocks, apparently situated at a considerable distance. They were subsequently found to be sixty miles away (Organ Pipe Cliffs, near Cape Blake).

Presently our course ended abruptly at the edge of a precipitous fall. We skirted round this for a while, but were ultimately forced to camp owing to the uncertainty of the light and the proximity of several large crevasses.

At 11 PM the sky cleared and a better idea could be gained of what lay ahead. In a line between our elevated position and the distant rocky outcrops the ice fell in a steep descent to a broad, glacial valley, undulating and in places traversed by torn masses of sérac-ice. We examined the country to the east very carefully with a view to selecting a track for the journey next day and finally resolved to pass to the south of a large ice-capped island— Dixson Island, which was only about ten miles to the north-east, set within Ninnis Glacier near its western border

On the 27th Mertz and I roped up, reconnoitred for a while and returned to the sledges. We then spent several hours in advancing a mile over badly broken ground, arriving at a slope covered with sastrugi and descending steeply for one thousand feet into the bed of the glacier.

In order the more safely to negotiate this, the dogs were all let loose excepting two in each sledge. Even then the sledges were often uncontrollable, rolling over and over many times before the bottom was reached.

When the dogs were re-harnessed it was found that Betli was missing and was not to be seen when we scanned the slopes in our rear with binoculars. It was expected that unless she had fallen into a crevasse she would turn up at the camp that night. However, she did not reappear, and we saw no more of her. Two other dogs, Jappy and Fusilier, had been previously killed, as neither was of any use as a puller. Blizzard, who had been always a great favourite with us, had to be shot next day.

When it had reached the edge of the glacier, our path led over a solid ocean rising and faring in billows, two hundred and fifty feet in height; no doubt caused by the glacier in its northward movement being compressed against the southern side of Dixson Island. Still, the "caravan" made considerable progress, ending with a day's journey of sixteen miles.

During the small hours of November 28 the wind rose to a velocity of sixty miles per hour, but gradually diminished to a twenty-knot breeze as the day advanced. Light snow fell from a sky which was densely clouded.

We still pursued a devious track amid rolling waves of ice, encountering beds of soft snow through which the sledges moved slowly. By 6 PM pinnacles and hummocks stood around on every side, and the light was such that one could not distinguish crevasses until he was on top of them. We had to camp and be satisfied with seven miles "to the good." By this time the dogs were in good training and grew noticeably ravenous. In the evening, before they were properly tethered, Shackleton seized a one-week provision bag, ripped it open and ate a block of butter weighing more than two and a half pounds. This was a loss to us, as butter was regarded as a particular delicacy.

The sun was shining brightly next day and it was at once evident that we were in a zone of tumbled and disrupted ice.

For many hours a way was won through a mighty turmoil of sérac and over innumerable crevasses with varied fortune. Just before lunch my two sledges were nearly lost through the dogs swinging sharply to one side before the second sledge had cleared a rather rotten snow-bridge. I was up with the dogs at the time, and the first intimation I received of an accident was on seeing the dogs and front sledge being dragged backwards; the rear sledge was hanging vertically in a crevasse. Exerting all my strength I held back the front sledge, and in a few moments was joined by Ninnis and Mertz, who soon drove a pick and ice-axe down between the runners and ran out an anchoring rope.

It was a ticklish business recovering the sledge which hung suspended in the crevasse. It could not be lifted vertically as its bow was caught in a V-shaped cornice formed by an overhanging mass of snow. To add to our troubles the ground all about the place was precarious and unsafe.

Mertz and Ninnis therefore lowered me down and I attached a rope to the tail-end of the sledge. The bow-rope and tail-rope were then manipulated alternately until the bow of the sledge was manoeuvred slowly through the gaping hole in the snow-lid and was finally hauled up on to level ground. No more remarkable test of the efficiency of the sledge straps and the compactness of the load could have been made.

After lunch Mertz ascended a high point and was able to trace out a route which conducted us in a few hours to a better surface.

We were now at an elevation of from four hundred to five hundred feet above sea-level, running across a beam-wind on our right which increased during the afternoon. A rising blizzard made it necessary to camp after a day's run of ten and one-third miles.

The wind blew up to seventy miles an hour during the night, but eased in strength early on November 30. At 10 AM we tried to make a start, but the dogs refused to face the drift. On the wind becoming gusty in the afternoon, it was once more possible to travel, and we set out.

Dense drift was still to be seen pouring over the highlands to the south-east. Above the glacier ahead whirlies, out-lined in high revolving columns of snow, "stalked about" in their wayward courses.

The sledges ran through a sea of crevassed, blue ice, over ridges and past open chasms. Seven miles brought us to the "foot-hills" on the eastern border of the Ninnis Glacier, where we pitched camp.

The first day of December was still and hot, with brilliant sunshine. The shade temperature reached 34° F. and the snow became so sticky that it was as much as we and the dogs could do to move the sledges up the slopes. As the evening lengthened and the sun sank lower the surface froze hard and our toil was lightened. At midnight we reached an altitude of nine hundred feet.

December 2 was another warm, bright day. The surface was atrociously bad; hard, sharp sastrugi, never less than two feet high and in many instances three feet six inches from crest to trough. The dogs were not able to exert a united pull for there were never more than half of them in action at a time.

Once more we were at a comparatively high altitude and a fine view presented itself to the north. One could look back to the mainland slopes descending on the western side of the Ninnis Glacier. Then the glacier, tumultuous and broken, was seen to extend far out into the frozen sea and, sweeping round to the north-east, the eye ranged over a great expanse of floe-ice dotted with bergs. To the east there was a precipitous coastline of dark rock which for a while we thought of visiting. But then it seemed likely that Madigan's party would reach as far east, so we set our faces once more to the rising plateau in the south-east.

At midnight the sun was peering over the southern sky-line, and we halted at an elevation of one thousand five hundred and fifty feet, having covered eight and a half miles in the day. The temperature was 5° F.

"*December 3.*—We were not long on the way before the sky became overcast and light snow fell. The surface was becoming flatter. Camp was pitched at 11 PM after eleven and two-thirds miles.

"*December 4.*—Another day of bad light but the surface improved and good headway was made on an easterly course at an elevation of between two thousand and two thousand eight hundred feet. The crevasses were practically past. The day's march was fifteen miles.

"*December 5.*—A bad day; overcast, snowing and a gale of wind from the east-south-east. However, we plugged on blindly into it until 7.30 PM and then camped, having done eleven and a half miles.

"*December 6, 7 and 8.*—During these days a dense blizzard raged, the wind reaching seventy miles per hour. There was nothing to do but lie in our bags and think out plans for the future. Each morning Ninnis and Mertz took it in turns to go out and feed their charges, who were snugly buried in the deep snow.

"One day in the sleeping-bag does not come amiss after long marches, but three days on end is enough to bore any one thoroughly.

"Ninnis was not so badly off with a volume of Thackeray, but Mertz had come to the end of a small edition of 'Sherlock Holmes' when blizzard-bound near Aladdin's Cave, and his only diversion on these days was to recite passages from memory for our mutual benefit."

I was troubled with an inflammation in the face just at this time, while Ninnis suffered pain owing to a "whitlow" on one of his fingers.

As usual the food ration was reduced. This caused us to have more than ordinarily vivid dreams. I happened to be awake one night when Ninnis was sledging in imagination, vociferously shouting, "Hike, hike," to the dogs; our equivalent of the usual "Mush, mush."

Despite considerable wind and drift we got away at 8 AM on December 9. The sky was overcast and there was nothing to be seen except a soft carpet of newly fallen snow into which we sank half-way to the knees. The sledges ran deeply and heavily so that the dogs had to be assisted. Ahead Mertz glided along triumphant, for it was on such occasions that skis were of the greatest assistance to him.

During the day a snow petrel circled above us for a while and then returned to the north.

The course was due east at an elevation of two thousand three hundred feet and the total distance we threw behind during the day was sixteen and a half miles.

On the 10th light wind and low drift were the order of things. Our spirits rose when the sky cleared and a slight down grade commenced.

During the morning Ninnis drew our attention to what appeared to be small ice-capped islets fringing the coast, but the distance was too great for us to be sure of their exact nature. Out near the verge of the horizon a tract of frozen sea with scattered bergs could be seen.

Next day more features were distinguishable. The coast was seen to run in a north-easterly direction as a long peninsula ending in a sharp cape—Cape

Freshfield. The north appeared to be filled with frozen sea though we could not be certain that it was not dense pack-ice. Little did we know that Madigan's party, about a week later, would be marching over the frozen sea towards Cape Freshfield in the north-east.

At 10 PM on the 11th, at an altitude of one thousand eight hundred feet, the highland we were traversing fell away rapidly and sea-ice opened up directly in front of us. The coastal downfalls to the south-east fell in rugged masses to a vertical barrier, off the seaward face of which large, tabular bergs were grouped within environing floe.

Throughout December 12 a somewhat irregular course was made to the south-east and south to avoid the broken area ahead. We had had enough of crevasses and wished to be clear of sérac-ice in the future.

For some days Ninnis had been enduring the throbbing pain of a whitlow and had not been having sufficient sleep. He always did his share of the work and had undoubtedly borne a great deal of pain without showing it. On several nights I noticed that he sat up in his sleeping-bag for hours puffing away at a pipe or reading. At last the pain became so acute that he asked me to lance his finger. This was successfully accomplished after breakfast on the 13th and during the day he had much relief.

While Ninnis rested before we made a start, Mertz and I re-arranged the sledges and their loads. A third sledge was no longer necessary, so the one usually driven by Ninnis, which had been damaged, was discarded and all the gear was divided between the other two sledges in nearly equal amounts. When the work was completed, the rear sledge carried an extra weight of fifty pounds. As, however, both food for men and dogs were to come from it, we reckoned that this superadded load would soon diminish.

On we went, during the afternoon, up a steep ascent. Crevasses were so numerous that we took measures to vent them. Some were as much as a hundred feet in width, filled with snow; others were great open holes or like huge cauldrons. Close to the windward edge of some of the latter high ramps of névé with bluff faces on the windward side stood up like monoliths reaching twenty-five feet in maximum height.

In the evening a field of névé was reached and we felt more placid after the anxiety of the preceding hours.

During the passage of a snow-filled valley a dull, booming sound like the noise of far-distant cannon was heard. It was evidently connected with the subsidence of large areas of the surface crust. Apparently large cavities had formed beneath the snow and the weight of ourselves and the sledges caused the crust to sink and the air to be expelled.

Sledging in Adelie Land. *From a crayon by Van Waterschool van der Gracht*

The sun appeared late in the day and, as it was almost calm, the last few hours of marching were very pleasant. At midnight we camped at an altitude of one thousand nine hundred feet.

A light east-south-east wind was blowing as the sledges started away eastward on the morning of December 14. The weather was sunny and the temperature registered 21° F.

Mertz and I were happy to know that Ninnis had slept well and was feeling much better.

Our march was interrupted at noon by a latitude observation, after which Mertz went ahead on skis singing his student songs. The dogs rose to the occasion and pulled eagerly and well. Everything was for once in harmony and the time was at hand when we should turn our faces homewards.

Mertz was well in advance of us when I noticed him hold up his ski-stick and then go on. This was a signal for something unusual so, as I approached the vicinity, I looked out for crevasses or some other explanation of his action. As a matter of fact crevasses were not expected, since we were on a smooth surface of névé well to the southward of the broken coastal slopes.

Lieutenant B. E. S. Ninnis, R.F., in Uniform

Mertz, Ninnis, and Mawson Erecting the Tent in a High Wind

A Later Stage in Erection of the Tent in a Wind (One Man Is Inside)

On reaching the spot where Mertz had signalled and seeing no sign of any irregularity, I jumped on to the sledge, got out the book of tables and commenced to figure out the latitude observation taken on that day. Glancing at the ground a moment after, I noticed the faint indication of a crevasse. It was but one of many hundred similar ones we had crossed and had no specially dangerous appearance, but still I turned quickly round, called out a warning word to Ninnis and then dismissed it from my thoughts.

Ninnis, who was walking along by the side of his sledge, close behind my own, heard the warning, for in my backward glance I noticed that he immediately swung the leading dogs so as to cross the crevasse squarely instead of diagonally as I had done. I then went on with my work.

There was no sound from behind except a faint, plaintive whine from one of the dogs which I imagined was in reply to a touch from Ninnis's whip. I remember addressing myself to George, the laziest dog in my own team, saying, "You will be getting a little of that, too, George, if you are not careful."

When I next looked back, it was in response to the anxious gaze of Mertz who had turned round and halted in his tracks. Behind me, nothing met the eye but my own sledge tracks running back in the distance. Where were Ninnis and his sledge?

I hastened back along the trail thinking that a rise in the ground obscured the view. There was no such good fortune, however, for I came to a gaping hole in the surface about eleven feet wide. The lid of a crevasse had broken in; two sledge tracks led up to it on the far side but only one continued on the other side.

Frantically waving to Mertz to bring up my sledge, upon which there was some alpine rope, I leaned over and shouted into the dark depths below. No sound came back but the moaning of a dog, caught on a shelf just visible one hundred and fifty feet below. The poor creature appeared to have broken its back, for it was attempting to sit up with the front part of its body while the hinder portion lay limp. Another dog lay motionless by its side. Close by was what appeared in the gloom to be the remains of the tent and a canvas tank containing food for three men for a fortnight.

We broke back the edge of the névé lid and took turns leaning over secured by a rope, calling into the darkness in the hope that our companion might be still alive. For three hours we called unceasingly but no answering sound came back. The dog had ceased to moan and lay without a movement. A chill draught was blowing out of the abyss. We felt that there was little hope.

Why had the first sledge escaped the crevasse? It seemed that I had been fortunate, because my sledge had crossed diagonally, with a greater chance of breaking the snow-lid. The sledges were within thirty pounds of the same weight. The explanation appeared to be that Ninnis had walked by the side of his sledge, whereas I had crossed it sitting on the sledge. The whole weight of a man's body bearing on his foot is a formidable load and no doubt was sufficient to smash the arch of the roof.

By means of a fishing line we ascertained that it was one hundred and fifty feet sheer to the ledge on which the remains were seen; on either side the crevasse descended into blackness. It seemed so very far down there and the dogs looked so small that we got out the field glasses, but could make out nothing more by their aid.

All our available rope was tied together but the total length was insufficient to reach the ledge and any idea of going below to investigate and to secure some of the food had to be abandoned.

Stunned by the unexpectedness of it all and having exhausted the few appliances we carried for such a contingency, we felt helpless. In such moments action is the only tolerable thing, and if there had been any expedient however hazardous which might have been tried, we should have taken all and more than the risk. Stricken dumb with the pity of it and heavy at heart, we turned our minds mechanically to what lay nearest at hand.

There were rations on the other sledge, and we found that there was a bare one and a half weeks' food for ourselves and nothing at all for the dogs. Part of the provisions consisted of raisins and almonds which had been taken as extras or "perks," as they were usually called.

Among other losses there were both spade and ice-axe, but fortunately a spare tent-cover was saved. Mertz's burberry trousers had gone down with the sledge and the best substitute he could get was a pair of thick Jaeger woollen under-trousers from the spare clothing we possessed.

Later in the afternoon Mertz and I went ahead to a higher point in order to obtain a better view of our surroundings. At a point two thousand four hundred feet above sea-level and three hundred and fifteen and three-quarter miles eastward from the Hut, a complete observation for position and magnetic azimuth was taken.

The coastal slopes were fearfully broken and scarred in their descent to the sea, which was frozen out to the horizon. No islands were observed or anything which could correspond with the land marked by Wilkes as existing so much farther to the north. Patches of "water sky" were visible in two places in the far distance. As we stood looking north a Wilson petrel suddenly appeared and after flitting about for a short time departed.

We returned to the crevasse and packed the remaining sledge, discarding everything unnecessary so as to reduce the weight of the load. A thin soup was made by boiling up all the old food-bags which could be found. The dogs were given some worn-out fur mitts, finnesko and several spare raw hide straps, all of which they devoured.

We still continued to call down into the crevasse at regular intervals in case our companion might not have been killed outright and, in the meantime, have become conscious. There was no reply.

A weight was lowered on the fishing line as far as the dog which had earlier shown some signs of life, but there was no response. All were dead, swallowed up in an instant.

When comrades tramp the road to anywhere through a lonely blizzard-ridden land in hunger, want and weariness the interests, ties and fates of each are interwoven in a wondrous fabric of friendship and affection. The shock of Ninnis's death struck home and deeply stirred us.

He was a fine fellow and a born soldier—and the end:—

Life—give me life until the end,
That at the very top of being,
The battle spirit shouting in my blood,
Out of very reddest hell of the fight
I may be snatched and flung
Into the everlasting lull,
The Immortal, Incommunicable Dream.

At 9 PM we stood by the side of the crevasse and I read the burial service. Then Mertz shook me by the hand with a short "Thank you!" and we turned away to harness up the dogs.

CHAPTER XIII

Toil and Tribulation

THE HOMEWARD TRACK! A FEW DAYS AGO—
only few hours ago-our hearts had beat hopefully at the prospect
and there was no hint of this, the overwhelming tragedy. Our
fellow, comrade, chum, in a woeful instant, buried in the bowels of the
awful glacier. We could not think of it; we strove to forget it in the necessity
of work, but we knew that the truth would assuredly enter our souls in
the lonely days to come. It was to be a fight with Death and the great
Providence would decide the issue.

On the outward journey we had left no depots of provisions en route,
for it was our bad fortune to meet such impossible country that we had
decided to make a circuit on our return to Winter Quarters sufficiently far
inland to avoid the coastal irregularities. As a matter of fact, on the very
day of the calamity, preparations had been made to cache most of the food
within twenty-four hours, as during the last few days of the journey we
were to make a dash to our "farthest east" point. Such were the plans, and
now we were ranged against unexpected odds.

With regard to the dogs, there were six very miserable animals left. The
best of them had been drafted into the rear team, as it was expected that if
an accident happened through the collapse of a snow-bridge the first sledge
would most probably suffer. For the same reason most of the food and
other indispensable articles had been carried on the rear sledge.

All the dogs which had perished were big and powerful; Basilisk, Ginger
Bitch, Shackleton, Castor, Franklin and John Bull. We had fully anticipated that
those at least would come back alive, at the expense of the six dogs in my sledge.

A silent farewell!—and we started back, aiming to reach our camping-
ground on December 12 before a snowstorm intervened, as several things
had been left there which would be of use to us in our straitened stances.
The weather still held good and there were no signs of approaching snow
or wind. So Mertz went ahead on skis, while we plodded slowly up the

hills and dashed recklessly down them. During the descents I sat on the sledge and we slid over long crevassed slopes in a wild fashion, almost with a languid feeling that the next one would probably swallow us up. But we did not much care then, as it was too soon after losing our friend.

At 2.30 AM on December 15 the discarded sledge and broken spade came into sight. On reaching them, Mertz cut a runner of the broken sledge into two pieces which were used in conjunction with his skis as a framework on which to pitch the spare tent-cover; our only tent and poles having been lost. Each time the makeshift shelter was erected, these props had to be carefully lashed together at the apex, which stood four feet from the ground. Inside, there was just room for two one-man sleeping-bags on the floor. However, only one man at a time could move about and neither of us could ever rise above a sitting posture. Still, it was a shelter which protected us from the bad weather, and, with plenty of snow blocks piled around it, was wonderfully resistant to the wind.

When we retired to rest, it was not to sleep but to think out the best plan for the return journey.

It was obvious that a descent to the frozen sea would be dangerous on account of the heavily crevassed nature of the falling glacier, delay would undoubtedly be caused and our distance from the Hut would be increased. To decide definitely for the sea-ice would be to take other risks as well, since, from the altitude at which we were placed, we could not be sure that the floe-ice which covered the sea would provide a good travelling surface. In any case it was likely to be on the point of breaking up, for the season was nearing midsummer. On the other hand, there was on the sea-ice a chance of obtaining seals for food.

After due consideration we resolved to follow the shorter route, returning inland over the plateau, for it was reckoned that if the weather were reasonable we might win through to Winter Quarters with one and a half weeks' rations and the six dogs which still remained, provided we ate the dogs to eke out our provisions. Fortunately neither the cooker nor the kerosene had been lost.

George, the poorest of the dogs, was killed and partly fed to the others, partly kept for ourselves. The meat was roughly fried on the lid of the aluminium cooker, an operation which resulted in little more than scorching the surface. On the whole it was voted good though it had a strong, musty taste and was so stringy that it could not be properly chewed.

As both mugs and spoons had been lost, I made two pannikins out of tins in which cartridges and matches had been packed, and Mertz carved wooden spoons out of a portion of the broken sledge. At this camp he also spliced the handle of the broken shovel which had been picked up, so as to make it temporarily serviceable.

It was midsummer, and therefore we found it easier to drag the sledge over the snow at night when the surface was frozen hard. Camp was not finally broken until 6 PM, when the long and painful return journey commenced.

For fourteen miles the way led up rising snow slopes to the north-west until an elevation of two thousand five hundred feet had been reached. After that, variable grades and flat country were met. Though the sledge was light, the dogs required helping and progress was slow. The midnight sun shone low in the south, and we tramped on through the morning hours, anxious to reduce the miles which lay ahead.

Early on December 16 the sky became rapidly overcast. The snowy land and the snowy sky merged to form an enclosed trap, as it seemed to us, while showers of snow fell. There were no shadows to create contrast; it was impossible to distinguish even the detail of the ground underfoot. We stumbled over unseen ridges of the hard névé, our gaze straining forward. The air was so still that advantage was taken of the calm to light the primus and melt some snow in the lee of the sledge. The water, to which were added a few drops of primus alcohol, helped to assuage our thirst.

The erection of the makeshift tent was a long and tedious operation, and so, on our return marches, we never again took any refreshment during the day's work excepting on this occasion.

At 6 AM, having done twenty miles and ascended to an elevation of about two thousand five hundred feet, we pitched camp.

There was very little sleep for me that day for I had an unusually bad attack of snow-blindness. During the time that we rested in the bags Mertz treated one of my eyes three times, the other twice with zinc sulphate and cocaine.

On account of the smallness of the tent a great deal of time was absorbed in preparations for "turning in" and for getting away from each camp. Thus, although we rose before 6 PM on December 16, the start was not made until 8.30 PM, notwithstanding the fact that the meal was of the "sketchiest" character.

On that night ours was a mournful procession; the sky thickly clouded, snow falling, I with one eye bandaged and the dog Johnson broken down and strapped on top of the load on the sledge. There was scarcely a sound; only the rustle of the thick, soft snow as we pushed on, weary but full of hope. The dogs dumbly pressed forward in their harness, forlorn but eager to follow. Their weight now told little upon the sledge, the work mainly falling upon ourselves. Mertz was tempted to try hauling on skis, but came to the conclusion that it did not pay and thenceforth never again used them.

Dr. Xavier Mertz

Close to the Magnetic Pole as we were, the compass was of little use, and to steer a straight course to the west without ever seeing anything of the surroundings was a difficult task. The only check upon the correctness of the bearing was the direction in which trended the old hard winter sastrugi, channelled out along a line running almost north and south. The newly fallen snow obliterated these, and frequent halts had to be called in order to investigate the buried surface.

At 2 AM on the 17th we had only covered eleven miles when we stopped to camp. Then Mertz shot and cut up Johnson while I prepared the supper.

Johnson had always been a very faithful, hard-working and willing beast, with rather droll ways of his own, and we were sorry that his end should come so soon. He could never be accused of being a handsome dog, in fact he was generally disreputable and dirty.

All the dogs were miserable and thin when they reached the stage of extreme exhaustion. Their meat was tough, stringy and without a vestige of fat. For a change we sometimes chopped it up finely, mixed it with a little pemmican, and brought all to the boil in a large pot of water. We were

Pages from Dr. Mertz' Diary

exceedingly hungry, but there was nothing to satisfy our appetites. Only a few ounces were used of the stock of ordinary food, to which was added a portion of dog's meat, never large, for each animal yielded so very little, and the major part was fed to the surviving dogs. They crunched the bones and ate the skin, until nothing remained.

A fresh start was made at 7.30 PM and a wretched, trying night was spent, when we marched without a break for twelve and a half hours. Overhead there was a dense pall of nimbus from which snow fell at intervals. None of the dogs except Ginger gave any help with the load, and Mary was so worn out that she had to be carried on the sledge. Poor Mary had been a splendid dog, but we had to kill her at the camp in the morning.

After a run of eighteen and a half miles we halted at 8 AM on December 18.

At 5.30 PM a light south-easter blew and snow fell from an overcast sky. Soon after a start was made, it became apparent that a descent was commencing. In this locality the country had been swept by wind, for none of the recent snow settled on the surface. The sastrugi were high and hard, and over them we bumped, slipping and falling in the uncertain light. We could not endure this kind of travelling for long and resolved to camp shortly after midnight, intending to go on when the day had advanced further and the light was stronger.

«*December 19.*—Up at noon and tried a few more miles in the snow-glare. Later in the afternoon the sky began to break and we picked our way with less difficulty. Camped at 5 PM, having done only twelve miles one thousand and fifty yards since the morning of December 18.

"Up at 8 PM again, almost calm and sun shining. Still continuing a westerly course we dropped several hundred feet, marching over rough, slippery fields of sastrugi."

In the early morning hours of the 20th the surface changed to ice and occasional crevasses appeared. It was clear that we had arrived at the head of the Ninnis Glacier above the zone of sérac we had traversed on the outward journey. It was very satisfactory to know this; to be certain that some landmark had been seen and recognized.

Soon after this discovery we came near losing Haldane, the big grey wolf, in a crevasse. Miserably thin from starvation the wretched dogs no longer filled their harness. As we pulled up Haldane, after he had broken into a deep, sheer-walled crevasse, his harness slipped off just as he reached the top. It was just possible to seize hold of his hair at that moment and to land him safely, otherwise we should have lost many days' rations.

He took to the harness once more but soon became uncertain in his footsteps, staggered along and then tottered and fell. Poor brutes! that was the way they all gave in—pulling till they dropped.

We camped at 4 AM, thinking that a rest would revive Haldane. Inside the tent some snow was thawed, and we drank the water with an addition of a little primus spirit. A temperature reading showed –1° F.

Outside, the hungry huskies moaned unceasingly until we could bear to hear them no longer. The tent was struck and we set off once more.

Haldane was strapped on the sledge as he could not walk. He had not eaten the food we had given him, because his jaws seemed too weak to bite. He had just nursed it between his paws and licked it.

Before the dogs became as weak as this, great care had to be taken in tethering them at each camp so as to prevent them from gnawing the wood of the sledge, the straps or, in fact, anything at all. Every time we were ready for a fresh start they seemed to regain their old strength, for they struggled and fought to seize any scraps, however useless, left on the ground.

The day's march was completed at 10.30 AM and fourteen and a half miles lay behind.

"We were up again at 11.20 PM Sky clear; fifteen-mile breeze from the south-south-east and the temperature 3° F. By midnight there was a thirty-mile wind and low, flying drift.

"*December 21.*—The night-march was a miserable one. The only thing which helped to relieve it was that for a moment Dixson Island was miraged up in the north, and we felt that we had met an old friend, which means a lot in this icy desolation. The surface was furrowed by hard, sharp sastrugi.

"We camped at 9 AM after only eleven miles. Haldane was finished off before we retired.

"We were up again at 9 PM, and when a start was made at 11 PM there was a strong south-south-east wind blowing, with low drift; temperature, zero Fahr.

"*December 22.*—The surface of hard, polished sastrugi caused many falls. The track was undulating, rising in one case several hundred feet and finally falling in a long slope.

"Pavlova gave in late in the march and was taken on the sledge.

"Camped at 6.40 AM in a forty-mile wind with low drift. Distance marched was twelve miles one thousand four hundred yards.

"Before turning in, we effected sundry repairs. Mertz re-spliced the handle of the shovel which had broken apart and I riveted the broken spindle of the sledge-meter. The mechanism of the latter had frozen during the previous day's halt, and, on being started, its spindle had broken off short. It was a long and tedious job tapping at the steed with a toy hammer, but the rivet held miraculously for the rest of the journey.

"Up at 11.30 PM, a moderate breeze blowing, overcast sky, light snow falling."

On December 28 an uphill march commenced which was rendered very heavy by the depth of the soft snow. Pavlova had to be carried on the sledge.

Suddenly, gaping crevasses appeared dimly through the falling snow which surrounded us like a blanket. There was nothing to do but camp, though it was only 4.30 AM, and we had covered but five miles one thousand two hundred and thirty yards.

Pavlova was killed and we made a very acceptable soup from her bones. In view of the dark outlook, our ration of food had to be still further cut down. We had no proper sleep, hunger gnawing at us all the time, and the question of food was for ever in our thoughts. Dozing in the fur bags, we dreamed of gorgeous "spreads" and dinner-parties at home. Tramping along through the snow, we racked our brains thinking of how to make the most of the meagre quantity of dogs' meat at hand.

The supply of kerosene for the primus stove promised to be ample, for none of it had been lost in the accident. We found that it was worth while spending some time in boiling the dogs' meat thoroughly. Thus a tasty soup was prepared as well as a supply of edible meat in which the muscular tissue and the gristle were reduced to the consistency of a jelly. The paws took longest of all to cook, but, treated to lengthy stewing, they became quite digestible.

On December 24 we were up at 8 AM just as the sun commenced to gleam through clouds. The light was rather bad, and snow fell as the track zigzagged about among many crevasses; but suddenly the sun broke forth. The sledge was crossing a surface of deep snow which soon became so sticky that the load would scarcely move. At last a halt was made after four miles, and we waited for the evening, when the surface was expected to harden.

A small prion visited us but went off in a moment. It is very remarkable how far some Antarctic sea-birds may wander inland, apparently at such a great distance from anything which should interest them. We were then more than one hundred miles south of the open sea. As the bird flew away, we watched it until it disappeared in the north, wishing that we too had wings to cross the interminable plateau ahead.

Lying in the sleeping-bag that day I dreamt that I visited a confectioner's shop. All the wares that were displayed measured feet in diameter. I purchased an enormous delicacy just as one would buy a bun under ordinary stances.

I remember paying the money over the counter, but something happened before I received what I had chosen. When I realized the omission I was out in the street, and, being greatly disappointed, went back to the shop, but found the door shut and "early closing" written on it.

Though a good daily average had been maintained on the march whenever conditions were at all favourable, the continuance of bad weather and the undoubtedly weaker state in which we found ourselves made it imperative to dispense with all but the barest necessities. Thus the theodolite was the only instrument retained, and the camera, photographic films (exposed and unexposed), hypsometer, thermometers, rifle, ammunition and other sundries were all thrown away. The frame of the tent was made lighter by constructing two poles, each four feet high, from the telescopic theodolite legs, the heavier pieces of sledge-runner being discarded.

We were up at 11 PM on December 24, but so much time was absorbed in making a dog-stew for Christmas that it was not till 2.80 AM that we got under way. We wished each other happier Christmases in the future, and divided two scraps of biscuit which I found in my spare kit-bag; relics of better days.

The surface was a moderately good one of undulating, hard sastrugi, and, as the course had been altered to north-west, the southerly wind helped us along. The sun shone brightly, and only for the wind and the low drift we might have felt tolerably comfortable. On our right, down within the shallow depression of the Ninnis Glacier, the low outline of Dixson Island, forty miles to the north, could be seen miraged up on the horizon.

The tent was raised at 9.30 AM after a run of eleven miles one hundred and seventy-six yards. An ounce each of butter was served out from our small stock to give a festive touch to the dog-stew.

At noon I took an observation for latitude, and, after taking a bearing on to Dixson Island, computed that the distance in an air-line to Winter Quarters was one hundred and sixty miles.

"*December 26.*—Got away at 2 AM; the surface undulating and hummocky with occasional beds of soft snow. Sun shining, wind ranged between thirty and forty miles per hour with much low drift; cold; camped about noon having done ten miles five hundred and twenty-eight yards.

"We have reached the western side of the Ninnis Glacier. Ahead are rising slopes, but we look forward to assistance from the wind in the ascent.

"I was again troubled with a touch of snow-blindness, but it responded to the usual treatment.

"At 11 PM we were at it again, but what with preparing dog-stew, packing up within the limited area of the tent and experimenting with a sail, it was five hours before the march commenced.

"The sail was the tent-cover, attached to the top of one ski lashed vertically as a mast and secured below to the other ski, lashed across the sledge as a boom."

A start was made at 4 AM on the 27th in a thirty-mile wind accompanied by low drift. The surface was smooth but grew unexpectedly soft at intervals, while the ascent soon began to tell on us. Though the work was laborious, notwithstanding some aid from the sail, the bright sunlight kept up our spirits, and, whenever a halt was called for a few minutes' spell, the conversation invariably turned upon the subject of food and what we should do on arrival on board the *Aurora*.

At noon the sledge-meter showed nine miles one thousand four hundred yards, and we agreed to halt and pitch camp.

The wind had fallen off considerably, and in the brilliant sunshine it was comparatively warm in the tent. The addition of the heat from the primus stove, kept burning for an unusually long time during the preparation of the meat, caused a thaw of drift-snow which became lodged on the lee side of the tent. Thus we had frequently to put up with an unwelcome drip. Moisture came from the floor also, as there was no floor-cloth, and the sleeping-bags were soon very wet and soggy. As soon as the cooking was finished, the tent cooled off and the wet walls froze and became stiff with icy cakes.

At this time we were eating largely of the dogs' meat, to which was added one or two ounces of chocolate or raisins, three or four ounces of pemmican and biscuit mixed together, and, as a beverage, very dilute cocoa. The total weight of solid food consumed by each man per day was approximately fourteen ounces. Our small supply of butter and glaxo was saved for emergency, while a few tea-bags which remained were boiled over and over again.

The march commenced on December 28 at 3 AM in a thirty-mile wind accompanied by light drift. Overhead there was a wild sky which augured badly for the next few days. It was cold work raising the sail, and we were glad to be marching.

Our faithful retainer Ginger could walk no longer and was strapped on the sledge. She was the last of the dogs and had been some sort of a help until a few days before. We were sad when it came to finishing her off.

On account of the steep up grade and the weight of Ginger on the sledge, we camped at 7.15 AM after only four miles one thousand two hundred and thirty yards.

We had breakfast off Ginger's skull and brain. I can never forget the occasion. As there was nothing available to divide it, the skull was boiled whole. Then the right and left halves were drawn for by the old and well-established sledging practice of "shut-eye," after which we took it in turns eating to the middle line, passing the skull from one to the other. The brain was afterwards scooped out with a wooden spoon.

On sledging journeys it is usual to apportion all food-stuffs in as nearly even halves as possible. Then one man turns away and another, pointing to a heap, asks "Whose?" The reply from the one not looking is "Yours" or "Mine" as the case may be. Thus an impartial and satisfactory division of the rations is made.

After the meal I went on cooking more meat so as to have a supply in readiness for eating. It was not till 2 PM that the second lot was finished. The task was very trying, for I had to sit up on the floor of the tent for hours in a cramped position, continually attending to the cooker, while Mertz in his Sleeping-bag was just accommodated within the limited space which remained. The tent was too small either to lie down during the operation or to sit up comfortably on a sleeping-bag.

At 9.30 PM Mertz rose to take a turn at the cooking, and at 11 PM I joined him at "breakfast."

At this time a kind of daily cycle was noted in the weather. It was always calmest between 4 PM and 6 PM During the evening hours the wind increased until it reached a maximum between four and six o'clock next morning, after which it fell off gradually.

We were away at 2.30 AM on the 29th in a thirty-mile wind which raised a light drift. The sail was found to be of great assistance over a surface which rose in terraces of fifty to one hundred feet in height, occurring every one to one and a half miles. This march lasted for six hours, during which we covered seven miles five hundred and twenty-eight yards.

On December 30 the ascent continued and the wind was still in the "thirties." After several hours we overtopped the last terrace and stood on flat ground—the crest of a ridge.

Tramping over the plateau, where reigns the desolation of the outer worlds, in solitude at once ominous and weird, one is free to roam in imagination through the wide realm of human experience to the bounds of the great Beyond. One is in the midst of infinities—the infinity of the dazzling white plateau, the infinity of the dome above, the infinity of the time past since these things had birth, and the infinity of the time to come before they shall have fulfilled the Purpose for which they were created. We, in the midst of the illimitable, could feel with Marcus Aurelius that "Of life, the time is a point."

By 9 AM we had accomplished a splendid march of fifteen miles three hundred and fifty yards, but the satisfaction we should have felt at making such an inroad on the huge task before us was damped by the fact that I suddenly became aware that Mertz was not as cheerful as usual. I was at a loss to know the reason, for he was always such a bright and companionable fellow.

At 10.15 PM the sky had become overcast, snow was falling and a strong wind was blowing. We decided to wait for better conditions.

On New Year's Eve at 5.30 AM the wind was not so strong, so we got up and prepared for the start.

Mertz said that he felt the dogs' meat was not doing him much good and suggested that we should give it up for a time and eat a small ration of the ordinary sledging food, of which we had still some days' supply carefully husbanded. I agreed to do this and we made our first experiment on that day. The ration tasted very sweet compared with dogs' meat and was so scanty in amount that it left one painfully empty.

The light was so atrocious for marching that, after stumbling along for two and a half miles, we were obliged to give up the attempt and camp, spending the day in sleeping-bags.

In the evening at 9.30 PM the sun appeared for a brief moment and the wind subsided. Another stage was therefore attempted but at considerable cost, for we staggered along in the bewildering light, continually falling over unseen sastrugi. The surface was undulating with a tendency to down grades. Two sets of sastrugi were found crossing one another, and, in the absence of the sun, we could not be sure of the course, so the camp was pitched after five miles.

"*January 1, 1913.*—Outside, an overcast sky and falling snow. Mertz was not up to his usual form and we decided not to attempt blundering along in the bad light, believing that the rest would be advantageous to him.

"He did not complain at all except of the dampness of his sleeping-bag, though when I questioned him particularly he admitted that he had pains in the abdomen. As I had a continuous gnawing sensation in the stomach, I took it that he had the same, possibly more acute.

"After New Year's Day he expressed a dislike to biscuit, which seemed rather strange. Then he suddenly had a desire for glaxo and our small store was made over to him, I taking a considerable ration of the dogs' meat in exchange.

"It was no use, however, for when we tried to cover a few more miles the exertion told very heavily on him, and it was plain that he was in a more serious condition than myself.

"*January 2.*—The same abominable weather. We eat only a few ounces of chocolate each day.

"*January 3.*—In the evening the sky broke and the sun looked through the clouds. We were not long in packing up and getting on the way. The night was chilly and Mertz got frost-bitten fingers, so camp was pitched after four miles one thousand two hundred and thirty yards.

"*January 4.*—The sun was shining and we had intended rising at 10 AM, but Mertz was not well and thought that the rest would be good for him. I spent the time improving some of the gear, mending Mertz's clothing and cooking a quantity of the meat.

"*January 5.*—The sky was overcast, snow was falling, and there was a strong wind. Mertz suggested that as the conditions were so bad we should delay another day.

"Lying in the damp bags was wretched and was not doing either of us any good, but what was to be done? Outside, the conditions were abominable. My companion was evidently weaker than I, and it was apparently quite true that he was not making much of the dogs' meat.

"*January 6.*—A better day but the sky remained overcast. Mertz agreed to try another stage."

The grade was slightly downhill and the wind well behind. Unfortunately the surface was slippery and irregular and falls were frequent. These told very much upon my companion until, after consistently demurring, he at last consented to ride on the sledge. With the wind blowing behind us, it required no great exertion to bring the load along, though it would often pull up suddenly against sastrugi. After we had covered two and a half miles, Mertz became so cold through inaction in the wind that there was nothing to do but pitch the tent.

Mertz appeared to be depressed and, after the short meal, sank back into his bag without saying much. Occasionally, during the day, I would ask him how he felt, or we would return to the old subject of food. It was agreed that on our arrival on board the *Aurora* Mertz was to make penguin omelettes, for we had never forgotten the excellence of those we had eaten just before leaving the Hut.

Reviewing the situation, I found that we were one hundred miles southeast of Winter Quarters where food and plenty awaited us. At the time we had still ordinary rations for several days. How short a distance it would seem to the vigorous, but what a lengthy journey for the weak and famished!

The skin was peeling off our bodies and a very poor substitute remained which burst readily and rubbed raw in many places. One day, I remember, Mertz ejaculated, "Just a moment," and, reaching over, lifted from my ear a perfect skin-cast. I was able to do the same for him. As we never took off our clothes, the peelings of hair and skin from our bodies worked down into our under-trousers and socks, and regular clearances were made.

During the evening of the 6th I made the following note in my diary:

"A long and wearisome night. If only I could get on; but I must stop with Xavier. He does not appear to be improving and both our chances are going now."

"*January 7.*—Up at 8 AM, it having been arranged last night that we would go on to-day at all costs, sledge-sailing, with Xavier in his bag on the sledge." It was a sad blow to me to find that Mertz was in a weak state and required helping in and out of his bag. He needed rest for a few hours at least before he could think of travelling. "I have to turn in again to kill time and also to keep warm, for I feel the cold very much now."

"At 10 AM I get up to dress Xavier and prepare food, but find him in a kind of fit." Coming round a few minutes later, he exchanged a few words and did not seem to realize that anything had happened. " . . . Obviously we can't go on to-day. It is a good day though the light is bad, the sun just gleaming through the clouds. This is terrible; I don't mind for myself but for others. I pray to God to help us."

"I cook some thick cocoa for Xavier and give him beef-tea; he is better after noon, but very low—I have to lift him up to drink."

During the afternoon he had several more fits, then became delirious and talked incoherently until midnight, when he appeared to fall off into a peaceful slumber. So I toggled up the sleeping-bag and retired worn out into my own. After a couple of hours, having felt no movement from my companion, I stretched out an arm and found that he was stiff.

My comrade had been accepted into "the peace that passeth all understanding." It was my fervent hope that he had been received where sterling qualities and a high mind reap their due reward. In his life we loved him; he was a man of character, generous and of noble parts.

For hours I lay in the bag, rolling over in my mind all that lay behind and the chance of the future. I seemed to stand alone on the wide shores of the world—and what a short step to enter the unknown future!

My physical condition was such that I felt I might collapse in a moment. The gnawing in the stomach had developed there a permanent weakness, so that it was not possible to hold myself up in certain positions. Several of my toes commenced to blacken and fester near the tips and the nails worked loose.

Outside, the bowl of chaos was brimming with drift-snow and I wondered how I would manage to break and pitch camp single-handed. There appeared to be little hope of reaching the Hut. It was easy to sleep on in the bag, and the weather was cruel outside. But inaction is hard to brook, and I thought of Service's lines:

Buck up, do your damndest and fight,

It's the plugging away that will win you the day.

If I failed to reach the Hut it would be something done to reach some prominent point likely to catch the eye of a search party, where a cairn might be erected and our diaries cached. And so I commenced to modify the sledge and camping gear to meet fresh requirements.

The sky remained clouded, but the wind fell off to a calm which lasted for several hours. I took the opportunity to set to work on the sledge, sawing it in halves with a pocket tool. A mast was made out of one of the rails of the discarded half of the sledge and a spar was cut from the other rail. The sledge-meter, very much battered, was still serviceable. Lastly, the load was cut down to a minimum by the elimination of all but the barest necessities.

Late on the evening of the 8th I took the body of Mertz, wrapped up in his sleeping-bag, outside the tent, piled snow blocks around it and raised a rough cross made of the two half-runners of the sledge.

On January 9 the weather was overcast and fairly thick drift was flying in a wind reaching about fifty miles an hour. As certain matters still required attention and my chances of re-erecting the tent were rather doubtful, if I had decided to move on, the start was delayed.

"I read the Burial Service over Xavier this afternoon. As there is little chance of my reaching human aid alive. I greatly regret inability at the moment to set out the detail of coastline met with for three hundred miles travelled and observations of glacier and ice-formations, etc.; the most of which latter are, of course, committed to my head.

"The approximate location of the camp is latitude 68° 2' S., longitude 145° 9' E. This is dead reckoning, as the theodolite legs have been out of action for some time, splinted together to form tent-props. I believe the truth lies nearer latitude 67° 57' S., longitude 145° 20' E., as the wind must have drifted us to the north."

During the afternoon I cut up Mertz's burberry jacket and roughly sewed it to a large canvas clothes-bag, making a sail which could be readily set or furled, so as to save delay in starting out or in camping.

January 10 was an impossible day for travelling on account of thick drift and high wind. I spent part of the time in reckoning up the amount of food remaining and in cooking the rest of the dogs' meat; the last device enabling me to leave behind some of the kerosene, of which there was still a good supply. Late in the afternoon the wind fell and the sun peered amongst the clouds just as I was in the middle of a long job riveting and lashing the broken shovel.

It was on January 11—a beautiful, calm day of sunshine—that I set out over a good surface with a slight down grade. From the start my feet felt lumpy and sore. They had become so painful after a mile of walking that I decided to make an examination of them on the spot, sitting in the sun on the sledge. The sight of my feet gave me quite a shock, for the thickened skin of the soles had separated in each case as a complete layer, and abundant watery fluid had escaped into the socks. The new skin underneath was very much abraded and raw.

I did what appeared to be the best thing under the stances: smeared the new skin with lanoline, of which there was a good store, and with bandages bound the skin soles back in place, as they were comfortable and soft in contact with the raw surfaces. Outside the bandages I wore six pairs of thick woollen socks, fur boots and a crampon over-shoe of soft leather. Then I removed most of my clothing and bathed in the glorious heat of the sun. A tingling sensation seemed to spread throughout my whole body, and I felt stronger and better.

When the day commenced with ideal weather I thought I would cover a long distance, but at 5.30 PM, after six and a quarter miles, I felt nerve-worn and had to camp, "so worn that had it not been a delightful evening, I should not have found strength to erect the tent."

Though the medical outfit was limited, there were a fair number of bandages and on camping I devoted much time to tending raw patches all over the body, festering fingers and inflamed nostrils.

High wind and much drift put travelling out of the question on January 12, and in any case my feet needed a rest.

"*January 13*.—The wind subsided and the snow cleared off at noon. The afternoon was beautifully fine. Descended hard ice-slopes over many crevasses—almost all descent—but surface cut my feet up; at 8 PM camped, having done five and three-quarter miles—painful feet—on camping find feet worse than ever; things look bad but shall persevere. It is now 11 PM and the glacier is firing off like artillery—appears to send up great jets of imprisoned air."

During the march Aurora Peak showed up to the west, about twenty miles away, across the Mertz Glacier. I felt happy at thus fixing my position, and at the sight of the far plateau which led onwards to Winter Quarters.

The glacier was the next obstacle to advance. To the south-west it descended from the plateau in immense broken folds. Pressing northward it was torn into the jumbled crush of sérac-ice, sparkling beneath an unclouded sun. The idea of diverging to the west and rounding the ice-falls occurred to me, but the detours involved other difficulties, so I strove to pick out the best track across the valley.

A high wind which blew on the morning of the 14th diminished in strength by noon and allowed me to get away. The sun was so warm that the puckered ice underfoot was covered with a film of water and in some places small trickles ran away to disappear into crevasses.

Though the course was downhill to the Mertz Glacier, the sledge required a good deal of pulling owing to the wet runners. At 9 PM, after travelling five miles, I pitched camp in the bed of the glacier.

Between 9.30 PM and 11 PM the "cannonading" heard on the previous night recommenced. The sounds, resembling the explosions of heavy guns, usually started higher up the glacier and ended down towards the sea. When I first heard them, I put my head outside the tent to see what was going on. The reports came at random from every direction, but there was no visible evidence as to how they were produced. Without a doubt they had something to do with the re-freezing and splitting of the ice owing to the evening chill; but the sounds seemed far too loud to be explained by this cause alone.

January 15—the date on which all the summer sledging parties were due at the Hut! It was overcast and snowing early in the day, and in a few hours the sun broke out and shone warmly. The travelling was so heavy over a soft snowy surface, partly melting, that I gave up, after one mile, and camped.

At 7 PM the surface had not improved, the sky was thickly obscured and snow fell. At 10 PM the snow was coming down heavily, and, since there were many crevasses in the vicinity, I resolved to wait.

On the 16th at 2 AM the snow was as thick as ever, but at 5 AM the atmosphere lightened and the sun appeared.

Without delay I broke camp. A favourable breeze sprang up, and with sail set I managed to proceed through the snowy "deluge" in short stages. The snow clung in lumps to the runners, which had to be scraped frequently. I passed some broken ridges and sank into several holes leading down to crevasses out of which it was possible to scramble easily.

After laboriously toiling up one long slope, I was just catching my breath at the top and the sledge was running easily when I noticed that the surface beneath my feet fell away steeply in front. I suddenly realized that I was on the brink of a great blue hole like a quarry. The sledge was following of its own accord and was rapidly gaining speed, so I turned and, exerting every effort, was just able to hold it back by means of the hauling-line from the edge of the abyss. I should think that there must have been an interval of quite a minute during which I held my ground without being able to make it budge. Then it slowly came my way, and the imminent danger was past.

The day's march was an extremely hard five miles. Before turning in I had an extra supper of jelly soup, made by boiling down some of the dogs' sinews, strengthened with a little pemmican. The acute enjoyment of eating under these circumstances compensates in a slight measure for the suffering of starvation.

January 17 was another day of overcast weather and falling snow. Delay meant a reduction in the ration which was low enough already, so there was nothing to do but go on.

When I got away at 8 AM I found that the pulling was easier than it had been on the previous day. Nevertheless I covered only two miles and had to consider myself fortunate in not winding up the whole story then and there. This is what happened, following the account in my diary.

"Going up a long, fairly steep slope, deeply covered with soft snow, broke through lid of crevasse but caught myself at thighs, got out, turned fifty yards to the north, then attempted to cross trend of crevasse, there being no indication of it; a few moments later found myself dangling fourteen feet below on end of rope in crevasse—sledge creeping to mouth—had time to say to myself, 'so this is the end,' expecting the sledge every moment to crash on my head and all to go to the unseen bottom—then thought of the food uneaten on the sledge; but as the sledge pulled up without letting me down, thought of Providence giving me another chance." The chance was very small considering my weak condition. The width of the crevasse was about six feet, so I hung freely in space, turning slowly round.

A great effort brought a knot in the rope within my grasp, and, after a moment's rest, I was able to draw myself up and reach another, and, at length, hauled myself on to the overhanging snow-lid into which the rope had cut. Then, when I was carefully climbing out on to the surface, a further section of the lid gave way, precipitating me once more to the full length of the rope.

Exhausted, weak and chilled (for my hands were bare and pounds of snow had got inside my clothing) I hung with the firm conviction that all was over except the passing. Below was a black chasm; it would be but the work of a moment to slip from the harness, then all the pain and toil would be over. It was a rare situation, a rare temptation—a chance to quit small things for great—to pass from the petty exploration of a planet to the contemplation of vaster worlds beyond. But there was all eternity for the last and, at its longest, the present would be but short. I felt better for the thought.

My strength was fast ebbing; in a few minutes it would be too late. It was the occasion for a supreme attempt. New power seemed to come as I addressed myself to one last tremendous effort. The struggle occupied some time, but by a miracle I rose slowly to the surface. This time I emerged feet first, still holding on to the rope, and pushed myself out, extended at full length, on the snow—on solid ground. Then came the reaction, and I could do nothing for quite an hour.

The tent was erected in slow stages and I then had a little food. Later on I lay in the sleeping-bag, thinking things over. It was a time when the mood of the Persian philosopher appealed to me:

Unborn To-morrow and dead Yesterday,

   Why fret about them if To-day be sweet?

I was confronted with this problem: whether it was better to enjoy life for a few days, sleeping and eating my fill until the provisions gave out, or to "plug on" again in hunger with the prospect of plunging at any moment into eternity without the great luxury and pleasure of food. And then an idea presented itself which greatly improved my prospects. It was to construct a ladder from alpine rope; one end of which was to be secured to the bow of the sledge and the other to be carried over my left shoulder and loosely attached to the sledge harness. Thus, if I fell into a crevasse again, it would be easy for me, even though weakened by starvation, to scramble out again by the ladder, provided the sledge was not also engulphed.

Notwithstanding the possibilities of the rope ladder, I could not sleep properly at all; my nerves had been so overtaxed. All night considerable wind and drift continued.

On the 19th it was overcast and light snow was falling. I resolved "to go ahead and leave the rest to Providence."

As they wallowed through the deep snow my feet and legs kept breaking through into space. Then I went right under, but the sledge was held back and the ladder "proved trumps." A few minutes later I was down again, but I emerged again without much exertion, half-smothered with snow. Faintness overcame me and I stopped to camp, though only a short distance had been covered.

All around me was a leaden glare, the snow clouds "corralling" me in. The sun had not shown up for some days and I was eager to see it once more, not only that it might show up the landscape, but for its cheerful influence and life-giving energy. A few days previously my condition had been improving, but now it was going back.

During the night of the 18th loud booming noises, sharp cracks and muffled growls issued form the neighbouring crevasses and kept waking me up. At times one could feel a vibration accompanying the growling sounds, and I concluded that the ice was in rapid motion.

The sun at last appeared on the 19th, and I was off by 8.30 AM The whole surface was a network of crevasses, some very wide. Along one after another of these I dragged the sledge until a spot was reached where the snow-bridge looked to be firm. Here I plunged across, risking the consequences.

After three hours' marching nothing serious had happened and I found myself on safer ground with a "pimply" surface visible ahead, close under the slopes of the highlands. Once on this I became over-reliant, and in consequence sank several times into narrow fissures.

At 1 PM the Mertz Glacier was at last crossed and I had reached the rising hills on its western side. Overlooking the camp, five hundred feet above the glacier, were beetling, crevassed crags, but I could trace out a good road, free from pitfalls, leading to the plateau, at an elevation of three thousand feet.

To lighten my load for the climb I threw away alpine rope, finnesko crampons, sundry pairs of worn crampons and socks, while I rubbed a composition on the sledge-runners which prevented them from sticking to wet snow.

January 20 was a wretched day; overcast, with wind and light drift. In desperation I got away at 2 PM in a wind which proved to be of considerable assistance. I could see nothing of my surroundings; one thing was certain, and that was that the ascent had commenced and every foot took me upward. The day's work amounted to about two and a half miles.

On the 21st the sun shone brightly and there was a good following wind. Through deep snow I zigzagged up for three miles before deciding to camp.

Wind and drift prevailed early on the 22nd but fell away towards noon, and I was then favoured with a glorious sunny day. Away to the north was a splendid view of the open sea; it looked so beautiful and friendly that I longed to be down near it. Six miles had been covered during the day, but I felt very weak towards the end on account of the heavy pulling.

During the early hours of the 23rd the sun was visible, but about 8 AM the clouds sagged low, the wind rose and everything became blotted out in a swirl of driving snow.

I wandered on through it for several hours, the sledge capsizing at times owing to the strength of the wind. It was not possible to keep an accurate course, for even the wind changed direction as the day wore on. Underfoot there was soft snow which I found comfortable for my sore feet, but which made the sledge drag heavily at times.

When camp was pitched at 4 PM I reckoned that the distance covered in a straight line had been three and a half miles.

Erecting the tent single-handed in the high wind was a task which required much patience and some skill. The poles were erected first and then the tent was gathered up in the proper form and taken to the windward side of the legs where it was weighted down. The flounce on the windward side was got into position and piled up with snow blocks. Other blocks of snow had previously been placed in a ring round the legs in readiness to be tumbled on to the rest of the flounce when the tent was quickly slipped over the apex of the poles. In very windy weather it was often as much as two hours after halting before I would be cozy within the shelter of the tent.

High wind and dense driving snow persisted throughout the 24th and I made five and a half miles, sitting on the sledge most of the time with the sail up.

The blizzard continued on the 25th, but after the trying experience of the previous two days, I did not feel well enough to go on. Outside, the snow fell in "torrents," piled up round the tent and pressed in until it was no bigger than a coffin, of which it reminded me.

I passed most of the day doctoring myself, attending to raw and inflamed places. Tufts of my beard and hair came out, and the snowy floor of the tent was strewn with it at every camp.

"*January 26.*—I went on again in dense, driving snow. There was no need of the sail. The wind, which was behind, caught the sledge and bundled it along so that, though over a soft surface of snow, the travelling was rapid. The snow was in large, rounded grains, and beat on the tent like hail. Altogether nine miles were covered.

"*January 27.*—Blizzard-bound again. The previous day's exertions were too much for me to undertake the same again without a long rest.

"*January 28,*—In the morning the wind had moderated very much but the sky remained overcast and snow continued to fall. It was a long job digging the tent out. Soon after the start the sun gleamed and the weather improved. The three-thousand-foot crest of the plateau had been crossed and I was bearing down rapidly on Commonwealth Bay, the vicinity of which showed up as a darker patch on the clouds of the north-west horizon.

"The evening was fine and I really began to feel that Winter Quarters were approaching. To increase my excitement Madigan Nunatak came into view for a time in the clear, evening light. Distance covered, over eight miles."

The calm of the previous evening was broken again, and I started on the morning of January 29 in considerable drift and a fairly strong wind. After going five miles I had miraculous good fortune.

I was travelling along on an even down grade and was wondering how long the two pounds of food which remained would last, when something dark loomed through the drift a short distance away to the right. All sorts of possibilities fled through my mind as I headed the sledge for it. The unexpected happened—it was a cairn of snow erected by McLean, Hodgeman and Hurley, who had been out searching for us. On the top of the mound was a bag of food, left on the chance that it might be picked up, while in a tin was a note stating the bearing and distance of the mound from Aladdin's Cave (E. 30° S., distance twenty-three miles), that the Ship had arrived at the Hut and was waiting, that Amundsen had reached the Pole, and that Scott was remaining another year in Antarctica.

It was rather a singular fact that the search party only left this mound at eight o'clock on the morning of that very day (January 29). It was about 2 PM when I found it. Thus, during the night of the 28th, our camps had been only about five miles apart.

With plenty of food, I speedily felt stimulated and revived, and anticipated reaching the Hut in a day or two, for there was then not more than twenty-three miles to cover. Alas, however, there was to be another delay. I was without crampons—they had been thrown away on the western side of Mertz Glacier—and in the strong wind was not able to stand up on the slippery ice of the coastal slopes. The result was that I sat on the sledge and ran along with the wind, nibbling at the food as I went. The sledge made so much leeway that near the end of the day, after fourteen miles, I reckoned that I had been carried to the east of Aladdin's Cave. The course was therefore changed to the west, but the wind came down almost broadside-on to the sledge, and it was swept away. The only thing to do was to camp.

On the 30th I cut up the box of the theodolite and into two pieces of wood stuck as many screws and tacks as I could procure from the sledge-meter. In the repair-bag there were still a few ice-nails which at this time were of great use. Late in the day the wind fell off, and I started westward over the ice-slopes with the pieces of nail-studded wood lashed to my feet.

After six miles these improvised crampons broke up, and the increasing wind got me into difficulties. Finally, the sledge slipped sideways into a narrow crevasse and was caught by the boom (which crossed from side to side at the lower part of the mast). I was not strong enough for the job of extricating it straight away, and by the time I had got it safely on the ice, the wind had increased still more. So I pitched camp.

The blizzard was in full career on January 31 and I spent all day and until late at night trying to make the crampons serviceable, but without success.

On February 1 the wind and drift subsided late in the afternoon, and I clearly saw to the west the beacon which marked Aladdin's Cave.

At 7 PM I reached this haven within the ice, and never again was I to have the ordeal of pitching the tent. Inside the cave were three oranges and a pineapple which had been brought from the Ship. It was wonderful once more to be in the land of such things!

I waited to mend one of the crampons and then started off for the Hut; but a blizzard had commenced. To descend the five miles of steep icy slopes with my miserable crampons, in the weak state in which I found myself, would only have been as a last resort. So I camped in the comfortable cave and hoped for better weather next day.

The high wind, rising to a hurricane at times, continued for a whole week with dense drift until the 8th. I spent the long hours making crampons of a new pattern, eating and sleeping. Eventually I became so anxious that I used to sit outside the cave for long spells, watching for a lull in the wind.

At length I resolved to go down in the blizzard, sitting on the sledge as long as possible, blown along by the wind. I was making preparations for a start when the wind suddenly decreased and my opportunity had come.

In a couple of hours I was within one mile and a half of the Hut. There was no sign of the Ship lying in the offing, but I comforted myself with the thought that she might be still at the anchorage and have swung inshore so as to be hidden by the ice-cliffs, or on the other hand that Captain Davis might have been along the coast to the east searching there.

But even as I gazed about seeking for a clue, a speck on the north-west horizon caught my eye and my hopes went down. It looked like a distant ship; it might well have been the *Aurora*. Well, what matter! The long journey was at an end-a terrible chapter of my life was finished!

Then the rocks around Winter Quarters began to come into view, part of the basin of the boat harbour appeared, and lo! there were human figures! They almost seemed unreal—I was in a dream—but after a brief moment one of them saw me and waved an arm, I replied, there was a commotion and they all ran towards the Hut. Then they were lost, for the crest of the first steep slope hid them. It almost seemed to me that they had run away to hide.

Minutes passed, and I slowly went along with the sledge. Then a head rose over the brow of the hill and there was Bickerton, breathless after a long run. I expect he considered for a while which one of us it was. Soon we had shaken hands and he knew all in a few brief words, and I learned that the Ship had left earlier in the day. Madigan, McLean, Bage and Hodgeman arrived, and then a new-comer—Jeffryes. Five men had remained behind to make a search for our party, and Jeffryes was a new wireless operator brought down by Captain Davis.

We were soon at the Hut where I found that full preparations had been made for wintering a second year. The weather was calm and the Ship was no distance away so I decided to recall her by wireless. The masts at the

Hut had been re-erected during the summer, and on board the *Aurora* Hannam was provided with a wireless receiving set. Jeffryes had arranged with Hannam to call up at 8, 9 and 10 PM for several evenings while the *Aurora* was "within range" in case there were any news of my party. A message recalling the Ship was therefore sent off and repeated at frequent intervals till past midnight.·

Next morning there was a forty-mile wind when we went outside, but away across Commonwealth Bay to the west the *Aurora* could be seen close to the face of the ice-cliffs. She had returned in response to the call and was steaming up and down, waiting for the wind to moderate.

We immediately set to work getting all the records, instruments and personal gear ready to be taken down to the boat harbour in anticipation of calm weather during the day.

The wind chose to continue and towards evening was in the sixties, while the barometer fell. During the afternoon Hodgeman went across to the western ridge and saw that the Ship was still in the Bay. The sea was so heavy that the motor-boat could never have lived through it.

That night Jeffryes sent another message, which we learned afterwards was not received, in which Captain Davis was given the option of remaining until calm weather supervened or of leaving at once for the Western Base. I felt that the decision should be left to him, as he could appreciate exactly the situation of the Western Base and what the Ship could be expected to do amid the ice at that season of the year. The time was already past when, according to my written instructions left for him on arrival at Commonwealth Bay, the *Aurora* should sail west to relieve Wild and his party.

On the morning of the 10th there was no sign of the Ship and evidently Captain Davis had decided to wait no longer, knowing that further delay would endanger the chances of picking up the eight men who had elected to winter on the shelf-ice one thousand five hundred miles to the west. At such a critical moment determination, fearless and swift, was necessary, and, in coming to his momentous decision, Captain Davis acted well and for the best interests of the Expedition.

A long voyage lay before the *Aurora* through many miles of ice-strewn sea, swept by intermittent blizzards and shrouded now in midnight darkness. We still fostered the hope that the vessel's coal-supply would be sufficient for her to return to Adelie Land and make an attempt to pick us up. But it was not to be.

The long Antarctic winter was fast approaching and we turned to meet it with resolution, knowing that if the *Aurora* failed us in early March, that the early summer of the same year would bring relief.

Mawson Emerging from His Makeshift Tent

The Half-Sledge Used in the Last Stage of Mawson's Journey

" . . . The long journey was at an end—a terrible chapter of my life was finished!"

CHAPTER XIV

The Quest of the South Magnetic Pole

By Dr. R. BAGE

> Send me your strongest, those who never fail.
> I'm the Blizzard, King of the Southern Trail!
> —*Sledging song*

O N THE AFTERNOON OF NOVEMBER 10, AT Aladdin's Cave, after a convivial hoosh, Webb, Hurley and I said good-bye to Dr. Mawson's party and made off south for the eleven and three-quarter mile cave where our Supporting Party, Murphy, Hunter and Laseron, were waiting for us. At 7 PM we started almost at a run over the smooth ice, to the accompaniment of hearty cheers from Dr. Mawson, Ninnis, and Mertz; two of whom we were never to see again.

Half a mile of this easy going, and we were on snow for the first time with a loaded sledge. Uphill snow, too, and the wind rising, so it was no small relief when we finally made the Cathedral Grotto at 11.30 PM, and found Murphy's tent pitched alongside it. The wind by this time was about forty-five miles per hour and, it being nearly dusk, the crevasses—a five-mile belt—had been fairly difficult to negotiate.

We soon had the cave clear of snow, had a good meal and then slept the sleep of the just, feeling well content with the first day's work—eleven and a half miles from home at an altitude of one thousand nine hundred feet. We were off at last on a search for the Magnetic Pole.

On the morrow some time was spent in rearranging the loads. Finally, both parties moved off south into heavy wind and fairly thick drift. What with the ground rising steadily, the pressure of the wind and our lack of

The Southern Supporting Party on the Plateau. Hunter, Murphy and Laseron

The Southern and Supporting Parties Building a Depot on the Plateau

condition, two and a quarter hours of solid work realized only two and a quarter miles; so we decided to camp.

All the night it blew hard, between seventy and eighty miles per hour, and next day it was still blowing and drifting heavily. Our tent was a good deal smaller than Murphy's, and, as Webb and Hurley are both six-footers, we always had to put all gear outside when the sleeping-bags were down. This is really a good thing when the weather is bad, as one is not tempted to stay in the bag all the time.

Early in the afternoon as we were all feeling hungry and had been in bags long enough to feel cold, although the weather was quite warm (10° F.), we rolled bags, and, when our frozen burberrys were once fairly on, quite enjoyed ourselves. After a boil-up and a few minutes' "run" round in the drift and wind, we did some stitching on our light drill tent, which was making very heavy weather of it, although pitched close under the lee of Murphy's strong japara tent. A little reading, some shouted unintelligible conversation with the other tent, another boil-up, and, last but not least, a smoke, found us quite ready for another sleep.

Next day (November 13), the wind having dropped to thirty-five miles per hour, we set out about 11 AM in light drift. The sky was still overcast, so the light was very trying. In the worst fogs at home one can at any rate see something of the ground on which one is treading; in Adelie Land, even when the air was clear of snow, it was easy to bump against a four-foot sastruga without seeing it. It always reminded me most of a fog at sea: a ship creeping "o'er the hueless, viewless deep."

When 6 PM arrived we had only covered five and a half miles, but were all thoroughly exhausted and glad to camp. Lunch had been rather barbarously served in the lee of the sledge. First came plasmon biscuit, broken with the ice-axe into pieces small enough to go into the mouth through the funnel of a burberry helmet; then followed two ounces of chocolate, frozen rather too hard to have a definite taste; and finally a luscious morsel—two ounces of butter, lovingly thawed-out in the mouth to get the full flavour. Lunches like these in wind and drift are uncomfortable enough for every one to be eager to start again as soon as possible.

By nine o'clock that night the wind had increased to a full gale. We were in camp all the 14th and the 15th, the wind rising to eighty-five miles per hour with very heavy drift during the small hours of the 15th. This was its maximum, and by the afternoon it was down to about seventy miles per hour with a clear sky and light drift. We donned our burberrys (I should like to give Hurley's "Ode to a Frozen Burberry") and dug out our sledges, both of which were completely buried in a ramp forty yards long; the shovel projecting nine inches above the surface.

While we were engaged on this work, I overheard the following conversation being shouted in the Supporting Party's tent:

> FIRST VOICE. I'm hungry. Who will go out and get the food-bag?
> SLEEPY VOICE. The food-weights **are in the cooker.
> FIRST VOICE. No they're not.
> SLEEPY VOICE. Saw them there yesterday, must be somewhere in
>   the tent.
> FIRST VOICE. No they're not . . . I ate them last night.

The exercise, a good hoosh and above all the clear sky made us take a less morbid view of the fact that we were six days out from the Hut and only nineteen and a half miles away.

Early on the 16th we could hear above the roar of the wind the drift still hissing against the tent, but it had diminished by nine o'clock breakfast.

By common consent it was agreed that our loads were too heavy for the conditions under which we were working. I accordingly decided to drop one hundred-pound bag. We had already saved nearly one week's food for three men and had not yet worked up our full sledging appetites. The bag was raised to the top of a six-foot snow mound, a thermograph being placed alongside. As we now seemed to be on plateau snow, I thought it wise to leave behind my heavy boots and Swiss crampons.

By 4 PM the wind had decreased to a light breeze. Work was very slow on a steeper up grade, and at six o'clock clouds came up quickly from the south-east and snow began to fall, so we camped at 7.30 PM thoroughly tired out. At twenty-four and a half miles the altitude was three thousand two hundred feet.

The snow was a false alarm. It ceased at 9 PM and the wind subsided to a dead calm!!

Good headway was being made against a strong breeze next day, when it was noticed that two gallons of kerosene were missing off the supporters' sledge. While Murphy and Laseron went back two miles to recover them, Webb secured a magnetic declination and I took sun observations for time and azimuth.

** *Until amounts were known by experience, rations were weighed by a small balance whose various weights were small calico bags filled with chocolate.*

We were off early on the 18th and for the first time were able to appreciate the "scenery." Glorious sunshine overhead and all around brilliant snow, dappled by livid shadows; very different from the smooth, soft, white mantle usually attributed to the surface of Antarctica by those in the homeland. Here and there, indeed, were smooth patches which we called bowling-greens, but hard and slippery as polished marble, with much the same translucent appearance. Practically all the country, however, was a jumbled mass of small, hard sastrugi, averaging perhaps a foot in height, with an occasional gnarled old veteran twice as high. To either side the snow rolled away for miles. In front, we made our first acquaintance with the accursed next ridge, which is always ahead of you on the plateau. Generally we passed from one ridge to another so gradually that we could never say for certain just when we had topped one; still the next ridge was always there.

The weather had lately been colder with the increased altitude. The temperature in daily range varied from −10° F. to 9° F. It was so hot in the sun, on the 18th, that lunching inside the tent was unbearable. We preferred its shadow outside in the breeze.

Wearing a minimum of clothes, we marched along gaily during the afternoon. The country changed in a wonderful manner, the sastrugi gradually becoming smaller and finally disappearing. The surface was so soft that a bamboo would easily penetrate it for a foot. Evidently it was fairly old and laid down in calm weather, for excavations showed that it became more compact without any hard wind-swept layers marking successive snowfalls.

It was proved that we were commencing a descent of one thousand five hundred feet down the north side of a valley feeding the Mertz Glacier. In order to explain the surface, smooth and unruffled by any wind, the question arose as to whether it is possible that there is a cushion of dead air more or less permanently over the north side of this depression.

On the soft surface we were able to dispense with crampons. Hitherto, it had been impossible to haul over a slippery surface in finnesko. Now we felt as light as air and were vastly cheered when some one calculated that the six of us were saving I don't know how many thousand foot-pounds of work every mile. With a run of twelve miles we were forty-two miles from Winter Quarters.

Another splendid day on the 19th. We had lunch in a curious cup-shaped hollow, estimated to be two miles wide and one hundred and fifty feet deep. Webb obtained here an approximate dip of 88° 44',** a very promising increase from the Hut (87° 27').

Snow-blindness had now begun to make itself felt for the first time. I for one had my first experience of it that afternoon. During the halt at lunch I put on yellow goggles in place of the smoked ones I had been wearing, and in a quarter of an hour the change of colour had 'settled' my eyes for the time being.

The afternoon was very hot. The thermometer stood at 10° F. at 4 PM, but the still air made it almost insupportable. By the time the load was hauled up out of the basin, we were streaming with perspiration.

Before halting, we sighted a dark, distant ridge, thirty miles away, and the course was corrected by its bearing. Our extravagant hopes of finding

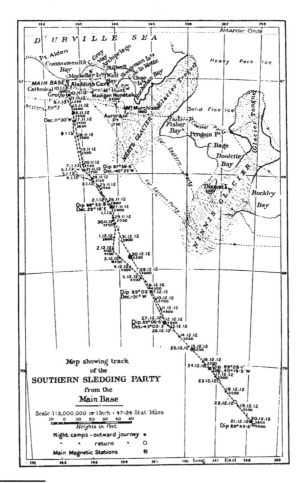

**At the South Magnetic Pole the dip is 90°.

306

a permanently calm region had been dwindling for the last few miles, as a hard bottom, a few inches under the surface, had become evident. They were finally dispelled by a south-west wind springing up during the night.

As every one was beginning to feel the hard work after another oppressive afternoon on the 20th, we decided to have an easy march next day and to build our first depot. Of course we had hoped to have been farther out before sending back the supporting party, but the weather had settled the question.

On the 21st, taking things as easily as a thirty-five mile wind would permit, we pulled on, up and down small undulations till 4 PM when we encountered a small rise, with the next ridge a considerable distance ahead. The depot was to be built here.

Webb at once proceeded to take full magnetic declination, time and azimuth observations, Laseron recording for him. Murphy put in a miserable hour over the primus melting snow. He was rather snow-blind and his eyes must have contributed a good deal of water to the pot. The water was poured into food-bags filled with snow, which were buried, encircled by wire slings, in holes. Here they froze, making excellent holdfasts for the depot flag. Depot flags had been exercising our ingenuity for months before the start, ordinary forms being destroyed by the wind in a few hours. Webb had finally built the perfect flag of the wind-vane type: a V of pieces of blackened Venesta board with light struts at the back and a piece of aeroplane tubing at the apex which slipped over the bamboo pole. The pole, of two bamboos, stood sixteen feet from the ground and was provided with two sets of flexible steel stays. Close by, Hurley and Hunter had built a snow mound ten feet in diameter and ten feet in height, finished off with a capping of snow blocks wrapped in black bunting.

Next day it was blowing a little harder and the sky was overcast, snow falling all day. What bad light means can be gathered from the fact that Laseron on crawling out of the tent in the morning raised an alarm that our tent had been blown away in the night. It turned out that our tent was hidden by a mound which he could not see, though only about ten yards from it.

I had been given the option of relieving the supporting party of any of their gear I coveted and I used it freely. The sledgemeter was the first thing commandeered, ours, made by Correll, having developed some slight complaint in its interior. Their cooker, being in good condition, was also taken. We all cast longing eyes at the roomy wind-proof tent but finally decided that it was too heavy—forty pounds as against our own of twenty-six pounds, including tent and poles.

At 7 PM we said good-bye to our supporters, Hurley exposed the last plate of his big reflex camera, which they carried back to the Hut, and a few minutes later Webb, Hurley, and I were standing alone watching three black specks disappearing in the drift; a stiff wind helping them along in great style. We were left to our own resources now, for better or for worse. "Weird" is how I described my feelings in the diary.

The same night it blew a hurricane and only dropped to sixty miles per hour during the 23rd, compelling us to remain in camp. Not an ideal birthday for Webb, but we made the most of it. I quote from my diary: "Turned out and rolled bags at 3 PM for lunch, for which we opened a wee tin of bacon ration brought for the occasion. Had some extra lumps of sugar (collared from the eleven-mile cave) in our tea. After the wine had been round (i.e. after a special second cup of tea), I gave Eric a pair of stockings from Murphy, and then 'Hoyle' and I smoked a cigar each which Webb produced. Dinner at 7 was also a special affair as we had the remains of the bacon ration in the hoosh, with great effect. Also an extra strong brew of cocoa boiled quite smooth. Burberrys on and a stroll outside in the wind for a yard or two to get up a circulation; then into bag where I am smoking a plebeian pipe which is very tame after the glories of the day, especially as I suspect my tobacco of being a bit damp."

Such was the first of the two "auspicious occasions" we had on the journey.

After going carefully through the gear, we discarded a pickaxe, one pair of big spiked boots and some odd clothing. We also decided, as the probability of leisure was not great, to leave our reading matter behind. It was with regret that I added my little *Virginibus Puerisque* to the small pile of "rejects." The load now amounted to seven hundred and forty-eight pounds in all. Not many days after, the floor-cloth (eight pounds) was left behind, as the japara sail afforded ample protection from damp in the low temperatures of the plateau.

The dip-circle, which was to yield the most important result of our journey, was housed after much thought on a conveniently shaped kerosene tray between the tins of oil. Four light leather straps, buckled tightly, made a solid mass of tray, oil tins, and dip-circle; very safe, and easy to undo.

My orders were to proceed inland, due south, taking magnetic, geographical, meteorological, and such other observations as were possible, returning to the Hut not later than January 15. Dr. Mawson had left it to my discretion, in the event of any great change occurring in the declination, to go either true or magnetic south.

At the Hut and up to about sixty miles south of it, the declination had proved fairly constant, but now at the Southern Cross Depot, as we had christened the sixty-seven-mile camp, the compass, from pointing a little to the east of south, had travelled to 40° east of south, so that it became obvious that there was considerable magnetic disturbance in the country over which we were travelling. Whether we went south or south-east seemed unlikely to affect the value of geographical and other information we might gather, while Webb was of the opinion that the best magnetic results would be obtained by marching directly towards the Magnetic Pole, particularly if there were disturbances over the intervening area. For these reasons the course was maintained magnetic south.

At 11 AM on Sunday, November 24, we moved off to the south-east in a wind of fifty miles an hour. The light was bad, and steering had to be done by sastrugi and wind. However, momentary glimpses of the sun served to check the course. The lunch camp was five miles from the depot, and a good mound with a top of black bunting was left there. At almost every halt, thus far on our journey, the snow cut for pitching the tent had been gathered up into a mound which, in addition to forming a landmark, could often be used as a back-mark for checking the course. Our depot thus had a mound four miles on the southern and five miles on the northern side of it. It was not marked as well as I had hoped, but under the circumstances we could not do better. Moreover, at intervals during the day, some very distinctive snow ramps had appeared in the valley, some five miles to the north-east, and their position was fixed relative to the course.

Our hopes for a good afternoon were disappointed, as the wind and drift came up again as strong as ever. The surface, too, grew worse; nothing but sastrugi eighteen inches to thirty inches high and very close together. We were marching a little to the east of the wind, and the sledge was continually blown sideways, making considerable leeway. By 8.30 PM it was blowing sixty miles per hour, so we halted, thoroughly tired out, having hauled our one-third of a ton eight and three-quarter miles.

When it is blowing hard, the end of the day's march is not the end of the day's work. As soon as a camping spot has been chosen, the sledge is pulled round head to wind. The straps round the load are loosened carefully, the shovel and tent removed and the straps retightened. One man starts breaking out chunks of snow, experimenting until he finds a place where

Depot Made by the Southern and Supporting Parties at a Point 67 Miles South of Commonwealth Bay. Murphy, Laseron, and Hunter Packing Sledge in the Foreground; Bage in the Distance

A Rough Sledging Surface of High Sastrugi Encountered by the Southern Party 200 Miles South-South-East of the Hut

large pieces come away readily. Lumps of forty pounds are the handiest and quickest, but often only smaller ones can be obtained. These are arranged in a circle round the tent-site, while the man with the tent places it on the ground pointing upwind, the bottom of the poles being just where the middle windward leg will be, and makes a hole for that leg.

When everything is ready, all three catch hold of the tent, one man crawling half into it, gripping hard the leather loop on the windward leg. The others sort out and grip their two side legs. "All ready? Up!" It almost takes one's breath away, the roar and the flap! The side legs are quickly separated as the tent rises, and before it can blow over, the leeward legs are more or less in position, taking the strain. The centre man is throwing all his weight on to the leather loop, while the other two outside each holds down his windward pole with one hand and with the other pulls blocks of snow on to the skirt to windward. Once this is done, the rest is simple: cutting holes in just the right positions for the other legs, pulling out the skirt and making it snug all round. Then in goes the floor-cloth, and, by the time that is spread out properly, the primus and cooker are passed in. The cooker is dissected and the two water vessels passed out to be filled with snow. The cook will have hard work to get the primus started if he does not shield the spirit flame from the wind, which blows through the tent, by putting the whole lamp inside the big cooker lid.

In come the pots filled with lumps of snow. The food tank is placed just outside the entrance, and the proper food-bags for the meal are passed in to the cook, the tank being retied to keep out drift. The cooker will now be going at full pressure, and the cook is ready to receive the gear. Sleeping-bags, "computation bag," hypsometer, "meat block" (a three-inch-square paper pad on which meteorological notes were taken); clothes-bag opened, three ditty-bags passed in and bag retied; a final temperature taken and aneroid read; sledge anchored securely by tow-rope to the ice-axe, and a final look round to see all gear is safely strapped down and snow-tight.

In calm weather, camping is a very different thing. On a fine day, half an hour after the halt would usually find us carefully scraping the last of the hoosh out of our pannikins, ready for the cocoa.

At the seventy-six-mile camp we tried the experiment of a break-wind. The tent was so small and light that it was necessary to protect it in the heavy winds. Hurley and I took about three-quarters of an hour to build the first one, but later we improved, getting into the knack of hewing snow with a sharp-pointed shovel.

That night in bag I wrote: "The result of the breakwind is that for once we have the wind bluffed. It is blowing seventy-five miles per hour—a full hurricane—but all the viciousness is taken out of the flapping and there will be no damage done to the tent by morning."

The wind was too strong for travelling early in the day (November 25). While outside we suddenly observed two snow petrels. It was hard to realize that they had actually flown seventy-six miles inland to a height of two thousand four hundred and fifty feet. I dashed inside for the fishing line; Hurley got out the camera. They were a beautiful sight, hovering with outspread wings just above the snow, tipping it with their feet now and then, to poise without a flutter in a sixty-five-mile gale. Hurley secured a couple of "snaps" at the expense of badly frost-bitten hands. Just as I arrived with the line hooked and baited, the birds flew away to the north-east; our visions of fresh meat went with them. The line was always ready after this.

Towards evening the wind dropped suddenly to twenty miles per hour. Our camp was stationed on the southern side of the large valley we had entered on the 18th, and we could identify the ridge crossed on that date, blue and dim, forty miles away to the north. To the north-east could be seen a distinct dip in the skyline, indicating the bed of the valley, on whose northern side the dip met the higher skyline in a steep bluff, twenty-five miles off. This bluff under the glasses was of heavily crevassed, blue ice.

The wind did not rise again much until 10 PM, when we had moved on seven and a half miles, rising about three hundred feet over several ridges and practically losing our view to the north.

A steady breeze on the 26th, and, on the whole, good light, allowed us to make twelve miles.

Each day, now, Webb took an approximate magnetic dip and declination in the lee of the break-wind. This was necessary in order to get some idea of local disturbances. Also, it gave us some vague idea as to the direction in which lay the South Magnetic Pole. For instance, at the eighty-three-and-three-quarter-mile camp, the needle showed the Pole to be 18° east of true south, while at our lunch camp that day, six miles farther on, it was given as 50° east of south. The dip was so great that our prismatic compass would not set closer than about 15°, but the long compass needle of the dip-circle, though of course sluggish, continued to give excellent results.

Under these conditions it is obvious that the magnetic needle is quite useless for steering purposes. The sun compass proved itself a more than efficient substitute. On a snowfield there is usually a total absence of landmarks of any kind, so the direction of wind, sastrugi, or perhaps a low cloud is found with the sun-compass, frequently checked, and the course kept accordingly. On camping we would generally carefully note the direction in which the sledge was left, in case the next day proved overcast. Thus we would march in the morning by the wind's direction till the sun, gleaming through the clouds for a few moments, enabled us to use the compass again.

Sastrugi, only six inches high, seen on the 26th, showed the effects of wind-erosion exquisitely. In an individual case the windward end of a sastruga might be completely undercut for six or nine inches, leaving a hard crust, sometimes only one-eighth of an inch in thickness and a couple of inches wide. This would sag downwards under its own weight in a fine curve till the tip rested on the snow beneath. It is marvellous how such a delicate structure can withstand the heavy wind.

November 27 proved a very hard day. The wind kept up sixty miles per hour all the time, so that, after taking four hours to do four and three-quarter miles, we were all thoroughly exhausted. It was not a great run, but the century was hoisted—one hundred and three-quarter miles by sledge-meter; altitude two thousand nine hundred feet. There was a mild celebration that night over a square of butter-scotch and half an ounce of chocolate, besides the regular hoosh and cocoa.

Next day the light was very bad and the wind fifty miles per hour. Observations were therefore made inside the tent. Webb, Hurley and the instrument occupied all available space, while I spent three hours digging a shaft eight feet deep in the snow, taking temperatures every foot. It appeared that the mean annual temperature of the snow was approximately −16° F.

The dip was 88° 54'; certainly rather too large a rise from 88° 20' of twenty miles back. The declination had actually changed about 80° in the last ten miles. This one-hundred-mile station was badly disturbed. From the evidence, it is possible that a subsidiary "pole" or area of almost vertical dip may exist close by this spot to the west or south-west.

Going straight up wind into a "blow" which varied from forty to fifty miles per hour, we were able to make eight miles after the previous day's rest. At lunch a hole was dug five feet square and two feet deep. It served three purposes. First, it gave a good shelter for a longitude observation; secondly, with the mast, yard and floor-cloth we converted it into a shelter snug enough to house the primus and to lunch comfortably; and thirdly, a mound was left as a back-mark which was picked up on the return journey.

By experience we found that a warm lunch and a rest enabled one to "peg" along a good deal farther than would otherwise be possible.

The "scenery" in the afternoon became if possible more desolate— very few new sastrugi, the surface appearing generally old and pitted. In some places it was rotten and blown away, disclosing coarse granulated substrata. At the top of one ridge the snow merged into névé split into small crevasses, nine inches wide and four or five yards apart. The camp was pitched, here, at 11 PM. The latitude was 68° 32' S., and we saw the midnight sun for the first time that summer, about one-quarter of its rim remaining above the horizon.

A full hurricane came up and kept between fifty and sixty miles per hour all day on the 30th. Before moving off, Webb found that the magnetic needle had "waltzed" back 60° since the one-hundred-mile camp, now pointing 30° east of south. Still, to allow the needle to make up its mind, we steered into the wind at 2 PM, losing the névé and meeting very rough country. By 6 PM, with four miles to our credit, we were nearly played out. It was being discussed whether we should go on when the discovery was made that the theodolite legs were missing; probably having slipped out in one of the numerous capsizes of the sledge.

The solemn rites of "shut-eye" determined that Webb was to stay and make camp while Hurley and I retraced our steps. It was no easy matter to follow the trail, for on hard snow the sledge runners leave no mark, and we had to watch for the holes of the crampon-spikes. About two and a half miles back, the legs were found, and there only remained a hard "plug" against the wind to camp and hoosh.

While we were lying half-toggled into the sleeping-bags, writing our diaries, Hurley spent some time alternately imprecating the wind and invoking it for a calm next day. As he said, once behind a break-wind one could safely defy it, but on the march one is much more humble.

Whether it was in honour of Queen Alexandra's birthday, or whether Hurley's pious efforts of the evening before had taken effect, December 1 turned out a good day. By noon, the wind had dropped sufficiently for us to hoist the Jack and Commonwealth Ensign for the occasion.

After four miles of battling, there came into sight a distinct ridge, ten miles to the west and south—quite the most definitely rising ground observed since leaving the coast. In one place was a patch of immense crevasses, easily visible to the naked eye; in another, due south, were black shadows, and towards these the course was pointed.

At a point more than one hundred and twenty-five miles from the sea, a skua gull paid an afternoon call, alighting a few yards from the track. I immediately commenced to stalk it with a fishing-line, this time all ready and baited with pemmican. However, it was quite contemptuous, flying off to the south-south-east as far as we could follow it. Was it taking a short cut to the Ross Sea?

December 2 saw us through "Dead-Beat Gully" to a rise, in sight of the shadows towards which we had been steering. Two miles away they appeared like the edge of the moon seen through a large telescope. The shadows were due to large mounds of snow on the south side of a steep escarpment. Three main prominences were cross-connected with regular lines of hillocks, giving the impression of a subdivided town-site. The low evening sun threw everything up in the most wonderful relief.

On the morning of the 3rd we were in a valley running west-north-west and east-south-east. The southern side rose steeply and from it projected three large mounds, about two hundred feet from the bottom of the valley, into which they fell just like tailings-heaps from a mine. They were christened "The Nodules."

Going due south uphill over névé we found ourselves in a regular network of crevasses. They were about ten feet wide and well bridged. Most noticeable were "hedges" of ice up to six feet in height on either side of the crevasses which ran southward. It was now nearly calm and in every crack and chink in the snow-bridges beautiful fern-like ice-crystals were seen. These must have been just forming, as a very light puff of wind was seen to destroy many of them.

We spent three hours exploring the locality. On nearing the top of the ridge, roped together, we found that the crevasses were becoming much wider, while the "hedges" were disappearing. The centre "nodule" was found to be immediately north or to the leeward of the intersection of two crevasses, each about forty feet wide. The bridge of one crevasse had dropped some thirty feet for a length of eighty yards. Doubtless, an eddy from this hole accounts for the deposit of snow and, by accretions, for the erection of the nodule. Webb went down at the end of the alpine rope and found the bridge below quite solid.

For about half a mile the summit of the slope was practically level, three hundred feet above the bed of the valley. The surface was still of névé, intersected by canals forty, sixty and eighty feet wide, in which the snow-bridge was generally four or five feet from the brink.

On the south-west horizon, perhaps twenty miles away, was a salient crest streaked by three dark vertical bars; evidently another crevassed area.

Returning to the sledge, we toggled-on and worked it up over the top of the ridge, much regretting that time would not allow us to examine the other two large "nodules." Hurley was in the lead, lengthening his line by thirty feet of alpine rope, but even then all three of us and the sledge were often on the lid of a crevasse. Luckily, the lids were fairly sound, and none of us went in beyond the waist. Finally, the trail emerged on to ordinary sastrugi once more, where a halt was made for lunch. We were all glad to have seen the place, but I think none of us has any wish to see another like it.

That night, after following the magnetic needle towards the south-east, we were fairly on the plateau at one hundred and forty miles, with an altitude of four thousand four hundred feet. The dip, however, had steadily decreased, standing now at 88° 30'. There was some consolation in the hope that a big, sudden rise was stored up for us somewhere along the way ahead.

December 4 and 5 were fine days, giving only twenty-two miles, as we met with a rough surface; a large quantity of very hard, razor-backed sastrugi, generally about two feet high, like groined vaulting inverted, on a small scale. Sledge and sledge-meter both had a very rough passage. The sledge, for instance, balances itself on the top of a sastruga for a moment, with an ominous bend in the runners, crashes down the slope and jams its bow into the next one, from which it has to be lifted clear.

During this run the needle again misbehaved itself, changing its direction some 85° in ten miles, but by the night of the 5th we were getting past the disturbed locality and the dip had increased considerably.

For the first time on the trip the wind veered round to the south-east. Snow had fallen overnight (December 5) and had drifted in long ramps diagonally across the sastrugi. In two and a half hours we covered two and a quarter miles, blindly blundering in an uncertain light among crests and troughs and through piles of soft, new snow. Then we stopped; Webb filling in the afternoon with a full set of dip observations.

That night the break-wind played its one possible trick. Waking on the 8th, we found that the heavy snowfall, with only a moderate wind, had drifted us up. Of course Hurley and I, who slept on the 'outsides,' had known it most of the night. Before we could extricate ourselves from the bags Webb had to turn out from the middle to dig away the drift which was weighing down the walls of the tent on top of us.

It was hopeless weather for travelling. In the afternoon a snow cave was dug, seven feet deep and enlarged to seven feet square at the bottom. The whole was covered with mast, yard and sail. It was very snug from the outward aspect, but we soon found that there were two objections to the "Sarcophagus," as it was named. There was very little light except a ghastly blue half-tone filtering through the snow, and the place was not over warm, surrounded by walls at a much lower temperature than that of the surface.

Webb commenced a declination "quick-run," consisting of half-hourly observations of the direction in which the compass was pointing. In ordinary latitudes, during the day, the compass needle moves over a few minutes of arc, but here, being so close to the Magnetic Pole, its movement is greatly magnified, the range being about 5° on this occasion. Webb carried on readings till midnight, and at 4 AM, December 9, I turned out, being relieved at 8 AM by Hurley, who carried on until the twenty-four hours were completed. This observation should be especially valuable when it is compared with continuous magnetic records obtained at the same time at Winter Quarters and by the Scott expedition at McMurdo Sound.

It was not till 1.30 PM on December 10 that the sixty-mile wind had subsided sufficiently for us to get away. Every yard of our quota of seven miles was hard going. A fine example of a typical old sastruga was passed on the way. In order to secure a photograph of it, Hurley had to waste eighteen films before he could persuade one to pull into place correctly. The film-packs had been carefully kept in an airtight tin, but the cold was too much for them. The tags which should pull each film round from the back to the front of the pack usually tore away with a small piece of film. In fact, out of one hundred and twenty films only forty-five exposures were made.

On the 11th a good deal of "piecrust" cut down the day's march to eight and a half miles. Sledge runners are usually supported by this surface, but one's feet break through in a most annoying and tiring manner. The drift eased off for a few hours and we managed to dry some of our gear. At the Sarcophagus, things which had all been wet enough before became saturated with drift which turned to ice. Felt mitts are perhaps the worst in this respect, and it is no exaggeration to say that you could easily brain a man with one after it had been worn in drift for a couple of days.

That night I decided that one more day must see us at our depot. Allowing three days' grace for contingencies, there were thirty-one days for us to attain our farthest southerly point and back to the Hut.

On the 12th we planned to reach a spot for the depot, two hundred miles out, and by 11.30 PM came on a fine site at one hundred and ninety-nine and three-quarter miles; altitude four thousand eight hundred and fifty feet, latitude 69° 33.1' south; longitude 140° 20' east. Everything possible was left behind, the sledge-decking being even cut away, until only three light bamboo slats remained. A pile, including ten days' food and one gallon of kerosene, was placed on a small mound to prevent it being drifted over. A few yards distant rose a solid nine-foot cairn surmounted by a black canvas-and-wire flag, six feet higher, well stayed with steel wire.

I took on food for seventeen days, three days more than I intended to be out, partly so that we could keep on longer if we found we could make very fast time, and also as a safeguard against thick weather when returning to the depot.

Late in the evening we set off against a stiff breeze. The sledge ran lightly for three and a half miles, and we camped. The depot showed up well in the north-west as a bright golden spot in the low midnight sun.

Next day the piecrust was so bad that, despite the lessened load, we only covered twelve miles. The surface was smoothly polished, and we either crashed through it from four inches to a foot or else slipped and came down heavily on knees, elbow, or head. New finnesko were largely responsible for such an accident.

At 11 PM a remarkable ramp, five chains long, was passed. On its windward side was a tangled cluster of large sastrugi. They made one imagine that the wind, infuriated at finding a block of snow impeding its progress, had run amok with a giant gouge, endeavouring to pare it down. Every now and then, the gouge, missing its aim, had taken great lateral scoops from the surface, leaving trenches two and three feet deep.

In bags that night we had a talk (not the first by any means) over our prospects. Up to the one hundred-and-seventy-four-mile camp, four hundred miles seemed dimly possible, but now we saw we would be lucky to reach three hundred miles. Moreover, the dip at this spot was 89° 11', practically what it had been ever since one hundred and fifty miles. Sixty-five miles for nothing! How far for the other forty-nine minutes which were needed for a vertical dip and the South Magnetic Pole? This problem was insoluble, so each toggled himself into his bag in a rather depressed state of mind.

December 16 was a glorious day; only a fifteen-mile wind, and for ten miles an improved surface. There was no drift, consequently opportunity was taken to turn the sleeping bags inside out. They needed it, too. The upper parts were not so bad as they had been propped open occasionally, but the lower halves were coated with solid ice. For the first time for weeks we did not wear burberrys, as the weather was so warm. Fourteen miles was the total work, the previous day's being twelve.

All three of us were having trouble with snow-blindness; the "zinc and cocaine" tabloids being in great demand.

Latitude 70° south was passed on the 17th and we were another fourteen miles to the good. The dip was on the increase 89° 25' and the declination swung to 40° east of the magnetic meridian. At two hundred and fifty-six miles the altitude was five thousand five hundred feet.

The temperature was getting lower; the minimum being −21° F. on the night of the 17th, rising to a maximum of 3° F. on the following day.

There was dead calm and a regular heat wave on December 19. As the sun rose higher and higher, the tent became absolutely oppressive. The rime coating the walls inside thawed and water actually trickled into our finnesko. Usually we awoke to find them frozen hard, just as we had shaped them on the previous night, but on this particular morning they were pathetically limp and wet. The temperature inside the tent was 66° F., heated, of course, by the sun's rays which raised our black bulb thermometer to 105° F. We were not used to this sort of thing and struggled out hurriedly for a breath of fresh air.

Once into harness, we began to feel the effects of exertion. By degrees we got rid of our clothing, but unfortunately soon came to bedrock in that respect, as the underclothing was sewn on and immovable. At lunch time, with the thermometer at −2° F. in the shade, we reluctantly dressed knowing how soon we would cool off. About 9 PM clouds moved over rapidly from the south-east and the landscape faded into the blank, shadowless nothing of an overcast day. The camp was pitched at two hundred and eighty-three miles amidst a jumble of ramps and sastrugi. The dip had seen fit to rise to 89° 35'.

In the morning the wind was doing thirty miles per hour, which certainly seemed to be the normal thing. It fell to a nice sailing breeze, but, at the time, we were not very appreciative of anything as the course was uphill. Again, it was to be the last day's run, so we were "all out" when the halt came after a good fifteen miles—the longest day's march on the outward journey. Nevertheless, Webb unpacked the theodolite after hoosh and took an altitude of the sun at midnight.

On December 21 the load on the sledge was stripped down to tent, dip-circle, theodolite, cooker and a little food. For two and a half miles we went south-east over rising ground until the sledge-meter showed three hundred and one miles.

While Hurley and I pitched the tent, Webb built a breakwind for his instrument fifty yards away. Then followed a long set of magnetic observations. About 5 PM the magnetic work was interrupted; the theodolite replacing the dip-circle on the legs, while I took a longitude shot. I was seeing double, being slightly snow-blind, and had some difficulty in choosing the correct combination from the assortment of suns and cross-wires visible in the telescope. Setting the vertical and horizontal wires simultaneously on the sun was beyond me; Webb taking the observations for the true meridian, which also checked my longitude shot.

Magnetic work under these conditions is an extremely uncomfortable operation. Even a light wind will eddy round the break-wind, and it is wind which makes low temperatures formidable. Nearly all the work has to be done with bare fingers or thin instrument-gloves, and the time taken is far greater than in temperate climates, owing to the fingers constantly "going" and because of the necessity of continually freeing the instrument from the condensed moisture of the breath. Considering that the temperature was −12° F. when he had finished his four hours' work, it may be imagined that Webb was ready for his hot tea. The dip proved to be 89° 43.5', that is, sixteen and a half minutes from the vertical. The altitude was just over five thousand nine hundred feet, in latitude 70° 36.5' south and longitude 148° 10' east.

After lunch the Union Jack and the Commonwealth Ensign were hoisted and three cheers given for the King—willing but rather lonesome away out there! We searched the horizon with glasses but could see nothing save snow, undulating in endless sastrugi. To the south-east the horizon was limited by our old enemy, "the next ridge," some two miles away. We wondered what could be beyond, although we knew it was only the same featureless repetition, since one hundred and seventy-five miles on the same course would bring us to the spot where David, Mawson and Mackay had stood in 1909.

After Hurley had taken a photograph of the camp, the tent was struck and the sledge repacked. At last the sail was rigged, we gave a final glance back and turned on the homeward trail.

My diary of that night sums up: "We have now been exactly six weeks on the tramp and somehow feel rather sad at turning back, even though it has not been quite a Sunday school picnic all along. It is a great disappointment not to see a dip of 90°, but the time is too short with this 'climate.' It was higher than we expected to get, after the unsatisfactory dips obtained near the two-hundred-mile depot. The rate of increase since that spot has been fairly uniform and indicates that 90 degrees might be reached in another fifty to sixty miles, if the same rate held, and that means at least another week. It's no good thinking about it for 'orders are orders.' We'll have our work cut out to get back as it is. Twenty-five days till we are overdue. Certainly we have twenty-three days' food, eight days' with us, ten

Farthest South Camp of Southern Party, 17 "Minutes" (About 50 Miles) from the South Magnetic Pole. Bage Near Sledge; Webb Taking Set of Magnetic Observations Behind Snow Barricade

Sastrugi Furrowed by the Mighty Winds of the Plateau, 250 Miles S.S.E. of Winter Quarters, Adelie Land

Under Reefed Sail. Southern Party 290 Miles S.S.E. of Winter Quarters, Adelie Land

days' at two hundred miles, and five days' at sixty-seven miles, so with luck we should not go hungry, but Webb wants to get five more full sets of dips if possible on the way back, and this means two and a half days."

That night the minimum thermometer registered its lowest at −25° F. It was December 21 and Midsummer Day, so we concluded that the spot would be a very chilly one in the winter.

At this juncture we were very short of finnesko. The new ones we had worn since the two-hundred-mile camp had moulted badly and were now almost "bald." The stitching wears through as soon as the hair comes off and frequent mending is necessary.

We rose earlier than usual on the 22nd, so as to get more advantage from the wind, which each evening had always tended to die down somewhat. With forty-two square feet of sail, the twenty-mile wind was too much for us, the sledge capsizing on the smallest pretext. Instead of hanging the yard from the top of the mast, we placed it across the load, reversing the sail and hooking the clews over the top of the mast. Three or four pieces of lampwick at intervals served as reefing-points by which the area of the sail could be quickly cut down by bunching the upper part as much as was necessary.

During the day we frequently saw our tracks in patches of snow left during a previous snowfall, but they were much eroded, although only three days old. After sledging in Adelie Land it is hard to realize that on certain parts of the Ross Barrier tracks a year old may remain visible.

After passing the two-hundred-and-eighty-three-mile mound, the sledge-meter became very sickly. Spoke after spoke had parted and we saw that nothing we could do would make it last very much longer. As we intended in one place to make a cross-country run of seventy miles, so as to cut off the detour to the "Nodules," the meter was carried on the sledge. We had now the mounds to check distances.

On December 23 we were lucky enough to catch sight of the two-hundred-and-sixty-nine-mile mound and later the one at two hundred and sixty-one miles, though there was a good deal of drift. The day's run was twenty and a half miles.

A thing which helped us unexpectedly was that, now with the wind behind, we found it unnecessary to wear the stiff, heavy, frozen, burberry trousers. Thick pyjama trousers took their place in all except the worst weather.

At our old two-hundred-and-forty-nine-mile camp, Webb took a complete set of magnetic observations and another time-shot for watch-rate. It was late when these were over, so we did only two and a half miles more, halting for Christmas Eve, well content with a run of fourteen miles in addition to a set of observations.

On Christmas Day the country was very rough, making sailing difficult. Still, eighteen and a half miles were left behind. The wind was practically along the sastrugi and the course was diagonal to both. As the sledge strikes each sastruga, it skids northwards along it to the discomfort of the wheelers and the disgust of the leader.

For Christmas dinner that night we had to content ourselves with revising the menu for the meal which was to celebrate the two-hundred-mile depot. But now it was all pretty well mapped out, having been matured in its finer details for several days on the march. Hors d'oeuvre, soup, meat, pudding, sweets and wine were all designed, and estimates were out. Would we pick up the depot soon enough to justify an "auspicious occasion"?

Next day the wind was due south at thirty miles per hour. Dodging big ramps and overturning on sastrugi, at the same time dragging well upwind of the course to save leeway, twelve miles went by without the two-hundred-and-fifteen-mile mound coming into sight. Finally, a search with the glasses through falling snow revealed it a good two miles back. As we particularly wanted some photos of the ramps at this camp, we made across to it and had lunch there, Hurley exposing the last of the films.

At two hundred and nine miles "Lot's Wife" appeared—a tall, thin mound which Hurley had erected during a lunch-camp on the way out.

On the 27th, with a thirty-five-mile wind and a good deal of drift, we did not see the two-hundred-and-three-mile mound until we almost ran into it. By three o'clock the great event occurred—the depot was found! We determined to hold the Christmas feast. After a cup of tea and a bit of biscuit, the rest of the lunch ration was put aside.

Webb set up his instrument in the lee of the big mound and commenced a set of observations; I sorted out gear from the depot and rearranged the sledge load; Hurley was busy in the tent concocting all kinds of dishes. As the tableware was limited to three mugs and the Nansen cooker, we had to come in to deal with each course the moment it was ready. Aiming at a really high-class meal, Hurley had started by actually cleaning out the cooker.

The absence of reindeer-hair and other oddments made everything taste quite strange, though the basis was still the same old ration with a few remaining "perks." After the "raisin gliders," soup and a good stiff hoosh, Webb finished his observations while I recorded for him. It is wonderful what sledging does for the appetite. For the first week of the journey, the unaccustomed ration was too much for us; but now when Hurley announced "Pudding!" we were all still ravenous. It was a fine example of ye goode olde English plum-pudding, made from biscuit grated with the Bonsa-saw, fat picked out of the pemmican, raisins and glaxo-and-sugar, all boiled in an old food-bag.

This pudding was so filling that we could hardly struggle through a savoury, "Angels on runners," and cocoa. There was a general recovery when the "wine" was produced, made from stewed raisins and primus alcohol; and "The King" was toasted with much gusto. At the first sip, to say the least, we were disappointed. The rule of "no heel taps" nearly settled us, and quite a long interval and cigars, saved up for the occasion by Webb, were necessary before we could get courage enough to drink to the Other Sledging Parties and Our Supporting Party.

The sun was low in the south when, cigars out and conversation lagging, we finally toggled in for the finest sleep of the whole journey.

The cook, under a doubtful inspiration, broke forth, later on, into a Christmas Carol:

> I've dined in many places but never such as these-
>
> It's like the Gates of Heaven when you find you've lost the keys.
>
> I've dined with kings and emperors, perhaps you scarce believe;
>
> And even they do funny things when round comes Christmas Eve.
>
> I've feasted with iguanas on a lonely desert isle;
>
> Once in the shade of a wattle by a maiden's winsome smile.
>
> I've "grubbed" at a threepenny hash-house, I've been at a counter-lunch,
>
> Reclined at a slap-up café where only the "swankers" munch.
>
> In short, I've dined from Horn to Cape and up Alaska-way
>
> But the finest, funniest dinner of all was on that Xmas Day.

For the first ten miles on the afternoon of the 28th, the sail was reefed down to prevent the sledge overrunning us on smooth patches. Not far past the one-hundred-and-ninety-mile mound, which was missed in the drift, we picked up some of the outward tracks—a bas-relief of three footsteps and a yard of sledge-meter track, raised half an inch and undercut by the wind. It was not very much, but quite a comfort when one is navigating in blinding weather.

At 11.30 PM we had marched twenty-one miles, and both light and surface were improving, so I proposed making a long run of it. Hurley and Webb eagerly agreed, and we had a preparatory hoosh. Ten miles scudded by monotonously without a sign of the mounds around the one-hundred-and-seventy-mile camp. As we were in the vicinity of a point where we had determined to diverge from our outward track, a course was laid direct for the one-hundred-and-thirteen-mile mark. The sledge-meter, which had been affixed, made its presence evident from time to time by ringing like a cash register, as still another broken spoke struck the forks. We would halt for a moment and extract the remains. Out of the original thirty-six wire spokes, only twelve wire and one wooden one remained. At 11.30 AM on December 29, a halt was called and the sledge-meter was then lying over on its side with a helpless expression. It indicated twenty-two miles, making, so we thought, a total of forty-three miles in the twenty-two and a quarter hours since leaving the depot. Observations for position next day proved that in its dying effort it exaggerated the truth; the total run being 41.6 miles.

We were now well ahead of schedule time, there being four and a half days' surplus food; above what was probably required to reach the sixty-seven-and-a-half-mile depot. It was decided to hold three days of this and to use one and a half days food as a bonus during the coming week, as long as we were ahead of our necessary distance. The sledging ration is quite enough to live on, but for the whole of the journey we had felt that we could have done more distance on a slightly larger ration. This may be partly explained by our comparatively high altitude.

Next morning the sledge-meter was cut away and stuck in the snow. It looked very forlorn sitting askew in its forks, with a pair of worn-out finnesko hanging over it.

After twelve miles with a favourable wind, Webb took more observations; Hurley and I recording by turns. There were several small holes in the tent which needed mending, and I experimented with adhesive plaster from the medical kit with great success. Heated over a fusée and pressed hard down between the bottoms of mugs, held outside and inside, the patches adhered well and made a permanent job.

Early on December 31, 1912, snow was falling. The light gave Hurley an attack of snow-blindness and a miserable day. Crampons were worn to give some security to the foothold on the uneven track. The position, after a trudge of fifteen miles, was estimated at five miles east of the one-hundred-and-twenty-three-mile mound.

On New Year's Day, 1913, the wind was fresher and the surface improved. Estimation placed us to the north of one hundred and thirteen miles, but we were not hopeful in the light falling snow of seeing a mound. Soon, however, the snow ceased, and Webb made out a hillock two miles ahead. It was identified as the one at one hundred and nine miles.

It had been my turn to be snowblind. I was so bad that the only thing to do was to camp or ride on the sledge. The trail changed here to straight downwind, so Webb and Hurley undertook the job, hauling the sledge with me as a passenger for three and a half miles to the one-hundred-and-five-mile mound. It must have been a trying finish to a run of twenty miles.

In spite of the spell, which was a sleepless one, I was no better in the morning and again had to ride. The others pulled away for five miles with a good helping wind, but in a provoking light. The camp was made where the one-hundred-mile mound was judged to be. We spent longer over lunch, hoping that the clouds would clear. At last we moved on, or rather *I* was moved on. After two miles the surface became heavier. My eyes were better now on account of the rest and a snow "poultice" Webb had invented. I harnessed-in for five miles over light, unpacked snow, with piecrust underneath. The day's work was twelve miles.

The snow-clouds broke at noon on January 3, and a reliable latitude was obtained. It agreed with our reckoning. Persevering over the same trying surface as on the previous day, we sighted the ninety-mile-mound in the rear as a rift broke in the sky. We must have passed a few hundred yards from it.

We were still eleven miles from the depot, so at breakfast on the 4th the rations were reduced by one-half to give plenty of time to locate our goal. On the 4th the sky was clear, but surface drift prevented us from seeing any mounds till, in the afternoon, the ramps near the sixty-seven-mile depot were discovered in fitful glimpses. They bore too much to the north, so we altered course correspondingly to the west, camping in rising wind and drift, with great hopes for the morrow.

A densely overcast sky on the 5th; light snow falling! We moved on two miles, but not being able to see one hundred yards, camped again; then walking as far as seemed safe in various directions. One could do nothing but wait for clear weather. The clouds lightened at 6 PM and again at 9 PM, when altitudes of the sun were secured, putting us four miles south of the depot.

With only one chronometer watch, one has to rely entirely on dead reckoning for longitude, the rate of a single watch being very variable. The longitude obtained on this occasion from our latest known rate moved us several miles to the east of the depot, so I concluded that our distances since the camp at ninety miles had been overestimated, and that we were probably to the south-east of it. Accordingly, we shifted four miles to the north-west, but by this time it had again clouded over and nothing could be seen.

On the 6th the sky was still overcast, but a lucky peep at noon aligned us on the exact latitude of the depot. We walked east and west, but it snowed persistently and everything was invisible.

It is weary work waiting in the tent for weather to improve. During this time Hurley amused himself and us by composing a Christmas carol on the Christmas dinner; a fragment from which has already appeared. I whiled away a whole afternoon, cutting up the remains of two cigars which had refused to draw. Sliced up with a pair of scissors and mixed with a few of Hurley's cigarettes, they made very good smoking tobacco.

On the 7th the sky was immovable, and we trekked four miles due east, camped once more and walked about without finding our goal.

I now decided that if the weather did not improve by the morning, we should have to dash for the north. It was a risk, but matters were coming to a serious pass. On broaching the subject to Webb and Hurley, they unconditionally agreed with me.

At 3 AM the sky cleared rapidly and we turned out and saw the ramps plainly to the east. Webb set up the theodolite while Hurley and I paced out a half-mile base-line to find out the intervening distance. Just as we got to the end of it, however, the clouds came over again and the ramps faded.

There was only one thing for it now, and that was to make a break for the coast. Of food, there was one full day's ration with enough pemmican for half a hoosh, six lumps of sugar and nine raisins, rather the worse for wear, oil for two days, and, last but not least, a pint of alcohol. After four days on half-rations we felt fairly fit, thanks no doubt to the good meals of the previous week.

There were sixty-seven miles to go, and in case we did not happen on the narrow descent to the Hut, the food was apportioned to last for five days. Everything unessential was stripped off the sledge, including dip-circle, thermometers, hypsometer, camera, spare clothing and most of the medical and repair kits.

Hurley in Sledging Gear

At 7 AM we set off on the final stage of the journey. The sky was densely overcast and snow was falling, but there was a strong wind almost behind. We would march for an hour by my wrist-watch, halt for five minutes and on again till all agreed that we had covered ten miles; when it was lunch time. Each man's share of this consisted of one-third of a biscuit, one-third of an ounce of butter and a drink made of a spoonful of glaxo-and-sugar and one of absolute alcohol, mixed in a mug of lukewarm water. We could not afford oil enough to do much more than thaw the water, but the alcohol warmed us splendidly, enabling us to get a good rest.

After an hour's spell we started again, luckily seeing just enough of the sun to check the course. The wind grew stronger in the afternoon and several times dense fog-banks drove down on us. Meeting one steep rise, we sidled round it for what seemed hours, but my chief memory of that afternoon was of the clouds of the northern horizon. They were a deep bluish-grey colour—a typical "water-sky"—but I have never seen clouds moving so fast. It was like trying to steer by one particular phase in a kaleidoscope. When all were satisfied that twenty miles had been covered we camped.

Dinner consisted of a very watery hoosh, followed up by a mug of alcohol and water. We were all very thankful for the forethought of Dr. Mawson in providing absolute alcohol for lighting the primus, instead of methylated spirit.

Breakfast on the 9th was of about the same consistency as dinner on the night before, except that cocoa replaced the alcohol. In fact, breakfast was possibly even more watery, as I was in charge of the food-bag and surreptitiously decided to make the rations last six days instead of five.

This was the worst day's march of the journey. The wind was booming along at sixty miles per hour with dense drift and falling snow. What made it worse was that it came from the south-east, forcing us to pull partly across it. I was the upwind wheeler and had to hitch on to the side of the sledge to reduce the leeway as much as possible. The sledge was being continually jammed into big, old, invisible sastrugi and we fell about in the wind until crampons became absolutely necessary.

At 4 PM we were disgusted to find that the wind had veered to south-by-east. So for possibly several hours we had been doing Heaven only knows how many times the amount of work necessary, and for any time up to four hours might have been marching three points off our course. Being blown straight downwind, the sledge made rapid progress, and about 6 PM a halt was called for lunch. This was over almost as soon as it was begun, but we had a good rest, sheltering ourselves with the floor-cloth from the wind which blew through the tent.

Off again, we "plugged" away until midnight when we were much surprised to find the usual snow surface merging into blue ice. The tent was pitched on the latter, snow being procured from the bridge of a crevasse as we had no pick: even the ice-axe having been left behind.

Turning out on the morning of the 10th, we were delighted to find the sky clearing and the wind moderating. And then, far away on the northern horizon a beautiful line of blue sea dotted with bergs!

We now officially considered ourselves to be twenty-seven miles from the Hut. As we should not have met blue ice on the proper course till we were only thirteen miles out, it was thought that we had edged a long way to the east the day before. When a start was made, we manoeuvred to the west in looking for a crossing-place at each crevasse.

It was not long before the bergs on the horizon were noticeably enlarging, and at last we realized that in reality it was only a few miles to them. Suddenly the grade increased, the ice becoming much lacerated; and we had some trouble getting the sledge along. Hurley was snow-blind and had one eye covered. He looked very comical feeling his way over the crevasses, but he probably did not feel over-humorous.

I was in the lead, and suddenly coming over a ridge above a steep ice-fall, I caught sight of the Mackellar Islets and the old "Piano" berg. Just at the same instant the spur of ice on which I was standing collapsed, and down I went into a crevasse. The others quickly had me out, and, as soon as I was in the upper air, I gave them the news: "There are the Islands!" Being twenty feet farther back on the rope they had not yet seen them.

We were now able to place ourselves about three miles west of Aladdin's Cave. The last camp must have been thirteen miles from the Hut, and we had really done twenty-seven miles each day instead of our conservative twenty.

We tried to work along to the east, but the ice was too much broken, so the camp was made on a patch of snow. In view of our good fortune, I produced that evening's ration of hoosh in addition to our usual lunch. Even this meagre spree went against Hurley's feelings, for, being snow-blind, he had not been able to see the islands and positively would not believe that we were nearly home.

After lunch it was necessary to retrace our way upwind to get out of the rough country. About midnight, Webb recognized Aladdin's Cave. Hurley and I had a competition as to who should see it first, for I was also getting a little blind again. We had a dead-heat at one hundred and fifty yards.

The first thing to arrest our attention was a tin of dog biscuits. These kept things going till we dug out a food tank from which was rapidly extracted a week's supply of chocolate. After that we proceeded in a happier frame of mind to open up the cave and have a meal.

The journey of more than six hundred miles was now practically over. After a carousal lasting till 5 PM on the 11th, we went down hill, arriving just after dinner and finding all well.

We three had never thought the Hut quite such a fine place, nor have we ever since.

Correll on the Edge of a Ravine in the Ice-Sheet

Madigan's, Murphy's, and Stillwell's Parties Breaking Camp at Aladdin's Cave at the Commencement of the Summer Journeys

CHAPTER XV

Eastward Over the Sea-Ice

By C. T. MADIGAN

> Harnessed and girt in his canvas bands,
> Toggled and roped to his load;
> With helmeted head and bemittened hands,
> This for his spur and his goad:
>
> "Out in the derelict fastnesses bare
> Some whit of truth may be won."
> Be it a will o' the wisp, he will fare
> Forth to the rising sun.
> —*The Sledge Horse*

THE EASTERN COASTAL PARTY CONSISTED OF Dr. A. L. McLean, P. E. Correll and myself. For weeks all preparations had been made; the decking put on the sledge, runners polished, cooker- and instrument-boxes attached, mast erected, spar and sail rigged, instruments and clothing collected, tent strengthened—all the impedimenta of a sledge journey arranged and rearranged, and still the blizzard raged on. Would we never get away? November arrived, and still the wind kept up daily averages of over fifty miles per hour, with scarce a day without drifting snow.

At last it was decided that a start must soon be made even though it ended in failure, so that we received orders to set out on November 6, or the first possible day after it.

Friday November 8 broke, a clear driftless day, and Murphy's party left early in the morning. By noon, Stillwell's party (Stillwell, Hodgeman and

Close), and we, were ready to start. The former were bound on a short journey to the near east and were to support us until we parted company.

All was bustle and excitement. Every one turned out to see us off. Breaking an empty sauce-bottle over the bow of our sledge, we christened it the M.H.S. Championship (Man-Hauled Sledge). The name was no boastful prevision of mighty deeds, as, at the Hut, a "Championship" was understood to mean some careless action usually occasioning damage to property, while our party included several noted "champions."

Mertz harnessed a dog-team to the sledge and helped us up the first steep slope. With hearty handshakes and a generous cheer from the other fellows, we started off and were at last away, after many months of hibernation in the Hut, to chance the hurricanes and drifting snow and to push towards the unknown regions to the east.

At the steepest part of the rise we dismissed our helpers and said good-bye. McLean and Correll joined me on the sledge and we continued on to Aladdin's Cave.

As we mounted the glacier the wind increased, carrying surface drift which obscured the view to within one hundred yards. It was this which made us pass the Cave on the eastern side and pull up on a well-known patch of snow in a depression to the south of our goal. It was not long before a momentary clearing of the drift showed Aladdin's Cave with its piles of food-tanks, kerosene, dog biscuit and pemmican, and, to our dismay, a burberry-clad figure moving about among the accumulation. Murphy's party were in possession when we expected them to be on the way south to another cave—the Cathedral Grotto—eleven and three-quarter miles from the Hut. Of course the rising wind and drift had stopped them.

It was then 5 PM, so we did not wait to discuss the evident proposition as to which of the three parties should occupy the Cave, but climbed down into it at once and boiled up hoosh and tea. Borrowing tobacco from the supporting parties, we reclined at ease, and then in that hazy atmosphere so dear to smokers, its limpid blue enhanced by the pale azure of the ice, we introduced the subject of occupation as if it were a sudden afterthought.

It was soon decided to enlarge the Cave to accommodate five men, the other four consenting to squeeze into Stillwell's big tent. McLean volunteered to join Stillwell's party in the tent, while Correll and I were to stay in the Cave with Murphy and company.

I went outside and selected ten weeks' provisions from the pile of food-tanks and piled them beside the sledge. McLean attended to the thermograph which Bage and I had installed in the autumn. Meanwhile, in a fifty-mile wind, Stillwell and his men erected the tent. Hunter and

Laseron started with picks and shovels to enlarge the Cave, and, working in relays, we had soon expanded it to eight feet by seven feet.

The men from the tent came down to "high dinner" at eight o'clock. They reported weather conditions unimproved and the temperature –3° F.

Early next morning I dug my way out and found that the surface drift had increased with a wind of fifty-five miles per hour. It was obviously impossible to start.

After breakfast it was arranged that those outside should have their meals separately, digging down at intervals to let us know the state of the weather. It was not pleasant for us, congested as we were in the Cave, to have visitors sliding down through the opening with a small avalanche of snow in their train. Further, to increase their own discomfort, they arrived covered in snow, and what they were unable to shake off thawed and wet them, subsequently freezing again to the consistency of a starched collar.

The opening was, therefore, kept partly closed with a food-tank. The result was that a good deal of snow came in, while the hole diminished in size. For a man to try to crawl out in stiff burberrys appeared as futile as for a porcupine to try to go backwards up a canvas hose.

The day passed slowly in our impatience. We took turns at reading The *Virginian*, warmed by a primus stove which in a land of plenty we could afford to keep going. Later in the afternoon the smokers found that a match would not strike, and the primus went out. Then the man reading said that he felt unwell and could not see the words. Soon several others commented on feeling "queer," and two in the sleeping-bags had fallen into a drowsy slumber. On this evidence even the famous Watson would have "dropped to it," but it was some time before it dawned on us that the oxygen had given out. Then there was a rush for shovels. The snow, ice and food-tank were tightly wedged, at the mouth of the entrance, and it took some exertion to perforate through to the outside air with an ice-axe. At once every one speedily recovered. Later, another party had a worse experience, not forgetting to leave a warning note behind them. We should have done the same.

The weather was no better by the evening, and during the night the minimum thermometer registered –12° F.

At six o'clock on Sunday morning, November 10, McLean dug down to us with the news that the wind had abated to thirty miles per hour with light surface drift.

We hurried through breakfast, rolled up the bags and started packing the sledge. Three 100-lb. food-tanks, one 50-lb. bag opened for ready use, and four gallons of kerosene were selected. Stillwell took for us a 50-lb.

food-tank, a 56-lb. tin of wholemeal biscuits, and a gallon of kerosene. With the 850 lbs. of food, 45 lbs. of kerosene, three sleeping-bags of 10 lbs. each, a tent of 40 lbs., 86 lbs. of clothing and personal gear for three men, a cooker, primus, pick, shovel, ice-axe, alpine rope, dip-circle, theodolite, tripod, smaller instruments such as aneroid, barometer and thermometer, tools, medical outfit and sledge-fittings, our total load amounted to nearly 800 lbs., and Stillwell's was about the same.

All were ready at 9 AM, and, shaking hands with Murphy's party, who set off due south, we steered with Stillwell to the south-east. The preliminary instructions were to proceed south-east from the Cave to a distance of eighteen miles and there await the arrival of Dr. Mawson and his party, who were to overtake us with their dogteams.

The first few miles gave a gradual rise of one hundred feet per mile, so that, with a heavy load against wind and drift, travelling was very slow. The wind now dropped to almost calm, and the drift cleared. In the afternoon progress was hampered by crevasses, which were very frequent, running east and west and from one to twenty feet in width. The wider ones were covered with firm snow-bridges; the snow in places having formed into granular and even solid ice. What caused most delay were the detours of several hundreds of yards which had to be made to find a safe crossing over a long, wide crevasse. At 6.30 PM we pitched camp, having only made five miles from the Cave.

We got away at 9 AM the next morning. Throughout the whole journey we thought over the same mysterious problem as confronted many another sledger: Where did the time go to in the mornings? Despite all our efforts we could not cut down the interval from "rise and shine" to the start below two hours.

Early that day we had our first experience of the treacherous crevasse. Correll went down a fissure about three feet wide. I had jumped across it, thinking the bridge looked thin, but Correll stepped on it and went through. He dropped vertically down the full length of his harness—six feet. McLean and I soon had him out. The icy walls fell sheer for about sixty feet, where snow could be seen in the blue depths. Our respect for crevasses rapidly increased after this, and we took greater precautions, shuddering to think of the light-hearted way we had trudged over the wider ones.

At twelve miles, blue, wind-swept ice gave place to an almost flat snow surface. Meanwhile the sky had rapidly clouded over, and the outlook was threatening. The light became worse, and the sastrugi indistinguishable. Such a phenomenon always occurs on what we came to call a "snow-blind day." On these days the sky is covered with a white, even pall of cloud, and cloud and plateau seem as one. One walks into a deep trench or a sastruga

two feet high without noticing it. The world seems one huge, white void, and the only difference between it and the pitch-dark night is that the one is white and the other black.

Light snow commenced at 2.30 PM, the wind rising to forty-five miles per hour with heavy drift. Thirteen miles out we pitched camp.

This, the first "snow-blind day" claimed McLean for its victim. By the time we were under cover of the tent, his eyes were very sore, aching with a throbbing pain. At his request I placed a zinc-cocaine tablet in each eye. He spent the rest of the day in the darkness of his sleeping-bag and had his eyes bandaged all next day. Up till then we had not worn goggles, but were careful afterwards to use them on the trying, overcast days.

For four and a half days the weather was too bad to travel. On the 14th the wind increased and became steady at sixty miles per hour, accompanied by dense drifting snow. We found it very monotonous lying in the tent. As always happens during heavy drifts, the temperature outside was high, on this day averaging about 12 degrees F.; inside the tent it was above freezing-point, and the accompanying thaw was most unpleasant.

Stillwell's party had pitched their tent about ten paces to the leeward side of ours, of which stratagem they continually reminded us. Going outside for food to supply our two small meals per day was an operation fraught with much discomfort to all. This is what used to happen. The man on whom the duty fell had to insinuate himself into a bundle of wet burberrys, and, as soon as he was outside, they froze stiff. When, after a while, he signified his intention of coming in, the other two would collect everything to one end of the tent and roll up the floor-cloth. Plastered with snow, he entered, and, despite every precaution, in removing burberrys and brushing himself he would scatter snow about and increase the general wetness. On these excursions we would visit Stillwell's tent and be hospitably, if somewhat gingerly, admitted; the inmates drawing back and pulling away their sleeping-bags as from one with a fell disease. As a supporting party they were good company, among other things, supplying us with tobacco *ad libitum*. When we parted, five days after, we missed them very much.

During the night the wind blew harder than ever—that terrible wind, laden with snow, that blows for ever across the vast, mysterious plateau, the "wind that shrills all night in a waste land, where no one comes or hath come since the making of the world." In the early hours of the morning it reached eighty miles per hour.

Not till 9 next morning did the sky clear and the drift diminish. Considering that it had taken us eight days to do thirteen miles, we decided to move on the 16th at any cost.

Our library consisted of *An Anthology of Australian Verse*, Thackeray's *Vanity Fair* and *Hints to Travellers* in two volumes. McLean spent much of the time reading the Anthology and I started *Vanity Fair*. The latter beguiled many weary hours in that tent during the journey. I read a good deal aloud and McLean read it afterwards. Correll used to pass the days of confinement arranging rations and costs for cycling tours and designing wonderful stoves and cooking utensils, all on the sledging, "cut down weight" principle.

On the 16th we were off at 9 AM with a blue sky above and a "beam" wind of thirty-five miles per hour. Up a gentle slope over small sastrugi the going was heavy. We went back to help Stillwell's party occasionally, as we were moving a little faster.

Just after lunch I saw a small black spot on the horizon to the south. Was it a man? How could Dr. Mawson have got there? We stopped and saw that Stillwell had noticed it too. Field-glasses showed it to be a man approaching, about one and a half miles away. We left our sledges in a body to meet him, imagining all kinds of wonderful things such as the possibility of it being a member of Wild's party—we did not know where Wild had been landed. All the theories vanished when the figure assumed the well-known form of Dr. Mawson. He had made a little more south than we, and his sledges were just out of sight, about two miles away.

Soon Mertz and Ninnis came into view with a dog-team, which was harnessed on to one sledge. All hands pulled the other sledge, and we came up fifteen minutes later with Dr. Mawson's camp at eighteen and a quarter miles. In the good Australian way we sat round a large pot of tea and after several cups put up our two tents.

It was a happy evening with the three tents grouped together and the dogs securely picketed on the great plateau, forming the only spot on the limitless plain. Every one was excited at the prospect of the weeks ahead; the mystery and charm of the "unknown" had taken a strange hold on us.

Ninnis and Mertz came into our tent for a short talk before turning in. Mertz sang the old German student song:

> *Studio auf einer Reis'*
> *Immer sich zu helfen weis*
> *Immer fort durch's Dick und Dunn*
> *Schlendert es durch's Leben hin.*

We were nearly all University graduates. We knew that this would be our last evening together till all were safely back at the Hut. No thought was farther from our minds than that it was the last evening we would ever spend with two companions, who had been our dear comrades for just a year.

Before turning into sleeping-bags, a messenger brought me dispatches from the general's tent—a letter on the plateau. This proved to be the instructions to the Eastern Coastal Party. Arriving back at the Hut by January 15, we were to ascertain as much as possible of the coast lying east of the Mertz Glacier, investigating its broad features and carrying out the following scientific work: magnetic, biological and geological observations, the character, especially the nature and size of the grains of ice or snow surfaces, details of sastrugi, topographical features, heights and distances, and meteorology.

On Sunday, November 17, we moved on together to the east with the wind at fifteen miles an hour, the temperature being 9° F. The sun shone strongly soon after the start, and with four miles to our credit a tent was run up at 1 PM, and all lunched together on tea, biscuit, butter and chocolate. Up to this time we had had only three *al fresco* lunches, but, as the weather seemed to be much milder and the benefit of tea and a rest by the way were so great, we decided to use the tent in future, and did so throughout the journey.

In the afternoon, Dr. Mawson's party forged ahead, the dogs romping along on a downhill grade. We took the bit in our teeth as we saw them sitting on their sledges, growing smaller and smaller in front of us. We came up with them again as they had waited to exchange a few more words at a point on the track where a long extent of coast to the east came into view.

Here we bade a final adieu to Dr. Mawson, Mertz and Ninnis. The surface was on the down grade towards the east, and with a cheer and farewell wave they started off, Mertz walking rapidly ahead, followed by Ninnis and Dr. Mawson with their sledges and teams. They were soon lost to view behind the rolling undulations.

A mile farther on we pitched camp at 8 PM in a slight depression just out of sight of the sea. Every one slept soundly after a good day's pulling.

November 18 was a bright dazzling day, the sky dotted with fleecy alto-cumulus. At 6 AM we were out to find Stillwell's party moving in their tent. There was a rush for shovels to fill the cookers with snow and a race to boil hoosh.

At this camp we tallied up the provisions, with the intention of taking what we might require from Stillwell and proceeding independently of him, as he was likely to leave us any day. There were fifty-nine days to go until January 15, 1913, the latest date of arrival back at the Hut, for which eight weeks' rations were considered to be sufficient. There were seven weeks' food on the sledge, so Stillwell handed over another fifty-pound bag as well as an odd five pounds of wholemeal biscuit. The total amount of kerosene was five gallons, with a bottle of methylated spirit.

Shortly after eight o'clock we caught sight of Dr. Mawson's camp, and set sail to make up the interval. This we did literally as there was a light westerly breeze—the only west wind we encountered during the whole journey.

The sledge was provided with a bamboo mast, seven feet high, stepped behind the cooker-box and stayed fore and aft with wire. The yard was a bamboo of six feet, slung from the top of the mast, its height being varied by altering the length of the slings. The bamboo was threaded through canvas leads in the floor-cloth which provided a spread of thirty square feet of sail. It was often such an ample area that it had to be reefed from below.

With the grade sloping gently down and the wind freshening, the pace became so hot that the sledge often overran us. A spurious "Epic of the East" (see *Adelie Blizzard*) records it:

> Crowd on the sail—
> Let her speed full and free "on the run"
> Over knife-edge and glaze, marble polish and pulverized chalk
> The finnesko glide in the race, and there's no time for talk.
> Up hill, down dale,
> It's all in the game and the fun.

We rapidly neared Dr. Mawson's camp, but when we were within a few miles of it, the other party started in a south-easterly direction and were soon lost to sight. Our course was due east.

At thirty-three and a half miles the sea was in sight, some fine flat-topped bergs floating in the nearest bay. Suddenly a dark, rocky nunatak sprang into view on our left. It was a sudden contrast after ten days of unchanging whiteness, and we felt very anxious to visit this new find. As it was in Stillwell's limited territory we left it to him.

According to the rhymester it was:

> A rock by the way—
> A spot in the circle of white—
> A grey, craggy spur plunging stark through the deep-splintered ice.
> A trifle! you say, but a glow of warm land may suffice
> To brighten a day
> Prolonged to a midsummer night.

After leaving Aladdin's Cave, our sledge-meter had worked quite satisfactorily. Just before noon, the casting attaching the recording-dial to the forks broke—the first of a series of break-downs. Correll bound it up with copper wire and splints borrowed from the medical outfit.

The wind died away and the sail was of little use. In addition to this, we met with a slight up grade on the eastern side of the depression, our rate diminishing accordingly. At 7 PM the tent was pitched in dead calm, after a day's run of fifteen miles with a full load of almost eight hundred pounds—a record which remained unbroken with us till near the end of the outward journey. Looking back, the nunatak and bergs were still visible.

Both parties were under way at 8 AM next day (November 19) on a calm and sunny morning. The course by sun-compass was set due east.

At noon I took a latitude "shot" with the three-inch Cary theodolite. This little instrument proved very satisfactory and was easily handled in the cold. In latitude 67° 15' south, forty-six and a half miles east of the Hut, we were once more on level country with a high rise to the north-east and another shallow gully in front.

A fog which had been moving along the sea-front in an opaque wall drifted over the land and enveloped us. Beautiful crystals of ice in the form of rosettes and small fern-fronds were deposited on the cordage of the sail and mast. One moment the mists would clear, and the next, we could not see more than a few hundred yards.

We now parted with Stillwell, Hodgeman and Close, who turned off to a rising knoll—Mount Hunt—visible in the north-east, and disappeared in the fog.

After the halt at noon the sastrugi became much larger and softer. The fog cleared at 2 PM and the sun came out and shone very fiercely. A very inquisitive skua gull—the first sign of life we had seen thus far—flew around the tent and settled on the snow near by. In the calm, the heat was excessive and great thirst attacked us all the afternoon, which I attempted to assuage at every halt by holding snow in my hands and licking the drops of water off my knuckles—a cold and unsatisfactory expedient. We travelled without burberrys—at that time quite a novel sensation—wearing only fleece suits and light woollen undergarments. Correll pulled for the greater part of the afternoon in underclothing alone.

At forty-nine and a half miles a new and wonderful panorama opened before us. The sea lay just below, sweeping as a narrow gulf into the great, flat plain of debouching glacier-tongue which ebbed away north into the foggy horizon. A small ice-capped island was set like a pearl in the amethyst water. To the east, the glacier seemed to fuse with the blue line of the hinterland. Southward, the snowy slope rose quickly, and the far distance was unseen.

We marched for three-quarters of a mile to where a steep down grade commenced. Here I made a sketch and took a round of angles to all prominent features, and the conspicuous, jutting, seaward points of the glacier. McLean and Correll were busy making a snow cairn, six feet high, to serve as a back-sight for angles to be taken at a higher eminence southward.

We set out for the latter, and after going one and a half miles it was late enough to camp. During the day we had all got very sunburnt, and our faces were flushed and smarting painfully. After the long winter at the Hut the skin had become more delicate than usual.

Under a clear sky, the wind came down during the night at forty-five miles per hour, lashing surface drift against the walls of the tent. It was not till ten o'clock that the sledge started, breaking a heavy trail in snow which became more and more like brittle piecrust. There was at first a slight descent, and then we strained up the eminence to the south over high sastrugi running almost north and south. Capsizes became frequent, and to extricate the heavy sledge from some of the deep furrows it was necessary to unload the food-bags. The drift running over the ground was troublesome when we sat down for a rest, but, in marching, our heads were just clear of it.

It was a long laborious day, and the four miles indicated by the inexorable sledge-meter seemed a miserable result. However, near the top of the hill there was a rich reward. A small nunatak slanted like a steel-blue shadow on the side of a white peak to the south-west. There was great excitement, and the sledge slid along its tracks with new life. It was rock without a doubt, and there was no one to dispute it with us. While speculating wildly as to its distance, we came unexpectedly to the summit of the hill.

The wind had subsided, the sky was clear and the sun stood low in the south-west. Our view had widened to a noble outlook. The sea, a delicate turquoise-blue, lay in the foreground of the low, white, northern ice-cliffs. Away to the east was the dim suggestion of land across the bed of the glacier, about which circled the southerly highlands of the plateau, buried at times in the haze of distance. Due south, twenty miles away, projecting from the glacier, was another island of rock. The nunatak first seen, not many miles to the south-west, was a snowy mountain streaked with sprouting rock, rising solitary in an indentation of the land. We honoured our Ship by calling it Aurora Peak, while our camp stood on what was thenceforth to be Mount Murchison.

It was obvious that this was the place for our first depot. I had decided, too, to make it the first magnetic station and the point from which to visit and explore Aurora Peak. None of us made any demur over a short halt. Correll had strained his back during the day from pulling too hard, and was troubled with a bleeding nose. My face was very sore from sunburn, with one eye swollen and almost closed, and McLean's eyes had not yet recovered from their first attack of snow-blindness.

November 21 was a day in camp. Most of the morning I spent trying, with Correll's help, to get the declination needle to set. Its pivot had been destroyed in transit and Correll had replaced it by a gramophone needle, which was found too insensitive. There was nothing to do but use the three-inch theodolite, which, setting to one degree, would give a good result, with a mean of thirty-two settings, for a region with such variable magnetic declination. A latitude "shot" was made at noon, and in the afternoon I took a set of dip determinations. These, with a panoramic sketch from the camp, a round of angles to conspicuous points and an observation at 5.30 PM for time and azimuth completed the day's work. Correll did the recording.

Meanwhile, McLean had built an eight-feet snow mound, erected a depot flag upon it and taken several photographs.

The next day was devoted to an excursion to Aurora Peak. The weather was, to our surprise, quite clear and calm. Armed with the paraphernalia for a day's tour, we set off down the slope. Correll put the primus stove and the inner pot of the cooker in the ready food-bag, McLean slung on his camera and the aneroid barometer, while I took my ruck-sack with the rations, as well as field-glasses and an ice-axe. In case of crevasses, we attached ourselves to an alpine rope in long procession. According to the "Epic" it was something like this:

> We saddled up, adventure-bent;
> Locked up the house—I mean the tent—
> Took "grub" enough for three young men
> With appetite to equal ten.
> A day's outing across the vale.
> Aurora Peak! What ho! All hail!
>
> We waltzed a'down the silvered slope,
> Connected by an Alpine rope;
> "Madi" in front with ice-axe armed,
> For fear that we should feel alarmed.
> Glad was the hour, and—what a lark!
> Explorers three? "Save the mark!"

The mystery of the nunatak was about to be solved. Apparently it rose from the level of the glacier, as our descent showed its eastern flank more clearly outlined. It was three miles to the bottom of the gully, and the aneroid barometer registered one thousand one hundred and ninety feet. The surface was soft and yielding to finnesko crampons, which sank through in places till the snow gripped the knees.

Ascending on the other side we crossed a small crevasse and the peak towered above us. The northern side terminated in a perpendicular face of ice, below which a deep basin had been "scalloped" away; evidently kept clear by eddies of wind. In it lay broken fragments of the overhanging cliff. The rock was a wide, outcropping band curving steeply to the summit on the eastern aspect.

After a stiff climb we hurried eagerly to the rock as if it were a mine of inexhaustible treasure. The boulders were all weathered a bright red and were much pitted where ferruginous minerals were leached out. The rock was a highly quartzose gneiss, with black bands of schist running through it. Moss and lichens were plentiful, and McLean collected specimens.

The rocky strip was eighty feet wide and three hundred feet high, so, making a cache of the primus, provisions and burberrys, we followed it up till it became so steep that it was necessary to change to the snow. This was in the form of hard névé with patches of ice. I went first, cutting steps with the ice-axe, and the others followed on the rope. The last ten of more than one hundred steps were in an almost vertical face, which gave a somewhat precarious foothold.

At 11.30 AM we stood on the summit at an altitude of one thousand seven hundred and fifty feet, while across the valley to the north-east rose Mount Murchison, one hundred and fourteen feet higher. The top of the ridge was quite a knife-edge, with barely space for standing. It ran mainly north and south, dipping in the centre, to curve away sharply westward to a higher eminence. At the bend was an inaccessible patch of rock. The surrounding view was much the same at that on Mount Murchison.

The Union Jack and the Australian flag were erected on a bamboo, and photographs taken. At the same time, low, threatening clouds rapidly emerged from the southeast, covering the sun and creating the "snow-blind" light. This was rather alarming as the climb had been difficult enough under a clear sky, and the descent was certainly much more difficult. So we hastily ate some chocolate and discussed the best way down.

Prospecting to the north, in search of a long snow ramp which appeared to run away in that direction, we scrambled down to the edge of a wide snowy crevasse full of blue chinks.

Turning back, we considered the chances of sliding down a steep scoured hollow to the west and finally decided to descend by the track we had cut.

McLean started off first down the steps and was out of sight in a few moments. When the rope tightened, Correll followed him and then I came last. It was very ticklish work feeling for the steps below with one's feet, and, as we signalled to one another in turn after moving a step, it took more than an hour to reach a safe position on the rocks. With every step I drove my axe into the ice, so that if the others had fallen there would still have been a last chance.

There was no time to be wasted; light snow was falling with the prospect of becoming thicker. In the gully the snowfall became heavy, limiting the view to within a few hundred yards. We advanced up the hill in what seemed to be the steepest direction, but circled half-way round it before finding out that the course was wrong. Aimlessly trying to place the broad flat summit I came across tracks in the snow, which were then carefully followed and led to the tent. The wind was rising outside and the hoosh in steaming mugs was eaten with extra relish in our snug retreat.

Specimens were labelled to be deposed and provisions were arranged for the rest of the journey. It was evident that we had superfluous clothing, and so the weight of the kit-bags was scrupulously cut down. By the time we crawled into sleeping-bags, everything dispensable was piled alongside the depot-flag.

We slept the sleep of the weary and did not hear the flapping tent nor the hissing drift. At 6 AM the wind was doing forty miles per hour and the air was filled with snow. It must have been a new climate, for by noon the sun had unexpectedly broken through, the wind was becoming gusty and the drift trailed like scud over the surface.

With six weeks' food we set off on a new trail after lunch. The way to the eastern glacier—Mertz Glacier—issued through the mouth of the gully, which ran in an easterly direction between Aurora Peak and Mount Murchison. On Mount Murchison ice-falls and crevasses began a short distance east of our first line of descent, but yet I thought a slight deviation to the east of south would bring us safely into the valley, and, at the same time, cut off a mile. Alas! it proved to be one of those "best-laid schemes."

The load commenced to glide so quickly as we were leaving the crest of the mountain that Correll and McLean unhitched from the hauling line and attached themselves by the alpine rope to the rear of the sledge, braking its progress. I remained harnessed in front keeping the direction. For two miles we were going downhill at a running pace and then the slope became suddenly steeper and the sledge overtook me. I had expected crevasses, in view of which I did not like all the loose rope behind me. Looking round, I shouted to the others to hold back the sledge, proceeding a few steps while doing so. The bow of the sledge was almost at my feet, when—whizz! I was dropping down through space. The length of the hauling rope was twenty-four feet, and I was at the end of it. I cannot say that "my past life flashed before me." I just had time to think "Now for the jerk—will my harness hold?" when there was a wrench, and I was hanging breathless over the blue depth. Then the most anxious moment came—I continued to descend. A glance showed me that the crevasse was only four feet wide, so the sledge could not follow me, and I knew with a thankful heart that I was safe. I only descended about two feet more, and then stopped. I knew my companions had pulled up the sledge and would be anchoring it with the ice-axe.

I had a few moments in which to take in my surroundings. Opposite to me was a vertical wall of ice, and below a beautiful blue, darkening to black in that unseen chasm. On either hand the rift of the crevasse extended, and above was the small hole in the snow bridge through which I had shot.

Soon I heard McLean calling, "Are you all right?" And I answered in what he and Correll thought an alarmingly distant voice. They started enlarging the hole to pull me out, until lumps of snow began to fall and I had to yell for mercy. Then I felt they were hauling, and slowly I rose to daylight.

The Surface of the Continental Ice-Sheet in the Coastal Region Where It Is Badly Crevassed

Working the Sledge Through Broken Sea Ice, 46 Miles off King George V Land. Madigan, Correll and Mclean

The crevasse ran westward along the gully, forcing us to make a detour through a maze of smaller cracks. We had to retreat up the hill in one place, throwing off half the load and carrying it on in relays. There was a blistering sun and the work was hard. At last the sledge came to a clear run and tobogganed into the snow-filled valley, turning eastward towards its outlet.

At the evening camp the sledge-meter indicated that our distance eastward of the Hut was sixty miles, one thousand two hundred yards. The northern face of the gully was very broken and great sentinel pillars of ice stood out among the yawning caves, some of them leaning like the tower of Pisa, others having fallen and rolled in shattered blocks. Filling the vision to the south-west was Aurora Peak, in crisp silhouette against a glorious radiant of cirrus cloud.

Reviewing the day through our peaceful smoke-rings, I was rather comforted by the fact that the fall into the crevasse had thoroughly tested my harness. Correll expressed himself as perfectly satisfied with his test. McLean seemed to feel somewhat out of it, being the only one without a crevasse experience; which happy state he maintained until the end, apparently somewhat to his disappointment.

On the 24th we broke camp at 9 AM, continuing down the gully towards the glacier. A lofty wall of rocks, set within a frame of ice, was observed on our left, one mile away. To it we diverged and found it to be gneiss similar to that of Aurora Peak. Several photos were taken.

The land was at our back and the margin of the glacier had been crossed. Only too soon we were in the midst of terribly crevassed ground, through which one could only thread a slow and zig-zag course. The blue ice was riven in every direction by gaping quarries and rose smooth and slippery on the ridges which broke the surface into long waves. Shod with crampons, the rear of the sledge secured by a tail-rope, we had a trying afternoon guiding the load along the narrow ridges of ice with precipices on either hand. Fortunately the wind was not above twenty miles per hour. As the frivolous "Epic" had it:

> Odds fish! the solid sea is sorely rent,
> And all around we're pent
> With quarries, chasms, pits, depressions vast,
> Their snow-lids overcast.
>
> A devious track, all curved and serpentine
> Round snow-lids superfine.
> On jutting brinks and precipices sheer
> Precariously we steer.

We pushed on to find a place in which to camp, as there was scarcely safe standing-room for a primus stove. At seventy miles the broken ice gave way to a level expanse of hard sastrugi dotted all over with small mounds of ice about four feet high. After hoosh, a friendly little Wilson petrel came flying from the northern sea to our tent. We considered it to be a good omen.

Next day the icy mounds disappeared, to be replaced by a fine, flat surface, and the day's march amounted to eleven and a quarter miles.

At 11 AM four snow petrels visited us, circling round in great curiosity. It is a cheerful thing to see these birds amid the lone, inhospitable ice.

We were taking in the surroundings from our position off the land scanning the far coast to the south for rock and turning round to admire the bold contours of Aurora Peak and Mount Murchison at our back. Occasionally there were areas of rubbly snow, blue ice and crevasses completely filled with snow, of prodigious dimensions, two hundred to three hundred yards wide and running as far as the eye could travel. The snow filling them was perfectly firm, but, almost always along the windward edge, probing with an ice-axe would disclose a fissure. This part of the Mertz Glacier was apparently afloat.

The lucky Wilson petrel came again in the evening. At this stage the daily temperatures ranged between 10° F. and near freezing-point. The greater part of November 26 was passed in the tent, within another zone of crevasses. The overcast sky made the light so bad that it became dangerous to go ahead. At 5.30 PM we started, and managed to do five and a half miles before 8 PM.

It was rather an eventful day, when across the undulating sastrugi there appeared a series of shallow valleys running eastward. As the valleys approached closer, the ground sloped down to meet them, their sides becoming steeper, buckled and broken. Proceeding ahead on an easterly course, our march came to an abrupt termination on an ice-bluff.

In front lay a perfectly flat snow-covered plain—the sea-ice. In point of fact we had arrived at the eastern side of the Mertz Glacier and were about fifteen miles north of the mainland. Old sea-ice, deeply covered in snow, lay ahead for miles, and the hazy, blue coast sank below the horizon in the south-east, running for a time parallel to the course we were about to take. It was some time before we realized all this, but at noon on the following day there came the first reminder of the proximity of sea-water.

An Adelie penguin, skiing on its breast from the north, surprised us suddenly by a loud croak at the rear of the sledge. As astonished as we were, it stopped and stared, and then in sudden terror made off. But before starting on its long trek to the land, it had to be captured and photographed.

To the south the coast was marked by two faces of rock and a short, dark spur protruding from beneath the ice-cap. As our friendly penguin had made off in that direction, we elected to call the place Penguin Point, intending to touch there on the return journey. During the afternoon magnetic dips and a round of angles to the prominences of the mainland were taken.

The next evidence on the sea-ice question came in the shape of a line of broken slabs of ice to the north, sticking out of the snow like the ruins of an ancient graveyard. At one hundred and fifteen miles the line was so close that we left the sledge to investigate it, finding a depression ten feet deep, through which wound a glistening riband of sea-water. It reminded one of a creek in flat, Australian country, and the illusion was sustained by a dark skua gull—in its slow flight much like a crow. It was a fissure in old thick sea-ice.

Sunday, and the first day of December, brought good weather and a clear view of the mainland. A bay opened to the east of Penguin Point, from which the coast trended to the south-east. Across a crack in the sea-ice we could just distinguish a low indented line like the glacier-tongue, we had already crossed. It might have been a long promontory of land for all we knew. Behind it was a continuous ice-blink and on our left, to the north, a deep blue "water sky." It seemed worth while continuing on an easterly course approximately parallel with the coast.

We were faced by another glacier-tongue; a fact which remained unproven for a week at least. From the sea-ice on to the glacier—the Ninnis Glacier—there was a gentle rise to a prominent knoll of one hundred and seventy feet. Here our distance from the Hut amounted to one hundred and fifty-two miles, and the spot was reckoned a good situation for the last depot.

In taking magnetic observations, it was interesting to find that the "dip" amounted to 87° 44', while the declination, which had varied towards the west, swung at this our most northerly station a few degrees to the east. We were curving round the South Magnetic Pole. Many points on the coast were fixed from an adjoining hill to which Correll and I trudged through sandy snow, while McLean stayed behind erecting the depot-mound, placing a food-bag, kerosene tin, black cloth and miner's pick on the top.

With four weeks' provisions we made a new start to cross the Ninnis Glacier on December 3, changing course to E. 30° N., in great wonderment as to what lay ahead. In this new land interest never flagged. One never could foresee what the morrow would bring forth.

Across rolling "downs" of soft, billowy snow we floundered for twenty-four miles, on the two following days. Not a wind-ripple could be seen. We were evidently in a region of comparative calms, which was a remarkable thing, considering that the windiest spot in the world was less than two hundred miles away.

After several sunny days McLean and I had very badly cracked lips. It had been often remarked at the Hut that the standard of humour greatly depreciated during the winter and this caused McLean and me many a physical pang while sledging, as we would laugh at the least provocation and open all the cracks in our lips. Eating hard plasmon biscuits was a painful pleasure. Correll, who was immune from this affliction, tanned to the rich hue of the "nut-brown maiden."

On December 5, at the top of a rise, we were suddenly confronted with a new vision—"Thalassa!" was our cry, "the sea!" but a very different sea from that which brought such joy to the hearts of the wandering Greeks. Unfolded to the horizon was a plain of pack-ice, thickly studded with bergs and intersected by black leads of open water. In the north-east was a patch of open sea and above it, round to the north, lowering banks of steel-blue cloud. We had come to the eastern side of Ninnis Glacier.

At this point any analogy which could possibly have been found with Wilkes's coastline ceased. It seems probable that he charted as land the limits of the pack-ice in 1840.

The excitement of exploring this new realm was to be deferred. Even as we raised the tent, the wind commenced to whistle and the air became surcharged with snow. Three skua gulls squatted a few yards away, squawking at our approach, and a few snow petrels sailed by in the gathering blizzard.

Through the 6th, 7th and 8th and most of the 9th it raged, during which time we came definitely to the conclusion that as social entertainers we were complete failures. We exhausted all the reserve topics of conversation, discussed our Universities, sports, friends and homes. We each described the scenery we liked best; notable always for the sunny weather and perfect calm. McLean sailed again in Sydney Harbour, Correll cycled and ran his races, I wandered in the South Australian hills or rowed in the "eights," while the snow swished round the tent and the wind roared over the wastes of ice.

Avoiding a few crevasses on the drop to sea-level on December 10, the sledge was manoeuvred over a tide-crack between glacier and sea-ice. The latter was traversed by frequent pressure-ridges; hummocks and broken pinnacles being numerous.

The next six days out on the broken sea-ice were full of incident. The weather was gloriously sunny till the 13th, during which time the sledge had to be dragged through a forest of pinnacles and over areas of soft, sticky slush which made the runners execrable for hours. Ponds of open water,

The "Organ-Pipes" of Horn Bluff (1000 Feet in Height) Pushing Out from the Mainland

Madigan, Correll, and Mclean Camped Below the Cliffs of Horn Bluff (1000 Feet in Height). Columnar Dolerite Is Seen Surmounting a Sedimentary Series Partly Buried in the Talus-Slope

by which basked a few Weddell seals, became a familiar sight. We tried to maintain a south-easterly course for the coast, but miles were wasted in the tortuous maze of ice—"a wildering Theban ruin of hummock and serrac."

The sledge-meter broke down and gave the ingenious Correll a proposition which he ably solved. McLean and I had a chronic weakness of the eyes from the continual glare. Looking at the other two fellows with their long protruding goggles made me think of Banquo's ghost: "Thou hast no speculation in those eyes that thou dost glare with."

I had noticed that some of the tide-cracks had opened widely and, when a blizzard blew on December 13, the thought was a skeleton in my brain cupboard.

On the 15th an Emperor penguin was seen sunning himself by a pool of water, so we decided to kill the bird and carry some meat in case of emergency. McLean found the stomach full of fish and myriads of cestodes in the intestines.

By dint of hard toil over cracks, ridges and jagged, broken blocks, we came, by diverging to the south-west, to the junction between shifting pack and fast bay-ice, and even there, we afterwards shuddered to find, it was at least forty-five miles, as the penguin skis, to the land.

It was a fine flat surface on which the sledge ran, and the miles commenced to fly by, comparatively speaking. Except for an occasional deep rift, whose bottom plumbed to the sea-water, the going was excellent. Each day the broken ice on our left receded, the mainland to the south grew closer and traces of rock became discernible on the low, fractured cliffs.

On December 17 a huge rocky bluff—Horn Bluff—stood out from the shore. It had a ram-shaped bow like a Dreadnought battleship and, adjoining it, there were smaller outcrops of rock on the seaward ice-cliffs. On its eastern side was a wide bay with a well-defined cape—Cape Freshfield—at the eastern extremity about thirty miles away.

The Bluff was a place worth exploring. At a distance of more than fifteen miles, the spot suggested all kinds of possibilities, and in council we argued that it was useless to go much farther east, as to touch at the land would mean a detour on the homeward track and time would have to be allowed for that.

At a point two hundred and seventy miles from the Hut, in latitude 68° 18' S., longitude 150° 12' E., we erected our "farthest east" camp on December 18, after a day's tramp of eighteen miles. Here, magnetic "dips" and other observations were made throughout the morning of the 19th. It was densely overcast, with sago snow falling, but by 3 PM of the same day the clouds had magically cleared and the first stage of the homeward journey had commenced.

CHAPTER XVI

Horn Bluff and Penguin Point

By C. T. MADIGAN

What thrill of grandeur ours
When first we viewed the column'd fell!
What idle, lilting verse can tell
Of giant fluted towers,
O'er-canopied with immemorial snow
And riven by a glacier's azure flow?

A S WE NEARED HORN BLUFF, ON THE FIRST STAGE
of our homeward march, the upper layers of snow were observed
to disappear, and the underlying ice became thinner; in corrugated
sapphire plains with blue reaches of sparkling water. Cracks bridged with flimsy
snow continually let one through into the water. McLean and I both soaked
our feet and once I was immersed to the thighs, having to stop and put on dry
socks and finnesko. It was a chilly process allowing the trousers to dry on me.

The mountain, pushing out as a great promontory from the coast amid
the fast sea-ice, towered up higher as our sledge approached its foot. A great
shadow was cast on the ice, and, when more than a mile away, we left the
warm sunshine.

Awed and amazed, we beheld the lone vastness of it all and were mute.
Rising out of the flat wilderness over which we had travelled was a mammoth
vertical barrier of rock rearing its head to the skies above. The whole face
for five miles was one magnificent series of organ-pipes. The deep shade
was heightened by the icy glare beyond it. Here was indeed a Cathedral of
Nature, where the "still, small voice" spoke amid an ineffable calm.

357

Far up the face of the cliff snow petrels fluttered like white butterflies. It was stirring to think that these majestic heights had gazed out across the wastes of snow and ice for countless ages, and never before had the voices of human beings echoed in the great stillness nor human eyes surveyed the wondrous scene.

From the base of the organ-pipes sloped a mass of debris; broken blocks of rock of every size tumbling steeply to the splintered hummocks of the sea-ice.

Standing out from the top of this talus-slope were several white "beacons," up to which we scrambled when the tent was pitched. This was a tedious task as the stones were ready to slide down at the least touch, and often we were carried down several yards by a general movement. Wearing soft finnesko, we ran the risk of getting a crushed foot among the large boulders. Amongst the rubble were beds of clay, and streams of thaw-water trickled down to the surface of a frozen lake.

After rising two hundred feet, we stood beneath the beacons which loomed above to a height of one hundred and twenty-eight feet. The organ-pipes were basaltic** in character but, to my great joy, I found the beacons were of sedimentary rock. After a casual examination, the details were left till the morrow.

That night we had a small celebration on raisins, chocolate and apple-rings, besides the ordinary fare of hoosh, biscuit and cocoa. Several times we were awakened by the crash of falling stones. Snow petrels had been seen coming home to their nests in the beacons, which were weathered out into small caves and crannies. From the camp we could hear their harsh cries.

The scene in the morning sun was a brilliant one. The great columnar rampart ran almost north and south and the tent was on its eastern side. So what was in dark shadow on the day before was now radiantly illumined.

Correll remained behind on the sea-ice with a theodolite to take heights of the various strata. McLean and I, armed with aneroid, glasses, ruck-sack, geological hammer (ice-axe) and camera, set out for the foot of the talus-slope.

The beacons were found to be part of a horizontal, stratified series of sandstones underlying the igneous rock. There were bands of coarse gravel and fine examples of stream-bedding interspersed with seams of carbonaceous shale and poor coal. Among the debris were several pieces of sandstone marked by black, fossilized plant-remains. The summits of the beacons were platforms of very hard rock, baked by the volcanic overflow. The columns, roughly hexagonal and weathered to a dull-red, stood above in sheer perpendicular lines of six hundred and sixty feet in altitude.

After taking a dozen photographs of geological and general interest and stuffing the sack and our pockets with specimens, we picked a track

---

** *To be exact the igneous rook was a very thick sill of dolerite.*

An Outcrop of a Sedimentary Formation Containing Bands of Coal Projecting Through the Talus Slope Below the Columnar Dolerite at Horn Bluff

The Face of a Granite Outcrop Near Penguin Point. At Its Base Is a Tide Crack and Ice Foot.

down the shelving talus to a lake of fresh water which was covered with a superficial crust of ice beneath which the water ran. The surface was easily broken and we fetched the aluminium cover of the cooker, filling it with three gallons of water, thus saving kerosene for almost a day.

After McLean had collected samples of soil, lichens, algae and moss, and all the treasures had been labelled, we lunched and harnessed-up once more for the homeward trail.

For four miles we ran parallel to the one-thousand-foot wall of Horn Bluff meeting several boulders stranded on the ice, as well as the fragile shell of a tiny sea-urchin. The promontory was domed with snow and ice, more than one thousand two hundred feet above sea-level. From it streamed a blue glacier overflowing through a rift in the face. Five miles on our way, the sledge passed from frictionless ice to rippled snow and with a march of seven miles, following lunch, we pitched camp.

Every one was tired that night, and our prayer to the Sleep Merchant in the book of Australian verse was for:

Twenty gallons of balmy sleep,
Dreamless, and deep, and mild,
Of the excellent brand you used to keep
When I was a little child.

For three days, December 22, 23 and 24, the wind soughed at thirty miles per hour and the sky was a compact nimbus, unveiling the sun at rare moments. Through a mist of snow we steered on a north-west course towards the one-hundred-and-fifty-two mile depot. The wind was from the south-east true, and this information, with hints from the sun-compass, gave us the direction. With the sail set, on a flat surface, among ghostly bergs and over narrow leads we ran for forty-seven miles with scarce a clear view of what lay around. The bergs had long ramps of snow leading close up to their summits on the windward side and in many cases the intervals between these ramps and the bergs were occupied by deep moats.

One day we were making four knots an hour under all canvas through thick drift. Suddenly, after a gradual ascent, I was on the edge of a moat, thirty feet deep. I shouted to the others and, just in time, the sledge was slewed round on the very brink.

We pushed on blindly:
The toil of it none may share;
By yourself must the way be won

Through fervid or frozen air
Till the overland journey's done.

Christmas Day! The day that ever reminds one of the sweet story of old, the lessons of childhood, the joys of Santa Claus—the day on which the thoughts of the wildest wanderer turn to home and peace and love. All the world was cheerful; the sun was bright, the air was calm. It was the hometrail, provisions were in plenty, the sledge was light and our hearts lighter.

The eastern edge of Ninnis Glacier was near, and, leaving the sea-ice, we were soon straining up the first slope, backed by a line of ridges trending north-east and south-west, with shallow valleys intervening. On the wind-swept crests there were a few crevasses well packed with snow.

It was a day's work of twelve miles and we felt ready for Christmas dinner. McLean was cook and had put some apple-rings to soak in the cooker after the boil-up at lunch. Beyond this and the fact that he took some penguin-meat into the tent, he kept his plans in the deepest mystery. Correll and I were kept outside making things snug and taking the meteorological observations, until the word came to enter. When at last we scrambled in, a delicious smell diffused through the tent, and there was a sound of frying inside the cooker-pot. We were presented with a menu which read:

"Peace on earth, good will to men."

Xmas 1912   KING GEORGE V. LAND

200 miles east of Winter Quarters.

MENU DU DÎNER

Hors d'oeuvre

Biscuit de Plasmon   Ration du lard glacé

Entrée

Monsieur l'Empereur Pingouin fricassé

Pièce de Résistance

Pemmican naturel à l'Antarctique

Dessert

Hotch-potch de pommes et de raisins

Chocolat au sucre glaxoné

Liqueur bien ancienne de l'Ecosse

Cigarettes   Tabac

The *hors d'oeuvre* of bacon ration was a welcome surprise. McLean had carried the tin unknown to us up till this moment. The penguin, fried in lumps of fat taken from the pemmican, and a little butter, was delicious. In the same pot the hoosh was boiled and for once we noted an added piquancy. Next followed the plum-pudding—dense mixture of powdered biscuit, glaxo, sugar, raisins and apple-rings, surpassing the finest, flaming, holly-decked, Christmas creation.

Then came the toasts. McLean produced the whisky from the medical kit and served it out, much diluted, in three mugs. There was not three ounces in all, but it flavoured the water.

I was asked to call "The King." McLean proposed "The Other Sledgers" in a noble speech, wishing them every success; and then there were a few drops left to drink to "Ourselves," whom Correll eulogized to our complete satisfaction. We then drew on the meagre supply of cigarettes and lay on our bags, feeling as comfortable as the daintiest epicure after a twelve-course dinner, drinking his coffee and smoking his cigar.

We talked till twelve o'clock, and then went outside to look at the midnight sun, shining brightly just above the southern horizon. Turning in, we were once more at home in our dreams.

By a latitude shot at noon on Boxing Day, I found that our position was not as far north as expected. The following wind had been probably slightly east of south-east and too much westing had been made. From a tangle of broken ridges whose surface was often granular, half-consolidated ice, the end of the day opened up a lilac plain of sea-ice ahead. We were once more on the western side of Ninnis Glacier and the familiar coast of Penguin Point, partly hidden by an iceberg, sprang into view. The depot hill to the north-west could be recognized, twenty miles away, across a wide bay. By hooch-time we had found a secure path to the sea-ice, one hundred and eighty feet below.

The wind sprang up opportunely on the morning of the 27th, and the sun was serene in a blue sky. Up went the sail and with a feather-weight load we strode off for the depot eighteen miles distant. Three wide rifts in the sea-ice exercised our ingenuity during the day's march, but by the time the sun was in the south-west the sledge was sawing through the sandy snow of the depot hill. It was unfortunate that the food of this depot had been cached so far out of our westerly course, as the time expended in recovering it might have been profitably given to a survey of the mainland east of Penguin Point. At 6.20 PM, after eighteen and a quarter miles, the food-bag was sighted on the mound, and that night the dinner at our one-hundred-and-fifty-two-mile depot was marked by some special innovations.

Penguin Point, thirty miles away, bore W. 15° S., and next day we made a bid for it by a march of sixteen miles. There was eleven days' ration on the sledge to take us to Mount Murchison, ninety miles away; consequently the circuitous route to the land was held to be a safe "proposition."

Many rock faces became visible, and I was able to fix numerous prominent points with the theodolite.

At three miles off the coast, the surface became broken by ridges, small bergs and high, narrow cupolas of ice surrounded by deep moats. One of these was very striking. It rose out of a wind-raked hollow to a height of fifty feet; just the shape of an ancient Athenian helmet. McLean took a photograph.

As at Horn Bluff, the ice became thinner and freer of snow as we drew near the Point. The rocky wall under which the tent was raised proved to be three hundred feet high, jutting out from beneath the slopes of ice. From here the coast ran almost south on one side and north-west on the other. On either hand there were dark faces corniced with snow.

The next day was devoted to exploration. Adelie penguins waddled about the tide-crack over which we crossed to examine the rock, which was of coarse-grained granite, presenting great, vertical faces. Hundreds of snow petrels flew about and some stray skua gulls were seen.

Near the camp, on thick ice, were several large blocks of granite which had floated out from the shore and lay each in its pool of thaw-water, covered with serpulae and lace coral.

Correll, our Izaak Walton, had brought a fishing-line and some penguin-meat. He stopped near the camp fishing while McLean and I continued down the coast, examining the outcrops. The type of granite remained unchanged in the numerous exposures.

I had noticed a continuous rustling sound for some time and found at length that it was caused by little streams of ice-crystals running down the steep slopes in cascades, finally pouring out in piles on the sea-ice. The partial thaw in the sunlight causes the semi-solid ice to break up into separate grains. Sometimes whole areas of the surface, in delicate equilibrium, would suddenly flow rapidly away.

For three miles we walked, and as the next four miles of visible coast presented no extensive outcrops, we turned back for lunch.

During the afternoon, on the summit of the Point, it was found that an uneven rocky area, about a quarter of a mile wide, ran backwards to the ice-falls of the plateau. The surface was very broken and weathered, covered in patches by abundant lichens and mosses. Fossicking round in the gravel, Correll happened on some tiny insect-like mites living amongst the moss or on the moist under side of slabs of stone. This set us all insect-hunting. Alcohol was brought in a small bottle from the tent, and into this they were swept in myriads with a camel's-hair brush. From the vantage-point of a high rock in the neighbourhood the long tongue of Mertz Glacier could be seen running away to the north.

At 8.30 AM, on New Year's Eve, we set off for another line of rocks about four miles away to the west. There were two masses forming an angle in the ice-front and consisting of two main ridges rising to a height of two hundred and fifty feet, running back into the ice-cap for a mile, and divided by a small glacier.

This region was soon found to be a perfect menagerie of life. Seals lay about dozing peacefully by the narrow lanes of water. Adelie penguins strutted in procession up and down the little glacier. To reach his rookery, a penguin would leap four feet on to a ledge of the ice-foot, painfully pad up the glassy slope and then awkwardly scale the rocks until he came to a level of one hundred and fifty feet. Here he took over the care of a chick or an egg, while the other bird went to fish. Skua gulls flew about, continually molesting the rookeries. One area of the rocks was covered by a luxuriant growth of green moss covering guano and littered skeletons—the site of a deserted rookery.

Correll and I went up to where the ridges converged, selecting numerous specimens of rock and mineral and finding thousands of small red mites in the moist gravel. Down on the southern ridge we happened on a Wilson petrel with feathered nestlings. At this point McLean came along from the west with the news of silver-grey petrels and Cape pigeons nesting in hundreds. He had secured two of each species and several eggs. This was indeed a discovery, as the eggs of the former birds had never before been found. Quite close to us were many snow petrels in all kinds of unexpected crevices. The light was too dull for photographing, but, while I took magnetic "dips" on the following morning, McLean visited the silver-grey petrels and Cape pigeons and secured a few "snaps."

The last thing we did before leaving the mainland was to kill two penguins and cut off their breasts and this meat was, later, to serve us in good stead.

Crossing the Mertz Glacier at any time would have been an unpleasant undertaking, but to go straight to Mount Murchison (the site of our first depot on the outward journey) from Penguin Point meant spanning it in a long oblique line. It was preferable to travel quickly and safely over the sea-ice on a north-westerly course, which, plotted on the chart, intersected our old one-hundred-mile camp on the eastern margin of the glacier; then to cross by the route we already knew.

The Granite Cliffs at Penguin Point Where Cape Pigeon and Silver Petrel Rookeries Were Found; the Site of New Year's Camp

By January 2 we had thrown Penguin Point five miles behind, and a spell of unsettled weather commenced; in front lay a stretch of fourteen miles over a good surface. The wind was behind us, blowing between thirty and forty miles per hour, and from an overcast sky light snow was falling. Fortunately there were fleeting glimpses of the sun, by which the course could be adjusted. Towards evening the snow had thickened, but thanks to the splendid assistance afforded by a sail, the white jutting spurs of the edge of Mertz Glacier were dimly visible.

A blizzard took possession of the next day till 7 PM, when we all sallied out and found the identical gully in which was the one-hundred-mile camp of the outward journey. The light was still bad and the sky overcast, so the start was postponed till next morning.

There was food for five days on a slightly reduced ration and the depot on Mount Murchison was forty miles away.

Once we had left the sea-ice and stood on the glacier, *Aurora* Peak with its black crest showed through the glasses. Once there, the crevasses we most dreaded would be over and the depot easily found.

A good fourteen and a quarter miles slipped by on January 4— a fine day. On January 5 the "plot began to thicken." The clouds hung above like a blanket, sprinkling light snow. The light was atrocious, and a few open rents gave warning of the western zone of pitfalls. All the while there was a shifting spectral chaos of whiteness which seemed to benumb the faculties and destroy one's sense of reality. We decided to wait for a change in the weather.

During the night the snow ceased, and by lunch time on the 6th the sledge-meter recorded ten miles. The strange thing was that the firm sastrugi present on the outward journey were now covered inches in snow, which became deeper as we marched westward.

It was now a frequent occurrence for one of us to pitch forward with his feet down a hidden crevasse, sometimes going through to the waist. The travelling was most nerve-racking. When a foot went through the crust of snow, it was impossible to tell on which side of the crevasse one happened to be, or in what direction it ran. The only thing to do was to go ahead and trust in Providence.

At last we landed the sledge on a narrow ridge of hard snow, surrounded by blue, gaping pits in a pallid eternity of white. It was only when the tent was pitched that a wide quarry was noticed a few yards away from the door.

It was now fourteen miles to the top of Mount Murchison and we had only two more days' rations and one and a half pounds of penguin-meat.

On January 7th the light was worse than ever and snow fell. It was only six miles across the broken country between us and the gully between Mt. Murchison and *Aurora* Peak, where one could travel with some surety. A sharp look-out was kept, and towards 11 PM a rim of clear sky overtopped the southern horizon. We knew the sun would curve round into it at midnight, so all was made ready for marching.

When the sun's disc emerged into the rift there was light; but dim, cold and fleeting. The smallest irregularity on the surface threw a shadow hundreds of yards long. The plain around was a bluish-grey checquer-board of light and shade; ahead, sharp and clear against the leaden sky, stood beautiful Aurora Peak, swathed in lustrous gold—the chariot of the goddess herself. The awful splendour of the scene tended to depress one and make the task more trying. I have never felt more nervous than I did in that ghostly light in the tense silence, surrounded by the hidden horror of fathomless depths. All was covered with a uniform layer of snow, growing deeper and heavier at every step. I was ahead and went through eight times in about four miles. The danger lay in getting the sledge and one, two, or all of us on a weak snow-bridge at the same time. As long as the sledge did not go down we were comparatively safe.

At 1.30 AM the sun was obscured and the light waned to dead white. Still we went on, as the entrance of the gully between Aurora Peak and Mount Murchison was near at hand and we had a mind to get over the danger-zone before a snowstorm commenced.

By 5.30 AM we breathed freely on "terra firma," even though one sunk through a foot of snow to feel it. It had taken six hours to do the last five and three-quarter miles, and, being tired out with the strain on muscles and nerves, we raised the tent, had a meal, and then slept till noon on the 8th. It was eight miles to the depot, five miles up the gully and three miles to the summit of Mount Murchison; and no one doubted for a moment that it could not be done in a single day's march.

Advancing up the gully after lunch, we found that the surface became softer, and we were soon sinking to the knees at every step. The runners, too, sank till the decking rested on the snow, and it was as much as we could do to shift the sledge, with a series of jerks at every step. At 6 PM matters became desperate. We resolved to make a depot of everything unnecessary, and to relay it up the mountain afterwards.

The sledge-meter, clogged with snow and almost submerged, was taken off and stood up on end to mark a depot, whilst a pile was made of the dip-circle, theodolite and tripod, pick, alpine rope, ice-axe, all the mineral and biological specimens and excess clothing.

Even thus lightened, we could scarcely move the sledge, struggling on, sinking to the thighs in the flocculent deluge. Snow now began to fall so thickly that it was impossible to see ahead.

At 7 PM we finished up the last scraps of pemmican and cocoa. Biscuit, sugar and glaxo had given out at the noon meal. There still remained one and a half pounds of penguin meat, several infusions of tea and plenty of kerosene for the primus.

We staggered on till 10.30 PM, when the weather became so dense that the sides of the gully were invisible. Tired out, we camped and had some tea. In eight hours we had only made four and a half miles, and there was still the worst part to come.

In our exhausted state we slept till 11 PM of January 9, awaking to find the sky densely overcast and a light fog in the air. During a rift which opened for a few minutes there was a short glimpse of the rock on Aurora Peak. Shredding half the penguin-meat, we boiled it up and found the stew and broth excellent.

At 1.30 AM we started to struggle up the gully once more, wading along in a most helpless fashion, with breathing spells every ten yards or less. Snow began to fall in such volume that at last it was impossible to keep our direction with any certainty. The only thing to do was to throw up the tent as a shelter and wait. This we did till 4.30 AM; but there must have been a cloud-burst, for the heavy flakes toppled on to the tent like tropical rain. We got into sleeping-bags, and tried to be patient and to forget that we were hungry.

Apparently, during our seven weeks' absence, the local precipitation had been almost continual, and snow now lay over this region in stupendous amount. Even when one sank three feet, it was not on to the firm sastrugi over which we had travelled out of the valley on the outward journey, for these lay still deeper. It was hoped that the "snowdump" did not continue over the fifty miles to the Hut, but we argued that on the windy plateau this could scarcely be possible.

It was evident that without any more food, through this bottomless, yielding snow, we could never haul the sledge up to the depot, a rise of one thousand two hundred feet in three miles. One of us must go up and bring food back, and I decided to do so as soon as the weather cleared.

We found the wait for clearer weather long and trying with empty stomachs. As the tobacco-supply still held out, McLean and I found great solace in our pipes. All through the rest of the day and till 5 PM of the next, January 10, there was not a rift in the opaque wall of flakes. Then to our intense relief the snow stopped, the clouds rolled to the north, and, in swift transformation—a cloudless sky with bright sunshine! With the rest of the penguin-meat—a bare half-pound—we had another thin broth. Somewhat fortified, I took the food-bag and shovel, and left the tent at 5.30 AM

Often sinking to the thighs, I felt faint at the first exertion. The tent scarcely seemed to recede as I toiled onwards towards the first steep slope. The heavy mantle of snow had so altered the contours of the side of the gully that I was not sure of the direction of the top of the mountain.

Resting every hundred yards, I floundered on hour after hour, until, on arriving at a high point, I saw a little shining mound standing up on a higher point, a good mile to the east. After seven hours' wading I reached it and found that it was the depot.

Two feet of the original eight-foot mound projected above the surface, with the bamboo pole and a wire-and-canvas flag rising another eighteen inches. On this, a high isolated mountain summit, six feet of snow had actually accumulated. How thankful I was that I had brought a shovel!

At seven feet I "bottomed" on the hard snow, without result. Then, running a tunnel in the most probable direction, I struck with the shovel the kerosene tin which was on the top of the food-bag. On opening the bag, the first items to appear were sugar, butter and biscuits; the next quarter of an hour I shall not forget!

I made a swag of five days' provisions, and, taking a direct route, attacked the three miles downhill in lengths of one hundred and fifty yards. Coming in sight of the tent, I called to my companions to thaw some water for a drink. So slow was progress that I could speak to them a quarter of an hour before reaching the tent. I had been away eleven and a half hours, covering about seven miles in all.

McLean and Correll were getting anxious about me. They said that they had felt the cold and were unable to sleep. Soon I had produced the pemmican and biscuit, and a scalding hoosh was made. The other two had had only a mug of penguin broth each in three days, and I had only broken my fast a few hours before them.

After the meal, McLean and Correll started back to the cache, two miles down the gully, to select some of the geological and biological specimens and to fetch a few articles of clothing. The instruments, the greater part of the collection of rocks, crampons, sledge-meter and other odds and ends were all left behind. Coming back with the loads slung like swags they found that by walking in their old footsteps they made fair progress.

By 8 PM all had rested, every unnecessary fitting had been stripped off the sledge and the climb to the depot commenced. I went ahead in my old trail, Correll also making use of it; while McLean broke a track for himself. The work was slow and heavy; nearly six hours were spent doing those three miles.

It was a lovely evening; the yellow sun drifting through orange cloudlets behind Aurora Peak. We were in a more appreciative mood than on the last midnight march, exulting in the knowledge of ten days' provisions at hand and fifty-three miles to go to reach the Hut.

In the manner of the climate, a few wisps of misty rack came sailing from the south-east, the wind rose, snow commenced to fall and a blizzard held sway for almost three days. It was just as well that we had found that depot when we did.

The fifty-three miles to the Hut melted away in the pleasures of anticipation. The first two miles, on the morning of January 14, gave us some strenuous work, but they were luxurious in comparison with what we expected; soon, however, the surface rapidly and permanently improved. A forty-mile wind from the south-east was a distinct help, and by the end of the day we had come in sight of the nunatak first seen after leaving the Hut (Madigan Nunatak).

In two days forty miles lay behind. Down the blue ice-slopes in slippery finnesko, and Aladdin's Cave hove in sight. We tumbled in, to be assailed by a wonderful odour which brought back orchards, shops, people—a breath of civilization. In the centre of the floor was a pile of oranges surmounted by two luscious pineapples. The Ship was in! There was a bundle of letters— Bage was back from the south—Wild had been landed one thousand five hundred miles to the west—Amundsen had reached the Pole! Scott was remaining in the Antarctic for another year. How we shouted and read all together!

CHAPTER XVII

With Stillwell's and Bickerton's Parties

L EAVING MADIGAN'S PARTY ON NOVEMBER 19, when forty-six miles from the Hut, Stillwell, Hodgeman and Close of the Near-Eastern Party diverged towards a dome-shaped mountain—Mount Hunt. A broad valley lay between their position on the falling plateau and this eminence to the north-east. Looking across, one would think that the depression was slight, but the party found by aneroid that their descent was one thousand five hundred feet into a gully filled with soft, deep snow. After skimming the polished sastrugi of the uplands, the sledge ran heavily in the yielding drifts. Then a gale of wind rose behind them just as the ascent on the other side commenced, and was a valuable aid in the pull to the summit.

From the highest point or cap of what proved to be a promontory, a wide seascape dotted with bergs was unfolded to the north. To the west the eastern cape of Commonwealth Bay was visible, and sweeping away to the north-east was the Mertz Glacier with sheer, jutting headlands succeeding one another into the distance. True bearings to these points were obtained from the camp, and, subsequently, with the help of an observation secured on the *Aurora* during the previous year, the trend of the glacier-tongue was determined. Hodgeman made a series of illustrative sketches.

On November 21 the party commenced the return journey, moving directly towards Madigan Nunatak to the south-west. This nunatak had been sighted for the first time on the outward march, and there was much speculation as to what the rock would prove to be. A gradual descent for seven miles brought them on to a plain, almost at sea-level, continuous with the valley they had crossed on the 19th further to the east. On the far side of the plain a climb was commenced over some ice-spurs, and then a broad field of crevasses was encountered, some of which attained a width of fifty yards. Delayed by these and by unfavourable weather, they did not reach Madigan Nunatak until the evening of November 20.

The outcrop—a jagged crest of rock—was found to be one hundred and sixty yards long and thirty yards wide, placed at an altitude of two thousand four hundred feet above sea-level. It is composed of grey quartzose gneiss.

There were no signs of recent glaciation or of ice-striae, though the rock was much weathered, and all the cracks and joint-planes were filled with disintegrating material. The weathering was excessive and peculiar in contrast with that observed on fresh exposures near the Hut and at other localities near sea-level.

After collecting specimens and placing a small depot of food on the highest point, the party continued their way to the Hut, reaching it on November 27.

At Winter Quarters noticeable changes had taken place. The harbour ice had broken back for several hundred yards and was rotten and ready to blow out in the first strong wind; marked thawing had occurred everywhere, and many islands of rock emerged from the snow; the ice-foot was diminishing; penguins, seals, and flying birds made the place, for once, alive and busy.

Bickerton, Whetter and Hannam carried on the routine of work; Whetter as meteorologist and Hannam as magnetician, while Bickerton was busied with the air-tractor and in preparations for sledging. Thousands of penguins' eggs had been gathered for the return voyage of the *Aurora*, or in case of detention for a second winter.

Murphy, Hunter and Laseron arrived from the south on the same day as Stillwell, Hodgeman and Close came in from the east. The former party had plodded for sixty-seven miles through a dense haze of drift. They had kept a course roughly by the wind and the direction of sastrugi. The unvarying white light of thick overcast days had been so severe that all were suffering from snow-blindness. When, at length, they passed over the endless billows of snow on to the downfalls near the coast, the weather cleared and they were relieved to see once more the Mecca of all sledging parties—Aladdin's Cave.

A redistribution of parties and duties was made. Hodgeman joined Whetter and Bickerton in preparation for the air-tractor sledge's trip to the west. Hunter took up the position of meteorologist and devoted all his spare time to biological investigations amongst the immigrant life of summer. Hannam continued to act as magnetician and general "handy man." Murphy, who was also to be in charge during the summer, returned to his stores, making preparations for departure. Hourly meteorological observations kept every one vigilant at the Hut.

Islets Fringing the Mainland: View Looking West from Stillwell Island. *Adelie Land*

In pursuance of a plan to examine in detail the coast immediately east of Commonwealth Bay, Stillwell set out with Laseron and Close on December 9. The weather was threatening at the start, and they had the usual struggle with wind and drift to "make" Aladdin's Cave.

Forewarned on the first journey of the dangers of bad ventilation, they cleared the entrance to the cave of obstacles so that a ready exit could be made, if, as was expected, the opening became sealed with snow-drift. This did happen during the night, and, though everything seemed all right the next morning, the whole party was overpowered during breakfast by foul air, the presence of which was not suspected.

Hoosh was cooked and about to be served, when Stillwell, who was in charge of the primus, collapsed. Close immediately seized an ice-axe, stood up, thrust its point through the choked entrance, and fell down, overcome. Laseron became powerless at the same time. An hour and a half later—so it was reckoned—the party revived and cleared the opening. The hole made by the ice-axe had been sufficient to save their lives. For a day they were too weak and exhausted to travel, so the tent was pitched and the night spent outside the Cave.

On December 11 they steered due south for a while and then eastward for three days to Madigan Nunatak; delayed for twenty-four hours by a blizzard.

Stillwell goes on to describe: "Part of the 15th was spent in making observations, taking photographs and collecting specimens of rocks and lichens. Breaking camp, we set out on a northerly course for the coast down gently falling snowfields. Gradually there opened up a beautiful vista of sea, dotted with floes and rocky islets (many of which were ice-capped). On December 16 camp was pitched near the coast on a stretch of firm, unbroken ice, which enabled one to venture close enough to the edge to discover an islet connected by a snow-ramp with the icy barrier. Lying farther off the shore was a thick fringe of islets, among and beyond which drifted a large quantity of heavy floe. The separate floes stood some ten or fifteen feet above the water-level, and the lengths of several exceeded a quarter of a mile. Every accessible rock was covered with rookeries of Adelie penguins; the first chicks were just hatched."

A theodolite traverse was run to fix the position of each islet. The traverse-line was carried close to the ice-cliff, so that the number of islets hidden from view was as few as possible. Snow mounds were built at intervals and the intervening distances measured by the sledge-meter.

The party travelled west for seven and a quarter miles round a promontory—Cape Gray—until the Winter Quarters were sighted across Commonwealth Bay. They then turned eastward over the higher slopes, meeting the coast some three miles to the east of the place where they had first encountered it. The surface was for the most part covered with snow, while crevasses were frequent and treacherous.

In the midst of the survey the sledge-meter broke down, and, as the party were wholly dependent upon it for laying out base-lines, repairs had to be made.

On the 27th another accessible rocky projection was seen. Over it and the many islands in the vicinity hovered flocks of snow petrels and occasional Antarctic and Wilson petrels. Masses of Adelie penguins and chicks constituted the main population, and skua gulls with eggs were also observed. The rock was of garnet gneiss, traversed by black dykes of pyroxene granulite.

A great discovery was made on December 29. On the abrupt, northern face of some rocks connected to the ice-cap of the mainland by a causeway of ice a large colony of sea-birds had nested. Cape pigeons, the rare silver-grey and snow petrels were all present. Amongst these Laseron made a collection of many eggs and birds.

The traverse-line was then carried back to Madigan Nunatak along a series of connecting mounds. After being held up for three and a half days

Madigan Nunatak—Close and Laseron Standing by the Sledge

in a blizzard from December 31 to January 4, the party were home once more late on January 5, 1913.

Returning to the fortunes of the air-tractor sledge, which was to start west early in December. Bickerton has a short story to tell, inadequate to the months of work which were expended on that converted aeroplane. Its career was mostly associated with misfortune, dating from a serious fall when in flight at Adelaide, through the southern voyage of the *Aurora,* buffeted by destructive seas, to a capacious snow shelter in Adelie Land—the Hangar— where for the greater part of the year it remained helpless and drift-bound.

Bickerton takes up the story:

I had always imagined that the air-tractor sledge would be most handicapped by the low temperature; but the wind was far more formidable. It is obvious that a machine which depends on the surrounding air for its medium of traction could not be tested in the winds of an Adelie Land winter. One might just as well try the capabilities of a small motor-launch in the rapids at Niagara. Consequently we had to wait until the high summer.

With hopes postponed to an indefinite future, another difficulty arose. As it was found that the wind would not allow the sea-ice to form, breaking up the floe as quickly as it appeared, the only remaining field for manoeuvres was over the highlands to the south; under conditions quite different from those for which it was suited. We knew that for the first three miles there was a rise of some one thousand four hundred feet, and in places the gradient was one in three and a half. I thought the machine would negotiate this, but it was obviously unsafe to make the venture without providing against a headlong rush downhill, if, for any reason, power should fail.

Suggestions were not lacking, and after much consideration the following device was adopted:

A hand rock-drill, somewhat over an inch in diameter, was turned up in the lathe, cut with one-eighth-inch pitched, square threads and pointed at the lower end. This actuated through an internal threaded brass bush held in an iron standard; the latter being bolted to the after-end of a runner over a hole bushed for the reception of the drill. Two sets of these were got ready; one for each runner.

The standards were made from spare caps belonging to the wireless masts. The timely fracture of one of the vices supplied me with sufficient ready-cut thread of the required pitch for one brake. Cranked handles were fitted, and the points, which came in contact with the ice, were hardened and tempered. When protruded to their fullest extent, the spikes extended four inches below the runners.

Sledging Rations for Three Men for Three Months

Stillwell Island—A Haunt of the Silver-Grey Petrel

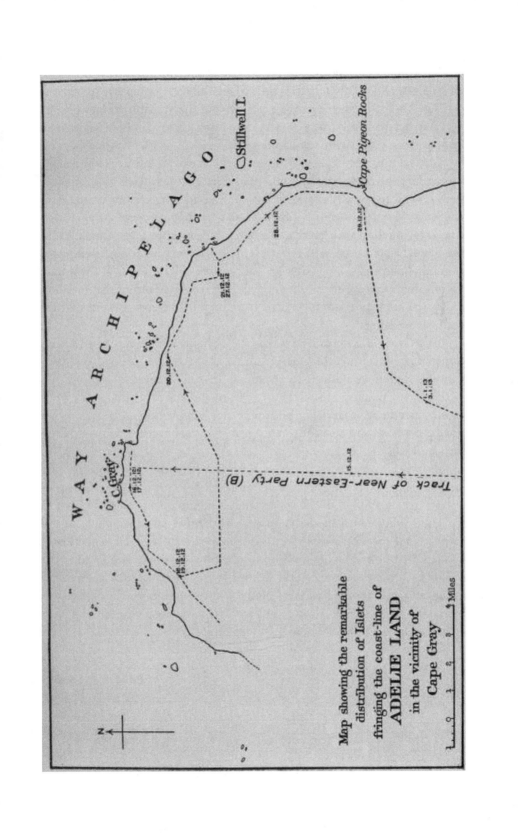

Map showing the remarkable
distribution of Islets
fringing the coast-line of
ADÉLIE LAND
in the vicinity of
Cape Gray

The whole contrivance was not very elegant, but impressed one with its strength and reliability. To work the handles, two men had to sit one on each runner. As the latter were narrow and the available framework, by which to hold on and steady oneself, rather limited, the office of brakesman promised to be one with acrobatic possibilities.

To start the engine it was necessary to have a calm and, preferably, sunny day; the engine and oil-tank had been painted black to absorb the sun's heat. On a windy day with sun and an air temperature of 30° F., it was only with considerable difficulty that the engine could be turned—chiefly owing to the thickness of the lubricating oil. But on a calm day with the temperature lower –20° F. for example—the engine would swing well enough to permit starting, after an hour or two of steady sun. If there were no sun even in the absence of wind, starting would be out of the question, unless the atmospheric temperature were high or the engine were warmed with a blow-lamp.

It was not till November 15 that the right combination of conditions came. That day was calm and sunny, and the engine needed no more stimulus than it would have received in a "decent" climate.

Hannam, Whetter and I were the only inhabitants of the Hut at the time. Having ascertained that the oil and air pumps were working satisfactorily, we fitted the wheels and air-rudder, and made a number of satisfactory trials in the vicinity of the Hut.

The wheels were soon discarded as useless; reliance being placed on the long runners. Then the brakes were tested for the first time by driving for a short distance uphill to the south and glissading down the slope back to the Hut. With a man in charge of each brake, the machine, when in full career down the slope, was soon brought to a standstill. The experiment was repeated from a higher position on the slope, with the same result. The machine was then taken above the steepest part of the slope (one in three and a half) and, on slipping back, was brought to rest with ease. The surface was hard, polished blue ice. The air-rudder, by the way, was efficient at speeds exceeding fifteen miles per hour.

On the 20th we had a calm morning, so Whetter and I set out for Aladdin's Cave to depot twenty gallons of benzene and six gallons of oil. The engine was not running well, one cylinder occasionally "missing." But, in spite of this and a head wind of fifteen miles per hour, we covered the distance between the one-mile and the two-mile flags in three minutes. This was on ice, and the gradient was about one in fifteen. We went no farther that day, and it was lucky that we did so, for, soon after our return to the Hut, it was blowing more than sixty miles per hour.

"The Bus," the Air-Tractor Sledge

Bickerton and His Sledge with Detachable Wheels

On December 2 Hodgeman joined us in a very successful trip to Aladdin's Cave with nine 8-gallon tins of benzene on a sledge; weighing in all seven hundred pounds.

After having such a good series of results with the machine, the start of the real journey was fixed for December 3. At 3 PM it fell calm, and we left at 4 PM, amid an inspiriting demonstration of goodwill from the six other men. Arms were still waving violently as we crept noisily over the brow of the hill and the Hut disappeared from sight.

On the two steepest portions it was necessary to walk, but, these past, the machine went well with a load of three men and four hundred pounds, reaching Aladdin's Cave in an hour by a route free of small crevasses, which I had discovered on the previous day. Here we loaded up with three 100-lb. food-bags, twelve gallons of oil (one hundred and thirty pounds), and seven hundred pounds of benzene. Altogether, there was enough fuel and lubricating oil to run the engine at full speed for twenty hours as well as full rations for three men for six weeks.

After a few minutes spent in disposing the loads, our procession of machine, four sledges (in tow) and three men moved off. The going was slow, too slow—about three miles an hour on ice. This would probably mean no movement at all on snow which might soon be expected. But something was wrong. The cylinder which had been missing fire a few days before, but which had since been cleaned and put in order, was now missing fire again, and the speed, proportionately, had dropped too much.

I made sure that the oil was circulating, and cleaned the sparking-plug, but the trouble was not remedied. A careful examination showed no sufficient cause, so it was assumed to be internal. To undertake anything big was out of the question, so we dropped thirty-two gallons of benzene and a spare propeller. Another mile went by and we came to snow, where forty gallons of benzene, twelve gallons of oil and a sledge were abandoned. The speed was now six miles an hour and we did two miles in very bad form. As it was now 11 PM and the wind was beginning to rise, we camped, feeling none too pleased with the first day's results.

While in the sleeping-bag I tried to think out some rapid way of discovering what was wrong with the engine. The only conclusion to which I could come was that it would be best to proceed to the cave at eleven and three-quarter miles—Cathedral Grotto—and there remove the faulty cylinder, if the weather seemed likely to be favourable; if it did not, to go on independently with our man-hauled sledge.

On December 4 the wind was still blowing about twenty miles per hour when we set to work on the machine. I poured some oil straight into the

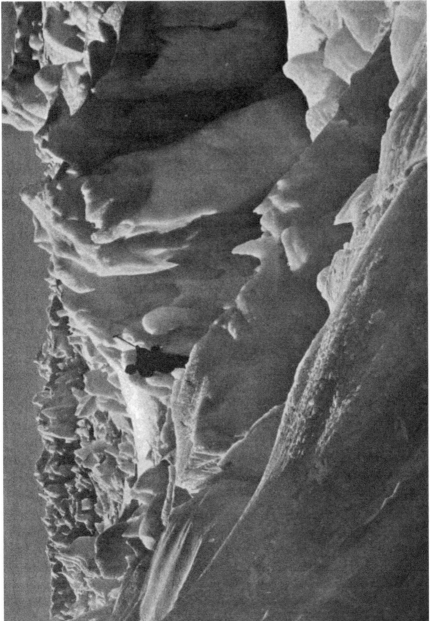

Amongst the Splintered Ice Where the Ice-Sheet Descends to the Sea Near Cape Denison

crank-case to make sure that there was sufficient, and we also tested and improved the ignition. At four o'clock the wind dropped, and in an hour the engine was started. While moving along, the idle cylinder was ejecting oil, and this, together with the fact that it had no compression, made me hope that broken piston-rings were the source of the trouble. It would only take two hours to remove three cylinders, take one ring from each of the two sound ones for the faulty one, and all might yet be well!

These thoughts were brought to a sudden close by the engine, without any warning, pulling up with such a jerk that the propeller was smashed. On moving the latter, something fell into the oil in the crank-case and fizzled, while the propeller could only be swung through an angle of about 30°. We did not wait to examine any further, but fixed up the man-hauling sledge, which had so far been carried by the air-tractor sledge, and cached all except absolute necessities.

We were sorry to leave the machine, though we had never dared to expect a great deal from it in the face of the unsuitable conditions found to prevail in Adelie Land. However, the present situation was disappointing.

Having stuffed up the exhaust-pipes to keep out the drift, we turned our backs to the aero-sledge and made for the eleven-and-three-quarter-mile cave, arriving there at 8 PM There was a cheering note from Bage in the "Grotto," wishing us good luck.

To avoid crevasses we steered first of all to the southwest on the morning of the 5th, which was clear and bright. After six miles the sastrugi became hard and compact, so the course was changed to due west. Shortly afterwards, a piece of rock** which we took to be a meteorite, was found on the surface of the snow. It measured approximately five inches by three inches by three and a half inches and was covered with a black scale which in places had blistered; three or four small pieces of this scale were lying within three inches of the main piece. Most of the surface was rounded, except one face which looked as if it had been fractured. It was lying on the snow, in a slight depression, about two and a half inches below the mean surface, and there was nothing to indicate that there had been any violent impact.

At eight o'clock that night we had done twelve miles, losing sight of the sea at a height of about three thousand feet. All felt pleased and looked forward to getting over a ridge ahead, which, from an altitude of four thousand feet, ran in pencilled outline to the western point of Commonwealth Bay.

On December 6 it was drifting hard, and part of the morning was spent theorizing on our prospects in an optimistic vein. This humour gradually wore off as the thick drift continued, with a fifty-mile wind, for three days.

** *This has since been examined by Professor E. Skeats and Stillwell, who report it to be an interesting form of meteorite, containing amongst other minerals, plagioclase felspar. This is, we believe, the first occasion on which a meteorite has been found in the Antarctic regions.—Ed.*

At 5 PM on December 8 a move was made. The drift was what our Hut-standard reckoned to be "moderate," but the wind had fallen to thirty miles an hour and had veered to the east; so the sail was hoisted. The going was difficult over a soft surface, and after five hours, by which time the drift had perceptibly thickened, we had done eight miles.

The thirst each one of us developed in those earlier days was prodigious. When filling the cooker with snow it was hard to refrain from packing it "up to the knocker" in order to obtain a sufficient supply of water.

The next day it blew harder and drifted thicker. Above the loud flapping of the tent and the incessant sizzling of the drift we discussed our situation. We were one week "out" and had travelled thirty-one miles. Future progress depended entirely on the weather—unfortunately. We were beginning to learn that though the season was "meteorologically" called summer, it was hardly recognizable as such.

December 10 was Whetter's birthday. It was heralded by an extra strong wind and the usual liberal allowance of drift. I was cook, and made some modifications in the meal. Hodgeman (who was the previous cook) used to make hoosh as thick as a biscuit, so we had some thin stuff for a change—two mugs each. Then really strong tea; we boiled it for some time to make sure of the strength and added some leaves which had already done good service.

Several times fault had been found with the way the tent was pitched. I had not yet tried my hand at being the "man inside" during this operation. One day, while every one was grumbling, I said I would take the responsibility at the next camp; the proposal being received with grunts of assent. When the job was finished and the poles appeared to be spread taut, I found myself alone in what seemed to me a cathedral. Feeling pleased, I called for the others to come in, and arranged myself in a corner with an "I-told-you-so" expression on my face, ready to receive their congratulations. Hodgeman came in first. He is not a large man, though he somehow gives one the impression that he is, but after he had made himself comfortable the place seemed smaller. When half-way through the "spout," coming in, he gave a grunt which I took to be one of appreciation. Then Whetter came in. He is of a candid disposition: "Ho, ho, laddie, what the dickens have you done with the tent?"

I tried to explain their mistake. But it was no good. When we were all inside, I couldn't help seeing that the tent was much smaller than it had ever been before, and we had to huddle together most uncomfortably. And there were three days like this.

At nine o'clock one morning Hodgeman woke me with, "What about getting a move on?" The wind had dropped to forty miles an hour, and through a tiny hole in the tent the ground could be seen. Amid a thinning fog of drift, the disc of the sun was just visible.

We made a start and then plodded on steadily till midnight over a soft and uncomfortable surface. Shortly after that hour I looked at the sledge-meter and found that it had ceased working; the sprocket had been knocked off. Repair was out of the question, as every joint was soldered up; so without more ado we dropped it. In future we were to estimate our speed, having already had some good experience in this way.

No sooner had Friday December 13 come on the scene than a catastrophe overtook us. The superstitious might have blamed Fate, but on this occasion there was no room for doubt; the fault was mine. The sail was up and, while braking the load upwind, I slipped and fell, allowing the sledge to collide with a large sastruga. The bow struck the solid snow with such force that it was smashed.

Next day a new bow was manufactured from a spare bamboo which had been brought as a depot pole. It took some time splitting and bending this into position and then lashing it with raw hide. But the finished article fully justified the means, and, in spite of severe treatment, the makeshift stood for the rest of the journey.

While on the march on December 16, the wind dropped and the drift ceased for the first time since December 5; for eleven days it had been heavy or moderate. Before we got into harness on the same day, a Wilson petrel flew above us. This little touch of life, together with the bright sun, light wind and lack of drift enabled us to start away in better spirits than had been our wont.

The next four days passed in excellent weather. The surface was mainly hard and the clusters of large sastrugi could generally be avoided. Patches of softer "piecrust" were met but only lasted for two or three miles. Making up for lost time, we did a few miles short of one hundred in five days.

Unfortunately there was always drift at midday, so that it was impossible to get a latitude "shot" with a sextant and artificial horizon.

On December 19 camp was pitched at 1 AM before a glorious view; an horizon of sea from west to north-east and white fields of massive bergs. In the extreme west there was something which very closely resembled pack-ice.

On the 20th the surface was softer and the snow more recent, but the wind was behind us and for part of the day the track led downhill into a peculiar saucer-shaped depression which, on our first entry, looked like a valley closed at the far end, while when we came to the middle it resolved itself once more into a saucer.

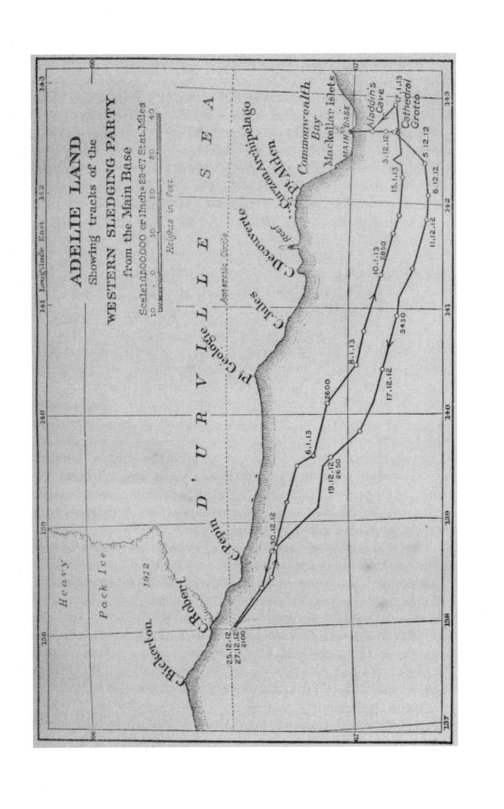

ADELIE LAND

Showing tracks of the

WESTERN SLEDGING PARTY

from the Main Base

Scale 1,500,000 or 1 Inch = 23·67 Stat.Miles

Heights in Feet

Camping here, I managed to get a good time-shot, so that, provided we occupied this camp on the return journey, I reckoned that I could get the watch-rate and fix the approximate longitude of the pack-ice, which for two days had been clearly within view.

December 21 marked the end of the good weather, for drift and wind came on apace lasting four days, the wind attaining about eighty miles an hour. Sleeping-bags and tent-cloth were soon in a wretched state, sodden with moisture. Christmas Day was not very enjoyable in cramped quarters, the tent having encroached on us owing to drift settling around it. Still, by the evening, it was clear enough to break camp and we made a spurt of thirteen miles.

From the next camp there was a good view to the northwest, the pack extending beyond the limit of vision. The land trended to the west-north-west and we could see it at a distance of fifty miles from our altitude.

All things considered, I thought it right to turn back at this stage. In twenty-six days we had done one hundred and fifty-eight miles, and ninety-seven miles of that distance had been covered on the only five consecutive good days. We waited some time until the sun appeared, when I was able to get an observation while Hodgeman made a sketch of the view.

By December 30 we reoccupied the camp of the 20th, sixteen miles on the return journey. A time-shot was successful, and observations were also taken for magnetic declination.

As the weather was fine, Hodgeman and Whetter went to investigate two odd-looking pyramids about five miles away. These turned out to be high snow-ramps, two hundred yards long, on the lee side of open crevasses.

The last day of 1912 was calm and "snow-blind"—the first of this particular variety we had experienced without drift. A New Year pudding was made of soaked biscuit, cocoa, milk, sugar, butter, and a few remaining raisins, and it was, of course, an immense success.

On January 1 and the two succeeding days the drift was so thick that we had to lie up and amuse ourselves discussing various matters of individual interest. Hodgeman gave us a lecture on architecture, explaining the beauties of certain well-known buildings. Whetter would describe some delicate surgical operation, while I talked about machinery. I also worked up the time-shots, and the hours passed quickly. If only our sleeping-bags had been drier we might have enjoyed ourselves at intervals.

The evening of the 4th found us camped ten miles nearer home, beside a large crevasse and with a closer view of the bay seen on December 20. This time we were greatly excited to see rocks outcropping near the water-line, and an investigation of them was resolved upon for the following day.

The morning broke overcast and ghostly white. Although only ten yards away from it, we could not see the huge crevasse in our vicinity. Thus our expedition to the rocks had to be abandoned.

After a week's travelling, during which obscured skies and intermittent drift were the rule, we were once more in the neighbourhood of Madigan's spring depot, forty-five miles west of Aladdin's Cave. It had been passed without our seeing any signs of it on the outward journey, and, as we never relied on finding it, we did not mind about missing it again.

Thick drift and a fifty-mile wind on January 12 kept us confined for thirty-six hours. It was clear enough after noon on the 13th, and five miles were covered in four hours through thick surface drift. What the course was we did not care as we steered by the sastrugi. If ever a man had any "homing instinct" it would surely show itself on such an occasion as this.

Travelling in driving snow used to have a curious effect on me. I always imagined that we were just coming to an avenue of trees running at right angles to our course. What produced this idea I have not the slightest suspicion, but while it lasted, the impression was very strong.

To avoid the drift, which was thickest by day, travelling had for some time been conducted at night. On the evening of the 14th, during a clear spell, a ridge rose up behind, and, in front, a wide bay was visible with its far eastern point rising in mirage. This was taken to be Commonwealth Bay, but the fact could not be verified as the drift came on thickly once more. The day's march was twelve miles by concerted reckoning.

Next day we went three miles to the north to see if any recognizable bergs would come in sight, but were stopped by crevasses. The eastward course was therefore resumed.

After continuing for about a mile Hodgeman told us to stop, flung down his harness and dashed back to the sledge, rummaging in the instrument-box till he found the glasses. "Yes, it's the aeroplane," he said.

This remark took us by surprise as we had not expected it for eight miles at least. It was about midnight—the time when mirage was at a maximum. Consequently, all agreed that the machine was about twelve miles away, and we went on our way rejoicing, steering towards the Cathedral Grotto which was two miles south of the aero-sledge. After three miles we camped, and, it being my birthday, the two events were celebrated by "blowing in" the whisky belonging to the medical outfit.

On the 16th the weather was thick, and we marched east for ten miles, passing a tea-leaf, which it was afterwards found must have come downwind from the Grotto. For eight hours nothing could be done in thick drift, and then, on breaking camp, we actually came to a flag which had been planted by Ninnis in the spring, thirteen miles south-east of Aladdin's Cave. The distance to the air-tractor had been over-estimated, and the Grotto must have been passed quite close.

We made off down the hill, running over the crevasses at a great pace. Aladdin's Cave with its medley of boxes, tins, picks and shovels, gladdened our eyes at 10 PM on the 17th. Conspicuous for its colour was an orange, stuck on a pick, which told us at once that the Ship was in.

CHAPTER XVIII

The Ship's Story

By CAPTAIN J. K. DAVIS

> *By sport of bitter weather*
> *We're warty, strained, and scarred*
> *From the kentledge on the kelson*
> *To the slings upon the yard.*
> *—Kipling*

D R. MAWSON'S PLANS, AS LAID BEFORE THE ROYAL Geographical Society in 1911, provided for an extensive oceanographical campaign in the immense stretch of ocean to the southward of Australia. Very little was known of the sea-floor in this area, there being but a few odd soundings only, beyond a moderate distance from the Australian coast. Even the great *Challenger* Expedition had scarcely touched upon it; and so our Expedition had a splendid field for investigation.

The first discovery made in this connexion on board the *Aurora* was the fact that deep-water work is more intricate than books would make it appear. Although text-books had been carefully studied on the subject, it was found that most of them passed over the practical side of the work in a few words, insufficient to give us much help in carrying out difficult operations with the vessel rolling and tumbling about in the heavy seas of the Southern Ocean.

So it was only after a good deal of hard work and many disappointments that the experience was gained which enabled us, during the later stages of the Expedition, to do useful and successful work.

Before passing on to the operations of the *Aurora* during the winter of 1912, I shall briefly refer to the equipment provided for oceanographical work.

The Lucas Automatic Sounding Machine was situated on the port side of the forecastle head. It was suitable for depths up to six thousand fathoms, being fitted with a grooved wheel so as to be driven by a rope belt from a steam-winch or other engine. The wire was wound in by means of a small horizontal steam-engine which had been specially designed for the *Scotia*, of the Scottish Antarctic Expedition (1902) and was kindly lent to us by Dr. W. S. Bruce.

The wire as it is paid out passes over a measuring wheel, the revolutions of which record on a dial the number of fathoms out. A spring brake, which is capable of stopping the reel instantly, is kept out of action by the tension of the wire, but when the sinker strikes the bottom, the loss of tension allows the brake to spring back and stop the reel. The depth can then be read off on the dial.

A hollow iron tube called a driver is attached to a piece of hemp line spliced into the outer end of the sounding wire. This driver bears one or two weights to the bottom and detaches them on striking it; a specimen of the bottom being recovered in the hollow part of the tube which is fitted with valves to prevent water from running through it on the way up. Immediately the driver and weight strike the bottom, the reel automatically stops paying out wire.

The Big Winding-Drum for the Deep-Sea Dredging Cable

Fletcher with the Driver Loaded Ready to Take a Sounding

To obtain a deep-sea sounding on the *Aurora*, the vessel was stopped, turned so as to bring the wind on the port-bow and kept as nearly stationary as possible; the engines being used to balance any drift of the vessel due to wind or sea.

The difficulties of sounding in the Southern Ocean were much increased by the almost constant, heavy swell. The breaking strain of the wire being only two hundred and forty pounds and the load it had to carry to the bottom weighing nearly fifty-six pounds in air, it could easily be understood that the sudden strain imposed by the violent rolling of the vessel often resulted in the parting of the wire. We soon learnt to handle both vessel and sounding machine in such a way as to entail the least possible strain on the wire.

Of all the operations conducted on board the *Aurora*, deep-sea trawling was the one about which we had most to learn. Dr. W. S. Bruce gave me most valuable advice on the subject before we left England. Later, this was supplemented by a cruise in Australian waters on the *Endeavour*, of the Commonwealth Fisheries Investigation. Here I was able to observe various trawling operations in progress, subsequently applying the information gained to our own requirements on the *Aurora*.

At the Provision Depot for Castaways Provided by the New Zealand Government, Camp Cove, Carnley Harbour, Auckland Island. Primmer on the Right

The Brick Pier Erected at Port Ross, Auckland Islands, by the Magneticians of Sir James Clarke Ross's Expedition

A short description of our trawling arrangements may be useful to those who are engaged in this work on board a vessel not specially designed for it.

We were provided with three thousand fathoms of tapered steel wire (varying from one and three-quarters to one and a half inches in circumference and weighing roughly a ton to the thousand fathoms in air); this was kept on a large iron reel (A) mounted on standards and controlled by a friction-brake. This reel was situated on the starboard side of the main deck, the wire being wound on to it by means of a chain-drive from the forward cargo-winch.

For heaving in, our steam-windlass was fitted with a specially constructed drum (B), which absorbed the crushing strain and then allowed the slack wire to be wound on the reel (A), which was driven as nearly as possible at the same speed; the windlass usually heaving at the rate of four hundred and fifty fathoms per hour.

A wooden derrick (D), provided with topping lift and guys, was mounted on the foremast by means of a band and goose-neck. At the outer end of the derrick, the dynamometer and a fourteen-inch block were attached. The maximum strain which could be supported was ten tons. In paying out, the wire was led from the head of the derrick to a snatch-block on the quarter (E), constructed so as to admit of its disengagement from the wire when it was necessary to heave in. This block kept the wire clear of the propeller and allowed us to have the vessel moving slow or fast as required, while the trawl was being paid out. The positions of the various parts of the trawling gear are shown in the plan on the next page.

Before trawling in deep water the vessel was stopped and a sounding obtained; then the derrick was hoisted, the wire rove through the various blocks, the trawl shackled on, and the men distributed at their stations. When all was ready, the engines were put at half-speed (three knots), a course was given to the helmsman and the trawl lowered into the water. When it was flowing nicely just astern, the order, "Slack away," was given; the wire being paid out evenly by means of the friction-brakes. In one thousand five hundred fathoms of water, after the two-thousand-fathom mark had passed out, the order was given, "Hold on and make fast." Speed was now reduced to one and a half knots and the wire watched until it gave a decided indication of the trawl dragging over the bottom. The strain was now taken by the windlass-barrel, controlled by a screw-brake, backed if necessary by a number of turns round the forward bitts. A slow drag over the bottom was generally continued for one hour. The engines were then stopped, and the order came, "Stand by to heave away." This was quickly

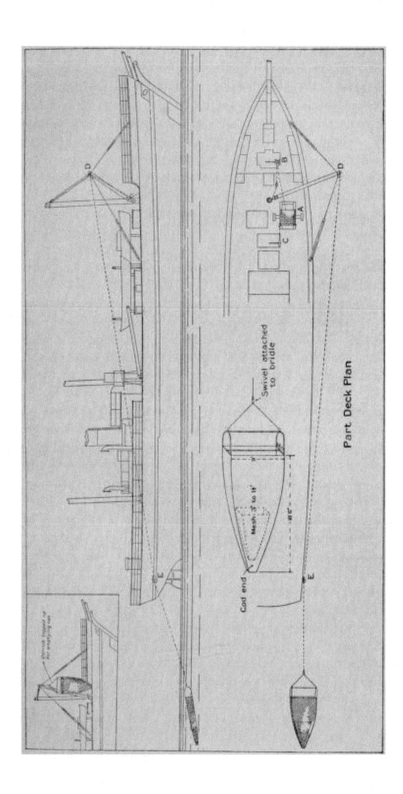

Swivel attached to bridle

Cod end

Mesh 3" to 11"

6'0"

Part Deck Plan

followed by "Knock out," which meant the disengaging of the after-block from the wire and allowed the vessel to swing round head-on to the wire. "Vast heaving" indicated the appearance of the net at the surface, and, when the mouth of the net was well above the bulwarks the derrick was topped up vertically, the lower part of the net dragged inboard and the cod-end untied, the catch being thus allowed to empty itself on deck. The contents of the haul supplied the biologists with the work of sorting and bottling for the next twelve hours or more.

The form of trawl used on board the *Aurora* was known as a Monagasque trawl, of a type employed by the Prince of Monaco. As will be seen from the sketch, it is of simple construction and possesses the advantage of having both sides similar so that it is immaterial which lands on the bottom.

The winter cruise in the Sub-Antarctic began on May 18, 1912, after we had refitted in Sydney and taken on board all the oceanographic apparatus, during the previous month. Leaving Port Jackson, we proceeded to Port Kembla, N.S.W., and took in four hundred and eleven tons of coal.

The following was the personnel of the ship's officers on this and the two following cruises: Chief Officer, F. D. Fletcher; Chief Engineer, F. J. Gillies; Second Officer, P. Gray; Third Officer, C. P. de la Motte.

During the first dredging cruise, Mr. E. R. Waite, from the Canterbury Museum, Christchurch, was in charge of the biological work.

My plan was to go through Bass Strait and then to sail towards the Royal Company Islands as given on the French chart, before heading for Macquarie Island. From thence we should steam across to the Auckland Islands. At both the latter places Mr. Waite would be able to secure specimens. It was not expected that the weather would permit of much trawling, but we anticipated some good soundings. As a matter of fact, sub-antarctic weather in the winter may be predicted with some certainty: strong winds, heavy seas, much fog and general gloom.

We had a fine run through Bass Strait with a light south-east breeze, arriving off King's Island at noon on May 28. The trawling gear was got ready for the following day, but the sea was too high and the ship continued south towards the position of the Royal Company Islands.

On June 1 we were in latitude 53° south, longitude 152 degrees east, and had been cruising about fruitlessly in heavy weather for days waiting for an opportunity to dredge. After being at sea for a whole fortnight we had only three soundings to our credit, and it was, therefore, resolved to make for Macquarie Island.

On the 7th we reached the island and anchored at North-East Bay in twelve fathoms, about one mile from land.

After a stiff pull ashore, next day, we landed and found the party all well. They had built a comfortable hut and were enjoying life as far as possible, despite the constant gales and continuous days of fog.

We then climbed up the hill to the wireless station, where everything was in splendid order. Two small huts had been erected, one for the engine and the other for the receiving apparatus. Sandell and Sawyer, the two operators, were to be congratulated on the efficient way the station had been kept going under very considerable difficulty. In addition to the routine work with Hobart and Wellington they had occasionally communicated with stations over two thousand miles distant.

I was able to send the following message to Professor David: "*Aurora* arrived Macquarie Island; all well, June 7; constant gales and high seas have prevented dredging so far. Royal Company Islands not found in the position indicated on the chart."

We were able to land some stores for the use of the land party under Ainsworth. Meteorological, biological and geological work were all in progress and the scientific records should be of great value. Up to the date of our arrival, no wireless messages had been received from Adelie Land. As Dr. Mawson was in ignorance of its exact location, the position of the Western Base under Wild was given to Ainsworth to forward to Adelie Land in case communication should be established.

After Mr. Waite had obtained several birds, it was decided to move down to Lusitania Bay to secure some Royal penguins and a sea-elephant. Two days later, the *Aurora* anchored in the bay, three-quarters of a mile from the beach, in sixteen fathoms; the weather was very misty. Mr. Waite and Mr. Haines, the taxidermist, were rowed ashore.

The island, above a height of three hundred feet from sea-level, was shrouded in mist throughout the day, and, before dark, all signs of the land had disappeared. The mist did not clear until 6 PM on the 15th.

We stayed for a whole fortnight at Macquarie Island, during which time the highest velocity of the wind recorded on shore was thirty-five miles per hour, although, during the winter, gales are almost of daily occurrence. On June 22, the date of departure, a course was set for the Auckland Islands, which lie in the track of homeward-bound vessels from Australia via Cape Horn.

The group was discovered in 1806 by Captain Bristow of the *Ocean*, owned by Samuel Enderby. It comprises one main island and several smaller ones, separated by narrow channels. There are two spacious harbours; a northern, now called Port Ross, and a southern, Carnley Harbour. The islands are situated about one hundred and eighty miles south of Stewart Island (New Zealand).

After a run of three hundred and forty miles on a northeast course, we entered Carnley Harbour and anchored off Flagstaff Point. A breeze blew strong from the west-northwest. Next day, June 25, we stood up to Figure of Eight Island and found good holding for the anchor in nine and a half fathoms.

The eastern entrance to Carnley Harbour is formed by two bluff points, about two miles apart; its upper extremity terminating in a lagoon. The site of Musgrave's house ("Epigwaith") is on the east side of this lagoon. Here he spent twenty months after the wreck of the *Grafton*.

We set off in the motor-launch on the 26th to visit Camp Cove, where we found the two huts maintained by the New Zealand Government for the benefit of castaways. In the larger hut there were potatoes, biscuits, tinned meats and matches. The smaller hut was empty but on the outside were carved many names of shipwrecked mariners. The *Amakura* had visited the depot in November 1911. The various depots established on the island by the New Zealand Government are visited every six months.

While in Carnley Harbour we were able to make several hauls with the small dredge.

After passing up the eastern coast of the main island we entered Port Ross and anchored west of Shoe Island. On June 30 the depot on Erebus Cove was visited, where three white sheds contain the usual necessaries for unfortunate castaways. The New Zealand Government steamer, *Hinemoa*, while on a scientific expedition to the Sub-Antarctic in 1907, rescued the sixteen survivors of the barque *Dundonald*, two thousand two hundred and three tons, which had been wrecked on Disappointment Island. The captain and ten men had been drowned and the chief officer had died from the effects of exposure and starvation.

On July 2 we went to Observation Point, finding there a flat stone commemorating the visit of the German Scientific Expedition of 1874.

The biologist found various kinds of petrels on Shoe Island, where the turf was riddled in all directions by their burrows.

At Rose Island, close by, there are some fine basaltic columns, eighty feet high, weathered out into deep caverns along their base.

In Sandy Bay, Enderby Island, there was an extensive depot. Among the stores I found a Venesta case marked SY *Nimrod*, which contained dried vegetables and evidently formed part of the stores which were sold on the return of the British Antarctic Expedition of 1907.

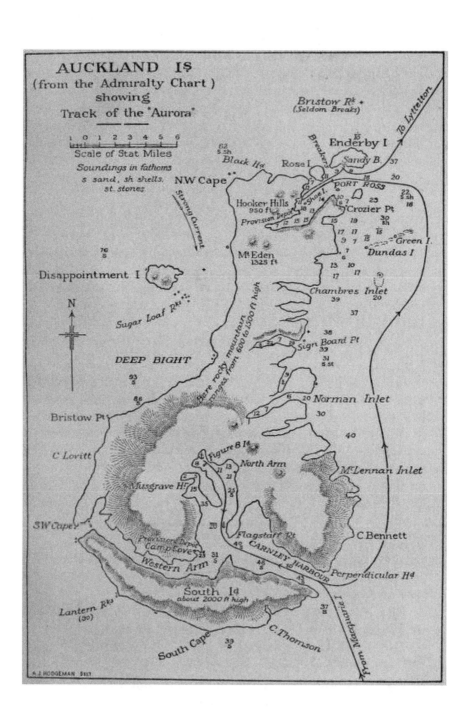

AUCKLAND IS
(from the Admiralty Chart)
showing
Track of the "Aurora"

Bristow Rk +
(Seldom Breaks)

To Lyttelton

1 0 1 2 3 4 5 6
Scale of Stat Miles

Soundings in fathoms
s sand, sh shells,
st. stones

62
s sh
Black Hd

Enderby I

Rose I

Sandy B.   37

Breakers

NW Cape

PORT ROSS
23

Hooker Hills
950 ft

Shoal I

Crozier Pt

Provision Depôt

Strong Current

Green I

Mt Eden
1325 ft

Dundas I

Disappointment I

Chambres Inlet
39

37

N

Sugar Loaf Rks

Sign Board Pt
39

DEEP BIGHT

93
s

Bare rocky mountain
ranges from 600 to 1500 ft high

Norman Inlet
30

Bristow Pt

Figure 8 Id

40

C Lovitt

North Arm

McLennan Inlet

Musgrave Hd

SW Cape

Flagstaff Pt

C Bennett

Provision Depôt
Camp Cove

CARNLEY HARBOUR

Western Arm

Perpendicular Hd

South Id
about 2000 ft high

From Macquarie I

Lantern Rks
(30)

C Thomson

South Cape

A.J. HODGEMAN DELT

After leaving the Auckland Islands for New Zealand, we were fortunate in having fairly good weather. Five soundings were taken, and, on July 9, the trawl was put over in three hundred and forty-five fathoms. The net unfortunately fouled on a rocky bottom and so we gained nothing but experience in the operation.

The *Aurora* arrived at Port Lyttleton on July 11 and we received a very kind welcome from the people of Christchurch. Mr. J. J. Kinsey, well known in connexion with various British Antarctic expeditions, gave us valuable assistance during our stay. We were back again in Melbourne on the 17th of the month.

While the first oceanographical cruise of the *Aurora* did not prove very fruitful in results, chiefly on account of the stormy weather, it provided the necessary training for officers and men in the handling of the deep-sea gear, and we were able to realize later how much we had learnt on our first cruise.

The ship, after undergoing a thorough overhaul at the State dockyard at Williamstown, Victoria, undertook a second deep-sea cruise.

Leaving Hobart on November 12, 1912, she laid her course to the southward in order to obtain soundings for a complete section of the sea-floor, as nearly as possible on the meridian of Hobart. Our time was limited to one month, during which a visit to Macquarie Island for the purpose of landing stores and mail had to be made. Professor T. Flynn of Hobart University accompanied the vessel in charge of the biological work.

An interesting discovery was made two hundred miles south of Tasmania. Here it was proved that a rocky ridge rose like a huge mountain from depths of more than two thousand fathoms to within five hundred and forty fathoms of the surface. A great number of soundings were taken in the vicinity of this rise, subsequently named the Mill Rise, until a heavy gale drove us far from its situation.

On November 21 we were not far from Macquarie Island and, at 7 PM, sounded in one thousand four hundred and fifty fathoms. As the weather was remarkably fine for these latitudes we decided to lower the trawl. Before dark it was being towed slowly towards the east with one thousand nine hundred fathoms of wire out.

We spent an anxious night hoping that the weather would remain fine long enough to permit us to get the gear on board again. We had been driving before a light westerly wind, when the trawl caught on the bottom and stopped the vessel.

A very heavy strain was imposed on the wire as the vessel rose in the swell; the dynamometer registering up to seven tons. I decided to wait

The *Aurora* at Anchor in Port Ross, Auckland Islands

The Monagasque Trawl Hoisted on the Derrick: Gray Standing By

for daylight before attempting to heave in the trawl. At 3 AM we cast the wire off the after-block and started to heave away; it was two hours before the trawl cleared the bottom and the strain was reduced.

At 8 AM the trawl was once more on board, the frames being bent and twisted and the net badly torn. On sounding, the depth was found to be only six hundred and thirty-six fathoms, so that we had evidently put over the trawl on to the edge of a steep rise and then drifted across it.

In view of our position—only thirty miles from Macquarie Island—this accident might have been expected. But opportunities of trawling had been so few that risks had to be taken when the weather quieted down for a few hours. Our only consolation on this occasion was that we recovered the gear.

The following evening, at 7.30, the anchor was dropped in North-East Bay, Macquarie Island, and we were immediately boarded by our land party who were all well. They had become very clever boatmen during their stay, using a small dinghy to make coastal journeys.

On November 24 we left the anchorage at 9 AM and spent the day in its vicinity. More than one hundred soundings were taken, which Blake, the geological surveyor, was to plot on the chart of the island which he had almost completed.

Some idea of the steepness of the submarine mountain of which Macquarie Island forms the crest may be gathered from a sounding, taken ten and a half miles east of the island, which gave two thousand seven hundred and forty-five fathoms and no bottom. In other words, if the sea were to dry up, there would be a lofty mountain rising from the plain of the ocean's bed to a height of nearly eighteen thousand feet.

A great deal of work still required to be done off Macquarie Island, but, as the uneven and rocky nature of the bottom prevented dredging, I decided to sail on the 25th, continuing the voyage towards the Auckland Islands.

Several people had expressed belief in a submarine ridge connecting Macquarie Island with the Auckland group. Three soundings which we obtained on this voyage did not support the suggestion, ranging as they did from one thousand eight hundred and fifty-five to two thousand four hundred and thirty fathoms, eighty-five miles south-west of the Auckland group. We were the more glad to obtain these soundings, as, during the winter cruise, in the same waters, the weather had forced us to abandon the attempt.

On November 28 we took several soundings on the eastern side of the Auckland Islands, but did not prolong our stay as we wished to investigate the ridge south of Tasmania—the Mill Rise. The course was therefore directed westward with a view to outlining the eastern edge of this submarine elevation.

The first sounding to indicate that we were once more approaching the Mill Rise was in one thousand and seventy-six fathoms. Continuing west we secured the next record in one thousand three hundred fathoms, limiting the southern extremity of the ridge which extends northward for nearly one hundred miles. From this sounding the water shoaled quickly as we steered north. Thus, on the same day, we were in eight hundred and thirty-five fathoms at noon, in seven hundred and thirty-five fathoms at 3.40 PM and in seven hundred and ten fathoms at 7.30 PM After the last sounding we lowered the rock-gripper. On the first trial, however, it failed to shut and, on the second, only a little fine sand was recovered. As it was blowing hard most of the time, we were very fortunate in being able to do this piece of work.

An inspection of the chart reveals the fact that the main direction of the shallowest water is in a north-west and south-east direction, but the number of soundings obtained was too small to give more than a general outline. Later, we were able to add to these on the voyage southward to relieve the Antarctic Bases.

The weather was so bad and the sea so heavy that we were unable to obtain soundings on December 9, and, as dredging under such conditions was out of the question, I decided to steer for the east coast of Tasmania, where dredging might be possible under the lee of the land. The constant gales were very disheartening, the last having continued for four days with only short intervals of moderate weather.

On December 12 and 13, in calmer water, some thirty miles off the east coast of Tasmania, trawlings were made successfully in one thousand three hundred fathoms and seventy-five fathoms respectively. From the deeper trawling were obtained a large octopus and several interesting fish.

Just before noon on December 14 we arrived in Hobart and immediately began preparations for the voyage to the Antarctic.

On December 24, 1912, preparations for sailing were complete. For ten days every one connected with the *Aurora* had been working at high pressure, and Christmas Day, our last day ashore, was to be celebrated as a well-earned holiday.

There was on board a good supply of coal, five hundred and twenty-one tons, and a very heavy mail of letters and packages for the members of the Expedition who had been isolated in the far South for more than twelve months. We were to take thirty-five sheep on board as well as twenty-one dogs, presented by Captain Amundsen upon his return from his South Polar expedition. Captain James Davis, of Hobart, of long whaling experience, was to accompany us to give an expert opinion upon such whales as we might meet. Mr. Van Waterschoot van der Gracht, who had had previous experience in the Antarctic, joined as marine artist, and Mr. S. N. Jeffryes as wireless operator. With C. C. Eitel, Secretary of the Expedition, the whole party on board numbered twenty-eight.

A very pleasant Christmas was spent ashore. The ship's company of twenty-three men met for dinner, and we did not forget to wish a "Merry Christmas" to our leader and his twenty-six comrades who were holding their celebration amid the icy solitudes of Antarctica. I was glad, on this festive occasion, to be able to congratulate officers and men on their willing and loyal service during the previous twelve months; every one had done his best to advance the objects of the Expedition.

The attractions of Hobart, at this season, are so numerous, and Tasmanian hospitality so boundless, that it gives me great pleasure to place on record that every man was at his post on the *Aurora* at 10 AM on Boxing Day.

As we drew away from the wharf amid the cheers of those who had come to wish us God-speed, the weather was perfect and the scene on the Derwent bright and cheering. Captain James Davis acted as pilot.

At 11.30 AM we had embarked the twenty-one dogs, which were brought off from the Quarantine Station, and were steaming down Storm Bay. Outside there was a heavy swell, and the wind was freshening from the west. The course was laid south 50° west, true.

For the next two days there was a westerly gale with a very high sea, and the dogs and sheep had a bad time, as a good deal of water came aboard. Two of the sheep had to be killed. By the afternoon of the 29th it had moderated, and a sounding was secured.

This storm was followed by another from the west-northwest. The *Aurora* weathered it splendidly, although one sea came over everything and flooded the cabins, while part of the rail of the forecastle head was carried away on the morning of the 31st. At this time we were in the vicinity of the reputed position of the Royal Company Islands. A sounding was taken with great difficulty, finding two thousand and twenty fathoms and a mud bottom.

January 4, 1918, was a fine day, with a fresh westerly breeze and a high sea. Occasionally there were snow squalls. At night the wireless operator was able to hear HMS *Drake* at Hobart, and also the station at Macquarie Island; the ship having been fitted to receive wireless signals before sailing.

Rafts of Floe-Ice

Next day the sun was bright and there was only a moderate westerly swell. Large bunches of kelp were frequently seen drifting on the surface. "Blue Billys"** flew in great numbers about the ship. Two soundings were obtained in one thousand nine hundred fathoms.

On the 8th a heavy swell came from the south-east. During the morning a sounding realized two thousand two hundred and seventy fathoms and the sample of mud contained a small, black manganese nodule. At 8 PM a floating cask was sighted and taken aboard after much difficulty. It turned out to be a ship's oil cask, empty, giving no clue from whence it came.

The first ice was observed about 6 PM on the 10th. The water was still deep—more than two thousand fathoms.

By noon on January 11 loose pack came into view, with a strong blink of heavier pack to the south. The course was changed to south-west. At 7 PM the ship was steaming west in clear water, a few bergs being in sight and a marked ice-blink to the south. Several whales appeared which Captain James Davis reported were "blue whales" (finners or rorquals).

After we had been steering westward until almost midnight, the course was altered to south-west in the hope of encountering the shelf-ice barrier (met in 1912) well to the east of the Main Base station. On the 12th we sailed over the position of the ice-tongue in 1912 without seeing a trace of it, coming up with heavy broken floe at 10 AM

For four hours the *Aurora* pushed through massive floes and "bergy bits," issuing into open water with the blink of ice-covered land to the south. At nine o'clock Adelie Land was plainly visible, and a course was set for the Main Base. In squally weather we reached the Mackellar Islets at midnight, and by 2 AM on the 13th dropped anchor in Commonwealth Bay under the ice-cliffs in twenty fathoms.

At 6 AM Fletcher, the chief officer, reported that a heavy gust of wind had struck the ship and caused the chain to carry away the lashing of the heavy relieving-tackle. The chain then ran over the windlass, and, before anything could be done, the pointer to which the end of the chain was attached had been torn from the bolts, and our best ground-tackle was lost overboard. It was an exasperating accident.

At seven o'clock the port anchor was dropped in ten fathoms, about eight hundred yards west of the first anchorage, with ninety fathoms of chain. The wind shifted suddenly to the north, and the

---

** *Prion Banksii.*

Aurora swung inshore until her stern was within one hundred yards of the cliffs; but the depth at this distance proved to be seventeen fathoms. After a few northerly puffs, the wind shifted to the south-east and then died away.

At 2.30 PM the launch was hoisted over and the mail was taken ashore, with sundry specimens of Australian fruit as "refreshment" for the shore-party. The boat harbour was reached before any one ashore had seen the *Aurora*. At the landing-place we were greeted most warmly by nine wild-looking men; some with beards bleached by the weather. They all looked healthy and in very fair condition, after the severe winter, as they danced about in joyous excitement.

We learned that five sledging parties had left the Hut: Bage, Webb and Hurley had returned from the south, Stillwell, Close and Laseron from the east, and the others were still out. In Dr. Mawson's instructions, all parties were to be back at the Hut by January 15, 1913.

The launch made some trips to and from the ship with specimens during the afternoon. I returned on board and had a look at the cable. The weather was fine, but changes were apt to occur without much warning. At midnight it was blowing a gale from the south-east, and the chain was holding well. The launch was hoisted up in the davits and communication with the shore was suspended until 8 AM on January 15.

The lull was of two hours' duration, during which Murphy came aboard and furnished me with some particulars about the sledging parties still away.

Dr. Mawson, with Ninnis and Mertz, had gone to the south-east. They were well provisioned and had taken eighteen dogs for transport purposes. Bickerton, Hodgeman and Whetter had been out forty-three days to the west and had food for forty days only. Madigan, McLean and Correll had been away for seventy days in an easterly direction.

Dr. Mawson had left a letter for me with instructions to take charge if he failed to return to time, that is not *later* than January 15, 1913.

On January 16 a party was observed from the ship coming in over the slope. There was much speculation as to its personnel since, at a distance, the three figures could not be recognized. The launch took us ashore and we greeted Madigan, McLean and Correll who had returned from a very successful expedition along the eastern coast over sea-ice.

Madigan and Bage came on board during the forenoon of the 17th and we had a long consultation about the position of affairs owing to the non-return of two parties. It was decided to re-erect the wireless mast and stay it well while the ship was waiting, so that, in case of any party being left at the Main Base, the wireless station would be in working order.**

At one o'clock on the morning of January 18, de la Motte, the officer on watch, reported that a party could be seen descending the glacier. This proved to be Bickerton, Hodgeman and Whetter returning from their trip along the west coast. Thus Dr. Mawson's party was the only one which had not yet returned.

All day work on the wireless mast went along very satisfactorily, while Captain James Davis and Chief Officer Fletcher spent their time in the launch dragging for the cable lost on the morning of our arrival. The launch returned at 10.30 PM and Captain Davis reported that the grapnel had been buoyed until operations could be resumed.

On January 19 we tried to recover the chain, and to this end the *Aurora* was taken over to the position where the grapnels had been buoyed and was anchored. All efforts to secure the chain were unsuccessful. At 7 PM we decided to return to our former position, having a hard job to raise the anchor, which appeared to have dragged under a big rock. Finally it broke away and came up in a mass of kelp, and with the stock "adrift." The latter was secured and we steamed back, "letting go" in eleven fathoms with ninety fathoms of chain.

When Dr. Mawson's party was a week overdue, I considered that the time had arrived to issue a provisional notice to the members of the Expedition at Commonwealth Bay concerning the establishment of a relief party to operate from the Main Base.

A party of four left the Hut on the 20th, keeping a sharp look-out to the south-east for any signs of the missing party. They travelled as far as the air-tractor sledge which had been abandoned ten miles to the south, bringing it back to the Hut.

I decided to remain at Commonwealth Bay until January 30. If the leader's party had not returned by that day, a search party was to proceed eastward while the *Aurora* sailed for Wild's Base. From the reports of the gales which prevailed during the month of March in 1912, and considering the short daylight there was at that time, I felt that it would be risking the lives of all on board to return to the Main Base after relieving Wild's party. I resolved, therefore, to wait *as long as possible*. As a result of a consultation

---

** *It should be borne in mind that during the summer months (November, December, January and part of February) wireless communication with the outside world is impossible owing to continuous daylight reducing the effective range. In summer the range was only a few hundred miles, and the effective working distance for all times of the day probably not above one hundred miles.*

with Madigan and Bage, I had a provisional notice drafted, to be posted up in the Hut on January 22.

This notice was to the effect that the non-arrival of the leader's party rendered it necessary to prepare for the establishment of a relief expedition at Winter Quarters and appointed Bage, Bickerton, Hodgeman, Jeffryes and McLean as members, under the command of Madigan; to remain in Antarctica for another year if necessary.

On the same evening I went ashore to inspect the wireless mast, which was practically complete. The work had been done thoroughly and, provided the mast itself did not buckle, the stays were likely to hold. Hannam, Bickerton and Jeffryes were busy placing the engine and instruments in position.

I then went up the slope for about a mile. The Winter Quarters looked like a heap of stones; boundless ice rose up to the southern skyline; the dark water to the north was broken by an occasional berg or the ice-covered islands. This wonderful region of ice and sea looks beautiful on a fine day. But what a terrible, vast solitude, constantly swept by icy winds and drift, stretches away to the south! A party will go out to-morrow to visit the depot at the top of the slope. This is the seventh day we have been waiting and hoping to welcome the absentees!

On the 23rd the breeze was very strong in the forenoon, but the wind moderated about 4 PM, when the launch was able to leave for the shore. We could see a search party (Hodgeman, Stillwell, and Correll) marching against a strong south-east wind on their way to examine the depot at Aladdin's Cave and its vicinity.

Though there was a moderate south-easter blowing, communication with the land went on during the day. I went ashore early, but the search party did not return until noon. They had remained at Aladdin's Cave overnight and marched farther south next morning, approaching a line of dense drift, without seeing anything.

It was arranged that another party of three men should start next morning (January 25) and, going in a southeasterly direction, make a search for five days, laying a depot at their farthest point. Hodgeman, Hurley and McLean made preparations to set out. I left instructions that a flag should be flown on the wireless mast if Dr. Mawson returned.

I now went through the supplies of provisions and coal which were to be landed for the use of the Relief Party. I intended to try and have everything on shore by January 29, taking advantage of any short interval of fair weather to send a boatload to the landing-place.

On the 25th there was a hard south-east gale blowing until the afternoon, when it moderated sufficiently to send off the launch with thirteen bags of

A Portal Worn Through a Berg by the Waves

A Remarkable Berg, Two Cusps Standing on a Single Basement. Note That It Has Risen Considerably Out of the Sea, Exposing Old Water Lines

A Turreted Berg

coal, Gillies being in charge. The boat harbour was reached in safety, the wind freshening to a gale before 6 PM

Terrific gusts followed in rapid succession and, without warning, the cable parted sixty fathoms from the anchor at 9 PM Having cleared the reefs to leeward, we managed to get in the rest of the chain and then stood along the coast to the north-west. By keeping about three miles from the shore, we seemed to be beyond the reach of the more violent gusts, but a short sea holding the ship broadside to the wind during the squalls, rendered it difficult to maintain a fixed course.

With reefs and bergs around, the increasing darkness about midnight made our position unpleasant. The engines had to be stopped and the ship allowed to drift with the wind, owing to a bearing becoming hot, but in a quarter of an hour they were moving once more.

Early on January 26 the *Aurora* was about half-way between Winter Quarters and the western point of Commonwealth Bay, when the wind suddenly ceased, and then came away light from the north-west. We could see that a south-east gale was still raging close inshore. Over the sea, towards the north, dark clouds were scudding with great rapidity along the horizon: the scene of a violent disturbance.

We returned towards our late anchorage. On reaching it, the south-east wind had moderated considerably, and we let go our spare anchor and what had been saved of the chain.

To the north, violent gusts appeared to be travelling in various directions, but, to our astonishment, these gusts, after approaching our position at a great rate, appeared to curve upwards; the water close to the ship was disturbed, and nothing else. This curious phenomenon lasted for about an hour and then the wind came with a rush from the south-east, testing the anchor-chain in the more furious squalls.

The gale was in its third day on the 27th, and there was a "hurricane sky" during the morning. The wind would die away, only to blow more fiercely than before. The suddenness with which the changes occurred may be gathered from the following extracts from my journal:

"*January 27.* 6 AM A whole gale blowing from the south-east.

"9 AM Light airs from north to east. Launch taking coal ashore.

"11 AM Last cargo of coal had just left ship when the wind freshened from the south-east. The launch had just got inside the boat harbour when a terrific gust struck the vessel and our chain parted. We were blown out to sea while heaving in thirty fathoms of chain which remained.

"4 PM We have been steaming backwards and forwards until the wind died away. The launch has just come off and taken another load of stores to the boat harbour.

"7 PM The weather is moderating with rising barometer. Nearly everything required by the Relief Party is now ashore. Two or three trips will take the remainder.

"We shall steam about for a few hours, and make the anchorage early to-morrow morning."

Next morning a kedge-anchor (about five hundred-weights) was lowered with the remainder of the chain. For a time this held the ship, but a gust of wind from the southeast caused it to drag. It was, therefore, hauled up and, on coming to the surface, was seen to have lost a fluke.

All equipment, coal and food were now on shore for the use of the Relief Party. I had given them everything that could be spared from the provisions set apart for the use of the ship's company. Next day I purposed to cruise along the coast to the east, if the weather were clear.

January 29 was fine, so we steamed off at 6.30 AM As no flag was seen on the wireless mast, we knew that Dr. Mawson had not returned. A course was kept two or three miles from the ice-cliffs beyond the fringe of rocky islets.

At 4 AM on the 30th we were alongside the Mertz Glacier and reached the head of the bay at the confluence of glacier with land-ice. Mount Murchison was only dimly visible, but the weather was clear along the glacier-tongue. Signals were fired and a big kite flown at a height of about five hundred feet to attract attention on shore in case the missing party were near.

"1.30 PM We are now about half a mile from the head of the inlet. From the appearance of the country (heavily crevassed) approach to the sea by a sledging-party would be extremely difficult. There is no floe-ice at the foot of the cliff.

"10.30 PM We are approaching the end of the glacier-tongue around which there is a collection of pack. There is some drift ahead and it is difficult to see far. We have passed the eastern limit of coast to be searched.

"10.35 PM The glacier-tongue is trending to the east and a line of heavy pack extends to the north, with many large bergs. No sign of flag or signal on the end of the barrier.

"*January 31.* We left the glacier-tongue at 8 AM and steered back to Winter Quarters.

"At noon we could see Madigan Nunatak, a rocky patch, high up on the slope.

"4.15 PM Sighted the large grounded berg, fifteen miles from the Main Base.

"9 PM Off Main Base. There is no flag to be seen on the wireless mast!

"Dr. Mawson's party is now sixteen days overdue; there must be something seriously amiss. But from our examination of the line of coast as far as 64° 45' south, 146° 19' east, there does not appear to be any probability of finding traces along the shore line at the base of vertical ice-cliffs."

No communication with the shore was possible until the wind, which had again risen, had moderated. We could just stand off and on until a favourable opportunity occurred. Once the returning ten members of the Expedition were embarked it was imperative to hasten towards Wild's Base.

A week's gale in Commonwealth Bay! The seven days which followed I do not think any of us will forget. From February 1 to 7 it blew a continuous heavy gale, interrupted only when the wind increased to a full hurricane ** (eighty miles an hour).

We endeavoured to maintain a position under the cliffs where the sea had not room to become heavy. This entailed a constant struggle, as, with a full head of steam during the squalls, the vessel drove steadily seaward to where the rising waves broke on board and rendered steering more perplexing. Then, when it had moderated to a mere "howl," we would crawl back, only to be driven out again by the next squall. The blinding spray which was swept out in front of the squalls froze solidly on board and lent additional difficulty to the operation of "wearing ship."

It was on this occasion that we realized what a fine old vessel the *Aurora* was, and, as we slowly moved back to shelter, could appreciate how efficiently our engine-room staff under Gillies were carrying out their duties. The ordinary steaming speed was six knots, yet for the whole of this week, without a hitch, the ship was being driven at an equivalent of ten knots. The fact of having this reserve power undoubtedly saved us from disaster.

A typical entry from my diary reads:

"*February 6*. Just as the sun was showing over the ice-slopes this morning (4 AM) the wind became very violent with the most terrific squalls I have ever experienced. Vessel absolutely unmanageable, driving out to sea. I was expecting the masts to go overboard every minute. This was the

---

** *The maximum wind-velocity recorded at this time by the anemometer on shore was approximately eighty miles an hour.*

A Midsummer View of the Hut and Its Neighbourhood, Looking S.E.

Forging Through Pack-Ice

worst, I think, lasting about two hours. At 6 AM, still blowing very hard but squalls less violent, gradually made shelter during the morning. . . ."

On February 8 the weather improved after 1 AM The gusts were less violent and the lulls were of longer duration. At 9 AM there was only a gentle breeze. We steamed in towards the boat harbour and signalled for the launch to come off with the ten members of the shore-party. The latter had been instructed to remain at the Hut until the vessel was ready to sail. Here, while the gale had been in full career, they had helped to secure enough seal and penguin-meat to keep the Relief Party and their dogs for another year.

The good-byes were brief while the launch discharged the men and their belongings. Instructions were handed over to Madigan directing him to follow the course believed to have been taken by Dr. Mawson and to make an exhaustive search, commencing as soon as the *Aurora* left Commonwealth Bay. Madigan gave me a letter containing a report of the work done by the party which had left on the 25th.

It appears that they had been confined in Aladdin's Cave for twenty-four hours by dense drift and then, in moderate drift, made four miles to the south-east. Here they camped and were not able to move for thirty-six hours in a high wind with thick snow.

On the 28th the drift decreased in amount and, though it was only possible to see a few hundred yards and crevasses were frequent, they kept a course of east 30° south for six miles. A snow-mound was built and on top of it were placed provisions and a note giving the bearing and distance from Aladdin's Cave.

In the afternoon the wind subsided and it became clear. Eight miles on the same course brought them to their farthest camp, twenty-three miles from the Hut. A mound of eleven feet was erected here, provisions and a note being left and some black bunting wound among the snow-blocks. The depot was on a ridge and, with glasses, several miles could be swept to the south-east.

The party consisted of McLean, Hodgeman and Hurley.

De la Motte and Hannam took the Relief Party ashore in the launch and, as soon as they had returned—at 11.30 AM—we steamed out of the bay. The weather had calmed and there were light airs and a smooth sea.

The members of the Relief Party were as follows: C. T. Madigan (leader), R. Bage, F. H. Bickerton, A. J. Hodgeman, Dr. A. L. McLean and S. N. Jeffryes (wireless operator). The remaining ten members of the Main Base Party returned to Australia: J. H. Close, P. E. Correll, W. H. Hannam, J. G. Hunter, J. F. Hurley, C. F. Laseron, H. D. Murphy, F. L. Stillwell, E. N. Webb and Dr. L. A. Whetter.

Throughout the afternoon we steered north-west and at 8.30 PM were approaching heavy pack. Just then Hannam received a wireless message from the Main Base informing us that Dr. Mawson had reached the Hut alone, his two comrades having perished, and instructing me to return at once and pick up all hands. We turned round and steered back immediately.

At 8 AM on February 9 the ship entered Commonwealth Bay steaming against a strong southerly breeze with some snow. We were right up near the anchorage about noon and the Pilot Jack could be seen flying from the wireless mast. Instructions were signalled for, but our efforts were unobserved. We then steamed to and fro across the bay. At 6 PM it was blowing a hard gale and showed signs of becoming worse.

At 6 PM the wind was growing in strength and the barometer was falling. Not having received any reply to my signal for instructions, I felt it was necessary to decide whether I was justified in remaining any longer.

After considering the position in all its bearings I decided to sail westward without further delay and for the following reasons:

1. Dr. Mawson and his companions were in safety, comfortably housed and fully equipped for another winter.
2. Any further delay was seriously endangering our chance of being able to relieve Wild's party that year. The navigation of the fifteen hundred miles to the Shackleton Ice-Shelf was becoming, daily, more dangerous on account of the shortness of daylight and the conditions of the ice.
3. The only vessel which had wintered in the vicinity of the Western Base (the *Gauss*) had been frozen in as early in the season as February 22, spending more than twelve months in the ice. The *Aurora* was not provisioned for a winter in the ice.
4. It had been ascertained from the records at the Main Base that gales were often protracted at the close of the short summer season. We had just experienced one such gale, lasting seven days.
5. As a seaman, I had realized the difficulties encountered in approaching and getting away from the Western Base in 1912. It was then three weeks later in the year.

I felt convinced that in leaving the Main Base, without further delay, I was acting as Dr. Mawson would have wished, if I had been able to acquaint him with the position of the Western Party.

At 6.30 PM we steamed out of the bay, the wind moderating as the ship got well out to sea. At midnight there was a moderate breeze from the south, with some snow.

Members of the Main Base Party Homeward Bound, January 1913. From Left to Right: Back Row, Whetter, Hurley, Webb, Hannam, Laseron, Close; Front Row, Stillwell, Hunter, Correll, Murphy

"Wireless" Corner in the Workshop. Our Link with Civilization

On February 10 heavy pack was met, about fifty miles north of Commonwealth Bay. After coasting along its margin for a while, we pushed among the floes and, after three hours, reached a patch of fairly open water about 1 PM

One hour later a large ice-formation was sighted, which tallied with that met on January 3 of the previous year (1912) and which, on this occasion, was no longer in its original position. We came to the conclusion that the whole must have drifted about fifty miles to the north-west during the intervening year. The face of this huge berg, along which the *Aurora* coasted, was about forty miles in length.

Hannam heard fragments of a message from Dr. Mawson during the evening. The words, "crevasse," "Ninnis," "Mertz," "broken" and "cable" were picked up.

Good progress was made on the 11th against a high westerly sea. The sun set in a clear sky and the barometer was slowly rising. Our position was evidently north of the pack and, if unimpeded by ice, there was a chance of the ship arriving at her destination in time.

Poor headway was made for nearly three days against an adverse wind and sea. Then, late on the 14th, a breeze sprang up from the east-south-east and, under all sail, the *Aurora* made seven knots.

Next morning we were driving along before an easterly gale in thick snow, and at noon the day's run was one hundred and eighty miles.

The journal describes the following week:

"*February 16*. The weather cleared up this morning and the sun came out, enabling us to fix our position.

"We are doing about eight knots under topsails and foresail. The sky looked threatening this evening but improved considerably before midnight.

"*February 17*. There were frequent snow squalls today, making it difficult to see. Only a few scattered pieces of ice were about.

"*February 18*. Bright, clear weather to-day enabled us to get good observations. There are a great many 'blue whales' round the ship, and the many bergs in sight are suggestive of heavy pack to the south. A great many petrels and Cape pigeons have been seen.

"*February 19*. The ship was brought up this morning at 8.45 by a line of heavy pack extending across the course. The weather was misty, but cleared up before noon. We have been obliged to steer a northerly course along the edge of the pack.

"The margin of this pack is some sixty miles farther north than that which we followed in 1912.

"At midnight we were steering north-north-west; many bergs in sight and a line of pack to port.

"*February 20*. At daylight we were able to steer southwest, being at noon about twenty miles north of Termination Ice-Tongue. Pushing through the looser edge of pack for a couple of hours we saw the loom of the ice-tongue to the southward. The pack becoming closer, we turned back to the north in order to try and push through farther west, where the sky looked more promising.

"At dark we were in a patch of clear water, with ice all around. It began to snow and, as the wind remained a light easterly, the ship was allowed to drift until daylight.

"*February 21*. The morning was very foggy up till 11 AM We steered west until noon and then entered the pack; there was a promising sky towards the south. Fair progress was made through the ice, which became looser as we advanced to the south. At 8 PM we passed through leads by moonlight, having a favourable run throughout the night.

"*February 22*. At 4 AM the wind freshened from the south-east with some snow; the floes were getting heavier and the advent of a blizzard was not hailed with joy. About noon the ship approached open water and the snow ceased.

"We were now on the confines of the sea of bergs where navigation had proved so dangerous in 1912.

"At 8 PM the driving snow and growing darkness made it impossible to see any distance ahead. The next seven hours were the most anxious I have ever spent at sea. Although the wind blew hard from the south-east, we passed through the sea of bergs without mishap, guided and protected by a Higher Power.

"*February 23*. At 4 AM the loom of an ice-tongue was sighted and we were soon standing in to follow this feature until we reached the Shackleton Shelf.

"At 8 AM we found that we were some miles south of our reckoning.

"At 11 AM we sighted a depot-flag on the slope. Soon after the ship was up to the fast floe at the head of the bay, the ice being nearly a mile farther north than on the previous year. In fact, the ice-conditions as a whole had changed considerably.

"At noon we reached the Base and found the party all well."

Wild and his comrades were as glad to see the *Aurora* as we were to see them. They had commenced to lay in a stock of seal-meat fearing that they might have to pass another winter on the glacier.

All the afternoon every one was busy getting baggage on board and watering ship. The weather was good and I had intended to sail on the same evening by moonlight, following the glacier-tongue northward in clear water for sixty miles.

As we turned northward, "all well" on board, I felt truly thankful that Wild's party had been relieved and anxiety on their account was now at an end. The party included F. Wild (leader), G. Dovers, C. T. Harrisson, C. A. Hoadley, Dr. S. E. Jones, A. L. Kennedy, M. H. Moyes and A. D. Watson.

Early on the 24th there was a fresh easterly breeze, while the ship steamed among fields of bergs, for the most part of glacier-ice. It is marvellous how a vessel can pass through such an accumulation in the dark and come off with only a few bumps!

Pack consisting of heavy broken floe-ice was entered at four o'clock on the same day, and at 8 AM on the 25th we were clear of it, steering once more among bergs, many of which were earth-stained. The day was remarkably fine with light winds and a smooth sea.

After we had passed through three hundred miles of berg-strewn ocean, large masses of ice, water-worn in most instances, were still numerous, and on February 27, though our position was north of the 80th parallel, they were just beginning to diminish in numbers. At noon on that day a sounding was made in two thousand two hundred and thirty fathoms.

Any hope we may have had of steaming to the east with the object of attempting to relieve the seven men at Adelie Land had to be definitely abandoned on account of the small supply of coal which remained.

There was now a clear run of two thousand miles through the zone of westerly gales and high seas, and on March 14 we reached Port Esperance. Mr. Eitel, Secretary of the Expedition, landed here and caught the steamer Dover to Hobart. We heard of the disaster to Captain Scott and it was learned that wireless messages had been received from Dr. Mawson, which had been forwarded on to Australia through the Macquarie Island party.

The *Aurora* Anchored to the Floe off the Western Base

The Establishment of the Western Base. Hauling Stores to the Top of the Ice-Shelf

CHAPTER XIX

The Western Base—
Establishment and Early
Adventures

By F. WILD

A
T 7 AM ON FEBRUARY 21, 1912, THE *AURORA* STEAMED
away to the north leaving us on the Shackleton Ice-Shelf, while cheers
and hearty good wishes were exchanged with the ship's company. On
the sea-ice, that day, there stood with me my comrades—the Western Party;
G. Dovers, C. T. Harrisson, C. A. Hoadley, S. E. Jones, A. L. Kennedy, M. H.
Moyes and A. D. Watson.

We proceeded to the top of the cliff, where the remainder of the stores and
gear were hauled up. Tents were then erected and the work of hut-building at
once commenced. The site selected for our home was six hundred and forty
yards inland from the spot where the stores were landed, and, as the edge
of the glacier was very badly broken, I was anxious to get a supply of food,
clothing and fuel moved back from the edge to safety as soon as possible.

Of the twenty-eight Greenland dogs that had reached Antarctica in the
Aurora, nineteen were landed in Adelie Land and nine with us. So far, none
of these had been broken in for sledging, and all were in poor condition.
Their quarters on the ship had been very cramped, and many times they
had been thoroughly soaked in salt water, besides enduring several blizzards
in Antarctic waters.

Harrisson, Hoadley, Kennedy and Jones "turned the first sod" in the
foundations of the hut, while Dovers, Moyes, Watson and I sledged
along supplies of timber and stores. Inward from the brink of the
precipice, which was one hundred feet in height, the surface was fairly

good for sledges, but, owing to crevasses and pressure-ridges, the course was devious and mostly uphill.

Until the building was completed, the day's work commenced at 6 AM, and, with only half an hour for a midday meal, continued until 7 PM Fortunately, the weather was propitious during the seven days when the carpenters and joiners ruled the situation; the temperature ranging from −12° F. to 25° F., while a moderate blizzard interrupted one day. The chief trouble was that the blizzard deposited six feet of snow around the stack of stores and coal at the landing-place, thereby adding considerably to our labour. As evidence of the force of the wind, the floe was broken and driven out past the foot of the "flying-fox," tearing away the lower anchor and breaking the sheer-legs on the glacier.

An average day's work on the stores consisted in bringing thirteen loads over a total distance of nine and a half miles. First of all, the cases had to be dug out of the snow-drifts, and loading and unloading the sledges was scarcely less arduous.

On February 27, while working on the roof, Harrisson made an addition to our geographical knowledge. Well to the north of the mainland, and bearing a little north of east, he could trace the outline of land. Subsequently this was proved to be an island, thirty-two miles distant, and seventeen miles north of the mainland. It was twenty miles long and fifteen miles wide, being entirely ice-covered. Later on, it was charted as Masson Island.

On the 28th, the hut was fit for habitation, the stove was installed, and meals were cooked and eaten in moderate comfort. The interior of the house was twenty feet square, but its area was reduced by a lobby entrance, three feet by five feet, a dark-room three feet by six feet situated on one side, and my cabin six feet six inches square in one corner. The others slept in seven bunks which were ranged at intervals round the walls. Of the remaining space, a large portion was commodiously occupied by the stove and table.

On three sides, the roof projected five feet beyond the walls and formed a veranda which was boarded up, making an excellent store-room and work-room. This was a splendid idea of Dr. Mawson's, enabling us to work during the severest storms when there was no room in the hut, and incidentally supplying extra insulation and rendering the inside much warmer. The main walls and roof were double and covered with weather-proof felt. Daylight was admitted through four plate-glass skylights in the roof.

A blizzard effectually prevented outdoor work on February 29, and all hands were employed in the hut, lining the roof and walls and fixing shelves for cooking and other utensils.

An attack was made on the transport of stores next day. As a result of twelve hours' work, five and a half tons of coal were dragged up and stowed under the veranda. It was Hoadley's birthday, and the cook made a special feature of the dinner. With extra dainties like figs, cake and a bottle of wine, we felt that the occasion was fitly celebrated. On March 2, more stores were amassed round the house; Hoadley, Harrisson and I doing odd jobs inside, opening cans, sorting out stores, fitting bunks, shelves and the acetylene gas plant.

While undoing some packages of small boards, Hoadley found that a space had been arranged in the centre of one of the bundles, and a box of cigars inserted by some of the men originally employed upon the construction of the hut in Melbourne. Enclosed was a letter of hearty good wishes.

During the afternoon, Dovers and Kennedy lowered a small sledge down to the floe and brought up a seal and three Adelie penguins. These served for a while as fresh food for ourselves and the dogs.

Sunday March 3 was the finest day we had up till then experienced, and, since the work was now sufficiently advanced to make us comparatively comfortable and safe, I determined to make a proper Sunday of it. All hands were called at 8.30 AM instead of 6 AM After breakfast a few necessary jobs were done and at noon a short service was held. When lunch was over, the skis were unpacked, and all went for a run to the east in the direction of Masson Island.

The glacier's surface was excellent for travelling, but I soon found that it would be dangerous to walk about alone without skis, as there were a number of crevasses near the hut, some of considerable size; I opened one twenty-five feet wide. They were all well bridged and would support a man on skis quite easily.

A heavy gale, with falling snow and blinding drift, came on early the next day and continued for forty-eight hours; our worst blizzard up to that time. The temperature, below zero before the storm, rose with the wind to 30° F. Inside, all were employed preparing for a sledging trip I intended to make to the mainland before the winter set in. We were greatly handicapped by the want of a sewing machine.** When unpacked, the one which had been brought was found to be without shuttles, spools and needles. Large canvas bags, made to contain two weeks' provisions for a sledging unit of three men, were in the equipment, but the smaller bags of calico for the different articles of food had

---

** *By accident the small sewing machine belonging to Wild's party was landed at the Main Base—Ed.*

to be sewn by hand. Several hundred of these were required, and altogether the time consumed in making them was considerable.

Emerging on the morning of the 6th, after the blizzard had blown itself out, we found that snow-drifts to a depth of twelve feet had collected around the hut. For entrance and exit, a shaft had to be dug and a ladder made. The stores, stacked in heaps close by, were completely covered, and another blizzard swooping down on the 7th made things still worse. This "blow," persisting till the morning of the 9th, was very heavy, the wind frequently attaining velocities judged to reach ninety miles per hour, accompanied by drift so thick that it was impossible to go outside for anything.

Beyond the erection of the wireless masts, everything was now ready for the sledging journey. On the day when the wind abated, a party set to work digging holes for the masts and stay-posts. The former were to be fifty-two feet high, four and a half feet being buried in the ice. Unfortunately, a strong breeze with thick drift sprang up just as hoisting operations had started, and in a few minutes the holes were filled up and the workers had to run for shelter. Meanwhile, four men had succeeded in rescuing all the buried stores, some being stowed alongside the hut, and the remainder stacked up again on a new level.

On came another severe blizzard, which continued with only a few minutes' interval until the evening of the 12th. During the short lull, Jones, Dovers and Hoadley took a sledge for a load of ice from a pressure-ridge rather less than two hundred yards from the hut. While they were absent, the wind freshened again, and they had great difficulty in finding a way to the entrance.

It was very disappointing to be delayed in this manner, but there was consolation in the fact that we were better off in the hut than on the glacier, and that there was plenty of work inside. The interior was thus put in order much earlier than it would otherwise have been.

In erecting the hut, it was found that a case of nuts and bolts was missing, and many places in the frame had in consequence to be secured with nails. For a while I was rather doubtful how the building would stand a really heavy blow. There was, however, no need for uneasiness, as the first two blizzards drifted snow to such a depth in our immediate vicinity that, even with the wind at hurricane force, there was scarcely a tremor in the building.

The morning of Wednesday March 13 was calm and overcast. Breakfast was served at six o'clock. We then set to work and cleared away the snow from the masts and stay-posts, so that by 8.30 AM both masts were in position. Before the job was over, a singular sight was witnessed. A large section of the glacier—many thousands of tons—calved off into the sea. The tremendous waves raised by the fall of this mass smashed into fragments all the floe left in the bay. With the sea-ice went the snow-slopes which were the natural roadway down. A perpendicular cliff, sixty to one hundred feet above the water, was all that remained, and our opportunities of obtaining seals and penguins in the future were cut off. Of course, too, the old landing-place no longer existed.

The whole of the sledging provisions and gear were brought out, weighed and packed on the sledges; the total weight being one thousand two hundred and thirty-three pounds. Dovers, Harrisson, Hoadley, Jones, Moyes and myself were to constitute the party.

It was necessary for two men to remain behind at the base to keep the meteorological records, to wind chronometers, to feed the dogs and to bring up the remainder of the stores from the edge of the ice-cliff. Kennedy, the magnetician, had to stay, as two term days** were due in the next month. It was essential that we should have a medical man with us, so Jones was included in the sledging party; the others drawing lots to decide who should remain with Kennedy. The unlucky one was Watson.

To the south of the Base, seventeen miles distant at the nearest point, the mainland was visible, entirely ice-clad, running almost due east and west. It appeared to rise rapidly to about three thousand feet, and then to ascend more gradually as the great plateau of the Antarctic continent. It was my intention to travel inland beyond the lower ice-falls, which extended in an irregular line of riven bluffs all along the coast, and then to lay a depot or depots which might be useful on the next season's journeys. Another reason for making the journey was to give the party some experience in sledging work. The combined weight of both sledges and effects was one thousand two hundred and thirty-three pounds, and the total amount of food carried was four hundred and sixty pounds.

While the sledges were being loaded, ten skua gulls paid us a visit, and, as roast skua is a very pleasant change of food, Jones shot six of them.

At 1 PM we left the hut, making an east-south-east course to clear a pressure-ridge; altering the course once more to south-east. The coast in this direction looked accessible, whereas a line running due south would have brought us to some unpromising ice-falls by a shorter route.

The surface was very good and almost free from crevasses; only one, into which Jones fell to his middle, being seen during the afternoon's march. Not wishing to do too much the first day, especially after the "soft" days

---

** *Days set apart by previous arrangement for magnetic "quick runs."*

431

we had been forced to spend in the hut during the spell of bad weather, I made two short halts in the afternoon and camped at 5 PM, having done seven and half miles.

On the 11th we rose at 5 AM, and at 7 AM we were on the march. For the two hours after starting, the surface was tolerable and then changed for the worse; the remainder of the day's work being principally over a hard crust, which was just too brittle to bear the weight of a man, letting him through to a soft substratum, six or eight inches deep in the snow. Only those who have travelled in country like this can properly realize how wearisome it is.

At 9 AM the course was altered to south, as there appeared to be a fairly good track up the hills. The surface of the glacier rose and fell in long undulations which became wider and more marked as the land approached. By the time we camped, they were three-quarters of a mile from crest to crest, with a drop of thirty feet from crest to trough. Despite the heavy trudging we covered more than thirteen miles.

I made the marching hours 7 AM to 5 PM, so that there was time to get the evening meal before darkness set in; soon after 6 PM.

The Western Base Hut in Winter. Note the Entrance; a Vertical Hole in the Snow in the Foreground

The Western Base Hut—the Grottoes—in Summer

An Evening Camp, Queen Mary Land

A Man-Hauled Sledge

The march commenced about seven o'clock on March 15, the thermometer registering −8° F., while a light southerly breeze made it feel much colder. The exercise soon warmed us up and, when the breeze died away, the remainder of the day was perfectly calm.

A surface of "pie-crust" cut down the mileage in the forenoon. At 11 AM we encountered many crevasses, from two to five feet wide, with clean-cut sides and shaky bridges. Hoadley went down to his head in one, and we all got our legs in others.

It became evident after lunch that the land was nearing rapidly, its lower slopes obscuring the higher land behind. The crevasses also became wider, so I lengthened the harness with an alpine rope to allow more room and to prevent more than two men from being over a chasm at the same time. At 4 PM we were confronted with one sixty feet wide. Crevasses over thirty feet in width usually have very solid bridges and may be considered safe, but this one had badly broken edges and one hundred yards on the right the lid had collapsed. So instead of marching steadily across, we went over singly on the alpine rope and hauled the sledges along in their turn, when all had crossed in safety. Immediately after passing this obstacle the grade became steeper, and, between three and five o'clock, we rose two hundred feet, traversing several large patches of névé.

That night the tent stood on a field of snow covering the lower slopes of the hills. On either hand were magnificent examples of ice-falls, but ahead the way seemed open.

With the exception of a preliminary stiffness, every one felt well after the toil of the first few days.

In bright sunlight next morning all went to examine the ice-falls to the east, which were two miles away. Roping up, we made an ascent half-way to the top which rose five hundred feet and commanded a grand panorama of glacier and coast. Soon the wind freshened and drift began to fly. When we regained the tents a gale was blowing, with heavy drift, so there was nothing to do but make ourselves as comfortable as possible inside.

All through Saturday night the gale raged and up till 11.30 AM on Sunday March 16. On turning out, we found that the tents and sledges were covered deeply in snow, and we dug continuously for more than two hours before we were able to pack up and get away. Both sledges ran easily for nearly a mile over névé, when the gradient increased to one in ten, forcing us to relay. It was found necessary to change our finnesko for spiked boots. Relaying regularly, we gradually mounted six hundred feet over névé and massive sastrugi. With a steep slope in front, a halt was made for the night. The sunset was a picture of prismatic colours reflected over the undulating ice-sheet and the tumbling cascades of the glacier.

On the evening of March 18 the altitude of our camp was one thousand four hundred and ten feet, and the slope was covered with sastrugi ridges, three to four feet in height. Travelling over these on the following day we had frequent capsizes.

The outlook to the south was a series of irregular terraces, varying from half a mile to two miles in breadth and twenty to two hundred feet in height. These were furrowed by small valleys and traversed by ridges, but there was not a sign of rock anywhere.

The temperature varied from 4° to 14° F. during the day, and the minimum recorded at night was −11° F.

Another nine miles of slow ascent brought us to two thousand feet, followed by a rise of two hundred and twenty feet in seven and three-quarter miles on March 21. Hauling over high broken sastrugi was laborious enough to make every one glad when the day was over. The rations were found sufficient, but the plasmon biscuits were so hard that they had to be broken with a geological hammer.

There now swept down on us a blizzard** which lasted for a whole week, on the evening of March 21. According to my diary, the record is as follows:

"*Friday, March 22.* Snowing heavily all day, easterly wind: impossible to travel as nothing can be seen more than ten to twelve yards away. Temperature high, 7° to 18° F.

"*Saturday, March 23.* Blowing hard at turn-out time, so did not breakfast until 8.30. Dovers is cook in my tent this week. He got his clothes filled up with snow while bringing in the cooker, food-bag, etc. The wind increased to a fierce gale during the day, and all the loose snow which fell yesterday was shifted.

"About 5 PM the snow was partially blown away from the skirt or ground cloth, and the tent bulged in a good deal. I got into burberries and went out to secure it; it was useless to shovel on snow as it was blown off immediately. I therefore dragged the food-bags off the sledge and dumped them on. The wind and drift were so strong that I had several times to get in the lee of the tent to recover my breath and to clear the mask of snow from my face.

"We are now rather crowded through the tent bulging in so much, and having cooker and food-bag inside.

"*Sunday, March 24.* Had a very bad night. The wind was chopping about from south-east to north and blowing a hurricane. One side of the tent was pressed in past the centre, and I had to turn out and support it with bag lashings. Then the ventilator was blown in and we had a pile of snow two feet high over the sleeping-bags; this kept us warm, but it was impossible to prevent some of it getting into the bags, and now we are very wet and the bags like sponges. There were quite two hundredweights of snow on us; all of which came through a hole three inches wide.

"According to report from the other tent they are worse off than we are; they say they have four feet of snow in the tent. All this is due to the change of wind, making the ventilator to windward instead of leeward.

"*March 25, 26* and *27.* Blizzard still continues, less wind but more snowfall.

"*Thursday, March 28.* Heavy falling snow and drift, south-east wind. At noon, the wind eased down and snow ceased falling, so we slipped into our burberry over-suits and climbed out to dig for the sledges.

** *It is a singular fact that this blizzard occurred on the same date as that during which Captain Scott and his party lost their lives.*

"Nothing could be seen except about two feet of the tops of the tents, which meant that there was a deposit of five feet of freshly fallen snow. The upper two feet was soft and powdery, offering no resistance; under that it was still soft, so that we sank to our thighs every step and frequently to the waist. By 4.30 PM both sledges were rescued, and it was ascertained that no gear had been lost. We all found that the week of idleness and confinement had weakened us, and at first were only able to take short spells at the digging. The sky and barometer promise fine weather to-morrow, but what awful work it will be pulling!"

At 5.30 AM on March 29 the weather was bright and calm. As a strong wind had blown throughout the night, a harder surface was expected. Outside, we were surprised to find a fresh wind and thick, low drift; owing to the tents being snowed up so high, the threshing of the drift was not audible. To my disgust the surface was as soft as ever. It appeared that the only resort was to leave the provisions for the depot on the nearest ridge and return to the Base. The temperature was −20° F., and, while digging out the tents, Dovers had his nose frost-bitten.

It took six of us well over an hour to drag the necessary food half a mile up a rise of less than one hundred feet; the load, sledge included, not being five hundred pounds. Nearly all the time we were sinking thigh-deep, and the sledge itself was going down so far that the instrument-box was pushing a mass of snow in front of it. Arriving on the ridge, Moyes found that his foot was frozen and he had to go back to camp, as there was too much wind to bring it round in the open.

Sufficient food and oil were left at this depot for three men for six weeks; also a minimum thermometer.

In a fresh breeze and flying drift we were off at 10 AM next day. At first we were ambitious and moved away with two sledges, sinking from two to three feet all the time. Forty yards was as much as we could do without a rest, and by lunch time nine hundred yards was the total. Now the course was downhill, and the two sledges were pulled together, creeping along with painful slowness, as walking was the hardest work imaginable. After one of the most strenuous days I have ever experienced, we camped; the sledge-meter recorded one mile four hundred and fifty yards.

A spell of two days' blizzard cooped us up once more, but improved the surface slightly. Still, it was dreadfully soft, and, but for the falling gradient, we would not have made what we did; five miles six hundred and ten yards, on April 2. On that and the following day it was fortunate that the road chosen was free of crevasses.

At the foot of the hills I had decided to reduce the rations but, as the track had grown firm once more, and we were only twenty-five miles from the hut, with a week's food, I thought it would be safe to use the full allowance.

Soon after leaving the hills (April 4), a direct course to the hut was made. There was no mark by which to steer, except a "water-sky" to the north, the hinterland being clouded over. During the afternoon, the sun occasionally gleamed through a tract of cirro-stratus cloud and there was a very fine parhelion: signs of an approaching blizzard. At 4.30 PM we had done seventeen and a half miles, and, as all hands were fresh and willing, I decided to have a meal and go on again, considering that the moon was full and there were only six miles to be done.

After supper the march was continued till 8.30 PM, by which time we were due for a rest. I had begun to think that we had passed the hut.

April 5 was far from being a Good Friday for us. At 2 AM a fresh breeze rose and rapidly increased to a heavy gale. At 10 AM Hoadley and I had to go out to secure the tent; the weather-side bulged in more than half the width of the tent and was held by a solid load of drift, but the other sides were flapping so much that almost all the snow had been shaken off the skirt. Though only five yards away from it we could not see the other tent. At noon Hoadley again went out to attend to the tent and entirely lost himself within six feet of it. He immediately started to yell and I guessed what was the matter at once. Dovers and I shouted our best, and Hoadley groped his way in with a mask of snow over his face. He told us that the wind which was then blowing a good eighty miles an hour, knocked him down immediately he was outside, and, when he struggled to his feet again, he could see nothing and had no idea in what direction lay the tent.

The space inside was now so limited by the combined pressure of wind and snow that we did not light the primus, eating lumps of frozen pemmican for the evening meal.

The blizzard continued with unabated violence until eleven o'clock next morning, when it moderated within an hour to half a gale. We turned out and had a good hot meal. Then we looked to see how the others had fared and found that their tent had collapsed. Getting at once into wind-proof clothing, we rushed out and were horrified to see Harrisson in his bag on the snow. He quickly assured us that he was all right. After carrying him, bag and all, into our tent, he emerged quite undamaged, but very hungry.

Jones and Moyes now had to be rescued; they were in a most uncomfortable position under the fallen tent. It appears that the tent had blown down on the previous morning at ten o'clock, and for thirty-six hours they had had nothing to eat. We did not take long to dig them out.

The wind dropped to a moderate breeze, and, through the falling snow, I could make out a "water-sky" to the west. The three unfortunates said that they felt fit to travel, so we got under way. The surface was soft and the pulling very heavy, and I soon saw that the strain was largely due to the weakness of the three who had been without food. Calling a halt, I asked Jones if it would do to go on; he assured me that they could manage to go on with an effort, and the march was resumed.

Not long after, Dovers sighted the wireless mast, and a quarter of an hour later we were safely in the hut, much to the surprise of Kennedy and Watson, who did not expect us to be travelling in such weather, and greatly to our own relief. According to the sledge-meter, the last camp had only been two miles one hundred yards from home, and if anything had been visible on the night of April 4, we could have got in easily.

I was very pleased with the way all the party had shaped. They had worked splendidly and were always cheerful, although conditions had been exceptionally trying during this journey. No one was any the worse for the hardships, except for a few blistered fingers from frost-bites. The party lost weight at the average of two and a half pounds; Harrisson was the greatest loser, being reduced six pounds. Out of the twenty-five days we were away, it was only possible to sledge on twelve days. The total distance covered, including relay work, was nearly one hundred and twenty-two miles, and the greatest elevation reached on the southern mainland was two thousand six hundred feet above sea-level.

Kennedy and Watson had been very busy during our absence. In a few days they had trained five of the dogs to pull in harness, and transported the remainder of the stores from the landing-place, arranging them in piles round the hut. The weather at the Base had been quite as bad as that experienced by us on the land slopes.

In the first blizzard both wireless masts were broken down. Watson and Kennedy managed to repair and re-erect one of the masts, but it was only thirty-seven feet in height. Any final hopes of hearing wireless signals were dispelled by the discovery that the case containing the detector and several other parts necessary for a receiving-station were missing.

Watson had fitted up a splendid dark-room, as well as plenty of shelves and racks for cooking utensils.

Kennedy was able to secure a series of observations on one of his term days, but, before the next one, the tent he was using was blown to ribbons.

In the Veranda of the Western Base Hut—the "Grottoes"—Looking Towards the Entrance Dug Vertically Down Through the Snow Drift

The Wind-Weathered Igloo Built for Magnetic Observations—Western Base

Nunatak—Queen Mary Land: Showing Remarkable Moat on Windward Side and Ramp on Lee

CHAPTER XX

The Western Base—Winter and Spring

O N EASTER SUNDAY, APRIL 7, 1912, A FURIOUS blizzard kept us close prisoners. To meet the occasion, Dovers prepared a special dinner, the principal item being roast mutton, from one of the six carcases landed with the stores. Divine service was held in the forenoon.

The blizzard raged with such force all Sunday and Monday that I dared not let any one go out to feed the dogs, although we found, later, that a fast of three days did not hurt them at all.

I now thought it time to establish a winter routine. Each member had his particular duties to perform, in addition to general work, in which all hands were engaged. Harrisson took charge of the lamps and checked consumption of oil. Hoadley had the care of the provisions, making out lists showing the amount the cook might use of each article of food, besides opening cases and stowing a good assortment on convenient shelves in the veranda. Jones and Kennedy worked the acetylene plant. In connexion with this, I should mention that several parts were missing, including T-pieces for joints and connexions for burners. However Jones, in addition to his ability as a surgeon, showed himself to be an excellent plumber, brazier and tinsmith, and the Hut was well lighted all the time we occupied it. Moyes's duties as meteorologist took him out at all hours. Watson looked after the dogs, while Dovers relieved other members when they were cooks. The duty of cook was taken for a week at a time by every one except myself. A night watch was kept by each in turn. The watchman went on duty at 9 PM, usually taking advantage of this night to have a bath and wash his clothes. He prepared breakfast, calling all hands at 8.30 AM for this meal at nine o'clock. The cook for the week was exempt from all other work. In the case of Kennedy, whose magnetic work was done principally at night, arrangements were made to assist him with the cooking.

Work commenced during the winter months at ten o'clock and, unless anything special had to be done, finished at 1 PM, when lunch was served. The afternoon was usually devoted to sport and recreation.

The frequent blizzards and heavy snowfall had by this time buried the Hut so deeply that only the top of the pointed roof was visible and all the outside stores were covered.

My diary for April 9 says:

"The blizzard" (which had commenced on the evening of the 6th) "played itself out during the night and we got to work immediately after breakfast. There was still a fresh breeze and low drift, but this gradually died away.

"We were an hour digging an exit from the Hut. The day has been occupied in cutting a tunnel entrance, forty feet long, through the drift, so that driving snow cannot penetrate, and we shall be able to get out with less trouble.

"As we get time I intend to excavate caverns in the huge drifts packed round the house and stow all our stores inside; also a good supply of ice for use during blizzards.

"I had intended to make a trip to Masson Island before the winter properly set in, but with the weather behaving as it does, I don't think it would be wise."

The 10th, 11th and 12th being fine, good progress was made in digging out store-rooms on either side of the tunnel, but a blizzard on the 13th and 14th stopped us again.

On going to feed the dogs during the afternoon of the 14th, Watson found that Nansen was dead; this left us with seven, as Crippen had already died. Of the remainder, only four were of any value; Sweep and the two bitches, Tiger and Tich, refusing to do anything in harness, and, as there was less than sufficient food for them, the two latter had to be shot. Sweep would have shared the same fate but he disappeared, probably falling down a crevasse or over the edge of the glacier.

Until the end of April almost all our time was spent in making store-rooms and in searching for buried stores; sometimes a shaft would have to be sunk eight to twelve feet. Bamboo poles stuck in the snow marked the positions of the different stacks. The one marking the carbide was blown away, and it was two days before Dovers finally unearthed it. By the 30th, caves roomy enough to contain everything were completed, all being connected by the tunnel. We were now self-contained, and everything was accessible and immune from the periodic blizzards.

The entrance, by the way, was a trap-door built over the tunnel and raised well above the outside surface to prevent it being drifted over. From below it was approached by a ladder, but the end of the tunnel was left open, so that in fine weather we could run sledges in and out with loads of ice. With each blizzard the entrance was completely choked, and it gave two men a day's work to clear it out once more.

On April 16 Kennedy had a term day. A fresh breeze was blowing and the temperature was –20° F. Some of his observations had to be taken in the open and the remainder in a tent. The series took three hours to complete and by that time he was thoroughly chilled through, his feet and fingers were frost-bitten and his language had grown more incisive than usual.

Between the 10th and the 19th we made a search for penguins and seals. Hoadley and Moyes staying behind, the rest of us with tents and equipment journeyed along the edge of the glacier to the south, without seeing the smallest sign of life. The edge of the shelf ice was very much fissured, many of the breaches giving no sign of their presence, in consequence of which several falls were sustained. It should be remarked that the Shackleton Shelf-Ice runs mainly in a southerly direction from the Winter Quarters, joining the mainland at a point, afterwards named Junction Corner. The map of Queen Mary Land illustrates this at a glance.

From the 25th to the 29th, Kennedy, Harrisson and Jones were employed building an igloo to be used as a magnetic observatory. On the afternoon of the 30th, the magnetician invited every one to a tea-party in the igloo to celebrate the opening. He had the place very nicely decorated with flags, and after the reception and the formal inspection of the instruments, we were served with quite a good tea. The outside temperature was –33° F. and it was not much higher inside the igloo. As a result, no one extended his visit beyond the bounds of politeness.

On May 1, Harrisson, Hoadley and Watson went away south towards the land at the head of the bay, which curved round to Junction Corner, to examine icebergs, take photographs and to search for seals. They took the four dogs with them and, as the load was a light one—three hundred and forty-two pounds—the dogs pulled it easily.

I went with the others to the north, hoping that we might find a portion of the glacier low enough to give access to the sea-ice. There were several spots where the ice-cliffs were not more than forty to fifty feet high, but no convenient ramps led down from the cliffs. In any case neither penguins nor seals were to be had in the vicinity. A great, flat sheet of frozen sea stretched away to the north for quite thirty miles.

May 2 was fine, but the 3rd and 4th were windy once more and we had to remain indoors. Saturday, the 4th, was clean-up day, when the verandas, tunnel and cave were swept and tidied, the stove cleaned, the hut and darkroom scrubbed and the windows cleared. The last was a job which was generally detested. During the week, the windows in the roof collected a coat of ice, from an inch to three inches thick, by condensation of moisture. Chipping this off was a most tedious piece of work, while in the process one's clothes became filled with ice.

One Sunday, Harrisson, Hoadley and Watson returned from their short trip; they had missed the strong winds which had been blowing at the Base, although less than twenty miles away. Some very fine old icebergs were discovered which were of interest to the two geologists and made good subjects for Harrisson's sketches. Watson had had a nasty fall while crossing a patch of rough ice, his nose being rather badly cut in the accident.

On May 7 another blizzard stopped all outside work. Moyes ventured as far as the meteorological screen at noon and got lost, but luckily only for a short time. The barometer behaved very strangely during the blow, rising abruptly during a little more than an hour, and then slowly falling once more. For a few hours on the 8th there was a lull and the store of ice was replenished, but the 9th and 10th were again spent indoors, repairing and refitting tents, poles and other sledging gear during the working hours, and reading or playing chess and bridge in the leisure time. Harrisson carved an excellent set of chessmen, distinguishing the "black" ones by a stain of permanganate of potash.

Bridge was the favourite game all through the winter, and a continuous record of the scores was kept. Two medals were struck: a neat little thing for the highest scorer and a huge affair as large as a plate, slung on a piece of three-and-a-half-inch rope, with "Jonah" inscribed on it, to be worn by the player at the foot of the list.

Divine service was held every Sunday, Moyes and I taking it in turn. There was only one hymn book amongst the party, which made it necessary to write out copies of the hymns each week.

The sleeping-bags used on the first sledging journey had been hung up near the roof. They were now taken down to be thoroughly overhauled. As a consequence of their severe soaking, they had shrunk considerably and required enlarging. Dovers's bag, besides contracting a good deal, had lost much hair and was cut up to patch the others. He received a spare one to replace it.

May 15 was a beautiful bright morning and I went over to an icy cape two miles southward, with Harrisson, Hoadley, Dovers and Watson, to find a road down to the sea-ice. Here, we had good fortune at last, for, by following down a crevasse which opened out at sea-level into a magnificent cave, we walked straight out on to the level plain. Along the edge of the glacier there was not even a seal's blow-hole. Watson took some photos of the cave and cliff.

It was Kennedy's term night; the work keeping him in the igloo from 10 PM until 2.30 AM He had had some difficulty in finding a means of warming the observatory—an urgent necessity, since he found it impossible to manipulate delicate magnetic instruments for three or four hours with the temperature from −25° F. to −30° F. The trouble was to make a non-magnetic lamp and the problem was finally solved by using one of the aluminium cooking pots; converting it into a blubber stove. The stove smoked a great deal and the white walls were soon besmirched with a layer of soot.

The 17th, 18th and 19th were all calm but dull. One day I laid out a ten-hole golf course and with some homemade balls and hockey sticks for clubs played a game, not devoid of interest and excitement.

During a blizzard which descended on the evening of the 20th, Zip and Sweep disappeared and on the 21st, a search on the glacier having been in vain, Dovers and Hoadley made their way down to the floe. They found Zip well and hearty in spite of having had a drop of at least forty feet off the glacier. A further search for Sweep proved fruitless. We were forced to conclude that he was either killed by falling over the precipice or he had gone far away hunting for penguins.

The regular blizzard immured us on May 22, 23 and 24; the wind at times of terrific force, approaching one hundred miles per hour. It was impossible to secure meteorological observations or to feed the dogs until noon on the 24th. Moyes and I went out during a slight cessation and, with the aid of a rope from the trap-door, managed to find the dogs, and gave them some biscuits. The drift was then so thick that six feet was as far as one could see.

We did not forget Empire Day and duly "spliced the mainbrace." The most bigoted teetotaller could not call us an intemperate party. On each Saturday night, one drink per man was served out, the popular toast being "Sweethearts and Wives." The only other convivial meetings of our small symposium were on the birthdays of each member, Midwinter's Day and King's Birthday.

On the 25th we were able to make an inventory of a whole series of damages effected outside. The dogs' shelter had entirely carried away; a short mast which had been erected some weeks previously as a holdfast for sledges was snapped off short and the sledges buried, and, worst of all, Kennedy's igloo had parted with its roof, the interior being filled with snow, underneath which the instruments were buried. The dogs were, however, all quite well and lively. It was fortunate for them that the temperature always rose during the blizzards. At this period, when on fine days it was usual to experience –25° to –37° F., the temperature rose in the snowstorms to 25° or even 30° F.

Monday the 27th was beautifully clear. The tunnel entrance was opened and some of the party brought in ice while others undid the rope lashings which had been placed over the hut. This was so compactly covered in snow that the lashings were not required and I wanted to make a rope ladder to enable us to get down to the sea-ice and also to be used by Watson and Hoadley, who were about to dig a shaft in the glacier to examine the structure of the ice.

Fine weather continued until June 2. During this time we were occupied in digging a road from the glacier down to the sea-ice in the forenoons and hunting for seals or skiing in the afternoons. Kennedy and Harrisson rebuilt the magnetic igloo. A seal-hole was eventually found near the foot of the glacier and this was enlarged to enable the seals to come up.

At the end of May, daylight lasted from 9 AM until 3 PM, and the sunrise and sunset were a marvel of exquisite colour. The nightly displays of aurora australis were not very brilliant as the moon was nearing the full.

On the days of blizzards, there was usually sufficient work to be found to keep us all employed. Thus on June 2, Watson and I were making a ladder, Jones was contriving a harpoon for seals, Hoadley was opening cases and stowing stores in the veranda, Dovers cleaning tools, Moyes repairing a thermograph and writing up the meteorological log, Harrisson cooking and Kennedy sleeping after a night-watch.

Between June 4 and 22 there was a remarkably fine spell. It was not calm all the time, as drift flew for a few days, limiting the horizon to a few hundred yards. An igloo was built as a shelter for those sinking the geological shaft, and seal-hunting was a daily recreation. On June 9, Dovers and Watson found a Weddell seal two and a half miles to the west on the sea-ice. They killed the animal but did not cut it up as there were sores on the skin. Jones

Midwinter's Dinner in Queen Mary Land, 1912. From Left to Right: Behind—Hoadley, Dovers, Watson, Harrisson, Wild. In Front—Jones, Moyes, Kennedy

went over with them afterwards and pronounced the sores to be wounds received from some other animal, so the meat was considered innocuous and fifty pounds were brought in, being very welcome after tinned foods. Jones took culture tubes with him and made smears for bacteria. The tubes were placed in an incubator and several kinds of organisms grew, very similar to those which infect wounds in ordinary climates.

The snowstorms had by this time built up huge drifts under the lee of the ice-cliffs, some of them more than fifty feet in height and reaching almost to the top of the ice-shelf. An exhilarating sport was to ski down these ramps. The majority of them were very steep and irregular and it was seldom that any of us escaped without a fall at one time or another. Several of the party were thrown from thirty to forty feet, and, frequently enough, over twenty feet, without being hurt. The only accident serious enough to disable any one happened to Kennedy on June 19, when he twisted his knee and was laid up for a week.

There were many fine displays of the aurora in June, the best being observed on the evening of the 18th. Curtains and streamers were showing from four o'clock in the afternoon. Shortly after midnight, Kennedy, who was taking magnetic observations, called me to see the most remarkable exhibition I have so far seen. There was a double curtain 30° wide unfolded from the eastern horizon through the zenith, with waves shimmering

A Bevy of Emperor Penguins on the Floe

along it so rapidly that they travelled the whole length of the curtain in two seconds. The colouring was brilliant and evanescent. When the waves reached the end of the curtain they spread out to the north and rolled in a voluminous billow slowly back to the east. Kennedy's instruments showed that a very great magnetic disturbance was in progress during the auroral displays, and particularly on this occasion.

Hoadley and Watson set up a line of bamboos, a quarter of a mile apart and three miles long, on the 20th, and from thence onwards took measurements for snowfall every fortnight.

On Midwinter's Day the temperature ranged from −38° F. to −25° F. and daylight lasted from 10 AM until 4 PM We proclaimed a universal holiday throughout Queen Mary Land. Being Saturday, there were a few necessary jobs to be done, but all were finished by 11 AM The morning was fine and several of us went down to the floe for skiing, but after twelve o'clock the sky became overcast and the light was dimmed. A strong breeze brought along a trail of drift, and at 6 PM a heavy blizzard was in full career. Inside, the hut was decorated with flags and a savoury dinner was in the throes of preparation. To make the repast still more appetising, Harrisson, Hoadley and Dovers devised some very pretty and clever menus. Speeches, toasts and a gramophone concert made the evening pass quickly and enjoyably.

From this time dated our preparations for spring sledging, which I hoped would commence about August 15. Jones made some experiments with "glaxo," of which we had a generous supply. His aim was to make biscuits which would be suitable for sledging, and, after several failures, he succeeded in compressing with a steel die a firm biscuit of glaxo and butter mixed, three ounces of which was the equivalent in theoretical food value to four and a half ounces of plasmon biscuit; thereby affording a pleasant variety in the usual ration.

July came in quietly, though it was dull and cloudy, and we were able to get out on the first two days for work and exercise. On the 2nd a very fine effect was caused by the sun shining through myriads of fog-crystals which a light northerly breeze had brought down from the sea. The sun, which was barely clear of the horizon, was itself a deep red, on either side and above it was a red mock sun and a rainbow-tinted halo connected the three mock suns.

On the 5th and 6th the wind blew a terrific hurricane (judged to reach a velocity of one hundred miles per hour) and, had we not known that nothing short of an earthquake could move the hut, we should have been very uneasy.

All were now busy making food-bags, opening and breaking up pemmican and emergency rations, grinding biscuits, attending to personal gear and doing odd jobs many and various.

In addition to recreations like chess, cards and dominoes, a competition was started for each member to write a poem and short article, humorous or otherwise, connected with the Expedition. These were all read by the authors after dinner one evening and caused considerable amusement. One man even preferred to sing his poem. These literary efforts were incorporated in a small publication known as "The Glacier Tongue."

Watson and Hoadley put in a good deal of time digging their shaft in the glacier. As a roofed shelter had been built over the top, they were able to work in all but the very worst weather. While the rest of us were fitting sledges on the 17th and 18th, they succeeded in getting down to a level of twenty-one feet below the surface of the shelf-ice.

Sandow, the leader of the dogs, disappeared on the 18th. Zip, who had been missed for two days, returned, but Sandow never came back, being killed, doubtless, by a fall of snow from the cliffs. All along the edge of the ice-shelf were snow cornices, some weighing hundreds of tons; and these often broke away, collapsing with a thunderous sound. On July 31, Harrisson and Watson had a narrow escape. After finishing their day's work, they climbed down to the floe by a huge cornice and sloping ramp. A few seconds later, the cornice fell and an immense mass of hard snow crashed down, cracking the sea-ice for more than a hundred yards around.

July had been an inclement month with three really fine and eight tolerable days. In comparison with June's, which was −14.5° F., the mean temperature of July was high at −1.5° F. and the early half of August was little better.

Sunday August 11 was rather an eventful day. Dovers and I went out in the wind to attend to the dogs and clear the chimney and, upon our return, found the others just recovering from rather an exciting accident. Jones had been charging the acetylene generators and by some means one of them caught fire. For a while there was the danger of a general conflagration and explosion, as the gas-tank was floating in kerosene. Throwing water over everything would have made matters worse, so blankets were used to smother the flames. As this failed to extinguish them, the whole plant was pulled down and carried into the tunnel, where the fire was at last put out. The damage amounted to two blankets singed and dirtied, Jones's face scorched and hair singed, and Kennedy, one finger jammed. It was a fortunate escape from a calamity.

A large capsized berg had been noticed for some time, eleven miles to the north. On the 14th, Harrisson, Dovers, Hoadley and Watson took three days' provisions and equipment and went off to examine it. A brief account is extracted from Harrisson's diary:

"It was a particularly fine, mild morning; we made good progress, three dogs dragging the loaded sledge over the smooth floe without difficulty, requiring assistance only when crossing banks of soft snow. One and a half miles from 'The Steps,' we saw the footprints of a penguin.

"Following the cliffs of the shelf-ice for six and three quarter miles, we sighted a Weddell seal sleeping on a drift of snow. Killing the animal, cutting off the meat and burying it in the drift delayed us for about one hour. Continuing our journey under a fine bluff, over floe-ice much cracked by tide-pressure, we crossed a small bay cutting wedge-like into the glacier and camped on its far side.

"After our midday meal we walked to the berg three miles away. When seen on June 28, this berg was tilted to the north-east, but the opposite end, apparently in contact with the ice-cliffs, had lifted higher than the glacier-shelf itself. From a distance it could be seen that the sides, for half their height, were wave-worn and smooth. Three or four acres of environing floe were buckled, ploughed up and in places heaped twenty feet high, while several large fragments of the broken floe were poised aloft on the old 'water-line' of the berg.

"However, on this visit, we found that the berg had turned completely over towards the cliffs and was now floating on its side surrounded by large separate chunks; all locked fast in the floe. In what had been the bottom of the berg Hoadley and Watson made an interesting find of stones and pebbles—the first found in this dead land!

"Leaving them collecting, I climbed the pitted wave-worn ice, brittle and badly cracked on the higher part. The highest point was fifty feet above the level of the top of the shelf-ice. There was no sign of open water to the north, but a few seals were observed sleeping under the cliffs."

Next morning the weather thickened and the wind arose, so a start was made for the Base. All that day the party groped along in the comparative shelter of the cliff-face until forced to camp. It was not till the next afternoon in moderate drift that a pair of skis which had been left at the foot of "The Steps" were located and the hut reached once again.

After lunch on August 11, while we were excavating some buried kerosene, Jones sighted a group of seven Emperor penguins two miles away over the western floe. Taking a sledge and camera we made after them. A mile off, they saw us and advanced with their usual stately bows. It seemed an awful shame to kill them, but we were sorely in need of fresh meat. The four we secured averaged seventy pounds in weight and were a heavy load up the steep rise to the glacier; but our reward came at dinner-time.

With several fine days to give us confidence, everything was made ready for the sledge journey on August 20. The party was to consist of six men and three dogs, the object of the journey being to lay out a food-depot to the east in view of the long summer journey we were to make in that direction. Hoadley and Kennedy were to remain at the Base, the former to finish the geological shaft and the latter for magnetic work. There remained also a good deal to do preparing stores for later sledge journeys.

The load was to be one thousand four hundred and forty pounds distributed over three sledges; two hundred pounds heavier than on the March Journey, but as the dogs pulled one sledge, the actual weight per man was less.

The rations were almost precisely the same as those used by Shackleton during his Expedition, and the daily allowance was exactly the same— thirty-four ounces per man per day. For his one ounce of oatmeal, the same weighs of ground biscuit was substituted; the food value being the same. On the second depot journey and the main summer journeys, a three-ounce glaxo biscuit was used in place of four and a half ounces of plasmon biscuit. Instead of taking cheese and chocolate as the luncheon ration, I took chocolate alone, as on Shackleton's southern journey it was found more satisfactory than the cheese, though the food value was practically the same.

The sledging equipment and clothing were identical with that used by Shackleton. Jaeger fleece combination suits were included in the outfit but, though excellent garments for work at the Base, they were much too heavy for sledging. We therefore wore Jaeger underclothing and burberry wind clothing as overalls.

The weather was not propitious for a start until Thursday, August 22. We turned out at 5.30 AM, had breakfast, packed up and left the Hut at seven o'clock.

After two good days' work under a magnificently clear sky, with the temperature often as low as −34° F., we sighted two small nunataks among a cluster of pressure-ridges, eight miles to the south. It was the first land, in the sense of rocks, seen for more than seven months. We hoped to visit the outcrops—Gillies Nunataks—on our return.

The course next day was due east and parallel to the mainland, then ten miles distant. To the north was Masson Island, while at about the same distance and ahead was a smaller island, entirely ice-covered like the former—Henderson Island.

A blizzard of three days' duration kept us in camp between August 27 and 30. Jones, Moyes and I had a three-man sleeping-bag, and the temperature being high, 11° to 15° F., we were very warm, but thoroughly tired of lying down for so long. Harrisson, Dovers and Watson had single bags and therefore less room in the other tent.

The last day of August was beautifully bright: temperature –12° to –15° F. We passed Henderson Island in the forenoon, and, hauling up a rise to the south of it, had a good view of the surroundings. On the right, the land ran back to form a large bay, seventeen miles wide. This was later named the Bay of Winds, as a "blow" was always encountered while crossing it.

In the centre of the bay was a nunatak, which from its shape at once received the name of the Alligator. In front, apparently fifteen miles off, was another nunatak, the Hippo, and four definite outcrops—Delay Point and Avalanche Rocks—could be seen along the mainland. The sight of this bare rock was very pleasing, as we had begun to think we were going to find nothing but ice-sheathed land. Dovers took a round of angles to all the prominent points.

The Hippo was twenty-two miles away, so deceptive is distance in these latitudes; and in one and a half days, over very heavy sastrugi, we were in its vicinity. The sledges could not be brought very near the rock as it was surrounded by massive ridges of pressure-ice.

We climbed to the top of the nunatak which was four hundred and twenty feet high, four hundred yards long and two hundred yards wide. It was composed of gneissic granite and schists. Dovers took angles from an eminence, Watson collected geological specimens and Harrisson sketched until his fingers were frost-bitten. Moss and lichens were found and a dead snow petrel—a young one—showing that the birds must breed in the vicinity.

To the south, the glacier shelf appeared to be very little broken, but to the north it was terribly torn and twisted. At each end of the nunatak there was a very fine bergschrund.** Twenty miles to the east there appeared to be an uncovered rocky islet; the mainland turning to the southward twelve miles away. During the night the minimum thermometer registered –47° F.

An attempt to get away next morning was frustrated by a strong gale. We were two hundred yards from the shelter of the Hippo and were forced to turn back, since it was difficult to keep one's feet, while the sledges were blown sideways over the névé surface.

I resolved to leave the depot in this place and return to the Base, for our sleeping-bags were getting very wet and none of the party were having sufficient sleep. We were eighty-four miles from the hut; I had hoped to do

---

** *The term not used in the usual sense. Referring to a wide, imposing crevasse caused by the division of the ice as it presses past the nunatak.—Ed.*

Before Sunrise: Camped Near the Hippo Nunatak

one hundred miles, but we could make up for that by starting the summer journey a few days earlier. One sledge was left here as well as six weeks' allowance of food for three men, except tea, of which there was sufficient for fifty days, seventy days oil and seventy-eight days' biscuit. The sledge was placed on end in a hole three feet deep and a mound built up around it, six feet high; a bamboo and flag being lashed to the top.

On September 4 we were homeward bound, heading first to the mainland leaving Delay Point on our left, to examine some of the outcrops of rock. Reaching the coast about 3 PM, camp was shortly afterwards pitched in a most beautiful spot. A wall of solid rock rose sheer for over four hundred feet and was crowned by an ice-cap half the thickness. Grand ice-falls surged down on either side.

The tents were erected in what appeared to be a sheltered hollow, a quarter of a mile from Avalanche Rocks. One tent was up and we were setting the other in position when the wind suddenly veered right round to the east and flattened out both tents. It was almost as humorous as annoying. They were soon raised up once more, facing the other way.

While preparing for bed, a tremendous avalanche came down. The noise was awful and seemed so close that we all turned to the door and started out. The fastening of the entrance was knotted, the people from the other tent were yelling to us to come out, so we dragged up the bottom of the tent and dived beneath it.

The cliff was entirely hidden by a cloud of snow, and, though the crashing had now almost ceased, we stood ready to run, Dovers thoughtfully seizing a food-bag. However, none of the blocks had come within a hundred yards of us, and as it was now blowing hard, all hands elected to remain where they were.

Several more avalanches, which had broken away near the edge of the mainland, disturbed our sleep through the night, but they were not quite so alarming as the first one. A strong breeze was blowing at daybreak; still the weather was not too bad for travelling, and so I called the party. Moyes and I lashed up our bags, passed them out and strapped them on the sledge; Jones, in the meantime, starting the cooker. Suddenly a terrific squall struck the front of our tent, the poles burst through the apex, and the material split from top to bottom.

Moyes and I were both knocked down. When we found our feet again, we went to the aid of the other men, whose tent had survived the gust. The wind rushed by more madly than ever, and the only thing to do was to pull away the poles and allow the tent to collapse.

Looking around for a lee where it could be raised, we found the only available shelter to be a crevasse three hundred yards to windward, but the wind was now so strong that it was impossible to convey the gear even to such a short distance. All were frequently upset and blown along the surface twenty or thirty yards, and, even with an ice-axe, one could not always hold his own. The only resort was to dig a shelter.

Setting to work, we excavated a hole three feet deep, twelve feet long and six feet wide; the snow being so compact that the job occupied three hours. The sledges and tent-poles were placed across the hole, the good tent being laid on top and weighted down with snow and blocks of ice. All this sounds very easy, but it was a slow and difficult task. Many of the gusts must have exceeded one hundred miles per hour, since one of them lifted Harrisson who was standing beside me, clean over my head and threw him nearly twenty feet. Everything movable was stowed in the hole, and at noon we had a meal and retired into sleeping-bags. At three o'clock a weighty avalanche descended, its fearful crash resounding above the roar of the wind. I have never found anything which gave me a more uncomfortable feeling than those avalanches.

The gale continued on September 6, and we still remained packed in the trench. If the latter had been deeper and it had been possible to sit upright, we should have been quite comfortable. To make matters worse, several more avalanches came down, and all of them sounded horribly close.

We were confined in our burrow for five days, the wind continuing to blow with merciless force. Through being closed up so much, the temperature of the hole rose above freezing-point, consequently our sleeping-bags and clothes became very wet.

On Sunday September 8, Moyes went out to feed the dogs and to bring in some biscuit. He found a strong gusty wind with falling snow, and drift so thick that he could not see five yards. We had a cold lunch with nothing to drink, so that the primus should not raise the temperature. In the evening we sang hymns and between us managed to remember the words of at least a dozen.

The long confinement was over on the 10th; the sky was blue and the sun brilliant, though the wind still pulsated with racking gusts. As soon as we were on the ice, away from the land, two men had to hold on to the rear of each sledge, and even then capsizes often occurred. The sledge would turn and slide broadside-on to leeward, tearing the runners badly on the rough ice. Still, by 9.30 AM the surface changed to snow and the travelling improved. That night we camped with twenty miles one hundred yards on the meter.

There was a cold blizzard on the 11th with a temperature of –30° F. Confined in the tents, we found our sleeping-bags still sodden and uncomfortable.

With a strong beam wind and in moderate drift big marches were made for two days, during which the compass and sastrugi determined our course.

My diary of September 14 runs as follows:

"On the march at 7 AM; by noon we had done twelve miles one thousand five hundred yards. Lunch was hurried, as we were all anxious to get to the hut to-night, especially we in the three-man bag, as it got so wet while we were living underground that we have had very little sleep and plenty of shivering for the last four nights. Last night I had no sleep at all. By some means, in the afternoon, we got on the wrong course. Either the compass was affected or a mistake had been made in some of the bearings, as instead of reaching home by 5 PM we were travelling till 8 PM and have done thirty-two miles one thousand one hundred yards. Light loads, good surface and a fair wind account for the good travelling, the sail doing almost all the work on the man-hauled sledge.

"The last two hours we were in the dark, except for a young moon, amongst a lot of crevasses and pressure-ridges which none of us could recognize. At one time, we found ourselves on a slope within a dozen yards of the edge of the glacier; this decided me to camp. Awfully disappointing; anticipating another wretched night. Temperature –35° F."

Next day we reached home. The last camp had been four and a half miles north of the hut. I found that we had gone wrong through using 149° as the bearing of Masson Island from the Base, when it should have been 139°. I believe it was my own mistake, as I gave the bearing to Dovers and he is very careful.

Before having a meal, we were all weighed and found the average loss to be eight pounds. In the evening, Moyes and I weighed ourselves again; he had gained seven pounds and I five and three-quarter pounds.

Comparing notes with Hoadley and Kennedy, I found that the weather at the Base had been similar to that experienced on the sledging journey.

It was now arranged that Jones was to take charge of the main western journey in the summer. While looking for a landing-place in the *Aurora*, we had noted to the west an expanse of old, fast floe, extending for at least fifty miles. The idea was for Jones and party to march along this floe and lay a depot on the land as far west as was possible in four weeks. The party included Dovers, Harrisson, Hoadley and Moyes. They were to be assisted by the dogs.

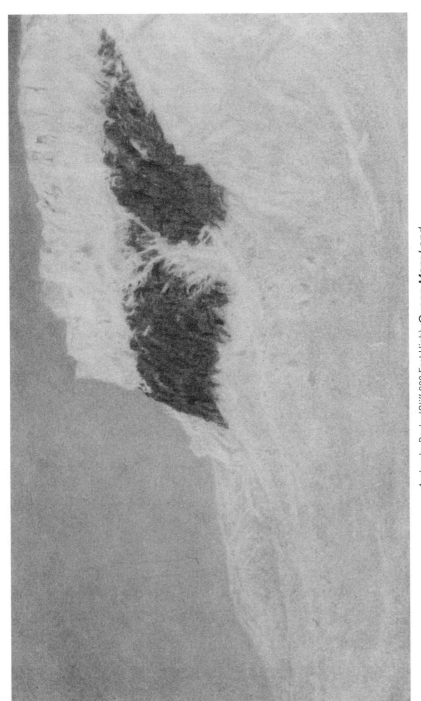

Avalanche Rocks (Cliff 600 Feet High). *Queen Mary Land*

It was my intention to take Kennedy and Watson up to the depot we had left on the hills in March, bringing back the minimum thermometer and probably some of the food. Watson was slightly lame at the time, as he had bruised his foot on the last trip.

Until Jones made a start on September 26, there were ten days of almost continuous wind and drift. The equinox may have accounted for this prolonged period of atrocious weather. No time, however, was wasted indoors. Weighing and bagging food, repairing tents, poles, cookers and other gear damaged on the last journey and sewing and mending clothes gave every man plenty of employment.

At 6 AM on the 26th, Jones reported that there was only a little low drift and that the wind was dying away. All hands were therefore called and breakfast served.

Watson, Kennedy and I assisted the others down to the sea-ice by a long sloping snow-drift and saw them off to a good start in a south-westerly direction. We found that the heavy sledge used for carrying ice had been blown more than five hundred yards to the edge of the glacier, capsized among the rough pressure-slabs and broken. Two heavy boxes which were on the sledge had disappeared altogether.

The rest of the day was devoted to clearing stores out of the tunnels. It was evident to us that with the advent of warmer weather, the roof of the caves or grottoes (by the way, the hut received the name of "The Grottoes") would sink, and so it was advisable to repack the cases outside rather than dig them out of the deep snow. By 6 PM nearly two hundred boxes were passed up through the trap-door and the caverns were all empty.

After two days of blizzard, Watson, Kennedy and I broke trail with loads of one hundred and seventy pounds per man. Right from the start the surface was so soft that pulling became very severe. On the first day, September 29, we managed to travel more than nine miles, but during the next six days the snow became deeper and more impassable, and only nineteen miles were covered. Crevasses were mostly invisible, and on the slope upwards to the ice-cap more troublesome than usual. The weather kept up its invariable wind and drift. Finally, after making laborious headway to two thousand feet, Kennedy strained his Achilles tendon and I decided to return to "The Grottoes."

At 2 PM on October 8, the mast was sighted and we climbed down into the Hut, finding it very cold, empty and dark. The sun had shone powerfully that day and Kennedy and Watson had a touch of snow-blindness.

Two weeks went by and there was no sign of the western depot party. In fact, out of sixteen days, there were thirteen of thick drift and high wind, so that our sympathies went out to the men in tents with soaking bags, waiting patiently for a rift in the driving wall of snow. On October 23 they had been away for four weeks; provisions for that time having been taken. I had no doubt that they would be on reduced rations, and, if the worst came, they could eat the dogs.

During a lull on October 24, I went to the masthead with the field-glasses but saw nothing of the party. On that day we weighed out provisions and made ready to go in search of them. It was my intention to go on the outward track for a week. I wrote instructions to Jones to hoist a large flag on the mast, and to burn flares each night at 10 PM if he should return while I was away.

There was a fresh gale with blinding drift early on the following morning; so we postponed the start. At 4 PM the wind subsided to a strong breeze and I again went up the mast to sweep the horizon. Westward from an icy cape to the south a gale was still blowing and a heavy cloud of drift, fifty to sixty feet high, obscured everything.

An hour later Watson saw three Adelie penguins approaching across the floe and we went down to meet them, bringing them in for the larder. Four Antarctic petrels flew above our heads: a sign of returning summer which was very cheering.

The previous night had promised a fine day and we were not disappointed on October 26. A sledge was packed with fourteen days' provisions for eight men and we started away on a search expedition at 10 AM

After doing a little over nine miles we camped at 5.30 PM Before retiring to bag, I had a last look round and was delighted to see Jones and his party about a mile to the south. It was now getting dark and we were within two hundred yards of them before being seen, and, as they were to windward, they could not hear our shouts. It was splendid to find them all looking well. They were anxious to get back to "The Grottoes," considering there was only one serviceable tent between them. Kennedy and I offered to change with any of them but, being too eager for warm blankets and a good bed, they trudged on, arriving at the Base at midnight.

Briefly told, their story was that they were stopped in their westerly march, when forty-five miles had been covered, by a badly broken glacier—Helen Glacier—on the far side of which there was open sea. There was only one thing to do and that was to set out for the mainland by a course so circuitous that they were brought a long way eastward, back towards "The

Grottoes." They had very rough travelling, bad weather, and were beset with many difficulties in mounting on to the land-ice, where the depot had to be placed. Their distance from the Base at this point was only twenty-eight miles and the altitude was one thousand feet above sea-level. On the ice-cap they were delayed by a blizzard and for seventeen days—an unexampled time—they were unable to move from camp. One tent collapsed and the occupants, Jones, Dovers and Hoadley, had to dig a hole in the snow and lower the tent into it.

These are a few snatches from Jones's diary:

"The next sixteen days (following Wednesday, October 9) were spent at this camp. . . . Harrisson and Moyes occupied one tent and Dovers, Hoadley and myself the other.

"On Saturday, the third day of the blizzard, the wind which had been blowing steadily from the east-south-east veered almost to east and the tents commenced to flog terrifically. This change must have occurred early in the night, for we awoke at 5 AM to find clouds of snow blowing under the skirt on one side: the heavy pile on the flounce having been cut away by the wind. As it would have been impossible to do anything outside, we pulled the tent poles together and allowed the tent to collapse. The rest of the day was spent in confined quarters, eating dry rations and melting snow in our mugs by the warmth of our bodies. . . . Although Harrisson and Moyes were no more than twenty feet from us, the noise of the gale and the flogging of our tents rendered communication impossible.

"The terrible flapping at last caused one of the seams of our tent to tear; we sewed it as well as we were able and hoped that it would hold till daylight.

"On Monday morning, the same seam again parted and we decided to let the tent down again, spending the day in a half-reclining position. . . .

"At 6.30 PM the gale eased and, during a comparative lull, Moyes came out to feed the dogs. Noticing our position, he helped us to re-erect the tent and Dovers then went out and piled snow over the torn seam. Moyes said that Harrisson and he had been fairly comfortable, although the cap of their tent was slowly tearing with the pressure of the wind and snow on the weather panels. . . .

"On Friday, the 18th, Swiss, one of the dogs, returned very thin after six days' absence from the camp.

"On the following Monday the blizzard moderated somewhat and we proceeded to make our quarters more roomy by digging out the floor and undercutting the sides, thus lowering the level about eighteen inches.

A Yawning Crevasse

Wild's Party Making Slow Progress in Dangerous Country

"Our tent now looks as if it were half blown over. To relieve the tremendous strain on the cap, we lowered the feet of the two lee poles on to the new floor. The tent now offered very little resistance to the wind. We were able to communicate with Harrisson and Moyes and they said they were all right."

When the snow and wind at last held up, they immediately made down to the sea-ice and back towards home, and, when they met us, had done nineteen miles. All were stiff next day, and no wonder; a march of twenty-eight miles after lying low for seventeen days is a very strenuous day's work.

Preparations were made on October 28 for the main eastern summer journey, the object of which was to survey as much coast-line as possible and at the same time to carry on geological work, surveying and magnetics. The party was to consist of Kennedy, Watson and myself.

Jones, Dovers and Hoadley were to start on the main western journey on November 2. I arranged that Harrisson and Moyes should remain at the Hut, the latter to carry on meteorological work, and Harrisson biology and sketching. Later, Harrisson proposed to accompany me as far as the Hippo depot, bringing the dogs and providing a supporting party. At first I did not like the idea, as he would have to travel one hundred miles alone, but he showed me that he could erect a tent by himself and, as summer and better weather were in sight, I agreed that he should come.

Each party was taking fourteen weeks' provisions, and I had an additional four weeks' supply for Harrisson and the dogs. My total load came to nine hundred and seventy pounds; the dogs pulling four hundred pounds with the assistance of one man and three of us dragging five hundred and seventy pounds.

C H A P T E R   X X I

The Western Base— Blocked on the Shelf-Ice

By F. WILD

WE STARTED AWAY ON THE MAIN EASTERN JOURNEY with a spurt of eleven miles on a calm and cloudless day, intending to follow our former track over the shelf-ice to the Hippo Nunatak. The surface varied; soft patches putting a steady brake on the ardour of the first, fresh hours of marching.

In the afternoon, it was only necessary to wear a shirt, singlet, heavy pyjama trousers, finnesko and socks, and even then one perspired freely. The temperature stood at 17 degrees F. The dogs pulled their load well, requiring help only over loose snow.

The evening of Friday November 1, 1912, saw us past Masson Island and about ten miles from the mainland. All day there had been a chill easterly breeze, the temperature being well below zero. The sky was hazy with cirro-stratus and a fine halo "ringed" the sun.

Looking out from the tent in the morning we saw that the clouds were dense and lowering, but the breezes were light and variable until 5 PM, when an east-north-east wind arose, bringing snow in its train. Travelling through foggy drift, we could just ascertain that the Bay of Winds had opened up on the right. The day's march was a good one of sixteen miles thirty-five yards.

The Bay of Winds did not belie its name. Throughout November 3 the wind veered about in gusts and after lunch settled down to a hard south-easter.

We had made a good start; more than sixty-two miles in a little over four days. The camp was half-way across the Bay of Winds, with the Alligator Nunatak six miles off on the "starboard bow" and the Rock of the Avalanches seventeen miles straight ahead. Passing glimpses were caught of the Hippo twenty-four miles distant.

On November 5, after a day's blizzard, there was much accumulated snow to shovel away from tents and sledges. Finding the hauling very arduous, we headed in for the land to find a better surface, passing the Alligator Nunatak close on its southern side.

At noon on the 6th, the sledges were running parallel to the Rock of the Avalanches, three miles away, and soon afterwards we came to a large boulder; one of four in a line from the rock-cliffs, from which they had been evidently transported, as they were composed of the same gneiss.

The Hippo was close at hand at four o'clock and, on nearing the shattered ice about the depot, we released the dogs and pulled the sledge ourselves. On being freed, they galloped over to the rock and were absent for over an hour. When they returned, Amundsen's head was daubed with egg-yolk, as we thought. This was most probable as scores of snow petrels were flying about the rocks.

A nasty shock was awaiting us at the depot. The sledge, which had been left on end, two feet buried in hard snow and with a mound six feet high built round it, had been blown completely away. The stays, secured to foodbags, were both broken; one food-bag weighing sixty-eight pounds having been lifted ten feet. This was a very serious loss as the total load to be carried now amounted to one thousand one hundred and eighty pounds, which was too great a weight to be supported by one sledge.

It appeared, then, that the only thing to do was to include Harrisson in the party, so that we could have his sledge. This would facilitate our progress considerably, but against that was the fact that Moyes would be left alone at the Base under the belief that Harrisson had perished.

A gale was blowing on the 7th, but as we were partly under the lee of the Hippo, it was only felt in gusts. A visit was made to the Nunatak; Harrisson to examine the birds, Watson for geology and photography, while I climbed to the summit with the field-glasses to look for the missing sledge. Kennedy remained at the camp to take a series of magnetic observations.

There were hundreds of snow petrels pairing off, but no eggs were seen in any of the nest-crevices. They were so tame that it was quite easy to catch them, but they had a habit of ejecting their partially digested food, a yellow oily mess, straight at one. This was the stuff we had thought was egg-yolk on Amundsen's head the previous night.

Upon returning to camp, the search for the sledge was continued. After prospecting with a spade in possible snow-drifts and crevasse-lids, we walked out fanwise, in the direction of the prevailing wind, but with no result. I decided, therefore, to take Harrisson with me. I was extremely sorry for Moyes, but it could not be helped.

On the way back towards the land to the south, we found that the surface had improved in the morning's gale. Camp was finally pitched on a slope close to the high land.

The coast, from the Base to this spot—Delay Point—runs almost due east and west and with no deep indentations except the Bay of Winds. To the west, the slope from the inland plateau is fairly gradual and therefore not badly broken, but still farther west it is much steeper, coming down from two thousand feet in a very short distance, over tumbling ice-fields and frozen cascades. Several outcrops of dark rock lay to the east, one of them only two miles away.

The wind-velocity fluctuated between sixty and eighty miles per hour, keeping us securely penned. Harrisson and Kennedy, after battling their way to our tent for a meal, used the second primus and cooker, brought for Harrisson, in their own tent. All we could do was to smoke and listen to the fierce squalls and lashing drift. I had brought nothing to read on the trip, making up the weight in tobacco. Watson had Palgrave's *Golden Lyrics*, Kennedy, an engineer's hand-book, and Harrisson, a portion of the *Reign of Mary Tudor*. There was a tiny pack of patience cards, but they were in the instrument-box on the sledge and none of us cared to face the gale to get them.

The wind, on the 10th, saw fit to moderate to half a gale; the drift creeping low and thick over the ground; the land visible above it. Donning burberrys, we made an excursion to the rocks ahead. Two miles and a climb of six hundred feet were rather exhausting in the strong wind. There were about eighty acres of rock exposed on the edge of the ice-cap, mainly composed of mica schists and some granite; the whole extensively weathered. A line of moraine ran from the rocks away in an east-north-east direction.

Most of the next day was broken by a heavy gale and, since the prospect ahead was nothing but bare, rough ice, we passed the day in making everything ready for a start and repaired a torn tent. The rent was made by Amundsen, who dragged up the ice-axe to which he was tethered and,

Delay Point: Ice-Fall on the Left, Morainic Deposit and Pool of Thaw-Water in the Foreground

in running round the tent, drove the point of the axe through it, narrowly missing Kennedy's head inside.

Tuesday November 12 was an interesting day. The greater part of the track was over rippled, level ice, thrown into many billows, through devious pressure-hummocks and between the inevitable crevasses. The coast was a kaleidoscope of sable rocks, blue cascades, and fissured ice-falls. Fifteen miles ahead stood an island twenty miles long, rising in bare peaks and dark knolls. This was eventually named David Island.

The dogs were working very well and, if only a little additional food could be procured for them, I knew they could be kept alive. Zip broke loose one night and ate one of my socks which was hanging on the sledge to dry; it probably tasted of seal blubber from the boots. Switzerland, too, was rather a bother, eating his harness whenever he had a chance.

On the 14th, a depot was formed, consisting of one week's provisions and oil; the bags being buried and a mound erected with a flag on top. Kennedy took a round of angles to determine its position.

At the end of two snowy days, after we had avoided many ugly crevasses, our course in an east-south-east line pointed to a narrow strait between David Island and the mainland. On the southern side of the former, there was a heaped line of pressure-ice, caused by the flow from a narrow bay being stopped by the Island. After lunch, on the 16th, there was an hour's good travelling and then we suddenly pulled into a half-mile of broken surface—the confluence of the slowly moving land-ice and of the more rapidly moving ice from a valley on our right, from which issued Reid Glacier. It was impossible to steer the dogs through it with a load, so we lightened the loads on both sledges and then made several journeys backwards and forwards over the more broken areas, allowing the dogs to run loose. The crevasses ran tortuously in every direction and falls into them were not uncommon. One large lid fell in just as a sledge had cleared it, leaving a hole twelve feet wide, and at least a hundred feet deep. Once over this zone, the sledges were worked along the slope leading to the mainland where we were continually worried by their slipping sideways.

Ahead was a vast sea of crushed ice, tossed and piled in every direction. On the northern horizon rose what we concluded to be a flat-topped, castellated berg. Ten days later, it resolved itself into a tract of heavy pressure ridges.

Camping after nine and a half miles, we were surprised, on moving east in the morning, to sight clearly the point—Cape Gerlache—of a peninsula running inland to the southwest. A glacier from the hinterland, pushing out from its valley, had broken up the shelf-ice on which we were travelling to such an extent that nothing without wings could cross it. Our object was to map in the coastline as far east as possible, and the problem, now, was whether to go north or south. From our position the former looked the best, the tumbled shelf-ice appearing to smooth out sufficiently, about ten miles away, to afford a passage east, while, to the south, we scanned the Denman Glacier, as it was named, rolling in magnificent cascades, twelve miles in breadth, from a height of more than three thousand feet. To get round the head of this ice-stream would mean travelling inland for at least thirty miles.

So north we went, getting back to our old surface over a heavy "cross sea," honeycombed with pits and chasms; many of them with no visible bottom. There was half a mile to safety, but the area had to be crossed five times; the load on the twelve-foot sledge being so much, that half the weight was taken off and the empty sledges brought back for the other half. Last of all came the dogs' sledge. Kennedy remarked during the afternoon that he felt like a fly walking on wire-netting.

The camp was pitched in a line of pressure, with wide crevasses and "hell-holes" within a few yards on every side. Altogether the day's march had been a miserable four miles. On several occasions, during the night, while in this disturbed area, sounds of movement were distinctly heard; cracks like rifle shots and others similar to distant heavy guns, accompanied by a weird, moaning noise as of the glacier moving over rocks.

November 18 was a fine, bright day: temperature 8° to 20° F. Until lunch, the course was mainly north for more than five miles. Then I went with Watson to trace out a road through a difficult area in front. At this point, there broke on us a most rugged and wonderful vision of ice-scenery.

The Denman Glacier moving much more rapidly than the Shackleton Shelf, tore through the latter and, in doing so, shattered both its own sides and also a considerable area of the larger ice-sheet. At the actual point of contact was what might be referred to as gigantic bergschrund: an enormous chasm over one thousand feet wide and from three hundred feet to four hundred feet deep, in the bottom of which crevasses appeared to go down for ever. The sides were splintered and crumpled, glittering in the sunlight with a million sparklets of light. Towering above were titanic blocks of carven ice. The whole was the wildest, maddest and yet the grandest thing imaginable.

The turmoil continued to the north, so I resolved to reconnoitre westward and see if a passage were visible from the crest of David Island.

The excursion was postponed till next day, when Kennedy, Watson and I roped up and commenced to thread a tangled belt of crevasses. The island was three and a half miles from the camp, exposing a bare ridge and a jutting bluff, nine hundred feet high—Watson Bluff. At the Bluff the rock was almost all gneiss, very much worn by the action of ice. The face to the summit was so steep and coarsely weathered that we took risks in climbing it. Moss and lichens grew luxuriantly and scores of snow petrels hovered around, but no eggs were seen.

Owing to an overcast sky, the view was not a great deal more enlightening than that which we had had from below. The Denman Glacier swept down for forty miles from over three thousand feet above sea-level. For twenty miles to the east torn ice-masses lay distorted in confusion, and beyond that, probably sixty miles distant, were several large stretches of bare rock-like islands.

On November 20, a strong north-east wind blew, with falling snow. Nothing could be seen but a white blanket, above, below and all around; so, with sudden death lurking in the bottomless crevasses on every hand, we stayed in camp.

A blizzard of great violence blew for two days and the tent occupied by Kennedy and myself threatened to collapse. We stowed all our gear in the sleeping-bags or in a hole from which snow had been dug for cooking. By the second day we had become extremely tired of lying down. One consolation was that our lips, which were very sore from exposure to the sun and wind, had now a chance of healing.

Next afternoon, the gale moderated sufficiently for us to go once more to David Island, in clearer weather, to see the outlook from the bluff. This time the sun was shining on the mainland and on the extension of the glacier past the bluff to the north. The distant southern slopes were seamed with a pattern of crevasses up to a height of three thousand feet. To the north, although the way was certainly impassable for twelve miles, it appeared to become smoother beyond that limit. We decided to try and cross in that direction.

We persevered on the 24th over many lines of pressure-ice and then camped near an especially rough patch. Watson had the worst fall on that day, going down ten feet vertically into a crevasse before his harness stopped him. After supper, we went to locate a trail ahead, and were greatly surprised to find salt water in some of the cracks. It meant that in two days our descent had been considerable, since the great bergschrund farther south was well over three hundred feet in depth and no water had appeared in its depths.

A few extracts from the diary recall a situation which daily became more serious and involved:

The Great Bergschrund of the Denman Glacier

"*Monday, November 25.* A beautiful day so far as the weather and scenery are concerned but a very hard one. We have been amongst 'Pressure,' with a capital P, all day, hauling up and lowering the sledges with an alpine rope and twisting and turning in all directions, with waves and hills, monuments, statues, and fairy palaces all around us, from a few feet to over three hundred feet in height. It is impossible to see more than a few hundred yards ahead at any time, so we go on for a bit, then climb a peak or mound, choose a route and struggle on for another short stage.

"We have all suffered from the sun to-day; Kennedy has caught it worst, his lips, cheeks, nose and forehead are all blistered. He has auburn hair and the tender skin which frequently goes with it. . . .

"*Tuesday, November 26.* Another very hard day's work. The first half-mile took three hours to cover; in several places we had to cut roads with ice-axes and shovels and also to build a bridge across a water-lead. At 1 PM we had done just one mile. I never saw or dreamt of anything so gloriously beautiful as some of the stuff we have come through this morning. After lunch the country changed entirely. In place of the confused jumble and crush we have had, we got on to névé slopes; huge billows, half a mile to a mile from crest to crest, meshed with crevasses. . .

"We all had falls into these during the day: Harrisson dropping fifteen feet. I received rather a nasty squeeze through falling into a hole whilst going downhill, the sledge running on to me before I could get clear, and pinning me down. So far as we can see, the same kind of country continues, and one cannot help thinking about having to return through this infernal mess. The day's distance—only one thousand and fifty yards.

"*Wednesday, November 27.* When I wrote last night about coming back, I little thought it would be so soon. We turn back to-morrow for the simple reason that we cannot go on any farther.

"In the morning, for nearly a mile along a valley running south-east, the travelling was almost good; then our troubles commenced again.

"Several times we had to resort to hand-hauling with the alpine rope through acres of pitfalls. The bridges of those which were covered were generally very rotten, except the wide ones. Just before lunch we had a very stiff uphill pull and then a drop into a large basin, three-quarters of a mile in diameter.

Wild, Kennedy, and Harrisson Amongst the Abysses of the Denman Glacier

"The whole was the wildest, maddest and yet the grandest thing imaginable"

"The afternoon was spent in vain searching for a road. . . . On every side are huge waves split in every direction by crevasses up to two hundred feet in width. The general trend of the main crevasses is north and south. . . .

"I have, therefore, decided to go back and if possible follow the road we came by, then proceed south on to the inland ice-cap and find out the source of this chaos. If we are able to get round it and proceed east, so much the better; but at any rate, we shall be doing something and getting somewhere. We could push through farther east from here, but it would be by lowering the gear piecemeal into chasms fifty to one hundred feet deep, and hauling it up on the other side; each crevasse taking at least two hours to negotiate. For such slow progress I don't feel justified in risking the lives of the party."

Snow fell for four days, at times thickly, unaccompanied by wind. It was useless to stir in our precarious position. Being a little in hand in the ration of biscuits, we fed the dogs on our food, their own having run out. I was anxious to keep them alive until we were out of the pressure-ice.

From this, our turning-point out on the shelf-ice, the trail lay over eighteen inches of soft snow on December 3, our former tracks, of course, having been entirely obliterated. The bridged crevasses were now entirely hidden and many weak lids were found.

At 9 AM Harrisson, Watson and I roped up to mark a course over a very bad place, leaving Kennedy with the dogs. We had only gone about one hundred yards when I got a very heavy jerk on the rope and, on looking round, found that Watson had disappeared. He weighs two hundred pounds in his clothes and the crevasse into which he had fallen was fifteen feet wide. He had broken through on the far side and the rope, cutting through the bridge, stopped in the middle so that he could not reach the sides to help himself in any way. Kennedy brought another rope over and threw it down to Watson and we were then able to haul him up, but it was twenty minutes before he was out. He reappeared smiling, and, except for a bruise on the shin and the loss of a glove, was no worse for the fall.

At 2.30 PM we were all dead-beat, camping with one mile one thousand seven hundred yards on the meter. One-third of this distance was relay work and, in several places, standing pulls with the alpine rope. The course was a series of Z's, S's, and hairpin turns, the longest straight stretch one hundred and fifty yards, and the whole knee-deep in soft snow, the sledges sinking to the cross-bars.

The 4th was a repetition of the previous day—a terribly hard two and a half miles. We all had "hangman's drops" into crevasses. One snow-bridge, ten feet wide, fell in as the meter following the twelve-foot sledge was going over behind it.

The 5th was a day of wind, scurrying snow and bad light. Harrisson went out to feed the dogs in the morning and broke through the lid of a crevasse, but fortunately caught the side and climbed out.

THE DIARY AGAIN:

"*Friday, December 6.* Still bad light and a little snowfall, but we were off at ten o'clock. I was leading and fell into at least a dozen crevasses, but had to be hauled out of one only. At 1.30 PM we arrived at the open lead we had crossed on the outward journey and found the same place. There had been much movement since then and we had to make a bridge, cutting away projections in some places and filling up the sea-water channels with snow and ice. Then Harrisson crossed with the aid of two bamboo poles, and hauled me over on a sledge. Harrisson and I on one side and Kennedy and Watson on the other then hauled the sledges backwards and forwards, lightly loaded one way and empty the other, until all was across. The shelf-ice is without doubt afloat, if the presence of sea-water and diatomaceous stains on the ice is of any account. We camped to-night in the same place as on the evening of November 25, so with luck we should be out of this mess to-morrow. Switzerland had to be killed as I cannot afford any more biscuit. Amundsen ate his flesh without hesitation, but Zip refused it."

Sure enough, two days sufficed to bring us under the bluff on David Island. As the tents were being pitched, a skua gull flew down. I snared him with a line, using dog's flesh for bait and we had stewed skua for dinner. It was excellent.

While I was cooking the others climbed up the rocks and brought back eight snow petrels and five eggs, with the news that many more birds were nesting. After supper we all went out and secured sixty eggs and fifty-eight birds. It seemed a fearful crime to kill these beautiful, pure white creatures, but it meant fourteen days' life for the dogs end longer marches for us.

Fresh breeze, light snow and a bad light on the 9th; we remained in camp. Two more skuas were snared for the evening's dinner. The snow petrels' eggs were almost as large as hens' eggs and very good to eat when fresh. Many of them had been under the birds rather too long, but although they did not look so nice, there was little difference in the taste. I was very glad to get this fresh food, as we had lived on tinned meat most of the year and there was always the danger of scurvy.

The light was too changeable to make a satisfactory start until the evening of December 11, when we managed to dodge through four and a half miles of broken ice, reaching the mainland close to our position on November 16, and camping for lunch at midnight. In front was a clear mile on a peninsula and then the way led across Robinson Bay, seven miles wide, fed by the Northcliffe Glacier.

Another night march was commenced at 8 PM The day had been cloudless and the sun very warm, softening the surface, but at the time of starting it was hardening rapidly. Crossing the peninsula we resolved to head across Robinson Bay as the glacier's surface was still torn up. We ended with a fine march of twelve miles one thousand two hundred yards.

The fine weather continued and we managed to cross three and a half miles of heavy sastrugi, pressure-ridges and crevasses, attaining the first slopes of the mainland at 10 PM on December 14. The discovery of two nunataks springing out of the piedmont glacier to the south, lured us on.

The first rock—Possession Nunataks—loomed ahead, two hundred feet above, up a slope of half a mile. Here a depot of provisions and spare gear was made, sufficient to take us back to the Hippo. The rock was found by Watson to be gneiss, rich in mica, felspar and garnets. We lunched in this place and resumed our march at midnight.

The second nunatak was on the course; a sharp peak in the south, hidden by the contour of the uprising ridges. In four miles we steadily ascended eight hundred feet. While we were engaged pitching camp, a Cape pigeon flew overhead.

There were advantages in travelling at night. The surface was firmer, our eyes were relieved from the intense glare and our faces no longer blistered. On the other hand, there were disadvantages. The skirt of the tent used to get very wet through the snow thawing on it in the midday sun, and froze solid when packed up; the floor-cloths and sleeping-bags, also, never had a chance of drying and set to the same icy hardness. When we had mounted higher I intended to return to work by day.

It was not till the altitude was three thousand feet that we came in sight of the far peak to the south. We were then pulling again in daylight. The ice-falls of the Denman Glacier on the left were still seen descending from the plateau, while down on the plain we saw that the zone of disrupted ice, into which the short and intricate track of our northern attempt had been won, extended for quite thirty miles.

The surface then softened in a most amazing fashion and hauling became a slow, dogged strain with frequent spells. A little over four miles was the most we could do on the 18th, and on the 19th the loads were dragging in a deluge of dry, flour-like snow. A long halt was made at lunch to repair a badly torn tent.

The peak ahead was named Mount Barr-Smith. It was fronted by a steep rise which we determined to climb next day. On the eastern margin of the Denman Glacier were several nunataks and higher, rising ground.

Following a twenty-four hours' blizzard, the sky was overcast, with the usual dim light filtering through a mist of snow. We set off to scale the mountain, taking the dip-circle with us. The horizon was so obscured that it was useless to take a round of angles. Fifteen miles south of Mount Barr-Smith, and a little higher there was another peak, to be subsequently called Mount Strathcona; also several intervening outcrops. Not a distinct range of mountains as we had hoped. The Denman Glacier sweeps round these projecting rocks from the south-west, and the general flow of the ice-sheet is thereby concentrated within the neck bounded by the two peaks and the higher land to the east. Propelled by the immense forces of the hinterland, this stream of ice is squeezed down through a steep valley at an accelerated speed, and, meeting the slower moving Shackleton Shelf, rends it from top to bottom and presses onward. Thus chaos, icequake, and ruin.

Our tramp to Mount Barr-Smith was through eighteen inches of soft snow, in many places a full two feet deep. Hard enough for walking, we knew from experience what it was like for sledging. There was only sufficient food for another week and the surface was so abominably heavy that in that time, not allowing for blizzards, it would have been impossible to travel as far as we could see from the summit of Mount Barr-Smith, while four miles a day was the most that could have been done. Our attempt to make east by rounding the Denman Glacier to the south had been foiled, but by turning back at that point, we stood a chance of saving our two remaining dogs, who had worked so well that they really deserved to live.

Sunday December 22 broke with a fresh breeze and surface drift; overhead a clear sky. We went back to Mount Barr-Smith, Kennedy taking an observation for latitude, Watson making a geological survey and collecting specimens, Harrisson sketching. The rocks at the summit were granites, gneisses and schists. The latitude worked out at 67° 10.4' S., and we were a little more than one hundred and twenty miles in an air-line from the hut.

In the next two days, downhill, we "bullocked" through eleven miles, reaching a point where the depot at Possession Nunataks was only sixteen miles away. The surface snow was very sticky in places, clogging the runners badly, so that they had to be scraped every half-mile. Stewed skua was the feature of our Christmas Eve supper.

Wild's Party Working Their Sledges Through the Crushed Ice at the Foot of Denman Glacier

The Hippo Nunatak

Dog-Sledging

FROM THE DIARY:

"*Christmas Day, Wednesday.* Turned out and got away at 8 AM, doing nine miles before lunch down a steep descent. The sun was very hot, and after lunch the surface became sticky, but at 5 PM we reached the depot, having done fifteen miles one hundred yards and descended two thousand three hundred feet.

"I am afraid I shall have to go back to travelling by night, as the snow is so very soft down here during the day; not soft in the same way as the freshly fallen powdery stuff we had on the hills, but half-thawed and wet, freezing at night into a splendid surface for the runners. The shade temperature at 5.30 PM to-day was 29° F., and a thermometer laid in the sun on the dark rocks went up to 87° F.

"Some time ago, a plum-pudding was found in one of our food-bags, put there, I believe, by Moyes. We ate it to-night in addition to the ordinary ration, and, with a small taste of spirits from the medical store, managed to get up quite a festive feeling. After dinner the Union Jack and Australian Ensign were hoisted on the rocks and I formally took possession of the land in the name of the Expedition, for King George V. and the Australian Commonwealth."

Queen Mary Land is the name which, by gracious sanction, was eventually affixed to that area of new land.

Night marches commenced at 1 AM on December 27. The sail was hoisted for the first time and the fresh breeze was of great assistance. We were once more down on the low peninsula and on its highest point, two hundred feet above the shelf-ice, Kennedy took a round of angles.

Along the margin of the shelf the crevasses were innumerable and, as the sun was hot and the snow soft and mushy, we pitched camp about six miles from the bluff on David Island.

At 6 AM on the 28th we rounded the bluff and camped under its leeward face. After lunch there was a hunt for snow petrels. Fifty-six were caught and the eggs, which all contained chicks, were given to the dogs.

It was my intention to touch at all the rocks on the mainland on the way home, as time and weather permitted. Under a light easterly breeze we scudded along with sail set and passed close to several outcrops. Watson examined them, finding gneiss and granite principally, one type being an exceptionally coarse granite, very much weathered. A mile of bad crevasses caused some delay; one of the dogs having a fall of twelve feet into one abyss.

Next day, the Hippo hove in sight and we found the depoted food in good condition. The course had been over high pressure-waves and in some places we had to diverge on account of crevasses and—fresh water! Many of the hollows contained water from thawed snow, and in others there was a treacherous crust which hid a slushy pool. The march of eighteen miles landed us just north of the Avalanche Rocks.

While we were erecting the tents there were several snow-slips, and Watson, Kennedy and I walked landwards after supper to try for a "snap" of one in the act of falling, but they refused to oblige us. It was found that one or more avalanches had thrown blocks of ice, weighing at least twenty tons, two hundred yards past the hole in which we spent five days on the depot journey. They had, therefore, travelled six hundred yards from the cliff.

The Alligator Nunatak was explored on January 2, 1913. It was found to be half a mile long, four hundred feet high and four hundred and fifty feet in width, and, like most of the rock we had seen, mainly gneiss.

There was half a gale blowing on the 4th and though the wind was abeam, the sail was reefed and we moved quickly. The dogs ran loose, their feet being very sore from pulling on rough, nobbly ice. The day's run was the record up to that time—twenty-two miles. Our camp was in the vicinity of two small nunataks discovered in August 1912. We reckoned to be at the Base in two days and wondered how poor Moyes was faring.

Early on the 5th, the last piece of broken country fell behind, and one sledge being rigged with full sail, the second sledge was taken in tow. Both dogs had bleeding feet and were released, running alongside. During the halt for lunch a sail was raised on the dogs' sledge, using tent poles as a mast, a floor-cloth for a sail, an ice-axe for an upper yard and a bamboo for a lower yard. Getting under way we found that the lighter sledge overran ours; so we cast off and Harrisson took the light sledge, the sail working so well that he rode on top of the load most of the time. Later in the afternoon the wind increased so much that the dogs' sledge was dismasted and taken in tow once more, the sail on the forward sledge being ample for our purpose.

At 4 PM we had done twenty miles, and, everybody feeling fresh, I decided to try and reach "The Grottoes," fifteen miles away. The wind increasing to a gale with hurtling drift, the sail was reefed, and even then was more than enough to push along both sledges. Two of us made fast behind and maintained a continual brake to stop them running away. At 9 PM the gale became so strong that we struck sail and camped. Altogether, the day's run was thirty-five miles.

An hour's march next morning, and, through the glasses, we saw the mast and soon afterwards the hut. Just before reaching home, we struck up a song, and in a few seconds Moyes came running out. When he saw there were four of us, he stood on his head.

As we expected, Moyes had never thought of Harrisson coming with me and had quite given him up as dead. When a month had elapsed—the time for which Harrisson had food—Moyes packed a sledge with provisions for Harrisson, himself and the dogs and went out for six days. Then, recognizing the futility of searching for any one in that white waste of nothingness, he returned. He looked well, after his lonely nine weeks, but said that it was the worst time he had ever had in his life. Moyes reported that the Western party were delayed in starting by bad weather until November 7.

The total distance sledged during our main summer eastern journey was two hundred and thirty-seven miles, including thirty-two of relay work, but none of the many reconnoitring miles. Out of seventy days, there were twenty-eight on which the weather was adverse. On the spring depot journey the travelling had been so easy that I fully expected to go four hundred or five hundred miles eastward in the summer. It was therefore, a great disappointment to be blocked as we were.

CHAPTER XXII

The Western Base—Linking up with Kaiser Wilhelm II Land

By Dr. S. E. JONES

ON OUR RETURN FROM THE WESTERN DEPOT journey towards the end of October 1912, we found preparations completed for the long western trip, towards Gaussberg in Kaiser Wilhelm II Land, which was discovered by the German Antarctic Expedition of 1902. The departure was delayed for several days, but came at last on November 7, Moyes bidding us adieu and wishing us good luck.

The party consisted of Dovers (surveyor), Hoadley (geologist), and myself (surgeon). We were hauling one sledge with rations for nine weeks. Our course, which was almost due south, lay over the glacier shelf practically parallel to the sea-cliffs. The surface was good, and we covered eleven miles by nightfall, reaching a point some two or three miles from the rising land slopes. As the high land was approached closer, the surface of the glacier-shelf, which farther north was practically level, became undulating and broken by pressure-ridges and crevasses. These, however, offered no obstacle to sledging.

Proceeding in the morning and finding that an ascent of the slopes ahead was rendered impracticable by wide patches of ice, we turned more to the west and steered for Junction Corner. Upon our arrival there, it was discovered that several bergs lay frozen within the floe close to where the seaward wall of the glacier-shelf joined that of the land ice-sheet. Some of these bergs were old and rotten, but one seemed to have broken away quite recently.

From the same place we could see several black points ahead; our course was altered towards them, almost due westward, about half a mile from the sea-cliffs. They proved to be rocks, six in number, forming a moraine. As it was then half-past five, we camped in order that Hoadley might examine them. There had been a halo visible all day, with mock suns in the evening.

In the morning a high wind was blowing. Everything went well for a little over a mile, when we found ourselves running across a steep slope. The wind having increased and being abeam, the sledge was driven to leeward when on a smooth surface, and when amongst soft sastrugi, which occurred in patches, was capsized. Accordingly camp was pitched.

The next day being less boisterous, a start was made at 9 AM There was still a strong beam wind, however, which carried the sledge downhill, with the result that for one forward step two had to be taken to the right. We were more fortunate in the afternoon and reached the depot laid on the earlier journey at 5.30 AM From this position we had a fine view of the Helen Glacier running out of a bay which opened up ahead.

Having picked up the depot next morning, we were disappointed to find that we should have to commence relay work. There were then two sledges with rations for thirteen weeks; the total weight amounting to one thousand two hundred pounds. By making an even division between the two sledges the work was rendered easy but slow. When we camped at 6 PM, five and a half miles had been covered. The surface was good, but a strong beam wind hindered us while approaching the head of Depot Bay. The ice-cap to the west appeared to be very broken, and it seemed inevitable that we should have to ascend to a considerable altitude towards the south-west to find a good travelling surface.

In the morning we were delayed by heavy wind, but left camp at ten o'clock after spending an hour digging out the sledges and tent. At lunch time the sun became quite obscured and each of us had many falls stumbling over the invisible sastrugi. At five o'clock the weather became so thick that camp was pitched. Hoadley complained of snow-blindness and all were suffering with cracked lips; there was consequently a big demand for hazeline cream in the evening.

On Wednesday November 13, we started early, and, finding a good firm track over a gently rising plateau, made fair progress. At three o'clock a gale sprang up suddenly; and fortunately the sledges were only a quarter of a mile apart as we were relaying them in stages up the rising plateau. The tent was pitched hurriedly, though with difficulty, on account of the high wind and drift. The distance for the day was four miles one thousand five hundred yards, the last mile and a half being downhill into a valley at the head of the bay. The morainic boulders visible from the camp at the depot were now obscured behind a point to the west of Depot Bay.

The next sixty hours were spent in sleeping-bags, a heavy snowstorm making it impossible to move. Owing to the comparatively high temperature, 20° to 26° F., the snow melted readily on the lee side of the tent, and, the water running through, things became uncomfortably wet inside. At midday of the 16th, however, we were able to go out, and, after spending two and a half hours digging out the tent and sledges, we made a start, travelling two and three-quarter miles on a south-westerly course.

During the morning of the 17th a slight descent was negotiated, but in the afternoon came the ascent of the slopes on the western side of Depot Bay. The ice-cap here was very badly crevassed, and spiked boots had to be worn in hauling the sledges up the steep névé slopes. In the latter part of the afternoon a course was made more to the west, and about the same time the south-east wind freshened and we travelled for a couple of hours through thick drift. The night's camp was situated approximately at the eastern edge of the Helen Glacier. The portion of the ice-cap which contributes to the glacier below is marked off from the general icy surface on either side by a series of falls and cascades. These appeared quite impassable near sea-level, but we hoped to find a smooth passage at an altitude of about one thousand feet.

A start was made at 7 AM. The surface consisted of ice and névé and was badly broken by pressure-mounds, ten to twenty feet high, and by numerous crevasses old and recent; many with sunken or fallen bridges. While crossing a narrow crevasse, about forty feet of the bridge collapsed lengthwise under the leading man, letting him fall to the full extent of his harness rope. Hoadley and myself had passed over the same spot, unsuspecting and unroped, a few minutes previously, while looking for a safe track. We were now nearing the approximate western edge of the Helen Glacier, and the broken condition of the ice evidently indicated considerable movement. Later in the morning a more southerly course was kept over an improving surface.

At midday Dovers took observations of the sun and found the latitude to be 66° 47′ S. Owing to the heat of the sun the fat in the pemmican had been melting in the food-bags, so after lunch the provisions were repacked and the pemmican was put in the centre of the large tanks. In the afternoon we hoisted the sail, and by evening had done four miles. From our camp the eye could range across the Helen Glacier eastward to the shelf-ice of "The Grottoes." Far away in the north-west was a wide expanse of open water, while a multitude of bergs lay scattered along the coast to the west of the Helen Glacier.

Where the Floe-Ice Meets the Shackleton Shelf

The Hummocky Floe on the Southern Margin of the Davis Sea

The next day was gloriously bright, with a breeze just strong enough to make hauling pleasant. Erecting a sail, we made an attempt to haul both sledges, but found that they were too heavy. It was soon discovered that a considerable detour would have to be made to cross the broken ice on the western edge of the Helen Glacier. By keeping to the saddles and valleys as much as possible and working to the south, we were able to avoid the rougher country, but at 4 PM we arrived at what at first appeared an *impasse*.

At this point three great crevassed ridges united to form the ice-falls on the western side of the glacier. The point of confluence was the only place that appeared to offer any hope of a passage, and, as we did not want to retrace our steps, we decided to attempt it. The whole surface was a network of huge crevasses, some open, the majority from fifty to one hundred feet or more in width. After many devious turns, a patch of snow between two large abysses was reached. As the ice in front seemed even more broken than that behind, camp was pitched. After tea a search was

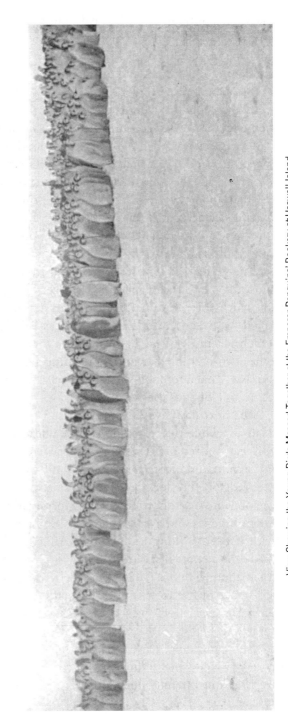

View Showing the Young Birds Massed Together at the Emperor Penguins' Rookery at Haswell Island

made for a way out, and it was found that by travelling along a narrow, knife-edge ridge of ice and névé, with an open crevasse on each side, a good surface could be reached within a mile of the camp. This ridge had a gradient of one in ten, and, unfortunately, also sloped down towards one of the open crevasses.

During the next four days a heavy blizzard raged. There was a tremendous snowfall accompanied by a gale of wind, and, after the second day, the snow was piled four feet high round the tent, completely burying the sledges and by its pressure greatly reducing the space inside the tent. On the 23rd, the fourth day, we dug out the floor, lowering the level of the tent about two feet, and this made things more comfortable. While digging, a crack in the ice was disclosed running across the floor, and from this came a considerable draught. By midday the weather had improved sufficiently to allow us to move.

The sledge and tent were excavated from beneath a great mass of soft snow; the new level of the snow's surface being four to five feet above that on which the camp had been made four days earlier. The wind having fallen, we went ahead with the sledges. While crossing the ridge of ice which led into the valley below, one man hauled the sledges while the other two prevented them from sliding sideways downhill into the open crevasse. That afternoon we noticed very fine iridescent colouring in cirro-cumulus clouds as they crossed the sun.

The next day gave us a pleasant surprise, there being a strong breeze dead aft, while the travelling surface ahead looked distinctly favourable. Sail was hoisted and the two sledges were coupled together. The course for a short distance was downhill, and we had to run to keep up with the sledges. The slopes on the far side of the valley we had entered on the previous afternoon were not so formidable as they had looked, for by lunch time six and a half miles had been covered. The surface was good, with occasional long undulations. After lunch a turn to the north was made for a short distance in order to come in touch with the coastline. Then the march west was resumed by travelling parallel to the shore at a distance of five to ten miles. At halting-time the extreme western edge of Helen Glacier was passed, and below lay young floe-ice, studded with numerous bergs.

In the morning, Dovers called attention to what appeared to be an ice-covered island lying to the north-north-west, thirty to forty miles away. We watched this carefully during the day, but found its form to be constant.

Through binoculars, icy patches and bluff points at the eastern and western ends were distinguishable.**

> As soon as camp was struck the march was resumed direct for what every one thought was a rocky outcrop, though nearer approach proved it to be merely the shady face of an open crevasse. The same course was maintained and the ridge of ice that runs down to the western point of Depot Bay was soon close at hand. From its crest we could see a group of about a dozen rocky islands, the most distant being five miles off the coast. All were surrounded by floe. Descending steeply from the ridge into a valley which ran out to the sea-cliffs, we pitched camp for lunch.

The meal completed, Hoadley and I descended to the edge of the glacier in order to see if there were a passable route to the sea-ice. Crossing wide areas of badly crevassed ice and névé during a descent of nine hundred feet, we reached the sea-front about one and a half miles from the camp. Below us there was a chaos of bergs and smaller debris, resulting from the disintegration of the land-ice, which were frozen into the floe and connected to one another by huge ramparts of snow. Following a path downward with great difficulty, we approached a small berg which was discovered to be rapidly thawing under the action of the heat absorbed by a pile of stones and mud. The trickling of the falling water made a pleasant relief in the otherwise intense silence. As it seemed impossible to haul sledges through this jumble of ice and snow, Hoadley suggested that he should walk across the floe and make a brief geological examination of at least the largest islet. I therefore returned to the camp and helped Dovers take observations for longitude and magnetic variation.

Hoadley returned at 9 PM and reported that he had seen an immense rookery of Emperor penguins near the largest islet, besides Adelie penguins, silver-grey, Wilson and Antarctic petrels and skua gulls. He also said that he thought it possible to take a sledge, lightly laden, through the drifts below the brink of the glacier.

Accordingly in the morning the eleven-foot sledge was packed with necessaries for a week's stay, although we intended to remain only for a

---

** *This was examined in detail from the* Aurora *in January 1913 and found to be an island, which was named Drygalski Island, for it is evidently the ice-covered "high-land" observed by Professor Drygalski (German Expedition, 1902) from his balloon.—Ed.*

day in order to take photographs and search for specimens. Erecting a depot flag to mark the big sledge, we broke camp at midday and soon reached the sea-front. Our track then wound among the snow-drifts until it emerged from the broken ice which was observed to border the land ice-sheet for miles. The travelling became unexpectedly good for a time over highly polished, green sea-ice, and thence on to snow, amid a field of numerous small bergs. Many of these showed a marked degree of ablation, and, in places, blocks of ice perched on eminences had weathered into most grotesque forms. There were numerous streams of thaw-water running from mud-covered bergs. Perspiring in the heat, we more than once stopped to slake our thirst.

Approaching the largest rock—Haswell Island, as it was called later—we saw more distinctly the immense numbers of Emperor penguins covering several acres of floe. The birds extended in rows even on to the lower slopes of several bergs. The sound of their cries coming across the ice reminded one of the noise from a distant sports' ground during a well-contested game. We camped at 5 PM on a snow-drift at the southern end of the island. A large rookery of Adelie penguins on a long, low rock, about a mile distant, soon made itself evident.

Although the stay was intended to occupy only about twenty-four hours, we were compelled to remain five days on the island on account of a snowstorm which continued for practically the whole of the time. This did not prevent us from leaving the tent and wandering about; Hoadley keen on the geology and Dovers surveying whenever the light was good enough. The temperature of the rock was well above freezing-point where it was exposed, and snow melted almost as soon as it fell. Our sleeping-bags and gear soon became very wet, but we rejoiced in one compensation, and that was a change in diet. It was agreed that five Adelie penguins or ten Cape pigeons' eggs made a good tasty entrée to the monotonous ration.

The camp was situated on the largest of a group of about twelve small islets, lying within five or six miles of the coast, on the lower slopes of which several outcrops of rock could be observed. Haswell Island was found to be roughly diamond-shaped; three-quarters of a mile in length, the same in width, and about three hundred feet on the highest point. It was surrounded by one season's floe, raised in pressure-ridges on the eastern side. On the northern, southern, and especially the eastern face, the rock was steep; on the western aspect, there was a more gentle slope down to the floe, the rock being almost concealed by big snow-drifts. There were signs of previous glaciation in the form of erratics and many examples of polishing and grooving. The rock was very rotten, and in many places, especially about the penguin rookeries, there were collections of soil. Two deep gorges cut through the island from north-west to south-east, in both of which there were small ponds of fresh water.

The most marked feature was the wonderful abundance of bird life, for almost all the birds frequenting the shores of the continent were found nesting there. Adelie penguins were in greatest numbers. Besides the large rookery on one of the smaller islets, there were numerous rookeries of fifty to one hundred birds each on Haswell Island. In most cases the penguins made their nests on the rock itself, but, failing this, had actually settled on snow-drifts, where they presented a peculiar sight, as the heat of their bodies having caused them to sink in the snow, their heads alone were visible above the surface. One bird was observed carrying an egg on the dorsal surface of his feet as the Emperor penguins do. Feathers were scattered broadcast around each rookery. These result from the numerous fights which occur and are also partly derived from the bare patch of skin at the lower part of the abdomen which provides the necessary heat for incubation when the bird is sitting. Most of the birds had two eggs in a well-advanced stage of incubation, and it was a difficult task to find a sufficient number fresh enough for culinary purposes. Attached to each rookery was a pair of skua gulls, who swooped down and quickly flew off with any eggs left for a moment untended.

The Emperor penguins had their rookery on the floe, about a mile from the island. The birds covered four to five acres, but there were undoubted signs that a much larger area had been occupied. We estimated the numbers to be seven thousand five hundred, the great majority being young birds. These were well grown, most of them standing as high as the shoulders of the adults. They were all very fat, covered by a grey down, slightly darker on the dorsal than on the ventral surface, with dark tails and a black, straight beak. The eyes were surrounded by a ring of grey plumage, and this again by a black band which extended over the skull to the root of the beak. Thus the markings on the young do not correspond with those of the adults. A few of the larger chicks had commenced to moult, the change of plumage being observed on the flippers.

Daily we watched large numbers of adults departing from and returning to the rookery. The direction in which they travelled was north, towards open water, estimated to be twenty miles distant. Although more than once the adults' return to the rookery was carefully noted, we never saw the young birds being fed, old birds as they entered the rookery quietly going to sleep.

Antarctic Petrels on the Nest

A Snow Petrel Chick on the Nest

A Silver-Grey Petrel on the Nest

Hoadley, on his first visit to the island, had seen Antarctic petrels flying about, and a search revealed a large rookery of these on the eastern side. The nesting-place of this species of petrel had never before been discovered, and so we were all elated at the great find. About three hundred birds were found sitting in the gullies and clefts, as close together as they could crowd. They made no attempt to form nests, merely laying their eggs on the shallow dirt. Each bird had one egg about the same size as that of a domestic fowl. Incubation was far advanced, and some difficulty was experienced in blowing the specimens with a blow-pipe improvised from a quill. Neither the Antarctic nor any other petrels offered any resistance when disturbed on their nests, except by the expectoration of large quantities of a pink or green, oily fluid.

The Cape pigeons had just commenced laying when we arrived at the island. On the first day only two eggs were found, but, on the fourth day after our arrival, forty were collected. These birds make a small shallow nest with chips of stone.

The silver-grey or Southern Fulmar petrels were present in large numbers, especially about the steep north-eastern side of the island. Though they were mated, laying had scarcely commenced, as we found only two eggs. They made small grottoes in the snow-drifts, and many pairs were seen billing and cooing in such shelters.

The small Wilson petrels were found living in communities under slabs of rock, and Hoadley one afternoon thought he heard some young birds crying.

Skua gulls were present in considerable force, notably near the penguin rookeries. They were breeding at the time, laying their eggs on the soil near the summit of the island. The neighbourhood of a nest was always betrayed by the behaviour of these birds who, when we intruded on them, came swooping down as if to attack us.

Although many snow petrels were seen flying about, we found only one with an egg. The nests were located in independent rocky niches but never in rookeries.

Vegetable life existed in the form of algae, in the pools, lichens on oversell rocks and mosses which grew luxuriantly, chiefly in the Adelie penguin rookeries.

Weddell seals were plentiful about the island near the tide-cracks; two of them with calves.

Though the continuous bad weather made photography impossible, Hoadley was able to make a thorough geological examination of the locality. On December 2 the clouds cleared sufficiently for photography, and after securing some snapshots we prepared to move on the next day.

Dovers built a small cairn on the summit of the island and took angles to the outlying rocks.

On the 3rd we packed our specimens and left for the mainland at 9.30 AM, arriving at the land ice-cliffs at 2 PM The snow surface was soft, even slushy in places, and the heat amongst the bergs along the coast of the mainland was very oppressive. After we had dug out the second sledge and re-arranged the loads, the hour was too late for sledging, so Dovers took another observation in order to obtain the rate of the half-chronometer watch. While on the island, we had examined the coast to the west with glasses and concluded that the only way to get westward was to ascend to a considerable altitude on the ice-cap, which, as far as the eye could reach, descended to the sea-level in long cascades and falls. We had expected to place a depot somewhere near Haswell Island, but such procedure was now deemed inadvisable in view of its distance from what would probably be our direct return route.

A start was made next day against an opposing wind, the sledges being relayed up a steep hillside. Later on, however, a turn was made more to the west, and it was then possible to haul both sledges at the same time. The surface was soft, so that after every halt the runners had to be cleared. The distance for the day was five and a half miles, and the night's camp was at an altitude of about one thousand five hundred feet, located just above the broken coastal ice.

During December 5 and 6 a snowstorm raged and confined us to our tent. The high temperature caused the falling snow to melt as it touched the tent, and, when the temperature fell, the cloth became thickly coated with ice.

On the 7th the march was resumed, by skirting a small valley at an approximate altitude of two thousand feet. The ice-cap ahead descended in abrupt falls to the floe. Having a fair wind and a smooth surface, we made good headway. In the afternoon we ran into a plexus of crevasses, and the surface was traversed by high ridges. The snowbridges in many cases were weak and several gave way while the sledge was crossing them. A chasm about fifty feet deep and one hundred feet long was passed, evidently portion of a crevasse, one side of which had been raised. Later in the afternoon the surface became impassable and a detour to the south was rendered necessary. This difficulty arose near the head of the valley, in which situation the ice-cap fell in a series of precipitous terraces for about one thousand feet.

At midday on the 8th we were compelled to continue the detour over a badly crevassed surface, ascending most of the time. On that night, camp was pitched again amongst crevasses. The sledge-meter showed only two miles one thousand one hundred yards for the afternoon, relaying having been necessary.

The sledges slipped along in the morning with a fresh breeze in their favour. The sky was covered with rapidly scudding, cirro-cumulus clouds which, by midday, quite obscured the sun, making surrounding objects and even the snow at our feet indistinguishable. After continuing for four and a half miles, we were forced to camp. In the afternoon a heavy snowstorm commenced and persisted throughout the following day.

Though snow was still falling on the morning of the 11th, camp was broken at 10 AM, and we moved off rapidly with a strong wind. During the morning the surface was gently undulating, but it mounted in a gradual ascent until nightfall. In the latter part of the afternoon the sun was clouded over, and steering had to be done by the aid of the wind. To the north we had a fine view of Drygalski's "High Land" (Drygalski Island), perceiving a distinct seaward ice-cliff of considerable height.

As there were no prominences on the ice-cap that could be used for surveying marks, Dovers had considerable difficulty in keeping a reckoning of our course. The trouble was overcome by building snow-mounds and taking back-angles to them with the prismatic compass. At this juncture we were about ten miles from the shore and could see open water some thirty miles to the north. Frozen fast within the floe were great numbers of bergs.

We started off early on December 12 with the aid of a fair breeze over a good surface, so that both sledges were easily hauled along together. The course was almost due west, parallel to the coast. Open water came within a few miles of the ice-cliffs, and, farther north, a heavy belt of pack was observed. When the sun sank lower, the bergs on the northern horizon were refracted up to such a degree that they appeared to be hanging from the sky.

The aid rendered by the sail under the influence of a fair breeze was well shown on the following day. In four hours, on a good surface, both sledges were transported seven miles. When we moved off, the wind was blowing at ten to fifteen miles an hour. By 10 AM the sky became overcast and the wind freshened. Camp was pitched for lunch at 11 AM, as we hoped that the weather would clear again later, but the wind increased and snow began to fall heavily in the afternoon, so we did not stir. The storm continued throughout the following day and it was impossible to march until the 15th.

The Symmetrically Domed Outline of Drygalski Island, Low on the Horizon. The Island Is 1200 Feet High and 9 Miles in Diameter.

The Main Western Party on Their Return to the "Grottoes." From the Left: Hoadley, Jones and Dovers

Continuing the ascent on the 16th out of a valley we had crossed on the previous day, we halted on the top of a ridge within view of German "territory"—a small, dark object bearing due west, evidently bare rock and presumably Gaussberg. The course was altered accordingly towards this object and everything went smoothly for ten miles. Then followed an area where the ice fell steeply in waves to the sea, crossed by crevasses which averaged fifty feet in width. The snow-bridges were deeply concave, and the lower side of each chasm was raised into a ridge five to ten feet high. Making fast the alpine rope on to the sledges, one of us went ahead to test the bridge, and then the sledges, one at a time, were rushed down into the trough and up on the other side. After crossing ten or more crevasses in this fashion, we were forced to camp by the approach of a rapidly moving fog driven before a strong westerly wind. While camp was being prepared, it was discovered that a tin of kerosene on the front sledge had been punctured causing the loss of a gallon of fuel. Fortunately, we were well within our allowance, so the accident was not serious. Soon after tea our attention was drawn to a pattering on the tent like rain, caused by a fall of sago snow.

In the morning the weather was clearer, and we saw that it was impossible to reach Gaussberg by a direct route. The ice ahead was cleft and split in all directions, and, in places, vertical faces stood up to a height of one hundred feet. The floe was littered with hundreds of bergs, and in several localities there were black spots which resembled small rocks, but it was impossible to approach close enough to be certain. Retracing the way out of the broken ice, we steered in a south-westerly direction, just above the line of sérac and crevassed ice. The coast here trended to the south-west, forming the eastern side of Drygalski's Posadowsky Bay. The going was heavy, the surface being covered by a layer of frost-crystals deposited during the night. A fog came up again early in the afternoon and had quite surrounded us at camping time. During the day there were fine clouds of ice-crystals in the air, and at 8 PM a fog-bow was seen in the east.

Turning out in the morning we saw Gaussberg peeping over a ridge to the west, but were still prevented from steering directly towards it by the broken surface. When we had advanced ten miles, a heavy fog brought us to a halt at 5 PM.

On Friday the 20th, in spite of a sticky surface, thirteen miles was covered on a west-south-west course. The ice-cap continued to be undulating but free of crevasses. The altitude was between two thousand five hundred and three thousand feet.

In the morning, after travelling two miles, we came in sight of Gaussberg again and steered directly towards it. The surface was good with a downward grade. At five and a quarter miles a depot was made of the small sledge and most of the food, in expectation of a clear run to the mountain. Not far ahead, however, were two broken-backed ridges intersecting the course, and a detour had to be made to the south to cross them higher up.

Midsummer's day, December 22, was spent in the tent, a move being impossible on account of the high wind. In the afternoon we walked ahead a short distance and reconnoitred six or seven crumpled ridges. Though the barometer had been falling ominously for twenty-four hours, the bad weather did not continue.

Gaussberg was reached in the afternoon, after our track had passed through seventeen miles of dangerous country. For the first few miles the surface consisted of a series of steep, buckled ice-ridges; later, it was snow-covered, but at times literally cut into a network of crevasses.

The only approach to Gaussberg from the plateau is from the south. To the east and west there are magnificent ice-falls, the debris from which litters the floe for miles around.

December 24 and Christmas Day were devoted to examining the mountain. Dovers made a long series of observations for longitude, latitude and magnetic variation, while Hoadley examined the rocks and took photographs.

On the southern side, the ice-cap abuts against this extinct volcano at an elevation of about four hundred feet above sea-level; the summit of the mountain rises another eight hundred feet. On the north, the rock descends to the floe. Gaussberg is pyramidal in shape, falling steeply, from a ridge at the summit. The sides are covered with a loose rubble of volcanic fragments, square yards of which commence to slide at the slightest disturbance. This renders climbing difficult and accounts for the large numbers of isolated blocks fringing the base.

At the summit two cairns were found, the bamboo poles which had previously marked them having blown over. Further examination revealed many other bamboos which had been used as marks, but no other record of the visit of the German expedition, ten years before, was met. Bird life was not plentiful, being limited to a few skuas, Wilson petrels and snow petrels; the latter nesting under slabs of rock. There were large quantities of moss where thaw-water had been running.

The ice and snow near the mountain showed evidences of marked thawing, and we had difficulty in finding a favourable spot for our camp.

Christmas Day was gloriously fine, with just sufficient wind to counteract the heat of the sun. At midday the Christmas "hamper" was opened, and it was not long before the only sign of the plum-pudding was the tin. In the afternoon we ascended the mountain and left a record in a cairn at the top. By the route followed, Gaussberg was two hundred and fifteen miles from "The Grottoes" but relay work had made the actual distance covered three hundred miles.

We had been away from home seven weeks, and, though there was sufficient food for an outward journey of another week, there was no indication that the country would change. Further, from the summit of Gaussberg one could see almost as far as could be marched in a week. Accordingly it was decided to commence our return on the 26th, making a course almost due east, thus cutting out numerous detours which had to be taken on the outward journey.

We left the mountain on December 26, pursuing a course to the south of our outward track so as to avoid some crevassed ridges. Ascending steadily against a continuous headwind, we picked up the second sledge at midday on the 28th.

Next day all the gear was transferred to one sledge and a course made direct to the Helen Glacier; the other sledge being abandoned.

On December 31, after a day's blizzard, the surface was found to be covered with sastrugi of soft snow eighteen inches to two feet in depth. In crossing a wide crevasse, the sledge became bogged in the soft snow of a drift which had a deceptive appearance of solidity. It took us ten minutes to extricate ourselves, and, after this, crevasses were negotiated at a run.

A violent blizzard raged during the following day—the first of the New Year 1913. This proved to be a blessing, for it made the surface more crisp and firm. In the morning the sun was obscured and nothing was visible but the snow at our feet, so that steering was very difficult. In the afternoon the sun broke through, a strong westerly wind sprang up and we moved along at a good pace, covering more than thirteen miles before camping.

On January 3 the track bordered on the edge of the plateau, the surface being almost level, rising gently towards the south.

After a violent blizzard of three days' duration, which confined us in the tent, we continued on the same course for four days, averaging about eleven miles each day. The surface was good, but a strong south-easter blew practically all the time and reduced our speed considerably.

At 10 AM on January 9, a fog-bank was observed in the east. This rapidly approached, and in fifteen minutes was quite close. There was now a splendid display of rings and arcs, caused apparently by minute ice-crystals which filled the air without obscuring the sun or sky. First an arc of prismatic colours appeared in the east, and in a few seconds the sky seemed literally to be covered with other arcs. At first they seemed to be scattered indiscriminately, but after a short time several arcs joined and we could discern a symmetrical arrangement. The sun was surrounded by a ring, the lower portion of which was broken by an inverted arc; two other arcs were visible on either side. A large ring appeared encircling the zenith, intersecting the first and passing through the sun. Two pairs of arcs were also seen, one pair in each ring. Excepting the arcs and ring about the zenith, which was grayish-white against the blue sky, the arcs showed prismatic colouring. The display lasted ten minutes and ended with the disappearance of the ice-crystals.

The diagram shows the arrangement of the arcs:

S = Sun. Z = Zenith.

At A, B, C, mock suns could be seen.

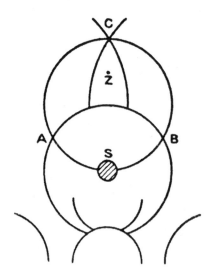

From our camp on the night of January 10, broken country could be seen ahead. To the north, open water was visible, and to the north-east the Shackleton Shelf, so that we were nearing home at last. Here, a heavy snowstorm delayed us for two and a half days, and it was not till the afternoon of January 13 that we were able to move ahead.

The next day was dull, the sun being quite obscured; and the only check upon the steering was the south-easterly wind. At midday the thermometer registered 35° F. in the shade, and the surface became quite sticky. After tea we walked ahead for a couple of hundred yards to the summit of a ridge where the full extent of the Helen Glacier was laid before us. It was evident that our position was some miles north of the true course, but, considering the absence of steering marks and the constant overcast weather, we considered ourselves lucky in being so close to it.

The bad weather continued and snow fell during the following day. On the 16th the light was better, and we pushed into a strong wind which freshened to the force of a moderate gale before we had travelled two miles. Approaching a steep ascent we were compelled to camp. The morning brought an improvement, and the crossing of the Helen Glacier was commenced a mile or two above the outward course.

At midday on January 18, over treacherous ice, in the face of strong winds, we were making good headway towards Junction Corner. Almost daily for a fortnight a Wilson petrel had visited us, the only form of life seen on the return journey.

On the 19th we were not able to move until 8.80 PM, when the wind, which had been blowing with the force of a gale, subsided. During the afternoon a magnificent view of the Helen Glacier was obtained, and in the west we could see Haswell Island and Drygalski Island.

Continuing on the same course, throughout the following day, we picked up the hut with the binoculars at 5 PM There now came a quick descent to Junction Corner.

On the lower levels there was clear evidence of thawing having occurred. The firm surface of snow which had been present on the outward journey was now converted into rough ice, over which we walked painfully in finnesko. Névé and ice surfaces were covered with sharp spicules, and the sides and bridges of crevasses were unmistakably thawed.

Leaving Junction Corner at 6 AM, we steered a course for the hut, running parallel to the edge of the glacier. At 3 PM the mast was sighted, and, later, the hut itself. When within half a mile of "The Grottoes" we saw three figures on the floe and guessed that the eastern party had returned. In a few minutes greetings were heartily exchanged and they had welcomed us home.

Instructions had been given that the Western Base should be in readiness to embark on the *Aurora* not later than January 30, 1913.

When Wild's party had arrived, preparations for departure were immediately made. Geological and biological collections were packed, stores were sorted out and cases containing personal gear were sledged to the edge of the glacier.

Harrisson contrived a winch for sounding and fishing. Fourteen-gauge copper wire was wound on it and, through a crack in the sea-ice a quarter of a mile from the glacier, bottom was reached in two hundred and sixty fathoms. As the water was too deep for dredging, Harrisson manufactured cage-traps and secured some fish, a squid, and other specimens.

At this time there was abundant evidence of life. Skua gulls frequently flew about the hut, as well as Cape pigeons, Antarctic, snow, Wilson, giant and silver-grey petrels. Out on the sea-ice, there were Adelie and Emperor penguins; the latter moulting. Hundreds of seals were seen with glasses on the edge of the floe, ten miles to the north.

On the whole, January was a very fine month. Some of the days seemed really hot; the shade temperature on one occasion reaching 37° F., and, in several instances, 33° F. It was quite a common thing for a man to work outside in loose, light garments; in fact, with nothing more than a singlet on the upper part of the body.

On January 26, while Kennedy took observations, Wild and the others went for a walk towards the open water. The surface was very rough and broken by leads, along which Weddell seals lay in great numbers. Three miles of ice were found to have drifted out, reducing the northern expanse to seven miles.

In view of the possibility of the *Aurora* not relieving them, the party went through their food-supplies, finding that these were sufficient for another year, with the exception of meat. With regard to coal, two tons of briquettes remained, which, augmented by good stock of seal-blubber, would provide sufficient fuel.

Laying in a store of seals' flesh and blubber now became the principal work, and every fine day saw a party out with a sledge. Unfortunately, the nearest crack on the sea-ice was nearly two miles away, so that the return journey, with a heavily laden sledge, was long and tedious. Two holes were dug in the glacier near the hut, one for blubber and the other for meat.

On January 31 six miles of sea-ice still remained, and, if the ship had arrived to time, a good deal of sledging would have been required to transport all the gear aboard.

In February, the weather altered for the worse, and there was not a single fine day until the 20th. A strong east-southeast wind with falling snow prevailed. As the days were shortening rapidly, all were beginning to feel anxious about the *Aurora*.

Wild erected a flagstaff on the highest ice-pinnacle near "The Grottoes" and flew a large flag on it whenever the wind moderated. On the 16th, a lamp-screen and reflector were fitted at the mast-head and each night a hurricane lamp was placed there, which could be seen eight miles with the naked eye.

On the 20th Dovers and Wild made a large signboard, taking it out to a prominent point on the glacier, three and a half miles to the north. It was lashed to a bamboo pole with a flag flying on it. The open water was then only three miles distant.

WILD WRITES:

"The 22nd February was the anniversary of the day the *Aurora* left us, but the weather was very different. A heavy blizzard was raging, the wind's velocity ranging up to eighty miles per hour. As it was Saturday, we kept the usual routine, scrubbing out and cleaning up the hut. We could not help speculating as to whether we should have to do it for another whole year. But every one had great faith in 'good old Davis,' and nobody was at all downhearted.

"When we 'turned out' on Sunday there was still a strong wind and drift, but this died away to a light breeze before breakfast was over, and the sun came out. I had a look round with the glasses and saw that the ice had broken away beyond a limit of one and a half miles. As there was a sledge, which Harrisson had been using for sounding, within a few yards of the water's edge, Jones and I went off to bring it in. We had gone less than half a mile when we saw what at first appeared to be a penguin, standing on some pack-ice in the distance, but which we soon saw was the mast-head of the *Aurora*.

"It was evident that she could not be alongside for some time, so Jones went back to the hut to tell the others to bring down a load of gear, and I went on to meet the ship. Before the *Aurora* had reached the fast ice, all the party were down with two sledge loads, having covered the mile and a half in record time.

"We were all anxious, of course, for news, and the first we received was the sad account of the deaths of Ninnis and Mertz; then of the wonderful march made by Dr. Mawson.

"Before closing, I should like to pay a tribute to the good-fellowship, unfailing industry, enthusiasm and unswerving loyalty which characterized my comrades. During the whole of the Expedition, whether carrying out monotonous routine work at the Base or under the trying conditions of sledging, all duties were performed with never-failing good temper and perseverance.

"Should it ever be my lot to venture on a like expedition I hope to have some, if not all, of the same party with me. But whether we meet again or not, I shall always think of every man of them with the greatest affection and respect."

CHAPTER XXIII

A Second Winter

URING THE FIRST BUSY YEAR IN ADELIE LAND, when the Hut was full of life and work, there were few moments for reflection. Yet, over the speculative pipe at home after a successful day's labour on the wireless masts, or out on the turbulent plateau when the hour of hoosh brought the strenuous day to a close, more than one man was heard to say, "One year in this country is enough for me." Still, in the early days, no one could predict what would happen, and therefore a change in the perverse climate was always considered probable. So great was the emulation, and so keen were all to extend our geographical boundaries, that the year sped away almost before the meagre opportunity came. With the cheery support of numbers, we did not find it a difficult matter "to drive dull care away."

Now there were only seven of us; we knew what was ahead; the weather had already given ample proof of the early approach of winter; the field of work which once stretched to the west, east and south had no longer the mystery of the "unknown"; the Ship had gone and there was scant hope of relief in March.

Against all this. There remained the Hut—a proven shelter from the wind; and, most vital of all, there was abundant food for another year. Every avenue of scientific work was not yet closed. Even the routine of meteorological and magnetic work was adding in no slight degree to the sum of human knowledge. Our short mile of rocks still held some geological secrets, and there were biological discoveries yet to make. A wireless telegraphic station had at last been established, and we could confidently expect communication with the outside world at an early date. These were some of the obvious assurances which no one had the heart to think about at first; and then there was always our comradeship, most enduring of all.

February, during 1912, was a tolerable month with a fair proportion of sunny, moderately calm days. A year later, the first eight days of this month

were signalized by the blizzard in which the *Aurora* had such a perilous experience. While the winter began in 1912 with the advent of March, now in 1913 it came on definitely in early February. Autumn was a term which applied to a few brilliant days which would suddenly intervene in the dense rack of drift-snow.

We set to work to make the Hut, if anything, safer and snugger. Bage put finishing touches to the break-wind of rock and cases, and with Hodgeman and McLean nailed battens of wood over a large sheet of canvas which had been stretched across the windward side of the roof, overlapping rolls of black paper, scraps of canvas and bagging, which were also battened down to make the eastern and western faces more air-tight.

Before the Ship left us, the remaining coal briquettes had been dug out of a bed of ice and carefully piled on a high point of the rocks. Round them all the spare timber and broken cases were gathered to provide sufficient fuel for the ensuing winter. The penguins' eggs, which had been stored in boxes, were stacked together on the windward side of the Hut, and a choice selection of steaks of seal and penguin for our own use were at the storeman's disposal in the veranda.

Madigan, in addition to his meteorological duties, took charge of the new sledging-dogs which had been presented by Captain Amundsen. A good many seals had been already killed, and a big cache of meat and blubber was made alongside the Hut to last throughout the winter.

Bickerton found many odd jobs to occupy his time in connexion with the petrol-engine and the wireless installations. He was also busied with the anemometer, which had broken down and needed a strong start for its second year of usefulness.

Bage, following the parting instructions of Webb, became the owner of the Magnetograph House and the Absolute Hut, continuing to keep the magnetic records. As storeman, Bage looked after the food-supplies. The canvas coverings had made the veranda drift-tight, so the storeman could arrange his tins and cases on the shelves with some degree of comfort, and the daily task of shovelling out snow was now at an end. Further, Hodgeman and he built an annex out of spare timber to connect the entrance veranda with the store. This replaced the old snow-tunnel which had melted away, and, when completed and padded outside with old mattresses, was facetiously styled the "North-West Passage." The only thing which later arose to disturb the composure of the storeman was the admission of the dogs to a compartment in the veranda on the eastern side. His constant care then became a heap of mutton carcases which the dogs in passing or during the occasional escapades from their shelter were always eager to attack.

Hodgeman helped to change the appearance of the living-hut by cutting the table in two and, since there was now plenty of room, by putting in more shelves for a larder on which the storeman displayed his inviting wares to the cook, who could think of nothing original for the next meal.

McLean undertook the duties of ice-cutting and coal-carrying throughout the year, kept the biological log and assisted in general observations. He also sent off sealed messages in bottles, regularly, on the chance of their being picked up on the high seas, thereby giving some indication of the direction of currents.

Jeffryes was occupied regularly every night listening attentively for wireless signals and calling at intervals. The continuous winds soon caused many of the wire stays of the main wireless mast to become slack, and these Jeffryes pulled taut on his daily rounds.

Looking back and forward, we could not but feel that the sledging programme of the previous summer had been so comprehensive that the broad features of the land were ascertained over a wide radius; beyond what we, with our weakened resources of the second year, could reach. The various observations we were carrying on were adding to the value of the scientific results, but we could not help feeling disappointed that our lot was not cast in a new and more clement region.

It was to be a dreary and difficult time for the five men who had volunteered to remain behind in order to make a thorough search for myself and comrades. They were men whom I had learned to appreciate during the first year, and I now saw their sterling characters in a new light. To Jeffryes all was fresh, and we envied him the novelties of a new world, rough and inhospitable though it was. As for me, it was sufficient to feel that

> . . . *He that tossed thee down into the Field,*
> *He knows about it all—He knows, He knows.*

On the night of February 15, Jeffryes suddenly surprised us with the exciting intelligence that he had heard Macquarie Island send a coded weather report to Hobart. The engine was immediately set going, but though repeated attempts were made, no answer could be elicited. Each night darkness was more pronounced and signals became more distinct, until, on the 20th, our call reached Sawyer at Macquarie Island, who immediately responded by saying "Good evening." The insulation of a Leyden jar broke down at this point, and nothing more could be done until it was remedied.

At last, on February 21, signals were exchanged, and by the 23rd a message had been dispatched to Lord Denman, Governor-General of the

Commonwealth, acquainting him with our situation and the loss of our comrades and, through him, one to his Majesty the King requesting his royal permission to name a tract of newly discovered country to the east, "King George V Land." Special messages were also sent to the relatives of Lieutenant B. E. S. Ninnis and Dr. X. Mertz.

The first news received from the outside world was the bare statement that Captain Scott and four of his companions had perished on their journey to the South Pole. It was some time before we knew the tragic details which came home, direct and poignant, to us in Adelie Land.

To Professor David a fuller account of our own calamity was sent and, following this, many kind messages of sympathy and congratulation were received from all over the world. On February 26 Lord Denman sent an acknowledgment of our message to him, expressing his sorrow at the loss of our two companions; and on March 7 his Majesty the King added his gracious sympathy, with permission to affix the name, King George V Land, to that part of the Antarctic continent lying between Adelie Land and Oates Land.

On February 23 there was a spell of dead calm; heavy nimbus clouds and fog lowering over sea and plateau. Fluffy grains of sago snow fell most of the day, covering the dark rocks and the blue glacier. A heaving swell came in from the north, and many seals landed within the boat harbour, where a high tide lapped over the ice-foot. The bergs and islands showed pale and shadowy as the snow ceased or the fog lifted. Then the wind arose and blew hard from the east-south-east for a day, swinging round with added force to its old quarter—south-by-east.

March began in earnest with much snow and monotonous days of wind. By contrast, a few hours of sunny calm were appreciated to the full. The face of the landscape changed; the rocky crevices filling flush with the low mounds of snow which trailed along and off the ridges.

On March 16 every one was relieved to hear that the *Aurora* had arrived safely in Hobart, and that Wild and his party were all well. But the news brought disappointment too, for we had always a lingering ray of hope that there might be sufficient coal to bring the vessel back to Adelie Land. Later on we learned that on account of the shortage of funds the Ship was to be laid up at Hobart until the following summer. In the meantime, Professors David and Masson were making every effort to raise the necessary money. In this they were assisted by Captain Davis, who went to London to obtain additional donations.

It was now a common thing for those of us who had gone to bed before midnight to wake up in the morning and find that quite a budget of wireless messages had been received. It took the place of a morning paper and we made the most of the intelligence, discussing it from every possible point of view. Jeffryes and Bickerton worked every night from 8 PM until 1 AM, calling at short intervals and listening attentively at the receiver. In fact, notes were kept of the intensity of the signals, the presence of local atmospheric electrical discharges—"static"—or intermittent sounds due to discharges from snow particles—St. Elmo's fire—and, lastly, of interference in the signals transmitted. The latter phenomenon should lead to interesting deductions, for we had frequent evidence to show that the wireless waves were greatly impeded or completely abolished during times of auroral activity.

Listening at the wireless receiver must have been very tedious and nerve-racking work, as so many adventitious sounds had to be neglected. There was, first of all, the noise of the wind as it swept by the Hut; then there was the occasional crackling of "St. Elmo's fire"; the dogs in the veranda shelter were not always remarkable for their quietness; while within the Hut it was impossible to avoid slight sounds which were often sufficient to interrupt the sequence of a message. At times, when the aurora was visible, signals would often die away, and the only alternative was to wait until they recurred, meanwhile keeping up calls at regular intervals in case the ether was not "blocked." So Jeffryes would sometimes spend the whole evening trying to transmit a single message, or, conversely, trying to receive one. By experience it was found easier to transmit and receive wireless messages between certain hours in the evening, while not infrequently, during the winter months, a whole week would go by and nothing could be done. During such a period auroral displays were usually of nightly occurrence. Then a "freak night" would come along and business would be brisk at both terminals.

It was often possible for Jeffryes to "hear" Wellington, Sydney, Melbourne and Hobart, and once he managed to communicate directly with the last-named. Then there were numerous ships passing along the southern shores of Australia or in the vicinity of New Zealand whose "calls" were audible on "good nights." The warships were at times particularly distinct, and occasionally the "chatter in the ether" was so confusing that Sawyer, at Macquarie Island, would signal that he was "jammed."

The "wireless" gave us another interest in life, and plenty of outside occupation when the stays became loose or an accident occurred. It served to relieve some of the tedium of that second year:

Day after day the same

Only a little worse.

Blizzard-Harassed Penguins, After Many Days Buried in the Snow

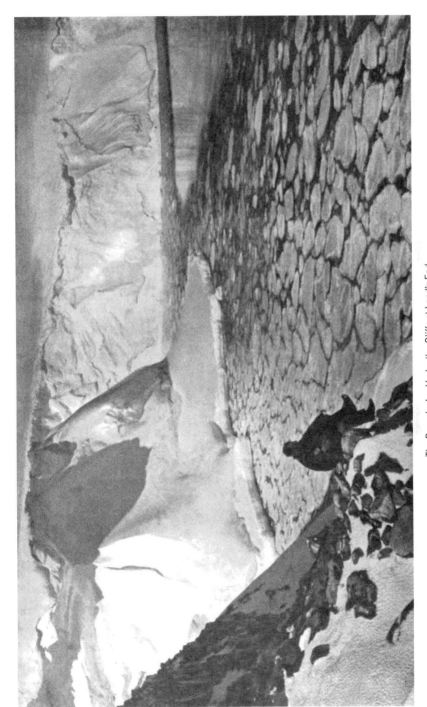

The Pancake Ice Under the Cliffs at Land's End

On March 13 there was a tremendous fall of snow, and worst "pea-souper" we had had during the previous year. Next day everything was deluged, and right up the glacier there were two-foot drifts, despite a sixty-mile wind.

It was very interesting to follow the changes which occurred from day to day. First of all, under the flail of the incessant wind, a crust would form on the surface of the snow of the type we knew as "piecrust," when out sledging. It was never strong enough to bear a man, but the sledge-runners would clear it fairly well if the load were not too heavy. Next day the crust would be etched, and small flakes and pellets would be carried away until the snow was like fleece. Assuming that the wind kept up (which it always did) long, shallow concavities would now be scooped out as the "lobules" of the fleece were carried away piecemeal. These concavities became deeper, hour by hour and day by day, becoming at last the troughs between the crests of the snow-waves or sastrugi. All this time the surface would be gradually hardening and, if the sun chanced to shine for even a few hours every day, a shining glaze would gradually form on the long, bevelled mounds. It was never a wise thing to walk on these polished areas in finnesko and this fact was always learnt by experience.

Above the Hut, where the icy slopes fell quickly to the sea, the snow would lie for a few days at the very most, but, lower down, where the glacier ran almost level for a short distance to the harbour ice, the drifts would lie for months at the mercy of the wind, furrowed and cut into miniature canyons; wearing away in fragments until the blue ice showed once more, clear and wind-swept.

Towards the end of March the wind gave a few exhibitions of its power, which did not augur well for the maximum periods of the winter. A few diary jottings are enough to show this:

"*March 23*. During the previous night the wind steadily rose to an eighty-mile 'touch' and upwards. It was one of those days when it is a perpetual worry to be outside.

"*March 24*. Doing at least seventy miles per hour during the morning. About 8 PM there was a temporary lull and a rise of .15 in the barometer. Now, 9.30 PM, it is going 'big guns.' The drift is fairly thick and snow is probably falling.

"*March 25*. Much the same as yesterday.

"*March 28*. In a seventy-five-mile wind, Hodgeman had several fingers frost-bitten this morning while attending to the anemograph.

"*March 29*. It was quite sunny when we opened the trap-door, though it blew about sixty miles per hour with light drift.

"*March 30.* The wind is doing itself full justice. About 8 PM it ranged between ninety-five and one hundred miles per hour, and now the whole hut is tremulous and the stove-pipe vibrates so that the two large pots on the stove rattle."

At the beginning of April, McLean laid the foundations of *The Adelie Blizzard* which recorded our life for the next seven months. It was a monthly publication, and contributions were invited from all on every subject but the wind. Anything from light doggerel to heavy blank verse was welcomed, and original articles, letters to the Editor, plays, reviews on books and serial stories were accepted within the limits of our supply of foolscap paper and type-writer ribbons.

It was the first Antarctic publication which could boast a real cable column of news of the day. Extracts from the April number were read after dinner one evening and excited much amusement. An "Ode to Tobacco" was very popular, and seemed to voice the enthusiasm of our small community, while "The Evolution of Women" introduced us to a once-familiar subject. The Editor was later admitted by wireless to the Journalists' Association (Sydney).

Many have asked the question, "What did you do to fill in the time during the second year?"

The duties of cook and night-watchman came to each man once every week, and meteorological and magnetic observations went on daily. Then we were able to devote a good deal of time to working up the scientific work accomplished during the sledging journeys. The wireless watches kept two men well occupied, and in spare moments the chief recreation was reading. There was a fine supply of illustrated journals and periodicals which had arrived by the *Aurora*, and with papers like the *Daily Graphic, Illustrated London News, Sphere* and *Punch*, we tried to make up the arrears of a year in exile. The "Encyclopaedia Britannica" was a great boon, being always "the last word" in the settlement of a debated point. Chess and cards were played on several occasions. Again, whenever the weather gave the smallest opportunity, there were jobs outside, digging for cases, attending to the wireless mast and, in the spring, geological collecting and dredging. If the air was clear of drift, and the wind not over fifty miles per hour, one could spend a pleasant hour or more walking along the shore watching the birds and noting the changes in "scenery" which were always occurring along our short "selection" of rocks. During 1912 we had been able to study all the typical features of our novel and beautiful environment, but 1913 was the period of "intensive cultivation" and we would have gladly forgone much of it. Divine service was usually held on Sunday mornings, but in place of it

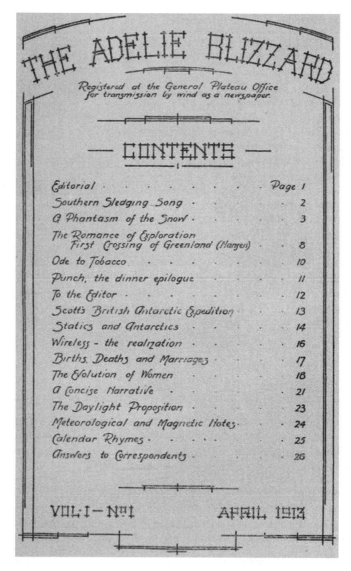

we sometimes sang hymns during the evening, or arranged a programme of sacred selections on the gramophone. There was a great loss in our singing volume after the previous year, which Hodgeman endeavoured to remedy by striking up an accompaniment on the organ.

Cooking reached its acme, according to our standard, and each man became remarkable for some particular dish. Bage was the exponent of steam puddings of every variety, and Madigan could always be relied upon for an unfailing batch of puff-pastry. Bickerton once started out with the object of cooking a ginger pudding, and in an unguarded moment used mixed spices instead of ginger. The result was rather appetizing, and "mixed-spice pudding" was added to an original list. McLean specialized in yeast waffles, having acquired the art of tossing pancakes. Jeffryes had come on the scene with a limited experience, but his first milk scones gained him a reputation which he managed to make good. Hodgeman fell back on the cookery book before embarking on the task of preparing dinner, but the end-product, so to speak, which might be invariably expected for "sweets" was tapioca pudding. Penguin meat had always been in favour. Now special care was devoted to seal meat, and, after a while, mainly owing to the rather copious use of onion powder, no one could say for certain which was which.

During the previous year, yeast had been cultivated successfully from Russian stout. The experiments were continued, and all available information was gathered from cookery books and the Encyclopaedia. Russian stout, barley wine, apple rings, sugar, flour and mould from potatoes were used in several mixtures and eventually fermentation was started. Bread-making was the next difficulty, and various instructions were tried in succession. The method of "trial and error" was at last responsible for the first light spongy loaf, and then every night-watchman cultivated the art and baked for the ensuing day.

On April 8 the snow had gathered deeply everywhere and we had some exercise on skis. Several of the morainic areas were no longer visible, and it was possible to run between the rocks for a considerable distance. A fresh breeze came up during the afternoon and provided a splendid impetus for some good slides. During the short calm, twenty-six seals landed on the harbour-ice.

On the morning of the same day Mary gave birth to five pups in the Transit House. The place was full of cracks, through which snow and wind were always driving, and so we were not surprised when four of them were found to have died. The survivor was named "Hoyle" (a cognomen for our old friend Hurley) and his doings gave us a new fund of entertainment.

The other dogs had been penned in the veranda and in tolerable weather were brought outside to be fed. Carrying an axe, Madigan usually went down to the boat harbour, followed by the expectant pack, to where there were several seal carcases. These lay immovably frozen to the ice, and were cut about and hacked so that the meat in section reminded one of the grain of a log of red gum, and it was certainly quite as hard. When Madigan commenced to chop, the dogs would range themselves on the lee side and "field" the flying chips.

On April 16 the last penguin was seen on a ledge overhanging an icy cove to the east. Apparently its moulting time had not expired, but it was certainly a very miserable bird, smothered in small icicles and snow and partly exposed to a sixty-five mile wind with the temperature close to −10° F. Petrels were

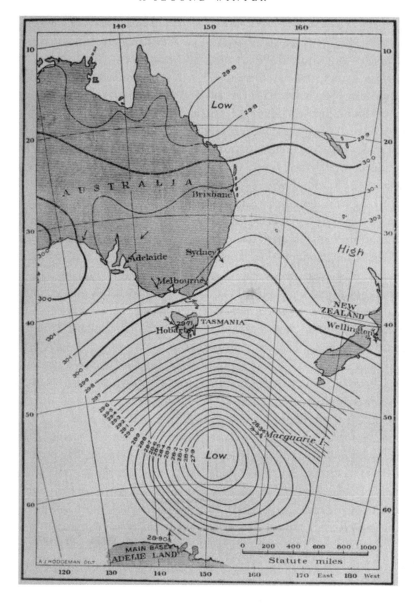

often seen flying along the foreshores and no wind appeared to daunt them. It was certainly a remarkable thing to witness a snow-petrel, small, light and fragile, making headway over the sea in the face of an eighty-mile hurricane, fluttering down through the spindrift to pick up a morsel of food which it had detected. Close to the western cliffs there was a trail of brash-ice where many birds were often observed feeding on Euphausia (crustaceans) in weather when it scarcely seemed possible for any living creature to be abroad.

The Meteorological Chart for April 12, 1913, Compiled by the Commonwealth Meteorological Bureau. Mr. Hunt appends the following explanation: "A very intense cyclone passing south of Macquarie Island, where the barometer fell on the 11th from 29.49 at 9 AM to 29.13 at 6 PM, and the next day to 28.34 at 9 AM and 27.91 at 6 PM At Adelie Land the barometer was not greatly affected, but rose in sympathy with the passage of the 'low' from 28.70 to 28.90 during the twenty-four hours. The influence of this cyclone was very wide and probably embraced both Adelie Land and Tasmania."

Throughout April news by wireless came in slowly and spasmodically, and Jeffryes was becoming resigned to the eccentricities of the place. As an example of the unfavourable conditions which sometimes prevailed: on April 14 the wind was steady, in the nineties, with light drift and, at times, the aurora would illumine the north-west sky. Still, during "quiet" intervals, two messages came through and were acknowledged.

A coded weather report, which had priority over all other messages, was sent out each night, and it is surprising how often Jeffryes managed to transmit this important intelligence. On evenings when receiving was an impossibility, owing to a continual stream of St. Elmo's fire, the three code words for the barometric reading, the velocity and direction of the wind were signalled repeatedly and, on the following night, perhaps, Macquarie Island would acknowledge them. Of course we had to use new signs for the higher wind velocities, as no provision had been made for them in our meteorological code-book. The reports from Macquarie Island and Adelie Land were communicated to Mr. Hunt of the Commonwealth Weather Bureau and to Mr. Bates of the Dominion Meteorological Office, who plotted them out for their daily weather forecasts.

It was very gratifying to learn that the Macquarie Island party to a man had consented to remain at their lonely post and from Ainsworth, their leader, I received a brief report of the work which had been accomplished by each member. We all could appreciate the sacrifice they were making. Then, too, an account was received of the great sledging efforts which had been made by Wild and his men to the west. But it was not till the end of the year that their adventurous story was related to us in detail.

On the 23rd Lassie, one of the dogs, was badly wounded in a fight and had to be shot. Quarrels amongst the dogs had to be quelled immediately, otherwise they would probably mean the death of some unfortunate animal which happened to be thrown down amongst the pack. Whenever a dog was down, it was the way of these brutes to attack him irrespective of whether they were friends or foes.

A Wonderful Canopy of Ice

Sastrugi Sculptured by the Incessant Blizzards

Among our dogs there were several groups whose members always consorted together. Thus, George and Lassie were friends and, when the latter was killed, George, who was naturally a miserable, downtrodden creature, became a kind of pariah, morose and solitary and at war with all except Peary and Fix, with whom he and Lassie had been associated in fights against the rest. The other dogs lived together in some kind of harmony, Jack and Amundsen standing out as particular chums, while the "pups," as we called them—D'Urville, Ross and Wilkes ("Monkey")—were a trio born in Adelie Land and, therefore, comrades in misfortune. Hoyle, as a pup, was treated benevolently by all the others, and entered the fellowship of the other three when he grew up. Among the rest, Mikkel stood out as a good fighter, Colonel as the biggest dog and ringleader against the Peary-Fix faction, Fram as a nervous intractable animal, and Mary as the sole representative of the sex.

It was remarkable that Peary, Fix and George in their hatred of the others, who were penned up in the dog shelter during bad weather, would absent themselves for days on a snow ramp near the Magnetograph House, where they were partly protected from the wind by rocks. George, from being a mere associate of Peary and Fix, became more amiable as the year went by, and at times it was quite pathetic to see his attempts at friendliness.

We became very fond of the dogs despite their habit of howling at night and their wolfish ferocity. They always gave one a welcome, in drift or sunshine, and though ruled by the law of force, they had a few domestic traits to make them civilized.

May was a dreaded month because it had been the period of worst wind and drift during 1912. On this occasion the wind velocities over four weeks were not so high and constant, though the snowfall was just as persistent. On the 17th and 18th, however, there was an unexpected "jump" to the nineties. The average over the first twenty-four hours was eighty-three, and on the 18th it attained 93.7 miles per hour. One terrific rise between 6.30 and 7.30 on the night of the 17th was shown as one hundred and three miles on the anemometer—the record up to that time.

Madigan was thrown over and had a hard fall on his arm, smashing a bottle of the special ink which was used for the anemograph pen. Bage related how he had sailed across the Magnetic Flat by sitting down and raising his arms in the air. He was accompanied by Fix, Peary and George, who were blown along the slippery surface for yards. McLean had a "lively time" cutting ice and bringing in the big blocks. Often he would slide away with a large piece, and "pull up" on a snow patch twenty yards to leeward.

On the 22nd there were hours of gusts which came down like thunderbolts, making us apprehensive for the safety of the wireless masts;

we had grown to trust the stability of the Hut. Every one who went outside came back with a few experiences. Jeffryes was roughly handled through not wearing crampons, and several cases of kerosene, firmly stacked on the break-wind, were dislodged and thrown several yards.

Empire Day was celebrated in Adelie Land with a small display. At 2.30 PM the Union Jack was hoisted to the topmast and three cheers were given for the King. The wind blew at fifty miles an hour with light drift, temperature –3° F. Empire greetings were sent to the Colonial Secretary, London, and to Mr. Fisher, Prime Minister of Australia. These were warmly reciprocated a few days afterwards.

Preceded by a day of whirlies on the 7th and random gusts on the same evening, the wind made a determined attack next morning and carried away the top and part of the middle section of the main wireless mast. It was a very unexpected event, lulled as we were into security by the fact that May, the worst month, had passed. On examination it was found that two of the topmast wire stays had chafed through, whilst another had parted. At first it seemed a hopeless task to re-erect the mast, but gradually ways and means were discussed, and we waited for the first calm day to put the theories into execution.

Meanwhile, it was suggested that if a heavy kite were made and induced to fly in the continuous winds, the aerial thus provided would be sufficient to receive wireless messages. To this end, Bage and Bickerton set to work, and the first invention was a Venesta-box kite which was tried in a steady seventy-mile wind. Despite its weight,—at least ten pounds —the kite rose immediately, steadied by guys on either side, and then suddenly descended with a crash on to the glacier ice. After the third fall the kite was too battered to be of any further use. Another device, in which an empty carbide tin was employed, and still another, making use of an old propeller, shared the same fate.

On the evening of the 19th a perfect coloured corona, three degrees in diameter, was observed encircling the moon in a sky which lit up at intervals with dancing auroral curtains. Coronae or "glories," which closely invest the luminary, are due to diffraction owing to immense numbers of very minute water or ice particles floating in the air between the observer and the source of light. The larger the particles the smaller the corona, so that by a measurement of the diameter of a corona the size of the particles can be calculated. Earlier in the year, a double corona had been seen when the moon was shining through cirro-cumulus clouds. Haloes, on the other hand, are wide circles (or arcs of circles) in the sky surrounding the sun or moon, and arising from light-refraction in myriads of tiny ice-crystals suspended in the atmosphere. They were very commonly noted in Adelie Land where the conditions were so ideal for their production.

Midwinter's Day 1913! we had reached a turning-point in the season. The Astronomer Royal told us that at eight o'clock on June 22 the sun commenced to return, and every one took note of the fact. The sky was overcast, the air surcharged with drifting snow, and the wind was forty miles an hour—a representative day as far as the climate was concerned. The cook made a special effort and the menu bore the following foreword:

> *Now is the winter of our discontent*
> *Made glorious summer. . . .*

On July 6 the wind moderated, and we set about repairing once more the fortunes of the "wireless." The shattered topmast used to sway about in the heavy winds, threatening to bring down the rest of the mast. Bickerton, therefore, climbed up with a saw and cut it almost through above the doubling. All hands then pulled hard, and the upper part cracked off, the lower section being easily removed from the cross-trees. The mast now looked "shipshape" and ready for future improvements.

It was decided to use as a topmast the mast which had been formerly employed to support the northern half of the aerial. So on the 29th this was lowered and removed to the veranda to be fitted for erection.

Almost a fortnight now elapsed, during which the weather was "impossible." In fact, the wind was frightful throughout the whole month of July, surpassing all its previous records and wearing out our much-tried patience. All that one could do was to work on and try grimly to ignore it. On July 2 we noted: "Thick as a wall outside with an eighty-five miler." And so it commenced and continued for a day, subsiding slowly through the seventies to the fifties and then suddenly redoubling in strength, rose to a climax about midnight on the 5th— one hundred and sixteen miles an hour! For eight hours it maintained an average of one hundred and seven miles an hour, and the timbers of the Hut seemed to be jarred and wrenched as the wind throbbed in its mightier gusts. These were the highest wind-velocities recorded during our two years' residence in Adelie Land and are probably the highest sustained velocities ever reported from a meteorological station.

With the exception of a few Antarctic and snow petrels flying over the sea on the calmer days, no life had been seen round the Hut during June. So it was with some surprise that we sighted a Weddell seal on July 9 attempting to land on the harbour-ice in a seventy-five-mile wind. Several times it clambered over the edge and on turning broadside to the wind was

The Terminal Moraine Near the Hut, Cape Denison

Disappearing in the Drift

The Hut Looming Through the Drift

actually tumbled back into the water. Eventually it struggled into the lee of some icy hummocks, but only remained there for a few minutes, deciding that the water was much warmer.

On the 11th there was an exceptionally low barometer at 27.794 inches. At the same time the wind ran riot once more—two hundred and ninety-eight miles in three hours. The highest barometric reading was recorded on September 3, 30.4 inches, and the comparison indicates a wide range for a station at sea-level.

To show how quickly conditions would change, it was almost calm next morning, and all hands were in readiness to advance the wireless mast another stage. Previously there had been three masts, one high one in three lengths, and two smaller ones of one length each, between which the aerial stretched; the "lead-in" wires being connected to the middle of the aerial. This is known as an "umbrella aerial." Since we were without one short mast it was resolved to erect a "directive" $\lceil$-shaped aerial. The mainmast was to be in two instead of three lengths, and we wondered if the aerial would be high enough. In any case, it was so calm early on the 11th that we ventured to erect the topmast and had hauled it half-way, when the wind swooped down from the plateau, and there was just time to make fast the stays and the hauling rope and to leave things "snug" for the next spell of bad weather.

In eight days another opportunity came, and this time the topmast was hoisted, wedged and securely stayed. Bickerton had fixed a long bolt through the middle of the topmast and just above it three additional wire stays were to be placed. Another fine day and we reckoned to finish the work.

From July 26 onwards the sky was cloudless for a week, and each day the northern sun would rise a fraction of a degree higher. The wind was very constant and of high velocity.

It was a grand sight to witness the sea in a hurricane on a driftless, clear day. Crouched under a rock on Azimuth Hill, and looking across to the west along the curving brink of the cliffs, one could watch the water close inshore blacken under the lash of the wind, whiten into foam farther off, and then disappear into the hurrying clouds of spray and sea-smoke. Over the Mackellar Islets and the "Pianoforte Berg" columns of spray would shoot up like geysers, and fly away in the mad race to the north.

Early in July Jeffryes became ill, and for some weeks his symptoms were such as to give every one much anxiety. His work on the wireless had been assiduous at all times, and there is no doubt that the continual and acute strain of sending and receiving messages under unprecedented conditions was such that he eventually had a "nervous breakdown." Unfortunately the weather was so atrocious, and the conditions under which we were placed so peculiarly difficult, that nothing could be done to brighten his prospects. McLean considered that as the spring returned and it became possible to take more exercise outside, the nervous exhaustion would pass off. In the meantime Jeffryes took a complete rest, and slowly improved as the months went by, and our hopes of relief came nearer. It was a great misfortune for our comrade, especially as it was his first experience of such a climate, and he had applied himself to work with enthusiasm and perhaps in an over-conscientious spirit.

July concluded its stormy career with the astonishing wind-average of 63.6 miles an hour. We were all relieved to see Friday, August 1, appear on the modest calendar, which it was the particular pleasure of each night-watchman to change. More light filtered day by day through the ice on the kitchen window, midwinter lay behind, and we were ready to hail the first signs of returning spring.

CHAPTER XXIV

Nearing the End

Seven men from all the world, back to town again,
Seven men from out of hell.
—Kipling

IT IS WONDERFUL HOW QUICKLY THE WEEKS SEEMED to pass. Situated as we were, Time became quite an object of study to us and its imperceptible drift was almost a reality, considering that each day was another step towards liberty—freedom from the tyranny of the wind. In a sense, the endless surge of the blizzard was a slow form of torture, and the subtle effect it had on the mind was measurable in the delight with which one greeted a calm, fine morning, or noted some insignificant fact which bespoke the approach of a milder season. Thus in August, although the weather was colder, there were the merest signs of thawing along the edges of the snow packed against the rocky faces which looked towards the sun; Weddell seals came back to the land, and the petrels would at times appear in large flocks; all of which are very commonplace events which any one might have expected, but at the time they had more than their face value.

August 5 was undoubtedly a great day from our very provincial point of view. On the 4th there had been a dense drift, during which the Hut was buttressed round with soft snow which rose above the eaves and half filled the entrance-veranda. The only way in which the night-watchman could keep the hourly observations was to dig his way out frequently with a shovel. In the early morning hours of the 5th the wind abated and veered right round from south through east to north-east, from which quarter it remained as a fresh breeze with falling snow. By 7 AM the air was still, and outside there was a dead world of whiteness; flocculent heaps of down rolling up to where glimpses of rock streaked black near the skyline of the ridges, striated masses of livid cloud overhead, and to the horizon the dark berg-strewn sea, over which the snow birds fluttered.

We did not linger over the scenery, but set to work to hoist to the head of the mainmast the aerial, which had been hurriedly put together. The job occupied till lunch-time, and then a jury-mast was fixed to the southern supporting mast, and by dusk the aerial hung in position. Bickerton was the leading spirit in the work and subsequently steadied the mainmast with eighteen wire stays, in the determination to make it stable enough to weather the worst hurricane. The attempt was so successful that in an ordinary fifty-mile "blow" the mast vibrated slightly, and in higher winds exhibited the smallest degree of movement.

At eight o'clock that night, Jeffryes, who felt so benefited by his rest that he was eager to commence operating once more, had soon "attuned" his instrument to Macquarie Island, and in a few minutes communication was re-established.

We learned from the Governor-General, Lord Denman, that her Majesty the Queen was "graciously pleased to consent to the name 'Queen Mary Land' being given to newly discovered land." The message referred to the tract of Antarctic coast which had been discovered and mapped by Wild and his party to the west.

On August 6 Macquarie Island signalled that they had run short of provisions. The message was rather a paradox: " Food done, but otherwise all right." However, on August 11, we were reassured to hear that the *Tutanekai*, a New Zealand Government steamer, had been commissioned to relieve the party, and that Sawyer through ill-health had been obliged to return to Australia. A sealing-ship, the *Rachel Cohen*, after battling for almost the whole month of July against gales, in an endeavour to reach the island, with stores for our party and the sealers, had returned damaged to port.

Marvellous to relate we had two calm days in succession, and on the 6th the snow lay so deeply round the Hut that progression without skis was a laborious flounder. The dogs plunged about in great glee, rolling in the snow and "playing off" their surplus energy after being penned for a long spell in the shelter.

On skis one could push up the first slopes of the glacier for a long distance. Soft snow had settled two feet thick even on the steep icy downfalls. The sea to the north was frozen into large cakes between which ran a network of dark water "leads." With glasses we could make out in the near distance five seals and two tall solitary figures which were doubtless Emperor penguins. During the whole day nimbus clouds had hung heavily from the sky, and snow had fallen in grains and star-like crystals. Gradually the nimbus lightened, a rift appeared overhead, and, the edges of the billowy cumulus were burnished in the light of the low sun. The sea-horizon came sharply into sight through fading mist. Bergs and islands, from being ghostly images, rose into sharp-featured reality. The masts and Hut, with a dark riband of smoke floating from the chimney, lay just below, and two of the men were walking out to the harbour-ice where a seal had just landed, while round them scampered the dogs in high spirits. That was sufficient to set us sliding downhill, ploughing deep furrows through the soft drift and reaching the Hut in quick time.

During August we were able to do more work outside, thus enlarging our sphere of interest. Bage, who had been busy up till August 8 with his daily magnetograph records, ran short of bromide papers and now had to be contented with taking "quick runs" at intervals, especially when the aurora was active. His astronomical observations had been very disappointing owing to the continuous wind and drift. Still, in September, which was marked by periods of fine weather, a few good star observations were possible. Shafts were sunk in the sea-ice and up on the glacier, just above the zone where the ice was loaded with stones and debris—the lower moraine. The glacier shaft was dug to a depth of twenty-four feet, and several erratics were met with embedded in the ice. In this particular part the crystalline structure of the ice resembled that of a gneiss, showing that it had flowed under pressure. I was able to make measurements of ablation on the glacier, to take observations of the temperature and salinity of the sea-water, and to estimate the forward movement of the seaward cliffs of the ice-cap.

Geological collecting now became quite a popular diversion. With a slight smattering of "gneiss," "felspar," "weathered limestone," "garnets," and "glacial markings" the amateurs went off and made many finds on the moraines, and the specimens were cached in heaps, to be later brought home by the dogs, some of which were receiving their first lessons in sledge-pulling.

Rather belated, but none the less welcome, our midwinter wireless greetings arrived on August 17 from many friends who could only imagine how much they were appreciated, and from various members of the Expedition who had spent the previous year in Adelie Land and who knew the meaning of an Antarctic winter. A few evenings later, Macquarie Islanders had their reward in the arrival of the *Tutanekai* from New Zealand with supplies of food, and, piecing together a few fragments of evidence "dropped in the ether," we judged that they were having a night of revelry.

The wind was in a fierce humour on the morning of August 16, mounting to one hundred and five miles per hour between 9 and 10 AM, and carrying with it a very dense drift.

A Wall of Solid Gneiss Near Winter Quarters

An Erratic on the Moraine. Cape Denison

We were now in a position to sit down and generalize about the wind. It is a tiresome thing to have it as the recurring insistent theme of our story, but to have had it as the continual obstacle to our activity, the opposing barrier to the simplest task, was even more tedious.

A river, rather a torrent, of air rushes from the hinterland northward year after year, replenished from a source which never fails. We had reason to believe that it was local in character, as apparently a gulf of open water about one hundred miles in width—the D'Urville Sea—exists to the north of Adelie Land. Thus, far back in the interior—back to the South Geographical Pole itself—across one thousand six hundred miles of lofty plateau—is a

Frozen Spray Built Up by the Blizzards Along the Shore

zone of high barometric pressure, while to the north lies the D'Urville Sea and beyond it the Southern Ocean—a zone of low pressure. As if through a contracted outlet, thereby increasing the velocity of the flow, the wind sweeps down over Adelie Land to equalize the great air-pressure system. And so, in winter, the chilling of the plateau leads to the development of a higher barometric pressure and, as the open water to the north persists, to higher winds. In summer the suns shines on the Pole for six months, the uplands of the continent are warmed and the northern zone of low pressure pushes southward. So, in Adelie Land, short spells of calm weather may be expected over a period of barely three months around the summer solstice. This explanation is intentionally popular. The meteorological problem is one which can only be fully discussed when all the manifold observations have been gathered together, from other contemporary Antarctic expeditions, from our two stations on the Antarctic continent, and from Macquarie Island; all taken in conjunction with weather conditions around Australia and New Zealand. Then, when all the evidence is arrayed and compared, some general truths of particular value to science and, maybe, to commerce, should emerge.

Of one thing we were certain, and that was that Adelie Land was the windiest place in the world. To state the fact more accurately: such wind-velocities as prevail at sea-level in Adelie Land are known in other parts of the world only at great elevations in the atmosphere. The average wind-velocity for our first year proved to be approximately fifty miles per hour. The bare figures convey more when they are compared with the following average annual wind-velocities quoted from a book of reference: Europe, 10.3 miles per hour; United States, 9.5 miles per hour; Southern Asia, 6.5 miles per hour; West Indies, 6.2 miles per hour.

Reference has already been made to the fact that often the high winds ceased abruptly for a short interval. Many times during 1913 we had opportunities of judging this phenomenon and, as an example, may be quoted September 6.

On that day a south-by-east hurricane fell off and the drift cleared suddenly from about the Hut at 11.20 AM On the hills to the south there was a dense grey wall of flying snow. Whirlies tracked about at intervals and overhead a fine cumulus cloud formed, revolving rapidly. Over the recently frozen sea there was an easterly breeze, while about the Hut itself there were light northerly airs. Later in the day the zone of southern wind and drift crept down and once more overwhelmed us. Evidently the "eye" of a cyclonic storm had passed over.

During September the sea was frozen over for more than two weeks, and the meteorological conditions varied from their normal phase. It appeared

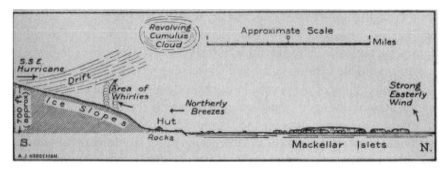

A Diagrammatic Sketch Illustrating the Meteorological Conditions at the Main Base, Noon, September 6, 1913

as if we were situated on the battlefield, so to speak, of opposing forces. The pacific influence of the "north" would hold sway for a few hours, a whole day, or even for a few days. Then the vast energies of the "south" would rise to bursting-point and a "through blizzard" would be the result.

On September 11, although there was a wind of seventy miles per hour, the sea-ice which had become very solid during a few days of low temperature was not dispersed. Next day we found it possible to walk in safety to the Mackellar Islets. On the way rushes of southerly wind accompanied by a misty drift followed behind us. Then a calm intervened, and the sun momentarily appeared and shone warmly. Suddenly from the north-west came breezy puffs which settled into a light wind as we went north. On the way home we could not see the mainland for clouds of drift, and, when approaching the mouth of the boat-harbour, these clouds were observed to roll down the lower slopes of the glacier and, reaching the shore, rise into the air in columns. They then sailed away northward at a higher altitude, almost obscuring the sun with a fine fog. On the same night the "south" had gained the mastery, and the wind blew with its accustomed strength.

Again, on September 24, McLean had a unique experience. He was digging ice in a fifty-mile wind with moderate drift close to the Hut and, on finishing his work, walked down to the harbour-ice to see if there were any birds about. He was suddenly surprised to leave the wind and drift behind and to walk out into an area of calm. The water lapped alongside the ice-foot, blue in the brilliant sunlight. Away to the west a few miles distant a fierce wind was blowing snow like fine spume over the brink of the cliffs. Towards the north-west one could plainly see the junction between calm water and foam-crested waves. To the south the drift drove off the hills, passed the Hut, and then gyrated upwards and thinned away seawards at an altitude of several hundred feet.

A View of the Mainland from the Mackellar Islets: Ice-Capped Islets in the Foreground: the Rock Visible on the Mainland Is Cape Denison

The wind average for September was 36.8 miles per hour, as against 53.7 for September of the previous year. There were nine "pleasant" days, that is, days on which it was possible to walk about outside and enjoy oneself. On the 27th there was a very severe blizzard. The wind was from the south-east: the first occasion on which it had blown from any direction but south-by-east at a high velocity. The drift was extremely dense, the roof of the Hut being invisible at a distance of six feet. Enormous ramps of snow formed in the vicinity, burying most of the cases and the air-tractor sledge completely. The anemograph screen was blown over and smashed beyond all repair. So said the Meteorological Notes in the October number of the *Adelie Blizzard*.

Speaking of temperature in general, it was found that the mean-temperature for the first year was just above zero; a very low temperature for a station situated near the Circle. The continual flow of cold air from the elevated interior of the continent accounts for this. If Adelie Land were a region of calms or of northerly winds, the average temperature would be very much higher. On the other hand, the temperature at sea-level was never depressed below –28° F., though with a high wind we found that uncomfortable enough, even in burberrys. During the spring sledging in 1912 the lowest temperature recorded was –35° F. and it was hard to keep warm in sleeping-bags. The wind made all the difference to one's resistance.

There was an unusually heavy snowfall during 1913. When the air was heavily charged with moisture, as in midsummer, the falls would consist of small (sago) or larger (tapioca) rounded pellets. Occasionally one would see beautiful complicated patterns in the form of hexagonal flakes. When low temperatures were the rule, small, plain, hexagonal stars or spicules fell. Often throughout a single snowfall many types would be precipitated. Thus, in September, in one instance, the fall commenced with fluffy balls and then passed to tapioca snow, sago snow, six-rayed stars and spicules.

Wireless communication was still maintained, though September was found to be such a "disturbed" month—possibly owing to the brilliant aurorae—that not a great many messages were exchanged. Jeffryes was not in the best of health, so that Bickerton took over the operating work. Though at first signals could only be received slowly, Bickerton gradually improved with practice and was able to "keep up his end" until November 20, when daylight became continuous. One great advantage, which by itself justified the existence of the wireless plant, was the fact that time-signals were successfully received from Melbourne Observatory by way of Macquarie Island, and Bage was thus able to improve on his earlier determinations and to establish a fundamental longitude.

During this same happy month of September, whose first day marked the event of "One hundred days to the coming of the Ship" there was a great revival in biological work. Hodgeman made several varieties of bag-traps which were lowered over the edge of the harbour-ice, and many large "worms" and crustaceans were caught and preserved.

On September 14 Bickerton started to construct a hand-dredge, which was ready for use by the next evening. It was a lovely, cloudless day on the 16th and the sea-ice, after more than two weeks, still spread to the north in a firm, unbroken sheet. We went out on skis to reconnoitre, and found that the nearest "lead" was too far away to make dredging a safe proposition. So we were contented to kill a seal and bring it home before lunch, continuing to sink the ice-shaft above the moraine for the rest of the day.

The wind rose to the "seventies" on September 17, and the sea-ice was scattered to the north. On the 19th—a fine day—there were many detached pieces of floe which drifted in with a northerly breeze, and on one of these, floating in an ice-girt cove to the west, a sea-leopard was observed sunning himself. He was a big, vicious-looking brute, and we determined to secure him if possible. The first thing was to dispatch him before he escaped from the floe. This Madigan did in three shots from a Winchester rifle. A long steel-shod sledge was then dragged from the Hut and used to bridge the interval between the ice-foot and the floe. After the specimen had been flayed, the skin and a good supply of dogs' meat were hauled across and sledged home. On the 30th another sea-leopard came swimming in near the harbour's entrance, apparently on the look-out for seals or penguins. Including the one seen during 1912, only three of these animals were observed during our two years' sojourn in Adelie Land.

A Wilson Petrel on the Nest, Mackellar Islets

The *Aurora* Lying at Anchor, Commonwealth Bay; in the Distance the Ice-Slopes of the Mainland Are Visible Rising to a Height of 3500 Feet. In the Foreground Is a Striking Formation Originating by the Freezing of Spray Dashed Up by the Hurricane Wind.

Dredgings in depths up to five fathoms were done inside the boat harbour and just off its entrance on five separate occasions between September 22 and the end of the month. Many "worms," crustaceans, pteropods, asteroids, gastropods and hydroids were obtained, and McLean and I had many interesting hours classifying the specimens. The former preserved and labelled them, establishing a small laboratory in the loft above the "dining-room." The only disadvantage of this arrangement was that various "foreign bodies" would occasionally come tumbling through the interspaces between the flooring boards of the loft while a meal was in progress.

Some Antarctic petrels were shot and examined for external and internal parasites. Fish were caught in two traps made by Hodgeman and myself in October, but unfortunately the larger of the two was lost during a blizzard. However, on October 11 a haul of fifty-two fish was made with hand-lines off the boat harbour, and we had a pleasant change in the menu for dinner. They were of the type known as Notothenia, to which reference has already been made.

By October 13, when a stray silver-grey petrel appeared, every one was on the qui vive for the coming of the penguins. In 1912 they had arrived on October 12, and as there was much floating ice on the northern horizon, we wondered if their migration to land had been impeded.

The winds were very high for the ensuing two days, and on the 17th the horizon was clearer and more "water sky" was visible. Before lunch on that day there was not a living thing along the steep, overhanging ice-foot, but by the late afternoon thirteen birds had effected a landing, and those who were not resting after their long swim were hopping about making a survey of the nearest rookeries. One always has a "soft spot" for these game little creatures—there is something irresistibly human about them—and, situated as we were, the wind seemed of little account now that the foreshores were to be populated by the penguins—our harbingers of summer and the good times to be. Three days later, at the call of the season, a skua gull came flapping over the Hut.

It was rather a singular circumstance that on the evening of the 17th, coincident with the disappearance of the ice on the horizon, wireless signals suddenly came through very strongly in the twilight at 9.30 PM, and for many succeeding nights continued at the same intensity. On the other hand, during September, when the sea was either firmly frozen or strewn thickly with floe-ice, communication was very fitful and uncertain. The fact is therefore suggested that wireless waves are for some reason more readily transmitted across a surface of water than across ice.

The weather during the rest of October and for the first weeks of November took on a phase of heavy snowfalls which we knew were inevitable before summer could be really established. The winds were very often in the "eighties" and every four or five days a calm might be expected.

The penguins had a tempestuous time building their nests, and resuming once more the quaint routine of their rookery life. In the hurricanes they usually ceased work and crouched behind rocks until the worst was over. A great number of birds were observed to have small wounds on the body which had bled and discoloured their feathers. In one case a penguin had escaped, presumably from a sea-leopard, with several serious wounds, and had staggered up to a rookery, dying there from loss of blood. Almost immediately the frozen carcase was mutilated and torn by skua gulls.

On October 31 the good news was received that the *Aurora* would leave Australia on November 15. There were a great number of things to be packed, including the lathe, the motor and dynamos, the air-tractor engine, the wireless "set" and magnetic and meteorological instruments. Outside the Hut, many cases of kerosene and provisions, which might be required for the Ship, had been buried to a depth of twelve feet in places during the southeast hurricane in September. So we set to work in great spirits to prepare for the future.

McLean was busy collecting biological specimens, managing to secure a large number of parasites from penguins, skua gulls, giant petrels, snow petrels, Wilson petrels, seals and an Emperor penguin, which came up on the harbour-ice. On several beautiful days, with a sea-breeze wafting in from the north, large purple and brown jelly-fish came floating to the ice-foot. Many were caught in a hand-net and preserved in formalin. In his shooting excursions McLean happened on a small rocky ravine to the east where, hovering among nests of snow and Wilson petrels, a small bluish-grey bird,** not unlike Prion Banksii, was discovered. Four specimens were shot, and, later, several old nests were found containing the unhatched eggs of previous years.

On the highest point of Azimuth Hill, overlooking the sea, a Memorial Cross was raised to our two lost comrades.

A calm evening in November! At ten o'clock a natural picture in shining colours is painted on the canvas of sea and sky. The northern dome is a blush of rose deepening to a warm terra-cotta along the horizon, and the water reflects it upward to the gaze. Tiny Wilson petrels flit by like swallows; seals shove their dark forms above the placid surface; the shore is

---

** *On arrival in Australia this bird proved to be new to science.*

lined with penguins squatting in grotesque repose. The south is pallid with light—the circling sun. Adelie Land is at peace!

For some time Madigan, Hodgeman and I had been prepared to set out on a short sledging journey to visit Mount Murchison and to recover if possible the instruments cached by the Eastern Coastal and the Southern Parties. It was not until November 23 that the weather "broke" definitely, and we started up the old glacier "trail" assisted by a good team of dogs.

Aladdin's Cave was much the same as we had left it in the previous February, except that a fine crop of delicate ice-crystals had formed on its walls. We carried with us a small home-made wireless receiving set, and arrangements were made with Bickerton and Bage to call at certain hours. As an "aerial" a couple of lengths of copper wire were run out on the surface of the ice. At the first "call" Madigan heard the signals strongly and distinctly, but beyond five and a half miles nothing more was received.

Resuming the journey on the following day, we made a direct course for Madigan Nunatak and then steered southeast for Mount Murchison, pitching camp at its summit on the night of November 28.

On the 29th Madigan and Hodgeman made a descent into the valley, on whose southern side rose Aurora Peak. The former slid away on skis and had a fine run to the bottom, while Hodgeman followed on the sledge drawn by Monkey and D'Urville, braking with an ice-axe driven into the snow between the cross-bars. Their object was to find the depot of instruments and rocks which the Eastern Coastal Party were forced to abandon when fifty-three miles from home. They were unsuccessful in the search, as an enormous amount of snow had fallen on the old surface during the interval of almost a year. Indeed, on the knoll crowning Mount Murchison, where a ten-foot flagpole had been left, snow had accumulated so that less than a foot of the top of the pole was showing. Nine feet of hard compressed snow scarcely marked by one's footsteps—the contribution of one year! To such a high isolated spot drift-snow would not reach, so that the annual snowfall must greatly exceed the residuum found by us, for the effect of the prevailing winds would be to reduce it greatly.

On the third day after leaving Mount Murchison for the Southern Party's depot, sixty-seven miles south of Winter Quarters, driving snow commenced, and a blizzard kept us in camp for seven days. When the drift at last moderated we were forced to make direct for the Hut, as the time when the Ship was expected to arrive had passed.

Descending the long blue slopes of the glacier just before midnight on December 12, we became aware of a faint black bar on the seaward horizon.

Soon a black speck had moved to the windward side of the bar—and it could be nothing but the smoke of the *Aurora*. The moment of which we had dreamt for months had assuredly come. The Ship was in sight!

There were wild cheers down at the Hut when they heard the news. They could not believe us and immediately rushed up with glasses to the nearest ridge to get the evidence of their own senses. The masts, the funnel and the staunch hull rose out of the ocean as we watched on the hills through the early hours of a superb morning. The sun was streaming warmly over the plateau and a cool land breeze had sprung up from the south, as the *Aurora* rounded the Mackellar Islets and steamed up to her old anchorage. We picked out familiar figures on the bridge and poop, and made a bonfire of kerosene, benzine and lubricating oil in a rocky crevice in their honour.

The indescribable moment was when Davis came ashore in the whale-boat, manned by two of the Macquarie Islanders (Hamilton and Blake), Hurley and Hunter. They rushed into the Hut, and we tried to tell the story of a year in a few minutes.

On the Ship we greeted Gillies, Gray, de la Motte, Ainsworth, Sandell and Correll. It was splendid to know that the world contained so many people, and to see these men who had stuck to the Expedition through "thick and thin." Then came the fusillade of letters, magazines and "mysterious" parcels and boxes. At dinner we sat down reunited in the freshly painted ward-room, striving to collect our bewildered thoughts at the sight of a white tablecloth, Australian mutton, fresh vegetables, fruit and cigars.

The two long years were over—for the moment they were to be effaced in the glorious present. We were to live in a land where drift and wind were unknown, where rain fell in mild, refreshing showers, where the sky was blue for long weeks, and where the memories of the past were to fade into a dream—a nightmare?

The Shack and Its Vicinity. *Macquarie Island*

Tussock Slopes and Misty Highlands. *Macquarie Island*

CHAPTER XXV

Life on Macquarie Island

By G. F. AINSWORTH

LEFT ON AN ISLAND IN MID-OCEAN!
It suggests the romances of youthful days—Crusoe, Sindbad and all their glorious company. Still, when this narrative is completed, imagination will be seen to have played a small part. In fact, it is a plain tale of our experiences, descriptive of a place where we spent nearly two years and of the work accomplished during our stay.

The island was discovered in 1810 by Captain Hasselborough of the ship *Perseverance*, which had been dispatched by Campbell and Sons, of Sydney, under his command to look for islands inhabited by fur seals. Macquarie Islands, named by Hasselborough after the Governor of New South Wales, were found to be swarming with these valuable animals, and for two years after their discovery was made known, many vessels visited the place, landing gangs of men to procure skins and returning at frequent intervals to carry the proceeds of their labours to the markets of the world.

The slaughter of the seals was so great that the animals were almost exterminated within a few years. One ship is known to have left Macquarie Island with a cargo of 35,000 skins during the first year of operations. High prices were obtained for them in London and China, and many American, British and Sydney firms were engaged in the enterprise.

The value of a skin is determined by the condition of the fur, which is often damaged by the animals fighting amongst themselves. Furthermore, at a certain season of the year, the seals moult, and if taken within a certain time of this natural process, the skin is almost valueless. These facts were ignored by the sealers, who killed without discrimination.

Again, both male and female, old and young were ruthlessly slaughtered, with the obvious result—the extermination of the species. If supervision had been exercised and restrictions imposed, there is no doubt that the island would still have been used by the fur seal as a breeding-ground. During our stay none were seen, but Mr. Bauer, who acts as sealing herdsman and who had visited the island in that capacity each summer for eleven years, stated that he had seen odd ones at infrequent intervals.

Associated as the island has been since the year 1812 with sealing and oil ventures, it follows that a history has been gradually developed; somewhat traditional, though many occurrences to which we shall refer are well authenticated.

It might be supposed from the foregoing, that a good deal is known about the place, but such is not the case, except in a general sense. Several scientific men from New Zealand, recognizing the importance of the island as a link between Australasia and Antarctica, visited it at different times within the past twenty years, only remaining long enough to make a cursory examination of the eastern side. They had to depend on the courtesy of the sealing ships' captains for a passage, and the stormy conditions which are ever prevalent made their stay too brief for any exhaustive work.

A Russian Antarctic expedition, under Bellingshausen's command, called there in 1821 and stayed for two days, collecting a few bird and animal specimens. They referred to the island as being "half-cooled down," in a short but interesting account of their visit, and remarked upon the large number of sea-elephants lying on the shores.

In 1840 the ship *Peacock*, one of the exploring vessels of the American Expedition under Wilkes, landed several men after much difficulty on the south-west of the island, but they remained only a few hours, returning to their ship after securing some specimens of birds. Expressing astonishment at the "myriad of birds," they remarked, "Macquarie Islands offer no inducement for a visit, and as far as our examination showed, have no suitable place for landing with a boat."

The next call of an Antarctic expedition was made by Captain Scott in the *Discovery* in November 1901. He, with several naturalists, landed on the eastern side to collect specimens, but remained only a few hours. He refers to the penguins, kelp-weed and tussock grass; certainly three characteristic features.

Captain Davis, during his search for charted sub-antarctic islands, when connected with Sir Ernest Shackleton's expedition, called there in the *Nimrod* in 1909. He landed a party of men who secured several sea-elephants and some penguins.

It will thus be seen that very little had been done which was scientifically important or generally interesting. Sealers came and went as a matter of business, and probably the arduous nature of their work and the rugged topography of the island combined to prevent the more curious from exploring far afield.

Captain Scott was desirous of establishing a base on Macquarie Island in 1910, but circumstances compelled him to abandon the idea. And so it came that we five men of Dr. Mawson's Expedition were landed on December 22, 1911, with a programme of work outlined by our leader. H. Hamilton was biologist, L. R. Blake surveyor and geologist, C. A. Sandell and A. J. Sawyer were wireless operators, the former being also a mechanic, and I was appointed meteorologist and leader of the party.

We stood on the beach in the dusk, watching the boat's party struggle back to the *Aurora*, which lay at anchor one and a half miles from the northwest shore. Having received a soaking landing in the surf and being tired out with the exertions of the day, we started back to our temporary shelter. We had not gone very far when a mysterious sound, followed by a shaking of the earth, made us glance at each other and exclaim, "An earthquake!" The occurrence gave rise to a discussion which carried us to bed.

Seeing that we were to spend a long time on the island, the question of building a hut was the first consideration. Through the kindness of Mr. Bauer, who had just left the island in the SS *Toroa*, we were able to live for the time being in the sealers' hut.

It was urgent to get the wireless station into working order as soon as possible. The masts and operating-hut had been erected during the stay of the *Aurora*, but there yet remained the building of the engine-hut and the installation of the machinery and instruments, as well as the construction and erection of the aerial. Accordingly we proceeded with the living-hut and the job on Wireless Hill at the same time, working on the hill most of the day and at the hut in the evening.

Wireless Hill rose to three hundred and fifty feet in height, and formed part of a peninsula running in a northeasterly direction from the main island. It had been chosen by Mr. Hannam of the Adelie Land party because of its open northerly aspect, and because "wireless" waves would probably have a good "set-off," southward to the Main Base in Antarctica.

Just a few yards from the base of the hill on its southwestern side was a huge rock, upon the easterly side of which we decided to build our dwelling. The timbers for the hut had been cut and fitted in Hobart, so all that remained for us was to put them together.

After working at high pressure until December 30, we were able to establish ourselves in a home. The doorway faced to the east, and the rock protected the small place from the strong westerly weather which is invariable in these latitudes. The dimensions were twenty feet by thirteen feet, the front wall being nine feet six inches high, sloping to seven feet six inches at the back. All the timbers were of oregon and deal, and particular attention was paid to bracing and strengthening the building, which rested on piles just clear of the sandy surface. The inside was lined and ceiled, and the roof of galvanized iron was set flush with the front wall, fascia boards along the front and sides being designed to keep the fine snow from blowing under the corrugations and lodging on the ceiling. "George V Villa" was fixed upon as the name, but the hut was never at any time referred to as the villa, and in future will always be known as the Shack.

Twelve live sheep had been landed, and these had been driven on to Wireless Hill so as to be accessible. We decided to kill one for Christmas, so on December 24 Sandell and I, leaving the others at work on the Shack, started out.

The hillsides are deeply ravined and the slopes covered with a dense growth of tussock, which renders progress uncertain and laborious. Our experience was a foretaste of many to come. We found the sheep huddled together in a deep gully on the eastern side, and drove them round to the front of the hill, where one was caught, killed and dressed.

Christmas Day dawned fine and sunny, and we decided to make some attempt at a dinner. Blake produced a plum pudding, and this, together with roast mutton and several kinds of vegetables, washed down with a little claret, constituted our first Christmas dinner.

The sealing schooner, *Clyde*, had been wrecked without loss of life on November 14, 1911, on the east coast, and was now lying on the beach nearly half a mile away. A two-hundred-gallon tank had been saved from the wreck and we managed on Christmas morning, after two hours of carrying and trundling, to place it at the end of the Shack. This was a valuable find, ensuring in the future a constant, convenient supply of rain water. Further, we made use of the timber of the wreck for building, and the broken pieces strewn about were stored up as firewood.

On the 26th we all went to the wireless station, and, as Sandell had the aerial made, we pulled it into position. In the afternoon I unpacked all my instruments and started them off so as to make sure that all were working correctly. I did not intend to record any observations till January 1, 1912, and therefore did not erect the meteorological screen until the 28th.

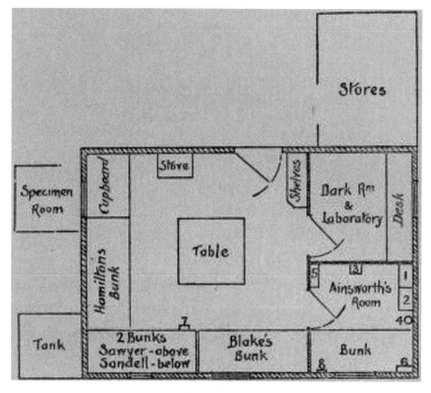

On moving into our abode domestic arrangements were made. With regard to cooking, each man took duty for a week, during which he was able to write up his work and to wash and mend clothes. To Hamilton and Sandell, who had had previous experience, frequent appeals were made as to methods of cooking various dishes, but by degrees each one asserted his independence. There were several cookery books for reference and each week saw the appearance of some new pudding, in each instance prefaced by the boast: "This is going to be the best pudding ever turned out on the island!" The promise was not always made good.

We had a good deal of difficulty at first in making bread and several batches were very "heavy" failures. This difficulty, however, was soon overcome and, after the first few months, the cooking standard was high and well maintained. Our stove was very small and only two loaves of bread could be cooked at once. It frequently happened, therefore, that the others, which would go on rising in the tins, overflowed; a matter which could only be set right by experience.

On New Year's Day, 1912, we carried timber in relays from the wreck to the top of Wireless Hill, so that the building of the engine-hut

550

The Shack: Showing the Natural Rocky Protection on the Windward Side

The Interior of the Operating Hut on Wireless Hill

Weka Pecking on the Beach

Chicks of the Dominican Gull

could be started. The next few days were occupied in getting food-stuffs, medicines, stationery, clothing and other necessaries over to the Shack from the landing-place on the beach. Blake and Hamilton unpacked their instruments and appliances, fitting up a small laboratory and photographic dark-room in one corner of the hut.

Some kind Hobart friend had sent four fowls to me on the day of sailing, requesting me to take them to Macquarie Island. They were housed in one of the meteorological screens, but on the third day from Hobart a heavy sea broke on board, upset the temporary fowl-house and crushed the rooster's head. The three hens were landed safely and appeared to be thoroughly reconciled to their strange surroundings, though the presence of so many large birds soaring about overhead had a terrifying effect on them for several days. They did not appear to pick up much food amongst the grass, but scratched away industriously all the same. I must say that they were very friendly and gave the place quite a homely aspect. One of them was christened "Ma" on account of her maternal and somewhat fussy disposition.

On the first Sunday in the new year all except myself went along the coast towards West Point. The party reported immense numbers of sea-elephants, especially young ones. They also saw many wekas and three ducks, shooting nine of the former for the kitchen.

The wekas or Maori hens are small, flightless birds, averaging when full grown about two and three-quarter pounds. They were introduced twenty-five years ago by Mr. Elder, of New Zealand, a former lessee of the island, and multiplied so fast that they are now very numerous. They live among the tussocks, and subsist for the most part upon the larvae of the kelp-fly, small fish and other marine life which they catch under the stones along the rocky shores at low tide. They are exceedingly inquisitive and pugnacious and may easily be caught by hand.

Usually, when disturbed, they will pop under a rock, and on being seized immediately commence to squeak. This is sufficient to bring every weka within a quarter of a mile hurrying to the spot, and, in a few minutes, heads may be seen poking out of the grass in every direction. The man holding the bird then crouches down, preferably just on the border of the tussock, holding the protesting bird in one hand. Soon there will be a rustle, then a rush, and another furious weka will attack the decoy. The newcomer is grabbed and, if the birds are plentiful, five or six of them may be taken in one spot.

Their call is peculiarly plaintive and wild and may be heard night and day. Though we saw and caught innumerable young ones of all sizes, we were never able to find the nests of these Maori hens.

A depot of stores had been laid by the *Aurora* at Caroline Cove, twenty miles from the Shack at the south end of the island, and it was deemed advisable to lay several more intermediate food-depots along the east coast.

The sealers had a motor-launch which they kindly placed at our disposal, and a supply of stores was put on board for transport. At 8 AM, January 9, Sandell, Blake, Sawyer and Hamilton started out accompanied by two sealers who offered to point out the positions of several old huts along the coast. These huts had been built by sealing gangs many years ago and were in a sad state of disrepair.

The first call was made at Sandy Bay, about five miles from the Shack. Stores were landed and placed in the hut, and the party proceeded to Lusitania Bay, eleven miles farther on, where they stayed for the night. At this place (named after an old sealing craft, the *Lusitania*) there were two huts, one being a work-hut and the other a living-hut. They had not been used for sixteen years and, as a result, were found to be much dilapidated. In the locality is a large King penguin rookery, the only one on the island, and two dozen eggs were obtained on this visit, some fresh and some otherwise.

As the next morning was squally, it was decided that the stores should be deposited in the hut at the south end; a distance of five miles across country. Through bog and tussock it took the party four hours to accomplish this journey. The hut was found in the same condition as the others and a rather miserable night was spent. A short distance from this spot is situated the largest penguin rookery on the island. On returning to the launch, the six men had a quick run of three hours back to the north end.

During the absence of the party I had been busy erecting a stand for the anemo-biagraph. Ordinarily, such an instrument is kept in a house, the upper section only being exposed through the roof. The Shack was in a position too sheltered for my purpose, so I built a place for the anemo-biagraph behind a low rock well out on the isthmus.

Sandell and Sawyer reported on the 16th that the wireless station was ready for testing. Therefore, on the following day, the three of us erected a small set on the farthest point of the peninsula—North Head. The set had been made in order to test the large station. Sawyer then returned to the operating-hut and received signals sent from North Head by Sandell, who in return received Sawyer's signals, thus showing that so far everything was satisfactory. It was thought, after the tests, that the "earth" was not by any means good and Sawyer erected a counterpoise, which, however, failed to give anything like the "earth" results. More "earths" (connexions by wire with the ground) were now put in from day to day, and on the 27th Sawyer

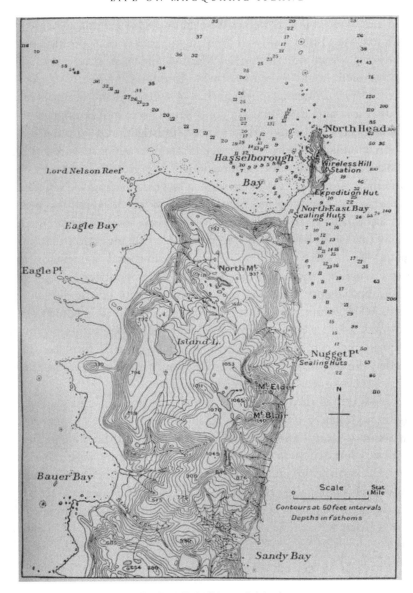

The North End of Macquarie Island

noted an improvement. Successful tests were again made on the 30th. The wireless men now expected communication with Australia.

Blake and Hamilton were soon making inroads, each on his own particular sphere of work. On the 17th a baseline was laid down on the plateau, and Blake was able to commence his survey of the island. He had already made some geological investigations in the vicinity of North

555

Head and West Point, as well as for a short distance along the east coast. Hamilton had visited nearly all the penguin rookeries in the vicinity, and already had several fine specimens. Marine collecting occupied part of his time and plant life promised to provide an interesting field.

From the intermediate position that Macquarie Island occupies relative to Australasia and the Antarctic continent, it was highly important that its biology should be fully determined. Investigation of the marine and terrestrial fauna and flora shows several facts indicating the part this island has played in the supposed connexion of the great land masses of the southern hemispheres. It is an established fact that the flora of New Zealand has strong sub-antarctic and South American affinities and the problem is to account for this distribution. Many forms of plant and animal life are circumaustral, being found in all suitable sub-antarctic situations. To account for this fact two theories have been advanced, namely, the Relict theory (Dahl, Schenck and others) and the Antarctic theory.

The first theory supposes that the inhabitants of the sub-antarctic islands are the remnants of groups of animals developed in some northern land-mass, and driven south by more highly developed forms. Again, that these sub-antarctic islands have always been separated from continents, and that the distribution of life on the former must have proceeded over wide stretches of sea.

The Antarctic theory accounts for the distribution and similarity of sub-antarctic fauna and flora by establishing a connexion between the sub-antarctic islands and the Antarctic continent. At the same period, the Antarctic continent was assumed to be connected by land with South America, South Africa and Australia, and the similar life forms now found in these continents were driven northward by a subsequent colder period. This theory is strengthened by several facts, chief of which are, (1) the existence of an Antarctic continent, and (2) the comparatively shallow waters between it, South Africa, Australia and South America.

Whichever theory is adopted, it is evident that our scientific opportunities were unique.

On the 28th, Sandell, Sawyer and I decided to climb on to the main ridge or plateau of the island. We had already discovered that the easiest way to get on to the hills was to follow up one of the many ravines or gullies which run down to the sea. This necessitates walking in water most of the way, but one soon gets accustomed to wet feet on Macquarie Island.

The slopes rise in a series of terraces which are generally soggy and covered with tussock (pleurophyllum) and with scattered cushions of Azorella. The summit of the ridge is a barren waste, over which loose rocks are scattered in every direction, while a wavy effect due to the action of wind is plainly visible over the surface of the ground. The steep, descending sides are very soft and sodden, supporting a scanty growth of vegetation, including the small burr known as the "biddy-bid."

Macquarie Island Skuas Feeding

Bull Sea Elephants Fighting

The Thermometer Screen, Macquarie Island

The Wind-Recording Instruments, Macquarie Island

"Feather Bed" Terrace Near Eagle Point, Macquarie Island

A Glacial Lake (Major Lake) on Macquarie Island, 600 Feet Above Sea Level

Hundreds of tarns and lakes are visible along the plateau-like ridge which extends throughout the length of the island. Several of the lakes are half a mile long and very deep. The tarns are, for the most part, shallow with hard stony bottoms. The water is beautifully fresh and apparently contains no life.

Skua gulls were plentiful and washed themselves, with a great flapping of wings, in the shallow waters at the edge of the lakes. They paid particular attention to our dog "Mac," swooping down and attempting to strike her with their wings. A yelp at intervals came from Mac if they were successful, though the former, if she were quick enough, would spring at the bird and retaliate by getting a mouthful of feathers.

We eventually came out on to a point about seven hundred feet high, overlooking the west coast, and it could be seen that the space between the base of the hills and the ocean was occupied by a plain which sloped very gradually to the beach. Here and there across its surface were huge mounds of earth and rock and, occasionally, a small lakelet fringed with a dense growth of tussock and Maori cabbage.

A descent was made to explore the place. A fairly large volume of water flowed rapidly downward by several deep gullies and, coming to the terrace, cut narrow, sinuous channels which were soon lost to view in the tussocks. Examination of the watercourses revealed that this tract was simply a raised beach covered with sodden peat and carrying a rather coarse vegetation. The ground was decidedly springy and shook to our tread; moreover, one sank down over the ankles at each step. Occasionally a more insecure area was encountered, where one of us would go down to the thighs in the boggy ground.

As the shore approached we came to thick tussock and Maori cabbage, and the travelling became much rougher. A group of earthy mounds and rock was sighted some distance away and we decided to reach them and have our lunch. A nearer view showed us a large opening in one of these prominences and we scrambled up to examine it.

Inside there was a small cave, high in front but sloping sharply towards the back for a distance of thirty-five feet. The roof and walls were blackened by smoke, and spikes and nails driven into crevices were evidences that the place had once been occupied. Eagle Cave it is called and its story was afterwards related to us.

Between thirty and forty years ago the schooner Eagle, in attempting to make the island, had been caught in a gale and wrecked on the rock-bound western coast. As far as can be learned, there were nine men and a woman on board, all of whom were saved. They lived in this cave for almost two years, subsisting upon what they could catch. Decayed tussock grass, a foot in depth, now covers the floor, showing that some attempt had been made to improve the comfort of the place, while bones lying strewn about in all directions indicate that gulls, penguins and cormorants must have supplied a good deal of their food. It is presumed that some of them made a journey to North Head periodically to look out for relief, as a well-defined track to that point is still visible in places.

The tale, however, has its tragic side, for the woman died on the very day when the rescuing ship called at the island. She was buried on the isthmus, not far from our Shack. One would think that death was rather a relief from such an existence as this unfortunate woman must have endured, but, at the same time, it seems hard that she did not live to participate in the joy of deliverance.

We ate our lunch and had a smoke, after which we decided to walk homewards along "Feather Bed" terrace. A few minutes after leaving the cave, Sawyer and Sandell caught three young ducks, which they carried back, intending to rear them, but they died several days later. A weary tramp brought us, thoroughly tired, to the Shack, where Hamilton had an excellent meal awaiting us.

The weather during January was rather trying. Precipitation in the form of either rain, hail, sleet or snow occurred on twenty-six days, sometimes all forms being experienced on the same day. As a result, the supply of water was well maintained; in fact, the amount caught exceeded the consumption and we finished the month with the tank almost full. Gales were experienced on eight days, the maximum wind-force being forty-two miles an hour. The sky was mostly heavily clouded or absolutely overcast and on many days the sun was not seen. Fog hung about the hills almost continuously, and driving mist accompanied the northerly winds.

January 24 was a glorious day, calm and sunny, with a maximum temperature of 51.3° F. The habit of former days induced Sandell and myself to have a dip in the surf, but as the temperature of the water was about 42° F., we stayed in as many seconds. The mean temperature for the month was 44.9° F.; the minimum being 35.5° F.

My first view of the island when the *Aurora* arrived in December 1911 left rather an agreeable impression. The day of our approach was marked by fine calm weather and the dark-green tussock-clad hillsides were rather attractive. On the other hand, one was immediately struck with the entire absence of trees, the steep precipices, cliffs and the exceedingly rugged nature of the coastline.

Victoria Penguins

Closer scrutiny shows that the tussock grass radiates closely from a semi-decayed mass of leaf-sheaths, with the blades of grass shooting upwards and outwards as high as three or four feet. Scattered through it are patches of Stilbocarpa polaris, locally known as Maori cabbage. It is of a more vivid green than the tussock and is edible, though somewhat stringy and insipid. Our sheep ate it readily, even nibbling the roots after the plant had been cropped down.

There were several Victoria penguin colonies round about the rocky faces of the hills in the vicinity of the Shack, and their hubbub and cackling uproar were something to remember. The rearing of the young appeared to be rather a busy process. The young ones look like bundles of down and seem to grow at a remarkable rate, while the attempt of the parent to shelter the usual two chicks is a very ludicrous thing to watch.

The material for the nest made by these birds seems to depend almost entirely on its immediate surroundings. The rookery is established on a broken rocky face close to the water's edge and the nests are made under rocks, in niches and passages, as well as amongst the tussock growing on the rocks. Those under the rocks are constructed of small stones and a few blades of grass, while those in the passages and fissures are usually depressions in soft mud. Amongst the tussock a hole is first made in the soft earth and then neatly lined with blades of grass.

The birds lay two or three eggs of a white or greenish-white colour, but I have never seen three chicks hatched. The eggs are edible, and we used many dozens of them during our stay.

The period of incubation is about five weeks, and male and female take turns at sitting. A young one is fed by placing its beak within that of the parent bird where the food—mainly crustaceans—is taken as it regurgitates from the stomach of the latter.

Although the smallest species on the island, the Victoria penguins are the most spiteful, and a scramble through the rookery invites many pecks and much disturbance. They have a black head and back, white breast and yellow crest, the feathers of which spread out laterally. During the moulting season they sit in the rookery or perched on surrounding rocks, living apparently on their fat, which is found to have disappeared when at last they take to the sea. They come and go with remarkable regularity, being first seen about the middle of October, and leaving during the first week of May. The same rookeries are occupied year after year, and the departure of the birds adds to the general desolation during the winter months.

Their destination on leaving the land is still a mystery. Although they are never seen, it is conjectured that they spend the winter at sea. Their natural enemy in the waters round Macquarie Island is the sea-leopard, and the stomachs of all specimens of this animal taken by us during the penguin season contained feathers.

The presence of numerous bones just at the rear of the Shack pointed to the fact that here must have been at one time the site of a King penguin rookery. As many of our potatoes and onions were sprouting in the bags, I determined to dig a portion of this area and plant the most «progressive» of these vegetables. The sandy soil did not appear to contain much nutriment, but I thought that something might be gained by giving it a trial.

On the night of February 2, Sawyer reported that he had heard the Wellington wireless operator calling Suva station, but, as no further signals were heard from anywhere, he was inclined to the idea that it was the experience of a «freak night.» In explanation of this term, I may say that it is used in reference to nights on which the atmospheric conditions are abnormally favourable for wireless work.

The news was particularly encouraging, and for the next few days we were on the tip-toe of expectation.

In the early morning of the 5th a howling gale sprang up and, increasing in force as the day wore on, rendered work impossible. A tremendous sea worked up, and the ocean for a distance of a mile from shore was simply a seething boil of foam. Huge waves dashed on shore, running yards beyond the usual marks, and threatening to sweep across the isthmus. Masses of tangled kelp, torn from the outlying rocks, washed backwards and forwards

View of the Wireless Station on the Summit of Wireless Hill

The Wireless Operating Hut

The Wireless Engine Hut

in the surf or were carried high up among the tussocks. The configuration of the shingly beach changed while one looked at it. The tops of the waves could be seen flying over Anchor Rock, seventy feet high, and spray was blowing right across the isthmus.

On the advice of the sealers we had shifted our stores farther back from the beach and it was just as well we did so, as the waves reached to within a few feet of the nearest box. Meanwhile I began to wonder how our benzine and lubricating oil were faring. Both had been stacked in cases among the tussock and rocks, well back from the waters of Aerial Cove on the western side of Wireless Hill.

Accordingly, Hamilton, Sandell and I went round in that direction the following morning, while Sawyer made his way up to the wireless station to see if there were any damages there. We worked along round the cliff-front through a cave rejoicing in the name of «Catch Me,» from the fact that the waves rushed into it, frequently catching and thoroughly wetting any unfortunate taken off his guard. A massive rock, evidently broken from the roof, lay right across its centre, while on either side of the obstruction were masses of greasy decaying kelp. We were «caught» and floundered about in the kelp while the water surged around us. Arriving at the Cove, we found that several cases were missing. One was discovered buried in kelp, and a little later we came upon a tin battered almost out of recognition. The loss was not serious, but the precaution was taken to shift the oil still farther back.

While we were engaged on this task, Sawyer appeared on the front of the hill above and signalled to us that the aerial had been blown down. The three-inch rope keeping the aerial taut had broken off close to the bridle and torn the halyard with it. It meant that some one would have to climb the mast to pass a rope through the block, and the wind was at this time too strong for anything to be done.

On February 7, Blake and Hamilton, who had been making preparations for several days past, set out for Sandy Bay, intending to do some work in that locality. Their blankets, sleeping-bag, instruments and other gear made rather heavy swags, but they shouldered them in true Murrumbidgee style and tramped away.

Sandell, Sawyer and I went up Wireless Hill to fix the aerial. Sandell, the lightest of the three, was being hoisted up the first section of the mast with some one-and-a-half-inch rope when the hauling-line gave way. Fortunately, he had a strap securing him to the mast, otherwise his fall would have been from twenty feet. This was the only rope we had, so we had to think of some other means of reaching the top. After a short discussion, I suggested that decking-spikes should be secured from the wreck of the Clyde and driven into the mast at intervals. The idea was followed with great success, and Sandell was able to run the halyard through the block at the top (ninety feet). The aerial was then hauled into position, the stay-wires were tightened, an extra "dead man" was put in and the station was once more ready for work.

Hamilton returned from Sandy Bay on the 11th laden with botanical trophies and four specimens of a small land bird which we had never before seen. He and Blake, who remained behind, had fixed up the hut there so that it afforded decent shelter.

On the night of the 13th what we had long expected happened. Wireless communication was established for the first time, with a ship—SS *Ulimaroa*. Sandell and Sawyer were complimented on their success.

On the following night communication was held with Sydney, SS *Westralia*, SS *Ulimaroa* and HMS *Drake;* the latter very courteously sending us time-signals. We heard that a wireless station had just been established in Melbourne, and that the Hobart station would be working in about one month. It was with the latter station that we expected to do most of our business. There was great joy in the camp now that this stage of practical efficiency was reached and because we were no longer isolated from the world.

Blake came back from Sandy Bay on the 16th with news that he had almost finished the survey of that section. Foggy or misty weather gave him a good deal of trouble in getting sights with the theodolite, and it became part of his future programme to devote the "impossible" days to plotting data, writing up field-notes, and making geological collections.

The afternoon of the 17th was fine, and I went along the beach towards West Point and found it very rough travelling. Hundreds of sea elephants, mostly of the season's young, lay about in the tussock or amongst the rocks. The young, silver-grey in colour, looked very sleek and fat. The adults consorted in groups of from eight to ten, packed closely and fast asleep. They seemed to fairly luxuriate in a soft, swampy place and were packed like sardines in some of the wallows.

Large numbers of skua gulls, creating a dreadful din, drew my attention to a spot amongst the rocks, and, on nearing it, I found them squabbling around the carcase of a xiphoid whale, about sixteen feet long, which had been cast up apparently only a few hours before.

The skuas, as they are commonly called, are large brown birds which resort to the island in great numbers for the purpose of breeding. They stay longer than any other migrant, being absent only three months during the depth of winter. Returning early in August, they do not start nesting until the beginning of October. The nests, nicely made of grass and plant leaves, are generally built on the terraces and slopes amongst the hills. The ideal site, however, is a pleurophyllum flat adjoining a penguin rookery. Two or three eggs of a brown or greenish-brown colour with darker spots or blotches are laid about the end of October, and, from this time till the chicks are reared, the parent exhibits much annoyance at the presence of any person in the vicinity. They utter shrill cries and swoop down continuously in an attempt to strike the invader with their wings. Several of our party received black eyes as a result of attacks by skuas.

The young grow rather quickly, and not much time elapses before they leave the nest to stagger round and hide amongst the vegetation. The parents fly down and disgorge food, which is immediately devoured by the young ones. The skuas are bare-faced robbers and most rapacious, harassing the penguins in particular. They steal the eggs and young of the latter and devour a great number of prions—small birds which live in holes in the ground. The skuas are web-footed, but are very rarely seen in the water.

Towards the end of the month, Blake spent two days at Sandy Bay and then returned to work up his results.

Hamilton, in order to get into close touch with another species of penguin, stayed several days at "The Nuggets," two and a half miles down the eastern coast. A creek flows into the sea at this point, and many Royal penguin rookeries are established along its course.

Meanwhile, many improvements had been effected in the interior of the Shack. Shelves lined the walls wherever it was convenient to have them, and many perishable foodstuffs had been brought inside. Comfort, after all, is but a relative matter, and, as far as we were concerned, it was sufficient.

Our clothing was all that could be desired, with the exception, perhaps, of the boots. In the equipment were included one pair of sea-boots, one pair of raw hide kneeboots and two pairs of rawhide hunting boots. The latter were not heavy enough, and soon showed the effect of travelling from a water-logged surface to one of rock and vice versa. In fact, our boots were very rarely dry on Macquarie Island.

An event of some moment occurred on the 28th. The fowls, in order to justify our confidence in them and as a return for our constant care, commenced to lay and, strange to say, all began to lay at the same time. Ma, who was greatly concerned during the turn of affairs, suffered from prolonged attacks of cackling.

During the opening days of March, Blake and Hamilton were engaged in field work down the island. They went as far as "The Brothers," a rocky promontory about two miles south of Sandy Bay. Wekas were so plentiful that they lived almost entirely on them. Blake, on returning to the Shack, had a badly blistered heel which kept him indoors for a few days. Hamilton, who had secured a goodly number of specimens, had to attend immediately to their preservation.

There were many rats on the island and we frequently heard them scuttling about on the ceiling of the Shack and slithering down between the lining and the wall. Hitherto they had contented themselves by doing this, but on the night of the 7th several of them flopped one after another into the hut, awakening the inmates. On getting out to investigate I found

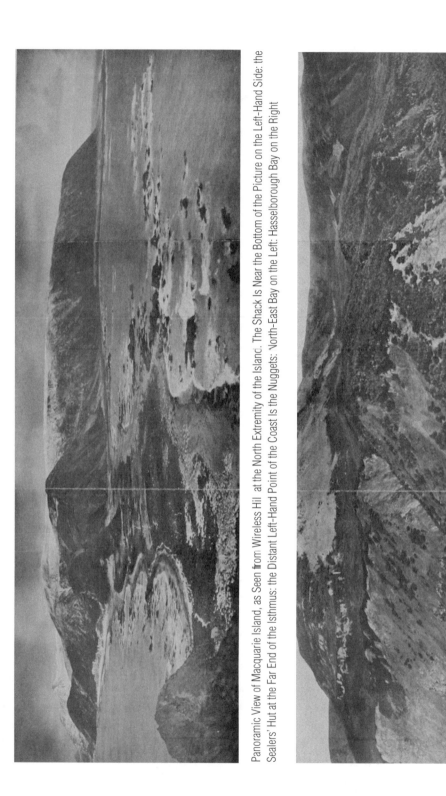

Panoramic View of Macquarie Island, as Seen from Wireless Hill at the North Extremity of the Island. The Shack Is Near the Bottom of the Picture on the Left-Hand Side: the Sealers' Hut at the Far End of the Isthmus: the Distant Left-Hand Point of the Coast Is the Nuggets: North-East Bay on the Left: Hasselborough Bay on the Right

a hole through the lining, about seven feet from the floor, and two or three were rustling about on the shelves. After much shifting of boxes and searching behind tins, the intruders were killed.

On March 10 our station held communication with Suva at a distance of two thousand four hundred miles; a remarkable performance for a one-and-a-half-kilowatt wireless set.

Hamilton and I set out for West Point and Eagle Cave on the 11th with the object of examining the flora of the locality and, incidentally, to shoot ducks which frequent the pools on the "Feather Bed" terrace. The weather was dull and misty and the walk very uncomfortable. We made our way across this treacherous tract, often sinking kneedeep. As we neared the first pool a duck rose and immediately paid the penalty. Although we saw at least two hundred, only one was shot, owing to the fact that there is no cover about and the ducks are too easily scared.

Close to Eagle Cave Hamilton gathered some plant specimens and, after lunching, we set off home. Light, steady rain set in about 3 PM and wet us thoroughly. We travelled back along the coast, finding it fearfully rough but not so tiring as walking on the terrace.

Heavy snow fell during the night of the 11th. Among other things we learnt by wireless that Amundsen had returned to Hobart with the news that he had reached the South Pole.

Blake had just recovered from his blistered heel when he had the misfortune to meet with a slight accident. He and Hamilton were engaged cutting a track through the tussock from the Shack to the beach, when the spade wielded by Hamilton struck Blake's foot, cutting through the boot and inflicting a wound on the great toe. It was treated antiseptically and bound up; Blake being laid up for a few days.

Cooking was still on the up grade. Everybody, as his turn arrived, embarked on something new. Blake turned out a magnificent meat pudding during his week, and Sawyer manufactured a salmon kedgeree. Sandell's treacle pudding and Hamilton's soda rolls and date pudding were all equally good, while I fairly surpassed myself with a roly-poly and some pancakes.

Hitherto, Sawyer and Sandell had been coming down to the Shack each night after finishing the wireless work, but on account of the bad weather they determined to sleep up there and, with that end in view, each built a bunk for himself; Sawyer, in the operating-hut, had ample room for the improvement, but Sandell had more difficulty in the engine-hut, finding it necessary to add a small structure to the original one.

Sooty Albatrosses Nesting

Good wireless work was now being done, and almost every ship trading to eastern Australian ports gave us a "call up." Much difficulty was experienced with the mast's stays, which frequently required tightening on account of the "deadmen" working loose in the yielding peaty soil. There were seven stays required for each mast, and Sandell spent much time in attending to them.

Hamilton had found, some weeks previously, several nests of the sooty albatross along the cliff-front on the eastern side of Wireless Hill, and on the 21st he visited them for the purpose of photographing the young in the nest. They were still in the downy stage, and vomited vigorously on being approached.

These birds build their nests on ledges along the face of a steep cliff and always betray the whereabouts of their nesting-place by wheeling and soaring around the vicinity. When sitting, the bird utters piercing calls for its mate and is thereby easily located. They make a nest of grass, generally at the root of a tussock growing on the cliff-front, and when the building is in progress the two birds sit side by side entwining their necks, rubbing beaks and at intervals uttering their harsh cries. One can approach and catch them quite easily, either at this time or when sitting. The female lays one large white egg, which has a peculiar and rather disagreeable odour. They have beautiful slaty or bluish-gray plumage with a dark soot-black head, while encircling the eye is a white ring which stands out conspicuously from the dark feathers surrounding it. Like most other sea-birds they have the rather revolting habit of vomiting quantities of partly digested food and fluid when an attempt is made to get close to them. In this respect old and young are alike. Their food is procured at sea, and consists of the small forms of marine life.

Sandell and Hamilton went round to Aerial Cove on the 25th to collect shells and to search for the missing lubricating oil. When coming home, after a successful day, they discovered a cave quite close to Catch Me. A lantern was secured from the Shack and they went back to examine it. It penetrated for a considerable distance and opened out on the hill side about eighty feet above sea-level. Many rocks hung down from overhead, and altogether it appeared a very unsafe place. Blake went along later and collected specimens from its floor.

We built a kind of annex to the Shack out of the cases of provisions; each case being numbered and a list being drawn out setting forth the contents of the case. This list was nailed on to the wall inside, and besides being convenient for procuring the provisions, gave the cook, in a coup-d'oeil, exact information and afforded him a glorious scope.

With regard to the coal-supply, our allowance at Macquarie Island had been reduced by one-half, on account of the large amount of wreckage lying on the beach. The weekly cook limited himself to three briquettes, and these he supplemented with sea elephant blubber and wood, which he gathered and cut up for use.

Each man commenced his cooking week on Saturday morning, and continued until the following Friday night, when, after having cleared up, washed the towels and cleaned the stove, he retired. The incoming cook, who for half an hour had been prowling about keenly observant of "overlooked" dirty "things" and betraying every sign of impatience to make a start, proceeded at once to set a batch of bread, sufficient for one week, which was baked early on Saturday morning. Five loaves had to be baked, and as only two could be dealt with at a time, the chance of producing at least one doughy loaf was reasonably high until every one became a master baker.

For a time we had been rather hard put to it in the matter of having baths, but the disability had been overcome by means of sawing a cask in two; an expedient which answered very well. The bath was also used as a wash-tub, each man taking charge as his cooking week came round. The clothes were dried inside the Shack along a number of strings arranged at the back of the stove. Darning and mending took a little time, and our experiences in this direction were such as to demonstrate the wisdom of putting in "a stitch in time."

In going over to the meteorological screen one morning I saw a giant petrel flapping about in the tussock, gorged to such an extent that it could not rise. I killed the loathsome bird with the rib-bone of a sea elephant, and Hamilton made a fine specimen of it later on.

These birds, properly called giant petrels, are usually known as "nellies" or "stinkers"; the latter title being thoroughly justified on account of the disagreeable smell which comes from them. As may be inferred from the name, they are the largest of all the petrels, and measure about seven feet from tip to tip when on the wing. The colour ranges through various shades from almost pure white to a dark greyish-brown; some even appearing almost black. Very large and ungainly when on the ground, they become most graceful when in the air, and soar about without the slightest effort even on the stormiest days. I have seen them flying into a forty-mile wind with absolute ease, never moving a wing, but occasionally adjusting their balance. They are gross scavengers, and eat apparently for the sake of eating. A carcase on the rocks or beach attracts them in large numbers, and very soon they can be seen pulling and tearing at it until thoroughly gorged,

A White Giant Petrel on the Nest

A Giant Petrel Rookery

when they waddle away into the water and sit there wholly unable to rise till digestion takes place. If disturbed, they immediately disgorge and fly off. They nest on the ground and lay one large white egg. When sitting, they are reluctant to leave the nest and will squat there, vomiting evil-smelling, partly digested food and fluid at any intruder. The young, even in the downy stage, have the same habit.

When mating they go on with a queer kind of performance, which consists of running around each other on the shore with wings outspread as if displaying their charms, finally flying off or waddling into the water.

The persistently windy weather during March had an effect on everything exposed to its force. Sandell discovered on the 29th that the rope holding the wireless aerial had cut through, leaving only one strand, which now bore all the strain. It was just a matter of days before it would part, and, with a view to preventing a repetition of February's happening, we went up to lower the aerial, but the frayed portion of the rope would not pass through the block, so we had to leave it as it was and wait for the inevitable.

Exceptionally low tides at the end of the month gave Hamilton a fine opportunity of collecting marine specimens, and he secured amongst many other things some striking anemones. Some difficulty was experienced in preserving them, as they lost colour and shrivelled up. But a special line of treatment was attended by fairly successful results. They were put in shallow dishes into which sea-water was poured. Very soon they attached themselves to the bottom and began to expand, finally opening out to the fullest extent. With a view to narcotizing them while in this condition, menthol was applied to the water but did not seem to have much effect. Chloral hydrate was found to give the best results. It killed them all, but, before dying, they elongated and detached themselves from the bottom of the dish; after which they were taken out and placed in formalin for preservation.

Blake had very little opportunity of doing much survey work during the month, as he was hampered by a sore foot and the weather was wretched. He therefore spent most of his time plotting data, making geological investigations and collecting and naming specimens.

He and Hamilton had so far confined their attention to the northern half of the island, and had resolved to complete the study of this area before tackling the southern half.

The weather throughout the month was rather severe, and only two days were really appreciated. Precipitation occurred on twenty-five days, but the worst feature was the continuity of strong winds, which however did not reach gale-force on more than three occasions. Much snow and hail fell, the former accompanying winds with a southerly component, while with the north-westers came the depressing mist or misty rain which is such a characteristic of the place. Temperatures, as might have been expected, were beginning to go down, and we experienced several very cold days. The average temperature for March was 41.8°, while the highest was 46.9° and the lowest 35.3° F. on the 24th.

At 10 PM on April 1 the rope supporting the aerial parted. Sawyer and Sandell were on duty at the time, but of course suspended operations immediately. As before, the halyard also carried away and Sandell henceforth resolved to shackle one end of the aerial to the mast, using a short length of chain instead of the rope. The wreck of the Clyde was once more our standby, providing a suitable length of chain and four shackles. After completing this job, they had very little subsequent trouble with the aerial.

Hamilton and Sawyer caught several three-pound fish on April 2, and Sandell served them in good style. They were good eating, but, unfortunately, were very much worm-infested. These parasitical worms are about an inch and a half long and taper to a point at each end. They penetrate right through the flesh and are plainly noticeable after the fish is cooked. One has to dodge the worms as the meal proceeds: either that or persuade oneself that they do not matter.

The flowing contours of the land in the vicinity of "The Nuggets" suggested glacial action to Blake, and on the 4th, while making geological investigations in that locality, he lit upon a well-defined basal moraine. Needless to say he was very interested in the discovery, and brought home a number of polished, striated boulders as convincing evidence of his theory.

It was rather disappointing to find that the vegetables we had planted were making little progress. They would shoot up at first very strongly, like the "seed which fell on stony ground," but, as soon as a gale arose, the tops turned black and shortly afterwards withered away. It was apparently an effect of the salt spray which, in rough weather, used to blow across the isthmus. Hamilton planted some willows and other cuttings, which shared the same fate.

The winter had now arrived in real earnest, and the months which followed were punctuated by a succession of gales, while we came to recognize that it was an exceptional day when the hills were not shrouded in mist. The only thing to do was to brace oneself up for the ordeal and to put a good foot forward.

The Macquarie Island Party. From Left to Right: Sandell, Ainsworth, Sawyer, Hamilton, Blake

CHAPTER XXVI

A Land of Storm and Mist

By G. F. AINSWORTH

A HEAVY NORTH-WEST GALE WAS EXPERIENCED on April 12, the wind attaining a force of over fifty miles an hour.

As usual, a tremendous sea worked up very quickly, and sheets of spray shredded across the isthmus. About 2 PM the wind shifted to west and later to south-west; these changes being accompanied by fierce hail and squalls of snow. During the night the wind moderated, heavy snow fell and, when morning dawned, all the pools were frozen over and the island was draped in white. It was the heaviest fall we had so far experienced.

On the 15th Hamilton and I shot several gulls for specimens.

The Dominican or black-backed gulls are very numerous and remain on the island all the year round. They are rather pretty, being snow-white, except on the upper part of the wings and back. Ordinarily their food is obtained from the water, but at Macquarie Island they live almost entirely upon the carcases left by the sealers, and are usually seen defending their rights against skuas and giant petrels. They build nests of tussock on rocks close to the water or maybe on the ground. Three eggs, much like those of the skua in colour, but with a greener tint and smaller, are laid, but generally only two are hatched. The young leave the nest early and hide amongst the rocks, whither the old ones come to feed them.

We now considered it advisable to prepare for the winter, and with that end in view papered the inside of the Shack in various places. As the cold winds were particularly searching, all faulty joints in the lining were pasted over with any kind of paper we could find. A leak down the outside of the stove-pipe was remedied, after a good deal of trouble, by soldering a collar round the pipe where it passed through the roof. Firing was an important consideration, so each man now brought home several loads of driftwood every day, until we had enough to keep us going for some months. There was a complete boot-mending outfit which was put to a good deal of use, for the weathered rocks cut the soles of our boots and knocked out the hobnails. Our supply of the last-named did not last long, and several of the party used strips of hoop-iron in their stead.

Blake found it necessary to make a kind of work-desk in his section, and accordingly had a thorough rearrangement. He shifted his bunk up to a height of about five and a half feet, very close to the ceiling; a fact which necessitated some wriggling and squirming on his part to get into the sleeping-bag. There was a fine open space left underneath, and he managed to fix up his table very neatly.

Although they had intended to leave the work on the southern half of the island until the spring, Hamilton and Blake set out for Lusitania Bay on April 28 to make a short reconnoitring trip. It was thought advisable to spend a few days down there, to improve the hut and generally speaking to have a look-round. Both men had already visited the place and depoted some provisions there. At 8 AM they started off, carrying their blankets, sleeping-bags and a few other articles. Their proposal was to go along the coast as far as Sandy Bay and from thence along the hill-tops for the remaining ten miles.

Hail and snow-squalls succeeded each other at frequent intervals, and by the time they reached Sandy Bay, all hope of proceeding along the hill-tops was dissipated. They therefore kept near the coast. The going was frightfully rough and the weather was very bad, so on making Green Valley they camped in a small cave for the night. The floor was covered with tussock, and, by searching amongst the rocks, enough pieces of wreckage were found to keep the fire going. On the whole they passed a fairly comfortable night. Mac proved a bit troublesome by persisting in her attempts to curl up on or between the sleeping-bags, and by finally eating the jam which had been saved for breakfast. The weather was quite as bad next morning, but, after a meal of dry biscuit and cocoa, they pushed on, taking four and a half hours to do the six miles. The next day was spent making the hut weather-proof and fixing up a couple of bunks. The provisions which had been cached were in good order and abundance of firewood lay around, in the shape of old barrel-staves. Just close to the living-hut was a works-hut containing boilers and digestors which years ago had been used for procuring penguin oil, while there was a rookery a few yards away from which the victims had come.

This rookery was the resort of King penguins, the largest of the four species which are to be found on the island. They are magnificently coloured birds, being bluish-grey on the back while the head is greenish-black and on each side of the neck there is a brilliant yellow band, shading to a greenish-yellow on the upper part of the breast, and gradually merging into the glossy white of the lower part of the body. They attain to a height of about three feet and weigh thirty pounds approximately. The site of their rookery is a stony flat about a hundred yards from the water, and here are collected between five and six thousand—all that remain on the island.

They make no nest, the single egg laid being supported on the feet, and kept in position and incubated in a kind of skin pouch which conceals it from view. One would never guess the egg was there, for, on being disturbed, the bird shuffles along, carrying it in the manner described. The egg is large, tapering very much at one end and resembling a pear in shape. They lay during December and January, and the young are hatched in about six weeks. A peculiar feature about the young birds is that the parents feed them for two seasons. They are covered with a coarse, greyish-brown furry growth, and a year-old chick looks bigger than the old bird. This furry growth is lost during the second year and the adult plumage replaces it. The young utter a peculiar sound, something between a squeak and a whistle. It is probable that the King penguins were never so numerous as the Royal or Victoria penguins, but the fact remains that they have not yet recovered from the wholesale slaughter to which they must have been subjected over sixteen years ago.

Down on a strip of shingly beach the birds parade, when not in the rookery or at sea getting food. Their proceedings strike one as being extraordinarily human, while the dignity and gravity of the participants are beyond description. On one occasion, a large number marching along the beach were seen to halt suddenly and talk excitedly. Three birds then left the main body, consulted together for a short time, and then separated. The other birds immediately separated into three companies, and each company stood behind one of the three already mentioned, who were now some distance apart. The individuals of each party then talked among themselves for several minutes, after which two parties joined forces and marched off, leaving the third party staring after them.

I have lost myself for the time being amongst the penguins and shall now return to Blake and Hamilton, who climbed on to the hill-tops the

King Penguins

following morning to spy out the land. The island is generally speaking higher, and all the more elevated peaks are on the southern half.

They saw numerous rabbits, of which many were black, and Mac had the day of her life amongst them. These animals were introduced to the island about

twenty-five years ago, and have gradually withdrawn to the lonelier southern part, though occasionally odd ones are seen about the northern end. They are very tame and live in holes amongst the rocks or make burrows in the gully banks and broken hill sides.

Many lakes, frozen over, were seen, several of which were fairly large. Altogether, the topography is similar to that of the northern end.

In an endeavour to improve the evening fare, a sweet broth consisting of biscuit, milk, jam and sugar was tried but it was not a success; Hamilton remarking that "even Blake had only one helping." On the following morning they started for the Shack and chose the route on the hilltops, as the ground was frozen hard; and, though there were frequent snow-drifts into which they floundered occasionally, the surface for travelling was much better than along the coast.

Hamilton slipped and hurt his ankle on the trip, and the boots of both were just about worn out. They apprehended no difficulty in completing their prospective work. Blake pointed out that the chart of the island shows Lusitania Bay as being rather a large indentation, whereas in reality it is almost a straight stretch of coast.

An earthquake shock was felt at 9.15 PM on the 27th. I was sitting in the Shack writing up records at the time, and it seemed as if somebody had struck the south-west end of the place a severe blow with a bag of sand. Immediately afterwards a crashing sound, apparently some distance away on the eastern side, indicated that some rocks on the cliff-front had been dislodged.

Much rough weather was experienced during the month, and it rained, hailed and snowed on twenty-five days. The wind attained moderate to fresh gale-force on six days, and fog and mist were almost invariable. The lowest temperature recorded was 32.7° F.

The average relative humidity for the four months ending April 30 was 93 per cent., leading to copious condensation on the instruments exposed to the air. It was necessary, therefore, constantly to attend and frequently clean the thermographs, hygrometers and the wireless plant. In the case of the latter, loss of power occurred in the form of "brush discharge," and Sawyer had to take great care in order to guard against this accident. He shellacked the condensers and other exposed parts and found the proceeding rather effective. I noticed that the drifting snow and misty rain managed to get down the opening leading to the liquid surface of the anemobiagraph, thus altering the zero of the recording apparatus. When this happened the instrument had to be dismantled and set right.

We found it necessary to use sea elephant blubber in the stove in order to warm the Shack, and a very small piece put on the fire at intervals always ensured a good heat. Sea elephants had become scarce, so, in order to lay in a supply of fuel for the next few weeks, we went round to Aerial Cove on the 3rd and killed the largest animal we could find, afterwards carrying the blubber round to the Shack. We came through Catch Me and had the same old experience. Hamilton examined the contents of the stomach of the sea elephant and found gravel, stones, cuttlefish, beaks and "worms" in abundance.

A violent north-west gale during the early morning hours of the 4th reached a maximum velocity of fifty-two miles an hour at 5.20 AM, but at 8 AM it began to weaken rapidly and an hour later had shifted to west-south-west, coming from that point as a moderate gale for the rest of the day. As was usual with winds having any southerly component, snow and squalls of soft hail were experienced. With the exception of the wind-vane, which was blown a few yards into the tussock, nothing was damaged.

In the afternoon Blake and I had a trip down to the moraine which he had found a few days previously. After a heavy one and a half hours' walk, the last half-mile of which was along a creek bed, with water ankle-deep all the way, we reached the spot: the site of one of the large penguin rookeries up on the hills at the back of "The Nuggets." The sun showed between squalls, and Blake took some interesting photographs of rocks showing striae and other glacial characteristics. We battled with one enormous boulder for some time before getting it into a suitable position for the camera, and afterwards walked right through the glacial area. The U-shaped character of the valleys was very pronounced, while boulder-clay obtruded itself everywhere on our notice.

Hobart wireless station was by this time in working order, a fact which greatly facilitated wireless business. Sandell took the engine to pieces early in the month and gave it, as well as the fittings, a thorough overhaul and cleaning. We received a message on the 7th, saying that the *Aurora* was leaving Hobart on the 13th for a sub-antarctic cruise and would call at the island. At the same time I was requested to send a list of articles required. I found, after going through the stock and consulting each member, that we needed nothing but strong boots, cartridges, dungaree trousers, coarse salt, cigarettes and fresh vegetables.

A persistent area of high pressure affected the weather conditions of the island to the extent of shrouding us in fog from the 6th to the 10th inclusive, and we did not catch a glimpse of the sun during that period.

The average daily temperature-range during this time was only 2.3°. Such conditions have a rather depressing effect on the spirits, but the cheering news we received on the 7th made some amends for the lack of sunshine.

The sun appeared at last on the 11th and shone strongly, so Blake and I went up to Wireless Hill to take some "shots" with the theodolite. I noticed four of our sheep on the front of the hill, and, as there should have been nine, Sandell and I, after finishing with Blake, walked out to North Head to see if the others were all right. We found them on the north-east side of the hill and drove them up to the rest of the flock.

From the hill-top we could see Hamilton engaged in skinning a large sea leopard on the coast, so we climbed down to render any necessary assistance. It was a beautifully marked animal, about eleven feet long, and made a fine specimen.

Sea leopards frequent Macquarie Island in great numbers from the late winter to the early summer, and may be seen lying about, sleeping close to the water and apparently always very tired. They do not give birth to the young there, and from observations I concluded that they were born at sea. We had taken female specimens on several occasions, apparently within a few hours of parturition, and as none had been seen with newly born young, and no islands lay within several hundred miles, it was presumed that the birth took place in the water. Until the young one is weaned, its habitat is evidently in the water as we never saw an adult suckling its offspring.

Sea leopards—long, lithe creatures with a reptilian cast of head—are remarkably quick in the water. If one is disturbed on shore it opens its mouth very wide, revealing a wicked-looking row of teeth in each jaw; the canine teeth or tusks being very long and slightly curved.

Unlike sea elephants and seals they are solitary animals, and should several of them be found on a small gravelly patch of beach they are seen to be as far as possible from one another. We have never seen them attempt to fight on the shore, but the gaping wounds and scars with which they are frequently covered indicate that they treat each other very severely in the water. They live on penguins, gulls, shags and fish.

I saw several shags on one occasion very busy fishing, and between diving intervals they would sit on the water. Suddenly one disappeared under the water and the rest flew off; but in a few seconds the one which had disappeared was thrown into the air and caught by a sea leopard, who played in this fashion with the maimed bird for several minutes before devouring it.

The Head of a Sea Leopard, Showing Fight

A Precocious Victoria Penguin

A few days previously we had received a request from Mr. D. C. Bates, the New Zealand Meteorologist, for a daily weather report, and from the 12th onwards a message was sent nightly to Wellington, a distance of about eleven hundred miles. In acknowledging these reports, subsequently, the office referred to their immediate value in the issue of daily forecasts, and expressed indebtedness to the Expedition.

The two species of penguins which leave the island during the winter months had disappeared, and silence now reigned where formerly were busy, noisy colonies. The departure of the migrants made the place seem lonelier and, during the depths of winter when snow covers the ground and the birds and animals are few in number, a more dreary spot would be difficult to find.

The weather conditions were now rather severe, and as Sawyer and Sandell worked from 8 PM till 2 or 3 AM every night and slept at the wireless station, they were exempted from the necessity of coming down to get breakfast during their cooking weeks. They now rested till about noon, and arrived at the Shack every day in time for lunch. Hamilton, Blake and I, each outside his own cooking week, took it in turns to prepare breakfast.

Blake's fieldwork at the north end, more particularly in the vicinity of West Point and North Head, was just about finished. West Point proved to be an area of gabbro, a coarse-grained eruptive rock representative of basic rocks, while North Head was composed of basic agglomerate, and volcanic bombs were numerous.

Hamilton had got together a good collection of bird specimens, and was now in quest of skeletons.

On the night of the 13th we witnessed a rather pretty auroral manifestation. It assumed the appearance of a Noah's ark cloud, that is, stretching from opposite points on the horizon and appearing to converge at each one of these points. The light was a pale yellow, no other tint being visible. In addition, a nebulous glow appeared at intervals in the south.

We heard on the 16th that the *Aurora* had sailed on that day from Hobart and would arrive at Macquarie Island in about three weeks; oceanographical work being carried out on the trip down. This was indeed cheerful news, and we began to look forward to her arrival.

A fresh west-south-west gale during the early morning hours of the 17th was accompanied by soft hail and snow-squalls, and the temperature at 9 AM was 31.2° F. The ground was covered with snow and all the pools were frozen over, but at 9 PM there was a rapid shift of the wind to the north-west and the snow almost disappeared. Soft hail, generally a little larger than tapioca and of the same shape, frequently fell. These little pellets are formed of compressed snow and are commonly supposed to be frozen cloud-particles mixed with raindrops compacted by a high wind.

On the following night, Blake and I went up to wireless Hill to take star observations. It was very dark and the hill-front was slippery, frequent falls being the rule. Just after setting up the instrument, the wind freshened to such an extent that it was impossible to do anything, so we descended very wet and muddy to the Shack, having had a rough passage. The reason for this was that I fell on the lantern and extinguished the light.

We were supplied with two hurricane lamps which do not by any means deserve their title as they blow out in even a moderately strong wind. Sandell made a lantern for his own use, declaring that it was impossible for any wind to blow it out. I firmly believed him, as it was a little binnacle lamp placed inside a small oatmeal tin into which a cleaned photographic plate had been fixed and with holes punched in the bottom and top of the tin for ventilation. It was thus a lamp with two covers, and frequent demonstrations of its ability to survive heavy blows were made by the inventor.

During the next three days a forty-mile wind accompanied by snow, hail and sleet was experienced and the maximum temperature on the 25th did not reach freezing-point, the ground being firmly frozen and snow-covered. During the evening of the last-named date the wind shifted to north-west, and by noon on the 26th no snow remained, except on the hills.

In anticipation of the *Aurora's* arrival, Blake and Hamilton collected some stores together in the hope that Captain Davis would transport them down to Lusitania Bay, thus obviating the necessity of carrying them down on foot. As Blake reckoned that he would remain there fully three months and Hamilton about two months, it was thought that such another opportunity might not present itself.

Through the courtesy of the naval officials, HMS *Drake* sent us time-signals twice a week, and though we had so far heard no sound from Adelie Land, there was a possibility that they could receive messages from us. Sawyer therefore sent out time-signals as a matter of routine.

Hamilton made a trip to the west coast on the 28th and returned with thirteen wekas. Sawyer did not care for these birds, but each of the others could account for one at a meal. They seem to be better eating if plucked like a fowl and roasted, but the plucking takes too long and we generally

skinned and boiled them. It is advisable to hang them for several days before cooking as it certainly makes them tender.

Rough, stormy weather prevailed during the greater part of the month and the wind reached the force of a gale on nine days. Much snow, soft hail and sleet fell and some very cold days were experienced. The average temperature was 40°, the maximum being 44.7° and the minimum 27.8° F.

A heavy snowfall occurred during the early morning hours of June 3, and the temperature was below freezing-point all day. In the afternoon we had rather an enjoyable time tobogganing down a steep talus-slope on the east coast. A considerable struggle was necessary in order to get the sledge to the top, but the lightning slide to the bottom more than compensated for the labour.

We made wireless inquiries concerning the *Aurora* at night, and were informed by Hobart that a search for the Royal Company Islands was included in her programme. It was therefore presumed that she was engaged in prosecuting this search and would probably not reach us for some days.

Hamilton killed a very fine sea leopard on the 5th and the skin, apart from being unscarred, was handsomely marked. It should make a splendid specimen. The stomach contained more than the usual number of worms and one specimen of tape-worm, seven inches long and three-eighths of an inch wide, was preserved.

Everything was going along in the usual placid manner on the 7th, when, as we were just taking our seats for lunch, some one rushed in with the information that the *Aurora* was in sight. There was a scramble to various points of vantage and she was soon observed coming up the east coast very slowly. At 2.30 PM she dropped anchor in North-East Bay, but, as it was blowing strongly and a nasty sea was running, no boat was launched, though one may imagine how anxiously we watched for some movement in that direction. As soon as it became dark a message was "Morsed" to us to the effect that a boat would bring mails and goods ashore in the morning if the weather moderated, and with that we had to be content. Needless to say, business ashore was for the time being paralysed, but a message was sent to the Secretary in Hobart advising him of the Ship's arrival.

True to his intimation of the previous night, Captain Davis brought a boat ashore at 9.30 AM and with him came several visitors who were to be our guests for some days. They were Mr. E. R. Waite, Curator of the Canterbury Museum and his taxidermist, and Mr. Primmer, a cinematographer. Conspicuous in the boat was a well-laden mail bag and no time was lost in distributing the contents. Letters, papers, and magazines were received by every member of the party, and all the news was "good."

Young Male Sea Elephants at Play

Some stores were brought along and, after getting these ashore, we took the visitors across to the Shack and invited them to make themselves at home.

Captain Davis also came along to the Shack and afterwards looked over the wireless station. He returned to the ship just after lunch, and Sandell, Sawyer and Blake took the opportunity of going on board. Hamilton, in the meantime, piloted the visitors on a short trip round to Aerial Cove, introducing them to Catch Me, where they were duly baptized. They afterwards climbed up Wireless Hill and had a look at the station, returning to the Shack much impressed with the rough nature of the country.

Blake went off to the ship again, taking the stores which had been got ready for transport to Lusitania Bay, as the captain had agreed to land them when he visited there in a few days' time.

Amongst the cases which were landed was one containing the recording apparatus for the tide-gauge. The other parts of this instrument had been left on the island in December, but for some reason the clock and charts had gone astray and were not found till the vessel was being unloaded in Adelie Land. Some thermometers and a Robinson anemometer had also been overcarried and, when they came to light, the latter was immediately placed in commission.

A Large Sea Leopard on the Beach

Captain Davis sent a boat ashore on the morning of the 12th with an invitation to come on board and lunch. I accordingly went out to the vessel and, after lunching, had a thorough look over her, mentally contrasting her spick-and-span appearance at the time with what it had been when I left her in December. I went ashore again in the afternoon and assisted the visitors to get their loads down to the boat, as they were returning to the ship, which was leaving next morning on a sounding trip down the island.

On the 14th we started to carry the stores across to the Shack on our backs. We soon realized that seventy or eighty pounds was not a light load over a half-mile stretch of rough, shingly beach, but succeeded in transporting the onions, apples and potatoes before finishing for the night. The other articles were brought over during the next two afternoons.

The tide-gauge pipe, weighing about six hundredweights, and the box for the housing of the recording gear had been landed in December round in Aerial Cove, where a site had been chosen for the erection of the gauge. Experience showed me that the place was unsuitable, so I took Hamilton, Sandell and Sawyer round to the cove on the 15th and we decided, as we had no boat, that it was impossible to carry the pipe round to the east coast.

A Sea Elephant

I had been making some tidal observations on an upright, fixed in a comparatively quiet spot on the east coast, and it was here that I contemplated erecting the gauge. Two snow-gauges, eight inches each in diameter, were amongst the meteorological equipment and it appeared that if these two were soldered together a suitable pipe could be made. Further, the pipe was to be protected from the violence of the seas by planks fixed round it. Sandell agreed with the idea and forthwith set about soldering the two together and making a suitable float, the one supplied being too wide. All that now remained was to erect the gauge.

The two following afternoons were devoted to stowing the new stores. We carried everything across and stacked them at the south-west end of the Shack. Unfortunately, the boots which we had ordered did not come, but Captain Davis let us have five pairs of light bluchers out of the ship's stores, and we reckoned that these with extra soles and a few hobnails would hold out till August or September, when a sealing vessel was expected.

The *Aurora* returned from the south of the island on the 19th and reported having had a rough experience in the north-east to south gale which blew on the two previous days. The wind came out of the north-east very suddenly on the 17th, and some very strong squalls were experienced. A calm prevailed for several hours in the evening, but a south-east gale then sprang up and blew all day on the 18th, gradually working into the south and dying away during the night.

Early on the 20th the *Aurora* steamed out of the bay, bound north as we thought, but she returned again in the evening, and we signalled to know if anything were wrong. They replied, "All well, but weather very bad outside." She lay at anchor in the bay all next day as it was snowing and blowing very hard from the south-west, but at 8.45 AM on the 22nd she disappeared in the north and we did not see her again for some months. A few hours after her departure the wind increased in force, and a continuous gale raged for the next five days.

Sandell and I now made a start at erecting the tide-gauge, and after the lapse of five days got the instrument into position. We could work on it only at low tide, for much rock had to be chipped away and numerous wire stays fixed. The work was therefore of a disagreeable character. Its appearance when finished did not by any means suggest the amount of trouble we experienced in setting it up, but the fact that it stood the heavy seas for the following eighteen months without suffering material damage was a sufficient guarantee that the work had been well done.

A tremendous sea was running on the 25th as a result of the previous two days' "blow" and a heavy gale still persisting. Spray was scudding across the isthmus, and the sea for a mile from the shore was just a seething cauldron. The wind moderated somewhat on the 26th, but strong squalls were experienced at intervals throughout the day, and on the 27th a strong wind from the south-west brought rather heavy snow.

On the following day a westerly gale sprang up which shifted suddenly to south-south-west and south-west in the evening and was accompanied by fierce hail and snow-squalls throughout the night. Without moderating to any extent the gale continued to blow on the 29th and passed through west to west-north-west, finally lasting till the end of the month.

Something in the nature of a "tidal" wave occurred during the night of the 28th, for, on rising the following morning, I was considerably astonished to see that the sea-water had been almost across the isthmus. To effect this, a rise of twenty or twenty-five feet above mean sea-level must have taken place and such a rise appeared abnormally high. Our coal heap, which we had hitherto regarded as perfectly safe from the sea, was submerged, as shown by the kelp and sand lying on top of it, and the fact that seven or eight briquettes were found fifteen feet away from the heap.

Nothing at the wireless station was damaged and work went on as usual. The wind used to make a terrific noise in the aerial wires, but this did not affect the transmission of messages. The howling of the wind round the operating-hut interfered with the receiving, at times making it extremely difficult to hear signals; particularly on nights not favourable for wireless work.

Hamilton was at this time concentrating his attention on shags or cormorants. This species of cormorant is peculiar to the island, being found nowhere else. They are blue-black, with a white breast, and on the head they have a small black crest. At the top of the beak are golden lobes, while the skin immediately round the eye is pale blue. They remain on the shores of the island all the year and nest on the rocks in or very close to the water. They form rookeries and build nests of grass, laying three eggs about the end of November. The period of incubation is six weeks. They live entirely on fish, and, on that account, neither the birds nor the eggs are palatable. They are very stupid, staring curiously till one gets almost within reach of them, when they flap heavily into the water. They are easily caught when sitting on the nest, but a shag rookery, like most other rookeries, is by no means a pleasant place in which to linger.

I had the satisfaction of getting the first record from the tide-gauge on the first day of July, but the clock worked erratically, requiring some attention.

Hamilton had a lobster-pot set some distance from the shore and anchored to a float, but unfortunately the pot was lost in the rough seas at the end of June. He had a couple of fish-traps also, but, in view of this disaster, he decided to set these in Aerial Cove, where the water was quieter. Having a couple of sea leopard heads which required macerating, he baited the trap with them and lowered it into the water, securing it to the rock with a steel wire.

Taking advantage of a bright sun on the following day, Blake and Hamilton went to "The Nuggets" and took some geological and biological photographs, which on being developed turned out well. They had occasion to enter one of the unoccupied huts down there and found a wild cat a little more than half grown, which they caught and carried home with them. He was of the usual tabby colour and by no means fierce, quickly yielding to the coaxing treatment of his captors. He made himself quite at home in the Shack, and we looked forward to a display of his prowess as a rat-catcher.

A bright display of the aurora occurred on the night of July 4, the ribbons and streamers of light being well defined and occasionally slightly coloured. We could establish no connexion between this extraordinary outburst and the fact that it occurred on American Independence night,

A Cormorant Rookery, Hasselborough Bay

but it was certainly the most energetic manifestation of the phenomenon we had so far witnessed. Many "glows" had been seen, and also a few displays of the arch-shaped form, but none had shown much activity or rapid movement.

A Sclater Penguin

A Young King Penguin

The operator was requested by the Pennant Hills high-power wireless station at Sydney to listen for signals tapped out during the daytime, and Sawyer spent a couple of hours on certain mornings assisting in these tests, which were attended with some success. We occasionally received press news from land stations or from ships passing across the Tasman Sea, but it was only a brief summary of the cable news: enough to whet one's curiosity, rarely ever satisfying it.

Very cold, rough weather was experienced on the 6th and 7th and a temperature of 26° F. occurred on the latter date, while the maximum did not reach freezing-point. Much snow and soft hail fell, and the ground set hard. The weather interfered to some extent with the tide-gauge clock, and it became so unsatisfactory that I took it to pieces on the 9th and gave it a thorough cleaning, after which it had a new lease of life.

We received a message on the 11th saying that the *Aurora* had arrived in Dunedin, "all well," but had experienced a very rough voyage which greatly interfered with the dredging and sounding programme.

Our tank water gave out for the first time on the 12th. The precipitation for a fortnight had been in the form of dry powdery snow and soft hail, the wind blowing it off the roof before it had a chance to thaw, thus robbing us of our usual water-supply. For a while we had to use swamp water, which contained a good many insects of various kinds and had a distinctly peaty flavour. Finding good water running from the hill-tops down a deep gully on the east coast, three-quarters of a mile away, we carried drinking water from there, using the other for washing up.

The 13th was a most delightful day—bright sun, very little wind and fresh exhilarating air. Blake and Hamilton went out early on a photographing excursion, and, later on, the latter shot and skinned a white giant petrel.

During the third week of July a very low tide exposed rocks, ordinarily submerged, and Hamilton was occupied all the week in collecting marine organisms, worms and plants and then preserving, bottling and labelling them.

A most peculiar sight was witnessed on the 17th. Aerial Cove is a favourite nesting-place for shags, and they may be seen in twos and threes flying round in that direction almost any time during the day; but on this particular day a kind of wholesale exodus from the cove took place, and large flocks of them followed each other for a couple of hours. They congregated on the rocks along the east coast, or settled in the water in scores; the latter fact suggesting that the probable reason for this extraordinary behaviour was the presence of unusual shoals of fish.

We used to relax and have a game of cards occasionally, while our small organ became a medium of much enjoyment. All the members except one played well enough to enjoy themselves and to give pleasure to the others. There was a distinct predilection in favour of "ragtime" and I must say I liked to hear that music at frequent intervals. Any one who plays a musical instrument knows that the mood of the player is generally reflected in the character of the music, particularly when he sits down and plays in a casual way.

The pursuit and killing of a sheep had now become something in the nature of an experience, and when Sandell and I went hunting for one on the 20th, we realized it before we reached home. The flock was very timid, and when disturbed on North Head invariably came past the wireless station close to the engine-hut. Sandell concealed himself there with a gun, while I went out to startle the animals. They did not fail to do their part, but Sandell missed and the shot frightened them. He then rushed out and fired another shot as they were running, managing to hit one, which immediately dropped behind and ran to the edge of the cliff. We did not want to shoot the sheep at this moment, as it would have fallen about two hundred feet, so we cautiously approached to drive it away. The poor creature simply took a leap out into space and landed on the talus below, down which it rolled to the water's edge. We scrambled down and skinned it, having to carry the carcase along the rocks at the base of the cliffs, and getting many duckings on the way.

On July 26 I went round to Aerial Cove with Hamilton to have a look at the fish-trap, but it had disappeared, the wire having broken, apparently through the continual friction against rock. He had previously caught some fish in it, and it was rather a misfortune to lose it so soon.

During the last week of the month we all had our hair cut. On arrival at the island, several of us had it shorn very closely with the clippers and had not trimmed it since then, growth being very slow. We had a proper hair-cutting outfit and either Blake, Hamilton or Sandell acted as barber.

Blake was an expert with the needle and did some really neat mending, while with the aid of some woollen thread and a mug he darned holes in his socks most artistically. He was the authority on how, when and where to place a patch or on the only method of washing clothes. The appearance of his articles when washed, compared with mine, made me wonder.

Hamilton was busy, about this time, dredging in swamp pools and securing specimens of the rockhopper or Gentoo penguin.

Royal Penguins on the Nest

Gentoo Penguin and Young

The small Gentoo penguins, like the King penguins, do not migrate and are few in numbers. They form diminutive colonies, which are always established on mounds amongst the tussock, or on the hill sides not far from the water. Their eggs, which are globular in shape, are about the best of the penguin eggs for eating, and if their nests are robbed the birds will generally lay again, although I think they could not lay more than four eggs. They build their nests of grass and plant leaves, and occasionally have been known to establish a fresh rookery after their first one has been robbed. They are more timid than any other species of penguin, and leave the nests in a body when one ventures into the rookery. The skuas take advantage of this peculiarity to the length of waiting about till a chance presents itself, when they swoop down, pick up an egg with their beak and fly off. The penguin makes a great fuss on returning to find that the eggs are gone, but generally finishes up by sitting on the empty nest. We have frequently put ten or a dozen eggs into one nest and watched the proprietress on her return look about very doubtfully and then squat down and try to tuck the whole lot under herself with her beak.

Weather conditions were rough enough during July, but occasionally a fairly quiet day would occur. High winds were experienced on ten days, the greatest hourly average for any twenty-four hours being thirty-two miles, but no day averaged less than ten miles. Precipitation occurred on twenty-one days, mostly in the form of snow and soft hail. The mean temperature was 37.7°, with extremes of 43.3° and 26° F. The average percentage of cloud was 78; somewhat less than usual and due to the greater frequency of south-west winds, which almost always bring a broken sky.

Now that our life was one of smooth routine I devoted a good deal of time to reducing the meteorological observations. Hourly pressure and temperature readings as well as descriptive remarks, averages and other details required to be summarized, and this occupied a considerable amount of time, so I made a practice of spending a couple of hours each day on the work, whenever possible, hoping thereby to pick up the "leeway." I did not take too kindly to inactive writing in the Shack, but the weather conditions were such that I was glad to stay indoors, though that meant enduring the inevitable cold feet. The floor of the Shack was never warm, and of course there were no carpets.

Mac developed a great animosity against the rats and thoroughly enjoyed rooting them out on all occasions. The only explanation of their presence on the island is that they had arrived in the ships which were wrecked along the coasts. They got into the Shack several times, and we simply brought in Mac and shifted things about till she caught them.

Rough weather occurred during the first week of August, and with occasional temporary weakenings a gale blew throughout, reaching fifty miles an hour at different times. Snow, hail and sleet fell every day, and on the 3rd the temperature was below freezing-point all day. The Shack, which always shook a little in exceptionally heavy gales, now vibrated a good deal in a forty-mile wind, no doubt feeling the effects of the beating it had undergone.

Blake found a cave running through North Head and went round, on the 5th, to examine it. He proved it to be about sixty yards from opening to opening, and to widen out very much inside; the roof being about fifteen feet above the floor.

Hamilton and Sandell went along the coast on the 6th and brought home a dozen Maori hens for the pot. Hamilton secured some spiders, parasites on birds and many beetles under the moss and stones on the site of a penguin rookery, besides shooting a few terns.

The tern is a very pretty bird with light grey plumage, a black head and red beak and feet. We found no nests on the island, though the fact that the birds remain throughout the year implies that they breed there. They fly very fast while not appearing to do so, but their movements are by no means graceful. They flit about over the water close to the shore, every now and then dipping down picking up morsels and keeping up a constant, shrill squeaking.

The sea was so high on the 7th that it reached the weight of the tide-gauge and, lifting it up, unshipped the recording gear, as the steel wire flew off the wheel before the latter could take up the slack. I deemed it advisable to use stout cord instead of wire in the future and made a protective slot for the weight. I had blocked up the seaward side of the pipe with rocks, but found that these caused a deposit of silt so I had to get into the water at low tide and shift them all out again to clean away the accumulation of sand.

Very heavy snow fell during the afternoon, the flakes being the size of half a crown. A fresh north-north-west wind dropped to a calm at 4 PM and almost immediately it began to snow, the island being quite white by 5.30 PM

Bright sunny intervals alternated with light snow-squalls on the 10th, and the temperature was below freezing-point all day. It was pleasant to be out of doors, and I walked along to the west coast to see if there were any signs of activity amongst the sea elephants.

An unmistakable sign of the near approach of the breeding season was the presence of an enormous old bull, almost too fat to move, lying on the beach. Very few small ones were seen, as, on the arrival of the adult males

A Cow Sea Elephant and Pup

The Head of a Bull Sea Elephant

and females for the breeding season, the young ones leave for a while, presumably in order to get fat for the moulting period, or because they are afraid of the bulls, who are particularly savage at this time. The full-grown bulls attain to a length of twenty feet, and have a fleshy proboscis about eight or ten inches in length hanging over the mouth, suggesting the trunk of an elephant. It is from this fact that they derive the name of sea elephant.

There is a considerable disparity in size between the adult male and female, the latter very rarely exceeding eleven feet, though we have seen a few twelve and thirteen feet long. The females have no snout development and some of them facially very much resemble a bull terrier. The adults are called bulls and cows, while, curiously enough, in the sealers' phrase, the offspring are referred to as pups. The places where large numbers of them gather together during the breeding season are known as rookeries! "Rookery" appears to me to be inapplicable to a herd of sea elephants, though "pup" supplies a more apt description of the young.

The pups, born during September or early October, are covered with a long, black, wavy fur, which they lose when about two months old, and in its place comes a growth of silver-grey hair, which changes later into the ordinary brown colour of the full-grown animal.

The old males and females leave the island about the end of January, and are not seen again (except a few stray ones) till August in the case of the males, and until September in the case of the females.

The fact that the bulls arrive first leads one to the conclusion that their feeding-grounds must lie at a considerable distance and, in the journey therefrom, the males, being the stronger, should arrive before the females, who are heavy with young and probably make a somewhat leisurely progress, feeding by the way.

The rookeries vary in size, containing from half a dozen to four or five hundred cows; in the last case, of course, being an aggregation of smaller rookeries, each with its proprietor, in the shape of an old bull, lying in or somewhere near the centre. The normal rookery, as far as I could judge, seemed to be one that contained about forty cows, but once the nucleus was formed, it was hard to say how many cows would be there before the season ended, as females keep arriving for a period of about three weeks.

The young vary in length from three and a half to four and a half feet, are born within a few days of arrival and suckled for about a month, becoming enormously fat. The cow, who has not eaten during the whole of this time and has become very thin, then leaves the pup, but remains in the rookery for about two days, after which she escapes to sea, remaining there till the

A Rookery of Sea Elephants Near the Shore at the Nelson Reef, Chiefly Cows and Pups

A Bull Sea Elephant in a Fighting Attitude

beginning of January, when she returns to the island to moult. The pups when weaned get such rough usage in the rookery that they soon make off into the tussock and sleep for about a month, living on their fat and acquiring a new coat. The noise in one of the large rookeries is something to remember—the barking of the pups, the whimpering and yelping of the mothers and the roaring of the bulls.

Another feature in connexion with the rookery is the presence of what may be called unattached bulls, which lie around at a little distance from the cows, and well apart, forming a regular ring through which any cow wishing to desert her pup or leave the rookery before the proper time has very little chance of passing, as one of these grips her firmly with his powerful flipper and stays her progress. The lord of the harem, in the meantime, hastens to the scene of the disturbance, whereupon the other bull decamps.

The sea immediately in the vicinity of a large rookery is generally swarming with unattached bulls, who may be seen with their heads out of the water eyeing each other and keeping a bright look out for escaping cows. Now and again one may see a bull in the water gripping a cow with his flipper, despite her struggles, and roaring at a couple of others who show up menacingly quite close to him.

It may be remarked that towards the end of the season changes in the proprietorship of a rookery are rather rapid, as continuous raids are made by individuals from the outside. The need of continuous vigilance and the results of many encounters eventually lead to the defeat and discomfiture of the once proud proprietor.

I have never seen two bulls fight without first indulging in the usual preliminaries, that is, roaring and advancing a few yards and repeating the performance till within striking distance. Then both animals rear high up, supporting themselves on the lower part of the body, and lunge savagely with their whole weight each at his opponent's head or neck, tearing the thick skin with their teeth and causing the blood to flow copiously. Several lunges of this kind generally finish the battle, whereupon the beaten one drops to his flippers and makes all haste towards the water, glancing fearfully behind him on the way. We have seen bulls with their snouts partly torn off and otherwise injured, but worse injuries must occur in the rare, desperate battles which sometimes take place between two very much enraged animals.

When a bull in the centre of a rookery has occasion to rush at an interloper, he does so without regard to anything in his way, going over cows and pups alike and very often crushing some of the latter to death.

Again, it seems as if all the outlying bulls recognize the noise of the rookery bull, because each time he roars they all lift up their heads and take notice, whereas others who have just been roaring have not the slightest regard paid to them, except perhaps by one immediately concerned.

The bull, during the breeding season, will on provocation attack a man, and it is surprising how quickly the former covers the ground. But on the whole he is an inoffensive animal. It is, of course, impossible to venture into a rookery, as the cows are very savage when they have the pups with them, but one can approach within a few yards of its outskirts without danger. Their food consists of cuttlefish, crabs and fish, and it is probable that they frequent the ocean where this food is plentiful, when they are absent from the island.

It has been stated that these animals are nearly extinct, but a visit to Macquarie Island during the breeding season would be enough to convince anybody to the contrary. There are thousands of them, and though about seven hundred are killed during a season, the increase in numbers each year, on Macquarie Island alone, must be very great.

The skuas were now returning to the island and their numbers and corresponding clamour were daily increasing. They were the noisiest and most quarrelsome birds we had, but their advent, we hoped, marked the return of less rigorous weather.

Blake left for Lusitania Bay on the 17th, intending to spend several months there in order to survey and geologically examine the southern end, so we gave him a send-off dinner. He had a very rough trip to the place, having to spend two nights in a cave about six miles from his destination, as a result of getting lost in a dense fog.

Hamilton made a wire fish-trap to replace the one which he had lost, and succeeded in getting a few fish on lowering it for the first time. He discovered parasitical mites all over them on the outside, and the flesh contained many worms.

A heavy north-north-west gale was experienced on the 26th, but the weather during the last three days of August was very quiet, either calms or light winds prevailing, and we took the opportunity to do some work on Wireless Hill. All the wire stays were tightened, and various ropes which appeared to require attention were renewed, while, as a final improvement, the aerial was hauled as tight as we could make it.

We heard on July 31 that the *Rachel Cohen*, a sealing-vessel, had sailed for Macquarie Island and was bringing a few articles for us, so there was something to which we could look forward in the immediate future.

The most remarkable feature of the month's weather was the wind, as gales blew on eleven days, and on seven other days the velocity reached twenty-five miles per hour. Precipitation occurred on twenty-seven days, and the average percentage of cloud was eighty-four. The mean temperature was 38.1° with extremes of 45.3° and 26° F. A prolonged display of auroral light occurred on the night of the 17th, though no colours other than the light lemon-yellow of the arch and streamers could be seen.

Bull elephants were now arriving in great numbers, and these monsters could be seen lying everywhere on the isthmus, both up in the tussock, on the beaches, and among the heaps of kelp. Now and again one would lazily lift a flipper to scratch itself or heave its great bulk into a more comfortable position.

The island is the habitat of two kinds of night-birds, one kind—a species of petrel (Lesson's)—being much larger than the other, both living in holes in the ground. They fly about in the darkness, their cries resembling those made by a beaten puppy. The smaller bird (apparently indigenous and a new species) was occasionally seen flying over the water during the day, but the larger ones come out almost exclusively at night. A light attracts them and Hamilton, with the aid of a lantern and a butterfly-net, tried to catch some. Others swooped about, well out of range, shrieking the while in an uncanny way. Numbers of them were secured afterwards by being dug out of their holes, Mac being just as keen to locate them as Hamilton was to secure them. They cannot see well during the day, and seem to have almost lost the use of their feet. They lay two small, white, thin-shelled eggs at the end of their burrow; and in certain parts of the island, where the burrows are numerous, the sound made by hundreds of them at once, during the nesting season, somewhat resembles that made by a high-power Marconi wireless set at close range.

Before Blake left Lusitania Bay, I promised to see that the hut on Sandy Bay was re-stocked with provisions by the middle of the month, so, on the 8th, Hamilton, Sandell and I carried a supply of stores down there, leaving a note which informed him that we expected the *Rachel Cohen* to arrive any day, and asking him to return to the Shack. On the way down we came upon a vast quantity of wreckage piled up on the beach, midway between "The Nuggets" and Sandy Bay. This was all that remained of the sealing schooner, *Jessie Nichol*, which had been wrecked on December 21, 1910. Three men were drowned, their bodies being interred among the tussock, each marked by a life belt and a small board on which the name was roughly carved.

On our homeward trip we caught some wekas for the pot and duly arrived at the Shack, tired, wet and hungry.

Next day, while sitting in the Shack reducing records, I heard a yell from Hamilton to the effect that the *Rachel Cohen* was in sight, and about an hour later she dropped anchor in North-East Bay.

The sea was fairly smooth and no time was lost in bringing a boat ashore with the mails, of which each man received a share. A gang of sealers was landed with a view to obtaining sea elephant and penguin oil. I had wirelessed asking for a dinghy to be sent down, which would enable Hamilton to do more marine work; and it now came to hand. Further, we received an additional supply of photographic material and some rubber tubing for the anemometer, but the much needed boots did not arrive.

On the 18th a strong southerly gale sprang up and compelled the *Rachel Cohen* to seek safety in flight; so she slipped her cable and put to sea. She had not yet landed all the sealers' stores and was forced to hang about the island till the weather moderated sufficiently for her to return to an anchorage.

The Gentoo penguins, which had been observed at the beginning of the month building their nests, commenced to lay, and the first ten eggs were collected by us on September 18. Many sea elephant rookeries were now well-formed as the cows began to arrive about the 11th and were soon landing in large numbers. The first pups were heard on the 20th, and Bauer and I walked along to the rookery from which the barking came and had a look at the newcomers. There were only four, none of which was more than a few hours old, but they yapped their displeasure, and the mothers made frantic lunges at us when we approached to get a close view of them.

The sealers always gave the animals time to form their rookeries and then killed the bulls for oil. A well-conditioned full-grown animal yields about half a ton of oil, and as the commodity when refined has a market value of from £20 to £25 per ton, it will be seen that the industry is a profitable one. The cows being small never have a very thick coating of blubber, but I have seen bulls with blubber to a depth of eight inches, and some of them yield nearly two thousand pounds, though I should estimate the average yield at about one thousand one hundred pounds. The sealers in the early days used to obtain the oil by cutting the blubber up into very small pieces and melting it down in "try " pots. These pots, many of which may be still seen about the island, were made of very thick iron and the fuel used was the refuse taken from the pot itself. In the present method

steam digestors are used, and the oil from the melted blubber is drawn off, after steam has been passing for twelve hours. Coal is brought down by the sealing-vessel to be used as fuel. The "elephant season" lasts only about three months, and within about four weeks of its conclusion, the "penguin season" begins; the same gang of men being employed as a rule. The most difficult operation in connexion with both of these industries is undoubtedly the loading and unloading of the vessel. If auxiliary power were used, the ship could then steam to within half a mile of the shore, but as it is, a sailing-vessel has to anchor about two miles off and the oil is towed in rafts over that distance.

We heard sounds from Adelie Land wireless station for the first time on September 25, 1912, but the signals were very faint and all that we could receive was: "Please inform Pennant Hills." Sawyer called them repeatedly for several hours, but heard no acknowledgment. Every effort was made to get in touch with them from this time forward, Sawyer remaining at the instrument until daylight every morning.

The Royal penguins returned to the island on the 27th and immediately commenced to make their way to the rookeries. They had been absent since April and were very fat after their long migration.

On the 28th Blake and Hamilton started out in the dinghy for Lusitania Bay. They had already made a step and sprit, and, with a calico sail hoisted, the frail craft ran before a light breeze. Having a fair wind they made good headway along the coast, dropping in at a Gentoo penguin rookery *en route*, and collecting about two hundred and twenty eggs. Mac was a passenger and was a very sick dog all the trip.

Shortly after their departure, the *Rachel Cohen*, which had been blown away on the 18th, reappeared and again anchored. The captain reported having seen numerous icebergs, some of which were very large, about thirty miles to the eastward of the island. The sealers immediately commenced to get away the rest of their stores and coal and also to put some oil aboard the vessel, but on the following day the wind increased to such an extent that, in attempting to reach the ship with a raft of oil, they were blown down the coast and had to beach the boat several miles away.

On the night of the 29th Adelie Land wireless station was again heard tapping out a message apparently with the hope that some station would receive it. All we got was: "Having a hell of a time waiting for calm weather to put up more masts." Sawyer again repeatedly called, but they evidently could not hear him as no reply was received, and the above message was repeated time after time.

A Cormorant and Young on Nest

The Wild West Coast of Macquarie Island

The weather during September was not quite so rough as that of the previous two or three months, but misty days were very frequent. Gales were experienced on six days and strong winds on nine days, but several quiet periods occurred. The average temperature was 38.6°, with extremes of 44.7° and 26° F.

October was ushered in by a strong gale and rather heavy rain-squalls. The *Rachel Cohen* had a severe buffeting, though she was lying on the lee side of the island.

Just about three-quarters of a mile to the west of the Shack were two large sea elephant rookeries, very close to each other, and on the 3rd Sandell and I went along to see what was happening there. We found about two hundred and fifty cows in the nearer one, and, as closely as we could count, about five hundred in the adjacent colony. The babel of sounds made one feel thankful that these noisy creatures were some distance from the Shack. Nearly all the cows had pups, some of which had reached a fair size, while others were only a few hours old. We saw several dead ones, crushed out almost flat, and some skuas were busily engaged gorging themselves on the carcases. These birds are indeed professional plunderers, and will venture almost anywhere in pursuit of food.

During the evening we again heard Adelie Land station working, and the burden of their message to an apparently chance audience was: "We do not seem able to get Macquarie Island, all is well, though bad weather has so far prevented any attempt at sledging."

Sawyer again called them at regular intervals for the rest of the night, but, as before, got no response.

Hamilton and Blake were busy at Lusitania Bay during the first two weeks of October securing sea elephant specimens and collecting eggs. They visited Caroline Cove where is established a giant petrel rookery containing about four hundred birds, and gathered a large number of eggs—purely specimens, as they are no use otherwise.

The *Rachel Cohen* finally left us on the 8th, expecting to pay another visit in December for the purpose of taking off the sea elephant oil procured by the sealers. Sandell and I visited the Gentoo penguin colony in Aerial Cove during the afternoon, for the purpose of getting a few eggs. We found plenty there and collected as many as we required. On returning to the empty nests, the birds would first of all peer round to assure themselves that the eggs were really missing, and then throw their heads back, swaying them from side to side to the accompaniment of loud, discordant cries.

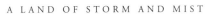
Several of us started out on the 10th to visit the west coast for the purpose of getting some wekas and, incidentally, to make any observations possible. We saw thousands of sea elephants along the coast and passed many rookeries of various sizes. There were a large number of wekas about, but after shooting fourteen we were satisfied with our bag.

A westerly gale during the night proved too much for the aerial, and down it came. Blake and Hamilton were away, so Sawyer, Sandell and I went up, and after much battling and frequent use of the "handy billy" succeeded in fixing things. We also re-tightened the wire stays and thoroughly overhauled the ropes. Snow and sleet fell all the time, making the task most disagreeable.

About the middle of the month the Royal penguins commenced to lay, and on the 17th Sandell and I went to their rookeries at "The Nuggets" and collected about fifteen dozen eggs, which we buried in a hole in the bank of the creek for preservation. This species of penguin is the one which is killed for oil, not because it is any fatter than the others, but because it lives in such large colonies. There is one rookery of these birds on the south end of the island which covers an area of sixteen and a half acres, whilst at "The Nuggets" there are numbers of them scattered along the banks of a creek which reaches the sea, aggregating ten acres. At the latter place are situated the oil works belonging to the sealers.

From careful observation I should say that the number of birds killed during the season would not total one hundred and fifty thousand. The method of killing—by blows from a heavy club—is about as humane as any that could be adopted, and the yearly increase in numbers in the only rookeries that are being worked is certainly greater than the decrease due to the depredations of the sealers. Apart from this, there are acres of rookeries on the island from which not a single bird is taken, and they go on year after year adding thousands upon thousands to their already vast numbers.

This species resembles the others in habits, and I shall not describe them at any length. They are of the same colour as the Victoria penguins, but have a more orderly crest. Their rookeries are always on or very close to a running stream which forms the highway along which they travel to and fro. There is no policeman on duty, but a well-ordered procession is somehow arranged whereby those going up keep to one side and those coming down keep to the other. Once they are in the rookery, however, different conditions obtain. Here are fights, squabbles and riots, arising from various causes, the chief of which appears to be a disposition on the part of some birds to loiter about. During the nesting time much

A Royal Penguins Rookery

disorder prevails, and fights, in which beaks and flippers are energetically used, may be seen in progress at various places throughout the rookery. The nests are made of small stones, and occasionally, a bone or two from the skeleton of some long-dead relative forms part of the bulwarks. The attempt on the part of some birds to steal stones from surrounding nests is about the most fruitful cause of a riot, and the thief generally gets soundly thrashed, besides which all have a peck at him as he makes his way with as much haste as possible from the danger-zone. As the season advances, these rookeries become covered with filthy slush, but it seems to make no difference to the eggs, as the chicks appear in due course. When the moulting process is in full swing the rookeries are very crowded, and feathers and slush then become mixed together, making the place anything but fragrant.

A fifty-four mile gale from the west-north-west blew down on us on the 20th, but shortly after noon it weakened, and, towards evening, with the shifting of the wind to southwest, came squalls of sleet and snow and a drop in temperature. Hamilton returned from Lusitania Bay in the dinghy on the 21st, but Blake stopped there as he had not yet finished his work in that locality. The dinghy was well laden with specimens of various kinds and, on the way up, some wood and pickets were left at Green Valley for future requirements.

On the 25th Sandell and I visited the west coast, but, instead of going the usual way, we walked down the east coast and went up the creek at "The Nuggets" with a view to having a look at the penguin colonies along its course, finally crossing over the hills and getting into another creek, which we followed all the way down to the west coast. Along this creek were numerous waterfalls, one of which was quite sixty feet in height with wind-blown spray frozen white on the rocks on either side. We came across several giant petrel rookeries, and were treated to a display of the "stinker's" ability to make himself objectionable. A pair of sooty albatrosses were seen nesting on the front of a rocky steep, but on climbing up we found that they had not yet laid. After catching some wekas and taking a few photographs we returned to the Shack.

On the last day of the month several of us crossed the hills to the west coast in search of plants and birds' eggs. We secured a number of plant specimens—a further sign of the arrival of spring—including two which bore a very small flower, and were most successful in obtaining skuas', giant petrels' and sooty albatrosses' eggs.

During the evening I received a message from Captain Davis stating that the *Aurora* would visit us in about three weeks' time and inquiring if we needed any supplies. This was entirely unexpected, as we thought that no more would be seen of the Ship until she came to take us home at the end of March 1913.

Earthquake shocks were felt at 1.55 AM and 9.35 AM on October 28, but did no damage other than to bring down some loose rock. Auroral displays were rather frequent but not very pronounced, and in most cases could only be classed as "glows."

A bright sunny morning on the 3rd induced Hamilton and me to make a photographic excursion along the coast. Hitherto only still-life photos had been taken, but with the sunlight we were then having, any work was possible, so we determined to have some "shots" at the sea elephants. They were rather difficult subjects, strange to say, but we spent some time amongst them and did famously, till a snow-squall made us suspend operations.

We heard the discordant but mournful cry of a sooty albatross coming from the cliff-front, so Hamilton climbed up and, after scrambling about for a while, succeeded in finding a nest, which contained one egg. This led him to look along the cliffs fronting the east coast, and on the following morning he found several nests and caught two birds, both of which were taken by hand while on the nest. They had beautiful plumage and made very fine specimens.

The Wreck of the *Gratitude* on the Nuggets Beach

Blake returned from Lusitania Bay during the afternoon of the 4th and reported that he required only four or five days to complete the survey. The configuration of the island at the southern end is vastly different to that shown in the published charts, and this became more apparent as Blake's figures were plotted.

The news that Piastre had won the Melbourne Cup was flashed about all over the southern ocean during the evening, and we picked it up; but as this was the first we had heard of the animal, nobody seemed much interested. It certainly gave a turn to the conversation, and quite a sporting tone permeated the discussions of the ensuing two or three days.

The subjects of discussion were usually those of environment, and most of our talk centred round sea elephants, sea-leopards, penguins, temperatures, wind, wireless telegraphy, fish, aurorae, exploration, ships, Queensland and New Zealand. Sea elephants and penguins do offer scope for a considerable amount of conversation, as one observes them under such different circumstances, and they are so odd that something remarkable is always associated with the sight of them. The weather, being practically the *bête noire* of our existence, came in for a good deal of abuse. Wireless telegraphy is a mighty interesting subject at all times, and we passed many hours of our stay in discussing its future. All the members were, allegedly, fishermen of some calibre, and when I have said that, anybody with a knowledge of the man who claims ability as an angler will know what all the others, in turn, had to receive with restrained and respectful admiration. The advantages of settlement in Queensland were so apparent to at least one member of the party that he simply could not understand why thousands were not annually killed in the rush to get to this, "the greatest of all the Australian States." Good old silky oak!

The scenery of New Zealand was almost as well known to us as to anybody who has lived in the country all his life, and three of us had never been there. We have sat round the Shack sometimes and only the roar of a sea elephant outside reminded us that we were not, as we imagined, at a Maori "tangi." The wages to be earned there, the delights of travelling, the legislators, Rotorua, kauri pine, and the moon they've got in Auckland—we've heard of all these and marvelled at them. "Kapai te Maori!"

Blake and Hamilton went to Sandy Bay in the dinghy on the 6th in order to complete some work. They improved the hut there, to the extent of making a fire-place and laying barrel-staves on the floor, afterwards bringing a boat-load of timber from the *Jessie Nichol* wreck and rigging up a board bunk sufficiently large to accommodate both of them.

While walking down to the *Clyde* wreck for some wood on the 7th I saw a strange bird on the beach, and, returning to the Shack for the gun, I got him at the second shot. He was a land bird and had evidently been blown out of his course, as none of his kind had been seen before on the island.

On getting up on the following morning I found poor old Ma lying dead, and the feathers which lay about indicated that she had been the victim of a savage assault, but whether at the teeth of a dog or the beak of a skua I was unable to determine. This was most unfortunate, as the hens had all started to lay again two days previously; but apart from this she was a funny old creature and one could almost hold a conversation with her, so we regretted her loss. However, to make amends for this disaster the Victoria penguins started to lay on the same day, and as several of their rookeries were only a few minutes' walk from the Shack, the position was much the same as if we owned a poultry farm.

Hamilton returned from Sandy Bay on the 17th and immediately set about collecting shags' eggs. He visited Aerial Cove for the purpose but did not get enough, and was compelled to go to West Point, where he gathered twenty-four dozen for specimens. He now had a collection of eggs of all birds which nest on the island, with the exception of the weka and the tern.

At 6.30 PM on November 22 the *Aurora* steamed into North-East Bay and dropped anchor. Hamilton, Blake and Sawyer launched the dinghy and pulled out to receive the mails, which they brought ashore for distribution. All on board were well and Captain Davis sent word to say he would land in the morning, bringing our goods and some visitors—Professor Flynn of Hobart and Mr. Denny.

The *Aurora* next day steamed round North Head and took a series of soundings between the main island and the Judge and Clerk. These latter islets lie about eight miles to the north of North Head, and are merely rocks about eighty feet high upon which thousands of shags and other birds have established rookeries. On the following morning we said good-bye to the Ship, which weighed anchor and steamed away, leaving us once more to our own devices.

All the flowering plants were now showing their extremely modest blooms, and the tussock looked like a field of wheat, each stem having a decided ear. The Gentoo penguins, as well as the giant petrels, had hatched their eggs, and the parent birds were shouldering full responsibilities.

Blake and Hamilton were now prepared for another visit to the southern end. Blake had almost completed the chart of the island, and the difference between it and the published chart was very striking. In the latter case the

Kerguelen Cabbage

Flowering Plant

south end was shown as being six miles wide, whereas it is in reality only a little more than two miles across, and the width of the island is nowhere more than three and a half miles. About twenty miles from the southern end lie two islets known as the Bishop and Clerk. The former, which is the larger, is covered with a growth of tussock, while the latter is mainly bare rock.

A distinct rise in temperature was noticeable during November and the mean worked out at 41.6°, while the extremes were 49° and 32° F. Strong winds were recorded on thirteen days and six short-lived gales occurred. We had less precipitation than during any previous month, as thirteen dry days were experienced. The average cloudiness was 93 percent.; largely due to the frequent foggy or misty weather.

On December 2, at 10 AM, Blake and I packed our sleeping-bags and blankets and started for Sandy Bay. The swags weighed only thirty-five pounds each and we made a rather quick trip.

After repairing the dilapidated shack, we sallied out for the purpose of catching our evening meal, and with the aid of Mac soon succeeded in getting eight wekas. A sea elephant was then killed, and the blubber, heart and tongue taken; the first-named for use as fuel and the others for food. We cleaned the wekas and put them in the pot, cooking the whole lot together, a proceeding which enabled us to forgo cooking a breakfast in the morning. The beach was swarming with young sea elephants and many could be seen playing about in a small, shallow lagoon.

Just south of the hut there is a sandy spit and one of the only stretches of beach on the island, where thousands of penguins from the adjacent rookeries were congregated, amongst them being three King penguins, which were easily distinguishable on account of their great size.

Feeling a little weary, I sought the hut about 9 PM and turned into the sleeping-bag, which was placed on a board bottom covered with tussock, which was by no means uncomfortable. The old place smoked so much that we decided to let the fire die down, and as soon as the smoke had cleared away, the imperfections of the hut became apparent; rays of moonlight streaming through countless openings in the walls and roof.

We rose at 6.30 AM While Blake lit the fire, I went out to fill the billy at a small stream running out of the hills about sixty yards away. After breakfast we set out for Green Valley, but had not gone very far when it began to blow very hard from the south, straight in our faces, and we scrambled on towards our destination amidst squalls of snow, hail and sleet. Eventually we reached the valley and had a somewhat meagre lunch in a small cave. The title "cave" rather dignifies this hole in the rock, but it was the only friendly spot in a most inhospitable locality, and we were inclined to be generous,

On the whole, the length of coast we had traversed was found to be as rough as any on the island. There is not a stretch of one hundred yards anywhere that can be termed "good going." In many places we found that the steep cliffs approached very close to the water, and the mournful cry of the sooty albatross could be heard coming from points high on the face of the cliffs, while the wekas were so tame that one could almost walk up and catch them.

A large creek whose banks are overhung with a coarse growth of fern makes its way out of the hills and runs into Sandy Bay. Just a little to the south of this creek Blake discovered a terminal moraine about two hundred yards in length and fifty feet wide. It rests on sandstone about fifteen feet above the present sea-level and the boulders consist of polished and sub-angular blocks of sandstone and porphyry of various sizes. It evidently belongs to the valley or to a later stage of glaciation. The rocks along the coast are all a volcanic series, and basic dykes are visible in many places.

We arose at 7 AM next day and breakfasted on porridge, weka, fried heart, "hard-tack" and cocoa. Leaving the hut shortly afterwards we climbed on to the hills and travelled south for several miles in order to fix the position of some lakes and creeks. There was one lake in the vicinity about half a mile long and to all appearances very deep. It lay between two steep hills, and the grassy bank at one end and the small sloping approach at the other gave it an artificial appearance, while the water was beautifully clear and perfectly fresh. At the sloping end, dozens of skuas were busily engaged washing themselves and the flapping of their wings in the water made a remarkable noise, audible at a considerable distance on the hill-tops. On returning to the hut at Sandy Bay several rabbits secured by Mac were cleaned and put on to boil.

Next morning a dense mist shrouded the island till about 11 AM, but the weather becoming fine and bright, we started for the west coast about noon. During our progress along the bed of a creek, Blake discovered what was believed to be a glacial deposit containing fossil bones, and considerable time was spent in examining this and attempting to extract whole specimens, thereby making it too late to proceed to the west. On returning to the hut we decided to pack the swags. We reached home just in time for tea, finding that nothing unusual had occurred during our four days' absence.

Hamilton and Blake went out fishing in the dinghy on the 9th and made a remarkable haul of fish, sixty in number, ranging in size from a few ounces to twelve and a half pounds. They were all of the same species, somewhat resembling

Darby and Joan. Two Rare Examples of Penguins Which Visited the Shack, Macquarie Island. On the Left a Sclater Penguin, on the Right an Albino Royal Penguin

Large Erratics and Other Glacial Debris on the Summit of Macquarie Island

Pillow-Form Lava on the Highlands of Macquarie Island

rock cod, but as usual they were covered with external parasites, and their flesh was full of worm-cysts. Hamilton preserved a number of them and the rest were cooked, but we did not relish them very much and the one meal was enough.

On December 11 we had a hard gale all day, the anemometer recording "bursts" of over fifty miles an hour frequently, while the average exceeded forty miles an hour throughout. Twelve months ago on that day we had made our first landing on the island from the *Aurora*, but vastly different weather conditions prevailed at the time.

Christmas Day was now very close at hand, and as Blake and Hamilton were going to celebrate at the other end of the island, whence they had gone on the 10th, Sawyer, Sandell and I arranged a little "spread" for ourselves. Sawyer produced a cake which he had received in the recent mail, and some friend had forwarded a plum pudding to Sandell, so on Christmas Day these, with a boiled ham, some walnuts, mince rolls and a bottle of stout were spread on the table, which had been decorated with tussock stuck in sea elephants' tusks. The highest temperature registered on the island during our stay—51.8° F.—was recorded on Christmas Day, and the sun seemed so warm that Sandell and I ventured into the sea for a dip, but the temperature of the water was not high enough to make it an agreeable experience.

During the evening of the 26th we received a message saying that the *Aurora* had left Hobart on her trip south to bring back the two parties from Antarctica, but no mention of picking us up on the return journey was made.

The King penguins and "night birds" had laid by this time, and Hamilton added more eggs to his collection. He found for the first time a colony of mutton birds near the south end. He also came upon a mollymawk rookery on the south-western point of the island, and managed to take one of the birds by hand.

Blake and he had an accident in the dinghy on the 29th, fortunately attended by no serious results. They had gone from Lusitania Bay to the south end, and, while attempting to land through the surf, the boat struck a rock and capsized, throwing them into the water. They had many things in the boat but lost only two billies, two pannikins, a sounding line and Hamilton's hat, knife and pipe. Their blankets floated ashore in a few minutes, and the oars came floating in later in the day. After the capsize Hamilton managed to reach the boat and turn her over, and Blake made for a kelp-hung rock, but, after pulling himself up on to it, was immediately washed off and had to swim ashore. The boat was afterwards found to be stove-in in two places, though the breaks were easily patched up subsequently.

New Year's Eve came and with keen anticipations we welcomed the advent of 1913.

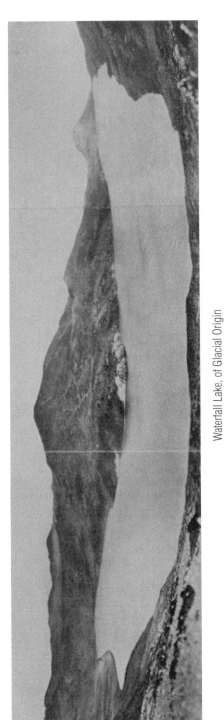

Waterfall Lake, of Glacial Origin

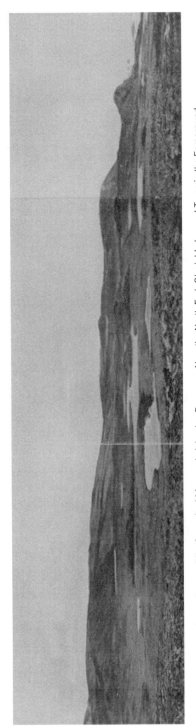

On the Plateau-Like Summit of Macquarie Island; a Panorama Near the North End. Glacial Lakes and Tarns in the Foreground

CHAPTER XXVII

Through Another Year

By G. F. AINSWORTH

W E HAD NOW THROWN A YEAR BEHIND AND the work we set out to accomplish was almost finished; so it was with pleasurable feelings that we took up the burden of completion, looking forward to the arrival of April 1913 which should bring us final relief and the prospects of civilisation. I shall deal with the first three months of the year as one period, since almost all the field-work, except photography, had been done, and, after the return of Blake and Hamilton from Lusitania Bay on January 8, our life was one of routine; much time being devoted to packing and labelling specimens in anticipation of departure.

The first business of the year was to overhaul the wireless station, and on the 6th, Sawyer, Sandell and I spent the day laying in a supply of benzine from Aerial Cove, changing worn ropes, tightening stay-wires, straightening the southern masts and finally hauling the aerial taut. These duties necessitated much use of the "handy billy," and one has but to form an acquaintance with this desirable "person" to thoroughly appreciate his value.

Blake and Hamilton returned on January 8 and reported that their work was finished at the southern end. Thenceforth they intended to devote their time to finishing what remained to be done at the northern end and in adding to their collections. Blake, for instance, resolved to finish his chart of the island, and, if time permitted, to make a topographical survey of the locality, as it was of great geological interest. Hamilton made the discovery that a number of bird specimens he had packed away were mildewed, and as a result he was compelled to overhaul the whole lot and attend to them. He found another colony of mutton birds on North

Head, the existence of which was quite unexpected till he dug one out of a burrow thought to contain "night-birds."

About the middle of January I endeavoured to do a little meteorological work with the aid of some box-kites manufactured by Sandell. But though a number of them were induced to fly, we had no success in getting them up with the instruments attached. They all had a habit of suddenly losing equilibrium and then indulging in a series of rapid dives and plunges which usually ended in total wreckage.

The *Rachel Cohen* again visited the island on January 26, but this time she anchored off "The Nuggets," whither the sealers had gone to live during the penguin season. We could see the ship lying about a mile offshore, and walked down to get our mails and anything else she had brought along for us. I received a letter from the Secretary of the Expedition saying that he had made arrangements for us to return by the *Rachel Cohen* early in April, and the news caused a little excitement, being the only definite information we had had concerning relief.

The end of the first month found Blake and Hamilton both very busy in making suitable boxes for specimens. Many of the larger birds could not be packed in ordinary cases, so Hamilton had to make specially large ones to accommodate them, and Blake's rock specimens being very heavy, extra strong boxes had to be made, always keeping in view the fact that each was to weigh not more than eighty pounds, so as to ensure convenient handling.

After a silence of about four months, we again heard Adelie Land on February 3, but the same old trouble existed, that is, they could not hear us. Sawyer called them again and again, getting no reply, but we reckoned that conditions would improve in a few weeks, as the hours of darkness increased.

Hamilton and I made a trip to the hill-tops on the 4th for the purpose of taking a series of plant and earth temperatures which were of interest biologically, and while there I took the opportunity of obtaining temperatures in all the lakes we saw. Hamilton also took some panoramic photographs from the various eminences and all of them turned out well.

During the evening Adelie Land sent out a message saying that Dr. Mawson had not yet returned to the Base from his sledging trip and Sawyer received it without difficulty, but though he "pounded away" in return for a considerable time, he was not heard, as no reply or acknowledgment was made.

The *Rachel Cohen* remained till the 5th, when a northerly gale arose and drove her away. As she had a good cargo of oil on board no one expected her to return. We had sent our mail on board several days previously as experience had shown us that the sailing date of ships visiting the island was very uncertain.

Sandell met with a slight though painful accident on the 7th. He was starting the engine, when it "backfired" and the handle flying off with great force struck him on the face, inflicting a couple of nasty cuts, loosening several teeth, and lacerating the inside of his cheek. A black eye appeared in a day or two and his face swelled considerably, but nothing serious supervened. In a few days the swelling had subsided and any anxiety we felt was at an end.

We now had only two sheep left, and on the 8th Blake and I went to kill one. Mac accompanied us. Seeing the sheep running away, she immediately set off after them, notwithstanding our threats, yells and curses. They disappeared over a spur, but shortly afterwards Mac returned, and, being severely thrashed, immediately left for home. We looked for the sheep during the rest of the day but could find no trace of them, and though we searched for many days it was not till five weeks had elapsed that we discovered them on a small "landing" about half-way down the face of the cliff. They had apparently rushed over the edge and, rolling down, had finally come to a stop on the ledge where they were found later, alive and well.

On the 8th Adelie Land was heard by us calling the *Aurora* to return at once and pick up the rest of the party, stating also that Lieutenant Ninnis and Dr. Mertz were dead. All of us were shocked at the grievous intelligence and every effort was made by Sawyer to call up Adelie Land, but without success.

On the following day we received news from Australia of the disaster to Captain Scott's party.

Blake, who was now geologizing and doing topographical work, discovered several lignite seams in the hills on the east coast; he had finished his chart of the island. The mainland is simply a range of mountains which have been at some remote period partly submerged. The land meets the sea in steep cliffs and bold headlands, whose general height is from five hundred to seven hundred feet, with many peaks ranging from nine hundred and fifty to one thousand four hundred and twenty feet, the latter being the height of Mount Hamilton, which rears up just at the back of Lusitania Bay. Evidence of extreme glaciation is everywhere apparent, and numerous tarns and lakes are scattered amongst the hills, the tops of which are barren, wind-swept and weather-worn. The hill sides are deeply scored by ravines, down which tumble small streams, forming cascades at intervals on their hurried journey towards the ocean. Some of these streams do not reach the sea immediately, but disappear in the loose shingly beaches of peaty swamps. The west coast is particularly rugged, and throughout its length is strewn wreckage of various kinds, some of which is now one hundred yards from the water's edge. Very few stretches of what may be called "beach" occur on the island; the foreshores consisting for the most part of huge water-worn boulders or loose gravel and shingle, across which progress is slow and difficult.

Apparently the ground shelves very rapidly under the water, as a sounding of over two thousand fathoms was obtained by the *Aurora* at a distance of eight miles from the east coast. The trend of the island is about eleven degrees from true north; the axis lying north by east to south by west. At either end are the island-groups already referred to, and their connexion with the mainland may be traced by the sunken rocks indicated by the breaking seas on the line of reef.

A very severe storm about the middle of the month worked up a tremendous sea, which was responsible for piling hundreds of tons of kelp on the shore, and for several days tangled masses could be seen drifting about like small floating islands.

On the 20th an event occurred to which we had long looked forward, and which was now eagerly welcomed. Communication was established with the Main Base in Adelie Land by wireless! A message was received from Dr. Mawson confirming the deaths of Ninnis and Mertz, and stating that the *Aurora* had not picked up the whole party. Sawyer had a short talk with Jeffryes, the Adelie Land operator, and among other scraps of news told him we were all well.

Hamilton killed a sea elephant on the 22nd. The animal was a little over seventeen feet long and thirteen and a half feet in girth just at the back of the flippers, while the total weight was more than four tons. It took Hamilton about a day to complete the skinning, and, during the process, the huge brute had to be twice turned over, but such is the value of the nautical handy-billy that two men managed it rather easily. When the skin had been removed, five of us dragged it to the sealers' blubber-shed, where it was salted, spread out, and left to cure.

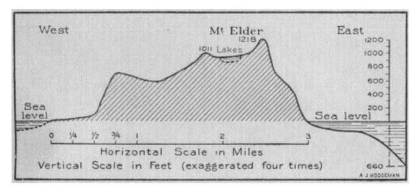

West · Mt Elder · East

1218

10II Lakes

Sea level · Sea level

0 ¼ ½ ¾ 1 · 2 · 3

Horizontal Scale in Miles

Vertical Scale in Feet (exaggerated four times)

660

A Section Across Macquarie Island Through Mt. Elder

We had communication with Adelie Land again on the 26th, and messages were sent and received by both stations. Dr. Mawson wirelessed to the effect that the *Aurora* would, after picking up Wild's party, make an attempt to return to Adelie Land if conditions were at all favourable.

Finding that provisions were running rather short on the last day of February, we reduced ourselves to an allowance of one pound of sugar per week each, which was weighed out every Thursday. Altogether there were only forty-five pounds remaining. Thenceforth it was the custom for each to bring his sugar-tin to the table every meal. The arrangement had its drawbacks, inasmuch as no sugar was available for cooking unless a levy were made. Thus puddings became rarities, because most of us preferred to use the sugar in tea or coffee.

March came blustering in, accompanied by a sixty-four-mile gale which did damage to the extent of blowing down our annexe, tearing the tarpaulin off the stores at the back and ripping the spouting off the Shack. A high sea arose and the conformation of the beach on the north-western side of the isthmus was completely changed. Numbers of sea elephants' tusks and bones were revealed, which had remained buried in the shingle probably for many years, and heaps of kelp were piled up where before there had been clean, stony beach. Kelp is a very tough weed, but after being washed up and exposed to the air for a few days, begins to decay, giving forth a most disagreeable smell.

At this time we caught numerous small fish amongst the rocks at the water's edge with a hand line about four feet long. It was simply a matter of dropping in the line, watching the victim trifle with destiny and hauling him in at the precise moment.

The King Penguins' Rookery, Lusitania Bay

Wireless business was now being done nightly with Adelie Land, and on the 7th I received a message from Dr. Mawson saying that the party would in all probability be down there for another season, and stating the necessity for keeping Macquarie Island station going till the end of the year. This message I read out to the men, and gave them a week in which to view the matter. The alternatives were to return in April or to remain till the end of the year.

I went through the whole of the stores on the 10th, and found that the only commodities upon which we would have to draw sparingly were milk, sugar, kerosene, meats and coal. The flour would last till May, but the butter allowance would have to be reduced to three pounds per week.

It was on the 12th that we found the lost sheep, but as we had some wekas, sufficient to last us for several days, I did not kill one till the 15th. On that day four of us went down towards the ledge where they were standing, and shot one, which immediately toppled off and rolled down some distance into the tussock, the other one leaping after it without hesitation. While Blake and Hamilton skinned the dead sheep, Sandell and I caught the other and tethered it at the bottom of the hill amongst a patch of Maori cabbage, as we thought it would probably get lost if left to

The Head of a Bull Sea Elephant Photographed in the Act of Roaring

roam loose. However, on going to the spot next day, the sheep was nearly dead, having got tangled up in the rope. So we let it go free, only to lose the animal a day or two later, for it fell into a bog and perished.

On March 22 a lunar eclipse occurred, contact lasting a little over three hours from 9.45 PM till within a few minutes of 1 AM on the 23rd. The period of total eclipse was quite a lengthy one, and during the time it lasted the darkness was intense. Cloud interfered for a while with our observations in the total stage. No coronal effect was noted, though a pulsating nebulous area appeared in front of the moon just before contact.

A message came on the 27th saying that the *Rachel Cohen* was sailing for Macquarie Island on May 2, and would bring supplies as well as take back the men who wished to be relieved, and this was forwarded in turn to Dr. Mawson.

He replied, saying that the *Aurora* would pick us up about the middle of November and convey us to Antarctica, thence returning to Australia; but if any member wished to return by the *Rachel Cohen* he could do so, though notification would have to be given, in order to allow of substitutes being appointed. All the members of the party elected to stay, and I asked

The Rookery of Royal Penguins at the South End, Viewed from a Cliff Several Hundred Feet Above It

each man to give an outline of the work he intended to pursue during the extended period.

During March strong winds were recorded on fourteen days, reaching gale-force on six occasions. The gale at the beginning of the month was the strongest we had experienced, the velocity at 5.40 AM on the 1st reaching sixty-four miles per hour. Precipitation occurred on twenty-six days and the average amount of cloud was 85 per cent. A bright auroral display took place on the 6th, lasting from 11.20 till 11.45 PM It assumed the usual arch-form stretching from the south-east to south-west, and streamers and shafts of light could be observed pulsating upwards towards the zenith.

We now started on what might be called the second stage of our existence on the island. In the preceding pages I have endeavoured to give some idea of what happened during what was to have been our full period; but unforeseen circumstances compelled us to extend our stay for eight months more, until the *Aurora* came to relieve us in November. As the routine was similar in a good many respects to that which we had just gone through, I shall now refer to only the more salient features of our life.

The loyalty of my fellows was undoubted, and though any of them could have returned if he had felt so inclined, I am proud to say that they all decided to see it through. When one has looked forward hopefully to better social conditions, more comfortable surroundings and reunion with friends, it gives him a slight shock to find that the door has been slammed, so to speak, for another twelve months. Nevertheless, we all found that a strain of philosophy smoothed out the rough realities, and in a short time were facing the situation with composure, if not actual contentment.

We decided now to effect a few improvements round about our abode, and all set to work carrying gravel from the beach to put down in front of the Shack, installing a sink-system to carry any waste water, fixing the leaking roof and finally closing up the space between the lining and the wall to keep out the rats.

We expected the *Rachel Cohen* to leave Hobart with our stores on May 2, and reckoned that the voyage would occupy two weeks. Thus, it would be six weeks before she arrived. I was therefore compelled on the 10th to reduce the sugar allowance to half a pound per week. We were now taking it in turns to go once a week and get some wekas, and it was always possible to secure about a dozen, which provided sufficient meat for three dinners. Breakfast consisted generally of fish, which we caught, or sea elephant in some form, whilst we had tinned fish for lunch.

Sandell installed a telephone service between the Shack and the wireless station about the middle of April, the parts all being made by himself; and it was certainly an ingenious and valuable contrivance. I, in particular, learned to appreciate the convenience of it as time went on. The buzzer was fixed on the wall close to the head of my bunk and I could be called any time during the night from the wireless station, thus rendering it possible to reply to communications without loss of time. Further, during the winter nights, when auroral observations had to be made, I could retire if nothing showed during the early part of the night, leaving it to Sandell, who worked till 2 or 3 AM to call me if any manifestation occurred.

We had heavy gales from the 12th to the 17th inclusive, the force of the wind during the period frequently exceeding fifty miles per hour, and, on the first-mentioned date, the barometer fell to 27.8 inches. The usual terrific seas accompanied the outburst.

Finding that there were only eight blocks of coal left, I reduced the weekly allowance to one. We had a good supply of tapioca, but neither rice nor sago, and as the sealers had some of the latter two, but none of the former, we made an exchange to the extent of twelve pounds of tapioca for eight pounds of rice and some sago. Only fifteen pounds of butter remained on the 20th, and I divided this equally, as it was now one of the luxuries, and each man could use his own discretion in eating it. As it was nearing the end of April, and no further word concerning the movements of the *Rachel Cohen* had been received, I wirelessed asking to be immediately advised of the exact date of the vessel's departure. A reply came that the ship would definitely reach us within two months. I answered, saying we could wait two months, but certainly no longer.

With a view to varying the menu a little, Blake and I took Mac up on the hills on April 26 to get some rabbits and, after tramping for about six hours, we returned with seven. In our wanderings we visited the penguin rookeries at "The Nuggets," and one solitary bird sat in the centre of the vast area which had so lately been a scene of much noise and contention.

On May 1 I took an inventory of the stores and found that they would last for two months if economically used. Of course, I placed confidence in the statement that the *Rachel Cohen* would reach the island within that time.

With the coming of May wintry conditions set in, and at the end of the first week the migrants had deserted our uninviting island. Life with us went on much the same as usual, but the weather was rather more severe than that during the previous year, and we were confined to the Shack a good deal.

The sealers who were still on the island had shifted back to the Hut at the north end so that they were very close to us and frequently came over with their dog in the evenings to have a yarn. The majority of them were men who had "knocked about" the world and had known many rough, adventurous years. One of them in particular was rather fluent, and we were often entertained from his endless repertoire of stories.

On the 23rd, finding that there were seventy-seven and a half pounds of flour remaining, and ascertaining that the sealers could let us have twenty-five pounds, if we ran short, I increased the allowance for bread to twelve and a half pounds per week, and this, when made up, gave each man two and three-quarter pounds of bread. Our supply of oatmeal was very low, but in order to make it last we now started using a mixture of oatmeal and sago for breakfast; of course, without any milk or sugar.

Just about this time Mac gave birth to six pups and could not help us in obtaining food. She had done valuable service in this connexion, and the loss in the foraging strength of the party was severely felt for several weeks. She was particularly deadly in hunting rabbits and wekas, and though the first-named were very scarce within a few miles of the Shack, she always managed to unearth one or two somewhere. Hut-slippers were made out of the rabbit skins and they were found to be a great boon, one being able to sit down for a while without his feet "going."

June arrived and with it much rough, cold weather. A boat was expected to come to our relief, at the very latest, by the 30th. We had a very chilly period during the middle of the month, and it was only by hand-feeding the "jacket" of the wireless motor that any work could be done by the station, as the tank outside was almost frozen solid.

The tide-gauge clock broke down towards the end of the month, and though I tried for days to get it going I was not successful. One of the springs had rusted very badly as a result of the frequent "duckings" the clock had experienced, and had become practically useless.

We had ascertained that the *Rachel Cohen* was still in Hobart, so on the 23rd I wirelessed asking when the boat was to sail. The reply came that the *Rachel Cohen* was leaving Hobart on Thursday, June 26.

Our supply of kerosene oil was exhausted by the end of the month, despite the fact that the rule of "lights out at 10 PM" had been observed for some time. Thus we were obliged to use sea elephant oil in slush lamps. At first we simply filled a tin with the oil and passed a rag through a cork floating on the top, but a little ingenuity soon resulted in the production of a lamp with three burners and a handle. This was made by Sandell out of an old tea-pot and one, two or three burners could be lit as occasion

Young Sea Elephants Asleep Amongst Royal Penguins, South End Rookery

Hamilton Inspecting a Good Catch of Fish at Lusitania Bay

Hamilton Obtaining the Blubber of a Sea Elephant for Fuel

demanded. During meal times the whole three burners were used, but, as the oil smoked and smelt somewhat, we generally blew out two as soon as the meal was finished. This was the "general" lamp, but each man had, as well, one of his own invention. Mine was scornfully referred to as the "house-boat," since it consisted of a jam tin, which held the oil, standing in a herring tin which caught the overflow.

At the end of June, Blake and I surveyed all the penguin rookeries round about "The Nuggets" and, allowing a bird to the square foot, found that there must have been about half a million birds in the area. The sealers kill birds from these rookeries to the number of about one hundred and thirty thousand yearly, so that it would seem reasonable to suppose that, despite this fact, there must be an annual increase of about one hundred thousand birds.

The end of the month arrived and, on making inquiries, we found that there was no news of the *Rachel Cohen* having left Hobart. We had enough flour to last a fortnight, and could not get any from the sealers as they possessed only three weeks' supply themselves. However, on July 8, Bauer came across and offered to let us have some wheatmeal biscuits as they had a couple of hundredweights, so I readily accepted twenty pounds of them. We now had soup twice a day, and managed to make it fairly thick by adding sago and a few lentils. Cornflour and hot water flavoured with cocoa made a makeshift blanc-mange, and this, with sago and tapioca, constituted our efforts towards dessert.

On the 12th I received a message stating that the *Rachel Cohen* had sailed on July 7; news which was joyfully received. We expected her to appear in ten or twelve days.

On the 18th we used the last ounce of flour in a small batch of bread, having fully expected the ship to arrive before we had finished it. Next day Bauer lent us ten pounds of oatmeal and showed us how to make oatmeal cakes. We tried some and they were a complete success, though they consisted largely of tapioca, and, according to the respective amounts used, should rather have been called tapioca cakes.

When the 22nd arrived and no ship showed up, I went across to see what the sealers thought of the matter, and found that they all were of opinion that she had been blown away to the eastward of the island, and might take a considerable time to "make" back.

On this date we came to the end of our meats, which I had been dealing out in a very sparing manner, just to provide a change from sea elephant and weka. We had now to subsist upon what we managed to catch. There were still thirty-five tins of soup, of which only two tins a day were used, so that there was sufficient for a few weeks. But we found ourselves running short of some commodity each day, and after the 23rd reckoned to be without bread and biscuit.

At this juncture many heavy blows were experienced, and on the 24th a fifty-mile gale accompanied by a tremendous sea beat down on us, giving the *Rachel Cohen* a very poor chance of "making" the island. Our last tin of fruit was eaten; twelve tins having lasted us since March 31, and I also shared the remaining ten biscuits amongst the men on the 24th. We were short of bread, flour, biscuits, meats, fish, jam, sugar and milk, but had twenty tins of French beans, thirty tins of cornflour, some tapioca, and thirty tins of soup, as well as tea, coffee and cocoa in abundance. We had not been able to catch any fish for some days as the weather had been too rough, and, further, they appeared to leave the coasts during the very cold weather.

Sea elephants were very scarce, and we invariably had to walk some distance in order to get one; each man taking it in turn to go out with a companion and carry home enough meat for our requirements. We were now eating sea elephant meat three times a day (all the penguins having migrated) and our appetites were very keen. The routine work was carried on, though a great deal of time was occupied in getting food.

Bauer very generously offered to share his biscuits with us, but we fellows, while appreciating the spirit which prompted the offer, unanimously declined to accept them. We now concluded that something had happened to the ship, as at the end of July she had been twenty-four days out.

On August 3 we had a sixty-three-mile gale and between 1 and 2 AM the velocity of the wind frequently exceeded fifty miles per hour. Needless to say there was a mountainous sea running, and the *Rachel Cohen*, if she had been anywhere in the vicinity, would have had a perilous time.

A message came to me on August 6 from the Secretary of the Expedition, saying that the *Rachel Cohen* had returned to New Zealand badly damaged, and that he was endeavouring to send us relief as soon as possible. I replied, telling him that our food-supply was done, but that otherwise we were all right and no uneasiness need be felt, though we wished to be relieved as soon as possible.

Splendid news came along on the 9th to the effect that the New Zealand Government's steamer *Tutanekai* would tranship our stores from the *Rachel Cohen* on the 15th and sail direct for the island.

Sawyer now became ill and desired me to make arrangements for his return. I accordingly wired to the Secretary, who replied asking if we could manage without an operator. After consulting Sandell, I answered that Sandell and I together could manage to run the wireless station.

Everybody now looked forward eagerly to the arrival of the *Tutanekai*, but things went on as before. We found ourselves with nothing but sea elephant meat and sago, with a pound-tin of French beans once a week and two ounces of oatmeal every morning.

We heard that the *Tutanekai* did not leave as expected on the 15th, but sailed on the afternoon of the 17th, and was coming straight to Macquarie Island. She was equipped with a wireless telegraphy outfit, which enabled us on the 18th to get in touch with her; the operator on board stating that they would reach us early on the morning of the 20th.

On the evening of the 19th we gave Sawyer a send-off dinner; surely the poorest thing of its kind, as far as eatables were concerned, that has ever been tendered to any one. The fare consisted of sea elephant's tongue "straight," after which a bottle of claret was cracked and we drank heartily to his future prosperity.

At 7.30 AM on the 20th the *Tutanekai* was observed coming up the east coast, and as we had "elephanted" at 6 AM we were ready to face the day. I went across to the sealers' hut and accompanied Bauer in the launch to the ship, which lay at anchor about a mile from the shore. We scrambled on board, where I met Captain Bollons. He received me most courteously, and, after discussing several matters, suggested landing the stores straight away. I got into the launch to return to the shore, but the wind had freshened and was soon blowing a fresh gale. Still, Bauer thought we should have no difficulty and we pushed off from the ship. The engine of the launch failed after we had gone a few yards, the boat was blown rapidly down the coast, and we were eventually thrown out into the surf at "The Nuggets." The Captain, who witnessed our plight, sent his launch in pursuit of us, but its engines also failed. It now became necessary for the crew of the whale-boat to go to the assistance of the launch. However, they could do nothing against the wind, and, in the end, the ship herself got up anchor, gave the two boats a line and towed them back to the former anchorage. The work of unloading now commenced, though a fairly heavy surf was running. But the whaleboat of the *Tutanekai* was so dexterously handled by the boatswain that most of our stores were landed during the day.

Sawyer went on board the *Tutanekai* in the afternoon, thus severing his connexion with the Expedition, after having been with us on the island since December 1911. On the following morning, some sheep, coal and flour were landed, and, with a whistled good-bye, the *Tutanekai* started north on her visit to other islands.

Our short period of stress was over and we all felt glad. From that time onwards we ate no more elephant meat "straight." A sheep was killed just as the *Tutanekai* left, and we had roast mutton, scones, butter, jam, fruit and rice for tea. It was a rare treat.

All the stores were now brought up from the landing-place, and as I had put up several extra shelves some weeks previously, plenty of room was found for all the perishable commodities inside the Shack.

The beginning of September found me fairly busy. In addition to the meteorological work, the results of which were always kept reduced and entered up, I had to work on Wireless Hill during the evening and make auroral observations on any night during which there was a display, attending to the stores and taking the week of cooking as it came along.

Blake and Hamilton went down the island for several days on September 3, since they had some special observations to make in the vicinity of Sandy Bay.

The sea elephant season was now in progress, and many rookeries were well formed by the middle of the month. The skuas had returned, and on the 19th the advance-guard of the Royal penguins arrived. The Gentoos had established themselves in their old "claims," and since the 12th we had been using their eggs for cooking.

Early in September time-signals were received from Melbourne, and these were transmitted through to Adelie Land. This practice was kept up throughout the month and in many cases the signals were acknowledged.

Blake and Hamilton returned to the Shack on the 24th, but left again on the 30th, as they had some more photographic work to do in the vicinity of Green Valley and Sandy Bay.

Blake made a special trip to Sandy Bay on October 30 to bring back some geological specimens and other things he had left there, but on reaching the spot found that the old hut had been burned to the ground, apparently only a few hours before, since it was still smouldering. Many articles were destroyed, among which were two sleeping-bags, a sextant, gun, blankets, photographic plates, bird specimens and articles of clothing. It was presumed that rats had originated the fire from wax matches which had been left lying on a small shelf.

On November 9 we heard that the *Aurora* would leave Hobart on the 19th for Antarctica, picking us up on the way and landing three men on the island to continue the wireless and meteorological work.

We sighted the *Rachel Cohen* bearing down on the island on November 18, and at 5.15 PM she came to an anchorage in North-East Bay. She brought down the remainder of our coal and some salt for Hamilton for the preservation of specimens.

On the next night it was learned that the *Aurora* had left Hobart on her way South, expecting to reach us about the 28th, as some sounding and dredging were being done *en route*.

Everybody now became very busy making preparations for departure. Time passed very quickly, and November 28 dawned fine and bright. The *Rachel Cohen*, which had been lying in the bay loading oil, had her full complement on board by 10 AM, and shortly afterwards we trooped across to say good-bye to Bauer and the other sealers, who were all returning to Hobart. It was something of a coincidence that they took their departure on the very day our ship was to arrive. Their many acts of kindness towards us will ever be recalled by the members of the party, and we look upon our harmonious neighbourly association together with feelings of great pleasure.

A keen look-out was then kept for signs of our own ship, but it was not until 8 PM that Blake, who was up on the hill side, called out, "Here she comes," and we climbed up to take in the goodly sight. Just visible, away in the north-west, there was a line of thin smoke, and in about half an hour the *Aurora* dropped anchor in Hasselborough Bay.

A Victoria Penguin on the Nest. *Macquarie Island*

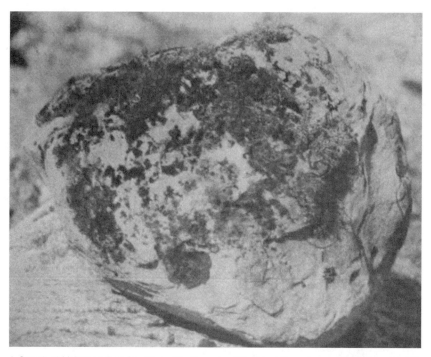

A Growth of Lichen on Red Sandstone (An Example of the Most Conspicuous Vegetation of Adelie Land). *Adelie Land*

CHAPTER XXVIII

The Homeward Cruise

We bring no store of ingots,
Of spice or precious stones;
But what we have we gathered
With sweat and aching bones.

—*Kipling*

AS WE SAT IN THE WARDROOM OF THE *AURORA* exchanging the news of months long gone by, we heard from Captain Davis the story of his fair-weather trip from Hobart. The ship had left Australian waters on November 19, and, from the outset, the weather was quite ideal. Nothing of note occurred on the run to Macquarie Island, where a party of three men were landed and Ainsworth and his loyal comrades picked up. The former party, sent by the Australian Government, were to maintain wireless communication with Hobart and to send meteorological reports to the Commonwealth Weather Bureau. A week was spent at the island and all the collections were embarked, while Correll was enabled to secure some good colour photographs and Hurley to make valuable additions to his cinematograph film.

The *Aurora* had passed through the "fifties" without meeting the usual gales, sighting the first ice in latitude 63° 33' S., longitude 150° 29' E. She stopped to take a sounding every twenty-four hours, adding to the large number already accumulated during her cruises over the vast basin of the Southern Ocean.

All spoke of the clear and beautiful days amid the floating ice and of the wonderful coloured sunsets; especially the photographers. The pack was so loosely disposed, that the ship made a straight course for Commonwealth Bay, steaming up to Cape Denison on the morning of December 14 to find us all eager to renew our claim on the big world up North.

There was a twenty-five-knot wind and a small sea when we pulled off in the whale-boat to the ship, but, as if conspiring to give us for once a gala-day, the wind fell off, the bay became blue and placid and the sun

645

beat down in full thawing strength on the boundless ice and snow. The Adelians, if that may be used as a distinctive title, sat on the warm deck and read letters and papers in voracious haste, with snatches of the latest intelligence from the Macquarie Islanders and the ship's officers. No one could erase that day from the tablets of his memory.

Late in the afternoon the motor-launch went ashore, and the first of the cargo was sent off. The weather remained serene and calm, and for the next six days, with the exception of a "sixty-miler" for a few hours and a land breeze overnight, there was nothing to disturb the embarkation of our bulky impedimenta which almost filled the outer Hut. Other work went on apace. The skua gulls, snow and Wilson petrels were laying their eggs, and Hamilton went ashore to secure specimens and to add to our already considerable collection of bird skins. Hunter had a fish-trap lowered from the forecastle, used a hand dredge from the ship, and did tow-netting occasionally from the launch in its journeys to and from the land. Hurley and Correll had bright sunshine to ensure good photographic results. Bage and Hodgeman looked after the transport of stores from the Hut, and Gillies, Bickerton and Madigan ran the motor-launch. McLean, who was now in possession of an incubator and culture tubes, grew bacteria from various sources—seals and birds, soils, ice and snow. Ainsworth, Blake and Sandell, making their first acquaintance with Adelie Land, were most often to be seen quarrying ice on the glacier or pulling loaded sledges down to the harbour.

On the 18th a party of us went off to the Mackellar Islets in the motor-launch, taking a tent and provisions, intending to spend two days there surveying and making scientific observations.

An Illustration of the Life of the Mackellar Islets

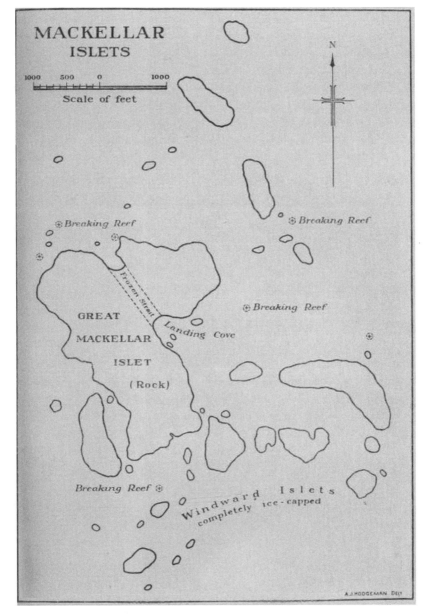

An Illustration of the Life on the Mackellar Islets

These islets, over thirty in number, are clustered mainly in a group about two miles off shore. The group is encircled by rocky "outposts," and there are several "links" to the southern mainland. Under a brilliant sun, across

An Ice Mushroom Amongst the Mackellar Islets

the pale blue water, heaving in a slow northerly swell, the motor-launch threaded her way between the granite knobs, capped with solid spray. The waves had undermined the white canopies so that they stood immobile, perched on the dark, kelp-fringed rocks, casting their pallid reflections in the turquoise sea. Steaming into a natural harbour, bordered by a low ice-foot on which scores of Weddell seals lay in listless slumber, we landed on the largest islet—a succession of salt-encrusted ridges covered by straggling penguin rookeries. The place just teemed with the sporadic life of an Antarctic summer.

It was calculated that the Adelie penguins exceeded one hundred and fifty thousand in number over an area of approximately one hundred acres. Near the landing-place there were at least sixty seals and snow petrels; skua gulls and Wilson petrels soon betrayed their nests to the biologists.

The islets are flat, and afford evidence that at one time the continental ice-cap has ridden over them. The rock is a hard grey gneiss. A rough plane-table map of the group was made by Hodgeman and myself.

Our scheme of local exploration was now continued to the west. For two years we had looked curiously at a patch of rocks protruding beneath the ice-cap eight miles away, within Commonwealth Bay. It had been inaccessible to sledging parties, and so we reserved Cape Hunter, as it was ultimately called, for the coming of the Ship.

The anchor was raised on the forenoon of the 22nd, and by midday the *Aurora* steamed at half-speed along the ramparts of the glacier, stopping about four miles from the Cape, after sounding in four hundred and twenty-four fathoms. Through field-glasses much had already been seen; enough to arouse an intense interest.

One could not but respond to the idea that here was a new world, flawless and unblemished, into which no human being had ever pried. Here were open secrets to be read for the first time. It was not with the cold eye of science alone that we gazed at these rocks—a tiny spur of the great unseen continent; but it was with an indefinable wonder.

In perfect weather a small party set off in the launch towards a large grounded berg which appeared to lie under the ice-cliffs. Approaching it closely, after covering two miles, we could see that it was still more than a mile to the rocks.

Penguins soon began to splash around; Wilson petrels came glancing overhead and we could descry great flocks of Antarctic petrels wheeling over cliff and sea. Reefs buried in frothing surge showed their glistening mantles, and the boat swerved to avoid floating streamers of brash-ice.

The rocky cliffs, about eighty feet in height at the highest point, were formed of vertically lying slate rocks—a very uniform series of phyllite and sericite-schist. At their base lay great clinging blocks of ice deeply excavated by the restless swell. One island was separated from the parent mass by a channel cut sheer to the deep blue water. Behind the main rocks and indenting the ice-cliff was a curving bay into which we steered, finding at its head a beautiful cove fringed with a heavy undermined ice-foot and swarming with Adelie penguins. Overhanging the water was a cavern hollowed out of a bridge of ice thrown from the glacier to the western limit of the rock outcrop.

Hurley had before him a picture in perfect proportion. The steel-blue water, paled by an icy reflection, a margin of brown rocks on which the penguins leapt through the splashing surf, a curving canopy of ice-foot and, filling the background, the cavern with pendent icicles along its cornice.

The swell was so great that an anchor had to be thrown from the stern to keep the launch off shore, and two men remained on board to see that no damage was done.

At last we were free to roam and explore. Over the first ridge of rocks we walked suddenly into the home of the Antarctic petrels! There had always been much speculation as to where these birds nested. Jones's party at our

View Looking Out of a Shallow Ravine at the Eastern Extremity of the Rocks at Cape Denison

"Hurley had before him a picture in perfect proportion . . ."

western base had the previous summer at Haswell Island happened upon the first rookery of Antarctic petrels ever discovered. Here was another spot in the great wilderness peopled by their thousands. Every available nook and crevice was occupied along a wide slope which shelved away until it met the vertical cliffs falling to the ocean. One could sit down among the soft, mild birds who were fearless at the approach of man. They rested in pairs close to their eggs laid on the bare rock or among fragments of slate loosely arranged to resemble a rest. Many eggs were collected, and the birds, losing confidence in us, rose into the air in flocks, gaining in feathered volume as they circled in fear above this domain of rock and snow which had been theirs for generations.

In adjoining rookeries the Adelie penguins, with their fat, downy cheeks, were very plentiful and fiercer than usual. Skuas, snow and Wilson petrels were all in their accustomed haunts. Down on the low ice-foot at the mouth of a rocky ravine, a few seals had effected a landing. Algae, mosses and lichens made quite a display in moist localities.

Before leaving for the ship, we "boiled the billy" on a platform of slate near the cove where the launch was anchored and had a small picnic, entertained by the penguins playing about in the surf or scaling the ice-foot to join the birds which were laboriously climbing to the rookeries

651

on the ridge. The afternoon was so peaceful and the calm hot weather such a novelty to us that we pushed off reluctantly to the *Aurora* after an eventful day.

Those on board had had a busy time dredging, and their results were just as successful as ours. A haul was made in two hundred and fifty fathoms of ascidians, sponges, crinoids, holothurians, fish and other forms of life in such quantity that Hunter and Hamilton were occupied in sorting the specimens until five o'clock next morning. Meanwhile the *Aurora* had returned to her old anchorage close to Cape Denison.

The sky banked up from the south with nimbus, and early on the 23rd a strong breeze ruffled the water. There were a few things to be brought off from the shore, while Ainsworth, Sandell and Correll were still at the Hut, so that, as the weather conditions pointed to a coming blizzard, I decided to "cut the painter" with the land.

An hour later the motor-launch, with Madigan and Bickerton, sped away for the last load through falling snow and a rising sea. Hodgeman had battened down the windows of the Hut, the chimney was stuffed with bagging, the veranda-entrance closed with boards, and, inside, an invitation was left for future visitors to occupy and make themselves at home. After the remainder of the dogs and some miscellaneous gear had been shipped, the launch put off and came alongside in a squally wind through thick showers of snow. Willing hands soon unloaded the boat and slung it in the davits. Every one was at last safe on board, and in future all our operations were to be conducted from the ship.

During the night the wind rose and the barometer fell, while the air was filled with drifting snow. On the 24th—Christmas Eve—the velocity of the wind gradually increased to the seventies until at noon it blew with the strength of a hurricane. Chief Officer Blair, stationed with a few men under the fo'c'sle-head, kept an anxious eye on the anchor chain and windlass.

About lunch time the anchor was found to be dragging and we commenced to drift before the hurricane. All view of the land and lurking dangers in the form of reefs and islets were cut off by driving snow.

The wind twanged the rigging to a burring drone that rose to a shriek in the shuddering gusts. The crests of the waves were cut off and sprayed in fine spindrift. With full steam on we felt our way out, we hoped to the open sea; meanwhile the chain cable and damaged anchor were slowly being hauled in. The ship's chances looked very small indeed, but, owing to the good seamanship of Captain Davis and a certain amount of luck, disaster was averted. Soon we were in a bounding sea. Each time we were lifted on a huge roller the motor-launch, swinging in the davits, would rise and then descend with a crash on the water, to be violently bumped against the bulwarks. Everything possible was done to save the launch, but our efforts proved fruitless. As it was being converted into a battering ram against the ship itself it had to be cut away, and was soon swept astern and we saw no more of it.

Most unexpectedly there came a lull in the wind, so that it was almost calm, though the ship still laboured in the seas. A clearance in the atmosphere was also noticeable for Cape Hunter became discernible to the west, towards which we were rapidly drifting. This sight of the coast was a great satisfaction to us, for we then knew our approximate position ** and the direction of the wind, which had veered considerably.

The lull lasted scarcely five minutes when the wind came back from a somewhat different quarter, north of east, as violent as ever. The "eye" of the storm had passed over us, and the gale continued steady for several days. That night the struggle with the elements was kept up by officers and crew, assisted by members of the shore party who took the lee-wheel or stood by in case of emergency.

"December 25. Christmas Day on the high seas off Adelie Land, everything wet and fairly miserable; incipient *mal de mer*, wind 55–60; snowing! When Davis came down to breakfast and wished us a Merry Christmas, with a smile at the irony of it, the ward-room was swaying about in a most bewildering fashion."

Towards evening, after the *Aurora* had battled for hours slowly to the east, the sea went down somewhat and some drifting ice was sighted. We continued under full steam, pushing forward to gain the shelter of the Mertz glacier-tongue. It was now discovered that the fluke of the anchor had broken off short, so great had been the strain imposed upon it during the height of the hurricane.

On Boxing Day the ship was in calmer water heading in a more southerly direction so as to come up with the land. Fog, fine snow and an overcast sky made a gloomy combination, but during the afternoon the fog lightened sufficiently for us to perceive the mainland—a ghostly cliff shrouded in diaphanous blink. By 10 PM the Mertz glacier was visible on the port bow, and to starboard there was an enormous tilted berg which appeared to be magnified in the dim light.

Allowing a day for the weather to become clearer and more settled, we got out the trawl on the 28th and did a dredging in three hundred fathoms

---

** *It should be borne in mind that compasses are unreliable in the vicinity of the magnetic pole.*

Antarctic Petrels Resting on the Snow

Silver-Grey Petrels Making Love

Looking Towards the Mainland from Stillwell Island: Silver-Grey Petrels Nesting in the Foreground

close to the glacier-tongue. Besides rocks and mud there were abundant crinoids, holothurians, corals, crustaceans and "shells." In addition, several pieces of fossilized wood and coaly matter were discovered scattered through the "catch."

Bage, under Davis's direction, took temperatures and collected water samples at fifty, seventy-five, one hundred, two hundred and three hundred fathoms, using the Lucas sounding-machine on the fo'c'sle. The temperature gradient from the surface downwards appeared to give some indication of the depth of ice submerged in the glacier-tongue alongside which we were lying.

On the 29th a cold south-easter blew off the ice-cliffs and the sun was trying to pierce a gauzy alto-stratus. The *Aurora* steamed north-east, it being our intention to round the northern limit of the Mertz Glacier. Gradually a distant line of pack, which had been visible for some time, closed in and the ship ran into a *cul-de-sac*. Gray, who was up in the crow's-nest, reported that the ice was very heavy, so we put about.

Proceeding southward once more, we glided along within a stone's throw of the great wall of ice whose chiselled headlands stood in profile for miles. There was leisure to observe various features of this great formation, and to make some valuable photographic records when the low south-western sun emerged into a wide rift. Hunter trailed the tow-net for surface plankton while the ship was going at half-speed.

At ten o'clock the ship had come up with the land, and her course was turned sharply to the north-west towards a flotilla of bergs lying to the east of the Way Archipelago, which we intended to visit.

On December 30, 1913, the *Aurora* lay within a cordon of floating ice about one mile distant from the nearest islet of a group scattered along the coast off Cape Gray.

Immediately after breakfast a party of eight men set off in the launch to investigate Stillwell Island. The weather was gloriously sunny and every one was eager at the prospect of fresh discoveries. Cape Hunter had been the home of the Antarctic petrels, and on this occasion we were singularly fortunate in finding a resort of the Southern Fulmar or silver-grey petrels. During the previous summer, two of the eastern sledging parties had for the first time observed the breeding habits of these birds among isolated rocks outcropping on the edge of the coast. But here there was a stronghold of hundreds of petrels, sitting with their eggs in niches among the boulders or ensconced in bowers excavated beneath the snow which lay deep over some parts of the island.

The rock was a gneiss which varied in character from that which had been examined at Cape Denison and in other localities. All the scientific treasures were exhausted by midday, and the whale-boat was well laden when we rowed back to the ship.

Throughout a warm summer afternoon the *Aurora* threaded her way between majestic bergs and steamed west across the wide span of Commonwealth Bay, some fifteen miles off the land. At eleven o'clock the sky was perfectly clear and the sun hung like a luminous ball over the southern plateau. The rocks near the Hut were just visible. Close to the "Pianoforte Berg" and the Mackellar Islets tall jets of fine spray were seen to shoot upward from schools of finner whales. All around us and for miles shoreward, the ocean was calm and blue; but close to the mainland there was a dark curving line of ruffled water, while through glasses one could see trails of serpentine drift flowing down the slopes of the glacier. Doubtless, it was blowing at the Hut; and the thought was enough to make us thankful that we were on our good ship leaving Adelie Land for ever.

On the morning of December 31, 1913, Cape Alden was abeam, and a strong wind swept down from the highlands. Bordering the coast there was a linear group of islets and outcropping rocks at which we had hoped to touch. The wind continued to blow so hard that the idea was abandoned and our course was directed towards the north-west to clear a submerged reef which had been discovered in January 1912.

The wind and sea arose during the night, causing the ship to roll in a reckless fashion. Yet the celebration of New Year's Eve was not marred, and lusty choruses came up from the ward-room till long after midnight. Next morning at breakfast our ranks had noticeably thinned through the liveliness of the ship, but it is wonderful how large an assembly we mustered for the New Year's dinner, and how cheerfully the toast was drunk to "The best year we have ever had!"

On January 2, 1914, fast ice and the mainland were sighted. The course was changed to the south-west so as to bring the ship within a girdle of loose ice disposed in big solid chunks and small pinnacled floes. A sounding realized two hundred fathoms some ten miles off the coast, which stretched like a lofty bank of yellow sand along the southern horizon. On previous occasions we had not been able to see so much of the coastline in this longitude owing to the compactness of the ice, and so we were able to definitely chart a longer tract at the western limit of Adelie Land.

The ice became so thick and heavy as the *Aurora* pressed southward that she was forced at last to put about and steer for more open water. On the way, a sounding was made in two hundred and fifty fathoms, but a dredging was unsuccessful owing to the fact that insufficient cable was paid out in going from two hundred and fifty fathoms to deeper water.

Our north-westerly course ran among a great number of very long tabular bergs, which suggested the possibility of a neighbouring glacier-tongue as their origin.

At ten o'clock on the evening of the 2nd, a mountain of ice with a high encircling bastion passed to starboard. It rose to a peak, flanked by fragments toppling in snowy ruin. The pyramidal summit was tinged the palest lilac in the waning light; the mighty pallid walls were streaked and blotched with deep azure; the green swell sucked and thundered in the wave-worn caverns. Chaste snow-birds swam through the pure air, and the whole scene was sacred.

A tropical day in the pack-ice! Sunday January 4 was clear and perfectly still, and the sun shone powerfully. On the previous day we had entered a wide field of ice which had become so close and heavy that the ship took till late in the evening to reach its northern fringe.

From January 5 onwards for two weeks we steamed steadily towards the west, repeatedly changing course to double great sheets of pack which streamed away to the north, pushing through them in other places where the welcome "water-sky showed strong" ahead, making "southing" for days following the trend of the ice, then grappling with it in the hope of winning through to the land and at last returning to the western track along the margin of brash which breaks the first swell of the Southern Ocean.

The weather was mostly overcast with random showers of light snow and mild variable winds on all but two days, when there was a "blow" of forty miles per hour and a considerable sea in which the ship seemed more active than usual.

Many soundings were taken, and their value lay in broadly [...] Of course, too, we were supplementing the ship's previous work in these latitudes.

Section Illustrating the Moat in the Antarctic Continental Shelf

One successful dredging in eighteen hundred fathoms brought up some large erratics and coaly matter, besides a great variety of animal life. It was instructive to find that the erratics were coated with a film of manganese oxide derived from the sea-water. Several tow-nettings were taken with large nets automatically closing at any desired depth through the medium of a "messenger." Small crustaceans were plentiful on the surface, but they were if anything more numerous at depths of fifty to one hundred fathoms.

Antarctic Petrels Nesting on the Rocky Ledges of the Cliffs Near Cape Hunter

Icing Ship in the Pack North of Termination Ice-Tongue

Amongst the latter were some strongly phosphorescent forms. The flying birds were "logged" daily by the biologists. Emperor and Adelie penguins were occasionally seen, among the floes as well as sea-leopards, crab-eater and Weddell seals.

Friday January 16 deserves mention as being a day full of incident. In the morning a thin, cold fog hung along the pack whose edge determined our course. Many petrels flew around, and on the brash-ice there were dark swarms of terns—small birds with black-capped heads, dove-grey backs and silvery-white breasts. They were very nervous of the ship, rising in great numbers when it had approached within a few hundred yards. One startled bird would fly up, followed by several more; then a whole covey would disturb the rest of the flock. Hamilton managed to shoot two of them from the fo'c'sle, and, after much manoeuvring, we secured one with a long hand-net.

Soon after, there was a cry of "killer whales!" from the stern. Schools of them were travelling from the west to the east along the edge of the pack. The water was calm and leaden, and every few seconds a big black triangular fin would project from the surface, there would be a momentary glimpse of a dark yellow-blotched back and then all would disappear.

We pushed into the pack to "ice ship," as the water-supply was running low. Just as the *Aurora* was leaving the open water, a school of finner whales went by, blowing high jets of spray in sudden blasts, wallowing for a few seconds on the surface, and diving in swirls of foam. These finners or rorquals are enormous mammals, and on one occasion we were followed by one for several hours. It swam along with the ship, diving regularly underneath from one side to another, and we wondered what would happen if it had chosen to charge the vessel or to investigate the propeller.

Close to a big floe to which the ship was secured, two crab-eater seals were shot and hauled aboard to be skinned and investigated by the biologists and bacteriologist. When the scientists had finished their work, the meat and blubber were cut up for the dogs, while the choicer steaks were taken to the cook's galley.

After lunch every one started to "ice ship" in earnest. The sky had cleared and the sun was warm and brilliant by the time a party had landed on the snow-covered floe with baskets, picks and shovels. When the baskets had been filled, they were hoisted by hand-power on to a derrick which had been fixed to the mizen mast, swung inboard and then shovelled into a melting tank alongside the engine-room. The melter was a small tank through which ran a coil of steam pipes. The ice came up in such quantity that it was not melted in time to keep up with the demand, so a large heap was made on the deck.

Later in the afternoon it was found that holes chipped in the sea-ice to a depth of six or eight inches filled quickly with fresh water, and soon a gang of men had started a service with buckets and dippers between these pools and the main hatch where the water was poured through funnels into the ship's tanks. The bulwarks on the port side of the main hatch had been taken down, and a long plank stretched across to the floe. At nine o'clock work was stopped and we once more resumed our western cruise.

It was found that as the region of Queen Mary Land approached, heavy pack extended to the north. While skirting this obstacle, we disclosed by soundings a steep rise in the ocean's floor from a depth of about fifteen hundred fathoms to within seven hundred fathoms of the surface, south of which there was deep water. It was named "Bruce Rise" in recognition of the oceanographical work of the Scottish Expedition in Antarctic seas.

On the 17th, in latitude 62° 21' S., longitude 95° 9' E., the course ran due south for more than seven hours. For the two ensuing days the ship was able to steer approximately south-west through slackening ice, until on the 19th at midday we were in latitude 64° 59' S., longitude 90° 8' E. At length it appeared that land was approaching, after a westward run of more than twelve hundred miles. Attempts to reach the charted position of Totten's Land, North's Land, Budd Land and Knox Land had been successively abandoned when it became evident that the pack occupied a more northerly situation than that of the two previous years, and was in most instances thick and impenetrable.

At 10 PM on the 19th, the ice fields still remaining loose and navigable, a dark line of open water was observed ahead. From the crow's-nest it was seen to the south stretching east and west within the belt of pack-ice—the Davis Sea. We had broken through the pack less than twenty-five miles north of where the *Gauss* (German Expedition, 1902) had wintered.

All next day the *Aurora* steamed into the eye of an easterly wind towards a low white island, the higher positions of which had been seen by the German Expedition of 1902, and charted as Drygalski's High Land. Dr. Jones's party had, the year before, obtained a distant view of it and regarded it as an island, which proved to be correct, so we named it Drygalski Island. To the south there was the dim outline of the mainland. Soundings varied between two hundred and three hundred fathoms.

On January 21, Drygalski Island was close at hand, and a series of soundings which showed from sixty to seventy fathoms of water deepening towards the mainland proved beyond doubt that it was an island. In shape it is like a flattened dome about nine miles in diameter and twelve hundred feet in height, bounded by perpendicular cliffs of ice, and with no visible evidence of outcropping rock.

The dredge was lowered in sixty fathoms, and a rich assortment of life was captured for the biologists—Hunter and Hamilton. A course was then made to the south amidst a sea of great bergs; the water deepening to about four hundred fathoms.

During the evening the crevassed slopes of the mainland rose clear to the south, and many islets were observed near the coast, frozen in a wide expanse of bay-ice. Haswell Island, visited by Jones, Dovers and Hoadley of the Western Party, was sighted, and the ship was able to approach within eight miles of it; at ten o'clock coming up to flat bay-ice, where she anchored for the night. Before we retired to bunk, a Ross seal was discovered and shot, three-quarters of a mile away.

Next day, January 22, an unexpected find was made of five more of this rare species of seal. Many Emperor penguins were also secured. It would have been interesting to visit the great rookery of Emperor penguins on Haswell Island, but, as the ship could only approach to within eight miles of it, I did not think it advisable to allow a party to go so far.

On the night of the 22nd, the *Aurora* was headed northeast for the Shackleton Ice-Shelf. In the early hours of the 28th a strong gale sprang up and rapidly increased in violence. A pall of nimbus overspread the sky, and blinding snow commenced to fall.

We had become used to blizzards, but on this occasion several factors made us somewhat apprehensive. The ship was at least twenty-five miles from shelter on an open sea, littered with bergs and fragments of ice. The wind was very strong; the maximum velocity exceeding seventy miles per hour, and the dense driving snow during the midnight hours of semi-darkness reduced our chances of navigating with any certainty.

The night of the 23rd had a touch of terror. The wind was so powerful that, with a full head of steam and steering a few points off the eye of the wind, the ship could just hold her own. But when heavy gusts swooped down and the propeller raced on the crest of a mountainous wave, Davis found it impossible to keep steerage-way.

Drift and spray lash the faces of officer and helmsman, and through the grey gloom misty bergs glide by on either hand. A long slow struggle brings us to a passage between two huge masses of ice. There is a shock as the vessel bumps and grinds along a great wall. The engine stops, starts

Sea-Urchins: A Shallow-Water Form (lower right); A Holothurian or "Sea-Cucumber": An Example of Animal Life from the Greatest Depths (upper right); Deep-Water Fish Living in the Vicinity of the Shackleton Ice-Shelf (left)

again, and stops once more. The yards on the foremast are swung into the wind, the giant seas are broken by the stolid barriers of ice, the engine commences to throb with its old rhythm, and the ship slowly creeps out to meet the next peril. It comes with the onset of a "bergy-bit" which smashes the martingale as it plunges into a deep trough. The chain stay parts, dragging loose in the water, while a great strain is put by the foremast on the bowsprit.

Early on the 24th the ship was put about and ran with the wind, while all hands assembled on the fo'c'sle. The crew, under the direction of Blair, had the ticklish job of replacing the chain stay by two heavy blocks, the lower of which was hooked on to the lug which secured the end of the stay, and the upper to the bowsprit. The running ropes connecting the blocks were tightened up by winding the hauling line round the capstan. When the boatswain and two sailors had finished the wet and chilly task of getting the tackle into position, the rest put their weight on to the capstan bars and the strain on the bowsprit was relieved. The fo'c'sle, plunging and swaying in the great waves, was encased in frozen spray, and along all the ropes and stays were continuous cylinders of ice. The *Aurora* then resumed her easterly course against the blizzard.

Saturday January 24 was a day of high wind, rough seas, watery decks, lively meals and general discomfort. At 11.30 PM the waves had perceptibly decreased, and it was surmised that we were approaching the berg, about thirty miles in length, which lay to the west of the Shackleton Ice-Shelf.

At 6 AM on the 25th the sun managed to glimmer through the low rack flying from the east, lighting up the carven face of an ice-cliff along which the *Aurora* was coasting. Up and down we steamed until the afternoon of the 26th, when the wind lulled away to nothing, and the grey, even pall of cloud rose and broke into fleecy alto-cumulus.

At the southern extremity of the long berg, fast bay-ice extended up to the land and for twenty miles across to the shelf on which the Winter Quarters of the Western Party had been situated. Further progress to the south was blocked, so our course was directed to the north along the western border of the berg.

When not engaged in sounding, dredging, or tow-netting members of the land party found endless diversion in trimming coal. Big inroads had been made in the supply of more than five hundred tons, and it now became necessary to shift many tons of it from the holds aft to the bunkers where it was accessible to the firemen. The work was good exercise, and every one enjoyed the shift below, "trucking" and "heaving." Another undoubted advantage, in the opinion of each worker, was that he could at least demand a wash from Chief Engineer Gillies, who at other times was forced to be thrifty with hot fresh water.

After supper on the 28th it was evident that we had reached a point where the shelf-ice veered away to the eastward and a wide tract of adhering sea-ice barred the way. The floe was exceedingly heavy and covered with a deep layer of soft snow. Emperor and Adelie penguins, crab-eater and Weddell seals were recognized through glasses along its edge. As there was a light obscuring fog and dusk was approaching, the *Aurora* "hung up" for the night.

On January 29 the ship, after a preliminary trawling had been done in three hundred and twenty fathoms, pushed into the floe and was made fast with an ice-anchor. Emperor penguins were so plentiful in the neighbourhood that many specimens were secured for skins.

A sea-leopard was seen chasing a crab-eater seal quite close to the bow of the ship. The latter, after several narrow escapes, took refuge on an ice-foot projecting from the edge of the floe.

Advantage was taken of a clearing in the weather to walk over the sea-ice to a berg two and a half miles away, from the summit of which it was hoped that some sign of land might be apparent. Away in the distance, perhaps five miles further on, could be seen an immense congregation of Emperor Penguins—evidently another rookery. No certain land was visible.

The cruise was now continued to the north-west in order to skirt a collection of bergs and floe, with the ultimate object of proceeding in an easterly direction towards Termination Ice-Tongue at the northern limit of the Shackleton Shelf-Ice.

A glance at the map which illustrates the work done by the Western Party affords the best idea of the great ice-formation which stretches away to the north of Queen Mary Land. It is very similar in character to the well-known Ross Barrier over which lay part of Scott's and Amundsen's journeys to the South Pole. Its height is remarkably uniform, ranging from sixty to one hundred feet above the water-level. When allowance has been made for average specific gravity, its average total thickness should approximate to six hundred feet. From east to west the formation was proved to be as much as two hundred miles, with one hundred and eighty miles between its northern and southern limits.

This vast block of ice originates fundamentally from the glacial flow over the southern hinterland. Every year an additional layer of consolidated snow is added to its surface by the frequent blizzards. These annual additions are clearly marked in the section exposed on the dazzling white face near the brink of the ice-cliff. There is a limit, however, to the increase in thickness, for the whole mass is ever moving slowly to the north, driven by the irresistible pressure of the land-ice behind it. Thus the northern face crumbles down into brash or floats away as part of a berg severed from the main body of the shelf-ice.

On the morning of January 30 we had the unique experience of witnessing this crumbling action at work—a cataclysm of snow, ice and water! The ship was steaming along within three hundred yards of a cliff,

Emperor Penguins Follow the Leader & Jumping on to the Floe (2)

when some loose drifts slid off from its edge, followed by a slice of the face extending for many hundreds of feet and weighing perhaps one million tons. It plunged into the sea with a deep booming roar and then rose majestically, shedding great masses of snow, to roll onwards exposing its blue, swaying bulk shivering into lumpy masses which pushed towards the ship in an ever-widening field of ice. It was a grand scene enacted in the subdued limelight of an overcast day.

During the afternoon the *Aurora* changed her north-westerly course round to north-east, winding through a wonderful sea of bergs grounded in about one hundred and twenty fathoms of water. At times we would pass through narrow lanes between towering walls and emerge into a straight wide avenue along which these mountains of ice were ranged. Several were rather remarkable; one for its exquisite series of stratification lines, another for its facade in stucco, and a third for its overhanging cornice fringed with slender icicles.

On January 31 a trawling was made in one hundred and twelve fathoms. Half a ton of life emptied on the deck gave the biologists occupation for several days. Included in the catch were a large number of monstrous gelatinous ascidians or "sea-squirts." Fragments of coal were once more found; an indication that coaly strata must be very widely distributed in the Antarctic.

The pack was dense and in massive array at the extremity of Termination Ice-Tongue. Davis drove the ship through some of it and entered an open lead which ran like a dark streak away to the east amid ice which grew heavier and more marked by the stress of pressure.

Our time was now limited and it seemed to me that there was little chance of reaching open water by forcing a passage either to the east or north. We therefore turned on our tracks and broke south-west back into the Davis Sea, intending to steam westward to the spot where we had so easily entered two weeks previously.

On February 4 the pack to the north was beginning to thin out and to look navigable. Several short-cuts were taken across projecting "capes," and then on February 5 the *Aurora* entered a zone of bergs and broken floe. No one slept well during that night as the ship bumped and ground into the ice which crashed and grated along her stout sides. Davis was on watch for long hours, directing in the crow's nest or down on the bridge, and throughout the next day we pushed on northwards towards the goal which now meant so much to us—Australia—Home!

At four o'clock the sun was glittering on the great ocean outside the pack-ice. Many of us climbed up in the rigging to see the fair sight—a prevision of blue skies and the calm delights of a land of eternal summer. Our work was finished, and the good ship was rising at last to the long swell of the southern seas.

On February 12, in latitude 55° S, a strong south-wester drove behind, and, with all sails set, the *Aurora* made eight knots an hour. The last iceberg was seen far away on the eastern horizon. Albatrosses followed in our wake, accompanied by their smaller satellites—Cape hens, priors, Lesson's and Wilson petrels.

Before leaving the ice, Sandell and Bickerton had fixed an aerial between the fore and mizen masts, while the former installed a wireless receiving-apparatus within the narrow limits of his cabin. There was no space on the ship to set up the motor-engine, dynamos and other instruments necessary for transmitting messages over a long distance.

As the nights began to darken, Sandell listened eagerly for distant signals, until on February 16, in latitude 47° S, the "calls" of three ships in the vicinity of the Great Australian Bight were recognized. After this date news was picked up every night, and all the items were posted on a morning bulletin pinned up in the ward-room.

The first real touch of civilization came unexpectedly early on the morning of February 21. A full-rigged ship on the southern horizon! It might have been an iceberg, the sails flashed so white in the morning sun. But onward it came with a strong south-wester, overhauled and passed us, signalling "*Archibald Russell*, fifty-four days out from Buenos Ayres, bound for Cape Borda." It was too magical to believe.

On February 26 we gazed on distant cliffs of rock and earth—Kangaroo Island—and the tiny cluster of dwellings round the lighthouse at Cape Borda. Then we entered St. Vincent's Gulf on a clear, hot day, marvelling at the sandy-blue water, the long, flat mainland with its clumps of trees and the smoke of many steamers.

The welcome home—the voices of innumerable strangers—the hand-grips of many friend—it chokes one—it cannot be uttered!

Appendix I

THE STAFF
The Ship's Officers

J. K. Davis	Master of SY *Aurora* and Second in Command of the Expedition.
J. H. Blair	First Officer during the later stages of the Expedition.
P. Gray	Second Officer.
C. P. de la Motte	Third Officer.
F. J. Gillies	Chief Engineer.

Macquarie Island Party

G. F. Ainsworth	Leader: Meteorologist.
L. R. Blake	Geologist and Cartographer.
H. Hamilton	Biologist.
C. A. Sandell	Wireless Operator and Mechanic.
A. J. Sawyer	Wireless Operator.

Main Base Party

Dr. D. Mawson	Commander of the Expedition.
Lieut. R. Bage	Astronomer, Assistant Magnetician and Recorder of Tides.
C. T. Madigan	Meteorologist.
Lieut. B. E. S. Ninnis	In charge of Greenland dogs.
Dr. X. Mertz	In charge of Greenland dogs.
Dr. A. L. McLean	Chief Medical Officer, Bacteriologist.
F. H. Bickerton	In charge of air-tractor sledge.
A. J. Hodgeman	Cartographer and Sketch Artist.
J. F. Hurley	Official Photographer.
E. N. Webb	Chief Magnetician.

P. E. Correll	Mechanic and Assistant Physicist.
J. G. Hunter	Biologist.
C. F. Laseron	Taxidermist and Biological Collector.
F. L. Stillwell	Geologist.
H. D. Murphy	In charge of Expedition stores.
W. H. Hannam	Wireless Operator and Mechanic.
J. H. Close	Assistant Collector.
Dr. L. A. Whetter	Surgeon.

Western Base Party

F. Wild	Leader.
A. D. Watson	Geologist.
Dr. S. E. Jones	Medical Officer.
C. T. Harrisson	Biologist.
M. H. Moyes	Meteorologist.
A. L. Kennedy	Magnetician.
C. A. Hoadley	Geologist.
G. Dovers	Cartographer.

In addition to these were the following gentlemen who accompanied the Expedition for a portion of the time only or who joined later.

S. N. Jeffryes	Wireless Operator, who relieved W. H. Hannam during 1913.
E. R. Waite	(Curator, Canterbury Museum, Christchurch), Biologist, first Sub-Antarctic cruise of *Aurora*.
Professor T. T. Flynn	(Hobart University), Biologist, second Sub-Antarctic cruise of *Aurora*.
J. van Waterschoot van der Gracht	Marine Artist, second Antarctic cruise of *Aurora*.
	Whaling Authority, second Antarctic cruise of *Aurora*.
Captain James Davis	Secretary, second Antarctic cruise of *Aurora*.
C. C. Eitel	Served in the capacity of Chief Officer
N. C. Toucher, and later F. D. Fletcher	on the *Aurora* during the earlier voyages.

G. F. AINSWORTH, thirty** years of age, single, was born in Sydney, New South Wales. His services were loaned to the expedition by the Commonwealth Meteorological Bureau, Melbourne. For a period of two years he acted as leader of the Macquarie Island Party, carrying out the duties of Meteorologist. In the summer of 1913–1914 he visited the Antarctic during the final cruise of the *Aurora*.

R. BAGE, twenty-three years of age, single, was a graduate in Engineering of Melbourne University and a lieutenant in the Royal Australian Engineers. A member of the Main Base Party (Adelie Land) and leader of the Southern Sledging Party, he remained in the Antarctic for two years. During the first year he was in charge of chronometers, astronomical observations and tidal records, and throughout the second year continued the magnetic work and looked after stores.

F. H. BICKERTON, F.R.G.S., twenty-two years of age, single, was born at Oxford, England. Had studied engineering: joined the Expedition as Electrical Engineer and Motor Expert. A member of the Main Base Party and leader of the Western Sledging Party, he remained in the Antarctic for two years, during which time he was in charge of the air-tractor sledge, and was engineer to the wireless station. For a time, during the second year, he was in complete charge of the wireless plant.

J. H. BLAIR, twenty-four years of age, single, was born in Scotland. For five years he served with the Loch Line of Glasgow as apprentice and third mate. As second mate he joined A. Currie and Company, of Melbourne, in the Australian-Indian trade, reaching the rank of first mate, in which capacity he acted during the final Antarctic cruise of the *Aurora* in the summer of 1913–14.

L. R. BLAKE, twenty-one years of age, single, was born in England, but had lived for many years in Queensland previous to joining the Expedition. Before accompanying the Macquarie Island Party as Geologist and Cartographer, he obtained leave from the Geological Survey Department, Brisbane. He visited the Antarctic during the final cruise of the *Aurora* in the summer of 1913–1914.

J. H. Close, F.R.G.S., forty years of age, married, was born in Sydney, New South Wales. During the South African War he saw active service in Rhodesia, and at the time of the Expedition's departure was a teacher of physical culture at Sydney. A member of the Main Base Party (Adelie Land)

and of several sledging parties, he spent two summers and one winter in the Antarctic.

P. E. CORRELL, nineteen years of age, single, was a student in Science of the Adelaide University. He joined the Expedition as Mechanician and Assistant Physicist. He was a member of the Main Base Party accompanying the Eastern Coastal Party during their sledging journey. He spent three summers and one winter in the Antarctic, acting as colour photographer during the final cruise of the *Aurora*.

J. E. DAVIS, twenty-eight years of age, single, was master of the *Aurora* and Second-in-Command of the Expedition. Born in Ireland and educated in England, he served his apprenticeship on the Liverpool owned sailing-ship, *Celtic Chief*, obtaining his certificate as second mate before joining the barque *Westland* trading between England and New Zealand. His next post was that of second officer on the training ship *Port Jackson*, following which he joined Sir Ernest Shackleton's Expedition (1907–1909) as chief officer of the *Nimrod*, acting subsequently as master. Throughout the whole period of the Australasian Antarctic Expedition (1911–1914) Captain J. K. Davis commanded the *Aurora* during five cruises.

G. DOVERS, twenty-one years of age, single, of Sydney, New South Wales, was completing his term for Licensed Surveyor in the service of the Commonwealth Government when he joined the Expedition. He was in the Antarctic for two summers and one winter, being stationed with the Western Party (Queen Mary Land). A member of several sledging parties, he acted as Cartographer to the party which reached Gaussberg.

F. J. GILLIES, thirty-five years of age, single, was born at Cardiff, Wales. He served his apprenticeship as an engineer on the steamers of John Shearman and Company and P. Baker and Company of Cardiff. For six years previous to joining the Expedition he was in the Indian trade. Throughout the five cruises of the *Aurora* between 1911 and 1914 F. J. Gillies was Chief Engineer.

P. GRAY, twenty-two years of age, single, was born and educated in England. He served on the *Worcester* as cadet captain for eighteen months and as apprentice on the *Archibald Russell*, of Glasgow, and in the New Zealand Shipping Company. In 1909 he entered the Peninsula and Oriental Company and reached the rank of third officer, joining the Australasian

Antarctic Expedition as second officer of the *Aurora*. Throughout five cruises, from 1911 to 1914, he served in this capacity.

H. HAMILTON, twenty-six years of age, single, was born at Napier, New Zealand. Graduate of the Otago University. Besides being employed on the New Zealand Geological Survey, he acted as Entomological Collector to the Dominion Museum at Wellington. A member of the Macquarie Island Party, of which he was the Biologist for two years, H. Hamilton visited the Antarctic during the final cruise of the *Aurora* in the summer of 1913–1914.

W. H. HANNAM, twenty-six years of age, single, was of Sydney, New South Wales, and joined the Expedition in charge of the arrangements for a wireless telegraphic system. He was in the Antarctic at the Main Base (Adelie Land) for two summers and a winter, and was successful in transmitting wireless messages for a short time during 1912 through Macquarie Island to Australia, assistant magnetician for a time.

C. T. HARRISSON, forty-three years of age, married, was born in Hobart, Tasmania. For many years previous to joining the Expedition he had done illustrative and artistic work and had been engaged on a survey and in botanical and other scientific observations on the west coast of Tasmania. Stationed with the Western Base (Queen Mary Land) he acted as Biologist and Artist, accompanying F. Wild on his main eastern journey and several other sledging parties.

C. A. HOADLEY, twenty-four years of age, single, was a graduate in Mining Engineering of Melbourne University. A member of F. Wild's Western Party (Queen Mary Land), he took part in several sledging journeys and was Geologist of the party who explored westwards to Gaussberg.

A. J. HODGEMAN, twenty-six years of age, single, was born at Adelaide, South Australia. For four years he was an articled architect, and for five years a draughtsman in the Works and Buildings Department, Adelaide. A member of the Main Base Party (Adelie Land), he took part in several sledging journeys, and throughout two years in the Antarctic acted in the capacity of Cartographer and Sketch Artist, as well as that of Assistant Meteorologist.

J. G. HUNTER, twenty-three years of age, single, was a graduate in Science of Sydney University, New South Wales. A member of the Main Base Party

(Adelie Land) he carried on the work of Biologist during two summers and one winter; and in the same capacity accompanied the *Aurora* in her final summer cruise 1911–1914.

J. F. HURLEY, twenty-four years of age, single, was of Sydney, New South Wales. He had been the recipient of many amateur and professional awards for photographic work before joining the Expedition. At the Main Base he obtained excellent photographic and cinematographic records and was one of the three members of the Southern Sledging Party. He was also present on the final cruise of the *Aurora*.

S. N. JEFFRYES, twenty-seven years of age, single, of Towoomba, Queensland, was a qualified operator of the Australasian Wireless Company. During the second year (1913) he took W. H. Hannam's place in charge of the wireless plant, wintering at the Main Base (Adelie Land).

S. E. JONES, twenty-four years of age, single, was a graduate in Medicine of Sydney University, New South Wales. A member and Medical Officer of F. Wild's Western Base (Queen Mary Land), he took part in several sledging journeys during 1912 and was leader of the party who explored westward to Gaussberg.

A. L. KENNEDY, twenty-two years of age, single, was a student in Science of Adelaide University, South Australia. Receiving special tuition, he acted as Magnetician at the Western Base (Queen Mary Land) during the year 1912. He was a member of several sledging parties and accompanied F. Wild on his main eastern journey as Cartographer.

C. F. LASERON, twenty-five years of age, single, had gained a Diploma in Geology at the Technical College, Sydney, New South Wales, and for some years was Collector to the Technological Museum. At the Main Base (Adelie Land), during 1912, he acted as Taxidermist and general Collector, taking part, as well, in sledging journeys to the south and east of Winter Quarters.

C. T. MADIGAN, twenty-three years of age, single, was a graduate in Science (Mining Engineering) of Adelaide University, South Australia. Through the courtesy of the Trustees of the Rhodes Scholarship, the necessary leave to accompany the Expedition was granted just as he was on the eve of continuing his studies at Oxford University. A member of the Main Base

Party (Adelie Land) he acted as Meteorologist for two years, and during the second year (1913) was also in charge of the Greenland dogs. An important journey in the spring and one to the east in the summer were made under his leadership, and the Party, left in Adelie Land in 1913, was to have been under his charge, but for my return.

D. MAWSON, thirty years of age, single, was the Organiser and Leader of the Australasian Antarctic Expedition and was, previous to it, a member of Sir Ernest Shackleton's Antarctic Expedition of 1907–1909, being one of the party under Professor David which reached the South Magnetic Pole. A graduate in Science and Engineering of Sydney and Adelaide Universities, he had filled for some time the post of Lecturer in Mineralogy and Petrology at the Adelaide University. The only survivor of a party sledging to the east from the Main Base in the summer of 1912–1913.

A. L. McLEAN, twenty-six years of age, single, was a graduate in Arts and Medicine of Sydney University, New South Wales. He acted as Chief Medical Officer at the Main Base (Adelie Land) and carried out observations in Bacteriology and Physiology during the first year. In 1913 (the second year) he was Biologist, Ice-Carrier and Editor of the *Adelie Blizzard*. He took part in a sledging journey along the eastern coast in the summer of 1912–1913.

X. MERTZ, twenty-eight years of age, single, of Basle, Switzerland, was a graduate in Law of the Universities of Leipzig and Berne. Prior to joining the Expedition he had gained the Ski-running Championship of Switzerland and was an experienced mountaineer. At the Main Base (Adelie Land) he was assisted by B. E. S. Ninnis in the care of the Greenland dogs. On January 7, 1913, during a sledging journey, he lost his life, one hundred miles south-east of Winter Quarters.

C. P. DE LA MOTTE, nineteen years of age, single, of Bulli, New South Wales, had early training at sea on the barque *Northern Chief* of New Zealand, obtaining his certificate as second mate in March 1911. During the eight months prior to joining the Expedition he served as fourth officer on the SS *Warrimoo* of the Union Steamship Company of New Zealand. Throughout the five cruises of the *Aurora* between 1911 and 1914, C. P. de la Motte was third officer with the Ship's party.

M. H. MOYES, twenty-five years of age, single, of Koolunga, South Australia, was a graduate in Science of Adelaide University. With the

Western Base Party (Queen Mary Land) he acted as Meteorologist and took part in several sledging journeys in the autumn and spring of 1912. During the summer of 1912–1913, through an unavoidable accident, he was left to carry on work alone at Winter Quarters for a period of nine weeks.

H. D. MURPHY, thirty-two years of age, single, of Melbourne, one-time Scholar in History of Oxford University. At the outset he was to have been leader of a third Antarctic Base which was eventually amalgamated with the Main Base (Adelie Land). Here he had charge of the stores and during the early summer of 1912 was leader of the Southern Supporting Party.

B. E. S. NINNIS, twenty-three years of age, single, was educated at Dulwich, England, and entered His Majesty's Army, having a commission as Lieutenant in the Royal Fusiliers prior to joining the Expedition in London. At the Main Base (Adelie Land) he was assisted by X. Mertz in the care of the Greenland dogs. On December 14, 1912, while on a sledging journey, he lost his life by falling into a crevasse three hundred miles east of Winter Quarters.

C. A. SANDELL, twenty-five years of age, single, of Surrey, England, studied electrical engineering for some years and then came to Australia in 1909 and entered the Commonwealth Branch of Telephony. Having a practical knowledge of wireless telegraphy he joined the Expedition as a Wireless Operator and Mechanic and was stationed with the Macquarie Island Party for two years. After the departure of A. J. Sawyer in August 1913, he was in complete charge of the wireless station. C. A. Sandell visited the Antarctic during the final cruise of the *Aurora* in the summer of 1913–1914.

A. J. SAWYER, twenty-six years of age, single, was born in New Zealand. Having had considerable experience in wireless telegraphy, he joined the Expedition as an operator from the Australasian Wireless Company. At the Macquarie Island Station he was chief wireless until August 1913, when on account of illness he returned to New Zealand.

F. L. STILLWELL, twenty-three years of age, single, was a graduate in Science of Melbourne University, Victoria. A member of the Main Base Party (Adelie Land) he acted as Geologist. F. L. Stillwell was leader of two sledging parties who did detail work for about sixty miles along the coast eastward of Winter Quarters.

A. D. WATSON, twenty-four years of age, single, was a graduate in Science of Sydney University, New South Wales. A member of the Western Base Party (Queen Mary Land) he acted as Geologist. A. D. Watson took part in several sledging journeys, accompanying F. Wild in his main eastern trip during the summer of 1912–1913.

E. N. WEBB, twenty-two years of age, single, was an Associate of Civil Engineering of Canterbury University College, and, for the five months previous to joining the Expedition, carried out magnetic observations under the Carnegie Institute of Washington, U.S.A. At the Main Base (Adelie Land) E. N. Webb was Chief Magnetician, accompanying the Southern Sledging Party.

L. A. WHETTER, twenty-nine years of age, single. He graduated at Otago University, New Zealand, and joined the Expedition as Surgeon, acting in that capacity at the Main Base (Adelie Land) during 1912. He accompanied a sledging party which explored to the westward of Winter Quarters.

F. WILD, thirty-eight years of age, single, was Leader of the Western Base Party (Queen Mary Land). He joined the Merchant Service in 1889 and the Navy in 1900, served on an extended sledge journey during the National Antarctic Expedition (Capt. R. F. Scott) of 1901–1904, and was one of the Southern Party of Sir Ernest Shackleton's Expedition from 1907–1909. During the Australasian Expedition he opened up a new tract of country— Queen Mary Land.

I desire to make special mention of the Ship's Party who faced the rigorous conditions of Antarctica and the stormy Southern Ocean, during five separate voyages, with a cheerfulness and devotion to duty which will always stand to their lasting credit. In regions of heavy pack-ice and sudden blizzard winds, Captain Davis piloted the Ship safely through many situations of extreme danger. In a report to me on the work of the Ship he writes an appreciative note:--

"I wish to draw particular attention to the loyal way in which the officers and men of the *Aurora* supported me. Messrs. Toucher, Fletcher, Blair, Gray, de la Motte, and Gillies, in their respective positions, carried out the duties assigned to them with ability and cheerfulness, often under very trying conditions.

Signatures of Members of the Land Parties

"Mr. Gillies not only looked after the engines but assisted materially in the deep-sea work by the invention of a new form of sounding driver which was used successfully during the various cruises of the *Aurora*.

"The Chief Officer was in charge of the stores and equipment of the Expedition on board the vessel, in addition to his ordinary executive duties. Messrs. Toucher, Fletcher and Blair served in this capacity on different voyages.

"Mr. P. Gray, as Second and Navigating Officer, and Mr. C. P. de la Motte, as Third Officer, acted capably and thoroughly throughout the Expedition."

Cape Hunter, Composed of Ancient Sedimentary Rocks (Phyllites)

Appendix II

Scientific Work

IT SHOULD BE REMARKED THAT THERE IS NO intention of furnishing anything more than a suggestion of the general trend of the scientific observations of the Expedition. The brief statement made below indicates the broad lines on which the work was conducted and in some cases the ground which was actually covered. It may thus give the general reader a clue to the nature of the scientific volumes which will serve to record permanently the results amassed during a period of more than two years.

Terrestrial Magnetism

1. *Field Work.*

(*a*) Dip determinations were made at Macquarie Island, on the eastern and southern journeys from the Main Base (Adelie Land) and on a short journey from the Western Base (Queen Mary Land).

(*b*) Declination by theodolite observations was determined at Macquarie Island and at intervals on all sledging journeys in the Antarctic.

(*c*) Rough observations of magnetic variation were made daily on the *Aurora* during her five cruises.

2. *Station Work.*

(*a*) Regular magnetograph records were kept at the Main Base (Adelie Land) for a period of eighteen months. A system of term days for quick runs was also followed; Melbourne, Christchurch, and other stations co-operating. In connexion with the magnetograph work, Webb conducted regular, absolute observations throughout the year 1912. Bage continued the magnetograph records for a further six months in 1913, observed term days, and took absolute observations.

(*b*) At the Western Base (Queen Mary Land) Kennedy kept term days in the winter, using a magnetometer and dip-circle.

Biology

1. *Station Collections.*

(*a*) At Macquarie Island, Hamilton worked for two years amongst a rich fauna and a scanty but interesting flora. Amongst other discoveries a finch indigenous to Macquarie Island was found.

(*b*) In Adelie Land, Hunter, assisted by Laseron, secured a large biological collection, notwithstanding the continuous bad weather. Dredgings from depths down to fifty fathoms were made during the winter. The eggs of practically all the flying birds known along Antarctic shores were obtained, including those of the silver-grey petrel and the Antarctic petrel, which were not previously known; also a variety of prion, of an unrecorded species, together with its eggs.

(*c*) At the Western Base (Queen Mary Land) eggs of the Antarctic and other petrels were found, and a large rookery of Emperor penguins was located; the second on record. Harrisson, working under difficulties, succeeded in trapping some interesting fish on the bottom in two hundred and fifty fathoms of water.

2. *Ship Collections.*

(*a*) A collection made by Mr. E. R. Waite, Curator of the Canterbury Museum, on the first Sub-Antarctic cruise.

(*b*) A collection made by Professor T. T. Flynn, of Hobart, on the second Sub-Antarctic cruise.

(*c*) A collection made by Hunter, assisted by Hamilton, in Antarctic waters during the summer of 1913–1914. This comprised deep-sea dredgings at eleven stations in depths down to one thousand eight hundred fathoms and regular tow-nettings, frequently serial, to depths of two hundred fathoms. Six specimens of the rare Ross seal were secured. A large collection of external and internal parasites was made from birds, seals and fish.

Geology

(*a*) A geological examination of Macquarie Island was made by Blake. The older rocks were found to be all igneous. The Island has been overridden in comparatively recent times by an ice-cap travelling from west to east.

(*b*) Geological collections at the Main Base. In Adelie Land the rocky outcrops are metamorphic sediments and gneisses. In King George V Land there is a formation similar to the Beacon sandstones and dolerites of the Ross Sea, with which carbonaceous shales and coaly strata are associated.

(*c*) Stillwell met with a great range of minerals and rocks in the terminal moraine near Winter Quarters, Adelie Land. Amongst them was red sandstone in abundance, suggesting that the Beacon sandstone formation extends also throughout Adelie Land but is hidden by the ice-cap. A solitary stony meteorite was found by a sledging party lying on the ice of the plateau.

(*d*) In the collections made by Watson and Hoadley at the Western Base (Queen Mary Land) gneisses and schists were ascertained to be the predominant types.

(*e*) A collection of erratics was brought up by the deep-sea trawl in the course of dredgings in Antarctic waters.

Glaciology

(*a*) Observations of the pack-ice, coastal glaciers and shelf-ice from the *Aurora* during her three Antarctic cruises.

(*b*) Observations of the niveous and glacial features met with on the sledging journeys from both Antarctic bases.

Meteorology

(*a*) Two years' observations at Macquarie Island by Ainsworth

(*b*) Two years' observations in Adelie Land by Madigan.

(*c*) One year's observations in Queen Mary Land by Moyes.

(*d*) Observations by the Ship on each of her five voyages.

(*e*) Observations during the many sledging journeys from both Antarctic Bases.

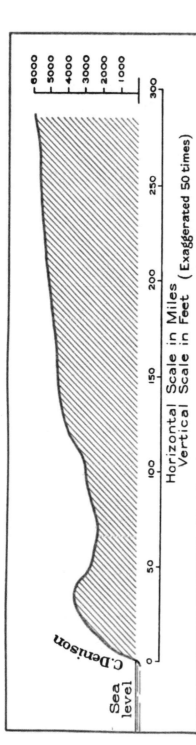

A Section of the Antarctic Plateau from the Coast to a Point Three Hundred Miles Inland, Along the Route Followed by the Southern Sledging Party (Adelie Land)

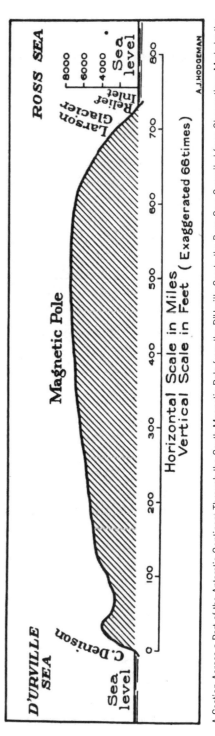

A.J.HODGEMAN

A Section Across a Part of the Antarctic Continent Through the South Magnetic Pole from the D'Urville Sea to the Ross Sea; Compiled from Observations Made by the British Antarctic Expedition (1907–1909) and by the Australasian Antarctic Expedition (1911–1914)

Bacteriology, etc.

In Adelie Land, McLean carried out many months of steady work in Bacteriology, Haematology and Physiology.

Tides

Self-recording instruments were run at Macquarie Island by Ainsworth and at Adelie Land by Bage.

Examples of Antarctic Marine Crustaceans

Wireless and Auroral Observations

A very close watch was kept upon auroral phenomena with interesting results, especially in their relation to the "permeability" of the ether to wireless waves.

Geographical Results

1. The successful navigation by the *Aurora* of the Antarctic pack ice in a fresh sphere of action, where the conditions were practically unknown, resulting in the discovery of new lands and islands.
2. Journeys were made over the sea-ice and on the coastal and upland plateau in regions hitherto unsurveyed. At the Main Base (Adelie Land) the journeys aggregated two thousand four hundred miles, and at the Western Base (Queen Mary Land) the aggregate was eight hundred miles. These figures do not include depot journeys, the journeys of supporting parties, or the many miles of relay work. The land was mapped in through 33° of longitude, 27° of which were covered by sledging parties.
3. The employment of wireless telegraphy in the fixation of a fundamental meridian in Adelie Land.
4. The mapping of Macquarie Island.

Oceanography

1. By soundings the fringe of the Antarctic Continent as well as the Continental Shelf has been indicated through 55° of longitude.
2. The configuration of the floor of the ocean southward of Australia and between Macquarie Island and the Auckland Islands has been broadly ascertained.
3. Much has been done in the matter of sea-water temperatures and salinities.

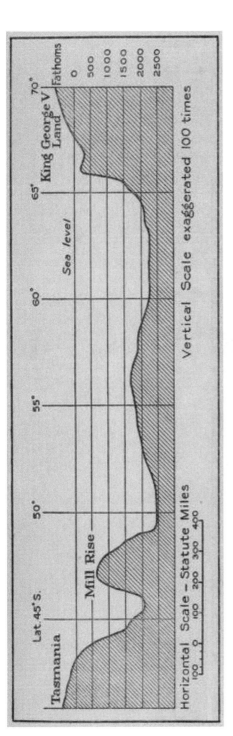

A Section of the Floor of the Southern Ocean between Tasmania and King George V Land

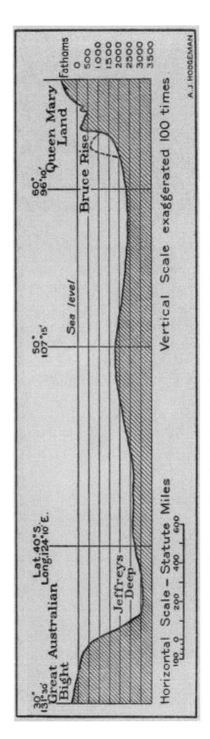

A Section of the Floor of the Southern Ocean between Western Australia and Queen Mary Land

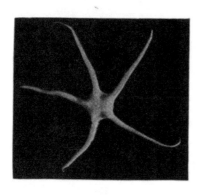

A "Cushion Star"

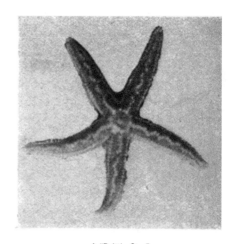

A "Brittle Star"

A "Haul" in 220 Fathoms off Queen Mary Land

A Starfish

Appendix III

An Historical Summary**

1775. James Cook circumnavigated the Globe in high southern latitudes, discovering the sub-antarctic island of South Georgia. He was the first to cross the Antarctic Circle.

1819. William Smith, the master of a merchant vessel trading between Montevideo and Valparaiso, discovered the South Shetland Islands.

1819. Fabian Gottlieb von Bellingshausen, despatched in command of an Expedition by the Emperor, Alexander I of Russia, with instructions to supplement the voyage of Captain Cook, circumnavigated the Antarctic continent in high southern latitudes. The first discovery of land south of the Antarctic Circle was made, namely, Peter I Island and Alexander I Land (also an island), in the American Quadrant of Antarctica.

1820. Nathaniel Palmer, master of an American sealing-vessel, sighted new land to the south of the South Shetland Islands. It seems clear that he was the first to view what is now known as the Palmer Archipelago (1820–21).

1823. James Weddell, a British sealer, sailing southward of the Atlantic Ocean, reached 74° 15' south latitude in the American Quadrant, establishing a "farthest south" record.

** *For this compilation reference has been largely made to Dr. H. R. Mill's "The Siege of the South Pole." Several doubtful voyages during the early part of the nineteenth century have been omitted.*

1830. John Biscoe, a whaling master of the British firm of Enderby Brothers, sailed on a voyage circumnavigating the Antarctic Regions. Enderby Land was discovered south of the West Indian Ocean in the African Quadrant of Antarctica. This was apparently a part of the Antarctic continent. New land was also met with to the south of America and charted as Graham's Land, Biscoe Island and Adelaide Island.

Kemp, a sailing master of Enderby Brothers, extended Biscoe's discoveries shortly after by the report of land east of, and adjacent to, Enderby Land.

Neither of these discoveries has yet been proved, though Enderby Land (Biscoe) undoubtedly exists.

1837. Jules Sebastian Cesar Dumont D'Urville, was despatched by King Louis Philippe of France for the prosecution of scientific researches on a voyage round the World. His cruise in the Antarctic resulted in the charting of Joinville Island and Louis Philippe Land to the south of America (American Quadrant) and the discovery of a portion of the Antarctic continent, named Adelie Land, southward of Australia (Australian Quadrant).

1838. Charles Wilkes, United States Navy, in accordance with a bill passed by Congress, set out on an exploring expedition to circumnavigate the World. His programme included the investigation of the area of the Antarctic to the south of Australia--the Australian Quadrant. The squadron composing this American expedition first visited the Antarctic regions in the American Quadrant, and then proceeded eastward round to the Australian Quadrant from which, after a long cruise, they returned, reporting land at frequent intervals in the vicinity of the Antarctic Circle between longitudes 157° 46' E. and 106° 19' E. He shares with D'Urville the full honour of the discovery of Adelie Land. Some of the supposed landfalls known to be non-existent.

1839. John Balleny, another of Enderby's whaling captains, discovered the Balleny Islands within the Antarctic Circle, in the Australian Quadrant of Antarctica, and gave a vague description of an appearance of land to the westward. This has been charted on maps, without adequate evidence, as Sabrina Land.

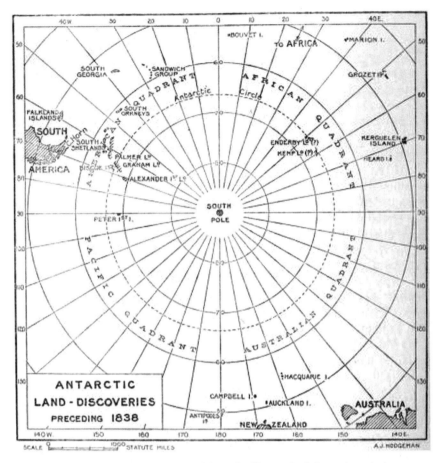

1839. James Clark Ross proceeded south in charge of a scientific expedition fitted out by the Admiralty at the instance of the British Association for the Advancement of Science and approved of by the Royal Society. His aim was to circumnavigate the Antarctic regions and to investigate the Weddell Sea. The geographical results were fruitful; the Ross Sea, the Admiralty Range and the Great Ice Barrier were discovered and some eight hundred miles of Antarctic coastline were broadly delineated.

1844. T. E. L. Moore was detailed by the Admiralty to supplement the magnetic work of Ross and to explore to the southward of Africa and of the Indian Ocean, but no additions were made to geographical knowledge.

1872. Eduard Dallmann, whilst engaged in whaling with a German steamer to the southward of America, added some details to the map of the Palmer Archipelago but did not go further south than 64° 45' S. latitude.

1874. The *Challenger* scientific expedition, under the command of George Strong Nares, in the course of their voyage from the Cape to Australia during the circumnavigation of the World penetrated within the Antarctic Circle in longitude 78° 22' E.

1892. A fleet of four Scottish whalers cruised through the north western part of the Weddell Sea. Scientific observations were made by W. S. Bruce and others, but no geographical discoveries were recorded.

1892. C. A. Larsen, master of a Hamburg whaler, added important details to the geography of the American Quadrant of Antarctica on the western side of the Weddell Sea.

1894. Evensen, master of another Hamburg whaler, brought back further information of the American Quadrant on the Pacific Ocean side.

1895. H. J. Bull organized a whaling venture and with Leonard Kristensen, master of the ship, revisited the Ross Sea area where a landing was made at Cape Adare (Australian Quadrant). This was the first occasion on which any human being had set foot on the Antarctic continent.

1897. Adrien de Gerlache sailed from Belgium on a scientific exploring expedition to the American Quadrant. Important additions were made to the map, but the ship became frozen into the pack-ice and drifted about for a whole year south of the Antarctic Circle. The members of this expedition were the first to experience an Antarctic winter. Antarctic exploration now entered upon a new era.

1898. Carstens Egeberg Borchgrevink led an expedition, fitted out by Sir George Newnes; its objective being the Ross Sea area. Further details were added to the map, but the most notable fact was that the expedition wintered at Cape Adare, on the mainland itself. The Great Ross Barrier was determined to be thirty miles south of the position assigned by Ross in 1839.

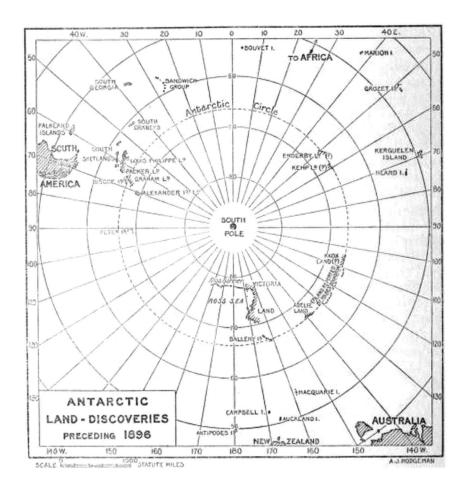

ANTARCTIC
LAND - DISCOVERIES
PRECEDING 1896

1898. Chun of Leipsig, in charge of the *Valdivia* Expedition, carried out oceanographical researches far to the south, in the vicinity of Enderby Land (African Quadrant), though he did not come within sight of the continent.

1901. Robert Falcon Scott, in command of the *Discovery* Expedition, organised by the Royal Geographical Society and Royal Society with the co-operation of the Admiralty, in accordance with a scheme of international endeavour, passed two winters at the southern extremity of the Ross Sea and carried out many successful sledging journeys. Their main geographical achievements were: the discovery of King Edward VII Land; several hundred miles of new land on a "farthest south" sledging journey to latitude 82° 17' S.; the discovery of the Antarctic plateau; additional details and original contributions to the geography of the lands and islands of the Ross Sea.

1901. A German national expedition, led by Erich von Drygalski, set out for the region south of the Indian Ocean. After a small party had been stationed on Kerguelen Island, the main party proceeded south close to the tracks of the *Challenger.* They came within sight of Antarctic shores but were frozen into the pack-ice for a whole year. Kaiser Wilhelm II Land was discovered close to the junction between the Australian and African Quadrants.

1901. A Swedish national expedition, planned and led by Otto Nordenskjold, wintered for two years on Snow Hill Island in the American Quadrant, and did much valuable scientific work.

1902. William Speirs Bruce organized and led a Scottish expedition to the Weddell Sea, southward of the Atlantic Ocean. The party effected notable oceanographic researches and wintered at the South Orkney Islands, but were foiled in their attempt to penetrate the pack-ice. During the second season, conditions were more favourable and the ship reached Coats Land in 74° 1' S. latitude.

1903. Jean Charcot organized and led a French expedition to the American Quadrant and there added many details to the existing chart.

1907. Ernest Henry Shackleton organized and led a British expedition with the main object of reaching the South Geographical Pole. His party wintered at Cape Royds, McMurdo Sound, and two main sledging parties set out in the early summer. E. H. Shackleton's party ascended the Antarctic plateau and penetrated to within ninety seven geographical miles of the South Pole, discovering new land beyond Scott's "farthest south." T. W. Edgeworth David's party reached the South Magnetic Polar Area, filling in many details of the western coast of McMurdo Sound.

1908. Jean Charcot organized and led a second French expedition to extend the work accomplished in 1903 in the American Quadrant. He was successful in discovering new land still further to the south. Loubet, Fallieres and Charcot Lands, towards and beyond Alexander I Land, were added to the map of Antarctica.

1910. Roald Amundsen organized an expedition for scientific research in the vicinity of the North Pole but changed his plans, eventually heading for the

South Pole. The expedition wintered on the Ross Barrier near King Edward VII Land, from which point he set out and attained the South Geographical Pole, mapping in new land on the way. Another party visited King Edward VII Land.

1910. Robert Falcon Scott led a second Antarctic expedition, the main object of which was to reach the South Geographical Pole. The principal party wintered near his old winter quarters at Hut Point, McMurdo Sound. A second party was landed at Cape Adare. Scott reached the Pole soon after the Norwegian Amundsen, but he and his party perished on the return journey. Other parties added details to the map of Victoria Land. Oates Land was sighted from the ship to the westward of Cape Adare in the Australian Quadrant.

1910. A Japanese expedition sailed to the Ross Sea, but on account of the lateness of the season was forced to turn back without landing. The winter was spent at Sydney, New South Wales. Next year a summer visit was made to the South, but no additional land discoveries were made.

1911. A German expedition, led by Wilhelm Filchner, proceeded to the Weddell Sea; the South Pole being its objective. The party succeeded in reaching further south in that region than any previous navigators and discovered new land, to be named Prince Luitpold Land. They were driven northwards amongst the pack in a blizzard and spent the winter frozen in south of Coats Land.

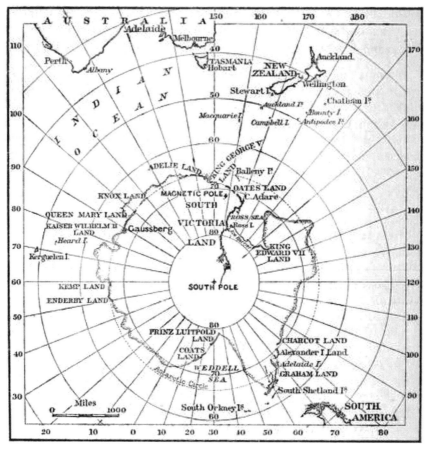

A Map of the Antarctic Regions as Known at the Present Day [1915]

Appendix IV

Glossary

Oceanography. The study of the ocean, including the shape and character of its bed, the temperature and salinity of the water at various depths, the force and set of its currents, and the nature of the creatures and plants which haunt its successive zones.

Névé. The compacted snow of a snow-field; a stage in the transition between soft, loose snow and glacier-ice.

Sastrugi. The waves caused by continuous winds blowing across the surface of an expanse of snow. These waves vary in size according to the force and continuity of the wind and the compactness of the snow. The word is of Russian derivation (from *zastruga* [sing.], *zastrugi* [pl.]), denoting snow-waves or the irregularities on the surface of roughly-planed wood.

Ice-foot. A sheath of ice adhering along the shores of polar lands. The formation may be composed of attached remnants of floe-ice, frozen sea-spray and drift-snow.

Nunatak. An island-like outcrop of rock projecting through a sheet of enveloping land-ice.

Shelf-ice. A thick, floating, fresh water ice-formation pushing out from the land and continuous with an extensive glacier. Narrow prolongations or peninsulas of the shelf-ice may be referred to as *ice-tongues* or *glacier-tongues*.

Barrier is a term which has been rather loosely applied in the literature of Antarctic Exploration. Formerly it was used to describe a formation, which is mainly shelf-ice, known as the Great Ross Barrier. Confusion arose when

"Barrier" came to be applied to the seaward ice-cliff (resting on rock) of an extensive sheet of land-ice and when it was also employed to designate a line of consolidated pack-ice. Spelt with a small "b" the term is a convenient one, so long as it carries its ordinary meaning; it seems unnecessary to give it a technical connotation.

Blizzard. A high wind at a low temperature, accompanied by drifting, not necessarily falling snow.

Floe or Floe-ice. The comparatively flat, frozen surface of the sea intersected by cracks and *leads* (channels of open water).

Pack or Pack-ice is a field of loose ice originating in the main from broken floe, to which may be added material from the disintegration of bergs, and bergs themselves.

Brash or Brash-ice. Small, floating fragments of ice—the debris of larger pieces—usually observed bordering a tract of pack-ice.

Bergschrund has been "freely rendered" in the description of the great cleft between the lower part of the Denman Glacier and the Shackleton Shelf-Ice (Queen Mary Land). In a typical glacier, "the upper portion is hidden by névé and often by freshly fallen snow and is smooth and unbroken. During the summer, when little snow falls, the body of the glacier moves away from the snow-field and a gaping crevasse of great depth is usually established, called a *Bergschrund,* which is sometimes taken as the upper limit of the glacier" ("Encyclopædia Britannica").

Sub-Antarctica. A general term used to denote the area of ocean, containing islands and encircling the Antarctic continent, between the vicinity of the 50th parallel of south latitude and the confines of the ice-covered sea.

Séracs are wedged masses of icy pinnacles which are produced in the surface of a glacier by dragging strains which operate on crevassed areas. A field of such pinnacles, jammed together in broken confusion, is called *sérac-ice.*

The following colloquial words or phrases occurring in the narrative were largely determined by general usage: To depot = to cache or to place a stock of provisions in a depot; drift = drift-snow; fifty-mile wind = a wind of fifty miles an hour; burberry = "Burberry gabardine" or specially prepared wind-proof clothing; whirly (pi. whirlies) = whirlwind carrying drift-snow and pursuing a devious track; night-watchman = night-watch; glaxo = "Glaxo" (a powder of dried milk); primus = primus stove used during sledging; hoosh = pemmican and plasmon biscuit "porridge"; tanks = canvas bags for holding sledging provisions; boil-up = sledging meal; ramp = bank of snow slanting away obliquely on the leeward side of an obstacle; radiant = an appearance noted in clouds (especially cirro-stratus) which seem to radiate from a point on the horizon.

The following appended list may be of biological interest:

BIRDS	AVES
Emperor penguin	*Aptenodytes forsteri*
King penguin	*Aptenodytes patagonica*
Adelie penguin	*Pygoscelis adelice*
Royal penguin	*Catarrhactes schlegeli*
Victoria penguin	*Catarrhactes pachyrynchus*
Gentoo or Rockhopper penguin	*Pygoscelis papua*
Wandering albatross	*Diomedea exulans*
Mollymawk or Black-browed albatross	*Diomedea melanophrys*
Sooty albatross	*Phoebetria fuliginosa*
Giant petrel or nelly	*Ossifraga gigantea*
MacCormick's skua gull	*Megalestris maccormicki*
Southern skua gull	*Megalestris antarctica*
Antarctic petrel	*Thalassoeca antarctica*
Silver-grey petrel or southern fulmar	*Priocella glacialoides*
Cape pigeon	*Daption capensis*
Snow petrel	*Pagodroma nivea*
Lesson's petrel	*Oestrelata lessoni*
Wilson petrel	*Oceanites oceanicus* '>
Storm petrel	*Fregetta melanogaster*
Cape hen	*Majaqueus cequinoctialis*
Small prion or whale bird	*Prion banksii*
Crested tern	*Sterna sp.*
Southern black-backed or Dominican gull	*Larus dominicanus*
Macquarie Island shag	*Phalacrocorax traversi*
Mutton bird	*Puffinus griseus*
Maori hen or " weka "	*Ocydromus scotti*

SEALS	PINNIPEDIA
Sea elephant	*Macrorhinus leoninus*
Sea-leopard	*Stenorhynchus leptonyx*
Weddell seal	*Leptonychotes weddelli*
Crab-eater seal	*Lobodon carcinophagus*
Ross seal	*Ommaiophoca rossi*

WHALES AND DOLPHINS	CETACEA
Rorqual, finner, or blue whale	*Balaenoptera sibbaldi*
Killer whale	*Orca gladiator*

Appendix V

Medical Reports

Western Base (Queen Mary Land)
By S. E. Jones, M.B., CH.M.

There was a very marked absence of serious illness during the whole period of our stay at the Base. After the *Aurora* left Adelie Land on January 19, 1912, for her western cruise, an epidemic of influenza broke out. It should be noted that one case occurred on the voyage south from Hobart, and then an interval of almost a month occurred before the infection spread. An interesting feature of the outbreak was the fact that the recovery of those who were convalescing, when we arrived at Queen Mary Land, was much more rapid than was the case with those whose convalescence occurred on the Ship.

By the careful use of snow-goggles during the summer, snow-blindness was practically prevented, and such cases as occurred yielded quickly when zinc and cocaine tablets were used and the eyes obtained rest. An undoubted factor in the causation of snow-blindness is the strain caused by the continual efforts at visual accommodation made necessary on dull days when the sun is obscured, and there is a complete absence of all light-and-shade contrast.

Although frostbites were frequent during the winter months, immediate attention to the restoration of circulation prevented the occurrence of after-effects, so that no one suffered the loss of any more tissue than the superficial epithelium. The nose, ears, fingers and toes were the parts which suffered first.

Our supplies of food were excellent in point of view of variety. Some tinned onions were responsible for several mild attacks of poisoning, but these were not used after our first experience. There was no sign of scurvy in any form.

Hoadley, on one occasion, had an unpleasant experience. He was alone in the hut sleeping one night when he awoke to find the room filled with smoke. On going outside he found that the chimney had become blocked with snow; as the fire was banked, the hut was filled with the gases from the imperfect combustion of the coal. It was three or four days before Hoadley recovered from his experience, having marked symptoms of carbon monoxide poisoning.

On my return from the Western Depot journey I found that Wild was suffering from an attack of herpes zoster. The illness came on while he was out sledging, and he suffered severely from the pain and irritation.

Beyond a few cases of minor illness, and one or two accidents, there was nothing of serious moment to report.

Main Base (Adelie Land)
By A. L. McLean, M.B., CH.M., B.A.

Throughout the whole period of the Expedition—from December 2, 1911, to February 26, 1914—the health of the expedition was remarkably good. Undoubtedly Antarctica has a salubrious climate, and it is simply because one returns in a measure to the primitive that such an ideal result is obtained.

The first thing to resist is the cold, and additional clothing is the first and adequate means to such an end. No one needs to be specially inured to a rigorous climate. If he has a normal circulation he immediately reacts to a new set of temperature conditions, and in a few weeks may claim to be acclimatized. Most of the members of the expedition were Australians, so that the change of latitudes was rather abrupt but none the less stimulating and healthful.

Appetite for food had suddenly a new piquancy, hard manual work was a pleasure in a novel and wonderful environment, the intellect and imagination were quickened and the whole man embodied the *mens sana in*

corpore sano. That is why illness was practically unknown for more than two years; and, further, it may be said with partial truth that in the high sense of physical and mental fitness he possessed for a time, lies the explanation of the proverbial desire of an explorer to return to the ice-lands.

Regular monthly examinations of the blood were made from the date of leaving Hobart in December 1911 until October 1912, with an interval of about nine weeks between the first and second examinations. The haemoglobin or red colouring-matter went up with a leap and then very steadily increased in amount during the winter months in Adelie Land. The blood pressure became slightly more marked, the weight increased, but as one might have expected, the resistance to ordinary civilized germs was decreased. With regard to weight, the maximum amount gained by a single individual during a period of eight weeks was almost two stones, and every one became heavier by as much as ten pounds. As clinical evidence of the loss in immunity may be quoted the epidemic of influenza to which Dr. S. E. Jones referred. As well, it was noted that several members had attacks of "boils" during the voyage southward; in Adelie Land during 1912 there were two instances of acute abscesses on the fingers (whitlows) and one jaw abscess. It appears as if, with its new and unbounded energy of function, the body attempts to throw oft its waste products. Then, too, experimental observations of opsonic index pointed towards the lowering of resistance, and, by the way, it was rather a remarkable fact that after a few months in Adelie Land, staphylococcus pyogenes aureus—a common germ in civilization—could not be cultivated artificially from the throat, nose or skin, of six individuals from whom monthly bacteriological cultures were made.

Within the Hut, at a temperature which ranged from 40° to 45° F., the number of micro-organisms continuously increased, if the exposure of agar plates at regular intervals (by night) gave a true indication. The organisms were staphylocci albi, bacilli, yeasts, and moulds; the latter overgrowing the plate after it had been for forty eight hours in the incubator.

Frostbites were common, but, perhaps for that reason, were not regarded seriously. No one suffered permanent harm from being frost-bitten, though in several cases rather extensive blisters formed and nails and skin were lost.

Whilst the Hut was being built, minor casualties often occurred; the common remedy being to cover the injured part with a small piece of gauze

surrounded by adhesive tape; for open wounds will not heal when exposed to the cold. The Greenland dogs had small accidents and ailments which often required treatment.

On sledging journeys snow-blindness was an affection which sooner or later caught every one in an unguarded moment. That moment was when he ceased to use goggles if the light were at all trying to his eyes. Prevention came first, and then the "zinc and cocaine" cure.

Adelie Land can only be regarded as an intolerable country in which to live, owing to the never-ceasing winds. Usage and necessity helped one to regard the weather in the best possible light; for the sake of a few hours of calm which might be expected to occasionally intervene between the long spells of the blizzards. It is, therefore, with regret and some diffidence that I speak of the illness of Mr. S. N. Jeffryes, who took up so conscientiously the duties of wireless operator during the second year (1913); but upon whom the monotony of a troglodytic winter life made itself felt. It is my hope that he is fast recovering his former vigour and enthusiasm.**

So many miles of sledging were done at both Antarctic Bases in a climate which is surely without a parallel in the history of polar travelling, the Ship was so often in jeopardy during her three main cruises to the South, that we feel the meagre comment should be made on our providential return to civilization with the loss of two comrades whose memory will ever be imperishable to each one of us.

** *With the advent of summer, Jeffryes became normal, but unfortunately suffered a temporary relapse upon his return to Australia.—D. M.*

Appendix VI

Finance

A General reference was made to the finances of the expedition in the Introduction. Here is an extended statement which, more fully amplified with a detailed list of donations, will be again published when additional funds have been raised to pay off the debit balance and establish equilibrium.

GRANTS AND DONATIONS

Australia, *January* 1911: £

Australasian Association for the Advancement of Science, £1000 ; R. Barr Smith (South Australia), £1000; Hugh Denison (Sydney), £1000; Samuel Hordern (Sydney), £1000 (subsequently increased to £2500)........................ 4,000

London, *June* 1911:

S. Hordern (Sydney), £1500 (second donation); Roderick Murchison (Melbourne), £1000; W. A. Horn (South Australia), £1000; Lord Strathcona, £1000; Eugene Sandow, £1050; Imperial Government, £2000; Royal Geographical Society, £500; Lionel Robinson (Sydney), £250; C. D. Mackellar, £150; G. P. Doolette, £150; G. Buckley, £150; Lord Denman, £100; Madame Melba (Melbourne), £100; S. Y. Buchanan, £100 (later increased to £200); *Daily Mail*, £100; Messrs. Bullivants £100, &c., aggregating an additional £593 9,843

Australia, *October* 1911:   £

Sydney: Government grant, £7000; collected by
    Professor David, £50; Sydney *Morning Herald*,
    £100; Professor David's own donation and
    lecture proceeds, £100.. 7,250

Melbourne: Government grant, £6000; collected
by Professor Masson, £70 6,070

Adelaide: Government grant, £5000; collected by
    Mr. Piper, £250 (including Angus £100,
    Simpson £85, Scarfe £50) 5,250

Hobart: Government grant,
£500; collected, £55.. 555

Commonwealth grant 5,000
                                                 24,125

                   Carried forward............................. 37,968
                                                        £
London, 1913:   Brought forward 37,968

Sir Lucas Tooth, £1000 (Sydney); Imperial Treasury, £1000;
    Royal Geographical Society, £100; S. Y. Buchanan,
    £100; Lady Scott, £100; Commander Evans, £100; other
    members of Scott Expedition and general subscriptions,
    £227 2,627

Australia, 1913:

Commonwealth grant, £5000; collected by Professor David
    (approximately), £50... 5,050

Australia, 1914:

Collected by Professor Masson (approximately), £80; G. J. R.
    Murray (Adelaide), £100; Sir Samuel Way, £50.............. 230

COLLECTED IN LONDON... 10

Total moneys donated   £45,885

ASSETS REALIZED AND ADDED TO THE FUND:

	£	£
Sale of photos and newspaper articles, £490; sale of ship and materials, £3699; lectures, films, &c., £726		4,915
BILLS OWING	5,932	5,932

ASSETS TO BE REALIZED:

	£		
In hand	560		
	340		
Owing..	570		
Anticipated sale of gear...........................	—	1,470	
Debit balance.................................	£4,462		
Total cost** of Expedition		£56,732

There is therefore a deficit of £4462 to be made up by the royalty on the sale of the book, lectures, donations, &c., and the cost of the publication of the scientific results, which will be approximately £8000, has yet to be defrayed.

** An estimate of the cost of the expedition should also take account of donations in kind, which, as can be gathered, were numerous. Facilities offered by harbour boards and valuable assistance extended in the matter of docking and repairing the Aurora, particularly in the case of the State of Victoria, and to a less extent in New South Wales.

Then there were valuable contributions of coal, particularly by Mr. J. Brown of Newcastle (N.S.W.), Mr. H. D. Murphy (Melbourne), and the Lithgow Collieries Company.

Appendix VII

Equipment

Clothing

With regard to the clothing, the main bulk was of woollen material as supplied by Jaeger of London. This firm is unexcelled in the production of camel's-hair garments and has supplied most polar expeditions of recent years with underclothing, gloves, caps, and the like. From the same firm we also secured heavy ski-boots, finnesko-crampons, and the blankets which were used at Winter Quarters at both Antarctic Bases. Some of the Jaeger woollens were damaged by sea water on the voyage from London to Australia and were replaced by Eagley goods; an Australian brand, which proved very satisfactory. The Ship's Party were outfitted with Kaipoi woollens (New Zealand).

Outer garments were made up to our design from Jaeger fleece by tailors in Hobart. The suit consisted of a single garment, to be worn with combination underclothing, and was calculated to meet the requirements of a severe climate.

An over-suit of wind-proof material, which may be worn when required, is a necessary adjunct to woollen clothing. Such a suit should have the additional properties of being light, strong, not readily absorbing moisture, and not affected by the cold. Burberry gabardine was found to possess all these properties, and two complete suits were made up for each man. One suit consisted of three pieces, whilst the other was made of two; the blouse-jacket and helmet of the latter being combined.

Furs, which were obtained from Norway, were restricted to sleeping bags, finnesko or fur-boots, and wolfskin mitts (Lapland).

The outfit of clothing for the party at Macquarie Island and on the Ship, respectively, differed from that used in the Antarctic. Warmer temperatures and wet conditions had to be taken into account, and so rubber boots, oilskins, and rubberized materials were provided as outer coverings.

Food

The food-stuffs were selected with at least as much consideration as was given to any of the other requisites. The successful work of an expedition depends on the health of the men who form its members, and good and suitable food reduces to a minimum the danger of scurvy; a scourge which has marred many polar enterprises. Thus our provisioning was arranged with care and as a result of my previous experience in the Antarctic with Sir Ernest Shackleton's Expedition.

A summary which may be of possible use to future expeditions is appended below:

In the matter of canned meats we had some six tons of the excellent Australian article supplied by the Sydney Meat Preserving Company, Ramornie Meat Company (N.S.W.), Baynes Brothers (Brisbane), and the Border (rabbit) Preserving Company of South Australia. For use on the Ship three tons of salt beef and pork served to replenish the "harness cask," largely obtained in Melbourne from Cook and Sons.

For a ton of sauces and pickles we were indebted to Brand and Company (London) and to Mason and Company (London).

Of course fresh meat was consumed as far as possible; a number of live sheep being taken by the *Aurora* on each cruise. Some of these were killed and dressed after reaching 60° south latitude and supplied our two Antarctic Bases with the luxury of fresh mutton about once a week throughout a year.

One ton of preserved suet came from the firms of Hugon (Manchester) and Conrad (Adelaide).

Almost all our bacon and ham, amounting to well over one ton, was of the Pineapple Brand (Sydney), and to the firm which supplied them we are indebted alike for the quality of its goods and for its generosity.

Soups in endless variety, totalling two tons, came chiefly from the Flemington Meat Preserving Company (Melbourne).

Fours tons of canned fish were supplied by C. & E. Morton (London).

Variety in vegetables was considered important. We decided to reduce the amount of dried vegetables in favour of canned vegetables. About six and a half tons of the latter in addition to one ton of canned potatoes were consumed; from Laver Brothers (Melbourne) and Heinz (Pittsburgh). There were one and a half tons of dried vegetables. In addition, large quantities of fresh potatoes and other vegetables were regularly carried by the *Aurora*, and many bags of new and old potatoes were landed at the Main Base. In the frozen condition, the former kept satisfactorily, though they were somewhat sodden when thawed. The old potatoes, on the other hand, became black and useless, partly owing to the comparatively high temperature of the ship's hold, and in part to the warmth of the sun during the first few weeks in Adelie Land.

Canned fruits, to the extent of five tons, were supplied by Jones Brothers (Hobart) and Laver Brothers (Melbourne). This stock was eked out by some two and a half tons of dried fruits, chiefly from South Australia.

The management of Hartley (London) presented us with two tons of jam, and James Keiller and Son (London) with one ton of marmalade.

Of the twelve tons of sugar and half a ton of syrup consumed, all were generously donated by the Colonial Sugar Refining Company (Sydney).

For milk we were provided with two tons of Glaxo (a dry powder) which was used at the land bases, and a ton and a half of Nestle's condensed variety for use on the ship.

Three tons of cereal meals, largely from Parsons (Sydney), were consumed.

As one might have expected, the amount of flour used was enormous. In the thirteen tons of this commodity from Colman (London) there were three varieties, self-rising, plain, and wheatmeal flour, encased in stout metal linings within strong, well-finished cases of a convenient size. Until required, the cases of flour were used to solidify the break-wind on the southern side of the Hut.

Bird and Company (Birmingham) more than satisfied our needs in the matter of baking powder, custard powder, jelly crystals, and the like.

There was over half a ton of fancy biscuits of excellent quality and great variety, for which we were indebted to Jacob and Company (Dublin), Arnott Brothers (Sydney), and Patria Biscuit Fabriek (Amsterdam). "Hardtack," the name by which a plain wholemeal biscuit of good quality, made by Swallow and Ariell (Melbourne) was known, constituted the greater part of the remaining two and a half tons of ordinary biscuits. "Hardtack" was much appreciated as a change from the usual "staff of life"—soda bread.

For sledging we had secured one ton of biscuits specially prepared by the Plasmon Company (London) containing 30 per cent. of plasmon. These, together with one ton of pemmican and half a ton of emergency ration prepared by the Bovril Company (London), are specially referred to in the chapter on sledging equipment.

Butter was an important item; the large stock of two and a half tons coming from the Colac Dairying Company (Melbourne). The butter was taken fresh in fifty-six lb. blocks, packed in the usual export cases. On the *Aurora* it was carried as deck-cargo, and at the Main Base was stacked in the open air on the southern side of the Hut. At the end of the second year (1913) it was still quite good; a fact which speaks well for the climate as a refrigerator. Of Australian cheese we used half a ton, and this was supplied in forty-pound blocks.

The firm of Messrs. Cadbury, well known for their cocoa and eating chocolate, supplied us with these commodities, and receive our unqualified praise for the standard of the articles and the way in which they were packed. The total consumption was one ton of cocoa and half a ton of chocolate.

The three-quarters of a ton of tea was donated by "Te Sol" (Guernsey) and Griffiths Brothers (Melbourne). In both cases the articles were well packed and much appreciated. Half a ton of coffee was used, partly supplied from London and partly donated by Griffiths Brothers.

Rose's (London) lime juice, as an antiscorbutic, was mainly reserved for consumption on the Ship. This lime juice was much in favour as a beverage.

Other supplies, taken in bulk, and for which we are indebted to the manufacturers, are: one ton of Cerebos Salt, half a ton of Castle salt, one ton of Sunlight Soap, our complete requirements in toilet soap from Pears, candles from Price, matches from Bryant and May including special sledging vestas, and dried milk from the Trufood Company.

Sweets, which were used for dessert and on special occasions, were presented by the firms of Fuller and Batger of London, and by Farrah of Harrogate, &c. There were also small quantities of aerated waters, ales, wines, and whisky for each Base.** At the Main Base, at least, there was no demand for whisky until penguin omelettes became fashionable.

The smokers were well provided for by a generous donation of Capstan tobaccos, cigarettes and cigars from the British American Tobacco Company in London. At a later date, when our Macquarie Island party was formed, the Sydney branch of the same firm met our added needs with the same generosity.

There are many other items which have not yet found a place in this summary which cannot be acknowledged severally, but for which we are none the less grateful. Mention is made of the following: Horlick's Malted

---

** *Acceptable donations of various articles were made by the firms of Ludowici, Sydney; Allen Taylor, Sydney; Sames and Company, Birmingham; Gamage, London; Gramophone Company, London; the Acetylene Corporation, London; Steel Trucks Ltd., &c.*

Milk, Neave's Health Diet, Brown and Polson's Cornflour, International Plasmon Company's Plasmon chocolate and Plasmon powder, Bovril and lime juice nodules manufactured by Bovril Limited, Colman's Mustard and Groats, Flemington Meat Company's desiccated soups, Seager's meats, Nestlé's nut-milk chocolate, Escoffier's soups, &c.

The cooking range which served us well for two years in the Hut at Adelie Land was from J. Smith and Wellstood (London); others were presented by Metters (Adelaide).

The total supply of foods purchased and donated aggregated quite one hundred tons, exclusive of packing. Much of this was assembled in London. In Australia the Government Produce Department of Adelaide rendered valuable assistance.

TABLE OF FOOD-SUPPLIES FOR A TWELVE-MAN BASE

The following are the food requirements for a party of twelve men wintering in the Antarctic. It is our own store list, with slight modifications where these are found desirable. The figures are based on the supposition that unlimited quantities of seal and penguin meat can be had on the spot, and, furthermore, are ample for a second year's requirements should the party be unavoidably detained. The fare during the second year might be somewhat less varied, but would otherwise be sufficient. Health was, of course, the first consideration in this selection, but economy was also studied. The quantities are stated in pounds weight.

Note. These weights are exclusive of packing. When high southern latitudes can be reached within three weeks, fresh eggs may be taken with advantage, preferably unfertilized, but care should be taken to freeze them as soon as possible, and not to allow them to thaw again until required for use. It is advisable to take small quantities of whisky, ale, wines and lime juice. Matches, candles, soap, and other toilet requirements, kerosene and fuel are not reckoned with here, appearing in a more general stores' list. Certain medical comforts, such as malted milk and plasmon, may also be included.

Medical Equipment

The medical equipment consisted of a complete outfit of Burroughs and Wellcome's drugs, dressings, &c., and Allen and Hanbury's surgical instruments. Sets, varying in character with particular requirements, were made up for the Ship and for each of the land parties. Contained within

	lbs.
Meats, tinned—Corned beef, 216; roast beef, 72; roast mutton, 72; boiled mutton, 72; Irish stew, 216; assorted meats, 168, including mutton cutlets, haricot mutton, ox tail, ox tongue, sausages, and brawn; sheep's tongues, 288; special meats, 192, including rabbit, hare, duck, fowl, and turkey....................	1296
Live sheep—16 sheep to be dressed south of 60° S. latitude (weight not included)......................	400
Suet, tinned—400.....................	250
Bacon and Ham—Bacon in sides, packed in salt, 250; ham, 250	
Fish, tinned—Salmon, 360; haddocks, 96; kippered herrings, 216; herrings in tomato sauce, 72; fresh herrings, 72; sardines, 300; cods' roe, curried prawns, &c., 72..............	1188
Soups, assorted tinned, 1152....................	1152
Vegetables, fresh, in wooden cases—new potatoes, 1200; onions, 360....................	1560
Tinned—potatoes, 864; onions, 216; peas, 450; French beans, 450; spinach, 360; cabbage, 144; beetroot, 288; carrots, 288; parsnips, 144; turnips, 108; celery, 144; leeks, 72; champignons, 144; Boston baked beans, 144; tomatoes, 288	3240
Cereals and Dried Vegetables, &c.—Split peas, 112; lentils, 56; marrowfat peas, 56; haricot beans, 56; barley, 72; rice, 252; tapioca, 144; semolina, 56; macaroni, 56; rolled oats, 648; cornflour, 156....................	1664
Flour, including plain, wholemeal, and self-rising..............	4480
Biscuits, &c.—Plasmon wholemeal, 1344; plain wholemeal, 560; assorted sweet, 560; cake tinned, 224; plum pudding, 224....................	1712
Fruit, tinned in syrup--peaches, 288; pears, 288; plums, 288; apricots, 288; pineapples, 288; apples, 288; gooseberries, 216; cherries, 216; mulberries, 48; strawberries, 48; red currants, 48; black currants, 48; raspberries, 48..............	2400

Dried fruits—Prunes, 112; apples, 112; peaches, 56; nectarines, 56; apricots, 56; raisins seeded, 224; currants, 112; figs, 224; dates, 112; candied peel, 56 1120

Sweets, &c.—Eating chocolate (chiefly for sledging) 504; assorted sweets, 168; crystallized fruits, 56; assorted nuts, 84 812

Milk—as dried powder, 2400 2400

Butter—in 56 lb. export cases, 1456 1456

Cheese—in original blocks or tins, 240 240

Cocoa, Tea, and Coffee—Cocoa, 576; tea, 288; coffee, 288...... 1152

Sugar, Jam, &c.—Sugar, 3584; jam, 1456; marmalade, 448; honey, 576; syrup, 288 6352

Sauces, Pickles, &c.—Tomato sauce, 180; Worcester sauce, 135; sweet pickles, 162; mango chutney, 81; assorted pickles (first quality) 216; vinegar, 210 984

Cooking requisites—Baking powder (in addition to that in selfrising flour) 56; sodium bicarbonate, 1; ground mixed spice, 3; ground ginger, 4; whole cloves, 1; nutmegs, 2; assorted essences, 10; desiccated cocoanut, 12; mixed dried herbs, 2; dried mint, 6; dried parsley, 1; onion powder, 9; curry powder, 30; mustard, 30; black pepper, 12; white pepper, 12; table salt, 784 975

Soap, &c.—Soap, 448; soda, 168 .... <u>616</u>

(16 tons approx.)   35,699

the fifty-five boxes was a wonderful assortment of everything which could possibly have been required on a polar expedition. There was in addition a set of Burroughs and Wellcome's medicines for the treatment of dogs.

Scientific Equipment

The scope of our projected scientific work necessitated extensive purchases, and these were amplified by loans from many scientific bodies and individuals.

Instruments for surveying and navigation were loaned by the Royal Geographical Society and by the Admiralty, while many theodolites, chronometers, and half-chronometer watches were manufactured to order.

An assortment of oceanographical gear was generously supplied through H. S. H. The Prince of Monaco, from the Institut Oceanographique of Monaco. Dr. W. S. Bruce made similar donations and supervised the construction of our largest deep-sea dredge. The three-thousand fathom tapered steel cables and mountings, designed to work the deep-water dredges, were supplied by Messrs. Bullivant. Appliances were also loaned by Mr. J. T. Buchanan of the *Challenger* Expedition and by the Commonwealth Fisheries Department. The self-recording tide-gauges we employed were the property of the New South Wales Government, obtained through Mr. G. Halligan.

The taxidermists' requirements, and other necessaries for the preservation of zoological specimens, were for the most part purchased, but great assistance was rendered through Professor Baldwin-Spencer by the National Museum of Melbourne and by the South Australian Museum, through the offices of Professor Stirling. Articles of equipment for botanical work were loaned by Mr. J. H. Maiden, Director of the Botanical Gardens, Sydney.

A supply of heavy cameras for base-station work and light cameras for sledging was purchased; our stock being amplified by many private cameras, especially those belonging to F. H. Hurley, photographer of the Expedition. Special Lumiere plates and material for colour photography were not omitted, and, during the final cruise of the *Aurora*, P. E. Correll employed the more recent Paget process for colour photography with good results.

The programme of magnetic work was intended to be as extensive as possible. In the matter of equipment we were very materially assisted by the Carnegie Institute through Dr. L. A. Bauer. An instrument was also loaned through Mr. H. F. Skey of the Christchurch Magnetic Observatory. A full set of Eschenhagen self-recording instruments was purchased, and in this and in other dispositions for the magnetic work we have to thank Dr. C. Chree, Director of the National Physical Laboratory, and Dr. C. C. Farr of University College, Christchurch. Captain Chetwynd kindly assisted in arrangements for the Ship's compasses.

Two complete sets of Telefunken wireless apparatus were purchased from the Australasian Wireless Company. The motors and dynamos were got from Buzzacott, Sydney, and the masts were built by Saxton and Binns,

Sydney. Manilla and tarred-hemp ropes were supplied on generous terms by Melbourne firms (chiefly Kinnear).

The meteorological instruments were largely purchased from Negretti and Zambra, but a great number were loaned by the Commonwealth Meteorological Department (Director, Mr. H. A. Hunt) and by the British Meteorological Office (Director, Dr. W. N. Shaw).

For astronomical work the following instruments were loaned, besides transit-theodolites and sextants: a four-inch telescope by the Greenwich Observatory through the Astronomer Royal: a portable transit-theodolite by the Melbourne Observatory through the Director, Mr. P. Baracchi; two stellar sidereal chronometers by the Adelaide Observatory through the Astronomer, Mr. P. Dodwell.

The apparatus for bacteriological and physiological work were got in Sydney, in arrangements and suggestions for which our thanks are due to Dr. Tidswell (Microbiological Laboratory) and Professor Welsh, of Sydney University.

Artists' materials were supplied by Winsor and Newton, London, while the stationery was partly donated by John Sands, Limited, Sydney

Geological, chemical, and physical apparatus were all acquired at the instance of the several workers.

Adjuncts, such as a calculating machine, a typewriter, and duplicator were not forgotten.

Apart from the acquisition of the instruments, there were long preparations to be made in the arrangement of the scientific programme and in the training of the observers. In this department the Expedition was assisted by many friends.

Thus Professor W. A. Haswell (Biology), Professor T. W. Edgeworth David (Geology), and Mr. H. A. Hunt (Meteorology), each drew up instructions relating to his respective sphere. Training in astronomical work at the Melbourne Observatory was supervised by Mr. P. Baracchi, Director, and in magnetic work by the Department of Terrestrial Magnetism, Carnegie Institute (Director, Dr. L. A. Bauer). Further, in the subject of magnetics, we have to thank especially Mr. E. Kidston of the Carnegie Institute for field tuition, and Mr. Baldwin of the Melbourne Observatory

---

** *Through the offices of Mr. C. A. Bang we are indebted to "De Forenede Dampskibsselskab," of Copenhagen, for the transport of the dogs from Greenland.*

for demonstrations in the working of the Eschenhagen magnetographs. Professor J. A. Pollock gave us valuable advice on wireless and other physical subjects. At the Australian Museum, Sydney, Mr. Hedley rendered assistance in the zoological preparations. In the conduct of affairs we were assisted on many occasions by Messrs. W. S. Dun (Sydney), J. H. Maiden (Sydney), Robert Hall (Hobart), G. H. Knibbs (Melbourne),and to the presidents and members of the councils of the several Geographical Societies in Australia--as well, of course, as to those of the Royal Geographical Society, London.

In conclusion, the proffered, disinterested help, of all the above and many other friends contrived to make our scientific equipment well-nigh complete and eminently up-to-date.

Index

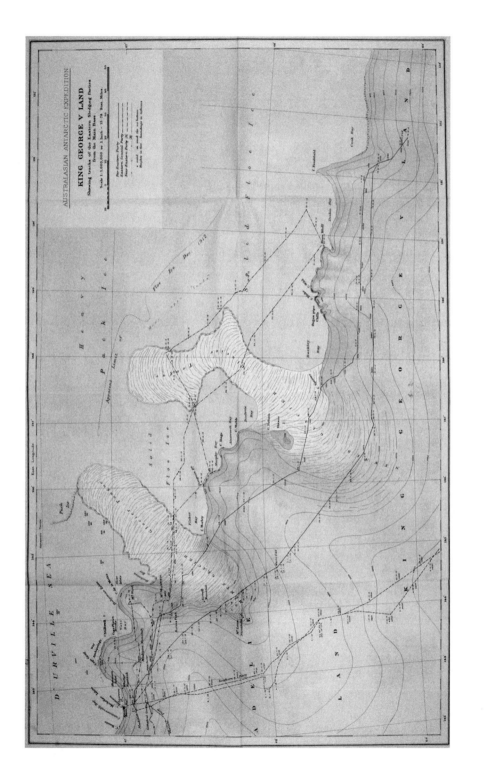

AUSTRALASIAN ANTARCTIC EXPEDITION

KING GEORGE V LAND
Showing tracks of the Eastern Sledging Parties
from the Main Base

Scale 1:3,000,000 or 1 inch : 47·78 Stat. Miles

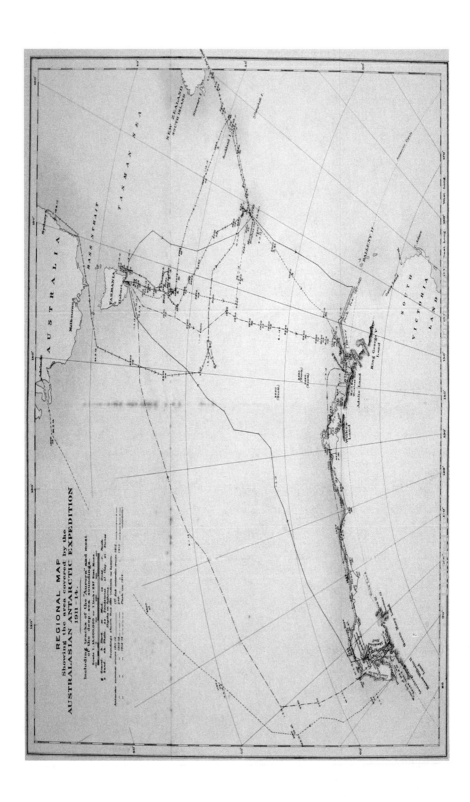

REGIONAL MAP
Showing the area covered by the
AUSTRALASIAN ANTARCTIC EXPEDITION
1911-14.

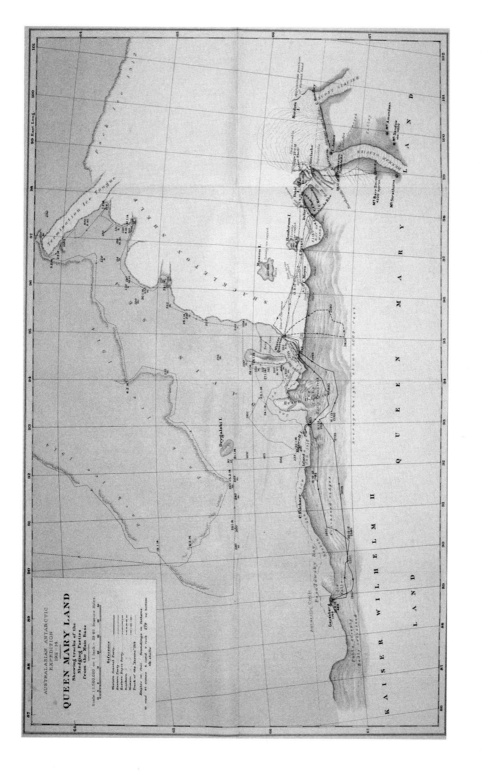